COULTER LIBRARY ONONDAGA COMM. COLL.
D0086909

Conflict in the Former Yugoslavia

Roots of Modern Conflict

Conflict in the Former Yugoslavia

An Encyclopedia

edited by

John B. Allcock,
Marko Milivojević,
and John J. Horton

foreword by Martin Bell, M.P.

ABC-CLIO

Denver, Colorado
Santa Barbara, California
Oxford, England

All maps by C. J. Bowers, University of Bradford

Library of Congress Cataloging-in-Publication Data
Conflict in the former Yugoslavia : an encyclopedia / edited by John B. Allcock,
Marko Milivojević, and John J. Horton.
p. cm.—(Roots of modern conflict)
Includes bibliographical references and index.
1. Yugoslavia—History—Dictionaries. 2. Yugoslav War, 1991–1995—
Dictionaries. 3. Former Yugoslav republics—History—Dictionaries.
I. Allcock, John B. II. Milivojević, Marko, 1957– . III. Horton,
John J. (John Joseph), 1940– . IV. Series.
DR1232.F67 1998
949.703—dc21 98-41772
CIP

ISBN 0-87436-935-5 (hc)
ISBN 1-57607-045-X (pbk)

04 03 02 01 00 99 10 9 8 7 6 5 4 3 2

ABC-CLIO, Inc.
130 Cremona Drive, P.O. Box 1911
Santa Barbara, California 93116-1911

This book is printed on acid-free paper ♾.

Manufactured in the United States of America

To our parents

Contents

Foreword

Martin Bell, M.P.

When the history of our time comes to be written, the wars of the dissolution of Yugoslavia will occupy a central place. The Bosnian war in particular dominated the politics and diplomacy of Europe in the mid-1990s. It challenged the New World Order following the end of the Cold War. It exposed the weakness of the Western democracies and the divisions between them. It raised questions about the role and responsibilities of the news media, especially television. It brought war and genocide home to people—the first war and genocide in Europe in 50 years. It caused its leading players and more marginal figures—soldiers, politicians, aid workers, and even journalists—to doubt their traditional practices and values and their ways of doing business. We were dealing with new realities.

As is the way with wars, too much blood was spilled in the first instance—and perhaps too much ink in the second. Over the years a literature of the wars of ex-Yugoslavia has come into being—some of it fiction, some nonfiction, and some occupying a middle ground between them. I must plead guilty to having written one of these books myself—I hope of the truthful variety. There seemed no point in living through such an ordeal without drawing from it the necessary lessons and trying to make them accessible to others.

The Dayton Agreements did not bring peace, but they brought a welcome respite from war. And if the respite holds, it will add to the growing library of books about what happened and why; about leaders and institutions that failed; about cowardice in the face of genocide; about the blame and the shame of it. The passage of time may also, however, provide more heat than light. Already I have sensed a tendency by those who were not present at the time to rewrite history according to their own prejudgments.

How useful then to have on hand a reference work—an A-to-Z of the Balkan wars—that can anchor these later theories in the facts. *The Former Yugoslavia* is that book.

Introduction

John B. Allcock,
Marko Milivojević,
and John J. Horton

As Yugoslavia was falling apart, Serb author Milorad Pavić achieved international fame for his novel *A Dictionary of the Khazars.* His book both is symptomatic of the process that is dealt with in our own work and resembles it. The Khazar khanate occupied an area to the north of the Black Sea between the early eighth and late tenth centuries, although little is known about it. Pavić's *Dictionary* is a fictional attempt to reconstruct the khanate's history and culture on the basis of the few scraps of knowledge that remain. The result is a parable, in Pavić's view, of the Serbs and the manner in which the distinctiveness of Serb culture was coming to be dissipated within modern Europe, to the extent that future generations would know as little of his own people as we do today of the Khazars. The sense of a crisis of identity that Pavić expresses is widely present among all of the peoples of former Yugoslavia and is an important dimension of the developments that are the subject of this book.

The unusual feature of Pavić's novel was that its form as a dictionary invited the reader to enter it at any point and to consult the entries in any order, in the expectation that following their random cross-referencing would enable a complete picture to eventually emerge. Abandoning the usual narrative structure of the novel, Pavić endeavored to convey an understanding of the situation by other means. This is precisely the hope and expectation of the editors of this book. Like Pavić, we also offer the reader a "dictionary." It is a work of reference, whose items may be consulted entirely in isolation from each other in the search for specific information. In the selection of the items that have been included here, however, and in the manner in which they are both consciously cross-referenced and treated internally (note that boldfaced terms in the text of the entries are cross-references to other entry titles), the editors have tried to convey a sense of the totality of the events, as well as their patterned interrelationship, leading to the eventual disintegration of the former Socialist Federation of Yugoslav Republics. The strategy that we have adopted in pursuit of this aim is to intersperse conceptual, historical, and interpretative items among the more narrowly factual ones and to ensure that entries convey something of the meaning of events as well as simply recording the events themselves.

Unlike the *Dictionary of the Khazars,* this is not the work of a single author. Indeed, in the attempt to provide material that is as authoritative as possible, the editors have sought the assistance of a range of specialists whose skills and experience more than complement their own. The reader who consults this volume regularly, or who reads many of the items in it, will naturally come to be aware that this is the work of many hands. Even within the editorial group, there are differences in the interpretation and evaluation of aspects of the story that is told here. The variety of contributing points of view, however, is a necessary feature of the situation in which we find ourselves.

Unlike Pavić, we do not have the benefit of several centuries of hindsight in the portrayal of our "Khazars." As we write, there is still no guarantee that the "Wars of the Yugoslav Succession" are over. The Dayton solution in Bosnia-Hercegovina is widely regarded as incomplete and unstable; many observers of the Balkan scene do not discount the possibility that the conflict may spread as a consequence of the still-unresolved problems of Kosovo in particular and the borders of the Albanian state in general. Although we have generally taken the Dayton Agreements as marking the limit of our material, it would be both presumptuous and foolish to attempt to tell the story of the Yugoslav conflict as if it were completed—and until the story has run its course there must remain room for a variety of interpretations.

While endeavoring to avoid contradiction in matters of fact, therefore, and while striving to ensure a reasonable harmony of style and consistency of presentation, the editors have not sought to impose an intepretative straitjacket upon the contributors. This approach is explicitly recognized in the fact that the authors of the entries are identified (as several of them have expressly wished) by initials at the end of each entry; these identifications are expanded upon in the *List of Contributors.*

Even so, it is a remarkable fact that a broad agreement has emerged among the contributors about a number of key points in the explanation of the tragic "death of Yugoslavia," and these points appear to be echoed in a wide range of work by specialists in the field. It is possibly useful to the reader for us to summarize the general lines of this agreement here.

Press treatment of the Yugoslav conflict has tended to be unbalanced in two directions. One approach to interpretation sees the violent disintegration of Yugoslavia as an almost inevitable outcome of the region's cultural diversity. The term *Balkan* in English has come to stand for fragmentation and confusion going beyond mere diversity. What else should one expect from the Balkans but conflict? The bloody collapse of Yugoslavia is depicted as the latest expression of a history of "age-old hatreds." In spite of the legacy of Cold War attitudes toward communism, the Tito regime was widely given credit for its ability to contain the presumed natural disorder of the region, which following the death of Tito welled up from its sources in popular culture.

By way of contrast, the other view takes as its focus the intentions and actions of powerful individuals. It is a natural outcome of "news values" that the reporting of events in the media of mass communication tends to focus on "personalities." Criticism of the press for its sensationalism often overlooks the fact that news reporting is often strongly moralizing in tone, addressing (even if tacitly) the question "Who is to blame?" rather than asking "Why did it happen?" Not surprisingly, in pursuit of answers to the former question, attention is directed toward political leaders, for example, Serbia's Slobodan Milošević, bizarre individuals like the paramilitary gangster "Arkan," or shadowy groups of conspirators such as the infamous "Hercegovina Lobby."

The editors find neither of these approaches satisfactory in themselves; though they may be founded upon grains of truth, they can be said at best to provide us with a very limited basis for an understanding of what has happened in Yugoslavia. Events as complex as the "death of Yugoslavia" grow out of a long history and an entanglement of a wide range of causes, much as the manner of the death of an individual can often be seen as encapsulating their whole life.

If asked to explain the disintegration of Yugoslavia, most informed people would probably refer to "nationalism." Indeed, by far the greater part of the social science literature produced on the topic over the past eight years has concentrated on this issue. This explanation begs the question, however, of why nationalism should have erupted there with such disruptive force at this time.

Reference is frequently made in this volume to the notion that the death of President Tito, in this context, released from control conflicts that had previously been held in check by his charismatic presence. This takes us little further forward, in that "The Old Man" died in 1980 (more than a decade before the collapse of the Yugoslav state), which suggests that there must have been other forces for cohesion that continued to act to good effect in addition to his role as a unifying symbol and source of authority. Any divisive forces must have been incompletely developed by the time of his death, and we are left with the problem of explaining them.

In fact, it is possible to identify a range of features in the recent history of Yugoslavia that constitute the roots of this particular conflict and that either contribute to the explanation of the rise of nationalism or have acted independent of it. These features also figure prominently in the entries of this volume.

It will be useful in reviewing these features to begin with the economic dimension. In 1987 Yugoslavia had a per capita gross domestic product (GDP) of U.S.$2,480, which placed it on a par with or ahead of most of its Eastern and Central European neighbors, such as Bulgaria, Czechoslovakia, Hungary, Poland, and Romania. This level of economic development was on a par with other "upper-middle-income countries" such as Argentina, Brazil, Portugal, and South Korea.

As significant as Yugoslavia's relative success in economic terms was the fact that, in comparison with other "real socialist" states, its citizens enjoyed the benefits of openness at a variety of levels. The growth of tourism after the mid-1960s made Yugoslavia (with 9 million foreign arrivals by 1988) one of Europe's primary tourist destinations. Reciprocally, Yugoslavs traveled abroad freely; it was common for the better-off Slovenes to shop in Trieste or for the Macedonians to shop in Thessaloniki. The country's relatively high standard of living was sustained in part by the remittances of Yugoslav workers abroad (estimated at U.S.$823 million in 1986). There was an absence of the intrusive personal surveillance to be found elsewhere in the region.

Although Yugoslavia was a one-party state, under the firm control of the League of Communists, its citizens enjoyed a relatively high degree of personal freedom of expression, movement, religion, and assembly. The major European newspapers were freely available on the newsstands of the larger cities. The domestic press was characterized by an independence unfamiliar in other socialist states on issues ranging from politics to sex. The arts were openly experimental, and areas such as the cinema and graphic arts acquired a worldwide reputation. It would be wrong to convey the impression that Yugoslavia before 1992 was idyllic, but by the death of Tito, Yugoslavs certainly had a lot to lose. The problem, however, was that this well-being rested upon rather shaky foundations.

Yugoslavia's economic problems are analyzed more fully in several entries in this volume, but a few points are appropriately made here in summary form. Economic security began to be undermined when the rapid rise of world energy prices in 1973–1975 and 1978–1979 hit Yugoslavia hard for several reasons. First, the country is not well supplied with sources of energy; with an economy that had developed to a large extent upon industrial manufacturing, the impact of this trend was serious. The problem was compounded by the fact that, to a significant extent, Yugoslav development was founded upon credit. Western sources were willing throughout the post-1945 period to support the success of this unusual model of socialism as an example of the advantages of a more open economy and society outside the Soviet bloc. During the 1970s, however, the problem of meeting these credit obligations mounted. By 1983, when the International Monetary Fund (IMF) demanded a reckoning and a review of Yugoslavia's credit position, the country owed abroad around U.S.$24 billion, or nearly $1,000 for every Yugoslav.

An adequate response to the economic crisis was made more difficult by Yugoslavia's political system. In spite of the much-heralded moves toward "market socialism," there were appreciable rigidities within an economic system that was still largely politicized. There were built-in pressures in particular toward inflation and low productivity that were rooted in large measure in the distinctive system known as workers' self-management. The political rigidities that prevented Yugoslavia from adapting successfully to its changing economic environment were broadly of two kinds.

The ruling League of Communists of Yugoslavia (LCY) was unwilling to contemplate the emergence of effective centers of organization outside its own control. Although the Yugoslav system was characterized by extensive devolution and decentralization, this feature remained within a framework very much under the control of LCY activists. In spite of the fact that the market was able to operate to some extent within the Yugoslav economy, market institutions enjoyed only limited autonomy from political control. The monopoly position of the LCY meant that proposals for reform could be formulated and implemented only from within the league itself—the very organization that was responsible for the problems in the first place.

Although by the late 1980s there were clear signs that the Communist leadership had grasped the need for urgent change—and that many people were convinced that the reform program proposed by Premier Ante Marković was capable of effectively addressing the issues—the regional party bosses were unable to create a sufficient consensus among themselves, especially in relation to those issues where change might have limited their own power.

Among the primary causes of Yugoslavia's woes was its system of workers' self-management, which was relevant to the breakdown of the Yugoslav state in three respects. First, a structure that devolved as much of the responsibility for policy and its implementation as the Yugoslav system did to regions, municipalities, and enterprises inevitably placed a huge burden upon those units. This burden can be measured in terms of time spent in meetings, the complexities of accounting requirements, duplication of effort, and the rigidities that are natural to all complex organizations. The Yugoslav economy carried an immense weight of "social and political organization" that depleted productivity and inhibited adaptation.

Second, it is generally recognized that a system that places so much responsibility for economic decisions in the hands of its workforce will tend to produce relatively high wage costs, low rates of investment, an irrational pattern of labor use, and a reluctance to innovate. The administrative costs of the system act to discourage the entry of new enterprises, especially small ones. Although there is still considerable disagreement among academics and policymakers about the precise importance of this point, self-management does seem to have contributed directly to the severity of Yugoslavia's economic problems.

Third, one of the less recognized but most important consequences of self-management, from the point of view of its part in the collapse of Yugoslavia, was its effect in fragmenting the political response to problems. The Yugoslav system—by focusing participation, responsibility, and identity within highly localized units (municipalities and enterprises)—prevented the creation of effective federation-wide structures through which alternative views could have been aired and consensus sought concerning new policies. All areas of economic, political, and cultural life were broken down into the same segments, which undermined the edifice of the state in this way. There were virtually no federation-wide organizations (except perhaps the army) that could act as vehicles for the aggregation and expression of common interests across the whole of society.

It is within this context that nationalism comes to be relevant to our search for the roots of conflict. The term *nationalism* has been used, confusingly, to refer to two different types of events. On the one hand, there is the development of policies that were directed toward protecting different republican interests and were advanced by political elites. On the other hand, there are sentiments distributed among the population at large, relating to their sense of collective identity. The two levels, although related, are not to be confused.

An important characteristic of the Yugoslav federation since 1945 was the steady growth of economic differences among its six republics and two provinces, not only in terms of their relative wealth but (equally important) in terms of the pattern of economic activity. This meant that the republics and provinces had strongly contrasting perceptions of the acceptability of proposals for economic reform.

At the same time, it became increasingly evident (especially during the ill-fated government of Branko Mikulić, who in 1988 earned the distinction of being the first Communist prime minister to resign because of a vote of no confidence in the legislature) that the LCY was incapable of implementing the kinds of reforms that would have facilitated adaptation to the economic realities of the world. A part of its incapacity lay in the manner in which it had become fragmented into a congeries of republican parties, each of which reflected a diversity of economic opinions and radical differences in attitude toward the kinds of political and constitutional changes that might also be required. Foremost in this respect were differences of view about the nature of the LCY itself and the defensibility of its historical claim to exercise a "leading role" in Yugoslav politics.

At issue as well was an irreconcilable conflict over the role of federal versus republican authority in every walk of life, especially politics. This conflict stemmed in large measure from the pattern of distribution of Yugoslavia's diverse ethnic groups, especially that of Serbs, who—as the largest group (around 36 percent of the total)—were widely distributed as minorities within other republics (especially Bosnia-Hercegovina and Croatia). Serbia was also troubled by the relationship between its own republican government and the two autonomous provinces (Kosovo and the Vojvodina) that it contained. The strengthening of both federal authority and the control of the LCY was seen as offering a defense of the interests of Serbs throughout the whole federation and as an effective means of disciplining the wayward provinces. Conversely, the tendencies toward pluralism and even confederalism, as advocated by some other republican leaderships, were construed as potentially reducing Serbs in other republics to the status of second-class citizens and even turning the government of Serbia itself into a hostage of the power of its own provinces.

The League of Communists was not able to negotiate solutions to any of these problems, and it fell apart at its extraordinary fourteenth (and final) congress in January 1989. This collapse opened the door to a new phase in Yugoslav politics, in which the emerging new generation of party leaders (together with many established figures in the Communist hierarchy anxious to hang on to their own power) resorted to nationalist rhetorics in order to create new political followings for themselves. The materials out of which nationalisms could be constructed were provided by the complex and troubled history of the region, extending over many centuries. However, they could be exploited only in circumstances where the country was faced with an economic crisis to which its Communist leadership was unequal and where the legitimacy of the post-1945 Communist order was collapsing.

Two additional factors need to be considered as having had a central part to play in the maturation of the Yugoslav crisis, even if they are not, strictly speaking, a part of its roots. The events within Yugoslavia would probably not have followed the course that they did had it not been for the general disintegration of the Soviet system. This factor is relevant in three respects. The wider failure of "real socialism" within Europe served to accentuate the failure of legitimacy of the League of Communists of Yugoslavia. A significant factor in promoting unity within the country across the post-1945 period had been the perception of an ever-present threat from the Soviet Union. Furthermore, the perception of Yugoslavia by the Western powers underwent a radical revision, as its potential strategic significance was suddenly downgraded. In the wake of the breakup of the Warsaw Pact, the North Atlantic Treaty Organization (NATO) was no longer clear about its own aims and function. Although the European Union (EU) was gradually feeling its way toward a common foreign policy, the eruption of the Yugoslav dispute served only to bring to light formerly unrecognized differences in the outlook of its members. Therefore, in spite of their ambitions to find a specifically European resolution to the issue, in this event the EU members were unready for the task at hand. Whereas under other circumstances external intervention to avert the slide toward disaster—or to moderate its more severe consequences—might have been possible, in the situation at hand efforts in this direction served only to exacerbate the problems.

There is no simple explanation of the roots of the Yugoslav conflict, only a complex braid of explanatory factors, the nature, interdependence, and significance of which still have to be fully evaluated. At the time of this writing, there is no firm assurance that the tale is told—indeed, the situation in Kosovo may be coming to a head at this moment as Richard Holbrooke tries to negotiate an agreement on withdrawal of Serb forces. There is a saying, however, that "to be forewarned is to be forearmed." The editors of this volume offer it in the hope that it might make a modest contribution to the wider understanding of the issues, so that any future engagement with them might be better informed and more clearly focused—and that perhaps, in this troubled region of Europe, it is not the case that the worst is yet to be.

Contributors

John B. Allcock is head of the Research Unit in Southeast European Studies at the University of Bradford, where since 1966 he has taught sociology, specializing in Yugoslavia and its successor states. He has published over 30 contributions in academic journals and books and is joint author or editor of the volumes *Black Lambs and Grey Falcons: Women Travellers in the Balkans* with Antonia T. Young (England: Bradford University Press, 1991); *Yugoslavia's Security Dilemmas* with M. Milivojević and P. Maurer (Oxford and New York: Berg, 1988), and *Yugoslavia in Transition* with M. Milivojević and J. Horton (Berg, 1992). He has been specialist adviser to the Select Committee on Foreign Affairs of the House of Commons, has extensive experience in advising the media on Yugoslav affairs, and is president of the Southeastern Europe Studies Association. He is currently working on a sociological study of the long-term transformation of the South Slav region, with particular interest in ethnic identities.

Ian R. Barnes obtained his Ph.D. from the London School of Economics and was tutor in politics at the Open University from 1974 to 1993. He is currently head of history at the University of Derby. His teaching interests include contemporary European history, Soviet and Russian history, and international relations; his research topics include neofascism, civil society, and Slovene affairs.

Will Bartlett is Reader in Social Economics at the School for Policy Studies, University of Bristol, where he is also coordinator of the Balkan Studies Resarch Programme of the Centre for Mediterranean Studies. He studied economics at Cambridge, London, and Liverpool, where he completed his Ph.D. in economic development in the former Yugoslavia. He has since worked at the Universities of Southampton, Bath, and Bristol and the European University Institute in Florence, Italy. He has written several articles on economic development issues in the former Yugoslavia and its successor states. His current research covers social policy and small and medium enterprise development in the transition economies of southeast Europe.

Milford Bateman is senior research fellow and head of the Local Economic Development in Transition Economies Unit, University of Wolverhampton. He lived for three years in the former Yugoslavia researching for his doctorate on the Yugoslav economy and has frequently returned as a consultant on small-enterprise development for the World Bank and European Commission and on relief activities in Bosnia and Croatia for the Red Cross. He is currently responsible for the Economist Intelligence Unit's *Quarterly Country Survey: Macedonia,* and his book on the economic reconstruction of the Yugoslav successor states is to be published by Edward Elgar (Cheltenham, England) in 1998.

Gavin R. Beckett studied social and political sciences at Churchill College, Cambridge, specializing in social theory, global security, and large-scale social and political change. He spent three years at the Department of Peace Studies, University of Bradford, researching his Ph.D. dissertation, which analyzed the conflict in Croatia and developed theoretical and practical perspectives on conflict transformation. His research highlighted the contribution of local grassroots antiwar groups to peacebuilding. His book *Constructing Peace in Croatia* will be published by Lynne Rienner Publishers (Boulder, CO) in 1998. His theory and practice as a peace researcher have been informed by, and in turn inform, his work as a mediator and activist in the UK conflict resolution movement. He has written on community mediation, social theory, the theory and practice of conflict resolution, and the conflict in Croatia. He works for Bristol City Council and is a mediator for Bristol Mediation Service and a member of the Mediation UK Accreditation Committee.

Leslie Benson teaches politics and sociology at Nene-University College, Northampton, England. After leaving Cambridge University in 1964 with a degree in history, he studied at the University of Kent for a Ph.D. in sociology, concentrating on socialism and class structure in Yugoslavia and traveling extensively throughout that country. He later taught at Massey University, New Zealand, and the University of Bath before moving to Northampton. He is currently engaged in writing a study of nationalism and state building in the South Slav state.

Alison Closs is a lecturer in special education at Moray House Institute of Education in Edinburgh. She has been involved with the former Yugoslavia, both personally and professionally, for nearly four decades and was honorary secretary of the Scottish Branch of the British-Yugoslav Society from 1981 to 1985. In 1984 she was awarded the Order of the Yugoslav Flag with Gold Star on Necklace for services to Yugoslav young people. Since the outbreak of hostilities, she has been actively involved with Edinburgh Direct Aid, serving on its committee and acting as interpreter on two convoys as well as undertaking analyses of the needs of institutionalized multiply disabled people and of the training of special-education teachers in Bosnia.

Andrew S. Cottey is a lecturer in the Department of Peace Studies at the University of Bradford (where he also received his doctorate), specializing in European security issues. He has been a NATO Research Fellow and has worked in the Warsaw office of the Institute for East-West Studies and as a researcher for Saferworld and the British American Security Information Council. He is author of *East-Central Europe after the Cold War: Poland, the Czech Republic, Slovakia and Hungary in Search of Security* (London: Macmillan, 1995) and editor of *Subregional Cooperation in the New Europe: Building Security, Prosperity and Solidarity from Barents to the Black Sea* (London: Macmillan, 1998).

Kyril Drezov is a lecturer in the politics of Southeast Europe at Keele University and an active member of the university's Southeast Europe Unit. He studied international relations at the Sofia School of Economics and was involved in research at the Bulgarian Academy of Sciences before taking up doctoral studies at Oxford. He has published articles on problems of transition, modernization, and nationalism in Bulgaria and Macedonia and on the Russian factor in Bulgarian politics.

Robert Elsie is a Canadian writer, translator, critic, and specialist on Albanian affairs. Born in Vancouver, he studied at the University of British Columbia, the Free University of Berlin, the Ecole Pratique des Hautes Etudes in Paris, and the Dublin Institute for Advanced Studies, finshing his doctorate in comparative linguistics at the University of Bonn in 1978. In addition to numerous translations, he is author of *Dictionary of Albanian Literature* (New York: Greenwood Press, 1986); *An Elusive Eagle Soars: Anthology of Modern Albanian Poetry* (London: Forest Books, 1993); *Albanian Folktales and Legends* (Tirana: Naim Frasheri, 1994); *History of Albanian Literature,* 2 vols. (Boulder and New York: East European Monographs, 1995); and the political reader *Kosovo: In the Heart of the Powderkeg* (Boulder and New York: East European Monographs, 1997).

Richard Evens is in his final year as a student in the Department of Peace Studies at the University of Bradford, where he is completing his dissertation on displaced persons and refugees in Croatia. He worked at various refugee camps in Croatia in 1993 and was a volunteer in a work camp in the Slavonian capital, Osijek, in 1997.

Tom Gallagher is professor of ethnic peace and conflict at the University of Bradford. He specializes in the politics and history of ethnicity in southeastern Europe and ethnicity's impact upon democratization processes in the 1990s. He has published widely in journals and edited volumes on these subjects. His own most recent book, *Romania after Ceausescu: The Politics of Intolerance* (Edinburgh: Edinburgh University Press, 1995) has now been updated in translation and published in Romania.

Nikolaos M. Glinias was born and lives in Crete. He holds degrees from Syracuse University, and as a doctoral candidate at the University of Bradford he is currently pursuing research into the military dimension of the breakup of the former Yugoslavia, in addition to his interest in relations between Yugoslavia's successor states and Greece.

Bulent Gokay is a lecturer in the international relations of Southeast Europe at Keele University, as well as an active member of the university's Southeast Europe Unit. He came to Keele in 1996 from Cambridge, where he had been a postdoctoral research fellow for three years as well as a supervisor and part-time lecturer. He was also visiting lecturer at the University of North London. He has coauthored with Richard Langhorne *Turkey and the New States of the Caucasus and Central Asia* (London: HMSO, 1996) and has edited seven volumes of *British Documents of Foreign Affairs—Turkey, 1923–39* (Bethesda, MD: University Publications of America, 1997). His book *A Clash of Empires: Turkey between Russian Bolshevism and British Imperialism* was published by IB Tauris (London) in 1997. He is currently preparing a book on Eastern Europe since 1970, to be published by Longman in 1999.

Celia Hawkesworth is senior lecturer in Serbo-Croatian language and literature in the School of Slavonic and East European Studies at the University of London. She has published widely in academic journals; her books include a major study of a Nobel Prize–winning novelist, titled *Ivo Andric: A Bridge between East and West* (Athlone Press, 1984), and *Colloquial Serbo-Croat* (Routledge, 1986). She has also translated the works of several writers from the former Yugoslavia, including most recently two works by Croatian writer Dubravka Ugrešić for Weidenfeld and Nicolson of London.

John J. Horton is deputy librarian at the University of Bradford and has been closely associated with that university's Postgraduate School of Yugoslav Studies and its successors since its establishment in 1967. He has contributed to several publications on Yugoslavia and was responsible for the *Yugoslavia* volume in the World Bibliographical Series from ABC-CLIO (Santa Barbara, Denver, and Oxford). He is also a representative on the Council of the Inter-University Center for Postgraduate Studies in Dubrovnik.

Amaury Hoste is a French research student who, after graduating from the Institut d'Etudes Politiques in Strasbourg, took his master's degree in European and Latin American relations at the University of Bradford. He has a special interest in the foreign policy of France.

Martyn Housden is lecturer in modern and contemporary history in the Department of European Studies at the University of Bradford, where he took his doctorate. He is researching the German occupation of Eastern Europe, 1939–1945, and subsequent international relations. His publications include *Helmut Nicolai and Nazi Ideology* (London: Macmillan, 1992) and *Resistance and Conformity in the Third Reich* (London: Routledge, 1997).

Barbara Jancar-Webster is professor of political science at the State University of New York at Brockport. She has long specialized in both environmental policy and the position of women in Eastern Europe and the former Yugoslavia. In addition to numerous articles in these fields, her more recent books have included *Environmental Management in the Soviet Union and Yugoslavia* (Durham, NC: Duke University Press, 1987); *Environmental Action in East Europe: Responses to Crisis* (Armonk, NY: Sharpe, 1993); and *Women and Revolution in Yugoslavia 1941–1945* (Denver: Arden, 1990).

Robert (Bob) Jiggins graduated in politics at Huddersfield Polytechnic in 1986 and received a master's degree in East European studies at the University of Bradford in 1993. After several years teaching sociology in Further Education colleges in the region, he is now a part-time lecturer in sociology in the Department of Interdisciplinary Human Studies, University of Bradford, and a freelance writer and researcher specializing in the politics and economics of Eastern Europe. He is also an honorary visiting research fellow at the Research Unit in Southeast European Studies at Bradford University and is currently pursuing research on Montenegrin history and identity.

Marko Milivojević studied at and received degrees from the Universities of Manchester and Warwick and the Manchester Business School. He is a freelance writer and consultant on former Yugoslav affairs, an associate editor of *South Slav Journal* (London), and an honorary visiting research fellow in the Research Unit in Southeast European Studies at the University of Bradford. He has published a number of monographs and, as sole author or coeditor, five books, the most recent being *Yugoslavia in Transition* (New York and Oxford: Berg, 1992). He writes regularly for publications such as *Jane's Intelligence Review, Conflict International, Construction Europe, South Slav Journal, World of Information,* and *World News.* He is presently working on the *Serbia* volume for ABC-CLIO's World Bibliographical Series.

David A. Norris graduated from the London School of Slavonic and East European Studies in Serbo-Croat language and literature and completed his Ph.D. dissertation on Serbian writer Miloš Crnjanski in 1989. He is author of *The Novels of Miloš Crnjanski: An Approach through Time* (Nottingham, England: Astra Press, 1990) and *Teach Yourself Serbo-Croat* (London: Hodder and Stoughton, 1993). He is currently lecturer in Serbian and Croatian studies at the University of Nottingham, teaching language, history, and culture.

Sava Peić is a curator and head of Southeast European collections at the British Library in London. He also teaches Serbo-Croatian language and literature at Kensington and Chelsea College. He has organized exhibitions in the United Kingdom and in many parts of the former Yugoslavia and the Balkans and has also been involved with the organization of donations to restore the stock of the National Library of Bosnia-Hercegovina in Sarajevo. He has compiled the volume *Balkan Crisis: Catalogue 1* (London: British Library, 1997) and is author of *Medieval Serbian Culture* (London: Alpine Fine Arts, 1995).

Oliver P. Ramsbotham and **Tom Woodhouse** are senior lecturers in peace studies at the University of Bradford, where they direct the work of the Conflict Resolution Centre. Their major research area is the relationship of peacekeeping to conflict resolution theory, in which they have recently focused on the former Yugoslavia. In addition to their numerous individual publications in the field of peace studies, they are the joint authors of the volume *Humanitarian Intervention in Contemporary Conflict* (Cambridge: Polity Press, 1996).

James D. D. Smith received his first degree in peace and war studies at the University of Calgary and his Ph.D. in war studies from King's College, London, in 1992. He was scholar in residence at Calgary for 1995–1996 and is currently lecturer in peace studies at the University of Bradford. He has published widely on cease-fires and the Yugoslav conflict, including the book *Stopping Wars* (Boulder, CO: Westview Press, 1995) and two studies: "Canada in Croatia" (Strategic and Combat Studies Institute Occasional Paper 15, 1992) and, with James Gow, "Peacemaking, Peacekeeping: European Security and the Yugoslav Conflict" (*London Defence Studies* 11, 1995).

Paul Stubbs is associate senior research fellow of the Globalism and Social Policy Programme (GASSP) at the University of Sheffield, UK, and STAKES (National Center for Health and Social Welfare Research) in Helsinki, Finland. He has worked with, and written on, nongovernmental organizations in post-Yugoslav countries since 1993 and has edited the book *Social Policy in Bosnia-Hercegovina,* due to be published by Školska knjiga of Sarajevo.

Michael J. Welton graduated in history at Middlesex University, England, in 1996. His current research is concerned with the psychology of revolution and the recourse to violence, with particular reference to the roots of the Yugoslav conflict.

Antonia T. Young is honorary research associate in sociology/anthropology at Colgate University and honorary research fellow in Southeast European studies at the University of Bradford. She has held an interest in the Balkans for four decades. With John Allcock she edited *Black Lambs and Grey Falcons: Women Travellers in the Balkans* (Bradford, England: Bradford University Press, 1991) and she has just completed *Albania* in the World Bibliographical Series for ABC-CLIO. She conducts an ongoing project concerned with peace and conflict resolution in Shkodra, was a member of the Organization for Security and Cooperation in Europe's team of observers for Albania's parliamentary election in June 1997, and was OSCE supervisor for the Serbian assembly elections in November the same year. Her cocontributor, **Nigel J. Young**, is Cooley Professor of Peace Studies at Colgate.

MAP 1:
THE FORMER YUGOSLAVIA AND ITS SUCCESSOR REPUBLICS IN THEIR REGIONAL CONTEXT

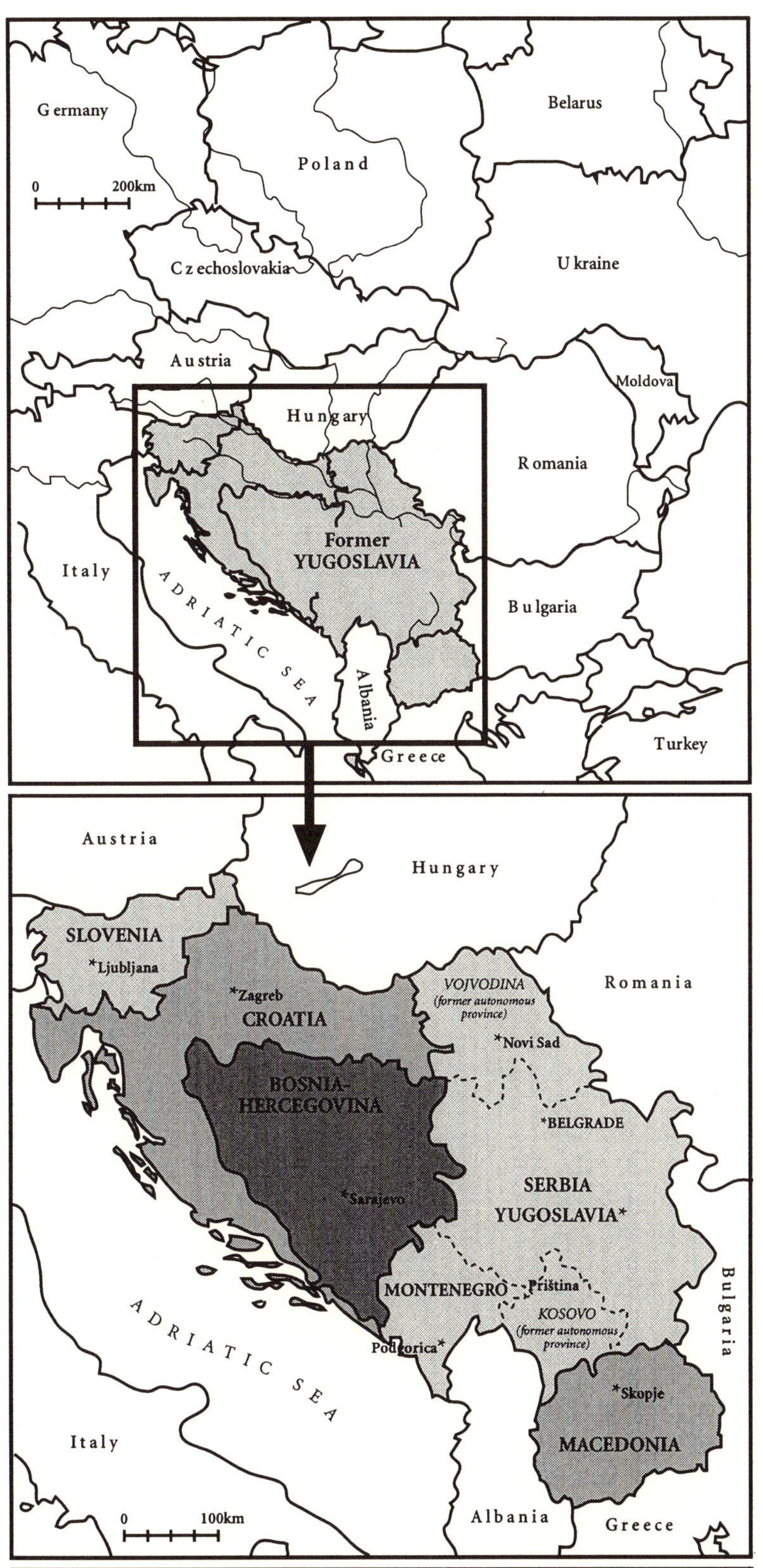

*Declared by Serbia and Montenegro in April 1992, the Federal Republic of Yugoslavia is not recognized internationally as being sole successor of the former Yugoslav Federation.

MAP 2:
PHYSICAL GEOGRAPHY, MAIN REGIONS, PRINCIPAL TRANSPORTATION ROUTES, AND MOST POPULOUS CITIES OF THE FORMER YUGOSLAVIA

MAP 3:
DISTRIBUTION OF PEOPLES IN THE FORMER YUGOSLAVIA, 1991

MAP 4:

SERB-, CROAT-, AND BOSNIAN MUSLIM-CONTROLLED TERRITORIES IN CROATIA AND BOSNIA-HERCEGOVINA, 1995

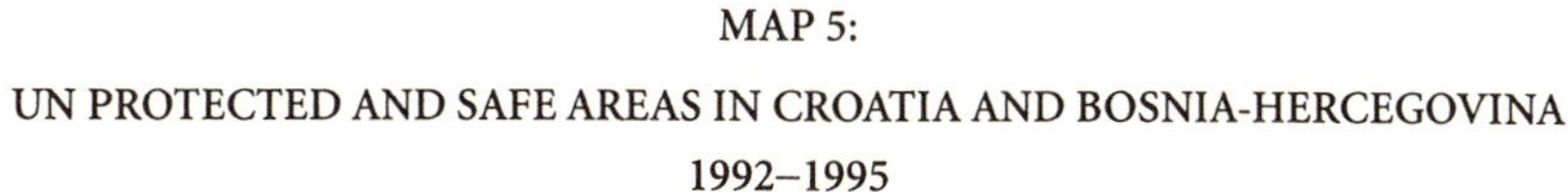

MAP 5:

UN PROTECTED AND SAFE AREAS IN CROATIA AND BOSNIA-HERCEGOVINA 1992–1995

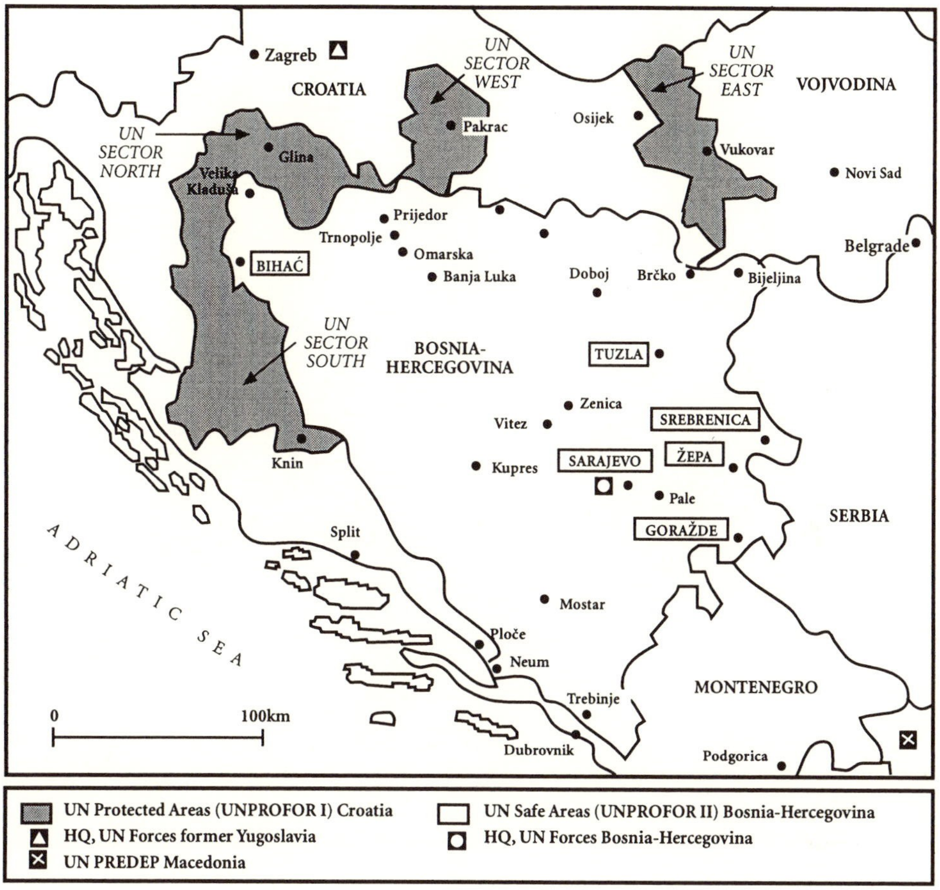

UN Protected Areas (UNPROFOR I) Croatia
UN Safe Areas (UNPROFOR II) Bosnia-Hercegovina
HQ, UN Forces former Yugoslavia
HQ, UN Forces Bosnia-Hercegovina
UN PREDEP Macedonia

MAP 6:

VANCE-OWEN PEACE PLAN, TERRITORIAL DISPENSATION AND AREAS TO BE CEDED UNDER ITS PROVISIONS, 1993

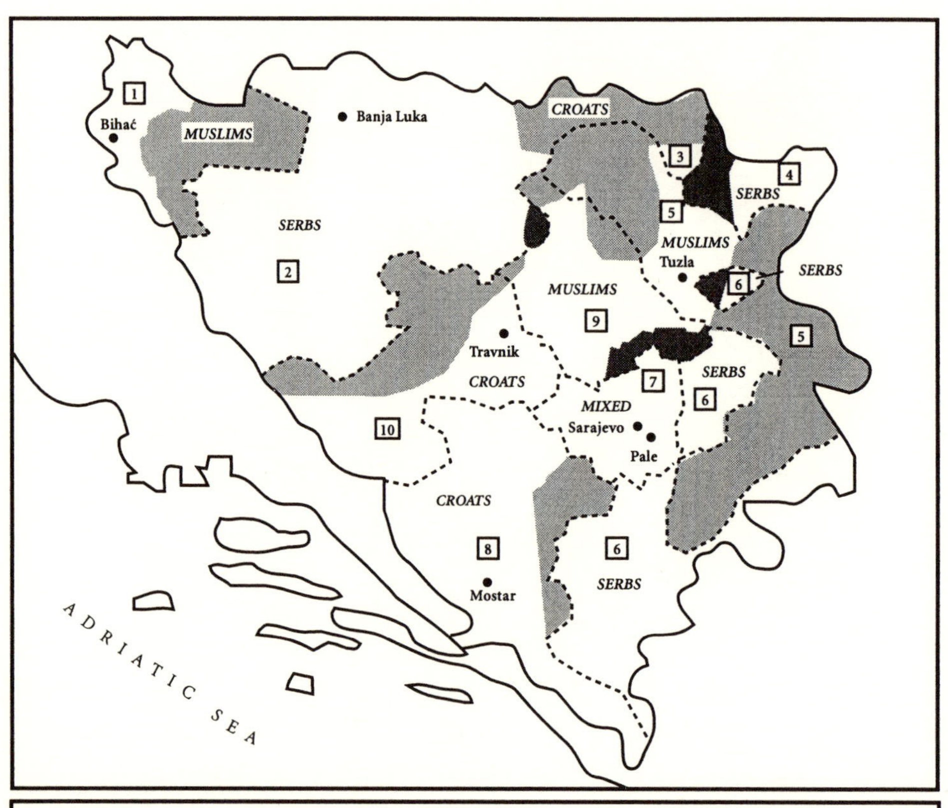

1,5,9 Muslim Provinces 2,4,6 Serb Provinces 3,8,10 Croat Provinces

Areas from which Bosnian Serb forces would need to withdraw according to the plan

Areas from which Muslim and Croat forces would need to withdraw according to the plan

MAP 7:
CONTACT GROUP PEACE PLAN TERRITORIAL DISPENSATION BETWEEN THE FEDERATION AND THE SERB ENTITY, 1994

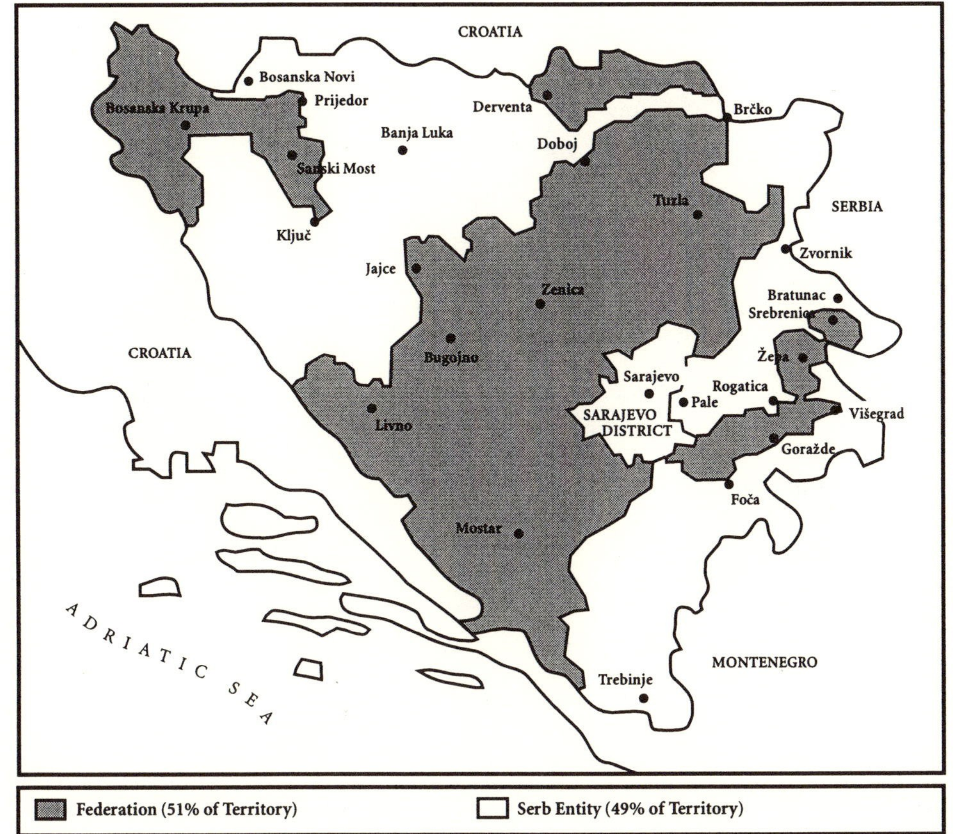

MAP 8:
SERB, CROAT, AND BOSNIAN MUSLIM GOVERNMENT-CONTROLLED TERRITORIES AND THEIR ESTIMATED POPULATIONS ON THE EVE OF THE DAYTON PEACE AGREEMENT, OCTOBER 1995

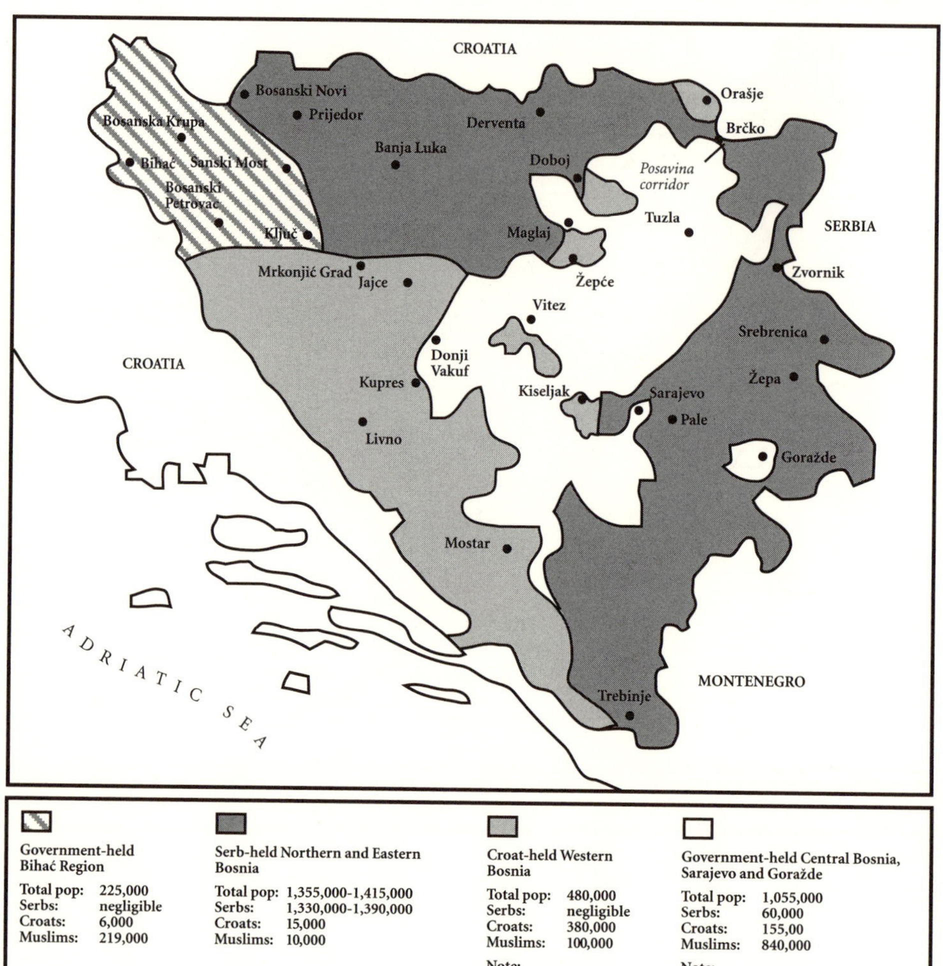

MAP 9:
DAYTON PEACE AGREEMENT TERRITORIAL DISPENSATION, INTERENTITY BOUNDARY LINE, AND I/SFOR OPERATIONAL ZONES, 1995–1998

IFOR AND SFOR OPERATIONAL ZONES: ❶ UK ❷ US ❸ French

MAP 10:

SERB-BOSNIAN GOVERNMENT FRONT LINES AND MAIN LOCATIONS IN BESIEGED SARAJEVO, 1992–1995

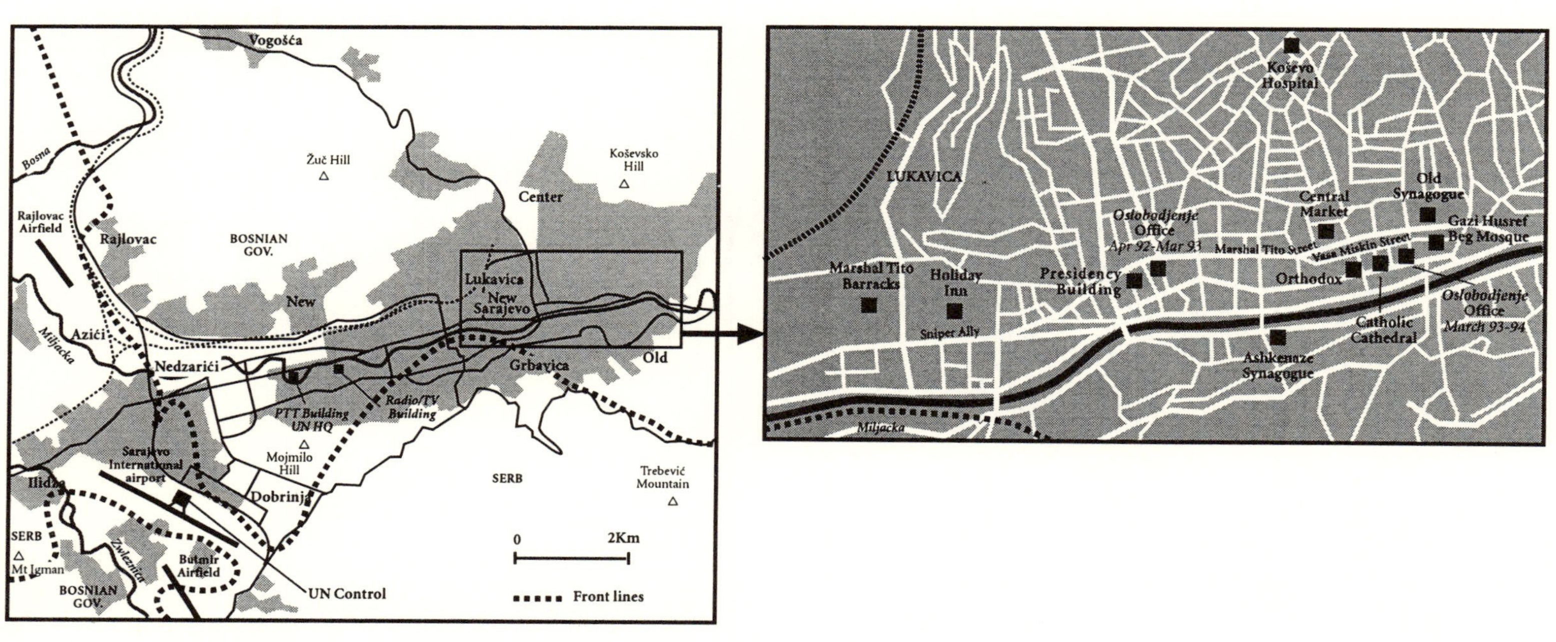

MAP 11:

BRČKO (BOSNIA-HERCEGOVINA) AND PREVLAKA (CROATIA)

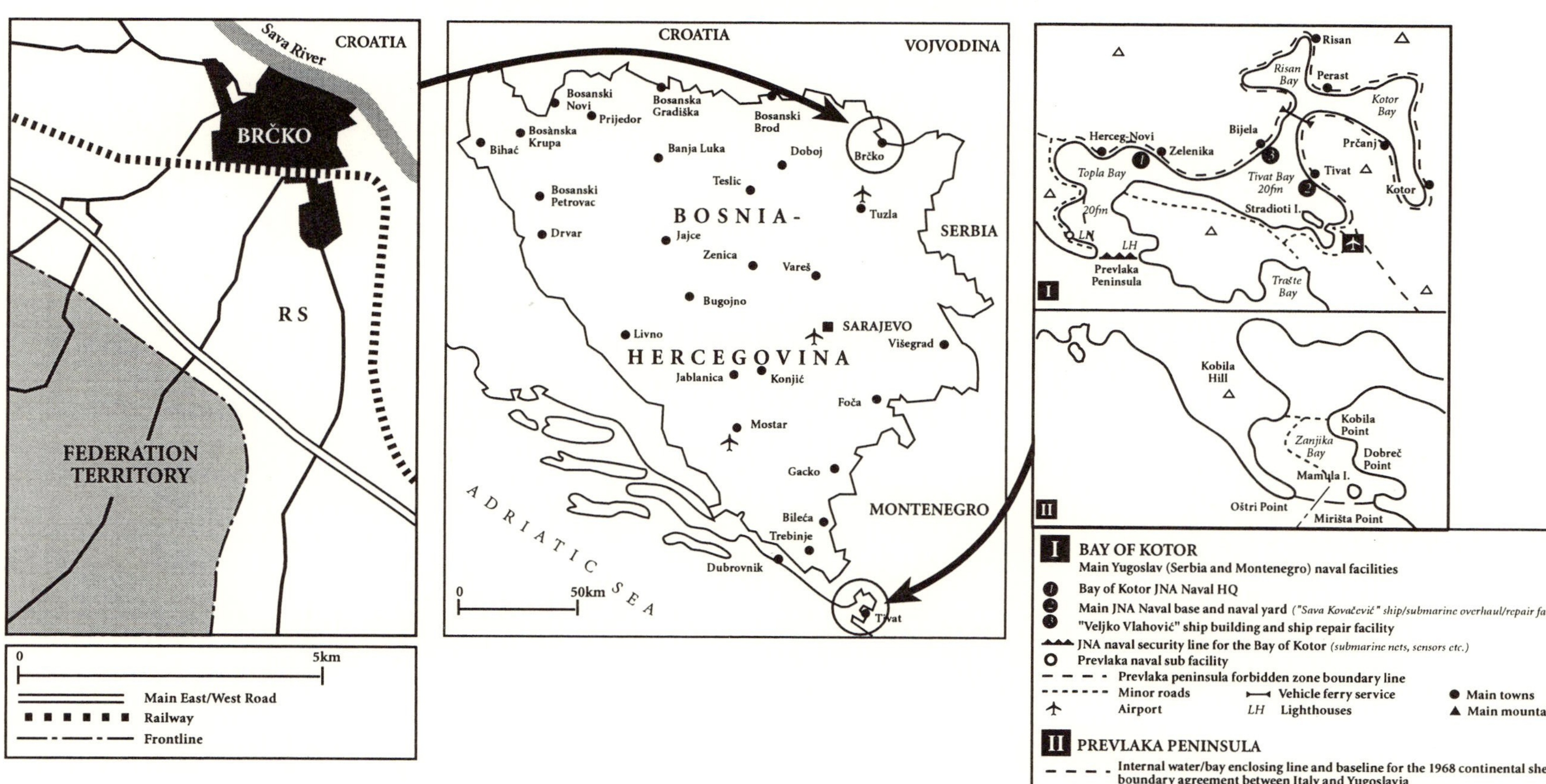

MAP 12:
ALBANIAN AND OTHER AREAS OF SETTLEMENT IN THE SOUTHERN BALKAN REGION

Conflict in the Former Yugoslavia

ABDIĆ, FIKRET

Fikret Abdić (born 1940) was a Muslim leader who turned the **Bihać** area into an independent enclave known as the **Autonomous Province of Western Bosnia** between 1992 and 1995. A leading Bosnian communist in the 1980s, he brought prosperity to Bihać with his dynamic, albeit corrupt, management of Agrokomerc, Yugoslavia's biggest food-processing company, based in Velika Kladuša. In 1987 he was sentenced to two years in prison for issuing a billion dollars' worth of unsecured promissory notes. In the presidential election of 1990, he won more votes than any other Muslim politician, although he failed to win a seat in the collective presidency. Abdić advocated acceptance of the **Owen-Stoltenberg** Plan of July 1993, which involved a union of republics in **Bosnia-Hercegovina** along ethnic lines. Accusing the Bosnian president, **Alija Izetbegović,** of intransigence, this consummate intriguer and tycoon declared the Bihać region to be self-governing on 27 September 1993 and formed his own Muslim Democratic Party in opposition to the **Party of Democratic Action.** He managed to keep the area out of the fighting for some time, selling food, arms, and fuel to the **Bosnian Serbs.** His militia even fought alongside them in 1994–1995 before his power base was overrun in August 1995. Abdić has resettled in the port of Rijeka, where he enjoys the protection of the Croatian authorities. His prominence illustrates the complexity of the war in Bosnia and suggests that it cannot be viewed as a religious conflict alone.

—*T. G.*

See also: arms transfers

ADRIATIC ISLANDS

There are over 1,000 islands lying off the eastern Adriatic coast, stretching from **Istria** in the north down to southern **Dalmatia**; only a small proportion of these islands are inhabited. Although they were virtually unaffected by the recent conflict, their importance during the 1941–1945 war meant that they were included in the recent strategic thinking of the armed forces of both **Croatia** and the international organizations; the islands would have played a larger role had the conflict spread into the naval arena. After a brief bombardment of coastal towns by ships of the Yugoslav navy in 1992, the coastal area ceased to play an active part in the conflict and its involvement was limited to international patrols.

—*J. J. H.*

See also: naval power

ADŽIĆ, BLAGOJE

Col.-Gen. Blagoje Adžić was chief of staff of the **Yugoslav Peoples' Army** (JNA) at the beginning of the Yugoslav wars in 1990–1991 and served briefly as acting federal defense minister in 1992. An ethnic Serb from Croatia, Adžić lost both his parents at the hands of the **Ustaša** during World War II. He joined Tito's **Partizans** in 1943. Adžić's career was spent entirely in the JNA, where he was to become a protégé of future Federal Defense Minister Col.-Gen. **Veljko Kadijević** during the 1970s and 1980s. Both officers were associated with Federal Defense Minister Admiral Branko Mamula, whom Kadijević replaced in 1988, when Adžić was also elevated to JNA chief of staff.

At the onset of the Yugoslav crisis in 1989–1990, Kadijević and much of the rest of the JNA high command were generally supportive of the federal premier at the time, **Ante Marković,** seeing in him and his policies the best and perhaps only hope of preserving a federal Yugoslavia. Once the federation began to unravel in 1990–1991, Adžić parted company from Kadijević, adopting an openly pro-Serb stance. Although weakened by illness, Adžić advocated a hard-line policy against both **Slovenia** and **Croatia**. Within the general staff, he was closely involved in controversial contingency plans, code-named Ram-1 and Ram-2, to deal with secessionist republics. Under Adžić the military counterintelligence service, KOS, was also used to covertly arm ethnic Serb militias in both Croatia and **Bosnia**. These activities were closely coordinated with the secret services controlled by Serbian president **Slobodan Milošević**.

The JNA leadership under Kadijević and Adžić failed either to preserve a communist Yugoslav federation by force or to maintain its own institutional autonomy, becoming little more than an instrument of Milošević. For all his bluster, Adžić was ineffective and confused at a critical moment in the Yugoslav crisis. Bereft as they were of a state to defend by 1991, both Kadijević and Adžić were easily manipulated by Milošević for his own political purposes, none of which had much to do with the survival of the JNA or, indeed, of Yugoslavia.

Upon the resignation of Kadijević in January 1992, Adžić briefly served as acting federal defense minister—a development that was widely regarded as a victory for the hard-line faction in the JNA. The fact that Milošević had de facto control of the JNA by this time, however, meant that he could easily disregard Adžić's views on any aspect of policy. Subsequently, Adžić was retired on medical grounds and replaced as federal defense minister by a more politically pliant figure, Col.-Gen. Života Panić.

—M. M.

AESTHETIC RESISTANCE

The expression "aesthetic resistance" came to be used to cover a wide range of actions intended to sustain morale among the besieged citizens of **Sarajevo** by insisting upon the maintenance of "normal" standards of self-presentation, including personal cleanliness, respectable clothing, shaving, and attention to hair care or makeup. Its use broadened to include the preservation of a "normal" artistic life in the community through the organization of concerts, exhibitions, and theater. During the siege of Sarajevo, supplies of basic utilities essential for sustaining standards of personal hygiene and appearance previously accepted as normal were often cut off or interrupted. People often had to carry water from sources at some distance from the home, facing considerable risk from snipers and artillery fire; once obtained, the water was difficult to heat. The idea of aesthetic resistance became important, however, to the city as a symbol of its image as an "oasis" of European civilization surrounded by forces of backwardness, ignorance, and intolerance.

—J. B. A.

AGOŠTAN, ANDRAŠ

A Yugoslav Magyar publisher and politician, Andraš Agoštan was born in 1952 in Subotica in the **Vojvodina**. He was educated at the University of Novi Sad and subsequently worked as a professional publisher. A deputy director of the *Forum* publishing enterprise by 1990, he cofounded the Democratic Community of Vojvodina Magyars (DCVM) in August of that year. As the main ethnic Hungarian party in the Vojvodina, the DCVM gained five seats in the Serbian assembly in the first postwar multiparty parliamentary **elections** in December 1990. Although often accused of irredentism in relation to neighboring Hungary, Agoštan's DCVM has campaigned for ethnic Hungarian minority rights in **Serbia** and the restoration of the Vojvodina's provincial autonomy, which was abolished by the Serbian government during 1988–1990. Agoštan has also been a prominent opposition critic of the policies of President **Slobodan Milošević** outside Serbia during the Yugoslav wars. A member of the Democratic Movement of Serbia (DEPOS), which contested elections in Serbia in December 1992 and December 1993, Agoštan and the DCVM have more recently been weakened by factional infighting among the Vojvodina's ethnic Hungarian community.

—M. M.

AHMIĆI

On 16 April 1993, a small band of Croatian militiamen from the **Croatian Council of Defense** (HVO) entered the central Bosnian village of Ahmići, a Muslim community of 500 people—swelled by recent refugees from the fall of **Jajce**—in an area of Croatian settlements. They destroyed over 50 homes with grenades and killed over 100 occupants (according to the United Nations High Commission for Refugees) regardless of age or gender; the fates of many others who fled or were captured are less certain. It is unlikely that the attack was planned as a clandestine operation. For one, it was a deadly mixture of unbridled ethnic opportunism and overt propagandistic violence at a time when international attention was focused on events in **Srebrenica.** In addition, it took place only three miles from the British regimental base representing the peacekeeping force **UNPROFOR** (United Nations Protection Force) at **Vitez.** The evidence for the Ahmići massacre was presented two days later in **Martin Bell**'s film of the scene for British Broadcasting Company (BBC) Television, which also records the personal encounter between an HVO commander and the commanding officer of the British troops in Bosnia, Lt. Col. **Bob Stewart.**

—J. J. H.

AID
See **humanitarian aid**

AIR POWER
Although never as decisive as its advocates claimed, the use of air power nevertheless played a major role in bringing the Yugoslav wars to an end in 1995. During the initial stages, air power did not figure prominently in the military strategy of local belligerents. The powerful air force of the **Yugoslav Peoples' Army** (JNA) was rarely used during the Ten Day War of June-July 1991 in **Slovenia** or the first Serb-Croat war in Croatia. Artillery rather than aerial bombardment caused most of the destruction in **Croatia** and **Bosnia-Hercegovina** in 1991–1992. In both Croatia and Bosnia, however, the departing JNA left a number of combat aircraft and helicopters, as well as military airfields, to the **Serb Army of the Krajina** (SAK) and the **Bosnian Serb Army** (BSA). At Udbina in the Serb Krajina, the SAK maintained a small military airfield from 1991 to 1995. In the **Republika Srpska** (RS), the departing JNA evacuated the main military aircraft factory at **Mostar** and destroyed the largest military air base at **Bihać** in 1991–1992, leaving a number of smaller military airfields for the BSA in eastern and northwestern Bosnia.

For most of the war, air power was not available to the **Bosnian Croat** and Muslim (Bošnjak) belligerents. Except for some relatively minor air operations in support of the BSA in Bosnia-Hercegovina, the Yugoslav air force was kept out of the Bosnian war, notwithstanding its proximity to this theater

NATO fighter aircraft in Bosnia-Hercegovina, Operation Deny Flight. (NATO photograph)

from its bases in **Serbia** and **Montenegro**. Most BSA military flights in 1992–1993 were used to transport troops and supplies.

In October 1992, when the United Nations Protection Force (**UNPROFOR**) mandate for Bosnia-Hercegovina was renewed, United Nations (UN) Security Council Resolution 781 banned all military flights in Bosnian airspace. Although this resolution authorized UNPROFOR to monitor compliance, the peacekeeping force lacked the power to enforce the **no-fly zone**. By March 1993, the number of violations of the no-fly zone by the BSA air force had reached 500, which prompted the UN finally to authorize the shooting down of all unauthorized military aircraft by **North Atlantic Treaty Organization** (NATO) forces operating under UNPROFOR command. Following the creation by the Security Council of six "**safe areas**" in June 1993, the same body authorized UNPROFOR to use force, including air power, to defend these areas from attack by the BSA. Around the Bosnian capital, **Sarajevo**, the UN secretary-general further authorized NATO forces to mount airstrikes against BSA artillery and other positions for the first time in February 1994.

Already involved in Operation Deny Flight over Bosnian and surrounding Serb-controlled territories, where the UN's no-fly zone was monitored by Airborne Warning and Control System (AWACS) aircraft and U.S. surveillance satellites, NATO air power was subsequently used in an offensive capacity to break the Bosnian Serb siege of Sarajevo. The strongest advocate of the tactical use of air power in Bosnia was the **United States**, which also favored the lifting of the 1991 UN arms embargo against the Bošnjaks in a policy that came to be known as "Lift and Strike." This U.S. emphasis on the use of air power was resisted for the most part by both the UN and the mainly British and French NATO forces that constituted the operational core of UNPROFOR II. Bombing the Bosnian Serbs at the behest of a NATO member that did not have ground forces in Bosnia, however, led to **hostage taking** of British, French, and other UNPROFOR troops. Only after the summer of 1995, when UNPROFOR II was more compactly deployed in Bosnia, was the ground clear for sustained and serious NATO air attacks against the BSA.

Using the NATO air base at Aviano in Italy, the U.S. carrier–based forces that were then deployed in the Adriatic Sea mounted airstrikes in the autumn of 1995, principally aimed at BSA air defenses, **communications** networks, and other military infrastructure and hardware. This sustained NATO air campaign played a major role in helping to bring the war to an end, although the fact that the BSA was also seriously weakened by the Bosnian Croat-Bošnjak offensive in western Bosnia was of equal significance in paving the way for the **Dayton Agreements** of December 1995.

—*M. M.*

AKASHI, YASUSHI

Born in Japan in 1931, Yasushi Akashi was educated at Japanese and U.S. universities before embarking upon an uninterrupted career as administrator and diplomat with the **United Nations** (UN) in 1957. Following a period as undersecretary general for disarmament affairs and a posting in Cambodia, he was appointed as the UN secretary-general's special envoy to Yugoslavia, succeeding **Thorvald Stoltenberg** in January 1994; he held the post until October 1995. His period of office thus spanned (coincidentally rather than intentionally) the most difficult period of the war for the United Nations, starting with the Serb assault on **Goražde** in early 1994 and the final fall of **Srebrenica** in August 1995. This involved him in disputes between the UN and the **North Atlantic Treaty Organization** (NATO) over airstrikes, between the UN and the **United States** on decision making, and within the UN itself as it sought to clarify its role. Akashi's generally cautious approach was a source of vehemently expressed frustration on the part of the Bosnian government as he sought in vain to initiate peace processes through shuttle diplomacy between Zagreb, Belgrade, **Pale**, and Sarajevo.

His constructive reflections on "The limits of UN diplomacy and the future of conflict mediation" with specific reference to the Yugoslav wars are set down in an article that appeared in the journal *Survival* (37[4]:83-98, Winter 1995–1996).

—*J. J. H.*

ALBANIA

The Republic of Albania (capital Tirana, which has a population of 600,000) is situated south of **Montenegro**, west of **Serbia** and of the Republic of **Macedonia**, north of **Greece**, and east of the

Adriatic and Ionian Seas. It is three-quarters mountainous. Its present population of 3.2 million is made up of 91 percent **Albanians**, 7 percent Greeks, and the remaining 2 percent Vlachs, Macedonians, Serbs, Roma, Bulgarians, and Montenegrins. After World War II, Albania had the highest population growth rate in Europe until 1990; since then the rate has fallen slightly. The Albanian language is spoken in two dialect forms: Geg to the north of the Shkumbin River and Tosk to the south. Geg is also the language of Kosovar Albanians in **Serbia**.

In 1967 Albania was proclaimed the world's first atheist state. After the ban was lifted at the end of 1990, however, the population was found to be, as before World War II, approximately 70 percent Muslim and 30 percent Christian (20 percent Orthodox and 10 percent Catholic), although levels of active observance are low and Albanians are very tolerant of one another's religions.

Albania has a primarily agricultural economy, with 65 percent of the population living in rural areas. Although rich in mineral resources, Albania lacks the technology and infrastructure to exploit these resources economically. Mining installations built during the periods of Soviet influence (1948–1961) and Chinese influence (1961–1978) have deteriorated beyond repair.

Albania was the last Balkan country to become free of **Ottoman** domination. Its present-day borders were defined in 1913 by the Great Powers (Austro-Hungary, France, Great Britain, and Russia), leaving as many Albanians outside Albania as within (most of those left outside fell within the borders of the former Yugoslavia). Last to gain freedom from communism, Albania held its first free elections in 1991, resulting in a majority Communist coalition government, which lasted only a few months. This coalition's collapse was followed by several months of anarchy. Thousands fled the country at this time to Italy, Greece, and the former Yugoslavia.

In March 1992 the Democratic Party won a sweeping victory under Sali Berisha and Aleksander Meksi. Economic recovery was initially assisted by international aid, and by 1993 Albania was shown to have the fastest-growing economy and lowest inflation rate in all the former communist Eastern European countries. Berisha's autocratic behavior soon disenchanted many of his former supporters, however, who created a new Democratic Alliance. After Berisha failed to win the referendum for a new constitution in November 1994, his efforts to silence opposition increased. Although national and international observers claimed that his party's victory in the May 1996 election was fraudulent, Berisha continued to receive strong U.S. and European support.

After 1992, individuals developed "pyramid" investment schemes that paid out very high interest rates to their first investors. These schemes grew rapidly, involving more than half the population as well as wealthy expatriates. Considerable sums of money were also made by illicit transport of oil through Albania to Montenegro in defiance of the trade embargo on Yugoslavia. Although this practice helped to support the pyramid schemes, it only delayed their eventual collapse. When investors began to panic in January 1997, demanding the return of their capital, police responded to peaceful demonstrations with violence. Cheated investors held the government to blame for condoning the schemes, and there were claims that members of the government were among the beneficiaries. As popular frustration rose, violence and looting rapidly got out of hand, armories were ransacked, and Berisha in turn supplied arms to all those he believed were his supporters. By May 1997 it was estimated that more than a million weapons were in the hands of the general population. Armed gangs took control of large areas of the country; 1,800 people are believed to have died violent deaths.

The solution to this state of anarchy was seen to lie in fresh, closely observed elections. In March 1997 a caretaker government of national reconciliation under Bashkim Fino of the Socialist Party took over. A state of emergency was introduced, backed by an Italian-led multinational force of 7,000; it lasted until the newly elected parliament met in July. The election of 29 June showed such a clear majority for the Socialist Party that, even allowing for some irregularities in voting propriety, it could not be disputed. Fatos Nano (who had spent four years in jail following his arrest on dubious charges of embezzlement) became prime minister and Rexhep Mejdani became president. Cautious optimism brought renewed international support to Albania.

The combination of Albania's internal instability, its long **border** with the former **Yugoslavia**, and its large Albanian minority ensured that Albania remained a focus of interest throughout the period of Yugoslavia's disintegration.

Concern within Albania for the Albanian population of **Kosovo** ("Kosova" in Albanian) varied throughout the communist period depending on Albania's relationship with Yugoslavia. **Tito**'s campaign of "Brotherhood and Unity" encouraged a bridge-building attitude that Albania accepted to varying degrees, depending in particular on the extent of isolationism pursued by Albania's communist leader, Enver Hoxha (head of state from 1945 until his death in 1985). During the early 1980s, Yugoslavia became one of Albania's major trading partners, and for some years the nations' ideological differences were minimized. A new railway between Titograd (**Podgorica**) and Shkodra was opened in 1986. In 1988 Albanian representatives attended the Balkan Foreign Ministers Conference in Belgrade and affirmed their friendship with Yugoslavia. At this time Albanian relations were better with the Yugoslav capital of Belgrade than with **Priština**, the capital of Kosovo.

As Serb-Kosovar relations deteriorated, however, the government of the Albanian capital city of Tirana protested against the treatment of Kosovars. Kosovars were encouraged by support from Albania itself in the face of increasingly frequent abuses of human rights. Albania gave official recognition to the September 1991 referendum declaring that the "Republic of Kosova" should be a sovereign and independent state. Berisha expected sympathy from the United States and Western Europe for his original support for unification, but he did not find it forthcoming. At the same time, Kosovars were regarded as unscrupulous and unpopular among the people of Albania, and domestic interest in unification declined. With encouragement from the U.S. ambassador in Tirana, William Ryerson, Berisha proposed a plan for the Kosovo issue involving the **North Atlantic Treaty Organization** (NATO) and the **United Nations**, for which he was commended for his restraint. Likewise in Macedonia, Berisha initially offered strong support to Albanians. Their oppression by Slav Macedonians was not as severe as that suffered by Kosovar Albanians, however, and Berisha was unable to maintain this support. Since the fall of Berisha, the Albanian and Macedonian governments have cooperated to reduce the flow of illicit weapons into Macedonia. The smaller Albanian population in Montenegro has been less well organized and has received less attention from the Albanian government.

—A. T. Y.

ALBANIANS

Like many of the peoples of the **Balkans**, the Albanians live along and across one of the great fault lines of Europe. They have both formed a frontier and lived on a battlefield. Their mountains have both unified and divided them. They have been conquered and reconquered, and their neighbors have coveted the strategic ports of the coast and the mineral wealth contained within their mountains. Their passes, especially the Egnatian Way, have served both as gateways for trade between East and West and as retreat routes. Ottomans and Greeks have conquered from the south, Bulgarians and Serbs from the east, and Italians from the west. All have played their part in the Albanians' conflictual history.

Albania is the only country whose population within its borders is almost equaled by the number around its borders. This situation resulted from the decision of the Great Powers at the London Conference of Ambassadors in 1912. Around two million Albanians live in the republics of the former Yugoslavia, particularly in **Serbia**'s province of **Kosovo** ("Kosova" in Albanian), where they make up 90 percent of the population. About 23 percent of the 1.9 million population of the Republic of **Macedonia** are Albanians. In **Montenegro** approximately 82,000 Albanians constitute 6 percent of the country's population.

The dramatic lack of correspondence between international **borders** and the pattern of ethnic settlement has been a focus of considerable local and international anxiety during the period of Yugoslavia's disintegration. There have been widespread expectations that the breakdown of the state in Yugoslavia could result in pressures for the unification of Albanians. In June 1991, Xhelil Gjoni, one of three secretaries who led the Albanian Party of Labor, likened the division of Albanians to that of Germans once separated by the Berlin Wall. Intervention from Albania is believed to be partly responsible for the splitting of the Macedonian Party of Democratic Prosperity in 1994, as well as for the emergence of a faction favoring unification and led by Menduh Thaçi and Arben Xhaferi. Thus far, the combination of external diplomatic pressure, the deterrent effect of Albania's internal disorder upon Yugoslav Albanians, and political divisions within the Albanian diaspora have prevented the realization of these expectations.

—A. T. Y. and N. J. Y.

ARK

See **peace movements**

ARKAN

See **Ražnjatović, Željko**

ARMS TRANSFERS

Throughout the Yugoslav conflict, the military balance among the various parties and arms transfers from other states were important issues. When war broke out in summer 1991, the Serb-dominated **Yugoslav Peoples' Army** (JNA) was militarily the most powerful force in the disintegrating country, enabling it (alongside Croatian Serb **paramilitary/irregular forces**) to seize significant parts of Croatia (particularly the **Krajina** region). When the conflict spread to **Bosnia-Hercegovina** in 1992, JNA support and arms supplies allowed **Bosnian Serb** forces to make substantial military advances. As it became clear that **United Nations** (UN) peacekeeping forces were unable to end the fighting or reverse Croatian and Bosnian Serb gains, external arms supplies came to be an important means of altering the military situation on the ground.

In an effort to limit the conflict, the UN Security Council imposed an arms embargo on all the former Yugoslav states in September 1991. Although the embargo was partially effective, it is widely believed that various states and companies violated its terms. The secrecy that surrounds the international arms trade, however, makes it difficult to ascertain which states and companies supplied arms to the various factions. Arms transfers became intertwined, with ties among the various parties to the Yugoslav conflict and their international supporters. **Russia** was reported to have supplied arms to the Croatian and Bosnian Serbs, partly based on support for its Slavic kin. Muslim states such as Saudi Arabia and **Turkey** were reported to have supplied arms to the Bosnian **Muslims**.

As the inability of the international community to halt the Yugoslav conflict became clear, debate emerged over whether to lift the UN arms embargo selectively. Critics of the embargo (particularly in the **United States** Congress) argued that if the international community was unable to defend the Bosnian Muslims, it should at least enable them to defend themselves by lifting the arms embargo. Supporters of the embargo argued that lifting the embargo would create not a "level playing field" but a "level killing field." In 1993, the Clinton administration came to power in the United States committed to a policy of "lift and strike": lifting the arms embargo against the Bosnian Muslims and supporting them with airstrikes against the Bosnian Serbs. It was, however, unable to persuade its allies, and the arms embargo remained in place. The Bosnian Muslim (and particularly Croatian) armed forces, however, were gradually strengthened, paving the way for both the reversal of earlier Serb military advances and the **Dayton Agreements** in 1995. The strengthening of the Croatian and Bosnian Muslim armed forces is widely thought to have been achieved-with U.S. acquiescence at least (if not covert support)-through such means as Military Professional Resources Incorporated (MPRI), a private U.S. company.

Dilemmas concerning arms transfers emerged during the course of the Dayton peace process. The United States argued that a stable peace required the strengthening of the Bosnian Muslim armed forces, and Congress passed legislation to "train and equip" these forces. However, the United States' Western European allies argued that there was a tension—if not an outright contradiction—between this policy and the military confidence-building and arms limitation elements of the Dayton Agreements.

—A. S. C.

ARMY

See **Bosnian army; Croatian Army; Serb Army of the Krajina; Slovenian Army; Yugoslav Peoples' Army**

ART TREASURES

The loss of artistic treasures from religious buildings, museums, and **libraries** in Croatia and Bosnia during the Yugoslav conflicts resulted from both indiscriminate destruction and targeted cultural vandalism. However, there is also evidence of looting for profit. Croatian authorities claim that a quarter of a million items are missing without trace

This 1991 image shows a deliberately destroyed and ransacked Catholic church in Vukovar. (Nikomoy Faynia)

from their museums; in addition, icons, as well as other religious artifacts, taken from both Catholic and Orthodox churches continue to appear for sale in catalogs unofficially distributed around Europe, particularly England. Items from churches in former Yugoslavia often bear no record of ownership and are therefore difficult to identify, intercept, and return to their original locations.

—J. J. H.

AUSTRIA

From a historical perspective, Austria should have been a central player in the Yugoslav crisis. As part of the Austro-Hungarian (**Habsburg**) Empire, **Slovenia** had been ruled from Vienna and **Croatia** from Budapest. **Bosnia-Hercegovina** had been annexed in 1908, and its capital, **Sarajevo**, provided the setting for the assassination of Archduke Franz Ferdinand by a member of Mlada Bosna (Young Bosnia, a Serb terrorist organization). The empire's subsequent attack on **Serbia** marked the start of World War I.

Initial signs indicated Austria was ready to exert a leading role in the area once again. As early as March 1991, Austrian foreign minister Alois Mock stated that should the Yugoslav republics demand independence, their cases should be considered urgently and seriously. Although committed to dealing with the federal authorities in Belgrade, the Austrian government made clear its wish to prevent the use of force in Yugoslavia. Within days of the secession of Slovenia from **Yugoslavia**, the Greens in Austria's legislature had presented to the foreign policy committee of the parliament a resolution calling for the full **recognition** of Slovenia. There was also some highly speculative talk about the possible creation of a "confederation" of the two nations.

Austrian prime minister Vranitzsky kept his distance from these more extreme enthusiasms, but he did his best to encourage his larger European neighbors to take seriously the burgeoning Yugoslav crisis. Austria recommended that a committee of experts be sent to the republics to help them settle their affairs throughout May and June 1991. Typically, however, Vranitzky and Mock found their initiatives brushed to one side, as happened at the meeting of the **Council for Security and Cooperation in Europe** held in Berlin in June 1991. In any event, although substantial sections of the Austrian electorate favored the cases of Croatia and Slovenia, the government proved sufficiently levelheaded not to embroil itself too deeply or unilaterally. Equally important, it lacked the international clout to lead European opinion, and as a result it played only a marginal political role in the evolving tragedy.

In terms of **arms transfers** and supply, however, Austria was not without significance. During the early summer of 1991, Austrian dealers, especially those in Styria and Kärnten, sold substantial quantities of weaponry to Yugoslav nationalists.

—M. H.

AUSTRO-HUNGARIAN EMPIRE

See **Habsburg Empire**

AUTONOMOUS PROVINCE OF WESTERN BOSNIA

The Autonomous Province of Western Bosnia is the title that was given to the enclave of the "**Bihać** pocket," which centered on the communes of **Cazin** and Velika Kladuša. In September 1993 this enclave, under the leadership of former businessman **Fikret Abdić**, attempted to detach itself from Bosnian government control. When negotiations over the **Owen-Stoltenberg** Plan for Bosnia of July 1993 collapsed, Abdić declared the autonomy of the Cazinska krajina. The project, called the Autonomous Province of Western Bosnia, was brought to an end when it was forcibly disbanded by the Bosnian Fifth Corps in August 1995. Nevertheless, this episode does underline the importance of not assuming homogeneity of political opinion on the basis of ethnic identity.

—J. B. A.

AVRAMOVIĆ, DRAGOSLAV

Dragoslav Avramović is a Yugoslav (Serbian) economist, former economic adviser to the World Bank, and governor of the National Bank of Yugoslavia (NBJ). Born in 1919 in Belgrade, he was educated at that city's university and participated in the National Liberation War (1941–1944). After the war, he worked as an academic economist and adviser, including 20 years at the World Bank in Washington, D.C. Well regarded internationally, Avramović was invited back to Belgrade to take up the position of governor of the NBJ in December 1993. Earlier the same year, the economy of the Federal Republic of **Yugoslavia** had experienced devastating hyper**inflation**. Through his radical financial and economic reforms, including the introduction of a new Yugoslav dinar linked to the German mark in January 1994, Avramović partially stabilized the Yugoslav economy. Although initially supported by Serbian president **Slobodan Milošević**, Avramović later came into conflict with him, notably after Avramović publicly advocated more radical structural reform of the Yugoslav economy in 1995. Following the lifting of the United Nations (UN) economic **sanctions** in December 1995, Avramović further clashed with Milošević over the issue of Yugoslavia's possible readmission to the **International Monetary Fund**. In May 1996, Avramović was dismissed as NBJ governor by a vote in the federal assembly.

—M. M.

See also: banking; economic dimension

B

BABIĆ, MILAN

Milan Babić (born 1956) was a leader of the Croatian Serbs during their struggle for autonomy. Babić was a dentist in **Knin** who broke away from the Croatian League of Communists in 1989 in order to found a new political party. Eventually joining **Jovan Rašković**'s Serbian Democratic Party (SDS), Babić worked his way up to become mayor of Knin and the second most important man in the SDS. He established his power base by creating the Association of Serbian Municipalities from areas in which Serbs were a majority.

SDS rallies eventually succeeded in forcing the moderates from the leadership. The association convened an assembly, which met on 25 July 1990, and decided to hold a referendum on Serb sovereignty in August. Babić made contacts in Belgrade and grew more outspoken in his opposition to Rašković's notions of cultural autonomy. Babić objected to Rašković's view that the Serbs in Croatia should be only culturally independent—Babić was for political independence. On 12 August 1990, Babić met Petar Gračanin, the federal interior minister, and **Borisav Jović**, the Serbian representative to the federal presidency and its head, in an attempt to get Serbia to publicly support the Croatian Serbs' stand on rejecting the symbols and authority of the new Croatian government. Gračanin rebuked the Croatian interior minister the next day, telling him that he should not attempt to take control of the Knin police station. Babić took this as a signal that he should go ahead with his plans to attain Croatian Serb sovereignty.

Babić led the resistance to the Croatian Police when they moved on Knin with armored vehicles and helicopters on 17 August 1990 in an attempt to quash the Serb rebellion. By February 1991 he was the effective political leader of the **Krajina** Serbs, with **Milan Martić** as his military commander.

Throughout 1991 Babić maintained his power as leader of the Krajina Serbs, but in January 1992 he found himself at odds with **Slobodan Milošević**'s purposes over the **Vance Plan**. He opposed the deployment of the peacekeeeping **UNPROFOR** (United Nations Protection Force) and refused to negotiate over the withdrawal of the **Yugoslav Peoples' Army** (JNA). Milošević organized a campaign against Babić, making use of differences between Babić, on the one hand, and Milan Martić and Mile Paspalj (speaker of the Krajina parliament)—who were both closer to the JNA and Belgrade's position—on the other. Babić was eventually deposed in favor of **Goran Hadžić**, secretary of the **Vukovar** branch of the SDS.

—G. R. B.

BADINTER COMMISSION

The Badinter Commission was the arbitration commission established by the **European Community** (EC) in November 1991; it was composed of five individual members under the chairmanship of Robert Badinter, a French judge and constitutional lawyer. Its purpose had been to advise upon the legal aspects of the dissolution of Yugoslavia (including the distribution of former federal assets) and specifically to prescribe the conditions that would have to be fulfilled by any republic in its bid for **recognition** of its independence by the EC. In its adjudication of the four "applicants," the commission recommended **Slovenia** and **Macedonia** for recognition; **Croatia** was to be conditional upon certain assurances concerning democratic principles, national minorities, and **border** protections; and **Bosnia** was to be subject to a referendum, which, crucially, was to be valid only if all three communities (Serb, Croat, and Muslim) were to participate in significant numbers. (The application from **Kosovo** was considered invalid because it did not come from a recognized republic.)

In the case of Croatia and Macedonia, the EC chose to be influenced by political expediency rather than legal advice. It waived the conditions on Croatia in the interests of **Germany**, and it rejected Macedonia outright in the interests of **Greece**. The Badinter Commission thus became symptomatic of Europe's inability to construct a common foreign policy on the basis of its own procedural structures, and an opportunity was lost to implement a set of recommendations that might not have found general disfavor either outside or inside Yugoslavia.

—J. J. H.

BALKANS

The Balkan Peninsula is the easternmost of the three great southern European peninsulas; the other two are the Iberian and the Apennine. It is bounded on the west by the Adriatic and Mediterranean Seas and on the east by the Black and Aegean Seas. The northern limit is more difficult to precisely characterize since the peninsula has a broad neck joining it to the continental landmass. Traditionally, Yugoslavia, **Bulgaria**, **Albania**, **Greece**, and European **Turkey** form the Balkan states; sometimes **Romania** is included as well. Others searching for natural features to designate the peninsula's northern border point to the river system formed by the **Danube** and **Sava** Rivers. This gives slightly different boundaries and on today's map would inscribe large parts of **Slovenia** and **Croatia** and the southeast corner of Romania, as well as **Bosnia-Hercegovina**, the Federal Republic of **Yugoslavia**, **Macedonia**, Bulgaria, Albania, Greece, and Turkey's territory on the west side of the Bosphorus Strait. This compact area of great contrasts contains numerous national groups speaking many different languages. The terrain is composed of high mountain ranges and fertile plains. It is a poor area, but the average figures hide huge differences between extreme poverty in Albania and the relative affluence of Slovenia.

Each of the Balkan nations can look to some period in the past as a "golden age," such as Dušan the Great's Serbian Empire (1331–1355) or Stefan Tvrtko's Bosnian Kingdom (1353–1391). For much of the postmedieval period, however, the peninsula has been a colonized space. The **Ottoman Empire** advanced into Europe via the Balkans, taking **Serbia** in 1459, Bosnia in 1463, and most of Croatia by the middle of the next century. Ottoman ambitions were eventually checked, and by the Treaty of Karlovci (1699) Croatia, **Slavonia**, and **Hungary** were ceded to the **Habsburg Empire**. The border between the two imperial powers ran through the Balkan region, leaving Serbia as far north as the Danube in Ottoman hands, as well as Bosnia and all territory to the south and east. This border roughly followed the border between the Eastern **Orthodox Church**, with its Byzantine cultural heritage, and the Roman **Catholic** world. For most of Europe, the Balkans remained an unknown place—a Eurasian territory marking the transitional point between Europe and the Orient, with numerous **cultural fault lines** running through it.

In the nineteenth century, all the Balkan nations experienced national revivals, fostering their separate historical and cultural identities. Some achieved political independence; first Serbia, then Greece, then Bulgaria. Colonial rivalry also continued, with the Ottoman Empire weakening while the Habsburg and Russian Empires became intent on spreading their influence. The Habsburg and Russian Empires appealed to the nations of the peninsula to win them over as client-states. The century of colonial expansion into the Balkans culminated in the assassination of Archduke Franz Ferdinand in **Sarajevo** in 1914 and the outbreak of World War I. The Balkan states named above appeared with their modern frontiers after 1918 but were submerged by the Axis Powers in World War II, during which time the peninsula figured again in the strategic geopolitical interests of foreign powers. The division between the Soviet Bloc and the West ran through the region, with Greece in the western sphere; Bulgaria, Romania, and Albania in the Soviet sphere; and Yugoslavia under **Tito** pursuing an independent line, exploiting a middle ground between the two blocs and gaining advantages from both sides. The end of communism and the related consequences will be instrumental in redefining Balkan political alliances.

The tension between the desires of the Balkan peoples to run their own affairs and international pressures from much stronger countries characterizes many developments in the Balkans. Outside interference tends to magnify internal differences, as each group realizes its dependence on patronage from abroad. There have been times when Balkan alliances have been successfully formed—such as in the 1860s and 1930—in pursuit of common regional interests. On other occasions individual interests have led to conflicts, such as the Balkan Wars, World War II, and most recently the Yugoslav Wars of 1991–1995. The West tends to see divisions within the region as a result of a broader cultural divisions between a sophisticated West and primitive East. This perspective ignores the influence of the West's presence, which is one of the decisive factors influencing the shape of internal alliances and conflicts.

The term *Balkans*, besides denoting a geographic region, has other historical and cultural echoes. The word was used by Ottoman geographers to refer to the chain of mountains in northern Bulgaria now known as Stara Planina. By the end of the eighteenth century, the term had been adopted by Western geographers to refer to the whole peninsula. By the end of the nineteenth century, it was used almost exclusively to refer to the Slavonic Orthodox and Muslim areas of the peninsula, thus excluding Greece with its classical civilization and the Catholic areas in the northwest. The Balkan Peninsula was reduced to that cultural space that was considered alien by Western Europe. Later dictionary definitions also included reference to the cognate forms *balkanize* and *balkanization.* These definitions refer to the division of an area into a number of small and hostile units, highlighting the instability, fragmentation, and aggression with which the region has become synonymous in the Western European mind. In this way, the Balkans have been transformed into a symbol of economic, cultural, and political inferiority. During the twentieth century, this myth, created by Western Europe, has helped to mask from foreign powers the consequences of their own actions in the region.

—D. A. N.

Reference: Todorova, Maria N. *Imagining the Balkans.* New York and Oxford: Oxford University Press, 1997.

BANJA LUKA

With a prewar population of about 195,000, Banja Luka is the second largest industrial and urban center in **Bosnia-Hercegovina.** Located 150 miles northwest of Sarajevo, its placement along the Vrbas River makes it a center for major road and rail routes, not only between **Sarajevo** and **Zagreb,** but also across Bosnia between the extended "arms" of **Croatia.** The city was taken early in the war by Serb forces, and because of its economic significance it became in several ways a rival to **Pale,** the **Bosnian Serb** capital. In many respects the city has a different political culture (of which the best-known representative is probably **Biljana Plavšić**) from that of the primarily rural Serb areas of Bosnia; representatives of Banja Luka have repeatedly found themselves at odds with the Bosnian Serb government in Pale. Serb troops based in Banja Luka mutinied briefly against their government in September 1993.

In spite of the fact that Serb forces controlled the city throughout the war, Banja Luka has a history of multiethnic settlement. In the census of 1991, it was estimated that Banja Luka was 55 percent Serb, 15 percent Muslim, 15 percent Croat, and 12 percent "Yugoslav," giving it the largest Croat population in Bosnia-Hercegovina after Sarajevo and **Mostar.** A feature of Serb control between 1992 and 1995 was the systematic destruction of public reflections of the city's former ethnic diversity, especially the destruction of its numerous mosques.

Such was the importance of the city to the Bosnian Serb political project that the imminent possibility of a direct attack on it by Croat and Bosnian government troops toward the end of September 1995 was a significant factor in persuading the Serbs to negotiate a peace settlement.

—J. B. A.

BANKING

Although often overlooked in recent analyses of the Yugoslav crises and wars of the 1990s, banking issues are of crucial importance in explaining the origins, dimensions, and economic consequences of the conflict.

Formerly presided over by the National Bank of Yugoslavia (NBJ) and the federation's six republican central banks, the Yugoslav banking and monetary system began to disintegrate under the impact of the economic and political crises of the late 1980s. Yugoslavia's U.S.$18 billion foreign debt problem forced a rescheduling of international liabilities in 1988. The **International Monetary Fund** (IMF) insisted upon accelerated economic stabilization and reform in return for its continuing financial support.

The IMF's related insistence on a strengthened federation—at the moment when the federation's very legitimacy was being openly contested by the constituent republics—proved to be highly problematic. Although economically rational, and in part successful, under the leadership of Federal Premier **Ante Marković** from 1989 to 1991, IMF-supported economic stabilization and reform came apart as a result of the opposition of all the federation's republican governments, that of **Serbia** in particular.

Because of the interference of the Serbian government, the autonomy of the Belgrade-based NBJ was effectively destroyed during 1990. Following the illegal appropriation of around U.S.$1.5 billion of hard currency and other assets by Serbia just before its parliamentary **elections** in December 1990, the Yugoslav crisis passed the point of no return. For **Slovenia** in particular, this blatant theft was the last straw a month before the **League of Communists of Yugoslavia** (SKJ) collapsed at its final congress in January 1991. In an equally serious development, through the NBJ the Serbian government seized over U.S.$5 billion of hard currency banked by private individuals throughout the imploding federation in 1991—a policy that was little more than theft and that was to lead to a serious crisis of confidence in all banks.

During 1991 further confusion ensued when what remained of the all-Yugoslav banking and monetary system completely collapsed, as Slovenia, **Croatia**, and **Macedonia** declared their independence from the federation. This process of disintegration was completed when **Bosnia-Hercegovina** declared its independence in April 1992. Thereafter, each of the successor states of the former Yugoslavia was to have its own central bank, currency, and banking system. All the former Yugoslav republics except Slovenia defaulted on their foreign debt liabilities at this time.

The newly declared Federal Republic of Yugoslavia (FRY—composed of Serbia and Montenegro) was also subjected to economic **sanctions** by the United Nations from 1992 to 1995. A policy of reckless fiscal and monetary expansionism at a time of declining output and trade, as well as under conditions of war and sanctions, resulted in hyperinflation, culminating in the highest **inflation** ever recorded in modern times: 1.3 trillion percent in 1993. In a desperate attempt to raise hard currency locally, the NBJ also allowed the operation of a number of semicriminal "private" banks involved in fraudulent pyramid selling schemes, resulting in losses of over U.S.$2 billion for their depositors by the time they collapsed in 1995. The FRY also used an elaborate network of offshore banking facilities linked to Cyprus to launder stolen moneys and to circumvent the UN economic sanctions before these sanctions were lifted in 1995. In a belated bid to avoid a complete economic collapse in 1994, the FRY introduced a new Yugoslav dinar tied to the German mark. Overseen by a new NBJ governor and former World Bank official, **Dragoslav Avramović**, this policy partly stabilized the economy and banking system of the FRY. Pending the lifting of the remaining "outer wall" of financial sanctions against the FRY, however, the rehabilitation of the republic's economy, banking system, and foreign debt position will remain incomplete.

Elsewhere in the former Yugoslavia, similar and inflationary fiscal and monetary expansionism under the impact of war and economic decline took place in all of the successor states during the early 1990s, followed by deflationary financial stabilization often supported by the IMF. Only in Slovenia has a properly functioning banking system emerged. In Croatia, a functioning banking and monetary system based on a new currency did not emerge until 1994. By 1997, however, Croatia was not far behind Slovenia in being able to borrow money abroad more or less normally. In Macedonia, financial stabilization did not begin until 1995, when a highly damaging economic blockade by **Greece** was finally lifted. In 1997 a major pyramid-selling banking scandal raised doubts about the integrity of Macedonia's financial system. Partitioned through war and economically devastated during the 1990s, Bosnia-Hercegovina has yet to create any sort of functioning economy and banking system. In practice, it remains completely dependent on foreign economic aid for its very survival.

—M. M.

See also: economic dimension

BATTLE OF KOSOVO

See **Kosovo, Battle of**

BAVČAR, IGOR

Igor Bavčar was born in Postojna, Slovenia, in 1955. Trained as a policeman and educated as a political scientist, he became a leading figure in the human rights movement in Slovenia in 1988, particularly in support of **Janez Janša** at the trial of the Ljubljana Four. By the time of the Ten Day War in summer 1991, when the **Yugoslav Peoples' Army** entered

Slovenia, Bavčar was head of police as minister for internal affairs in the DEMOS (Democratic Opposition of Slovenia) coalition government, of which his own party, the Slovene Democratic Alliance (SDZ), was a part. In 1992 he ran unsuccessfully for the post of prime minister, but he remained a member of Parliament for the Democratic Party of Slovenia, which had split from the SDZ in 1991.

—*J. J. H.*

See also: Mladina

BELGRADE

The capital city of the Federal Republic of **Yugoslavia** (FRY) and the Republic of **Serbia**, Belgrade (Beograd) is located in the north of "Inner Serbia" at the confluence of the **Sava** and **Danube** Rivers. As a center of communications, Belgrade is an important regional river-to-sea port, lies on the main road-rail route between Western Europe and the Middle East, and has an international airport at Surčin.

Around a third of the annual gross domestic product (GDP) of Serbia and the FRY is estimated to be produced in the Belgrade area. Sectorally, the city's economy has traditionally been dominated by metallurgy, machine building, electronics, food processing, trade, and financial services. However, during the period of United Nations (UN) economic **sanctions** against the FRY (1992–1995), Belgrade's economy experienced serious decline, hyper**inflation**, mass unemployment, and major social deprivation. Part of a wider all-Yugoslav trading and payments area prior to 1991, Belgrade now has a more uncertain economic future, mainly because of the loss of former Yugoslav and foreign markets, as well as a lack of capital for the modernization of its decaying infrastructure and productive capacity.

According to the last Yugoslav census in 1991, Belgrade had a total population of 1,087,915. Since 1991, however, there has reportedly been a significant increase in the number of the city's inhabitants, mainly because of the large influx of Serb **refugees** from **Croatia** and **Bosnia**. By 1993, the total number of residents was estimated at around 1.5 million, and more recent estimates have raised this to around 2 million, or a fifth of the total population of

An aerial view of Belgrade, capital of the former Yugoslav Federation and the Republic of Serbia. (Tanjug)

the current FRY. Most of the 600,000 Serbian refugees in Serbia at the present time are thought to be residing in the Belgrade area. The result of this influx of largely destitute people has been severe overcrowding, growing poverty, and serious pressure on local services. There has been a growing problem of street crime. In recent years a powerful local mafia has emerged, based initially on "sanctions busting" (principally involving oil) and linked to widespread official corruption on the part of the ruling **Socialist Party of Serbia** (SPS).

Belgrade has extensively benefited from large quantities of international **humanitarian aid.** The city has become an important regional distribution center for aid bound for neighboring Bosnia-Hercegovina.

Since coming to power in 1987, Serbian president **Slobodan Milošević** has overseen an extreme centralization of executive authority in Serbia. Around half of Serbia's 100,000 police personnel are thought to be deployed in and around Belgrade, which is also the operational headquarters of the Army of Yugoslavia (VJ—previously known as the **Yugoslav Peoples' Army**, or JNA) and of the VJ's First Army. Although now the seat of power in Serbia and the FRY, Belgrade has, in general, traditionally been politically hostile to the government and to Milošević. "**Yugonostalgia**" remains strong in Belgrade. Serbia's recently created independent media have also functioned only in the Belgrade area. In March 1991 and again in March 1993, major antigovernment demonstrations and riots took place. During successive parliamentary and presidential **elections**, the main Serbian opposition parties have performed best in the city. Once sympathetic to Milošević, the influential Serbian **Orthodox Church**, whose patriarch resides in Belgrade, has more recently openly come out against him. Should the SPS and Milošević ever lose power in Serbia, the process of political change will almost certainly begin and end in Belgrade.

—M. M.

BELGRADE INITIATIVE

The Belgrade Initiative in July 1991 was an early attempt by Serbian president **Slobodan Milošević** to prevent Bosnian Muslims from following Croatia and Slovenia into secession from Yugoslavia, on the prophetic grounds that Bosnia itself would be divided as a republic and would potentially face violent conflict with **Bosnian Serbs.** Bosnian president **Alija Izetbegović** became increasingly suspicious of the motives of the proposal and the consequences of agreeing to it; this led Milošević to bypass Izetbegović and to enlist the support of **Adil Zulfikarpăsić**, leader of the moderate **Muslim** Bošnjak Party, who duly signed the Belgrade Initiative to initial acclaim in Serbia but to little effect in Bosnia (particularly with the Bosnian Serb leadership). Within three months the initiative was effectively dead, and its limited potential can be measured only hypothetically against the subsequent alternative consequences.

—J. J. H.

BELL, MARTIN

Martin Bell (born 1938) worked as a journalist for British Broadcasting Company (BBC) Television from 1965 to 1997. Already well known as a foreign and war correspondent, he became the chief interface between television audiences and the Yugoslav wars as the reporter who stayed longest throughout, covering the Serb-Croat conflicts in **Vukovar**, the **Krajina**, and elsewhere, as well as the war in Bosnia. Nearly always reporting from the front line, he suffered serious wounding, which forced his temporary return home. The "man in the white suit," as he was called, was meticulous in his search for the truth while practicing his belief in what he called "the journalism of attachment": the journalist does not take sides but cannot be outside the tragedy—we are all part of it. These beliefs are eloquently expressed in his book *In Harm's Way* (rev. ed. Penguin, 1996). In May 1997 he successfully ran as an independent (anticorruption) parliamentary candidate in the UK general election.

—J. J. H.

Reference: Bell, Martin. *In Harm's Way: Reflections of a War-Zone Thug,* rev. ed. London: Penguin, 1996.

BIHAĆ

Located on the **Una River** and commanding road and rail communication important for both **Bosnia** and neighboring **Croatia**, Bihać played a significant part in the defense of the integrity of the Bosnian state. With a population of 71,000 (according to the 1991 census), two-thirds of whom declared themselves as **Muslims**, the town was the center of the "**Bihać** pocket" in the northwest of the republic (which also included the communes of **Bosanska**

Krupa, **Cazin**, and Velika Kladuša). Because of its strategically important location, Bihać was subjected to fierce pressure by the surrounding forces of the Serbian **Krajina** and the **Bosnian Serbs**, which resulted in its being declared a "**safe area**" by the United Nations on 6 May 1993. In spite of its status as a safe area, and because of the fact that the town had become the recipient of many thousands of **refugees** from surrounding rural areas, it was subjected to its most threatening assault in November 1994 (including air attacks launched from the base at Udbina, in defiance of the **no-fly zone**); during this assault, Serb forces briefly reached the suburbs. During late 1994 the Bihać pocket was contested by no fewer than five armies—**the Bosnian army**, the **Bosnian Serb Army**, Serb forces from the **Krajina**, units loyal to dissident Muslim leader **Fikret Abdić**, and the **Croatian Council of Defense** (HVO). Isolation of the pocket ended in August 1995 following the successful Croatian **Operation Storm**.

—J. B. A.

BIJELJINA

A town in the northeastern corner of Bosnia with a population of 97,000 (in 1991), Bijeljina marked the transition of the conflict from eastern Croatia into Bosnia. Events there served as the prelude to the Bosnian tragedy. On 1 April 1992, the much-feared Serb paramilitary unit headed by **Željko Ražnjatović** ("Arkan") subjected the town initially to a show of terror on and off the streets, followed by a targeted search for and execution of leaders of the Muslim population. Two days later the **Yugoslav Peoples' Army** (JNA) arrived, ostensibly to calm the situation but effectively to occupy the town and spur the exodus of all but the Serb population. This event finally brought home to the government in Sarajevo and the international community that war in Bosnia was virtually inevitable. One week later, the fighting moved with full intensity 20 miles south to **Zvornik**.

—J. J. H.

See also: ethnic cleansing

BILDT, CARL

Carl Bildt (born 1949), having been a member of the Swedish Parliament representing the Moderate Party since 1979, rose to become prime minister of Sweden from 1991 to 1994. In 1995 he was appointed by the **European Union** as cochair of the **International Conference on the Former Yugoslavia** (succeeding Lord **Owen**), with considerable input into the terms of the **Dayton Agreements** and their monitoring. He also had a high profile in subsequent negotiations between Europe and the Balkan states. His term as peace envoy expired in June 1997.

—J. J. H.

BLACK MARKET

Representing one of the key socioeconomic consequences of the Yugoslav wars of the 1990s, black-market activities of all types have now become common throughout the former Yugoslavia. Already a serious problem in the Yugoslav period, black markets became larger and more significant than officially recorded or taxed economic activities in many regions following the collapse of the federation and its descent into war. According to several recent estimates (which may not reveal the full scale of the problem), black markets in goods and services have accounted for around 50 percent of the officially declared gross domestic product (GDP) in all former Yugoslav republics during the war period. The main structural factors behind the rise of such markets were the collapse of recorded or taxed economic activities in conditions of war, international economic **sanctions**, and the related imposition of high nominal taxation on private-sector entrepreneurs by governments desperate for revenues at a time of declining economic activity.

Primarily a contest over territory and other economic resources, the Yugoslav wars of the 1990s also afforded opportunities for large-scale looting and other criminal enrichment. In both **Croatia** and **Bosnia-Hercegovina** in 1991 and 1992, respectively, much of this looting was done by **paramilitary/irregular forces**. The leaders of militia bands from **Serbia** became extremely wealthy war profiteers virtually overnight. A notorious example of these warlords-turned-businessmen was **Željko Ražnjatović** ("Arkan"), now one of the richest individuals in Serbia. Also in Serbia and **Montenegro**, the imposition of economic sanctions by the United Nations (UN) from 1992 to 1995 created lucrative opportunities for criminal black marketeers to enrich themselves by covertly trading in imported essential goods, such as oil. Similarly, in **Macedonia**, which was subjected to an economic blockade by **Greece** for much of the 1990s, black market traders and "sanctions busters" became economically very powerful. By the end of the Yugoslav wars in 1995, such was the power of criminal networks that local governments found it difficult to eliminate the gangsters that they had earlier tolerated—particularly in Serbia, Montenegro, Macedonia, and Bosnia-Hercegovina.

Other than the smuggling, trading, or looting of various types of goods, the key money earner for black marketeers was the provision of technically illegal but officially tolerated financial services. These activities became particularly significant in Serbia during its hyper**inflation** of the early 1990s, when the German mark became the only real repository of value and medium of exchange. Tolerated by the Serbian (and other) governments at a time when they were desperately short of hard currency, black-market money changing was to lead to more elaborate forms of financial fraud in the region. In Serbia and then Macedonia, these practices involved the establishment of a number of "private" pyramid-selling banking schemes designed to fleece depositors of hard currency resources. By 1997, when the last of these schemes collapsed in Macedonia, local depositors had reportedly lost in excess of U.S.$2.5 billion.

In retrospect, the rise of black markets in the region has had mainly negative consequences. Criminal networks are now well established and not easily removed, making lawful and normal socioeconomic development difficult. Peacetime socioeconomic conditions may lessen the centrality of black markets in the longer term, although this situation remains dependent in the last analysis on changes in government policy that have yet to be implemented. It has also been argued that black market provision of goods and services in the region in recent years has had some positive results by unintentionally making very difficult economic conditions more bearable than they might have been otherwise.

—M. M.

See also: economic dimension

BOBAN, MATE

The ferociously nationalist leader of the secessionist Croat region of **Herceg-Bosna**, Mate Boban, a former supermarket manager, emerged to prominence in February 1992. At this time, with the backing of the **Croatian Democratic Union** (HDZ) in Zagreb, he replaced the moderate **Stjepan Kljuić** as the principal political voice of Croats in **Bosnia-Hercegovina.** Kljuić's backing had been in the Croat communities of the more industrialized towns of central Bosnia; Boban's power base was the underdeveloped rural region of western **Hercegovina.**

Whereas the policy of Croat president **Franjo Tudjman** has vacillated between the hope of dividing Bosnia-Hercegovina between **Serbia** and **Croatia** (on the one hand) and support for a multiethnic Bosnian buffer state between the two (on the other), Boban has shared with his Serb counterpart **Radovan Karadžić** an unwavering commitment to division. In May 1992 he met Karadžić in the Austrian city of Graz, where they reached an agreement on a proposed sharing of the territorial spoils.

The summit of Boban's international credibility was his representation of **Bosnian Croats** during the **International Conference on the Former Yugoslavia** in August/September 1993. Starting in December of that year, it became increasingly evident that Boban's strident nationalism was seen as out of tune with President Tudjman's newly adopted stance of accommodation under growing pressure from the United States. Zagreb signed a **cease-fire** agreement on 23 February 1994, partly with U.S. brokerage, cementing an alliance between Bosnian Muslims and Croats that became the **Muslim-Croat Federation.** It is widely believed that Boban's resignation on 8 February was a precondition for that agreement. He was replaced by **Kresimir Zubak.**

Lord **Owen,** although usually restrained in his judgments on those with whom he dealt, described Boban as "to my mind a racist in much the same way as **Mladić.**"

—J. B. A.

Reference: Owen, David. *Balkan Odyssey.* London: Gollancz, 1995, p. 300.

BOBETKO, JANKO

Gen. Janko Bobetko was a Croatian military officer prominent in the **Croatian Spring** of 1970–1971, cofounder of the Croatian National Guard (HNS) in 1990, and a vocal critic of Croatian president **Franjo Tudjman** at the time of the first Serb-Croat war in Croatia in 1991. Deputy commander-in-chief of the **Yugoslav Peoples' Army** (JNA) Zagreb army corps at the time of the Croatian Spring, Bobetko was dismissed for publicly demanding the creation of a **Croatian Army**. Nearly 20 years later, when Tudjman's **Croatian Democratic Union** (HDZ) came to power in Croatia in 1990, Bobetko and the new defense minister, Gen. **Martin Špegelj**, cofounded the HNS.

In July 1991, because of his outspoken criticism of President Tudjman's policy with respect to the war, Bobetko was replaced as operational head of the HNS by Gen. **Antun Tus**, former commander of the Yugoslav federal air force. Although always a secondary figure to Špegelj, Bobetko was nevertheless a major influence during the early development of the post-Yugoslav Croatian armed forces.

—*M. M.*

BORDERS

The disintegration of the former Federal Republic of **Yugoslavia** brought to the surface several problems relating to the borders between the constituent republics. Whereas all the republics have been able to base their claims to territorial identity on historical precedent of one kind or another, none of them has been able to affirm its borders as an independent state without challenge. Problems relating to the delineation of borders with other states that were not previously part of the Yugoslav federation are touched upon in entries relating to the states in question (e.g., the disputed border in relation to Italy and Slovenia is treated in the entry relating to **Italy**). This entry confines itself to disputes between the states emerging from the former Yugoslav federation.

Disputes have arisen for two reasons. Yugoslavia was constructed upon the ruins of two large, multinational empires (the **Habsburg** and the **Ottoman**), which recognized no firmly defined internal boundaries among their component ethnic groups. This multiethnic character was to some extent perpetuated in both the First Yugoslavia (created in 1919) and the Second Yugoslavia (the communist era from 1945). The process of creating states along ethnic lines has run up against the problems created by these multiple diasporas. Even where it has been possible to identify former state boundaries of some historical longevity, their origins in the administrative or treaty boundaries imposed or negotiated in earlier times by states that no longer exist has tended to rob them of legitimacy.

Questions relating to the borders between the Yugoslav republics were to some extent swept under the carpet by the new communist government in 1945, which took the view that these were matters of internal administrative convenience to which no issue of principle was attached. A federal control commission set up in 1945 arbitrated upon the most urgent questions, particularly relating to the border between **Croatia** and **Slovenia** in Istria (which had been incorporated into **Italy** by the Treaty of Rapallo in 1920) and between Croatia and **Serbia**, in eastern **Slavonia**. Further minor boundary rectifications took place in 1947 and 1956.

The dissolution of Yugoslavia affected all the new, post-Yugoslav states to some degree. The case of **Bosnia-Hercegovina** is, generally speaking, of a quite different character from Slovenia, Croatia, or Serbia in that the issues over which the war has been fought have related to its very existence as a state, not to the details of its territorial limits. Four primary areas of controversy are worthy of note with respect to the creation of new states in the territory of the former Yugoslavia.

In **Istria** the border between Croatia and Slovenia was problematic because the historical boundaries (dating back to Habsburg times) of the Austrian lands of Küstenland, Carniola, and Styria did not reflect precise ethnic distribution. The problem was exacerbated in Istria because of the movement of populations after Italian rule was imposed following World War I and because the region was awarded to Yugoslavia in 1945. The significance of the problem became apparent only when Slovenia and Croatia became independent states, making competing claims upon what had previously been Yugoslav territorial waters in the Gulf of Trieste. Although substantial progress was made in the resolution of the problem in talks between the two governments in 1995, a number of outstanding issues remain to be settled.

In eastern Slavonia, the border between **Serbia** and Croatia presented the post-1945 boundary commissions with their most difficult problems. The historical Croatian province of Slavonia had extended eastward as far as Zemun. However, the pattern of ethnic settlement, reflecting the peculiar history of the Habsburg **Military Frontier**, had given the region a largely **Orthodox**/Serb population. This latter situation had been taken into account in the demarcation of the autonomous Banovina Hrvatska (i.e., Prefecture of Croatia) of 1939, but the former concept of the boundaries of

"Croatia" prevailed in the Nazi partition of Yugoslavia in 1941. Whereas something like a natural boundary could be said to be suggested by the **Danube** River north of Ilok, no similarly natural frontier can be traced southward to the Bosnian border. The extent of Serbian occupation of the region in 1992 was determined simply by force of arms, limited to some extent by United Nations (UN) mediation.

Although the UN-brokered restoration of eastern Slavonia to Croatian control implemented during 1998 is based upon a return to the status quo ante (i.e., a recognition of the former republican boundaries within Yugoslavia), the precise determination of frontiers in this region must be regarded as to some extent still in question, particularly in the light of the uncertainty that hangs over the future control of the Bosnian town of **Brčko**, which was left unresolved by the **Dayton Agreements**.

For similar reasons, the proprietorship of the **Prevlaka** Peninsula, which defines the northern edge of the Bay of Kotor, has also been called into question. The peninsula was (before the time of Napoleon) the southernmost reach of the Ragusan Republic and represented the frontier with Venetian territory. During the nineteenth century, the land on both sides of the Bay of Kotor was incorporated into Austria-Hungary, although subsequently (with brief intermissions) Prevlaka came to be accepted as marking the southernmost extent of Croatia. This was unproblematic for the most part after 1918, when the entire coastline belonged to a single state, but the disintegration of Yugoslavia suddenly endowed the locality with a previously unsuspected military significance.

The border between Serbia and **Macedonia** has no known definition in terms of historical kingdoms, in the distribution of dialects, or in geographical features such as a watershed. It does not correspond either to the former Ottoman provinces of Kosovo, Monastir, and Selanik or to the historical pattern of Orthodox ecclesiastical administration. No modern Macedonian state existed before its creation as one of Yugoslavia's socialist republics in 1945, and its borders were fixed in an apparently arbitrary fashion by the Federal Control Commission in 1945. Following the creation of an independent Macedonian state, the legitimacy of the border was challenged, and attempts were made in the summer of 1993 by Serb troops to control small areas of Macedonian territory in the region of Skopska Crna Gora, as well as north of **Kriva Palanka**. This attempted destabilization of the border was met with a prompt response from the international community, and in June 1993 the Macedonian government accepted an offer by the U.S. government to provide a small "preventive deployment" force under the auspices of the UN (**UNPREDEP**).

—*J. B. A.*

Reference: Allcock, John B., et al. *Border and Territorial Disputes*, 3rd ed. London: Longman, 1992.

BOROVO SELO

Borovo Selo, a village three miles north of **Vukovar** in eastern **Slavonia** on the banks of the **Danube River**, separating Croatia from Serbia, was the site of a watershed moment in Croats' perceptions of Serbs. In April 1992 a group of militants from the **Croatian Democratic Union** (HDZ) led by **Gojko Šušak** were escorted to the village by the moderate chief of police for the area, **Josip Reihl-Kir**. The group fired three rockets into the Serb village without apparent provocation. Unsurprisingly, the Serbs were prepared for another assault, which occurred at the start of May when four Croat policemen—at night and without Kir's permission—attempted to take down the Yugoslav flag flying in the village and to substitute the Croatian flag. Two of the police were wounded and taken prisoner; when reinforcements were sent the next morning to rescue them, armed Serbs (whether local or imported remains a matter of claim and counter) killed 12 of the Croat police. Borovo Selo was thus exploited to harden Croat public opinion against an already galvanized Serb population.

—*J. J. H.*

BOSANSKA KRUPA

Bosanska Krupa, a town of 58,000 inhabitants (as of 1991) in northwestern **Bosnia**, reflects the situation of many such settlements in Bosnia. Located on either side of a river (in this case the Krupa, from which it takes its name), its population was largely Muslim (74 percent) on one side and Serb (26 percent) on the other. By the late spring of 1992, the hostilities and consequences had reached a point of no return. Bosanska Krupa lies on the edge of the **Bihać** pocket, whose front line and crossing point for **refugees** is the Krupa River, in an area that became totally surrounded by Serb territory. It was a place unsafe to live in and unsafe to leave, most accurately and memorably described by the journalist Ed Vulliamy as a "trap within a trap." For a vivid account of conditions in Bosanska Krupa during 1992, see Vulliamy's book *Seasons in Hell* (New York and London: Simon and Schuster, 1994).

—J. J. H.

BOSANSKI BROD

Bosanksi Brod is a town on the northern border of Bosnia, lying on the opposite bank of the **Sava River** relative to the larger, Croatian town of **Slavonski Brod** (the location of **Yugoslav Peoples' Army** barracks). It was of strategic importance to the Serbs as a key point on the **Posavina Corridor**, which potentially linked Serbia itself with the Serbs in the west of Bosnia and **Krajina**. The 300-meter-long metal bridge linking the two towns was also vital in terms of potential reinforcements from Croatia in the defense of Bosanski Brod; it was badly damaged by a Yugoslav federal airstrike on 3 May 1992. Before the conflict the population was around 33,000, of whom one-third were Serb and the rest were mixed Croat and Muslim. At the beginning of March 1992, the local Serbs declared Bosanski Brod an autonomous Serb district, and the shelling began; the Croat-Muslim defenders were gradually confined to one sector and enclosed with their backs to the river. Casualties and the exodus of refugees reduced the town to less than a quarter of its previous number of inhabitants. Several sources have suggested that Bosanski Brod was the subject of a deal between the Croatian and Yugoslav leaders (whose common interests by late summer excluded the Bosnian Muslims) whereby the siege of **Dubrovnik** would be ended in return for Croatian withdrawal from Bosanski Brod.

—J. J. H.

BOSNA RIVER

In many ways the "heartland river" of Bosnia, as well as the longest, the Bosna River rises on the slopes of Mount **Igman** to the southwest of **Sarajevo** and flows for 200 miles northward, mainly through traditionally Bosnian Muslim areas, before joining the **Sava River** on the Croatian border. Because of the significance of its valley for **communications** by road and rail, the Bosna River experienced much conflict in the Bosnian war from its source to its mouth—from Igman itself; through towns such as **Zenica**, Žepće, **Maglaj**, and **Doboj**; to the iron bridge at Bosanski Šamac.

—J. J. H.

BOSNIA-HERCEGOVINA

Bosnia-Hercegovina (Bosna i Hercegovina) is one of the six republics of the former Yugoslav federation, and in many respects it provides the key to understanding the federation's collapse. With an area of 51,129 square kilometers and a population in 1991 of 4.36 million, it was the third largest and most populous of the republics. Bosnia-Hercegovina (B-H) held a special position in relation to the breakup of the federation for the following reasons.

Whereas in other republics there was a clear ethnic majority that could provide some kind of legitimation for the creation of separate nation-states, the population of B-H (according to the 1991 census) was approximately 17 percent Croat, 31 percent Serb, and 44 percent Muslim, with a further 5.5 percent declaring themselves to be "Yugoslavs." The successful creation of a state would have required sensitive balancing of different ethnic cultures. B-H was surrounded, however, by republics in which there were already serious conflicts among the constituent ethnic groups—in particular, between Croats and the large Serb minority in **Croatia** and between Serbs and the predominantly Albanian population of the province of **Kosovo** in **Serbia**. This had a marked impact on ethnic relations in B-H itself.

In both of these neighboring republics, historical traditions regarding the extent of the state included reference to medieval states that had incorporated large areas of B-H. The traditional **Greater Croatia** harkened back to the kingdom of Zvonimir, and that of **Greater Serbia** looked to the Empire of Dušan Nemanjić. The rise of nationalistic movements in both Croatia and Serbia made for an atmosphere of external threat, as well as for conflict between local Serbs and Croats within B-H. B-H was relatively rich in natural resources, including iron and nonferrous metals, coal, and the potential for hydroelectric **energy** generation. It contained an appreciable proportion of Yugoslavia's industrial manufacturing capacity. In the event of the disintegration of the federation, control of these resources was seen as a major prize by both Serbia and Croatia, each of which was deficient in these in one respect or another. Control of B-H was of particular importance for Croatia, because of Croatia's unusual shape. Essential **communication** links between northern cities such as **Zagreb** and **Osijek**, as well as coastal cities such as **Split** or **Dubrovnik**, lay across B-H. A vital outlet for landlocked Serbia's trade was provided by the **Neretva** Valley in B-H. In the face of all of these pressures for the division and assimilation of the region by its neighbors, however, there have been advocates of the continuing integrity of a state of B-H. As in all of the regions of former Yugoslavia, arguments about the natural, desirable, or necessary form of contemporary states have involved recourse to a range of often mutually incompatible historical accounts.

Proponents of the Croat interest in B-H rely heavily upon the role of Roman Catholic missionaries in the spread of Christianity to the region. They also look back to the achievements of early Croatian princes, especially Tomislav (910–928) and Zvonimir (1075–1089), whose territories included large parts of modern B-H. They also regard the fourteenth-century Bosnian Kotromanić dynasty as having been "Croatian" by virtue of its adherence to Roman Catholicism. Similarly, those who see the area as historically Serb are able to point to the steady expansion of the Serb principality of Raška, which grew between 1169 and 1355 to include for a time all of modern B-H.

"Autonomists," however, cite the twelfth-century despot Kulin and the fourteenth-century Tvrtvo Kotromanić (who was able to challenge Nemanjić power after 1353) as historical justification for the claims of a distinctively Bosnian state. In this endeavor they also appeal to the distinctive religious traditions of the area (the spread of the heretical Bogomil sect and the rise of a "Bosnian Church" in the Middle Ages) as representing the long history of a uniquely Bosnian culture.

The factor that imposed a uniform framework upon the history of the region was the region's conquest by the **Ottoman Empire** between the late fourteenth and early sixteenth centuries. This process also resulted in the conversion of large numbers of the indigenous Slav population to **Islam**, giving rise to the ethno-religious complexity of the area. Ottoman rule also bestowed a measure of political identity following the region's constitution as a separate province under an Ottoman governor after 1580 (although the boundaries of this province, particularly in relation to the status of **Hercegovina**, varied during the nineteenth century). An important characteristic of Ottoman order was the division of the population into confessional communities through which a great deal of administration, especially the administration of justice, was conducted (the *millet* system; a system of religious communities within the Ottoman Empire). Rebellion against Ottoman rule in 1874 spread from the province to become a wider war, which was brought to conclusion only in 1878 at the Congress of Berlin. B-H was then placed under an Austrian protectorate. This had far-reaching consequences for the entire South Slav area. Austrian administration fostered a sense of "Bosnian" identity by supporting the Muslim establishment, playing them off against both Roman **Catholic** and **Orthodox** communities. Austrian occupation (which became full-fledged annexation in 1908) also stimulated a degree of nationalistic speculation among Serbs and Croats about the possible eventual integration of at least part of the two provinces into their own emerging nation-states. It is only during this period that B-H began to emerge as the locus of interethnic rivalry between Serbs and Croats in the provinces. It was the action of representatives of a Serb terrorist organization, Mlada Bosna (Young Bosnia), that triggered the conflict between Serbia and Austria in 1914, which in turn rapidly escalated into World War I. The centralizing tendencies of the "First Yugoslavia," as created in 1919, sat poorly with Bosnians of all faiths, particularly under the royal dictatorship of 1929. The division of the state into prefectures *(banovine)* that cut across historical geographical, cultural, and political units eliminated B-H from the map and apportioned it among four new units. The arrangement was particularly offensive to Muslims because the boundaries were drawn in such a way as to divide the Muslims' settlements among units with either Serb or Croat majorities. The situation was not improved in that respect either by the creation of a unified Croatian *banovina* in 1931, to which a sizable proportion of B-H was allocated.

The onset of war in 1941 saw B-H incorporated into the new Independent State of Croatia under a puppet fascist regime, although divided between German and Italian military administrations. B-H possessed a combination of factors ensuring that it would be the locus of the fiercest and most protracted struggles of the war: its ethnic diversity; its terrain; its strategic location; and its experience of being incorporated into an indigenous fascist state that sponsored the most extreme persecution of its non-Croat citizens, especially Serbs.

After three decades of the denial of B-H's existence, however, the victory of the communists in 1945 saw the province designated as one of the new Yugoslav federation's six republics. B-H played a key role in the strategy of building a balanced constitution, preventing the monopolization of power by the federation's most numerous nationality (the Serbs) but ensuring their significant representation. The approach required two important developments: (1) the operation of a strict ethnic "key" in the allocation of career openings and positions of responsibility or authority, and (2) the building of the national consciousness of the "Muslim" population. Hence, in Yugoslavia the term ***Muslim*** came to be used to designate **ethnicity** or national identity, not simply religious identity.

Largely because of its sensitive location within the federation and partly because of its relative poverty, B-H became the preserve of a rather conservative faction of the **League of Communists** (LC), typically inclined to support a relatively strong federal center and suspicious of moves toward "market socialism." Liberalism largely passed the republic by, and the relative closure of its Communist elite eventually opened opportunities for "cronyism" and even corruption, as in the Agrokomerc scandal, involving **Fikret Abdić**. The positive side of this regime, however, was the suppression of any manifestation of ethnic hostility, as well as the creation of a highly secularized Muslim elite that was able to set standards of toleration and openness. It is symptomatic of Bosnian politics that the Yugoslav Communist elite failed their first serious test when, in 1988, the federal government under Branko Mikulić (the republic's representative in the collective presidium) was forced to resign, admitting its inability to grasp with sufficient firmness the imperative need for economic modernization. It is equally symptomatic that the rather belated attempt of Mikulić's successor, **Ante Marković**, to found a new political party—one that would lead the forces of modernization across all of Yugoslavia's republics and would represent all of its nations (Alliance of Reform Forces)—found its greatest support in B-H.

The tragedy of B-H during the breakup of Yugoslavia is that the discredit into which its Communist elite had fallen made the going relatively easy for the anti-Communist and nationalist alternative **political parties**. This tendency was reinforced by the geographic position of B-H, surrounded by other republics in which ethnic conflict had already become heightened. The political leadership that emerged following the first multiparty **elections** in December 1990 was consequently ill equipped to handle the difficult task of making a peaceful transition to a new **constitutional** order. Perhaps the task was impossible; but it was made particularly risky by the intransigence of the **Bosnian Serb** leadership, under **Radovan Karadžić**, and by the insensitive handling of the issues by the **European Community** (EC). It is clear that the EC's response to the report of the **Badinter Commission** demanded that the Bosnian government under **Alija Izetbegović** conduct a referendum that was seen as provocative by Bosnian Serbs; this forced the Bosnian government toward a declaration of independence at a point that they regarded as dangerously premature. By 6 April 1992, however, when Bosnia-Hercegovina was recognized as an independent state, armed conflict was already under way.

—J. B. A.

See also: Bosnian army; Bosnian Serb Army; Croatian Council of Defense; ethnicity; language question; Muslims in Yugoslavia; nationality; religion

Reference: Malcolm, Noel. *Bosnia: A Short History,* new ed. London: Macmillan, 1996.

BOSNIAN ARMY

The Army of the Republic of **Bosnia-Hercegovina** (ARBH, also known as the Armija) is the main armed force controlled by the Bosnian **Muslim** (Bošnjak)-dominated government in **Sarajevo**. It also has close links with the ruling **Party of Democratic Action** (SDA). Created out of a chaotic mixture of Territorial Defense Force (TDF) reservists, police, and militia volunteers, led by the Sarajevo-based volunteer force, the "zeleni bereti," or "Green Berets" in 1992, the ARBH was at first the weakest of the armed formations involved in the Bosnian conflict. It was powerless to prevent the 1992 seizure of 70 percent of Bosnia-Hercegovina by the **Bosnian Serb Army** (BSA) and its predecessor, the **Yugoslav Peoples' Army** (JNA), a move in which the **Croatian Council**

of Defence (HVO) also played a part. At this time the Bosnian government of **Alija Izetbegović** retained only a small triangle of territory bounded by **Sarajevo, Tuzla,** and **Travnik** in central Bosnia.

Having reportedly allowed the JNA to disarm the Bosnian TDF in 1991, the Izetbegović government found itself at a severe disadvantage when Bosnia descended into war in April 1992. Faced with the well-armed and well-prepared BSA, which was supported by the JNA even after the JNA declared withdrawal from Bosnia-Hercegovina in May 1992, the government forces' survival was at first extremely precarious. The improvised but successful defense of Sarajevo against the besieging BSA (commanded by Gen. **Ratko Mladić**) was to prove decisive for the Bošnjak cause; it began with the forced evacuation of the JNA garrison from the Bosnian capital in April 1992. Although the newly created ARBH was to make a number of attempts to break the siege of Sarajevo, it was constrained by its limited firepower and the failure of the HVO based at Kiseljak to cooperate. The Armija was thus forced to adopt an essentially defensive strategy for much of 1992 and 1993.

Under the command of Gen. **Rasim Delić**, who replaced Šefer Halilović as its chief of staff in 1992, the ARBH was reorganized into a modern and effective force. Delić and Deputy Defense Minister Hasan Čengić set about rearming the Armija, concentrating at first on **Turkey** and **Iran** as sources of arms. It was at this time that a number of foreign **Islamic** volunteer units (Mujaheddin) first became significant as elite assault troops in the ranks of the Armija. The last of the **paramilitary/irregular forces** that had bedeviled Izetbegović's control over his armed forces were eliminated in 1993.

Although still inferior in firepower to both the BSA and the HVO at this time, the Armija troops were well motivated, composed mainly of **refugees** from territories controlled by Serbs and Croats. These factors largely explain why the ARBH forced the HVO to sue for peace after a brief but intense Bošnjak-Croat civil war in central Bosnia in 1993–1994. Victory over the Bosnian Croats in central Bosnia was even more remarkable given that the better-armed HVO was supported by the **Croatian Army** (HV). On the other hand, the war with the HVO also resulted in the Croatian government in Zagreb temporarily cutting off the Armija's main arms supply route.

In relation to the BSA, which opportunistically aided the HVO in 1993, the **United Nations** (UN) Security Council decision to create **safe areas** in five Bošnjak-controlled enclaves indirectly aided the Armija, enabling it to launch offensive raids from **Goražde, Srebrenica,** and **Žepa** in eastern Bosnia without fear of serious reprisal. The provision of **humanitarian aid** by UN and other foreign agencies from 1992 onward also aided the military efforts of the Bošnjaks.

Following the end of the conflict with the Bosnian Croats and the creation of a **Muslim-Croat Federation** in March 1994, the Armija was free to concentrate on the BSA. Covert **arms transfers** restarted, this time also involving the **United States.** Within the outlying territories nominally controlled by the Bošnjak government in Sarajevo, however, a self-declared **Autonomous Province of Western Bosnia** (APWB) was set up under the leadership of **Fikret Abdić**. This led to a short war between Abdić's forces and the ARBH Fifth Corps in 1994, in which the APWB was eliminated. The fall of Abdić made communication and cooperation between the Bosnian Serbs and the **Krajina** Serbs more difficult and weakened the BSA in 1995.

This shift of balance had wider consequences. A Krajina Serb incursion into western Bosnia triggered the significant use of North Atlantic Treaty Organization (NATO) air power against the Bosnian Serbs. A joint ARBH-HVO-HV offensive was made possible against the BSA in western Bosnia and paved the way for the fall of the ethnic Serb enclaves in the Krajina and western **Slavonia** following **Operation Flash** and **Operation Storm.** This connected series of events nearly led to the complete collapse of the Bosnian Serb position in western Bosnia in 1995.

In eastern Bosnia, however, 1995 witnessed a number of defeats for the Armija, notably its loss of the **Srebrenica** and **Žepa** enclaves. Essentially indefensible and only nominally protected by **UNPROFOR** (United Nations Protection Force) since 1993, these enclaves may have been sacrificed by the Izetbegović government in return for Serb-held suburbs in Sarajevo, which was finally reunified in 1996. In the case of Srebrenica, the commander of the town's defense force, **Naser Orić**, was inexplicably ordered out of the enclave just before the BSA overran it. The fall of the eastern Bosnian enclaves (except Goražde) created considerable political controversy, although this development made for a more easily defensible national territory for the Bošnjaks.

At the time of the **Dayton Agreements** in late 1995, the ARBH fielded around 92,000 troops, plus some 100,000 reservists. It was then larger than the HVO (50,000 troops) and the BSA (85,000 troops). Subsequently cut to around 40,000 troops but keeping the same number of reservists (in accordance with the demilitarization provisions of the Dayton Agreements), the Armija remained larger than either the HVO (16,000) or the BSA (30,000) by the end of 1996. It continues to benefit from a large pool of available manpower, something its actual or potential enemies in Bosnia do not have.

In the event of a collapse of the Dayton Agreements, the ARBH could easily overwhelm the undermanned BSA, which suffers from low morale, political feuding among its leaders, and poor equipment. The ARBH's structure has been extensively modified since 1992, creating a flexible and modern armed force. As with the HV in nearby Croatia, its organization has been greatly influenced by U.S. thinking, emphasizing operational flexibility and fast offensive movement—the opposite of the JNA tradition.

Over the last five years, the Armija has had one headquarters (HQ)—Sarajevo, also the base for its First Corps—plus five other corps in Tuzla (Second Corps), **Zenica** (Third), Konjić and **Mostar** (Fourth), **Bihać** (Fifth), and Travnik (Seventh). There are two divisional HQs in Sarajevo and Tuzla. The Armija's order of battle includes around 40 infantry brigades, some of which are mechanized; one special forces brigade; and 19 artillery, antitank, and air defense brigades.

The ARBH military inventory and firepower have greatly improved in recent years. Since 1992, covert arms transfers may have been worth around U.S.$500 million, with Iran and Saudi Arabia providing most of this money. Since the lifting of the UN arms embargo in 1995, U.S. military aid and training programs have become increasingly important, providing (under the U.S.$400 million Equip and Train Program for Bosnia-Hercegovina) 273 main battle tanks (MBTs), 227 armored combat vehicles (ACVs), 1,000 artillery pieces, and 14 attack helicopters for the fiscal year 1996–1997. Over the same period, a further U.S.$40 million of military aid was provided by a number of Islamic states. Before the arrival of U.S. military aid, the ARBH had only 80 MBTs, 70 ACVs, 2,500 artillery pieces (most of which were mortars), and some antitank and air defense weaponry. This was comparable to what the HVO, if not the HV, had, but it was still inferior to the inventory of the BSA.

U.S. policy since 1996 has been to strengthen the Armija over the BSA, albeit within the context of the creation of a new **Muslim-Croat Federation** army. Projected under the **Washington Agreement** of 1994 and reiterated at Dayton in 1995, this integrated army has yet to be created, thereby threatening the future continuation of U.S. military aid. In 1996–1997, this situation was of increasing concern to the United States, which was then also strongly opposed to the continued presence of Mujaheddin in Armija ranks. As a result, U.S. arms deliveries were temporarily delayed and were subject to tight controls by the UN **Implementation Force** then deployed in Bosnia. The rearming of the Bošnjak armed forces will continue with or without the United States, however, with Iran likely to remain a key player.

The demographic displacements and radicalization of the Bošnjak community during the Bosnian civil war inevitably had an impact on the Armija. The general staff and officer corps have long been a key constituency of the hard-line nationalist and clerical wing of the ruling SDA. This politically dominant faction now regards the Dayton Agreements as little more than a glorified cease-fire prior to the final national liberation of the whole of Bosnia-Hercegovina. There has been a purging of non-Muslim officers and an imposition of compulsory SDA membership on all leading cadres in what is now a classic party militia. Initially quite significant in the Armija—where Delić's most senior deputy for many years has been an ethnic Serb, Gen. Jovan Divjak—non-Muslims have been gradually removed from the Bošnjak armed forces.

—M. M.

BOSNIAN CROATS

Although the 1991 census reported that, in the prewar period, 18 percent of the population of **Bosnia-Hercegovina** (about 822,000 people) were Croats, the exact definition of "Bosnian Croat" is far from easy. It might generally seem reasonable to assume that a "Croat" will adopt that title in declaring nationality and will be of the Roman **Catholic** faith, but things are not always so straightforward. Some Croats adopt secular identities, and not all Catholics define themselves as Croats.

The matter is complicated by **language**. Officially the language of Bosnia-Hercegovina could be described either as "Serbo-Croat" *(srpskohrvatski)* or "Croato-Serb" *(hrvatskosrpski)*, and in the census many people adopted other names for their maternal tongue, such as "Croatian" or "Bosnian." It is interesting to note that in communities where small numbers of Croats were mixed with other groups, a much smaller proportion tended to report their own language as "Croato-Serb" or "Croatian" than one might have expected on the basis of either religion or self-declared **nationality**. On the other hand, in communities with massive Croat majorities, even those who did not declare themselves to be "Croats" were likely to label their mother tongue in this "Croat" style. In short, there is an indistinctness surrounding the sense of national identity, and the extent of this fuzziness is all the greater in urban settlements with mixed **ethnicity** and a strongly secular dimension to culture.

Croats were the smallest of the three major national groups in Bosnia-Hercegovina; only 14 of the republic's 109 prewar communes had absolute Croat majorities, and another 7 had Croats as the dominant national group. With the exception of a few overwhelmingly Croat and relatively remote rural areas, Bosnian Croats were disproportionately located in the towns, dispersed among other nationalities. They also had high rates of **intermarriage**. Consequently, a clear sense of national identity was relatively weakly developed and expressed among them. The Croat community in Bosnia-Hercegovina has been acutely divided between (1) a predominantly rural, rather virulent nationalism bent upon a union with Croatia, which would redress the Croats' relative isolation and sense of being swamped by others, and (2) a more cosmopolitan willingness to accommodate a multiethnic state. In part, therefore, the fragility of the project of **Herceg-Bosna** and the possibility of creating a more durable political cooperation between Croats and Muslims in Bosnia-Hercegovina are founded upon these characteristics of the Bosnian Croat community.

—*J. B. A.*

See also: Bosnian Serbs; rural-urban differences

BOSNIAN MUSLIMS

See **Muslims in Yugoslavia**

BOSNIAN SERB ARMY

The most powerful of the parties to the Bosnian civil war of 1992–1995, the Bosnian Serb Army (BSA) was also the party militia of the ruling Serbian Democratic Party (SDS), formerly led by **Radovan Karadžić**. Officially known as Vojska Republike Srpske, the Bosnian Serb Army was formally constituted in May 1992, when the Federal Republic of **Yugoslavia** replaced the **Yugoslav Peoples' Army** (JNA) with a new Army of Yugoslavia (VJ). The BSA was created from 80,000 former JNA troops of Bosnian origin who had remained in **Bosnia-Hercegovina** after the JNA officially left the republic. The departing JNA also left the BSA with large quantities of armaments and ammunition, numerous military installations, and military industries. The JNA also provided the BSA with a high command, led by Gen. **Ratko Mladić**, a veteran officer who had formerly commanded the First **Krajina** Corps and served during the JNA's **Vukovar** campaign in Croatia.

In the lead-up to the outbreak of civil war in Bosnia in April 1992, the JNA managed to disarm the Bosnian Territorial Defense Force (TDF). Its military counterintelligence service (KOS) and the secret services controlled by Serbian president **Slobodan Milošević** had also secretly armed local ethnic Serbs. The end of the JNA's wars in **Slovenia** and **Croatia** led to the redeployment of large numbers of its troops and significant quantities of military equipment into Bosnia-Hercegovina. In nearby **Serbia**, where the JNA had experienced considerable difficulty in mobilizing conscripts for its campaigns

An improvised Bosnian Serb Army tank, Bosnia-Hercegovina, 1992. (Stevan Filipović)

in Slovenia and Croatia, a number of semicriminal **paramilitary/irregular** groups were recruited and armed for deployment in Bosnia, where they became nominally subject to BSA commanders.

The BSA and Karadžić's SDS leadership were in a dominant position at the beginning of the Bosnian civil war. During six months beginning in April 1992, the BSA carried out a ruthless and extremely violent blitzkrieg against its Bosnian **Muslim** (Bošnjak) enemies, taking 70 percent of the territory of **Bosnia-Hercegovina.** This campaign was dominated by the "**ethnic cleansing**" of the Bošnjak population from all Serb-controlled territories. Around **Sarajevo**, which it was incapable of taking without large casualties, the BSA began a long siege in May 1992. Beyond Bošnjak-controlled Sarajevo, plus a small triangular area of territory in central Bosnia, Mladić's BSA then faced serious opposition only from the **Croatian Council of Defense** (HVO), notably in **Hercegovina.**

The official position of the Milošević government, then and thereafter, was that it was not involved in the Bosnian civil war after the JNA left Bosnia-Hercegovina in May 1992. This claim was rejected by the international community, leading to the imposition in the same month of United Nations (UN) economic **sanctions** against Serbia and **Montenegro** for their role in the dismemberment of an internationally recognized state. In fact, the BSA continued to function as an offshoot of the Yugoslav armed forces for some time into the Bosnian war. Created and equipped by the JNA, the BSA was financed and supplied by the VJ and the Serbian government until well after the first public split between Karadžić and Milošević in 1993. At the level of its high command, the BSA commander, Mladić, and his chief of staff, Gen. Manojlo Milanović, always coordinated their strategy and operations with VJ headquarters (HQ) in Belgrade, to which they were connected by fiber-optic cables and microwave relays until at least 1995. In the key area of air defense, Bosnian Serb territory and airspace were closely integrated with the air defenses of nearby Serbia. It is believed that certain BSA operations, such as the attacks against the Bošnjak enclaves in eastern Bosnia in 1993 and 1995, involved the covert participation of regular VJ troops, Serbian special forces, and military police. The BSA has been an integral component of the Yugoslav armed forces for most of its existence, in much the same way that the HVO is part of the regular **Croatian Army** (HV). Only by 1994, and then only partially, did Milošević order a blockade of the BSA and its **Republika Srpska** (RS), following ever-worsening public splits between the Serbian president and his Bosnian counterpart.

Having forcibly seized much of what they wanted in 1992, Karadžić's government and the BSA were henceforth basically concerned with hanging on to their territorial gains. This broadly defensive strategy was partly dictated by the major operational weakness of the BSA, particularly its shortage of manpower. For the same reason, the chosen modus operandi of the BSA was **siege warfare** and the avoidance, if at all possible, of attacks by infantry and armor on open ground or in urban areas. The problem with this traditional and essentially static strategy, however, was that it passed the initiative to the Bošnjak side. The BSA was given temporary reprieve by the brief Bošnjak-Croat civil war of 1993–1994, during which it covertly aided the HVO in return for hard currency. Once this arrangement was ended by the creation of the **Muslim-Croat Federation** of March 1994, the hitherto dominant position of the BSA was seriously eroded and then all but eliminated.

The creation of the federation allowed the **Bosnian army** (Army of the Republic of Bosnia-Hercegovina, or ARBH) to concentrate on only one enemy. Furthermore, the longer the war went on, the stronger the ARBH and the Croatian armed forces became, so that by the summer of 1995, BSA control of the territory of Bosnia-Hercegovina had fallen to around 49 percent. In May 1995 BSA front lines with the Bosnian Armija and the HVO totaled around 1,500 kilometers, although this fell to well below 1,000 kilometers by the time of the **Dayton Agreements.** Overextended front lines were a major problem for the BSA, forcing its commanders to move its declining manpower pool to deal with enemy attacks when they arose.

In 1993, in response to BSA attacks, the UN Security Council created five **safe areas** in and around the Bošnjak enclaves of **Bihać**, **Tuzla**, **Goražde**, **Srebrenica**, and **Žepa**. This allowed the ARBH to go on the offensive in a number of places for the first time since 1992. With the progressive and ever deeper involvement of the **North Atlantic Treaty Organization** (NATO) in defending **UNPROFOR** (United Nations Protection Force) in

Bosnia, the Bosnian Serb military position was weakened still further, notably during 1994–1995. Having attempted an overambitious offensive with the **Krajina** Serbs in response to the fall of **Fikret Abdić**'s Bihać enclave in 1994, the BSA was confronted with an intensive NATO air-bombing campaign at the same time as a joint Bošnjak-Croat offensive in western Bosnia. In a related series of developments in nearby Croatia, the Serbs in northern **Dalmatia** and western **Slavonia** suffered complete defeat by the HV in the summer of 1995.

If not for the withdrawal of Croatian support and the pressure placed on the Bosnian government by the United States, the BSA would probably have been completely routed in western Bosnia in late 1995. Its only gains at this time were the Bošnjak enclaves at Srebrenica and Žepa, and even these came as part of a reported trade-off involving the abandonment of a number of Serb-held suburbs in **Sarajevo**.

The military defeats of 1995 were also the result of the internal disintegration and international isolation of the RS as a pariah state. Its only sponsor, Serbia, was also close to socioeconomic collapse. One of the results of this development was a serious mutiny by the BSA First Krajina Corps based in **Banja Luka** in 1994. Never particularly strong, troop morale was reportedly very low by 1995, when conscript desertion was rife. The RS and BSA leaderships were forced to sue for any peace agreement that Milošević could get them at Dayton in November 1995. The demilitarization provisions of the Dayton Agreements, strictly monitored by NATO's **Implementation Force** (IFOR), further weakened the BSA.

At the time of the Dayton Agreements, the BSA fielded around 85,000 troops, including reservists. Smaller than the ARBH but larger than the HVO at this time, the BSA was cut to around 30,000 troops one year after Dayton. By that time, it was still larger than the HVO (16,000 troops) but smaller than the ARBH (40,000 troops). Always a problem for the BSA, manpower shortages became critical after Dayton, when large numbers of its demoralized troops simply deserted. At its present manpower levels, the BSA is not a credible fighting force.

Equally serious, the indictment of Mladić and other senior BSA officers as alleged war criminals by the International **War Crimes Tribunal** in The Hague in 1996 effectively left the BSA without a proper command, disorganized and prey to the power struggle in the RS leadership. The BSA had earlier greatly depended on the charismatic figure of Mladić; without him, the BSA high command is in a state of collapse and in no state to fight another major war in Bosnia.

Post-Dayton, the BSA order of battle consists of four corps HQs, of which the most important is Han Pijesak (Sarajevo), followed by Banja Luka, base of the elite First Krajina Corps. The Drina Corps is based at **Višegrad** and the Hercegovina Corps at **Trebinje**. (Prior to Dayton a fifth corps HQ was based at Brčko-Bijeljina [Tuzla].)

Further down the chain of command, the BSA was subdivided into around 80 infantry and other brigades—this number was reduced to around 40 post-Dayton. Of these, around a third were mechanized or armored. This relatively highly mechanized force made it highly dependent on imported fuel supplies from Serbia. As the inheritor of much JNA military equipment in 1992, the BSA inventory consisted of around 600 main battle tanks (MBTs), 350 armored combat vehicles (ACVs), and around 4,000 pieces of artillery of all types, including over 2,000 heavy mortars and some mobile rocket artillery. Post-Dayton demilitarization has reduced this inventory by about half for all main weapons systems. In the air defense sphere, the BSA previously deployed around 1,000 air defense guns, plus a number of surface-to-air missiles (SAMs). During the major NATO air offensive of 1995, however, much of the BSA's air defense system was incapacitated. During the early stages of the Bosnian war, the BSA had a small air force consisting of 20 fixed-wing aircraft and 12 armed helicopters. Most of this was eliminated by NATO in 1995. **Air power** played a minor role in the Bosnian war. The main JNA air bases were either located in enemy territory (Tuzla) or destroyed by the retreating federal army (at Bihać) in 1992. The BSA also had a number of aging surface-to-surface missile (SSM) Frog-7 systems, reportedly manned by regular VJ specialist troops until destroyed by NATO air attacks in 1995.

Unlike the Bošnjak ARBH and the Croatian armed forces, which have been extensively modernized post-Dayton by the United States and other foreign arms suppliers, the isolated BSA is stuck with an aging and decrepit inventory that is unlikely to be replaced even by Serbia. At no time has Milošević allowed the VJ to supply its most modern weapons systems to the BSA. There have been unconfirmed rumors of secret Russian and other arms transfers to the Bosnian Serbs.

—*M. M.*

BOSNIAN SERBS

The pace of the war in **Bosnia-Hercegovina** has in large measure been set by the Bosnian Serbs, beginning with their creation of secessionist regions *(krajine)* in 1992. The communications **media** have also focused world attention upon the more brutal features of that war, such as **detention camps** and "**ethnic cleansing.**" For these reasons many people have formed the impression that the war came about because of an invasion of Bosnia by Serbs. This view has been reinforced by the prominent role that Serbian president **Slobodan Milošević** has played in negotiation on behalf of Serb interests in Bosnia. Certainly it is the case that forces from Serbia have played an active part in the war there, including collaboration between units of the **Yugoslav Peoples' Army** (JNA) and the depredations of Serb **paramilitaries.** Consequently, the war has frequently been described as a "war of aggression" rather than as a **civil war.**

The Serb population has very deep roots in Bosnia-Hercegovina. In the seventh century, the ancestors of modern-day Serbs first located themselves along the Adriatic coast between the mouth of the **Neretva River** and the modern Albanian city of Shkodra, in a proto-state known as Dioclea, or Duklija. During the Middle Ages, **Hercegovina** also was an important part of the early Serb kingdoms of Ras, Hum, and Zeta. It was only in the fourteenth century that the center of gravity of *srpstvo* (Serbdom) moved eastward and southward to **Kosovo** and **Macedonia.** The oldest Serb communities in the Balkans are therefore found in Hercegovina.

Serb settlement farther north stems partly from the assimilation of "Serb" identity by pastoral Vlahs who adopted Orthodox faith. In part it is a result of the historical stimulation of migration by the Ottoman authorities, who were anxious to replace the depleted population of regions disturbed by war. It is largely in these terms that we can explain the dense band of Serb settlement extending across the northern edge of Bosnia, from Bosanska Dubica to Doboj. Similarly, the Serb communities in the Semberija region (around Bijeljina) and on Mount Ozren (east of the **Bosna River**, between **Doboj** and **Maglaj**) are also believed to be of great antiquity. The **Ottoman Empire** tended to favor the **Orthodox Church** over the **Catholic Church** because the empire had an established political relationship with the patriarch in Istambul, and the Ottoman civil service was heavily influenced by the Greek-speaking Phanariotes. Roman Catholics, as followers of the pope, were suspect as possible agents of an outside power.

The culture of Serbs in Bosnia-Hercegovina has always exhibited important differences vis-à-vis that of the Serbs of Serbia "proper." Their **language** (taken by the great standardizer of the language, Vuk Karadžić, as exemplifying the "purest" Serbian) is generally that of the *ijekavski* group of dialects (as is that of **Montenegro** and the **Kosovo** Serbs), which distinguishes it from the *ekavski* of the central and northern Serb districts—and contrasts strongly with the speech of the Timok-Prizren dialects of southeast Serbia. During the time of the "First Yugoslavia" (created in 1919), the strength of the Democratic Party was found in Serbia itself (and in the Croatian ***krajina***), whereas Bosnian Serbs were far more likely to support the Radicals or the Agrarians. During the more recent turn toward multiparty politics, Bosnian Serbs have gone their own way. Slobodan Milošević's **Socialist Party of Serbia,** largely secularist and still explicitly appealing to continuity with the traditions of the **League of Communists**, has been eclipsed in Bosnia-Hercegovina by the Serbian Democratic Party (SDS). This party drew its inspiration from Croatian Serb leader **Jovan Rašković**, whose anti-communist mysticism, adopted by Bosnian Serb leader **Radovan Karadžić**, is much closer in many respects to the views of Serbia's **Vukašin Drašković** than to Milošević's opportunism and pragmatism. Although the hierarchy of the Orthodox Church has been cautious, indeed ambivalent, in its endorsement of Milošević, the SDS in Bosnia-Hercegovina has developed close and active links with the local Orthodox clergy.

Milošević's apparent "desertion" of the Serb cause in Bosnia, as well as his emergence as an agent of the imposition of the **Dayton Agreements** on a reluctant SDS, has been interpreted as a volte-face brought about by his need to lift the economic **sanctions** imposed on his country. It is equally likely that his holding at arm's length of the Bosnian Serbs is rooted in caution about the prospects of bringing into a Yugoslav federation another Serb political entity that does not share his own conception of politics—and which, in concert with dissident opinion in the **Vojvodina**, the **Belgrade** region, and even Montenegro, might topple him from power.

—*J. B. A.*

See also: political parties; religion

BOŠNJACI

See **Muslims in Yugoslavia**

BOUTROS-GHALI, BOUTROS

As **United Nations** (UN) secretary-general from 1991 to 1996, Boutros Boutros-Ghali was the individual ultimately responsible for the UN's peacekeeping, humanitarian, and other operations during the Yugoslav wars. Appointed to replace the outgoing Javier Perez de Cuellar as secretary-general just as the UN's role in the former Yugoslavia was becoming more central, Boutros-Ghali's involvement in the Yugoslav situation attracted considerable controversy. As an Egyptian Coptic Christian, he was accused by the Bosnian **Muslim** government in Sarajevo of holding pro-Serb sympathies. During his visit to **Sarajevo** in 1992, he remarked that the city's situation was better than that of several other war zones, implying that there was less suffering than in other areas also under attack by Bosnian Serbs. In general his handling of the second UN Protection Force (**UNPROFOR** II) operation in **Bosnia-Hercegovina** attracted criticism. Rather than being part of some pro-Serb or anti-Muslim conspiracy and an alleged appeaser of the **Bosnian Serbs**, however, Boutros-Ghali acted as a cautious professional diplomat. He was bound by the procedures of his organization and restricted by the mandates set out in resolutions of a UN Security Council reluctant to become militarily involved in the area. These political constraints greatly limited what the UN forces deployed in **Croatia** and Bosnia could realistically accomplish.

In the process of forming an interpretation of the conduct of UN operations in the former Yugoslavia, it is also difficult to separate the responsibility of Boutros-Ghali from that of his special representative in the region, **Yasushi Akashi**. Even taking account of the constraints under which the UN operated at this time, however, Boutros-Ghali and Akashi became noted for the caution of their efforts, notably so after the **North Atlantic Treaty Organization** (NATO) became more actively

Boutros Boutros-Ghali, UN secretary general during the Yugoslav wars of the 1990s. (United Nations photo)

involved in the Bosnian conflict under pressure from the **United States** in 1994. The secretary-general and his special representative were then accused of hampering the use of NATO firepower against the troublesome Bosnian Serbs.

After four years of UNPROFOR deployment, the Croatian war was ended by the independent action of the **Croatian Army**, sweeping aside the UN presence. Civil war in Bosnia-Hercegovina was finally ended by a mixture of enhanced NATO air power and a major Muslim-Croat offensive against the Bosnian Serbs in 1995, after which the UN forces were replaced by a purely NATO operation. Nevertheless, the success of UN peacekeeping operations under Boutros-Ghali's stewardship should not be judged only in relation to UNPROFOR. The deployments of the UN Preventive Deployment Force (**UNPREDEP**, in Macedonia) and the UN Transitional Administration for Eastern Slavonia, Baranja, and Western Sirmium (**UNTAES**) were unqualified successes. In terms of **humanitarian aid** and **refugees**, the records of the UN and of Boutros-Ghali were far more creditable than is often acknowledged, and the role of the UN High Commission for Refugees (**UNHCR**) was of great importance throughout the former Yugoslavia. Boutros-Ghali was also strongly in line with Western thinking in being in favor of the imposition of economic **sanctions** against **Serbia** and **Montenegro**. On other central issues, such as the Security Council's decisions to create a number of "**safe areas**" in Bosnia in 1993, he diplomatically accepted the official line even when he knew that it would fail and that he would be blamed for failures that were not of his own making.

At the end of his first five-year term as UN secretary-general, what should have been an automatic extension of his term of office was vetoed by the United States. Top policymakers took their revenge against a figure whom they had spent so much effort maligning for alleged failures in the former Yugoslavia—failures that were only partly of his making and that perhaps should have been laid at other doors, the United States included.

—M. M.

BRČKO

Brčko, a port on the south bank of the **Sava River** within the Republic of **Bosnia-Hercegovina**, was of considerable potential importance for all sides in the Bosnian war. Located astride a major east-west road, it commands the essential means of communication linking the northern parts of the **Republika Srpska**, including **Banja Luka**, both with its southern and eastern parts and with **Serbia** itself. Without control of the Brčko "corridor," the project of an integral **Bosnian Serb** state would be seriously damaged. The port is also seen as an essential **communications** link by the Bosnian government, providing an alternative access by the outside world to the **Neretva River** ports. The railway line through Brčko is also an important element of the Bosnian system of communication. Control by a hostile state would impose significant restrictions upon Bosnian trade. Croats also have an interest in the town. Although the largest component—44 percent—of its 88,000 population (1991 census) was Muslim in the prewar period, Brčko contained one of the largest Croat communities in Bosnia (22,000). In recognition of its importance in this respect, the area was included in the short-lived Banovina Hrvatska (i.e., Prefecture of Croatia) between 1939 and 1941. More significant, because of its location in relation to road and rail communication, **Croatia**, too, would wish to ensure an unhindered passage of goods and people across Bosnia between eastern **Slavonia** and **Dalmatia**.

As a consequence of its undoubted strategic importance, the area of the south bank of the Sava between Brčko and Orăsje was subjected to some of the most sustained and fierce fighting of the war, involving troops of all sides but with no decisive military result. Control of the area was one of the points over which negotiations broke down repeatedly during the long search for a settlement and turned out to be a stumbling block during the Dayton negotiations as well. Exceptionally, the **Dayton Agreements** expressly deferred a decision about the interentity boundary in this area, and an arbitrating commission headed by Robert W. Farrand of the United States was set up. On 14 February 1997, the commission issued a provisional judgment identifying a number of issues still to be addressed and postponing its final adjudication for another year. Decision was again deferred by the commission a year later. These deferrals of a final decision are an indication of the extreme sensitivity of the issue, but by the same token they are an indication of the leverage that can be asserted to ensure continuing compliance on the part of the various parties to the Dayton program.

—*J. B. A.*

See also: Posavina Corridor

BRIDGES

See **Maslenica Bridge; Mostar**

BRIONI ACCORD

Slovenia's declaration of independence from Yugoslavia on 25 June 1991 had provoked the immediate intervention of the **Yugoslav Peoples' Army** (JNA), which resulted in the Ten Day War. On 7–8 July, a meeting on the island of Brioni off the western coast of Istria, which had previously served as one of **Tito**'s retreats, was called by the European Community (EC) as mediator. This meeting was presided over by the minister of foreign affairs from the Netherlands, Hans van den Broek, and involved three ministers from the EC and delegates from Slovenia, Croatia, and Serbia. It resulted in agreement to uphold the **cease-fire,** to return both Yugoslav and Slovene troops and territorial defense units to their bases, and to restore Slovenia's control over its own entry points. It was also agreed that the Slovene and Croatian declarations of independence would not be implemented before a "cooling off" period of three months, with a further meeting to be held at the beginning of August, although this meeting did not transpire. Ostensibly this was an agreement brokered by the EC; in fact, though, it was an outcome of the already engineered agenda between the Slovene and Serbian presidents, **Milan Kučan** and **Slobodan Milošević**, and it effectively ensured both Yugoslav and international recognition of Slovenia's independence, at the same time allowing Milošević to pursue the Serbian cause. In this respect, for Croatia the Brioni agreement was an empty one.

—*J. J. H.*

BROD

See **Bosanski Brod; Slavonski Brod**

BROTHERHOOD AND UNITY MOTORWAY

See **communications and transport**

BROZ, JOSIP

See **Tito, Josip Broz**

BUKOSHI, BUJAR

Bujar Bukoshi is a leading **Kosovo Albanian** political figure. Born in 1947 in Suhareka/Suva Reka (Kosovo), Bukoshi studied medicine in Belgrade and Berlin. As a specialist in urology, he worked for a number of years as associate professor of surgery at the Faculty of Medicine of the University of Priština. In October 1991 he was elected to the post of prime minister of the self-proclaimed Republic of Kosovo. He leads his government from self-imposed exile in Germany.

—*R. E.*

BULATOVIĆ, MOMIR

Momir Bulatović was president of the Socialist Republic of **Montenegro** from 1989 to 1992 and of the Republic of Montenegro from 1992 to 1997. A Montenegrin by birth (1957), Bulatović studied at the University of Titograd and was a founding member of the **League of Communists** of Montenegro (LCM). He spent most of his working life was as a minor functionary of the LCM, but he rose to prominence on his election in 1989 to the Montenegrin presidency.

It is generally considered that his election owed much to the sponsorship of **Slobodan Milošević**, then president of Serbia. The old government in Montenegro was overthrown by a series of orchestrated protests as a part of the "antibureaucratic revolution" engendered by Milošević. Bulatović's youth and relative obscurity were an advantage in this context, confirming the image of a "new broom" in politics. In April 1989 a new government was formed with Bulatović at its head.

He has attempted to steer a difficult path between the proindependence, primarily liberal (and thus anti-Serb) lobby and the more "traditional" wing of Montenegrin politics, which views Belgrade as the ultimate guarantor of Montenegrin "Serbdom." Despite repeated vows that Montenegro would remain within the new Yugoslav federation, Bulatović has sought to pursue a number of alternative options, seeking relationships with other states, principally **Albania** and **Italy**. To this end he required his foreign minister to visit potential allies, and he himself conducted several visits abroad, sometimes surreptitiously. He created suspicion in Belgrade by making conciliatory gestures toward **Croatia** regarding the siege of **Dubrovnik** (where he appeared in a TV interview) and toward the **United**

Nations (UN) over the future of both Croatia and **Bosnia-Hercegovina.** Within the Federal Republic of **Yugoslavia,** Montenegro conducted a dogged resistance over its representation in government following the fall of the government of **Milan Panić.**

Nevertheless, Bulatović found himself in an increasingly difficult situation. On the one hand, he was regarded as Milošević's "man in **Podgorica**" and thus subject to centralizing pressure within the Yugoslav federation. On the other hand, he was compelled to act as the principal representative of Montenegro's interests, reflecting the traditional pride of Montenegrins in their independence, and as the defender of the republic's freedom of political maneuvering both within the federation and on the international scene.

As pressure toward pan-Serb solidarity eased following the settlement of the war in Bosnia-Hercegovina in 1995, Montenegrin premier **Milo Djukanović** emerged as a vocal source of opposition to **Serbia.** Neither Bulatović nor Djukanović have hidden their political and personal animosity, and the conflict between the two (and their respective views of the political future of the republic) quickly became more open and more vigorously pursued. After a hard-fought political battle during 1996 and 1997, the Democratic Party of Socialists of Montenegro (the successor to the LCM) split, and in the presidential election of December 1997 Bulatović was narrowly defeated.

—*R. J.*

BULGARIA

The 1990 multiparty elections in individual Yugoslav republics and the first signs of a likely disintegration of Yugoslavia polarized Bulgarian public opinion along Communist/anti-Communist lines. Although the Bulgarian Socialist Party (BSP) was generally sympathetic to the forces of the "old order," federalism, and **Slobodan Milošević,** the Union of Democratic Forces (SDS) expressed sympathy toward anti-Communist parties and politicians. This remained the case throughout the 1990s, with pro-Socialist and pro-**Serbian** attitudes being almost the exclusive preserve of the BSP.

With the advent of free speech after November 1989, there was a resurgence of traditional Bulgarian interest in Macedonian issues, as well as anti-Serbian and anti-Yugoslav attitudes. These attitudes were particularly evident in Pirin Macedonia and among Macedonian refugees and their descendants, most of whom in 1990 had united in the Internal Macedonian Revolutionary Organisation–Union of Macedonian Societies (VMRO-SMD). VMRO allied itself to the anti-Communist bloc/SDS in all elections throughout the 1990s and played an important role in Pirin local politics, although its nationwide influence remained negligible. Although VMRO succeeded in impressing its interpretation of Macedonian issues on the largely indifferent Bulgarian public and policymakers, Macedonian issues remained marginal in Bulgarian political discourse.

In January 1991 the Bulgarian Ministry of Foreign Affairs declared that in case of a legally correct process of dissociation of **Macedonia** from **Yugoslavia,** Bulgaria would recognize Macedonia as an independent state within its existing **borders**—this took place months before the Macedonian leadership could seriously consider independence. Events in Yugoslavia were hardly a priority for a Bulgarian government consumed by the difficulties of transition toward a market economy. When Slovenia and Croatia declared independence at the end of June 1991, VMRO staged sparsely attended demonstrations in front of the Yugoslav embassy in Sofia and urged their immediate recognition, but the official Bulgarian reaction faithfully followed the European Community's pattern: support for the preservation of a united Yugoslavia only gradually gave way to declarations about the right of Yugoslav republics to self-determination. In early September Bulgarian president Zhelyu Zhelev's official visit to Germany was preceded by a declaration by the Bulgarian Ministry of Foreign Affairs that spoke of the right to self-determination without mentioning anything about the preservation of federal Yugoslavia; the declaration resolutely condemned attempts to change the internal borders in Yugoslavia by force. In his press conference after talks with German chancellor Helmut Kohl and **Hans-Dietrich Genscher** in Bonn, Zhelev spoke about a "total unanimity of views" between Bulgaria and Germany concerning Yugoslavia, thus firmly allying Bulgaria with the countries most sympathetic toward the recognition of the independence of individual Yugoslav republics—**Austria, Hungary,** and **Germany.**

Bulgaria was the only neighboring country that hailed the Macedonian independence referendum on 8 September 1991, committing itself to recognizing the independence (when it would be declared) and territorial integrity of Macedonia. Moreover, after the referendum Bulgaria derailed a summit (organized by **Greece**) of Balkan **Orthodox** leaders by refusing to discuss questions related to Macedonia in the absence of Macedonian representatives.

Because of its European aspirations and severe economic and political problems, however, Bulgaria muted its Yugoslav policy and waited for an EC lead. Following the December recommendations of the **Badinter Commission** for the recognition of Slovenia and Macedonia, Sofia prepared to recognize these countries in mid-January 1992. The EC's backtracking on Macedonia split the ruling SDS government. Bulgarian foreign minister Stoyan Ganev favored fidelity to the EC stand and made promises to this effect to his German counterpart. Ganev's deputy, Stefan Tafrov, actively conspired to bring about a **recognition** of Macedonia, and in Ganev's absence he managed to sway President Zhelev and Prime Minister Philip Dimitrov. The recognition issue came to a head in the week between two rounds of presidential elections in Bulgaria, and VMRO and SDS politicians from Pirin Macedonia lost no time in impressing on Zhelev that recognition of Macedonia would increase his minimal electoral lead over the BSP contender. On 15 January, 1992 Dimitrov announced the recognition of Slovenia, Croatia, Macedonia, and Bosnia-Hercegovina to a standing ovation by the members of parliament (MPs) of the ruling majority, who booed the BSP MPs for remaining seated. Ganev learned about this recognition on returning to the Sofia airport from a visit to Germany, where he had just affirmed that Bulgaria would not recognize Macedonia before the EC countries. He did not rest until he secured the dismissal of Tafrov. Ganev was particularly incensed by the recognition of **Bosnia-Hercegovina** (included in the process to give it a veneer of "equidistance" and "principle" and to avoid placing emphasis on Macedonia), which came at a time when no other state had recognized Bosnia and before Bosnia itself had held a referendum on independence or asked any country for recognition.

Bulgaria's lead in the recognition of Macedonia under its constitutional name was well received in the Macedonian capital, Skopje. It reinforced latent pro-Bulgarian sentiments among VMRO-DPMNE (Democratic Party for Macedonian National Unity) supporters, while the traditionally anti-Bulgarian ex-Communist politicians and commentators were at a loss in terms of how to react.

In August 1992, while on an official visit to Sofia, Russian president Boris Yeltsin pledged an immediate recognition of Macedonia under its constitutional name and explained this act as "a support for the position of Bulgarian leaders" and their understanding of the issue. Yeltsin's recognition of Macedonia took by surprise the foreign policy establishment in Moscow, which for a day would neither confirm nor deny it. His explicit linkage of recognition to the position of the Bulgarian leadership caused mixed reactions in Skopje's ruling circles; gratitude to **Russia** was mixed with warnings against a revival of the Russian support that existed for Bulgaria in the nineteenth century.

Most of the advantages Bulgaria had gained from its head start in the process of recognition were squandered through a delay in opening a diplomatic office in Skopje for about a year, as well as through the emergence of a "**language** dispute" with Macedonia in 1993. Bulgaria's preferred formula was that bilateral documents were to be prepared "in the official languages of both countries," whereas Skopje insisted that these languages be explicitly named as Bulgarian and Macedonian. Trade between both countries temporarily surged during the economic **sanctions** on the remaining Yugoslavia in 1992–1995, as well as in the 18 months of the Greek blockade of Macedonia (February 1994–September 1995). Because there was no improvement in the poor infrastructure linking the countries, preembargo trade patterns were quick to reemerge after 1995.

The issue of the Bulgarian-populated borderlands in eastern Serbia was another problem reawakened by the disintegration of Yugoslavia. In December 1990 a Bulgarian minority party, Democratic Alliance of Bulgarians in Yugoslavia (DSBJ), was founded in Niš. It has since called for the restoration of Bulgarian-language schools and other cultural institutions closed in the 1960s–1980s, as well as for unobstructed cultural and economic contacts with Bulgaria. DSBJ has had a growing impact on the Bulgarian public and on the authorities in Sofia (mostly through the government Committee for Bulgarians Abroad, created in

1992). Ever since 1991, VMRO-SMD has argued that the post-1918 borders were open to revision after the disintegration of Yugoslavia. The official Bulgarian position throughout the 1990s, however, has been that border changes are inadmissible and that Bulgarians in Yugoslavia should enjoy full minority rights as loyal Yugoslav citizens. Yugoslav and Serbian authorities have reacted nervously to any signs of Bulgarian interest in the situation of the Bulgarian minority in Serbia. They have consistently refused to recognize the official Bulgarian term for the Bulgarian-inhabited Yugoslav borderlands ("Western Borderlands") and to engage themselves in talks about that region with Bulgarian and other foreign officials. They insist that there are no problems with minority rights there and no police persecution of Bulgarian activists. Accordingly, the Belgrade press regularly describes DSBJ as fascists and separatists. DSBJ, on its part, has successfully lobbied Serbian opposition parties for joint action against Slobodan Milošević and his **Socialist Party of Serbia.**

On 25 January 1995, a fact-finding mission from the Organization for Security and Cooperation in Europe (OSCE) visited Dimitrovgrad on the Bulgarian border in eastern Serbia for talks with representatives of the local authorities and the DSBJ. Its conclusions were that although the Yugoslav and Serbian constitution and laws give adequate protection to minority rights, in practice their implementation leaves much to be desired. Predictably, the OSCE mission was challenged by the Belgrade **media** and was approvingly described by the Sofia media. Since then the situation of the Bulgarian minority in Serbia has been regularly monitored by **human rights** missions to Yugoslavia.

Apart from the issues of Macedonia and the Bulgarian minority in Serbia, Bulgarian politicians largely followed the zigzags of Western and **United Nations** (UN) policies concerning the remaining Yugoslavia. There was no enthusiasm in Sofia concerning sanctions on Yugoslavia because these sanctions cut off Bulgaria's major route toward the West and forced reorientation toward longer and more difficult routes through Romania. Legitimate Bulgarian trade with Western Europe suffered heavy losses, while criminal companies reaped fortunes by "sanctions busting." For Bulgaria the lasting legacy of the economic sanctions from 1992 to 1995 was a dramatically increased physical isolation from Western Europe, heightened corruption of the state administration (particularly at the borders), and a wholesale criminalization of the economy.

—*K. D.*

C

CANTONS

Proposals for new **constitutional** structures for **Bosnia-Hercegovina** have all made provision in one way or another for a multiplicity of units joined in a federation, and these units have frequently been described as "cantons." The term derives from the constitution of Switzerland, which is composed of a confederation of 20 cantons and 6 half-cantons, reflecting the country's complex pattern of **ethnicity**—German, French, Italian, and Romance. It is fundamentally misleading, however, to describe the proposals that have been debated for Bosnia as "cantons" based on the Swiss model; the Swiss versions represent a union of preexisting free states, whereas the various plans for Bosnia have involved the enforced division of a formerly unified republic.

—J. B. A.

CARRINGTON, (LORD) PETER

Lord Carrington (born 1919), formerly foreign secretary in the British Conservative government in the 1980s, was the first to be appointed by the **European Community** (EC) as its peace envoy to Yugoslavia. Carrington chaired the EC Conference on Yugoslavia at The Hague in October 1991, which accepted that Yugoslavia as such no longer existed but urged caution in the matter of independence for its individual republics, justifiably anticipating that haste would engender deeper conflict. Carrington's reputation for detachment perhaps led him to underestimate the depth of feeling already engendered—though in less tense circumstances his plan for a mixture of independence and confederalism had much to commend it. In any event, the combination of Serbian president **Slobodan Milošević**'s refusal to condone the defederalization of Yugoslavia and German foreign minister **Hans-Dietrich Genscher**'s usurping of the EC collective role to force through early recognition of independence for Slovenia and Croatia effectively ended the Carrington peace plan. Carrington had already astutely warned of the potential implications for Bosnia, and three weeks after the outbreak of hostilities there in April 1992 he visited Sarajevo for talks with Bosnian president **Alija Izetbegović** in a vain search for a negotiated cease-fire. During his term, Carrington had presided over several **cease-fires,** which became increasingly superficial. He was succeeded in August 1992 by Lord **David Owen.**

—J. J. H.

See also: Badinter Commission

CARTOONS

See **media (domestic)**

CASUALTIES

No authoritatative or systematic attempt has yet been made to account for the casualties caused by the breakup of Yugoslavia. Estimates of casualties are complicated by three factors: the effects of the movement of **population**; the ambiguities in those figures that have been reported; and official secrecy.

The Ten Day War in **Slovenia** resulted in the deaths of 36 soldiers of the Yugoslav Peoples' Army (JNA) and 5 members of the Slovene armed forces. Five Slovene and 10 foreign civilians also lost their

A casualty of war, Bosnia-Hercegovina, 1992. (Stevan Filipović)

lives. A government estimate reported that the war in **Croatia** had left 13,583 people dead or missing and 37,180 wounded. A calculation by the U.S. Central Intelligence Agency (CIA) that fighting in **Bosnia-Hercegovina** claimed around 200,000 lives has been widely quoted. The figures for Bosnia, however, give an indication of the difficulty in assessing the realism and accuracy of published claims. The CIA judged that around 90 percent of casualties in Bosnia-Hercegovina were among "Muslims," although it is unclear as to whether this refers to ethnic Muslims or simply to supporters of the government regardless of their ethnicity. Croatian government sources report that in Bosnia-Hercegovina 9,909 Croats were killed or missing and 20,649 were wounded. Clearly these two assessments are mutually inconsistent. If the CIA is approximately correct in its assessment of the *proportionate* share of the burden of casualties, and if the Croatian estimate of *numbers* is at all credible, then the *overall total* of 200,000 must be too low. Other sources, however, suggest that the CIA figure for the total number of deaths at the very least conflates the dead and the missing and is possibly too high.

The problem of making accurate estimates in this area is rendered particularly difficult by the reticence of Serb sources, both in the **Republika Srpska** and in the Federal Republic of **Yugoslavia**, about casualties. It is believed that several actions during the war cost Serb armed forces dearly: the defense of **Trebinje**; the succession of clashes around **Maglaj/Ozren**; the several attempts to dislodge Bosnian government forces from the **Bihać** enclave; and the successful repulse of an attempt to break the seige of **Sarajevo** in June 1995. The constant struggle (particularly against Croatian forces) for control of the Orašje/**Brčko** area involved very heavy fighting including large losses for the Serbs, and **Operation Flash** in western **Slavonia** in May 1995 is also thought to have resulted in relatively high Serb casualties, including many civilians. The numbers of troops involved in these engagements were typically small, however, so that even proportionately large losses will have meant no more than a few hundred deaths on any occasion. A distinctive feature of the war in Yugoslavia has been a reversal of the normal pattern of casualties in wartime, in which the majority of those killed or injured are combatants. In Yugoslavia a clear preponderance of casualties has been from among the civilian, noncombatant population—more than 1,600 children were killed in Sarajevo alone. (None of the figures given include the costs of the terrorist suppression of the **Albanian** population in **Kosovo**.)

—*J. B. A.*

See also: disabled; land mines; rape

CATHOLIC CHURCH

Although the conflict in Yugoslavia has often been presented primarily in terms of religion (between nations that are largely characterized by their adherence either to the **Orthodox** or Roman Catholic traditions of Christianity or to **Islam**), the role of organized religion has everywhere been complex. This is nowhere more true than in the case of Catholicism.

Among the diverse ethnic groups in former Yugoslavia, Slovenes and Croats have been historically closely identified with Roman Catholicism. The nature and importance of this link, however, has been both historically and geographically variable. In **Slovenia** (the only South Slav area to be affected appreciably by the Reformation and Counter-Reformation), the clergy became central to the development of national consciousness during the nineteenth century. The University of Ljubljana was initially a religious institution. The principal voice of Slovene national identity during the "First Yugoslavia" (created in 1919) was the Slovene People's Party, led by Monsignor Anton Korošec.

In **Croatia**, on the other hand, the link was looser and more complex. The "**Yugoslav Idea**" was partly the creation of Bishop Josip Strossmayer. The Croatian Peasant Party, which emerged after 1908 as the dominant political voice of the Croat nation, was often quite outspokenly anticlerical. During the period of the "Second Yugoslavia" (communist Yugoslavia from 1945), relations between church and state in Croatia were further complicated by the experience of the wartime "Independent State of Croatia." During this period Catholics were acutely divided in their response to the political situation. Some ardently backed the fascist **Ustaša** regime; others fought with equal determination and commitment for the **Partizans**. These divisions affected the laity, ordinary clergy, and the hierarchy. After the war, when the communist regime took a rigidly antireligious stance, relations between Roman Catholics and the state were embittered by the trial of Archbishop **Alojzije Stepinac** in 1946. Although accused of active collaboration with the fascist regime, it seems most likely that the archbishop sought to remove the Catholic Church from a political role and that his crime was his subsequent refusal to countenance the creation of a compliant state church, which would reduce, if not sever, its links with the Vatican.

The communist victory in 1945 ushered in a period of mutual hostility between the Catholic Church and the regime. The property of religious communities composed a significant proportion of land sequestered under the land reform program; the church's role in education was curtailed, and its freedom to publish was circumscribed. Diplomatic links with the Vatican were severed in December 1952, and a freer atmosphere was not restored until the late 1960s, when the influential weekly *Glas Concila* was permitted to begin publication.

It is important not to oversimplify the situation, and the attitudes and experience of Catholics within former Yugoslavia cannot be reduced to the dimension of church-state relations or to relations between Belgrade and the Vatican. As in the Roman Catholic Church elsewhere, the church in Yugoslavia has been divided over issues of liturgy, morals, and social policy, which might be characterized as conflict between modernity and traditionalism. Its political stance has ranged from active participation in the official priests' associations and engagement in the lively debate between Christianity and Marxism in Slovenia during the late 1960s to obdurate anticommunism.

The disintegration of the Yugoslav federation has seen a continuation of this diversity. It is important in assessing the role of the church in this period to distinguish between the attempts made by nationalist politicians to co-opt religion to their own purposes and the part played in politics by either the clergy or laity. Only in Slovenia has there been anything approaching a significant "clerical party" (the Christian Democrats), although the immediate postindependence Croatian Sabor included three members of the clergy (two members of the **Croatian Democratic Union** and one Christian Democrat).

The Roman Catholic hierarchies in Croatia (especially Cardinal **Franjo Kuharić** of Zagreb) and **Bosnia-Hercegovina** have repeatedly called for interethnic and interfaith tolerance and have condemned the outrages sometimes committed in the name of religion. Joint statements on the war have been issued by the leaders of all faiths, calling for restraint and negotiated solutions to conflict.

The historical indentification of Slovene and Croat nationality with Catholicism must be balanced against low rates of regular religious observance in both republics. A study in 1985 study reported that only 33 percent of Croats and 26 percent of Slovenes declared themselves to be "believers." Another study in 1982 found only 12 percent of Slovenes to be "consistently religious," and a Croatian survey (also 1985) recorded only 10 percent of respondents declaring a "religious orientation," with the number falling to 4 percent of routine white-collar workers. If religion does function as a rather diffuse badge of identity, therefore, it should not be surprising to find that ecclesiastical guidance is not necessarily a good guide to either the attitudes or behavior of ordinary people.

—*J. B. A.*

See also: Medjugorje

References: Kristo, Jure. "Catholicism among Croats and Its Critique by Marxists." In Dennis J. Dunn (ed.), *Religion and Nationalism in Eastern Europe and the Soviet Union.* London: Lynne Rienner Publishers, 1987; Ramet, Sabrina Petra. *Balkan Babel: Politics, Culture, and Religion in Yugoslavia.* Boulder, CO: Westview Press, 1992, ch. 7.

CAZIN

With a population of 64,000 (1991 census), Cazin was an important center of Muslim resistance within the "**Bihać** pocket" of northwestern Bosnia throughout the war. As in the neighboring communes of Bihać, **Bosanska Krupa**, and Velika Kladuša, the prewar population of Cazin was overwhelmingly **Muslim** (97 percent); consequently, every internationally sponsored plan for the division, or "cantonization," of **Bosnia** placed Cazin at the heart of a specifically Muslim entity. The town generally benefited from the influence of **Fikret Abdić**, who managed until his fall in August 1994 to minimize the impact of the war on the locality. Because of its link with Abdić, the area came to be known mockingly as the Cazinska *krajina* (a term used by Serbs in territorial claims). In January 1995, however, the town became engulfed in the war as forces loyal to Abdić attempted, with Serb support, to retake the region from Bosnian government control. Fighting continued until the end of March.

Cazin was headquarters of the **Bosnian army**'s Fifth Corps, which emerged as one of the most effective formations of the war.

—*J. B. A.*

CEASE-FIRES

"God protect us from cease-fires."

—*Canadian general Lewis Mackenzie*

The Yugoslav conflict will be remembered for many reasons, including the level of brutality, the tragic legacy of **land mines**, and most certainly the seeming inability of third parties to stop the conflict. Depending on the definition used, there were 13 cease-fires in the first eight months of the conflict alone; the obvious question to ask is why this was the case. In general, the failure of these and subsequent agreements can be attributed to two main factors: (1) the coerced nature of many of the agreements and (2) technical imperfections.

Coerced Agreements

Most **conflict resolution** professionals believe that it is difficult, if not impossible, to successfully de-escalate or resolve a conflict when the participants do not desire such outcomes. If a solution is forced upon those in conflict and that solution is not one of their own making, it is in all likelihood doomed to failure. Nevertheless, it was clear in the Yugoslav conflict that not only were participants often being coerced into ceasing fire, but that solutions were often not of their own design. This is not to say a coerced solution can never work, and it should be admitted that the international community faced tremendous pressure to do something; the difficulty is that if a cease-fire is something that is coerced, the coercer needs to ensure that it has the means, and the willingness to use them, to guarantee that the belligerents will do what they say they will do.

The coercer, by imposing the cease-fire, will in many ways be expected to take responsibility for it, but this was something that rarely happened in the Yugoslav conflict. Guaranteeing a cease-fire requires at least one of two related things: adequate **monitoring** or adequate peacekeeping. The number of **European Community** cease-fire monitors in the advance group that went to **Slovenia** was 10. Over 200 were eventually in place, but even of that number only 120 were actual monitors—the remainder filled support roles. Even by 1994, and despite the presence of peacekeeping troops by that stage, the British **United Nations** (UN) commander in **Bosnia, Michael Rose**, reported that a shortage of troops, coupled with the unwillingness of the parties to negotiate, made it impossible to achieve a specific **safe area** agreement, since the presence of **UNPROFOR** (United Nations Protection Force) was limited to no more than eight observers. It is clear that because of the failure to guarantee provisions of the agreement, what ended up being coerced were not cease-fires but cease-fire agreements. The difference is crucial.

Technical Imperfections

Even if it is assumed that at certain points in the conflict there was some desire on the part of the belligerents to stop fighting—and there is some evidence for this—the agreements themselves were often flawed, mostly owing to a lack of specificity. In many cases, it was often not clear to either side what exactly it was they had agreed to. Belligerents made their own interpretations and undertook actions that the other side considered to be violations.

If any agreement is to be implemented fully (and if it is to last), dealing with perceived or actual violations means handing not only obvious violations such as shooting at the enemy, but also actions taken under the cease-fire that, although not specifically prohibited, could nevertheless be considered to be violations. None of the early agreements in the Yugoslav conflict made any attempt to address this sort of complication. (As an extreme example of the consequences, Gen. **Veljko Kadijević**, the minister of defense of the Yugoslav federation, complained in September 1991 that the latest cease-fire had been violated when a forest had been set alight.) It should be noted that this situation changed considerably once the United Nations became involved in early 1992. UN agreements were still imperfect, but they were clearer.

Lack of clarity in cease-fire agreements is a historical and as yet unresolved problem. If one lesson can be learned from the Yugoslav conflict, it is that a cease-fire agreement is a delicate and unstable instrument that needs to be carefully crafted if it is to be effective. There is much to be learned from past agreements. These lessons should not be ignored in the future. Distrust and cynicism increase with every failed agreement, and the chances of implementing a durable cease-fire, let alone a permanent settlement, decrease proportionally after each failure.

—*J. D. D. S.*

ÇETTA, ANTON (1925–1995)

Born at Prizren in southern Kosovo in 1925, Anton Çetta was one of the most eminent Albanian ethnographers. He was director of folklore at the Institute of Albanology at Priština University until 1985, an editor and prolific writer on folklore, and founder of the Movement for the Reconciliation of Blood Feuds. In areas of **Kosovo** and northern Albania, social organization is still to some extent based upon tribal structure, governed by customary rather than state law, where disputes are often best resolved through *besa* (the pledge of honor). Çetta came to be recognized as a reconciliatory patriarch, through whom families felt able to "forgive the blood." He succeeded in resolving over a thousand blood feuds. This work came to be seen as particularly significant during the Kosovo conflict of the 1980s, contributing to the culture of nonviolence that marked the **Albanian** response to the Serb attempts to suppress Albanian culture and exclude them from political life.

—*A. T. Y.*

CHETNIKS

Bands of irregular guerrilla fighters called "Chetniks" (from the Serbo-Croat term *četnici*) have come to be known for their ferocity in battle and their espousal of Serbian nationalism. The Chetnik tradition originated during the time of the **Ottoman Empire**, when bands of Chetniks were formed to fight the Turkish occupiers. These bands were first organized into recognizable military formations during the Balkan Wars (1912–1913). During World War I, they became an integral part of the Royal Serbian Army, often operating as special forces behind enemy lines. This army was one of the first in Europe to have such guerrilla detachments in its ranks. During World War II and the Axis occupation of Yugoslavia, Chetnik bands in Serbia and Montenegro emerged under the command of Gen. Draža Mihailović (1892–1946), who decided to stay on to fight the Germans and Italians after the capitulation of the government in April 1941. After liberating areas of Serbia toward the end of 1941, the Chetniks were driven into Montenegro and Bosnia by superior German forces.

A complicated and bitter civil war then broke out between the Chetniks and the communist **Partizans** led by Josip Broz **Tito**. Initially supported by the Western Allies, the Chetniks were later abandoned because of their alleged collaboration with the Axis occupiers. The British government also calculated that the entirely Serb Chetniks would not be able to resolve the deep divisions of the Yugoslav peoples in the postwar period. Increased Western political and military assistance was then made available to Tito's Partizans. By the end of 1944, Mihailović's Chetniks had been defeated and discredited by the communists. In April 1946 Mihailović was tried and executed as an alleged collaborator and traitor by the new communist Yugoslav government. In parts of Serbia, Chetnik anticommunist bands were in existence until the early 1950s. Large numbers of Chetniks fled Yugoslavia after the war and settled in North America and Western Europe; during the 1960s and 1970s, they occasionally undertook acts of terrorism in Yugoslavia.

A number of **paramilitary** forces calling themselves "Chetniks" emerged in **Serbia**, mainly in response to the rebellion of the **Krajina** Serbs in Croatia in 1990. These forces later fought in Croatia and Bosnia, where they are alleged to have committed many **war crimes** against non-Serbs.

These contemporary Chetniks, particularly those loyal to the Serbian Radical Party (SRS) and led by **Vojislav Šešelj**, claim to be the latter-day followers of Mihailović and one of his surviving commanders in exile, Momčilo Djuić. They have also called for the restoration of the exiled crown prince of Yugoslavia, Aleksandar Karadjordjević. Early supporters of the new nationalist agenda of Serbian president **Slobodan Milošević**, Šešelj's Chetniks later fell out with their onetime ally, mainly because of his alleged betrayal of the Bosnian and Croatian Serbs. Bitterly hostile toward both communism and Tito's Yugoslavia, which they claimed was opposed to the interests of the Serbs, Serbia's new Chetniks also strove to bring about the establishment of a royalist and **Orthodox** "**Greater Serbia**" on the ruins of the Yugoslav federation.

Modern Serb Chetniks have used insignia copied from earlier Chetnik models—a black flag with a white skull and crossbones, with the words "Freedom or Death" inscribed below it, and use of

A 1992 photograph of a Chetnik fighter, Brčko, in Bosnia-Hercegovina. (Stevan Filipović)

the three-fingered, or Orthodox, salute. A symbol of mourning for Chetniks in the past, beards have also been grown by today's Chetniks. Their oath has remained, as before: "For King and Country."

—*M. M.*

See also: monarchy

CHURKIN, VITALII

Russian diplomat Vitalii Churkin (born 1952) gained a high profile for a short period in the mid-1990s through his efforts to achieve **cease-fires** and peace agreements in the former Yugoslavia. Churkin was a Russian deputy foreign minister,

Russian delegate to the **International Conference on the Former Yugoslavia** (ICFY), and Russian delegate to the international **Contact Group**. In the spring of 1994, when the **Bosnian Serbs** were attacking **Sarajevo** and the other United Nations (UN) "**safe areas**" of Bosnia, Churkin brokered various cease-fires, in part by offering the deployment of Russian peacekeeping forces. These cease-fires were broken, however, and Churkin accused the Serbs of "using Russian politics as a shield"; he warned them that they were dealing with Russia, a "great state, not a banana republic." Churkin's diplomatic efforts were in the end unsuccessful—reflecting **Russia**'s limited influence over the conflict.

—A. S. C.

CINEMA

Although rarely seen abroad, many important feature films have been made throughout the former Yugoslavia on its wars of the 1990s, often under very difficult conditions. The period after the end of these wars in 1995 has seen a number of Western films on the same subject matter in response to growing media and public interest in the former Yugoslavia.

The upheavals of the 1990s resulted in the demise of what was once a large, innovative, and internationally renowned film industry in Yugoslavia. Local filmmaking became more modest in scope, as well as limited in its subject matter, under the pressure of contemporary political and economic developments. Of the bigger post-Yugoslav films, many were international coproductions, financed with foreign money and consequently slanted toward an international film audience. Local political and economic factors also forced a number of prominent Yugoslav filmmakers into exile. Of these, the most important was Emir Kusturica, a director from Sarajevo who first came to prominence in 1984 with his controversial and award-winning film *When Father Was Away on Business.* A decade later, Kusturica produced another prophetic film, *Underground* (1995), which won him his second Palme d'Or at the Cannes Film Festival. Like his previous award winner of 1984, *Underground* looks at the past in order to illuminate and reflect upon the present—the disaster that befell Yugoslavia during the 1990s. Always a self-declared "Yugoslav" filmmaker, Kusturica was forced to seek exile in France after he received politically motivated threats to his life in his native Sarajevo and then Belgrade.

Although nobody could have predicted their extent and savagery during the 1980s, the Yugoslav wars were hinted at in a number of key films of the late Yugoslav era. The tragic Bosnian story of Ademir Kenović's *Kaduz* (1989)—wherein a man is released from prison, fails to cope with his new-found freedom, and then murders those he loves—was collectively reenacted in the Bosnian civil war. Borders, divisions between people, and identity problems that result in violence figure prominently in Zoran Nasirović's feature *Border* (1990) and Srdjan Karnović's *Virginia* (1991).

Other films made in **Serbia** at this time revisit the **Tito**ist past, and hence the origins of the disaster that engulfed the Serbs under the rule of President **Slobodan Milošević**. Goran Marković's *Tito and Me* (1992) and Želimir Žilnik's *Tito for a Second Time amongst the Serbs* (1992) are two key films on the myth of Tito, his flawed legacy, and his heirs led by Milošević. In Vladimir Blaževski's 1992 feature film *The Boulevard of the Revolution,* the disaffected and lost youth of **Belgrade** are the protagonists at a time when they were being forced to fight in wars of aggression and plunder in which they did not believe. Boro Drašković's *A Love in Vukovar* (1994) directly and honestly faces up to the brutality and dishonesty of the first Serbo-Croat war in 1991; and the same subject matter is examined in *The Price of Life* (1994), a Croatian view of this conflict directed by Bogdan Žižić.

More so in **Croatia** than in Serbia, the battle for **Vukovar** in 1991 was also often treated in ways close to nationalist **propaganda**, most notably in *Vukovar Is Coming Home* (1994), a patriotic melodrama directed by Croatian Branko Schmidt. In Serbia, where denial of the reality of the Yugoslav wars of the 1990s was arguably as strong as realistic treatments of their horrors, many escapist and officially promoted feature films set in the distant past also appeared at this time, including Aleksandar Petrović's epic *Migrations* (1995).

Following the end of the wars in 1995, some of the darkest films about the conflicts appeared, notably in relation to **Bosnia-Hercegovina**. Although made in Serbia, Srdjan Dragojević's *Pretty Village, Pretty Flame* (1996) caused great controversy upon its release in Belgrade for its brutally honest view of **Bosnian Serb** atrocities in Bosnia. A big commercial success in Serbia, this virulently antiwar film was subsequently released internationally to major critical acclaim in 1997. Based on Slobodan Selenić's 1993 novel of the same name, *Premeditated Murder* (1997) is a tragic love story in Belgrade that brilliantly captures the city's descent into barbarism, poverty, and paranoia. It ends with the meaningless death of its male protagonist in the Serb **Krajina** and the related emigration of his fiancée to New Zealand.

In the West, the centrality of **Sarajevo** in media coverage of the Yugoslav wars of the 1990s has recently prompted a number of cinematic treatments of life in that city during the **siege** by the Bosnian Serbs. Based on the experiences of Independent Television News (ITN) reporter Michael Nicholson, Michael Winterbottom's *Welcome to Sarajevo* (1997) re-creates the horrors of a city under siege and under the spotlight of the international **media.** Like a number of other Western feature films and documentaries on wartime Sarajevo, however, this British film has been criticized in some quarters for attempting to simplify its complex subject matter and for placing foreign outsiders, in this case a British television reporter, at the center of its dramatic action. Its approach makes the foreign **media** more important than the war on which the media reports, and it unwittingly distorts the conflict in Sarajevo, where the suffering of the city's inhabitants was arguably more important than the travails of the foreign media correspondents who visited and reported upon the city.

—*M. M.*

CITIZENSHIP

The concept of citizenship is especially relevant in the context of the Yugoslav wars. Citizenship can be regarded as perhaps the focal concept in modern political life. In premodern societies, political rights and obligations usually belonged only to certain groups, usually an aristocracy, certain ruling clans, or often those who were regarded as qualified by the possession of property. Citizenship in its modern sense, in the words of T. H. Marshall, is "a status which is bestowed on those who are full members of a community"; "full membership" is increasingly defined by the fairly basic criteria of adulthood and residence. Everyone who meets these criteria is entitled to claim certain rights (such as voting or equal treatment before the law) and is expected to meet certain obligations (such as respect for the law and the payment of taxes).

The crumbling of the communist systems across Europe has posed a problem with respect to citizenship in that the countries' socialist pasts left a legacy of a different understanding of rights. The presumed movement toward a "dictatorship of the proletariat" tended both to make rights dependent upon labor and to remove the privileges of those who were regarded as the remnants of a historically outmoded order—those who owned "the means of production" or employed others. Commitment to a belief in the vanguard role of the Communist Party similarly tended to yield privileges for party members. Through its system of **workers' self-management**, the Yugoslav system generally involved people in political life and bestowed upon them rights such as access to social insurance through their place of work. It was only in the later years of its existence that the Yugoslav state extended social insurance provisions to private cultivators, and then only incompletely.

The disintegration and discredit of communism in Yugoslavia (as elsewhere) has confronted the state with an awkward process of adjustment, in which the definition of citizenship rights has often come to be a subject of great controversy. An important feature of the Western European and North American tradition of thinking about citizenship is that this status is the prerogative of *individuals.* This contrasts strongly with the highly *collectivist* traditions of political thought that have come to be entrenched within the cultures of central and eastern Europe. In rejecting the emphasis on *class* and *party* typical of communism, the new postcommunist states have often held onto collectivist ways of thinking. In these circumstances, the *nation* has come to replace the working class as the primary locus of identity and the point of reference with respect to rights and duties.

This tendency to think in terms of the primacy of a nation has been particularly problematic in Yugoslavia. Although a federation, the former **Yugoslavia** bestowed citizenship equally upon all of its peoples; they were citizens of *Yugoslavia,* whether or not they were Croats, Macedonians, or whatever. Even if citizenship brought with it limitations on activity that would be regarded as irksome elsewhere (such as limitations on freedom of speech), at least these restrictions applied equally to all citizens across the federation.

The disintegration of the federation changed this situation in that the newly independent republics each tended to define themselves first and foremost as the homeland of specific nations. For example, the constitution of **Croatia** sets out from the "millennial national identity of the Croatian nation." Article 3 of the constitution of **Slovenia** tells us that the state is "based on the permanent and inalienable right of the Slovenian people to self-determination." Members of national minorities in these states can regard this sort of language as implying that the state is, first and foremost, one that belongs to the nation in question, to whom full citizenship belongs, and one where the members of minority groups can expect to remain only second-class citizens.

The full meaning of citizenship is not defined exhaustively in constitutions; all of the newly created states (with the exception so far of **Bosnia-Hercegovina**) have enacted additional legislation that has set out in more detailed terms who is entitled to citizenship, as well as the means by which claims to it can be enforced. Debate has usually centered upon certain disqualifying conditions, such as the need to demonstrate an ancestor of the appropriate nationality or a lengthy period of residence. Regardless of the way in which legislation has been framed, accusations have been leveled everywhere that the implementation of registration procedures has been conducted unfairly.

The situation of **refugees** is particularly difficult when it comes to them registering citizenship. In cases where the possession of a Yugoslav passport was no longer accepted as evidence of entitlement to citizenship or where resort had to be made to residence to prove such entitlement, many of those subject to "**ethnic cleansing**" were compelled (as a condition of their safe departure) to sign away property—in which they might have been able to live and thereby comply with the conditions of residence—to thwart any attempts on their part to return to their former homes. The legal ambiguities and practical difficulties surrounding citizenship will contribute to problems in terms of reconstructing political normality in the former Yugoslavia for many years to come.

—J. B. A.

See also: ethnicity; nationality

Reference: Marshall, T. H. *Citizenship and Social Class.* London: Pluto Press, 1992, p. 18.

CIVIL WAR

International humanitarian law distinguishes between international and noninternational armed conflicts; the latter are frequently known colloquially as "civil wars." Whereas this distinction may appear to be straightforward, considerable controversy has surrounded the use of that term to describe war in Yugoslavia, and the governments of **Bosnia-Hercegovina**, **Croatia**, and **Slovenia** have repeatedly insisted on describing the conflict as a "war of aggression."

In part the difficulty stems from the international **recognition** of states. The states emerging from the former Yugoslav Federation had generally secured international recognition by the summer of 1992, including mutual recognition among themselves. The conspicuous exception was the new Federal Republic of **Yugoslavia** (consisting of **Serbia** and **Montenegro**), established in April 1992. The government of this newly formed republic continued to insist that it was the legal legatee of the former socialist federation. This claim was contested by all of the other partners to the former federation, who declined to recognize the republic's legitimacy. A consequence of this withholding of recognition has been that Yugoslavia has been granted the opportunity to deny that any of its military involvement in the war can be interpreted as "aggression" on the part of one state against another, preferring to present the conflict as "civil war."

This claim has been important in shaping the international response to the hostilities. Governments are normally reluctant to commit themselves to any action that might be construed as interference in the affairs of another sovereign state. In the case of Yugoslavia, there has been substantial disagreement within the international community about what might constitute an appropriate and effective form of involvement. Where governments have been either reluctant to involve themselves at all in the Yugoslav war or confused about the aims and methods of engagement, the claim that the conflict is civil war has provided a useful rhetorical device that has legitimated inaction.

A further consequence of describing the conflict as civil war has been a blurring of the focus of

A Yugoslav Peoples' Army (JNA) convoy under attack in Bosnia-Hercegovina. (Stevan Filipović)

humanitarian concern, particularly in that this view makes it harder to distinguish "combatants" from "noncombatants" in relation to international humanitarian law. This difficulty has consequences for the identification of **war crimes.**

—*J. B. A.*

COLONIZATION

Internal colonization is the opposite of **ethnic cleansing**, in that areas that are considered to be insufficiently populated are settled with new inhabitants, usually with the aim of changing the areas' ethnic composition. Colonization of this kind can come about by the more or less spontaneous movement of people, but it has usually been an instrument of state policy. It has been a common feature of policy in the **Balkans** for centuries. Land reform programs initiated in 1919 and 1945 both incorporated attempts to "correct" ethnic imbalances in certain areas by new settlement. Serbo-Croat speakers replaced the German Volksdeutsche in the **Vojvodina** and **Slavonia**, as well as **Turks** and other **Muslim** groups in **Macedonia**, after World War I. After World War II, similar policies were also attempted in the Vojvodina and **Kosovo**—in the latter case in order to reduce the numerical dominance of **Albanian** speakers.

Colonization has reemerged as a policy in the 1990s. In **Serbia**, ethnic Serbs displaced from **Croatia** and **Bosnia-Hercegovina** have been resettled in eastern **Slavonia** and in the Vojvodina on land taken from former Croat and Magyar inhabitants, and there have been renewed attempts at the "re-Serbianization" of Kosovo. In Croatia the Law on the Strategy of Organizing Croatian Space was drafted early in 1995; and immediately following the reclamation of the former **Krajina** from secessionist Serbs, a program of resettlement with ethnic Croats was commenced, although no figures are available at the time of this writing.

Very large areas have been depopulated as a result of the war in Yugoslavia, a fact that is unlikely to be remedied by the spontaneous return of **refugees** to their former homes. Colonization programs will undoubtedly be considered in various forms by governments in the region as components of reconstruction policies.

—*J. B. A.*

COMMUNICATIONS AND TRANSPORT

The communications and transport of the integrated and relatively well-developed all-Yugoslav territorial and economic area have been fragmented, disrupted, and damaged during the Yugoslav wars. These strategic assets were also extensively fought over.

In **Slovenia**, the Ten Day War of June-July 1991 was focused mainly on the country's border-crossing points to **Italy** and **Austria**. Seized by the **Slovenian Army** (SA), these were then easily isolated from the approaching and largely road-based **Yugoslav Peoples' Army** (JNA). Trapped on roads in Alpine **terrain** or besieged in urban garrisons, the JNA was quickly defeated. Later the same year in **Croatia**, JNA and rebel Serb operations against the Croatian armed forces in **Dalmatia** and **Slavonia** were largely directed against communications and transportation. The JNA contingency plans for the secession of the northern republics (code-named Ram-1 and Ram-2) envisaged that Croatia would be partitioned by the seizure of key sections of strategic roads and railways. In this way the Croatian government lost control of, and access to, a third of its national territory.

Formerly known as the Bratstvo i Jedinstvo (Brotherhood and Unity) motorway, the trans-European E7 road route between **Zagreb** and **Belgrade** was closed in 1991; it was not reopened until rebel Serbs were dislodged from western Slavonia in May 1995. Following the same route as this motorway, the Zagreb-Belgrade railway was also closed from 1991 to 1996. To the south of Zagreb, the capital of the self-declared **Serb Republic of the Krajina** (SRK), **Knin**, was of equal strategic importance to both the Croats and Serbs, commanding the only rail route from the capital to Croatia's second-largest seaport at **Split**. In addition, because of its geographic position, the SRK was able to cut and damage the oil import pipeline from Croatia's largest port, Rijeka. Other pipelines from Croatia's oil fields in eastern Slavonia were also cut and damaged in 1991. Not until the fall of the SRK in 1995 did Zagreb secure unimpeded

Securing control of major roads and other transportation and communication infrastructures has been a central strategy for all sides in the Yugoslav wars of the 1990s. (Stevan Filipović)

access to its **Adriatic** coastline, which had earlier been linked to the capital only by a long and tortuous route. Except for **Istria** to the north, Croatia's coastal motorway was threatened by the SRK for much of the war, the key point being the **Maslenica Bridge** near **Zadar**. This threat was also particularly serious in southern Dalmatia, where the city, port, and airport of **Dubrovnik** were briefly attacked by the Serbs in 1991.

Control of **Bosnia-Hercegovina**'s main north-south and east-west transportation routes was central to the Bosnian war of 1992–1995. One of the major reasons **Sarajevo** was besieged by the **Bosnian Serb Army** (BSA) and resolutely defended by the Bosnian government was that it was a road-rail nodal point for the whole of the republic. Handed over to the United Nations Protection Force (**UNPROFOR**) by the BSA in 1992, Sarajevo's international airport was a vital asset during the siege of the Bosnian capital. Southwest of Sarajevo, control of the **Neretva River Valley** road-rail routes to the Adriatic port of Ploče was also bitterly contested by all three parties to the Bosnian war from as early as 1991. Following the defeat of the Serbs by the Croats at **Mostar** in 1991–1992, Mostar became a major battleground in the war between the **Bosnian Croats** and **Muslims** in 1993. The key to Croatia's control over the current **Muslim-Croat Federation** remains the Neretva Valley. In central Bosnia, most of the major battles were fought over a number of road-rail routes in the Vrbas and Bosna Valleys. The largest town in the **Republika Srpska** (RS), **Banja Luka**, is second only to Sarajevo as a road-rail nodal point, controlling as it does the main east-west transportation routes to both Croatia and Serbia. Another key crossing point to the west, **Bihać** in the **Una River** Valley, was extensively fought over in the Bosnian war, including internecine fighting among the Bosnian Muslims themselves.

By far the most strategic point of the Bosnian war was the route through the **Posavina Corridor** focused on **Brčko**. Connecting the western and eastern territories of the RS, this route remains of central importance for the Bosnian Serbs. For this reason, the forces of the **Bosnian army** from **Tuzla**, as well as Bosnian Croat forces from the **Orašje** pocket on the **Sava River**, constantly attempted to cut the route. In addition to breaking the RS, such a scenario would open up a direct transportation route between Sarajevo and Croatia to the north across the Sava. The importance of the Brčko area for all three sides in the Bosnian conflict was revealed when disputes over the area very nearly led to the collapse of the **Dayton Agreements** of 1995.

In eastern Bosnia, in the strip of territory between the **Drina River** and the Mostar-Sarajevo-Tuzla triangle, control of bridge-crossing points and road-rail routes to Serbia proper from Bosnia has been a central strategic objective of the RS. Although this region was largely subjected to "**ethnic cleansing**" of Bosnian Muslims, the recapture of this region would be important to the Sarajevo government, which has managed to hold on only to **Goražde**. Control of this area offers the possibility of communication with the sensitive region of the **Sandžak** in **Serbia**.

The progress of the wars in Croatia and then Bosnia, as well the related imposition of economic **sanctions** by the **United Nations** against the Federal Republic of **Yugoslavia** (FRY) from 1992 to 1995, cut Serbia's main road-rail links to the west and closed Belgrade's international airport to all commercial traffic. During this period, reduced road-rail traffic from and through Serbia was rerouted through **Hungary** to the north. Montenegro's maritime links to the outside world were also cut by the sanctions from 1992 to 1994. Serbia's main road-rail route to **Greece** via **Macedonia** then became its "sanctions-busting" lifeline. Also involving **Bulgaria**, this route to the Greek port of **Thessaloniki** enabled Serbia to survive the worst effects of sanctions. In the case of **Montenegro**, sanctions busting took place through **Albania** via old smuggling routes over Lake Shkoder. In 1994–1995, Serbia also imposed limited sanctions against the Bosnian Serbs along the Drina River.

Physical damage to road and rail infrastructure during the war was extensive, and a good part of the effort of UNPROFOR and its **North Atlantic Treaty Organization** (NATO) successors has been devoted to the temporary restoration of disrupted communications, including the rebuilding of **bridges**. By 1996–1997, the main road-rail transportation routes between Croatia and Serbia had been partly reopened, although a complete restoration of prewar transportation and communications routes throughout the former Yugoslavia will probably not take place for many years to come.

Another consequence of note is the fact that civilian traffic, foreign or national, through what was formerly one country is now hampered by differing visa regimes.

—*M. M.*

See also: Neum

COMMUNISTS

See **League of Communists of Yugoslavia**

CONCENTRATION CAMPS

See **detention camps**

CONFEDERATION

See **constitutional models**

CONFLICT MANAGEMENT AND CONFLICT RESOLUTION

Since the very first days of violence in Croatia and Slovenia, there have been attempts to manage and resolve the conflict by peaceful means. The two different terms in the title of this entry refer to different strategies and techniques based on different theories about the nature of conflict in general, and the conflicts in Yugoslavia and its successors more specifically. Both approaches have been used by various intervenors in the seven years of the conflict.

Most well-known interventions by international organizations are attempts to manage the conflict. They aim to bring about a settlement on a set of concrete military and political issues, and they concentrate on enabling, persuading, and coercing the leaders of the states, armed forces, and other political constituencies to come to agreements through peace conferences and other types of bargaining processes. Clear examples of this approach are the original **European Community** (EC) mediation process, the **Vance-Owen Plan** (VOP) negotiations, the **London Conference**, the **International Conference on the Former Yugoslavia** (ICFY), and the conference that yielded the **Dayton Agreements**. Both the United Nations Protection Force in Yugoslavia (**UNPROFOR**) and the European Community **Monitoring** Mission (ECMM), as instruments of these wider negotiation and mediation processes, also represent tools of a conflict management approach. This strand of theory and practice emphasizes the structural, political context of conflict and the processes that are useful for dealing with it. It focuses on methods such as arbitration, mediation, peacekeeping, and power mediation, and it sees sanctions and rewards as important instruments of conflict management. Theorists of this approach see conflicts as being essentially objective phenomena, the settlement of which must involve bargaining over objective issues such as resource scarcity.

There have also been many less well known interventions that have used a conflict resolution approach. Resolution approaches aim to address the deeper roots of conflict; they try to identify the social, psychological, and structural reasons for the outbreak of conflict and generate creative strategies for solving these problems. The subjective elements of conflict are particularly important: the way it is understood by the parties, the methods used to prosecute it, and the parties' beliefs about how it could come to an end. Resolution approaches work on the relationships between the warring parties, dealing directly with the ordinary people who are in conflict as well as their leaderships. Many international **nongovernmental organizations** (NGOs) have been involved in this form of work in the Yugoslav successor states. Some of the most important organizations to use resolution approaches are the groups that form the **peace movements** in Slovenia, Croatia, Bosnia, Serbia, and Macedonia. In all the republics, concerned and courageous citizens organized in defense of cosmopolitanism, human rights, difference, and diversity. These groups attempted to maintain contacts among the different nationalities in the face of nationalist violence, and in the aftermath of war they worked on the creation of long-term reconciliation processes in an attempt to heal the psychological wounds of violence.

These two levels of peacemaking and peacebuilding complement rather than contradict one another. Both types of strategies are necessary in order to transform the conflict away from violence. Local work to reconstruct the social and physical infrastructure of the community is necessary in order to begin the process of reconciliation, but this work cannot go on unless there is some level of settlement among the political leadership. In addition, no amount of agreement between politicians can reduce the conflict between individuals and groups where the underlying relationship is unaddressed. Work on each dimension of the conflict supports work on the others.

The Yugoslav conflict became violent within a short space of time in 1991, and potential intervenors were unaware of the need for action until after the war had developed. Accordingly, most of the conflict management that took place had the aim of ending the violence. The public perception is generally that efforts to manage the conflict by outside mediators were unsuccessful—the string of broken **cease-fire** agreements in Croatia under the auspices of Lord **Carrington** and the inability of any international agency to effectively slow or halt the extreme violence in Bosnia for most of the three years of the war highlighted this view of conflict management. With the eventual move into enforcement via the **Rapid Reaction Force** and North Atlantic Treaty Organization (NATO) airpower to shell and bomb the Serbs into submission, as well as the strategic alliance between Croatia and Bosnia that brought about a shift in military power, the warring parties were coerced into the process that led to the Dayton peace accords. Coercion has always had a role to play in conflict management; mediators such as Henry Kissinger have used "sticks" as well as "carrots" in discussions with political leaders. However, public perceptions were that mediation had failed. This is a misunderstanding of the nature of mediation at the international political level.

Noncoercive, peaceful methods of mediation are part of the conflict resolution approach in which many NGOs (international and local) were involved. Even during the worst violence, when international publics believed that nothing could be achieved by peaceful means, there were pockets of resistance, where peace groups provided support to minorities under threat of violence, maintaining communication between villages in the face of external attempts to split them down national lines, working with refugees to help them regain some measure of control over their lives, and campaigning publicly for peace, reconciliation, and nonviolent means of settling the dispute between the political leaders of the warring groups. After the interstate organizations achieved the deployment of UNPROFOR and then later coerced the parties into agreeing to the Dayton plans, the work of the international NGOs and local peace groups became even more important. If the societies of the successor states are to develop in democratic and open ways, the scars left by this century's several nationalist movements have to be actively healed; this means that they must be addressed by local groups who can engage with ordinary people in their own contexts. Most of the governments of the successor states are actively nationalist and have made no effort to move toward an inclusive vision of state and society, where citizens can have diverse personal, social, and political identities and still remain equal with other citizens. The peace groups and the allied human rights groups work continuously to resist the national criterion for **citizenship** and to promote communication and dialogue about difference.

—G. R. B.

CONSTITUTIONAL MODELS

In several respects the collapse of the Yugoslav state can be said to have been rooted in the state's constitutional practice, as well as in the irreconcilability of divergent constitutional models.

Whereas in most states constitutional change is both relatively rare and difficult to accomplish, in the 45 years of communist Yugoslavia there were in effect five constitutions. The Soviet-modeled constitution of 1945 was replaced in 1953 by one that acknowledged the ideological changes that accompanied the introduction of **workers' self-management**. This process was repeated in 1963 in a document that laid the foundations for a radically decentralized system. Almost as soon as this system was adopted, the exigencies of the economic reform process led to pressure for further revision. The most dramatic change took place in 1974, with the introduction of what is said to be the longest constitution in the world (406 articles). Its principal innovation was to render political life in terms of a system of "delegation," which subsequent interpreters have identified as both an acute mystification and a reversion to Leninist democratic centralism. This document was followed shortly by an attempt to systematize and rationalize workers' self-management in the Law of Associated Labor (Zakon o Udruženom Radu—ZUR) of 1976. The complexity and partial incompatibility of these two documents set in motion the production of a series of 48 amendments, which when consolidated in 1981 virtually constituted a fifth postwar constitution.

This willingness to treat as a working draft a document that elsewhere might be regarded as a fundamental framework for action had its roots only partly in communism. The three decades of existence of the "First Yugoslavia" (created in 1919) also saw four constitutional revisions. The controversial Vidovdan constitution of 1921 was swept away by the proclamation of royal dictatorship by King

Aleksandar in 1929, during which period the **monarchy** governed through a number of *banovine* (prefectures). The attempt to return to a parliamentary system under the regency in 1934 was accompanied by a new constitution, which can be said to have led to a fourth when in 1938 the first tentative moves toward federalism were taken with the granting of semiautonomous status to the reorganized Prefecture of Croatia (Banovina Hrvatska).

To this tradition the League of Communists added a propensity to see constitutions as ideological statements—enshrining the current thinking of the regime about how best to present itself both domestically and to the outside world—rather than as legal documents. The timing of constitutional change in post–1945 Yugoslavia has been commented upon frequently: whenever the country ran into economic crisis, the response of the regime was an essentially political one that told a new story about the way things were and diverted energy from addressing the underlying problems. The political disagreements that had crystallized in Yugoslavia by the late 1980s presented themselves, not surprisingly, in terms of conflicts over the future constitutional structure of the state. Two types of problems came together in this respect: the problem of interrepublican economic differences and the problem of political liberalization.

The differences that had emerged in the level of economic development and economic structure of the six republics and two autonomous provinces of federal Yugoslavia are described elsewhere. Suffice it to say in this context that the difference between the economically most developed republic (**Slovenia**) and the least developed province (**Kosovo**) can be measured in terms of their gross material product (GMP). The ratio of the GMPs of these two areas in 1950 was 3:1. By 1960 this had risen to 5:1. By 1970 the ratio stood at 6:1 and by 1980 at 7:1. Controversy raged across most of the postwar period about the best means by which this issue could be addressed, particularly about the redistributive mechanisms that were designed to alleviate the problem. The differences between Yugoslavia's regions were not only those of wealth, however, but more significantly differences of economic structure. Consequently, by the time the regime was compelled to grasp the nettle of economic reform in the late 1980s, including the prospect of economic reconstruction along the lines of a market economy, which the proposals of Premier **Ante Marković** began to implement in 1989, there were radical differences among Yugoslavia's regions over the entire nature and direction of economic policy. Differences also emerged over the nature and limits of desirable political change. The collapse of the **League of Communists of Yugoslavia** (LCY), in terms of both the league's effectiveness and its legitimacy, raised the prospect of a transition to multiparty politics. The implications of any such change varied dramatically among the different republics. In **Slovenia** and **Croatia**, party pluralism could be presented largely in terms of the need for relegitimizing the political system and for creating an effective and modern system of government. In republics with very large ethnic minorities, however, the implications of pluralism looked quite different. Party pluralism here raised the prospect of transforming the electoral process into a contest between ethnic parties that would challenge the legitimacy of the state itself. This was a serious issue not only in **Serbia**, where democratic diversity was expected to result in a clear expression of preference on the part of the majority **Albanian** population in **Kosovo** for separation from the Serbian republic. A similar prospect faced **Macedonia**, in the predominantly Albanian communes along its western border. In **Bosnia-Hercegovina**, with its complex pattern of ethnic diversity, it was rapidly appreciated that the consequences of an electoral contest that largely revolved around differences of **ethnicity** would be potentially even more disastrous. Other local differences in the history and political practice of the LCY worked to promote radically divergent views about the desirable direction of political change.

Broadly speaking, during the late 1980s, two contrasting models of the future constitutional development of the country contended with increasing force. On the one hand, Slovenia and Croatia tended to favor a loosening of the ties between republics, as well as greater room for diversity in the political and economic practice of more autonomous republican governments. They tended to see the redistributive practices that had been developed in order to cope with differences of economic development as ineffective, as founded upon dubious principles, and as constituting an unjustifiable drain upon their own resources. The need to ensure that political change was imposed uniformly across the federation was seen as tying their future to the pace of change in the most recalcitrant of the republics. Consequently, they increasingly favored movement toward a "confederal" constitutional structure, which would have turned Yugoslavia into an association of relatively independent states within a minimal common institutional framework. On the other hand, other republics, most vocally Serbia, feared the consequences of a dramatic commitment to economic modernization and saw confederalism as surely opening the door to Albanian secessionism. Where criticism of the existing federal structure was advanced by these republics, it tended to focus on the demonstrated ineffectiveness of several federal institutions (such as the cumbersome collective presidency) and the weak central financial institutions. In place of confederalism these republics argued for a renewed federalism, which, if anything, would have placed the competing and divergent republican governments under greater control from effective central institutions.

As individual republics began to make unilateral moves toward party pluralism in 1989, a number of situations arose in which republican law and practice placed themselves above those of the federation, in a creeping movement toward confederalism. The succession of summit meetings among republican leaders during 1991 was directed principally toward the search for a last-minute resolution of these conflicting views about constitutional development, but it was overtaken by the declarations of independence by Slovenia and Croatia in June.

—J. B. A.

See also: democratization; economic dimension; political parties; regional inequality

References: Dimitrijević, Vojin. "The 1974 Constitution and Constitutional Process as a Factor in the Collapse of Yugoslavia." In Payam Akhavan and Robert Howse (eds.), *Yugoslavia, the Former and the Future: Reflections by Scholars from the Region.* Washington, DC: Brookings Institution, 1995; Ramet, Sabrina Petra. *Nationalism and Federalism in Yugoslavia, 1962–1991,* 2nd ed. Bloomington: Indiana University Press, 1992.

CONTACT GROUP

The Contact Group, which superseded the **International Conference on the Former Yugoslavia**, was established in April 1994 (the year after the demise of the **Vance-Owen Plan**) as a means of establishing a new peace initiative for **Bosnia-Hercegovina.**

Based in Geneva, it comprised high-level representation from five countries: the **United States of America** (Charles Redman), **Russia** (**Vitalii Churkin**), **Germany** (Michael Steiner), **France** (Jacques-Alain de Sedouy), and **United Kingdom** (David Manning). (**David Owen**'s original concept included only the first three—the latter two then lobbied for inclusion.) It was unlikely that the five would form a convincingly unified group for the purpose; although they were committed to peace, their agendas were at variance, and they were perceived by the warring parties in Bosnia as opportunistic. In the summer of 1994, the group emerged with its peace plan, which recognized the existing borders of Bosnia-Hercegovina as a whole, but more importantly allocated 51 percent of the territory to the **Muslim-Croat Federation** and 49 percent to the **Bosnian Serbs**, effectively reducing the latter's previous gains by one-third. The plan, along with two improbably intricate maps delineating territorial assignments for all communities except the capital, **Sarajevo,** which would come under **United Nations** (UN) control, was issued to all sides with a fortnight's deadline to reply. The subsequent maneuverings are vividly reported in Silber and Little's *Death of Yugoslavia.* The net result was not peace but an unintended, though ultimately significant, division between **Serbia** and the Bosnian Serbs.

However, the Contact Group did have the effects of (1) drawing the Americans positively into the resolution of the main conflict and (2) increasing the cooperation of the Russians. By 1997 the group was functioning on the basis of consensus rather than compromise.

—J. J. H.

Reference: Silber, Laura, and Alan Little. *The Death of Yugoslavia.* London: Penguin, 1995.

ĆOSIĆ, DOBRICA

One of the most widely known and respected Serbian and Yugoslav writers, Dobrica Ćosić served as president of the Federal Republic of **Yugoslavia** (FRY) in 1992–1993. Born in 1921 at Velika Drenova, Serbia, he was educated at the University of Belgrade and participated in the National Liberation War (1941–1945) as a political commissar. After the war, he attended the elite Higher Party School and subsequently held many high-ranking positions in the Communist Party of Yugoslavia (subsequently the **League of Communists of Yugoslavia**—LCY), including membership in its central committee. Working also as a professional journalist and writer, Ćosić subsequently published a number of novels, beginning with *Daleko je sunce* (*Far Away Is the Sun,* 1951), a fictional treatment of the wartime ***Partizan*** experience in Yugoslavia. With the publication of his major work, a two-volume historical epic on the Serb experience during World War I entitled *Vreme smrti* (*A Time of Death,* 1972–1977), his reputation as Serbia's greatest living novelist was confirmed. His most recent and more politically controversial two-volume work on wartime and postwar experience, *Vreme zla (A Time of Evil),* was published in 1985–1990.

During the 1950s and 1960s, Ćosić was involved in a number of literary, linguistic, and political controversies about Yugoslav culture and hence the postwar communist Yugoslav experience; these circumstances eventually resulted in his prosecution as a Serbian nationalist and his subsequent expulsion from the League of Communists. Although never openly proscribed as a novelist, he was nevertheless in the political wilderness until the 1980s, when a revived Serb nationalism led to his reinvolvement in politics. He reportedly coauthored the controversial "Memorandum of the Serbian Academy of Sciences and Arts" (SANU) on the question of Serbian nationalism in 1985.

Ćosić initially gave public support to **Slobodan Milošević**, who later reciprocated this important intellectual endorsement of his controversial rule and policies. Following the proclamation of a new Federal Republic of Yugoslavia in April 1992, Ćosić was elected to its presidency by a vote in the FRY assembly in June 1992. Supported by Milošević and the renamed League of Communists, the **Socialist Party of Serbia** (SPS), he subsequently parted company with the Serbian president over the latter's policies toward **Croatia** and **Bosnia**. In association with the federal prime minister at the time, **Milan Panić**, who had been invited by Ćosić to take up this post from exile in the United States, Ćosić attempted to pursue a more independent policy than that of Milošević, most notably in relation to Croatia. In October 1992 Ćosić and Panić effected a partial rapprochement with Croatia over the disputed **Prevlaka** Peninsula in southern Dalmatia. They then also tried to break the political impasse in the Serbian province of **Kosovo**. Ćosić then publicly backed Panić's unsuccessful bid against Milošević for the presidency of Serbia. The result of this effort was Ćosić's forced removal from office in June 1993; he was accused of plotting with discontented generals to get rid of Milošević through a military coup. Since then, Ćosić has not been formally involved in politics, but he remains an influential figure in **Serbia**.

—*M. M.*

See also: Serbian Academy Memorandum

References: Ćosić, Dobrica. *A Time of Death,* transl. M. Heppell. New York: Harcourt Brace Jovanovich, 1983; ———. *Far Away Is the Sun,* transl. M. Heppell and M. Mihajlović. Belgrade: Jugoslavia Publishing House, 1963.

COSTS OF WAR

See **war costs**

COUNCIL FOR SECURITY AND COOPERATION IN EUROPE

See **Organization for Security and Cooperation in Europe**

CRNA GORA

See **Montenegro**

CROATIA

Croatia is one of the former republics of federal **Yugoslavia**, lying along the east of the Adriatic Sea. In 1991 its population was 4,760,300, living on an area of 56,538 square kilometers. Of this population, 78.1 percent declared themselves as Croat and 12.2 percent as Serb, with over 10 other national minorities each accounting for less than 1 percent of the population. Croatia's main historical regions are the northwestern peninsula of **Istria**, the southern coastal strip of **Dalmatia**, Croatia proper in the north, and the eastern lands of **Slavonia**.

In 924 a Croatian Kingdom was established by Tomislav, centered around Nin in Dalmatia. Over the next 165 years, it fluctuated in size, covering an area of 100,000 square kilometers at its height. In 1102 Prince Kalman of Hungary took the Croatian crown and then succeeded to the Hungarian throne in 1106, unifying the two countries. The Hungarian crown eventually passed to the Habsburgs after the

Ottoman victory at Mohács in 1526, and Ferdinand I thereby became king of Croatia. Croatia remained a Habsburg possession for the next 392 years. It fluctuated in size during this period of its history, diminishing to 16,800 square kilometers at the height of the Turkish depredations.

As the Turks were driven south of the **Sava River** during the sixteenth and seventeenth centuries, the historic Croatian lands acquired a complex ethnic complexion. Severely depopulated by war, large areas were resettled by colonists brought from other parts of the **Habsburg Empire**. Large numbers of **Orthodox** Christian Slavs from south of the Sava migrated to Croatia-Slavonia and were formed into regiments of *graničari* (frontiersmen) along a **military frontier** *(vojna krajina)*. They were given land and exempted from feudal duties in return for their military service against the Ottoman Turks. The Adriatic coastal region came under the control of Venice, giving the cities a substantial Italian population. Until their reunification in 1918, therefore, the historic Croat lands remained divided between Austrian, Hungarian, Ottoman, and Venetian administrations.

Despite differences in religion and their experiences of imperial rule, Serbs and Croats in early modern Croatia had few reasons to be antagonistic. The Croat political elite was focused on resisting Magyar nationalism, and the Serbs were focused on their role as a bulwark against the Turks. The vast majority of Serb and Croat peasants in Croatia lived similar lives working the land. It was only during the nineteenth century that they came to see themselves as in conflict.

Three developments were significant in this respect. The rise of an independent Serbian principality stimulated the expectation of Serbs that they might achieve unification within a single state. The redefinition of relations between the Austrian and Hungarian parts of the empire in the Ausgleich (meaning "balance" or "reconciliation") of 1867 strengthened Magyar authority in Croatia-Slavonia. Moderate Hungarians realized the importance of a negotiated settlement of the constitutional issue with the Croats and concluded the following year the historic Nagodba (Compromise). Within the constitutional framework laid down by the Nagodba, Croatia received autonomy. The occupation of **Bosnia** and **Hercegovina** by Austrian armies after 1878 raised the possibility that a future Croatian state might extend to include the **Catholic** population of these provinces. The Bosnian crisis placed on the agenda the conflicting programs of a "**Greater Serbia**" and a "**Greater Croatia**," although the Croatian national movement remained divided throughout the nineteenth century between exponents of this vision and more modest expectations of the unification of the South Slav peoples within the empire as a third force to balance Austrian and Magyar domination (the so-called trialist solution).

With the collapse of the Habsburg Empire at the end of World War I, a wider reorganization of the pattern of states in the Balkans was required. The representatives of Croat interests negotiated the creation of a unified South Slav state: the "Kingdom of Serbs, Croats, and Slovenes," which drew together not only the former South Slav areas of Austria-Hungary, but also the Kingdoms of **Serbia** and **Montenegro**, under the Serbian dynasty. The Croat parties hoped that the new state would continue to respect the historical identities of the Croat regions, and they were severely disappointed by the heavily centralized constitution promulgated in 1921. The main Croat party (Stjepan Radić's Hrvatska Republička Seljačka Stranka [Croatian Republican Peasant Party]) boycotted the assembly in protest and began the pattern of Croat opposition to Yugoslavia that was to continue throughout the interwar period. In 1928, Radić and other Croat deputies were shot in the assembly, to which they had only recently returned. The king suspended the constitution and proclaimed a royal dictatorship under the title of "Yugoslavia," which lasted until 1931. Several Croat nationalists fled the country, including **Ante Pavelić** and set up the **Ustaša** movement in Italy, which was responsible for the assassination of King Aleksandar in 1934. In spite of the attempted return to a form of democratic politics, unrest continued. In 1939, Vladko Maček, leader of the Croatian Republican Peasant Party, was able to reach a *sporazum* (agreement) with the government, which partially met Croat aspirations by creating an autonomous Croatian *banovina* (governorship).

Whether this would have produced a stable constitutional settlement remains a historical speculation because in April 1941 Yugoslavia was drawn into war and was dismembered by the occupying Axis powers. An extreme nationalist Ustaša government was installed within an Independent State of Croatia (Nezavisna Država Hrvatska—NDH) by their Italian and German patrons. The record of atrocities committed by the Ustaša became a potent reason for fear on the part of Serbs during the recent breakup of Yugoslavia, particularly when the new Croatian government adopted the NDH as a part of the historic heritage of a Croat state.

Following the victory of the Communist Partizans led by Josip Broz (**Tito**), Croatia in 1945 became the Socialist Republic of Croatia, in a federal Yugoslavia. In the postwar period, Croatia developed a very different economic structure from several other regions of the country. Particularly after the economic and constitutional reforms of 1963–1965, its pattern of industrial development and thriving **tourism** trade tended to make Croatian political leaders advocates both of regional economic independence and of greater reliance upon the market, in place of communist centralization. Conflict over these and other issues (especially questions of **language** policy and cultural autonomy) came to a head after 1968 in events known as the **Croatian Spring**. The suppression of Croat demands in 1971—1972, as well as the disciplining of many Croatian political activists at that time (including the eventual president, **Franjo Tudjman**) laid up a store of resentment that was to fuel the campaign for independence between 1989 and 1992.

The program of reform undertaken in 1974–1976 did not address the principal underlying problems faced by Yugoslavia. There was a return to the politicization of the economy, and the radically decentralized structures adopted then merely served to deepen the problems of legitimating the regime, without addressing important problems such as **inflation** or the efficiency of production. Although Croatia remained quiescent during the 1980s, this surface quiet belied underlying dissatisfaction and growing disillusionment. As federal attempts to produce an adequate response to Yugoslavia's deepening crisis faltered and failed, pressure began to grow, particularly in Croatia, for a real alternative to the **League of Communists** (LC) and a fundamental redefinition of the structure of the federation.

Although the LC in Croatia was outspoken (along with the Slovenes) in its demands for reform, in the first multiparty **elections** in May 1990 it suffered a heavier electoral defeat than in any other republic except Bosnia-Hercegovina. The scale of this defeat was magnified by the "first past the post" electoral system, which brought Franjo Tudjman and the **Croatian Democratic Union** (HDZ) to power. The new government embarked upon an aggressive policy of "Croatization." The **media**, cultural, and educational institutions were purged; the language began to be "purified" of supposedly Serb words; and all references to socialism were removed from the name and emblem of the state.

Tudjman and the HDZ oscillated between attempting to persuade Serbs that their rights would be protected and using nationalist, anti-Serb rhetoric. Serbs were deeply disturbed by reports of firms requiring employees who were not ethnic Croats to sign loyalty oaths, as well as by the replacement of Serb officials. **Jovan Rašković**, leader of the Serbian Democratic Party (SDS), was offered a vice-presidential post but declined. The situation was not improved by the campaign of anti-Croatian **propaganda** emanating from the Belgrade **media** and Serbian government circles.

In May 1990 a referendum was held on the issue of the **constitutional** status of Croatia, ostensibly to strengthen the hand of Tudjman in his negotiation with other republics over the negotiation of a looser confederal system for the country. The Serb minority understood this as a prelude to secession, and the atmosphere of nationalist triumphalism in which the referendum was conducted tended to confirm this understanding. The referendum, boycotted by many Serbs, returned a yes vote of 94 percent. In December a new constitution was adopted that, in defining the state as embodying the millennial ambitions of the Croatian people for their own state, was read by national minorities as consigning them to second-class **citizenship**. Carried away with exuberance generated by their success, however, nationalists in Croatia failed to hear the warnings of what secession from Yugoslavia might bring. There is no evidence that they modified the negotiating stance of the Croatian government in the constitutional discussions that took place during the first half of 1991; and together with **Slovenia**, Croatia declared its independence from Yugoslavia on 25 June 1991, precipitating the decline into war.

—G. R. B. and J. B. A.

Reference: Tanner, Marcus. *Croatia: A Nation Forged in War.* New Haven, CT: Yale University Press, 1997.

CROATIA (GREATER)
See **Greater Croatia**

CROATIAN ARMY

The Croatian Army, known as Hrvatska Vojska (HV), was created out of the Croatian National Guard (HNS) in 1992. On first coming to power in **Croatia** in 1990, the government led by President **Franjo Tudjman** failed to make adequate military preparations for the defense of the independence it sought from the disintegrating Yugoslav federation. The HNS was no more than an ad hoc and underarmed paramilitary formation put together from former territorial defense reservists, police, and militia volunteers. Consequently, in the first Serb-Croat war of 1991, Croatia lost around one-third of its national territory to rebel ethnic Serb militias supported by the **Yugoslav Peoples' Army** (JNA) by the end of that year. Defeat left Croatia partitioned by the self-declared **Serb Republic of the Krajina** (SRK), which impeded Zagreb's access to both its Adriatic coastline and the resource-rich province of **Slavonia** to the east. The peace agreement that ended that war in late 1991 led to the deployment of the United Nations Protection Force (**UNPROFOR**) on the territory of the SRK, thereby helping to perpetuate an unstable situation of neither war nor peace.

As the war of 1991 unfolded into a disaster for Croatia, Tudjman was criticized by some of his top commanders. One of these critics was Gen. **Janko Bobetko**, who was dismissed as chief of staff in July 1991 and replaced by the former commander of the Yugoslav Federal Air Force, Gen. **Antun Tus**. The other cofounder of the HNS and Bobetko's political superior in 1990–1991, Defense Minister Gen. **Martin Špegelj**, also criticized Tudjman at this time but was not dismissed until 1993, mainly because of his high standing in the HDZ.

Over a five-year period beginning in 1990, Croatia was able to import around U.S.$1 billion worth of armaments. Its forces were extensively reorganized, and the HV came into being in 1992. The reorganization and consolidation of the Croatian armed forces began with the elimination of a number of unruly militias that had caused considerable problems for both the HNS and the government. Foremost among these was the party militia of the **Croatian Party of Rights**. With the elimination of these and other **paramilitary/irregular forces** in 1992, the HV became the sole armed force on the territories of Croatia controlled by the Zagreb government.

Unlike other former Yugoslav leaders, Tudjman (a former JNA officer) was the actual commander-in-chief of the Croatian armed forces, working through the National Security Council and taking a close interest in the organization and operations of the HV. Tudjman took his military experience seriously, and his affinity with the HV manifested itself in his public appearances in uniform, the presence of senior HV officers at HDZ congresses, and their open membership of the party. His belief that the problem of the SRK could be resolved only through the use of force resulted in high expenditure on national defense, with well over 50 percent of budgetary outlays devoted to the armed forces.

In **Bosnia-Hercegovina**, Tudjman's hopes of creating a **Greater Croatia** on the ruins of the Yugoslav republic also required the use of military force. Although Tudjman had agreed in principle to partition Bosnia-Hercegovina with Serbian president **Slobodan Milošević** as early as March 1991, the territorial aspects of this deal could be settled only by war. Having defeated the Serbs in **Mostar** in 1992, the HV-supported HVO went on the offensive against the Army of the Republic of Bosnia-Hercegovina (ARBH) in 1993. This policy was fully supported by Tudjman and the defense minister he appointed in 1993, **Gojko Šušak**. This aggressive HVO landgrab was partly encouraged by the **Vance-Owen Plan** for Bosnia and began in earnest with the seizure of **Travnik** in the summer of 1993.

Unfortunately for Tudjman and Šušak, the HVO was very nearly defeated by the ARBH in central Bosnia by November 1993, when its defense of Čapljina collapsed, necessitating the first major intervention by the HV in Bosnia. Tudjman's disastrous military strategy at this time pitted the HVO against the United Nations (UN) deployment in the former Yugoslavia (UNPROFOR-2) and gravely worsened Croatia's international isolation to the point where Croatia was threatened by UN economic **sanctions**. This threat forced Tudjman to agree to the U.S.-sponsored **Muslim-Croat Federation** in March 1994, which created a new military balance in Bosnia-Hercegovina.

The creation, reorganization, and strengthening of the HV in 1992–1993 also resulted in a more aggressive strategy toward the SRK. This began with low-level probing against the **Serb Army of the Krajina** (SAK) and UNPROFOR units, notably in the indeterminate **pink zones** in UN Sectors North and South. A number of such incidents in 1992 were followed by a larger assault against the **Medak pocket** north of Zadar. Although militarily insignificant and risky in relation to the United Nations, these operations were politically important and timed to bring the maximum advantage to the HDZ at a time when its popularity was declining. The negotiation of a cease-fire between the HV and the SAK in March 1994 also had the effect of bringing the problem of the **Krajina** back onto the international agenda after two years of relative quiet and political deadlock.

Under the terms of the **Washington Agreement**, Croatia was able to enter into a military alliance with the United States despite the UN arms embargo of 1991. The United States tacitly tolerated the illegal transfer of large quantities of armaments to Croatia, as well as the transit of weaponry over its territory into nearby Bosnia-Hercegovina. The U.S. government also allowed the signing of a military assistance contract in 1994 between the Croatian government and Military Professional Resources Incorporated (MPRI), a military consultancy with close ties to the Pentagon and the Central Intelligence Agency (CIA), which operated a number of secret surveillance facilities from Croatian territory for spying operations over nearby Bosnia-Hercegovina and Serbia. Following MPRI recommendations to the Croatian Defense Ministry and the general staff, it was agreed that the HV was to be further reorganized. It was to be given improved command, control, and intelligence capabilities; mobile and operationally flexible ground forces; the strongest navy in former Yugoslavia; and the beginnings of a significant air force and associated air defense capabilities. The weakest component of the HV was its lack of a modern air force relative to the air force of nearby Yugoslavia. This disadvantage was to be partly compensated for by the increasing use of the **air power** of the **North Atlantic Treaty Organization** (NATO) in Bosnia-Hercegovina and enforcement of an earlier UN **no-fly zone.**

For these reasons, 1994–1995 marked the turning point for both the Croatian and Bosnian conflicts, with the Serbs the losers in each of these theaters of war. Fortunately for Croatia and its sponsors in Washington, the declining military positions of the SAK and the BSA did not stop their overconfident leaderships from making a fatal miscalculation by going on the offensive in western Bosnia in 1994. This gave Tudjman the pretext he had been waiting for: beginning in 1994 and extending into 1995, a combined HV-HVO counteroffensive swept through western Bosnia, encircling the core of the Serb Krajina focused on Knin in the process.

Later reinforced by an intensive air-bombing campaign by NATO against the BSA in 1995, these Croatian operations in Bosnia were to mark the beginning of the almost total collapse of the **Bosnian Serb** position in Bosnia-Hercegovina. Bereft of support from either the BSA or Serbia, and plagued by shortages of manpower, the SRK then fell to two major HV assaults, beginning with **Operation Flash** against western Slavonia in May 1995 and ending with **Operation Storm** against the **Dalmatian** heartland of the Serb Krajina in August of the same year. Lasting only five days, Operation Storm led to the complete route of the SAK. Only a combination of U.S. pressure and the promise of full reintegration into Croatia by 1998 prevented a similar scenario from unfolding in eastern Slavonia in the winter of 1995.

At the time of the **Dayton Agreements** of late 1995, the HV fielded around 65,000 troops, reduced to around 58,000 troops post-Dayton, with a concomitant rise in the reserves to around 150,000 troops, plus 70,000 Home Defense Force soldiers. Croatia's paramilitary police forces totaled around 40,000 in 1996–1997. Capable of mobilizing somewhere between 350,000 and 400,000 troops, Croatia's armed forces were then the largest in the former Yugoslavia. A mainly conscript force with a relatively small core of military professionals, which is only now being expanded in line with MPRI recommendations, the HV is deployed over six military districts, the most important of which is **Zagreb**, followed by **Osijek**, **Knin**, **Split**, Pula, and **Dubrovnik**. Following the successful conclusion of the operations against the SRK in 1995, the HV high command underwent further reorganization, including a purge of officers deemed to be too closely associated with the former JNA.

With Tudjman acting as commander-in-chief, the HV general staff was reorganized into a new joint chiefs of staff on the U.S. model, consisting of separate general staffs for ground forces, the navy, and the air force. Although reduced in size from

63,000 to 50,000 troops regular troops in 1996–1997, the HV's ground forces remain its operational core, consisting of seven elite combined-arms brigades, ten infantry brigades (most of which are mechanized), seven artillery brigades, one multiple rocket launcher brigade, three antitank brigades, four air defense brigades, three special forces brigades, and one engineering brigade. Deployed at five major naval bases at Split, Pula, Šibenik, Ploče, and Dubrovnik (plus minor facilities at Lastovo and Vis), the navy was increased in size from 1,000 to 3,000 troops in 1996–1997. Consisting of only 600 troops at the time of Dayton, the air force has since been expanded to 5,000 troops.

Following its armaments procurement program of the 1990s, the HV equipment inventory in 1996–1997 consisted of around 300 main battle tanks, 300 armored fighting vehicles, 2,500 pieces of artillery (including 400 towed units and 200 MRLs (multiple rocket launches), 200 antitank guns, plus a larger number of portable antitank and antiair guided weapons, as well as 600 air defense guns for its ground forces), 1 submarine and 8 major naval combatant vessels for its navy, and 30 fixed-wing combat aircraft plus 15 armed helicopters for its air force. Since its military alliance with the United States became open following the lifting of the UN arms embargo against the former Yugoslavia in 1991, the HV has embarked upon an extensive and expensive reequipment program.

As the provider of U.S.$400 million via the Train and Equip military assistance program for the Muslim-Croat Federation, the United States is likely to remain a key armaments supplier for Croatia's armed forces, although Tudjman's ambivalence about the reunified Bosnia-Hercegovina envisaged by Dayton could well threaten future military assistance from the United States. Already Washington has been reluctant to supply Croatia with the sort of strategic weaponry that would give the HV a decisive military advantage in the former Yugoslavia. Croatia is now reportedly looking to China to supply long-range surface-to-surface missiles (SSMs). The Croatian air force is reportedly looking to **Russia** for the supply of MiG-29s, which are the frontline combat aircraft of the Yugoslav air force. With or without these weapons, Croatia is now well placed to defeat any of the other military forces in the region if the Dayton peace process collapses in the future.

—M. M.

CROATIAN COUNCIL OF DEFENSE

The Croatian Council of Defense (Hrvatsko Vijeće Odbrane—HVO) was the main armed force controlled by the Bosnian Croat entity **Herceg-Bosna.** It still serves as the party militia of the **Croatian Democratic Union** (HDZ).

In April 1992, international **recognition** of **Bosnia-Hercegovina** and the latter's consequent descent into civil war precipitated the creation of a **Bosnian Croat** statelet, Herceg-Bosna, centered on western **Hercegovina** and led by **Mate Boban.** The HVO was formally constituted in May 1992, incorporating a number of **paramilitary/irregular** militias created during the fighting against the Serbs in **Mostar** in 1991. The HVO also claimed sovereignty over the strategically important Orašje pocket in northern Bosnia, as well as a number of contested areas in central Bosnia, including the pivotal town of Kiseljak.

Despite the signing of a joint military cooperation agreement between Croatian president **Franjo Tudjman** and Bosnian **Muslim** leader and president **Alija Izetbegovič** in June 1992, Boban's forces at Kiseljak did little to help break the siege of **Sarajevo** by the **Bosnian Serb Army** (BSA). With Herceg-Bosna controlling around 20 percent of the territory of Bosnia-Hercegovina at this time, the Sarajevo government and the Bosnian army (Army of the Republic of Bosnia-Hercegovina—ARBH) were in a precarious situation. From its base at Kiseljak, the HVO was able to limit the transit of foreign armaments across its territory to the ARBH—and such transit that occurred did so only at a very high price.

The HVO drove out the BSA from Mostar in the summer of 1992, whereupon this largely Bošnjak (Muslim) city was declared to be the new capital of Herceg-Bosna, provoking a serious split between Boban and Izetbegović. The former flatly refused to hand over Mostar to the Sarajevo government. Throughout Bosnia, HVO operations against the BSA were motivated only by strictly Bosnian Croat interests, disregarding the Bošnjaci who by 1993 came to regard their supposed allies as an even more dangerous enemy than the Bosnian Serbs. Following the **Vance-Owen Plan** for Bosnia-Hercegovina, Herceg-Bosna began to expand its territories in central Bosnia aggressively, with the Bosnian Croats eventually controlling a quarter of Bosnia-Hercegovina.

A Croatian Council of Defense tank and roadblock in Bosnia-Hercegovina, 1992. (CICR)

Boban's first task after the creation of the HVO was the elimination of a rival militia, the Croatian Defense Force (HOS) controlled by the **Croatian Party of Rights** (HSP). Led by **Dobroslav Paraga**, the HOS played a major role in the fighting against the Serbs in both Croatia and Hercegovina in 1991–1992, but it subsequently incurred the enmity of Tudjman. The demise of the HOS in 1992 improved discipline within the HVO, which henceforth became an integral component of the regular **Croatian Army** (HV). Despite these changes, however, the HVO remained a semicriminal organization, bound both to the local HDZ and to powerful mafia structures in **Grude** and Mostar. Its failings were overlooked by Tudjman, while in Croatia the cause of Herceg-Bosna and the HVO were given a major boost in 1993 when an influential member of the "Hercegovina Lobby," **Gojko Šušak**, became the Croatian defense minister.

Forcibly driving the ARBH and Bošnjak civilians out of central Bosnian towns such as **Travnik**, the HVO entered into a brief civil war with its former allies in 1993–1994. Unexpectedly, the relatively well-armed HVO was defeated, and a complete rout of the Bosnian Croat position in Central Bosnia was prevented only by the intervention by the HV from Croatia. The HVO also failed to dislodge the ARBH from eastern Mostar, despite intensive bombardment from positions west of the city. Tudjman's and Boban's disastrous military strategy in 1993 also pitted the HVO against **UNPROFOR** II, raising the possibility of Croatia's international isolation.

Acting under strong pressure from the **United States**, Tudjman was forced to agree to the creation of a new **Muslim-Croat Federation** in March 1994. This development led to the removal of Boban and his replacement by **Kresimir Zubak**. The creation of the federation allowed the ARBH to concentrate on its main enemy, the BSA, which had formerly supported the HVO against the Bošnjak armed forces. Despite the federation's call for the unification of the ARBH and the HVO, this did not happen in the field, and Herceg-Bosna remained in being.

Extensively reequipped by the more powerful HV in 1994, the HVO was to play an important secondary role during the joint HV-HVO and ARBH offensives against the BSA in western Bosnia in 1994–1995, when the Bosnian Serbs were also subjected to **North Atlantic Treaty Organization** (NATO) air attacks. Begun from the Croatian side by the encirclement of the **Serb Republic of the Krajina** (SRK) from western Bosnia, these offensives led to major gains for the HVO, particularly the gain of towns such as Kupres and **Jajce**, the site of Bosnia's largest hydroelectric **energy** generation facilities. To the north, the fall of **Banja Luka** was prevented only by a combination of U.S. pressure against Izetbegović and Tudjman's unwillingness to have his forces aid the ARBH in the seizure of such an important prize. At the end of the major military offensives of 1995, a new balance of power had been created in Bosnia-Hercegovina, leading directly to the **Dayton Agreements** in December of the same year. By the time of Dayton, the Muslim-Croat Federation controlled around 51 percent of the territory of Bosnia-Hercegovina, more or less equally divided between its two sides.

As of May 1995, the HVO had around 400 kilometers of front lines with the BSA, later reduced by around half at the time of Dayton. Post-Dayton, in 1996, Herceg-Bosna was formally eliminated by Tudjman under U.S. pressure, although a Croatian sphere of influence remained very much in place in its old territories, including the still-divided city of Mostar. Dayton also called for a new federation army, but this has yet to be created mainly because of HVO unwillingness to be dominated by the ARBH in this proposed venture.

At the time of Dayton, the HVO had around 50,000 troops, including reservists. Smaller than both the BSA (85,000 troops, including reservists) and the ARBH (92,000 troops, plus around 100,000 reservists), the HVO was cut by two-thirds post-Dayton, numbering only 16,000 troops by the end of 1996, compared to the 40,000 troops then in the ARBH and the 30,000 troops of the BSA. During the Bosnian war, the HVO suffered from the same manpower shortages as the BSA, mainly because of high emigration out of Hercegovina and central Bosnia into Croatia. Even more than in the past, given the lack of full HV support, the HVO is not a credible fighting force. Like the BSA, the HVO command has been recently weakened by the indictment of some of its officers as war criminals by the International **War Crimes Tribunal.**

Deployed over four operational zones commanded by headquarters at Mostar, Tomislavgrad, **Vitez,** and Orašje, the pre-Dayton HVO order of battle consisted of around 40 infantry and other brigades (reduced to around 10 brigades post-Dayton) and some 24 home defense regiments that are no longer active. Unlike the BSA, the HVO has never been heavily mechanized or heavily armed, with the notable exception of artillery. Dependent on the HV for its heavier firepower, the HVO has also been reliant on the Croatian armed forces for new equipment, ammunition, fuel, and money.

Just as the ARBH was deprived of Yugoslav Peoples' Army (JNA) military supplies in 1992, the HVO equipment inventory by the time of Dayton consisted of around 100 main battle tanks, around 50 armored fighting vehicles, and 1,200 pieces of artillery, most of which were heavy mortars. Of the equipment recently provided by the HV, most was former JNA material seized in Croatia in 1991. From 1993 onward, however, the HVO received more modern antitank and antiaircraft missiles. The HVO has also deployed a number of helicopters in recent years. Under the post-Dayton U.S.$400 million Train and Equip program, the HVO could receive U.S. military assistance, but only if it agrees to join a new federation army. In practice, future HVO modernization will remain the responsibility of the HV.

—M. M.

CROATIAN DEMOCRATIC UNION

The Croatian Democratic Union (Hrvatska Demokratska Zajednica—HDZ) is the governing political party in **Croatia.** Led by **Franjo Tudjman,** it grew rapidly from a loose nationalist movement to a fully functioning party between 1989 and 1990, and it took power in the first multiparty **elections** held in Croatia.

In Croatia during the late 1980s, as the legitimation crisis affecting the whole of Yugoslavia developed, non-Communist **political associations** attracted more and more support. There was a revival of nationalist sentiment and of open support for the Roman **Catholic Church.** The leaders of the Croatian League of Communists (LC) had been carefully screened since the 1970s to eliminate a recurrence of the **Croatian Spring.** In 1989 the LC finally began to respond to public demand for the legalization of opposition parties, and in December it agreed to create a multiparty system in Croatia.

With only four months to prepare for the elections to be held in April 1990, the Communists were unable to successfully reorient themselves. They changed the name of the LC to League of

Communists: Party of Democratic Change, but such window dressing proved insufficient to stave off the nationalist challenge.

More than 35 parties and movements registered in Croatia in 1990, but the challenge came primarily from the HDZ, led by Franjo Tudjman. From the beginning the HDZ pulled ahead from the rest, being better financed and better managed. By early 1990 the HDZ had 116 offices, one in each of Croatia's townships. Its major advantage was the support among the Croatian diaspora cultivated by Tudjman, which raised an estimated $8.2 million for HDZ funds. These émigrés were a highly politicized community, having fled Yugoslavia in two major waves (one after World War II, the other after 1971), and by their collaboration with Tudjman they achieved influential positions within the party.

The HDZ campaigned on a platform of Croatian national autonomy, arguing that Croats should decide the future of Croatia. Croatian identity and sovereignty were argued to be paramount, and the HDZ proposed a restructured confederal Yugoslavia in which Croatia would gain the powers of an independent state, its relation to the center being similar to that of states within the European Union. Tudjman himself emphasized the cultural difference between Croats and Serbs and argued that this was why a unitary Yugoslavia could not work. While supporters said that he always spoke of change taking place only democratically, such statements increased the insecurity of Serbs in Croatia.

The elections brought victory for the HDZ, aided by the "first past the post" electoral system installed by the Communists; the HDZ gained 41.5 percent of the vote but 69 percent of the seats (205 out of 365 seats) in the legislature. Because the president was elected by the legislature and not directly by the electorate, this victory assured Tudjman's accession by a huge majority.

As the war went increasingly in favor of the Croatian Serbs (with the support of the **Yugoslav Peoples' Army**) in the summer of 1991, Tudjman began to lose support within the HDZ. In response he turned to the opposition to support him, forming a "government of democratic unity" on 1 August 1991, which included opposition politicians but in which the HDZ held 11 out of 27 posts. This is the only period since 1990 when non-HDZ politicians have held any power in the Croatian government.

The old tricameral Communist structure of the Sabor (Assembly) was reorganized, creating a chamber of deputies (Zastupnički Dom) and an upper chamber of districts (Županijski Dom). The first elections to this second (63-seat) chamber were held on 7 February 1993, just after the most intense fighting since 1991 in which the Croatian Army recaptured the **Maslenica Bridge**. The election resulted in the HDZ gaining a majority in all 21 districts except **Istria** and Medjumurje—both of which had developed strong regional identities. Prior to the offensive, the HDZ had been criticized heavily for its interference in the **media** and for its handling of the **privatization** program. This political situation was exacerbated by the desperate condition of the economy—the country had lost about 40 percent of its economic capacity; its main source of income, **tourism**, had shrunk to one-tenth of its pre-1991 levels; the cost of defense production had risen to some $250 million; and costs of supporting **refugees** were an even larger burden.

The political capital gained through military success could not last forever. In October 1993, opposition deputies walked out of the assembly in protest over the autocratic behavior of the HDZ, especially its refusal to enact legislation to liberalize broadcasting. Dissatisfaction was also growing within the HDZ owing to Tudjman's autocratic leadership style. On 5 April 1994, the first reports broke of the formation of a new party, the Croatian Independent Democrats (Hrvatski Nezavisni Demokrati—HND), by several highly placed members of the HDZ; this new party was led by **Stipe Mesić** and **Josip Manolić**. Several deputies from the liberal wing of the HDZ left in protest of the HDZ's support of the **Bosnian Croats**' war against the Bosnian **Muslims**, as well as subsequent measures by Tudjman against critics of the war, which Mesić denounced as "crude bolshevism." There was speculation that the creation of the HND would be a major turning point in Croatian politics, providing a clear focus for the previously divided opposition. In any event, though, the HND failed to attract many defectors, and the HDZ was able to carry on into 1995 without being significantly weakened.

Following the successes of **Operation Flash** and **Operation Storm**, retaking the **Krajina** and western **Slavonia**, elections for the Chamber of Deputies were announced in September 1995 to be held in October. Tudjman and the HDZ hoped to capitalize on their popularity as the deliverers of an independent and united Croatia. Despite the creation of a broad alliance of seven opposition parties to fight the elections, the HDZ was still able to win over 45 percent of the vote. Controversially, both Bosnian Croats and Croats living abroad were permitted to register to vote in Croatia, and they are believed to have voted disproportionately for Tudjman.

Although its vote has declined, the HDZ has maintained its dominance in Croatian politics, winning elections again in 1997 in large measure because of the failure of efforts to create a coherent and effective opposition.

—G. R. B.

CROATIAN PARTY OF RIGHTS

A political and military movement of the far right, the extreme nationalist Croatian Party of Rights (Hrvatska Stranka Prava-HSP) was refounded in 1990 by longstanding Croat dissident **Dobroslav Paraga** largely on the principles of **Ante Pavelić**'s Ustaša between 1929 and 1941. The party even went so far as to have its militants sport the blackshirts and initialed caps of the original **Ustaša**. As a political party, it attracted only minority support on a platform of a **Greater Croatia** (i.e., the inclusion, not the partition, of Bosnian Croats), but the actions of its military wing, the Croatian Defense Force (Hrvatska Obrambena Snaga—HOS), during the Serb-Croat conflict in eastern **Slavonia**, before the establishment of a fully organized **Croatian Army**, commanded greater public attention. On 29 February 1992, the party's headquarters in Vinkovci were blown up, but the movement continued its antipartitionist operations in the Bosnian war.

—J. J. H.

CROATIAN SPRING

The Croatian Spring is the name given to the upsurge of nationalism in Croatia between 1967 and 1972. It occurred in the context of a wave of nationalism across Yugoslavia, much of it anti-Serbian. The fall of Aleksandar Ranković, the Serb head of the state security apparatus, had unleashed tensions against Serbs, and the concomitant restraints placed upon UDBa, the secret police, enabled protests that previously would not have been possible. These protests included mass demonstrations among the **Albanians** in Kosovo and Macedonia during 1968; anti-Serb factions in **Montenegro** arguing against the pro-Serb conservatives; Slovenian nationalists concerned about the drain of resources to the south; and Serbs in Serbia and Croatia developing nationalist programs that at the most extreme called for an autonomous province within Croatia or even secession and attachment to Serbia.

The crisis came about partly as a result of the Croats' dismay at the lack of swift results from the economic reforms of the 1960s. Belgrade still seemed to control the vast majority of the money supply, with over half the total credits and over 81 percent of foreign credits controlled by the central banks. Croatian economists published figures showing that Croatia brought in 50 percent of foreign capital but disposed of only 15 percent of Yugoslav credits. The perception that Croatia and the Croats were being exploited by the Serbs began to grow through the mobilization of nationalist groups, led by the organization Matica Hrvatska, around a number of issues, as well as the dissemination of Croatian nationalist ideas through a variety of **media**.

The main economic issue was exacerbated by three others. First, there were demographic changes involving a proportionately older population in Croatia (which had the third lowest birth rate), a proportionately larger number of *gastarbeiter* (workers abroad) drawn from the Croatian working population than from other republics, and an increasing influx of Serbs into Croatia. Croatian nationalists recast the latter two factors as intentional actions by Serbian nationalists aimed at weakening Croatia. Second, there was some encouragement of **Dalmatian** separatism by Serbian nationalists. Third, there was the publication in 1967 of the first two volumes of a dictionary resulting from the 1954 Novi Sad agreement to collaborate on the creation of a common orthography and a definitive Serbo-Croatian dictionary. The "informed" Croatian public were outraged to find that the Croatian variants of words had been described as a local dialect and represented as deviations from the norm of the Serbian variants, thus underpinning the instatement of the Serbian form of Serbo-Croat as the official language of Yugoslavia to the detriment of the Croatian form.

Since 1969, spokespersons and media instruments of Croatian organizations such as the Croatian Literary Society and Matica Hrvatska had been arguing that Croatia was under attack and proposing measures to "defend" it. *Hrvatski književni list (Croatian Literary Gazette),* published weekly by Matica Hrvatska, was one of the first mouthpieces for Croatian nationalists and was soon followed by many others. The leadership of the League of Communists of Croatia (LCC) was divided, with Croatian conservatives attacking these manifestations of nationalism. In mid-1969 *Hrvatski književni list* was shut down, provoking an outpouring of criticism from the remaining publications. It was soon replaced with an even more radical nationalist paper that became the biggest-selling publication in Croatia. Even the daily newspaper, *Vjesnik (Herald)* and Radio-Television Zagreb were transformed from instruments of the Socialist Alliance of Workers of Croatia into de facto nationalist ones.

The divisions in the LCC leadership were settled in favor of the nationalists in January 1970. **Savka Dabčević-Kučar** attacked a leading conservative, Miloš Žanko, and succeeded in portraying the latter's behavior in deploring Croatian nationalism as part of a readiness to undermine the rest of the party leadership and bring in outside forces to achieve the downfall of the leadership. As a result, Žanko lost his party positions by decision of the LCC, and the rest of the LCC leadership moved closer to the position of Matica Hrvatska.

A number of figures from Croatian history were recast in a more positive light, including Stjepan Radić and Ban Josip Jelačić, with statues to them proposed. Traditional Croatian songs were promoted, and Matica Hrvatska used *Hrvatski tjednik* (the *Croatian Weekly*) to attack all examples of "Serbianization" of the language—in publications, on bus signs, and on train timetables. It was only natural that the vocal anti-Serbianism of the Croatian nationalists should have an impact on the large number of Serbs (15 percent of Croatia's population) living in Croatia.

The conflict that developed between Serbs in Croatia and Croats centered on the impact of the intensification of Croatian national consciousness on the rights of Serbs to national self-expression. While *Hrvatski tjednik* argued that Croats were only protecting their rights against outside pressure, the Croat nationalists failed to convince Serbs that the overall intention was not to isolate and oppress them. The Serb response was to look for allies amongst the Croatian conservatives and to call for changes to the Croatian constitution that would give Serbs cosovereignty.

Intense lobbying and counterlobbying on the part of the Serb and Croat cultural and political groups within Croatia introduced amendment after opposing amendment. In the end, official government draft amendments were passed, and Croatia was described as the state of the Serbian nation in Croatia as well as the Croatian national state.

The turmoil and infighting within the Croatian LCC during 1971 among conservatives, nationalists, and liberals ended with the ascendancy of a nationalist-liberal alliance. By November, Matica Hrvatska was over 40,000 strong, and a growing number of local papers were carrying nationalist stories. Serbian periodicals began to respond to the Croat nationalism by attacking it as extreme and anti-Yugoslav; the Croatian periodicals responded to these allegations equally vehemently, and Croats began to believe that there was a concerted campaign to undermine and then suppress Croatian nationalism, especially in the form of Matica Hrvatska.

President **Tito** was by now extremely concerned, criticizing the Croat leaders and nationalists. However, they escaped full censure and widened their demands, turning their attention outward to the Croats in Bosnia and Hercegovina. Matica Hrvatska tried to set up branches outside Croatia, arguing that the Bosnian Croats, who formed 20 percent of the Bosnian population, were discriminated against. Not surprisingly, the other republics denied these claims. In response Croat nationalists called for western **Hercegovina** and parts of Montenegro to be attached to Croatia. The insensitivity of this demand was incredible, given that most of Bosnia had been part of the **Ustaša** state during World War II. This was perhaps the major mistake of the Croatian leadership, which lost any residual support that they may have had from the Bosnian, Montenegrin, and Vojvodinan Leagues of Communists. Once again these events foreshadow those of the 1990s.

In the last two months of 1971, the troika of Savka Dapčević-Kučar, Mika Tripalo, and Pero Pirker returned to the original economic grievances of Croatia and began to increase the pressure on the federal level for settlement of their demands. To a large extent, they had been swept along by the nationalists, forced to choose an alliance with them because they could not surmount the barriers of mistrust with the conservatives and because they did share a common position on economic matters with the nationalists. But the latter had pushed the situation too far. Calls for secession were raised, and friction was increasing between Serbs and Croats at the local level in Croatia, with the suggestion that some communities may have been arming for a coming confrontation.

In response to Croat demands, as well as the 30,000-strong student strike that swept through Croatia at the end of November 1971, Tito called the party presidia of the **League of Communists of Yugoslavia** and the LCC together at Karadjordjevo in the Vojvodina, and on 1 December he and representatives of six of the other regions attacked the Croatian leaders. The latter were instructed to initiate severe measures against the increasingly extreme Croatian nationalists, and after several days of struggle the central troika were forced to resign. Protests by student militants enabled the use of riot police, and the climate turned fully against nationalism. Tens of thousands of members were expelled from the party; several nationalists (including ex-Partisan turned revisionist historian **Franjo Tudjman**) were imprisoned; Matica Hrvatska and 14 publications were suppressed; and the **media, student** organizations, and university departments were purged.

The main economic demands of the nationalists were granted, with retention quotas of earnings by Croatian enterprises rising, among other measures. However, although the expression of nationalism in organized forums had been suppressed, there were still incidents of Croatian nationalism throughout the 1970s, with a number of nationalist intellectuals returning to jail shortly after their initial releases. Tudjman was reimprisoned in 1981, as was former student leader **Dobroslav Paraga**. Many of the leading nationalists eventually ended up emigrating and were an important part of the diaspora support for Tudjman's **Croatian Democratic Union** (HDZ) in the 1990s.

In many ways the Croatian Spring was the prime intellectual, political, and economic resource for the nationalist programs of the 1990s; the constitutional and cultural changes made by the HDZ mirrored many of the Croatian Spring's elements, and the Serbs felt as threatened as they had in the late 1960s. Without a strong, legitimate center and the essential consensus among the elite that had existed in the suppression of the first crisis, there was nothing to stop the second Croatian crisis from escalating into the war of 1991.

—*G. R. B.*

CROATIAN WRITERS
Like other wars in Europe in the twentieth century, the recent war in Yugoslavia has given rise to a great deal of creative activity. The basic impulse underlying this activity is the need to bear witness, to remember, to give incomprehensible experience a form. For the individual who has direct experience of the suffering of war, the telling of the story is the issue. For the outsider, anxious to understand, the way the message is delivered is inevitably also an issue: the sheer power of the material may distort its meaning. The greater calm lent by distance is generally more conducive to an appropriate formulation of extreme experience. Hence, there will be more works of literature to emerge from this war over the coming years, especially from Bosnia and Croatia, the only two of the six former Yugoslav republics to endure extended conflict on their soil. In addition, Croatia's established publishing contacts with the West will help bring such literature to the international community.

Already several writers from Croatia dealing with the war have gained attention and respect abroad. The fact that they are women is mirrored by the fact that the **peace movements** that sprang up immediately throughout Croatia were run for the most part by women, as were many of the practical volunteer groups that have provided help for refugees and victims of the war. Some of these women are journalists who have maintained their integrity and spoken their minds at considerable personal risk. The impact of their words on frightened, isolated individuals can never be known, but it is certain that such writing has played a vital role in preserving basic human values and dignity.

Slavenka Drakulić is a Croatian journalist whose first books of essays to appear in English, *How We Survived Communism and Even Laughed* (1992) and *Balkan Express* (1993)(London, Hutchinson), are also commentaries on the current political situation. Drakulić was one of five women journalists and intellectuals attacked and vilified in the Croatian press as "witches" for their role in damaging Croatia's image abroad through their criticism of **Franjo Tudjman**'s regime. Rada Ivekovič, who taught philosophy at the University of Zagreb, subsequently chose a different medium through which to comment on the war: with three other women, she published, in Germany, a volume of letters that the four wrote to each other between 1991 and 1993 (*Briefe von Frauen über Krieg und Nationalismus*, 1993) Another Croatian journalist, Nada Prkačin from Vinkovci, published a work entitled *Tamo gdje nema rata* (*Where There Is No War*, 1993), which is a fictionalized account of her experience as a reporter visiting the Slavonian battlefields, talking to soldiers, the wounded, and the doctors tending them. The text speaks above all of the tragedy and the futility of war.

Dubravka Ugrešić is arguably the most important living woman writer in the Croatian language. Ugrešić, who has published two novels and two volumes of short stories, was working on her next book of fiction in summer 1991 when war broke out in Slovenia and thereafter Croatia. She stopped work on her novel and was unable to return to it in the same form. Instead she wrote two volumes of fictionalized essays, both colored by sharp irony and humor but expressing an increasingly desperate anger. One of the themes of the first book, *Američki fikcionar*, which appeared in English as *Have a Nice Day: From the Balkan War to the American Dream*, is the disjunction of personality that comes from having to try to reconcile the madness of wartime with all that one has known until that time: memories and expectations of "normality" combined with a kind of disbelief that violent destruction can in fact be real. This duality is concentrated in the case of Ugrešić's work by the fact that she is thinking about the destruction in her native Croatia from the quiet backwater of Middletown in Connecticut. From the United States Ugrešić returned to Croatia and endeavored to go on living her old life. This became increasingly impossible as she was incapable of subscribing to the prevailing ideology and the public image of Croatia as an entirely innocent victim. Since she could not publish in Croatia, her articles began to appear abroad and she became a "public enemy." She has now become one of the four million former Yugoslavs living in various kinds of exile. One of the main themes of her subsequent book of essays, *Kultura laži (The Culture of Lies)* is what she calls "autism": the incapacity of people to respond to blatant manipulation, their readiness to forget or deny all that belonged to the time "before the war," to forget their own experience of growing up and living in a state called Yugoslavia.

—*C. H.*

See also: Serbian writers

References: Iveković, R., B. Joanović, M. Krese, and R. Lazić. *Briefe von Frauen über Krieg und Nationalismus.* Frankfurt-am-Main: Suhrkamp, 1993; Prkačin, Nada. *Tamo gdje nema rata.* Vinkovci: Privlačica, 1993; Ugrešić, Dubravka. *Američki fikcionar.* Zagreb: Durrieux, 1993. *Have a Nice Day,* transl. C. Hawkesworth. London: Cape, 1994; ———. *The Culture of Lies,* transl. C. Hawkesworth. London: Weidenfeld and Nicolson, 1998.

CRVENA ZASTAVA

See **Kragujevac**

CRVENKOVSKI, BRANKO

Born the son of an officer in the Yugoslav Peoples' Army in Sarajevo in 1962, Branko Crvenkovski heads the Social Democratic Union of Macedonia—the successor to the former **League of Communists** of Macedonia. Graduating as an engineer in 1986, he began a career in industry before being elected to the assembly. His rise to power can be described only as meteoric: he became president of the Commission on Foreign Affairs, head of his party in 1991, and prime minister of **Macedonia** in 1992. Although his political success has been attributed to the patronage of **Kiril Gligorov**, he has undoubted political ability, as evidenced by his success in managing a succession of coalition governments, which have included the main **Albanian** party (the PDP).

—*J. B. A.*

See also: political parties

CSCE

See **Organization for Security and Cooperation in Europe**

ČUBRILOVIĆ, VASO (1897–1990)

A **Bosnian Serb** scholar and political figure, Vaso Čubrilović was born in Bosanska Gradiška. As a student, he participated in the assassination of Archduke Ferdinand of **Austria-Hungary** in **Sarajevo** in 1914—the event that precipitated World War I. Between the two wars, he was professor at the Faculty of Arts in Belgrade and a leading member of the **Serbian Academy** of Sciences and Arts. It was for the Serbian Academy of Sciences and Arts that

Čubrilović prepared a number of politically influential memoranda particularly in favor of the "**ethnic cleansing**" of national minorities, such as the **Albanians** in **Kosovo** and the Germans in the **Vojvodina.** Among these documents are "Iseljavanje Arnauta" ("The Expulsion of the Albanians"), presented in Belgrade on 7 March 1937, and "Manjinski problem u novoj Jugoslaviji" ("The Minority Problem in the New Yugoslavia"), presented in Belgrade on 3 November 1944. Čubrilović held several ministerial portfolios in the Yugoslav government after World War II. Of his major publications, mention must be made of the monograph *Istorija političke misle u Srbiji XIX veka (History of Political Thought in Serbia in the 19th Century),* presented in Belgrade in 1958.

—*R. E.*

CULTURAL FAULT LINE

Explanations for the breakup of Yugoslavia often resort to the idea that the creation of a unified South Slav state was an unnatural event, in that it sought to bring together in one political community peoples who are separated by a major "cultural fault line." Different versions of this thesis have been proposed, but in general terms the argument rests upon the historical division of the **Balkans** between the Roman and Byzantine traditions of Christianity, which are said to have laid incompatible cultural foundations.

Several historical events have been cited as defining this cultural fault line. The first is the division of the Roman Empire on the death of Theodosius I in 395. The second is the demarcation of the patriarchates of Rome and Constantinople in 451. The third is the definitive schism between the Eastern and Western churches, which did not take place until 1054. The lines that correspond to each of these events do not coincide, and they bear little relationship (if any) to the pattern of religious distribution that subsequently developed in the region, which saw the creation of substantial areas of **Orthodox** observance on the **Catholic** side of the "line."

Although there is clearly a range of cultural differences that distinguish the various Balkan peoples, explanations of contemporary political change in terms of the cultural fault line do not make consistent or clear reference either to which cultural patterns are rooted in this particular contrast or to the reasons why those cultural contrasts that are noted should be so significant as to prevent the creation of a common state.

Discussion of the importance of a cultural fault line based upon the historical schism within Christianity frequently becomes blurred by reference to two other supposed primary cultural contrasts. Sometimes the relevant line of contrast is taken to be that between **Islam and the West.** Croatian-American anthropologist Dinko Tomašić also developed a theory of the permanent opposition within the Balkan region between the "*zadruga*," or "extended family," and "dinaric," or "highland," cultural types (*Personality and Culture in Eastern European Politics,* New York, Stewart, 1948). This theory, which has enjoyed a revival of interest during the disintegration of Yugoslavia, basically postulates an inherent conflict between cultures deriving from (1) the ecology and family structures of settled agricultural peoples and (2) pastoral (especially seminomadic) peoples.

—*J. B. A.*

See also: religion; social character

CYRILLIC SCRIPT

One of the central symbols of cultural difference between the South Slav peoples is the Cyrillic script. This script has come to be associated particularly with communities in the **Orthodox** Christian tradition, as well as in the Balkans with Bulgarians, Macedonians, Montenegrins, and Serbs.

The Cyrillic alphabet derives from the efforts of Byzantine missionaries St. Cyril and St. Methodius in the mid-ninth century. In order better to communicate the gospel to the Slav peoples, the Greek alphabet was adapted to correspond more closely to the phonetics of the Slav languages. An important step in the process was the adoption of Christianity by the court of Mutimir, *župan* (Count) of Raška (north of modern Novi Pazar) sometime between 850 and 891.

The original script differed from modern versions of Cyrillic and is known as the Glagolitic script (based on Greek cursive letters). It was used primarily as a medium for writing ecclesiastical works, and because it antedates the definitive schism between the Eastern and Western churches, it was for a time also used in **Bosnia** and **Croatia,** associated in particular with the Franciscan order. It survived in liturgical use in parts of **Dalmatia** into the nineteenth century. The Cyrillic alphabet proper underwent a transition from Greek cursive to uncial characters during the eleventh century. There have been several variations in the orthography of the South Slav languages since then. In particular, scholars have noted regional peculiarities in the alphabet's use in Bosnia, **Bulgaria**, and **Macedonia**, which have provided a pretext for contemporary nationalists to affirm the antiquity of specific national identities of the peoples of these regions. The standardization of these differences took place mainly during the nineteenth century (differentiating Bulgarian from Serbian), although Macedonian orthography was standardized only after 1945 (differentiating it from both).

During the breakup of Yugoslavia, the right to use the Cyrillic script in public became a symbolic bone of contention for Serbs living in Croatia and **Bosnia-Hercegovina**, although in both of these areas there had been a long-term spontaneous drift toward the use of the Latin script. This was particularly the case in Dalmatia, where many local Serbs had difficulty in using the Cyrillic script, especially in writing. Nevertheless, the public display of signs in Cyrillic (or their suppression) has become one of the most important signals of local ethnic domination.

—J. B. A.

D

DABČEVIĆ-KUČAR, SAVKA

Savka Dabčević-Kučar (born on the Dalmatian island of Korčula in 1923) was a member, along with Mika Tripalo and Pero Pirker, of the troika that led Croatia's League of Communists (LC) during the nationalist upsurge of the **Croatian Spring** in 1971. In 1990 she and Mika Tripalo formed the Coalition for National Accord (KNS), which contested the first presidential elections in Croatia. The KNS argued for more autonomy for Croatia—but not full independence—and opposed any changes of borders. Dabčević-Kučar now heads the Croatian People's Party (HNS), which secured six seats in Croatia's first multiparty elections in 1990.

—*G. R. B.*

DALMATIA

Dalmatia is the southern region of **Croatia**, stretching from **Zadar** on the coast across to **Knin** in the hinterland, narrowing down to **Dubrovnik**, and ending in the **Prevlaka** Peninsula that overlooks the bay of Kotor. The flat plain between Zadar and Šibenik and thin strips of land along the coast and on the many islands have a Mediterranean climate, but the hinterland is dominated by the limestone Dinaric Mountains, which offer the problems of intermittent drainage; floods and droughts; and poor, stony soil.

Dalmatia was the heart of the medieval Croat kingdom of Tomislav during the tenth century, and the Croatian church and state were centered on Nin, some 20 miles north of Zadar. With the union with Hungary came conflict with Hungary's rival, Venice, and the Croats in Dalmatia found themselves under Venetian rule for much of the next four centuries. The Venetian-controlled cities of Zadar, Šibenik, and **Split** flourished, as did the independent city-state of Ragusa (Dubrovnik). In the coastal cities, the arts and sea trade both benefited from the influence of Venice. The population of the hinterland is much poorer, and as a result of the migration of Serbs during the period of the **Ottoman** conquest of the Balkans, there are many Serbs in the northern Dalmatian region, bordering onto Lika. Dalmatia was governed separately from the rest of Croatia and **Slavonia** under the **Habsburg Empire** and was integrated into a common state only after Yugoslavia itself was created. Its separate historical traditions, including the linguistic legacy of Venice, have made for continuing cultural contrasts with continental Croatia.

During the conflict in Croatia, many of the Dalmatian coastal cities were bombarded by the Yugoslav navy. Split and Dubrovnik were targeted in particular for their symbolic cultural value rather than for any military reasons. For a long time the Croatian Serbs succeeded in cutting southern Dalmatia off from road traffic by destroying the **Maslenica Bridge**, near Zadar. Rail links with the region were also severed when Knin (the main rail junction for the south) came under Serb control. Fighting continued sporadically from January 1993 until the cease-fire agreement of March 1994. Communications between the region and the rest of Croatia were completely reconnected after the offensive (**Operation Storm**) of August 1995, in which the Croats retook all the Serb-controlled land around Knin.

—*G. R. B.*

See also: naval power

DAMS

See **Peruča Dam**

DANUBE RIVER

The Danube, or Dunav, River flows for 588 of its 2,857 miles through **Serbia**, reaching its confluence with the **Sava River** at **Belgrade**. The Danube forms part of the western border of the Federal Republic of **Yugoslavia** (FRY) with **Croatia** and then flows eastward across the **Vojvodina** to form part of the eastern frontier of the FRY with **Romania.** A founding member of the Danube Commission of 1948 (a multilateral grouping of Danubian riverine states pledged to ensure free navigation of one of Europe's major international waterways), FRY has major river-to-sea ports at Novi Sad, Belgrade, and Pančevo.

During the period of the United Nations (UN) economic **sanctions** against the FRY (1992–1995), the Serbian government reportedly authorized blockades of its section of the Danube to foreign traffic. Serbia's Danubian border with Croatia has been highly militarized for most of the 1990s—indeed, it has been contested during this period, although the FRY agreed in late 1995 to return by late 1996 those areas of eastern **Slavonia** that it had earlier annexed to Croatia. The 1990s also witnessed disputes with Romania's government over the operation of the Yugoslav-Romanian hydroelectric **energy** generation facilities at the Iron Gates. With the lifting of the economic sanctions against the FRY, Serbia's use of the Danube River for its foreign trade is expected to revive rapidly.

—M. M.

DAYTON AGREEMENTS

This complex series of documents (sometimes referred to as the Dayton Accords) was negotiated at the Wright-Patterson Air Force Base of the U.S. Air Force, near Dayton, Ohio, between 1 and 21 November 1995. Following ratification by appropriate constitutional or political bodies in the former Yugoslav states, the documents were finally signed in Paris on 14 December. Although brokered by the state department of the **United States** (the initiative was led by **Richard Holbrooke**, assistant secretary of state for European and Canadian affairs, and Anthony Lake, presidential national security adviser), the agreements were signed by representatives of the Republic of **Bosnia-Hercegovina**, the Republic of **Croatia**, and the Federal Republic of **Yugoslavia.** The Dayton Agreements consisted of a general framework agreement of 11 articles and 11 annexes, together with a number of letters binding specific signatories in particular ways and a definitive collection of maps. Based upon the international **Contact Group**'s proposal of 1994, the territorial division into "entities" reflected in part the substantial territorial gains that had been made by the Bosnian government forces, with Croatian assistance, following the success of **Operation Storm** in August, as well as in the wake of NATO's (the **North Atlantic Treaty Organization**'s) Operation Deliberate Force in September.

The agreements reached at Dayton do not represent a major change of political position on the part of any of the signatories. Rather, they reflect the rapid readjustment of U.S. policy toward Bosnia following the second massacre at a marketplace in **Sarajevo**, on 28 August 1995, as well as the growing evidence of an imminent military collapse by Serb forces in Bosnia. The Serb leadership (both in Bosnia-Hercegovina and in Serbia itself) realized that failure to reach a negotiated settlement soon could have prejudiced the entire project of the Bosnian Serbs' **Republika Srpska.**

U.S. "brokerage" appears to have consisted in significant measure of extreme personal pressure applied to the negotiators, in addition to any political or military leverage that the United States may have enjoyed in the wake of the NATO intervention. Isolated in a U.S. military base and reduced to limited contact with the outside world, Presidents **Alija Izetbegović**, **Slobodan Milošević**, and **Franjo Tudjman**, plus their advisers, found themselves in circumstances that at every turn emphasized their own powerlessness.

The general framework agreement notes that "the agreement of August 29 1995 . . . authorized the delegation of the Federal Republic of Yugoslavia to sign on behalf of the Republika Srpska." In many respects this cleared the way for successful negotiation, replacing the intransigent **Radovan Karadžić** (who in any case may well not have been acceptable as a negotiating partner to the Bosnians) by the much more opportunistic Milošević (whose cooperation was stimulated by the possible removal of the United Nations [UN] program of economic **sanctions** against his own country). This ploy may well have delivered the goods in terms of signed agreements, but it left a legacy of difficulties in relation to implementation. None of the parties to Dayton have been wholehearted in their pursuit of implementation; nevertheless, resistance has been in general far more sustained and determined on the part of the Serbs, many of whom have been able to point to the imposition of the settlement upon them against their will.

The Dayton Agreements established the Republic of Bosnia-Hercegovina as a federation, composed of two "entities": the Federation of Bosnia-Hercegovina (populated predominantly by persons of Muslim and Croat **ethnicity**) and the Republika Srpska (Serb Republic). The agreements identified the two entities, proposed a constitution that was to frame their relationship, provided for an electoral process that would generate a legislative assembly, suggested the establishment of a variety of bodies to handle common business, and created an administration under the High Representative of the United Nations, the task of which was to supervise the transition to a peaceful and legitimate state. The process was to be enforced by an international military **Implementation Force** (IFOR).

The separation of the armed forces of the two entities, as well as their movement away from the newly defined interentity boundary, was achieved expeditiously and within the target date constraints. In spite of considerable anxiety about the feasibility of the exercise, elections were held for the legislative assembly in September 1996, although it took three months of subsequent negotiation to produce a government. Delays were encountered in relation to almost all other areas of agreement, however, which resulted in the postponement of the withdrawal of IFOR and its replacement by a longer-term Stabilization Force (SFOR).

Five areas presented the most serious difficulties. Whereas the agreements provided for complete freedom of movement within Bosnia-Hercegovina, this has not been realized either within the Republika Srpska or the Croat-controlled areas of **Hercegovina**. The expectation that **refugees** would be permitted to return to their homes has been frustrated in many areas. The creation of a new civic government in **Mostar** was achieved only after exceptional efforts by the local office of the UN High Representative. The surrender of indicted war criminals for trial at the International **War Crimes Tribunal** in The Hague has been subject to widespread obstruction, especially within the Serb entity. The Dayton negotiators could reach no agreement about the future of the **Brčko** area, and settlement of this issue was set aside for special negotiations.

It is widely agreed that the Dayton constitution cannot survive as the political framework for Bosnia-Hercegovina in the longer term. Aside from the issues mentioned, too many significant areas of activity (especially defense and taxation) remain outside the control of the federal government and in the hands of the entities. It is hard to credit the state with a stable future when one of its entities is fundamentally committed to its supersession. An environment in which the republic's two neighboring states each stand to gain from its collapse is not conducive to optimism. Whether these problems can be overcome by further negotiation or will be remedied only by further war remains to be seen.

The full text of the Dayton Agreements is given in the appendix to this volume.

—J. B. A.

DELIĆ, RASIM

A former officer in the **Yugoslav Peoples' Army** (JNA) and chief of staff of the **Bosnian army** (Armija Republike Bosnia-Hercegovina—ARBH), Gen. Rasim Delić was responsible for transforming the latter army into a modern and effective armed force.

Delić was one of the few Bosnian **Muslims** (Bošnjaks) to achieve a high rank in the Yugoslav armed forces. A veteran of the JNA campaign at **Vukovar** in late 1991, Delić deserted its ranks just before his native Bosnia descended into **civil war** in April 1992. He first came to prominence, and to the attention of Bosnian president **Alija Izetbegovič**, during the brief civil war between the newly established ARBH and the forces of the **Croatian Council of Defense** (HVO) in 1993–1994. Thereafter he was closely involved in the defense of **Sarajevo** from the besieging **Bosnian Serb Army** (BSA). A member of the ruling **Party of Democratic Action** (SDA) since 1991, Delić was then appointed chief of staff of the ARBH, which had recently been created out of a chaotic and undisciplined mixture of former Territorial Defense Force reservists, police, and militia volunteers.

Although loyal to Izetbegovič, Delić thereafter developed close ties with the hard-line nationalist wing of the SDA associated with Vice President **Ejup Ganić**. Working closely with Izetbegovič's chief procurer of foreign armaments in the Islamic world, Deputy Defense Minister Hasan Čengić, Delić has, since 1993, transformed the ARBH into an effective army.

—M. M.

DEMAÇI, ADEM

Adem Demaçi (born 1936) is a **Kosovo Albanian** prose writer, former political prisoner, and human rights activist. He is author of the controversial novel *Gjarpijt e gjukat (The Snakes of Blood)*, Priština, 1958, on the theme of vendetta. He was held for a total of 28 years, between 1958 and 1990, as a political prisoner of the Belgrade regime, and he was considered at the time one of Yugoslavia's most prominent political dissidents. Since his release from prison on 28 April 1990, he has been active in the field of human rights and is currently head of the Committee for the Protection of Human Rights and Freedoms in Priština, the capital of Kosovo. In 1991, Adem Demaçi was awarded the Sakharov Prize for Freedom of Thought by the European Parliament in Strasbourg, France.

—*R. E.*

DEMOCRATIC LEAGUE OF KOSOVO

As the leading political party of the **Albanian** community in **Kosovo**, the Democratic League of Kosovo (Lidhja Demokratike e Kosovës—LDK) was formed in December 1989 after the dissolution of the one-party **League of Communists of Yugoslavia** and soon received wide support among the Albanians in Kosovo. Other parties were also founded. Under **Ibrahim Rugova,** the LDK won the majority of votes in the Kosovo **elections** of 24 May 1992 (boycotted by the Serb minority and ignored by the Belgrade authorities), in which a total of 24 political parties and groups took part. Although the elected four-party parliament has not yet been able to meet, the LDK is regarded as the legal political representative of the majority Albanian community in Kosovo. The LDK has branch offices abroad (including Britain, Germany, Switzerland, Sweden, and the United States) to coordinate its political activities.

—*R. E.*

DEMOCRATIZATION

The fall of the Berlin Wall in 1989 stimulated expectation that the former Soviet satellite countries in Eastern Europe would become integrated into a wider European democratic culture. It was anticipated that the former "real socialist" system, characterized by state planning of economic activity, would give way to the initiative of the private entrepreneur. It was supposed that the domination of a single ruling party, the "dictatorship of the proletariat," would give way to democracy. A kind of historical necessity was attributed to these changes by academic commentators on the region, such as Samuel P. Huntington (*The Third Wave: Democratization in the Late Twentieth Century,* 1991) and Francis Fukuyama (*The End of History and the Last Man,* 1992).

Although Yugoslavia can be regarded as having been a part of the Soviet system only with some qualification, it is clear that the collapse of Soviet hegemony in Central and Eastern Europe was linked in important respects to the disintegration of the federation. The movement toward the creation of democratic political structures, which became evident across the region after 1988, was echoed within Yugoslavia. The ignominious collapse of the **League of Communists of Yugoslavia** (LCY) at its fourteenth congress, in January 1990, was interpreted as part of a general pattern.

The first stirrings of this movement were hailed in the formation of the Slovene Peasant League as early as May 1988. This was followed by the formation in Zagreb of the **Croatian Democratic Union** (HDZ) in June 1989, and in Belgrade of the Association for a Yugoslav Democratic Initiative in November. Following the disintegration of the LCY, arrangements were made across the federation to provide republican governments that were legitimated by popular election, beginning in Slovenia in April 1990 and ending in December in Serbia and Montenegro.

Although since that time it has come to be taken for granted that governments across the region will emerge as the result of contested popular elections, there are several good reasons why the various post-Yugoslav regimes should be regarded as incompletely democratic, or democratic only in form.

A feature of the creation of a multiparty system throughout Yugoslavia was the contrast between (1) those parties that grew up within the former framework of Communist political institutions and (2) those that were set up in opposition to it. The former were sometimes in a position to enter the electoral contest equipped with the inherited assets of the LCY and the Socialist Alliance. Although in **Croatia** (the CDU) and to some extent **Macedonia** (Internal Macedonian Revolutionary Organisation) émigré money provided a very effective counterweight, elsewhere (especially in **Serbia** and **Montenegro** but also to some extent in **Slovenia**) the "sitting tenants" of government set out with a clear economic advantage. A closely related asset was privileged access to the **media** of mass communication. The generally centralized structure of ownership and control over the media, together with historical traditions of their state regulation, have tended toward the effective control of the media of communication by established political elites in all republics.

There has been a tendency toward the monopolization of electoral choice by nationalistic parties, with the effect that parties that decline to present themselves in these terms—or, more particularly, those that identify themselves with ethnic minorities—stand in danger of being branded as disloyal to the state. Instead of being seen as a natural and necessary part of the electoral process, opposition tends to be regarded as illegitimate; hence, local commentators have suggested that the term *ethnocracy* rather than *democracy* better describes political systems across the former federation.

Largely as a result of the Communist system (though the roots of the problem go deeper than this), there has been a lack of a developed "civil society." Analysts of democratic politics have emphasized the belief that effective democracy does not depend upon **elections** and parties alone. Citizens exercise leverage upon political elites not only through the ballot box, but also through a number of other groups, such as churches or trades unions, as well as through the independence of institutions such as the judiciary or educational bodies. The lack of alternative sources of opinion provided by such intermediate groups, or of alternative sources of power provided by other securely established institutions, tends to make electoral politics more manipulative. At the extremes, this failure to provide independent checks upon the activity of party elites permits the resort to force, fraud, and intimidation in order to influence the electoral process.

—*J. B. A.*

See also: constitutional models; political associations; political parties

References: Fukuyama, Francis. *The End of History and the Last Man.* New York: Free Press, 1992; Huntington, Samuel P. *The Third Wave: Democratizations in the Late Twentieth Century.* Norman: University of Oklahoma Press, 1991.

DEMOGRAPHY

See **population**

DEMOS

See **political parties, in Slovenia; Slovenia**

DETENTION CAMPS

One of the defining characteristics of the war in **Bosnia-Hercegovina** has been the use of the chilling phrase *etničko čišćenje,* or **ethnic cleansing.** The reality of this policy as an aim of the conflict has come to public attention most strongly in the establishment of detention camps. Media images of the suffering experienced by thousands of Bosnia's inhabitants served to isolate the Serbs in world opinion and led to the widespread view that only the "traditional" Balkan propensity to violence could explain the cause and nature of the conflict. The camps have thus assumed a symbolic importance that is probably greater than their real significance and have played a substantial role in the **propaganda** war in the international **media.**

The overriding impression created by media treatment of the issue is that the camps were operated solely by **Bosnian Serbs** and run along the lines of the death camps of Nazi Germany. However, there is evidence that all sides in the conflict operated such camps and that there was considerable variation in their management, even among different camps operated by the same side. Thus, a myth has been created that will no doubt play an important role long into the future. There has already been an attempt to rewrite Yugoslav history from that period, with Croatian president **Franjo Tudjman**'s challenge of the previously accepted accounts of the Croatian **Ustaša** camps such as **Jasenovac.** We can expect to see further rewriting of history given the paucity of information about the camps of the Bosnian conflict.

According to the incomplete figures available, only a minority of people died actually within the camps. Many more were killed when they were shipped out of the camps to other locations to meet their deaths or when their villages were overrun. What is certain is that the Nazi camps' industrialized, conveyor-belt approach to killing was not a feature of the Bosnian war. Instead, the deaths that occurred were from poor hygiene, starvation, sustained beating, and "sport" deaths, in which the victims' tormentors practised sadistic, "imaginative," individualized killings. Furthermore, these camps were not purpose-built but were frequently located in former industrial units, probably the only sites available in most areas. Of the camps featured most often in media coverage, Manjača was a farm owned and operated by the **Yugoslav Peoples' Army,**

Bosnian Muslim detainees held by the Bosnian Serb Army, Bosnia-Hercegovina, 1992. (Stevan Filipović)

Keraterm was a former ceramics factory, and Omarska was an abandoned iron mine. There is evidence that in the Serb-run camps organization and management were chaotic, with different authorities responsible for different camps (Manjača was controlled by the **Bosnian Serb Army** and Omarska by the Commune of **Prijedor**) which led to difficulties and delays when aid agencies and other organizations such as **UNHCR** attempted to gain access. These delays inevitably led to the impression that the Bosnian Serbs were deliberately restricting access.

The existence of the camps, although known to various international agencies, did not become public knowledge and thus an issue of concern until the summer of 1992. The first person to break the news of their existence was Roy Guttman of New York's *Newsday,* closely followed by the *Guardian* newspaper's **Maggie O'Kane** and ITN. ITN's coverage of Manjača flashed around the world and is generally considered to be the reason for the camps' appearance on the international political agenda.

There is considerable evidence that many camps were established, although some were of a very temporary nature. By August 1993, for example, the International Committee of the **Red Cross** estimated that there were 6,474 inmates in 51 camps. These numbers probably represent only a portion of the total number of inmates and camps at that time, and the complete figures may never be known. The Bosnian Serbs certainly conceived of the camps as fulfilling one of their war aims: the creation of ethnically pure areas. Most of the inmates were civilians, as Croat and Muslim community leaders and soldiers were generally isolated and taken away (the evidence suggests for execution) when Bosnian Serb forces arrived in an area. Imprisoning civilians achieved several aims: ethnic cleansing, hostages for exchange (in one instance 400 Croats for diesel fuel), and the creation of fear, which further enabled ethnic cleansing by encouraging civilians to flee before advancing military forces.

The camps had varying impacts on the various sides and across socioeconomic classes. In the early stages of the war, when the Bosnian Serbs were securing large areas of territory, most of the camps, including Manjača and Omarska, were run by them. Under intense international pressure, camps that were known to the media and international agencies were gradually closed and the inmates transferred to holding centers in Croatia. Later stages of the war saw the creation of camps by the Muslims and Croats, and relatively little is known of these, as by then media attention had shifted to **Sarajevo** and the various Muslim enclaves. One Croat-run camp, **Mostar,** is known to have had conditions as bad or even worse than those of the Serb camps. Mostar was established by the Ustaša-inclined **Croatian Party of Rights** at the former Yugoslav Peoples' Army heliport near the town, and inmates were kept in fuel tanks. Many died from the fumes, and a considerable number of people were murdered for sport by guards (including women) stationed there.

Finally, evidence suggests that among the Serbs, captured non-Serb civilians were screened to determine their fate. Those who were highly literate (such as teachers) or who occupied relatively high socioeconomic positions in the area seem to have disappeared (presumably executed), and very few from these groups ever made it to the camps. One inmate of Trnopolje camp told Red Cross officials, "Only the working class lived."

Little is really known about the camps of the Bosnian war, and what is known is distorted by often sensationalist media reporting. Much investigative work needs to be done to obtain a more accurate picture of their purposes, roles, and consequences.

The following rough list of detention camps includes no names of Bosnian government camps, although they certainly existed. Although all the camps witnessed high levels of civilian deaths, some seem to have been actively utilized as killing centers. These are marked with an asterisk and "normal" concentration camps with a plus sign.

Bosnian Serb
Batković+
Brčko-Luka*
Čelopek
Foča
Keraterm*
Kotor Varoš
Lopare
Manjača+
Omarska*
Potočari
Sušica*
Trnopolje+

Bosnian Croat
Čapljina
Dretelj
Ljubuški
Mostar*
Rodoč

—*R. J.*

See also: hostage taking; rape

DINARA, MOUNT

The ridge of Mount Dinara extends from the southeast to the northwest between Livno and Bosansko Grahovo, along the border between **Bosnia-Hercegovina** and **Croatia.** The mountain's highest summit (1,831 meters) overlooks the city of **Knin,** which became the capital of the secessionist Serb **Krajina** within Croatia. It was the site of one of the most important military campaigns of the war, which went almost unmarked within the international press. During the early summer of 1995, Croatian forces executed a two-pronged movement that eventually placed artillery on the ridge only 10 miles from Knin. Units of the **Croatian Army** moving northward from Sinj were coordinated with units of the **Croatian Council of Defense (HVO)** from Livno. To the north, Croat units that had been deployed originally for the relief of **Bihać** and **Cazin** were able to force their way through Bosanski Petrovac toward Drvar. Laying the groundwork for an encirclement of Knin, the Dinara campaign constituted an extremely important part of the preparation for **Operation Storm,** which brought the Knin Krajina to an end.

—*J. B. A.*

DINARIC ALPS

See **Karst**

DISABLED

Prewar services for disabled people in the former Yugoslavia (about 2.6 percent of the nongeriatric population) followed the Eastern European "medical-utilitarian" model whereby disability was seen as originating only in the individual (i.e., as not being affected by societal attitudes and environmental factors such as poor access). Centralized social, educational, and medical services focused on remediating or compensating for defects and on optimizing individual economic productivity. There was a network of specialists, separate and residential hospitals/clinics, and schools and centers for further education and vocational training in the larger towns. Some of these institutions catered to citizens of their own republic, but many accepted those from other republics as well. This interrepublican activity also applied to the training of specialist professionals.

People with sensory and physical disabilities but without additional cognitive impairments benefited most from this inadequate system. The quality and effectiveness of service provisions were greatest in northern Yugoslavia. In Slovenia and Croatia, current Western trends toward a "social disability" model (the belief that societal attitudes and environmental aspects, such as poor access, are key disabling factors and that disabled people are different but not inferior, with a right to be fully included as valued community members) were beginning to have some influence on professional thinking and opinion. School integration and parents' and disabled peoples' associations were beginning to develop. In all republics most people with severe mental handicaps or with combined disabilities and mental illness were institutionalized, often from birth and far from home. The stigmatization of families, as well as the provision of basic physical care only in institutions in **Montenegro**, **Kosovo**, and **Macedonia**, reflected the even lower status of disabled people in the south.

The effects of war on the disabled population were most acute in **Croatia** and **Bosnia-Hercegovina** because of direct war action and the destruction of service infrastructures; however, the other emerging countries were also affected. Although economic **sanctions** did not include **humanitarian aid** to the disabled, the increasing isolation and poverty in **Serbia**, Montenegro, and Macedonia; the previously low standards of care; and the influx of disabled adults and children from the war zone all ensured a further reduction of the quality of life.

Specific effects included malnutrition, with reduced resistance to infections and no access to specialized diets. **United Nations High Commission for Refugees** (UNHCR) and **nongovernmental organizations** (NGOs) were unable to meet all dietary needs, even with donations from the United Nations Protection Force (**UNPROFOR**), and some rural institutions received little or no aid. Others became, collusively or otherwise, conduits through which aid intended for disabled people went to the army or the **black market**. There were substantial losses of professionals such as doctors, paramedical therapists, teachers, and occupational workers through emigration or flight, through voluntary or conscripted transfers to non-disability-related employment, and through leaving of posts due to nonpayment of salaries or transport problems. Life-sustaining and regulating medication was either irregularly supplied, unavailable, or of a poorer specification. The death rate, deterioration in health, and lack of meaningful employment for the disabled population rose directly as a result of these factors.

The level of morbidity also increased as a direct result of the war. The official Croatian government statistics of war victims as of 1996 indicated that of the total 37,190 wounded, including 971 children, about one-third to one-half would have lasting disabilities. In Bosnia the child statistics in 1995 from Naša Deca (Our Children, the national umbrella organization concerned with child welfare) estimated that of the 34,718 war-wounded children, about 10,000 would have long-term disabilities.

Prewar physical facilities and administrative systems were to a great extent destroyed in the war zones. Institutions were overrun, blasted, devastated, or "cleansed," and services and their records were destroyed. The School for the Blind in **Sarajevo**, used as a Serb Army base, was in ruins and nonfunctional. Drin and Bakovici Hospitals for disabled and mentally ill people in Fojnica were the battleground for Croatian/Muslim fighting in 1993, causing staff to flee and resulting in the deaths of seven patients and the destruction of the cooking, washing, and sanitation systems for over 600 people, many of them incontinent and nonambulant. In the same year, 300 severely mentally handicapped patients of the Vrlika Institute in the Krajina and their staff fled to safety in open trucks to the Juraj Bonači Institute in **Split**, already full with its own clients and previous refugees. The Institute for the Welfare of the Blind in **Mostar** lost its offices, resources including mobility and communication equipment, and all its records.

Some instances of deliberate maltreatment of disabled people were reported. The murder of a group of mentally handicapped people in the 1995 Croatian "**ethnic cleansing**" of the **Krajina**; the exclusion of mentally ill people from allocation of aid in parts of Bosnia; and the alleged sexual abuse/exploitation by Canadian UNPROFOR troops of patients and staff in Fojnica are examples.

Because provision and professional training were previously centralized, the emergence of the new separate countries, the flight of **refugees**, the ethnic separation, and the frozen **communications** have resulted in inequity of provision and the "trapping" of this vulnerable population either in provision across new national boundaries, separated from their families, or with no appropriate provision at all. It was estimated that there were 3,400 children with physical and multiple disabilities from Bosnia in special schools, training centers, and institutions in Serbia at the end of hostilities. Subsequent reunification programs by the International **Red Cross** and Save the Children have achieved much, but there remain 200 children for whom reunification with families or "home" institutions has not been possible. The lack of suitable provision applies across all disabilities throughout Bosnia. A specific example is that of blind children who were effectively without education throughout the war, except in the **Tuzla** region. Many of these children now have to go to school in Zagreb, where the Croatian authorities charge fees for nonnationals. Training of special education teachers was previously centered in Belgrade, Zagreb, and Ljubljana, and Bosnia is now struggling to establish its own special education faculty in Tuzla.

The surge of interest and involvement of outside aid agencies, albeit poorly coordinated, ill-informed, occasionally self-interested, and insensitive to local disability history, has nonetheless brought some new thinking to bear on the situation of disabled people in the former Yugoslavia. It has encouraged those who have a wider, more progressive vision of what may be done for—and above all, *by*—disabled people. The involvement in humanitarian aid of larger organizations such as Oxfam, Care, Handicap International, and smaller organizations (such as Edinburgh Direct Aid, Connect, War Child, and the Irish Refugee Trust) has enabled disability policies and practices to be revised. The presence of large numbers of rights-seeking young war-wounded should also have a catalytic effect on the actions of the relevant authorities.

—A. C.

Reference: Hastie, Rachel. *Disabled Children in a Society at War: Casebook from Bosnia.* Oxford: Oxfam, 1997.

DISPLACED PERSONS

See **refugees (external); refugees (internal)**

DJILAS, MILOVAN (1911–1995)

Milovan Djilas was a former **Partizan** leader, vice president of the Socialist Federal Republic of **Yugoslavia** (1945–1954), and subsequently known as a political dissident and writer. Born in a village in **Montenegro**, he became a communist in the interwar years and served a term in prison between 1933 and 1936, during which he became acquainted with several leading figures in the Communist Party. He came during World War II to occupy a position of one of the inner circle of Yugoslav Communists, as a close collaborator of the late President **Tito**, and he was appointed to high positions in both the party and government. During the conflict between Yugoslavia and the Soviet Union in 1948, he became disillusioned with the Communist Party, and in 1953 he published a series of articles in the party daily, *Borba*, in which he openly criticized several aspects of the political culture of Yugoslavia. (These articles were collected and published in English in 1959 as *Anatomy of a Moral.*) Disciplined by the party and sentenced to a term of imprisonment, he went on to write a critique of the emerging communist hierarchy that made his name in the West—*The New Class* (1959).

Many who have sought to explain the disintegration of the Yugoslav federation after 1989 have tended to dwell upon the primacy of the factor of **ethnicity** and ethnic differences, and to see the decisive divisions that broke the federation as results of its more recent history. Djilas is important as a reminder of the long history of political dissent in the country and of the fact that issues other than ethnic conflict, especially the suppression of democracy, have been at the heart of social and political conflict in the country since 1945. Djilas's longer-term reputation is likely to rest upon his autobiographical historical and literary studies.

—R. J. and J. B. A.

References: Djilas, Milovan. *Anatomy of a Moral.* New York: Praeger, 1959; ———. *The New Class.* New York: Praeger, 1959.

DJUKANOVIĆ, MILORAD

Although formerly prime minister of the Republic of **Montenegro**, and since December 1997 president of the republic, Milorad Djukanović is a relatively new and young figure in Montenegrin and Yugoslav politics. He unexpectedly won the presidential election in Montenegro in October 1997—an event of potentially great importance because it perhaps heralds the end of federal president **Slobodan Milošević's** power locally, as well as the political career of **Momir Bulatović**, the outgoing president.

Milo Djukanović was born in 1962 at Nikšić, the son of a high court judge. He graduated with a degree in economics from Titograd University and immediately started nurturing political ambitions within the youth division of the **League of Communists** (LC). His current high visibility owes much to the "antibureaucratic revolution" launched by Milošević, replacing the old guard of the LC with new, young politicians generally subservient to himself. Djukanović's rise to senior positions within the Montenegrin party is not dissimilar to that of Bulatović, and indeed for some time Djukanović was considered a political ally. Whereas Bulatović has sought to tread a careful path between Montenegrin aspirations and Milošević's line in Belgrade, Djukanović has increasingly distanced himself from both, emerging as the voice of Montenegrin autonomism. Initially his criticism of Bulatović was limited to minor observations, but from 1996 he began to openly challenge not only Bulatović but also Milošević. In this he has been aided by the declining fortunes of the latter (particularly since the Bosnian war) and by the willingness of the **Bosnian Serbs** to demonstrate their own independence from Belgrade. As Milošević has grown weaker, Djukanović has become more outspoken.

This tense relationship with Belgrade has been demonstrated through many and increasing references by Belgrade television (RTB) to Djukanović's background. (It is alleged that his money and influence derive primarily from the smuggling of cigarettes and arms with Italy and fuel with Albania.) The fact that such remarks are being made by a state television station (not to mention the print media) regarding an elected senior political figure is indicative of the bitterness surrounding the question of the relationship between Montenegro and the Yugoslav federation.

Djukanović has reveled in this notoriety, claiming that such attention by the Milošević-controlled **media** is proof of his commitment to Montenegrin interests. Although he publicly holds a commitment to continued Montenegrin membership in Yugoslavia and has not espoused the cause of total independence, he has been extremely critical of current arrangements and is therefore seen as a positive voice in Montenegro compared with the vacillation of Bulatović.

Since Djukanović's investiture as president, the Montenegrin relationship with **Serbia** has improved—largely, it would seem, because Milošević has recognized the inevitable. Prior to this event, cadres loyal to Bulatović organized demonstrations, perhaps sponsored (albeit indirectly) by Milošević, in an attempt to have Djukanović's election victory annulled by any means possible, including civil unrest. The situation is for the moment calmer, opening the way for more diplomatic methods of redefining Montenegrin/Serbian relations.

—R. J.

DOBOJ

The strategic importance of Doboj, a large town (population 103,000 in 1991) in northern Bosnia lying on the **Bosna River**, in the Bosnian war was as a railway town, at the crossing of the east-west line linking **Tuzla** with **Banja Luka** and the north-south line linking **Slavonski Brod** with towns down to **Sarajevo.** If Bosnian government forces had been able to take Doboj, they would have been able to enclose the Serb-dominated region of **Maglaj/Ozren** and use it as a bargaining factor, but the Serbs successfully held the town as a frontline location.

—J. J. H.

DRAŠKOVIĆ, VUKAŠIN

Vukašin (Vuk) Drašković heads the Serbian Renewal Movement (SPO) and is one of the principal figures in the Serbian political opposition. Born in 1946 in Novi Sad, Vojvodina, Drašković was educated at the University of Belgrade. At one time a member of the **League of Communists**, he subsequently became an extreme Serb nationalist. During the 1970s and 1980s, he published a number of controversial novels, foremost of which was the best-selling *Nož (The Knife),* a story set during World War II in occupied Yugoslavia.

As a self-declared Serbian nationalist of **Chetnik** sympathies, inspired by the wartime Serb anticommunist leader Gen. Draža Mihailović, Drašković cofounded the SPO in 1990. The SPO called for the

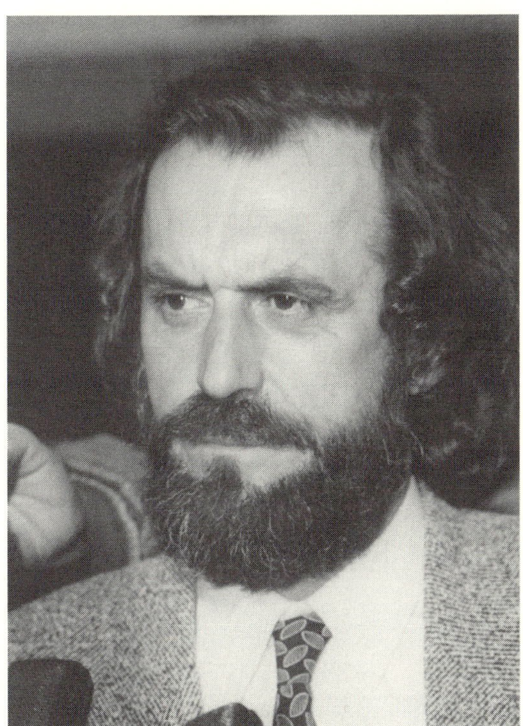

Vukašin Drašković, leader of the Serbian Renewal Movement. (Tanjug)

return to **Serbia** of the exiled crown prince Aleksandar of Yugoslavia. More controversially, the party was believed to sponsor a number of Chetnik militias at the beginning of the war in **Croatia.** Although also espousing the Serb nationalism then co-opted by Serbian president **Slobodan Milošević,** Drašković was hostile toward Milošević and the **Socialist Party of Serbia** (SPS) from an anticommunist and royalist perspective.

During the first postwar multiparty parliamentary **elections** in Serbia, in December 1990, the SPO was trounced by the SPS, partly because of the latter's tight control of the country's **media;** Drašković gained only 20 percent of the vote in the Serbian presidential elections, which Milošević overwhelmingly won. During the antigovernment demonstrations in **Belgrade** in March 1991, however, Drašković emerged as the leading Serbian opposition leader. Then the largest opposition group in the Serbian parliament, Drašković's SPO formed an electoral coalition, the Democratic Movement of Serbia (DEPOS), with other opposition parties to contest the parliamentary and presidential elections in Serbia in December 1992. Of the 49 seats then gained by DEPOS, most went to SPO candidates. In the concurrent presidential elections, Drašković stepped aside for another DEPOS candidate, **Milan Panić,** who lost to Milošević. Claiming widespread electoral fraud by the SPS, Drašković's SPO and DEPOS boycotted the Serbian parliament in February 1993.

During antigovernment demonstrations in Belgrade in June 1993, Drašković and his wife, Danica, were detained for five weeks and badly beaten by the Serbian police. After the Serbian parliamentary elections in December 1993, when DEPOS gained only 45 seats, the SPO parted company with the rest of the Serbian opposition.

Earlier, in 1991–1992, Drašković had also split with his former political ally, **Vojislav Šešelj,** who then went on to found the Serbian Radical Party (SRS), thereby further dividing the Serbian opposition. By 1994–1995 Drašković had moderated his Serb nationalist views, going so far as to publicly support Milošević's efforts to end the conflict in Bosnia at the time. The result of this move was the effective political collapse of the divided Serbian opposition in the run-up to the elections in Serbia in December 1996.

—*M. M.*

See also: paramilitary/irregular forces; political parties

Reference: Drašković, Vukašin. *Nož.* Belgrade: Zapis, 1982.

DRINA RIVER

The Drina is the most important of **Bosnia-Hercegovina's** many rivers. Rising near the border with **Montenegro** in the southeast, it flows tortuously northward for 200 miles, the latter half of its course forming the border with **Serbia,** before joining the **Sava River** on the border with **Croatia.** The settlements and towns along the Drina Valley historically had mainly **Muslim** populations; however, because they were close to the Serbian border, nearly all of them were taken by the Serbs in the Bosnian war—in particular **Foča, Višegrad,** and **Zvornik,** although **Goražde** ultimately remained under government control.

The river is also a symbol for Bosnians as the focus of Nobel Prize winner Ivo Andrić's novel *Bridge on the Drina (Na Drini ćuprija),* originally published in 1945.

—*J. J. H.*

Reference: Andrić, Ivo. *Bridge on the Drina,* transl. L. F. Edwards. London: Allen and Unwin, 1959. Reprint, Chicago: University of Chicago Press, 1977.

DRNOVŠEK, JANEZ

Born in Celje (Slovenia) in 1950, Janez Drnovšek obtained a Ph.D. in economics at the University of Maribor. He emerged from the first democratic elections in **Slovenia** (2 April 1989) as the Slovenian representative to the Yugoslav collective presidency, in which he held the post of president between May 1989 and May 1990. In this capacity he became head of the **Nonaligned Movement** and chaired its summit conference in Belgrade in September, continuing the foreign policy line established by former Yugoslav president **Tito**.

As president, Drnovšek attempted to build a modern market economic system on track for integration within the European Community (now known as the European Union). He freed all political prisoners in Yugoslavia and sought to introduce a pluralist, multiparty political system. Although he desired peaceful and negotiated solutions to political problems in the disintegrating Yugoslavia, obstructionism on the part of some political leaders, as well as their opposition to Western European forms of democracy, inflamed relationships between units of the federation. Following the Slovene plebiscite on the issue, independence was eventually declared on 25 June 1991, precipitating intervention by the **Yugoslav Peoples' Army** (JNA) and the Ten Day War of independence. A summer meeting between **European Community** peacebrokers and Serb and Slovene leaders on the island of **Brioni** was facilitated by Drnovšek's position as president of the Yugoslavian Presidency. This resulted in the withdrawal of the JNA from Slovene soil by 19 July.

Since then, Drnovšek's astute political maneuverings have established a broad political consensus behind his policies of winning international **recognition**, redirecting Slovenian international trade, and securing integration into the European Union (EU). His tenure of office has resulted in Slovenian integration into organizations and institutions such as the **United Nations** (UN), the **International Monetary Fund** (IMF), the World Bank, the General Agreement on Tariffs and Trade (GATT), and the Council of Europe. A major success was his signing of the Association Agreement between Slovenia and the EU.

On 27 February 1997, a new coalition government was approved by the Slovenian National Assembly, comprising Liberal Democrats and the Slovene People's Party, supported by the Democratic Party of Pensioners, the Italian and Hungarian minorities, and one independent. This is the third government that the popular Janez Drnovšek has led since independence, highlighting his contribution to the democratic and political development of Slovenia.

—I. R. B.

See also: political parties; Italy; Hungary

DUBROVNIK

Dubrovnik (Italian name Ragusa) lies on the Adriatic coast of **Dalmatian** Croatia, and for 13 centuries it has functioned as a heavily fortified seaport. Since the arrival of the Slavs in the seventh century, the city has in turn been part of the Roman, Byzantine, Venetian, Napoleonic, and Austrian empires, but for much of the time it has remained a virtually free city-republic pursuing independent commercial and cultural activity. In 1918 it became part of the original "Yugoslav" kingdom, and from the 1950s it sensitively developed a highly successful tourist industry based upon its architectural attractions and reputation as "the pearl of the Adriatic." Its population totaled 49,000 in the census of 1991.

In early October 1991, the Serb-Croat war spread to Dubrovnik (or as the Dubrovčani themselves prefer to describe it, the siege of Dubrovnik began) when the **Yugoslav Peoples' Army** (JNA) launched an offensive from the south. The motivation was quite different from that expressed in relation to other areas of the conflict: the Serb population of Dubrovnik amounted to barely 6 percent, and there had been no military presence to be protected. However, the capture of Dubrovnik and its port of Gruž could clearly provide maritime access for an enlarged Serbia through neighboring **Bosnia-Hercegovina.** More significant perhaps was Dubrovnik's international status as a city of cultural heritage, the capture of which would be of great propaganda and bargaining value; this gave credence to the earlier and variously attributed threat by Montenegrins that for every drop of Serb blood spilled a stone would be blasted from the walls of Dubrovnik. The villages to the south and east succumbed without real resistance to the Serb/Montenegrin advance, and by the end of the month the JNA was at the gates of the Old City.

Although parts of Dubrovnik outside the city walls were destroyed (many of the buildings being

Outlying areas of Dubrovnik under attack by the Yugoslav Peoples' Army (JNA) during the siege of Dubrovnik, 1991. (Stevan Filipović)

of more recent construction), it was the fate of the Old City that commanded the international headlines. Constant shelling, particularly from the sea, shattered most of the roofs and topped the towers of many of the famous buildings; many sections of the city and its old harbor were ablaze. The Old City walls (in places six meters deep) and their associated fortifications prevented more lateral damage, but the living conditions for the citizens besieged in their shelters became virtually intolerable with loss of all utilities, especially water supply. Several hundred citizens lost their lives through the shelling or the resulting conditions.

The **propaganda** value of the siege to Croatia was highlighted when a convoy of supply ships ("Convoy of Hope"), accompanied by several domestic and international celebrities headed by **Stipe Mesić**, reached the city on 31 October 1991. It became clear that the city was not forced into surrender, and in mid-November a **cease-fire** was signed. In May 1992 an agreement was reached between the Croats and the JNA for the latter's withdrawal from the Dubrovnik hinterland—attention of the Croats and the Serbs was now being diverted to Bosnia.

As Dubrovnik began the task of restoration, there remained one more tragic incident as late as April 1996, when a plane carrying 33 people on a flight from a U.S. military base in **Tuzla** crashed in stormy weather on approach to the Dubrovnik airport; all persons on board were killed, including the U.S. secretary of commerce, Ron Brown. This incident, too, had connection with the war in that the earlier attempts to destroy the airport had deprived it of the advanced tracking equipment that it is now believed might have guided the aircraft properly.

At the time of this writing, the reconstruction of Dubrovnik has been effected to such a degree that the authorities are predicting the return of 25 percent of the seaport's original **tourism** trade for 1998. The international annual summer festival of arts has continued throughout.

—*J. J. H.*

See also: Montenegro

ECONOMIC DIMENSION

Although often overlooked in recent analyses, the economic determinants, dimensions, and consequences of the Yugoslav crises and wars of the 1990s are of crucial importance.

Preceded by a serious economic and political crisis during most of the 1980s, Yugoslavia's final disintegration and its descent into **civil war** can be explained mainly in terms of a struggle over scarce resources: territory, productive capacity, infrastructure, and hard currency. Furthermore, the Yugoslav wars can be described as an economic catastrophe for most of the former federation. There have been vast cumulative economic losses of both output and foreign trade, as well as serious damage to economic and other infrastructure, the main results of which have been far lower living standards than hitherto and chronic uncertainty in all the successor states of the former Yugoslavia except Slovenia. Even if the Yugoslav wars are now coming to an end, reversing the economic dislocation and decline that they have caused will be extremely difficult and prolonged, and only Slovenia enjoys anything like economic normality at the present time.

A predominantly agricultural economy during the period 1918–1941, Yugoslavia experienced rapid socioeconomic change and development after 1945, based on forced industrialization, growing urbanization, and a gradual change from centralized economic planning toward a "socialist market economy." Postwar communist Yugoslavia's economic development resulted in high growth rates and significant improvements in living standards during the 1950s, 1960s, and 1970s. Although initially modeled on the Soviet experience, after 1953 Yugoslav development adopted innovative forms of industrial organization, notably **workers' self-management**. Earlier attempts at agricultural collectivization were also abandoned at this time.

Although subsequently partly reversed for political reasons, the economic reforms embarked upon in 1965 were then the most radical in the communist world, introducing to some extent market principles. During the 1960s and 1970s, the Yugoslav economy became increasingly integrated into the world economy through foreign trade and borrowing in the capitalist West, through the rapid development of international **tourism** and other service sectors, and through the export of surplus labor to other parts of Europe. These trends set Yugoslavia apart from the communist world in general and the COMECON (Council for Mutual Economic Assistance) countries of Eastern Europe in particular.

Following the increased transfer of political power from the federation to its constituent republics and autonomous provinces during the 1970s and 1980s, Yugoslavia became a de facto confederation, and economic development became more regionally focused than hitherto. The federation-wide market was curtailed, resulting in a degree of autarky in each of the federation's republics. These political developments had a number of adverse economic consequences, notably the creation of excess productive capacity and infrastructure, widening **regional inequalities** in incomes and living standards, and uncontrolled growth of the federation's foreign debt. Already a serious problem by the 1960s, unemployment grew rapidly in the 1970s and 1980s. Another persisting problem was **inflation** arising out of price liberalization and uncoordinated monetary/credit policy, which had the effect of reducing real incomes and living standards by the early 1980s. This period also witnessed serious disequilibrium in Yugoslavia's foreign trade.

Yugoslav economic growth declined sharply during the 1980s, when the federation experienced a major foreign debt crisis. First formally rescheduled in 1983 and then again in 1988, Yugoslavia's consolidated foreign debt exceeded U.S.$18 billion by the end of the 1980s. The deflationary consequences of the **International Monetary Fund**'s approved stabilization then lowered economic growth, adversely affecting both employment and living standards. This economic decline was highly uneven in its regional impact: by the end of the decade, per capita income in **Slovenia** was six times that in **Kosovo**.

Reversing this economic decline through stabilization and reform implied strengthening the federal government. Once the government of **Serbia**, under President **Slobodan Milošević**, achieved a dominant position in federal institutions after 1987; however, the other republics, led by Slovenia and **Croatia**, resisted moves toward the centralization of economic policymaking. The last major attempt to stabilize and reform the Yugoslav economy, by Federal premier **Ante Marković** in 1989–1991, ultimately failed for political reasons. All the federation's republics subverted the economic policies of the federal government at this time, culminating in illegal appropriations in 1990–1991 by the Serbian government from the National Bank of Yugoslavia and the onset of a full-scale trade war between Serbia and Slovenia.

With Yugoslavia's disintegration and descent into civil war in 1991, its successor states experienced major economic dislocation. In 1990, the last year of comparative economic normality, the federation had a combined gross domestic product (GDP) of around U.S.$55 billion. Slovenia's GDP per capita was then about twice the Yugoslav average of U.S.$2,679. Croatia's GDP per capita was just above this average. GDP per capita was well below the all-Yugoslav average in **Bosnia-Hercegovina**, **Macedonia**, and **Montenegro**. Serbian GDP per capita was then about the same as the all-Yugoslav average, although the poorest areas of Serbia, particularly Kosovo, recorded the lowest level of all.

Industrial manufacturing accounted for around 45 percent of all-Yugoslav GDP and employment in 1990. In the more developed northern republics, this level was even higher, above 50 percent. Economically central in the prewar period, agriculture played a relatively minor part as a source of GDP and employment, although it remained more important in the southern republics, with agriculture accounting for around 15 percent of Serbia's GDP and employment during the 1980s. After manufacturing, services were the second most important sector, notably in Croatia.

Foreign trade was of great significance for the Yugoslav economy (notably for Slovenia and Croatia), but Yugoslavia's persistently negative trade balance throughout the postwar years contributed to the accumulation of a foreign debt of more than U.S.$18 billion by 1990.

At the time when the domestic market and payments area collapsed in conditions of acute political crisis in 1990–1991, the country's former international markets also disappeared in Eastern Europe and the former Soviet Union. The successor states of the federation all experienced sharp falls in GDP and hence living standards. In Slovenia this fall was relatively slight. In Croatia, GDP fell by 20 percent in 1990–1991, with further sharp falls in 1992–1993, bottoming out only in 1994. In constant prices, Croatia's GDP per capita did not return to 1990 level until 1995. By then, Slovenia's GDP per capita was around three times the figure for Croatia. In Serbia, the GDP fell to 60 percent of its 1990 level by 1995 as a result of the loss of former Yugoslav and COMECON markets and the imposition of United Nations (UN) economic **sanctions**. Over the same period, Macedonia's GDP and GDP per capita declined by more than 50 percent in real terms because of the loss of federal fiscal transfers, the UN embargo against trade with Serbia, and the economic blockade of the country by **Greece**. Already the poorest and least developed of the Yugoslav republics in 1990, Bosnia-Hercegovina experienced the worst economic collapse in the region, with its 1995 GDP and GDP per capita at no more than 20 percent of their former levels.

Lost output, foreign trade and finance, and damaged infrastructure have been estimated at U.S.$100 billion–$150 billion during the 1990s, with the worst losses in Bosnia-Hercegovina, Serbia, and Macedonia. Damage to productive and other infrastructure in Bosnia has been estimated at around U.S.$40 billion–$50 billion. In Croatia, such losses have been estimated at around U.S.$20 billion. Serbian and Macedonian infrastructure and productive capacity have suffered because of a lack of capital for new investment. Other consequences of war have been bloated military expenditures throughout the region, politically motivated fiscal expansionism and resultant high inflation, and the growth of untaxed **black market** economies often dominated by mafia elements. These problems have been particularly acute in Croatia and the Federal Republic of Yugoslavia, with Serbia and Montenegro experiencing a return to hyperinflation in 1992–1993.

For 1995, Bosnian GDP has recently been estimated at around U.S.$3 billion (around U.S.$500 per capita), or no more than 20–30 percent of the levels in 1990. Most of Bosnia's remaining 3.5 million population remains dependent on international **humanitarian aid** for its survival. Bosnian industrial output in 1995 was no more than 10 percent of its level in 1990, resulting in unemployment rates over 80 percent in cities like **Sarajevo**. According to recent estimates, it will take Bosnia 15–20 years to reach its GDP and GDP per capita levels of 1990. The costs in Bosnia of reconstruction, which is initially to be focused on infrastructure rehabilitation, are expected to be in the region of U.S.$5 billion per annum for the rest of the 1990s. The costs of UN Protection Force (**UNPROFOR**) and international humanitarian aid to Bosnia since 1992 have been in the region of U.S.$5 billion. In 1995–1996, the costs of NATO's **Implementation Force** (IFOR) commitments are expected to exceed U.S.$5 billion.

In Serbia and Montenegro, estimated combined GDP in 1995 was around U.S.$15 billion (around U.S.$1,500 per capita). Output of goods and services in 1995 was only 60 percent of its 1990 level, and industrial output was no more than 20 percent of its 1990 level. This process of deindustrialization has resulted in unemployment of more than 60 percent. Agriculture has become ever more central in Serbia, where it may have accounted for up to 50 percent of GDP in 1995. Another high-growth area has been black market and "sanctions-busting" services. According to recent estimates, it will take "rump" Yugoslavia 10–15 years to reach its GDP and GDP per capita of 1990. Uncertainty continues to blight the economic prospects of Macedonia, where GDP and GDP per capita were U.S.$1.5 billion and U.S.$700, respectively, in 1995, with officially recorded unemployment exceeding 50 percent in 1995.

Croatia has relatively good economic prospects, although local output of goods and services is still only at 60 percent of its 1990 level. At more than 20 percent in 1995, Croatian unemployment remains relatively high. Annual GDP growth was 4 percent in 1995, mainly because of a revival of foreign trade with the **European Union** (EU), and Croatia's foreign trade turnover of U.S.$11.1 billion exceeded its 1990 level for the first time. Financial stabilization has been successful, resulting in a low inflation rate of 3.5 percent in 1995. With record hard currency reserves of U.S.$3 billion in 1995, Croatia is also well placed to service its agreed-upon U.S.$5 billion share of former Yugoslav foreign debt.

In Slovenia, GDP and GDP per capita in 1995 were U.S.$18 billion and U.S.$9,000, respectively—a performance that places Slovenia on par with the Czech Republic. At U.S.$18 billion in 1995, Slovene foreign trade turnover then equaled 100 percent of Slovenia's GDP. Over 80 percent of this trade was with the EU. In 1995, Slovene hard currency reserves reached a record U.S.$4 billion. At U.S.$3.5 billion in 1995, Slovenia's agreed-upon share of former Yugoslav foreign debt was the most manageable in the former Yugoslavia. As of 1995, only Slovenia and Croatia had regularized the servicing of their foreign debt liabilities to the point where they could resume normal borrowing abroad. Only Slovenia of the former Yugoslav republics is now in a position to be seriously considered for EU membership by the year 2000.

—*M. M.*

See also: banking; war costs

Reference: Vojnić, Dragomar. "The Economic Dimension of Yugoslavia's Demise." In Payam Akhavan and Robert Howse (eds.), *Yugoslavia, the Former and the Future: Reflections by Scholars from the Region.* Washington, DC: Brookings Institution, 1995.

ECONOMIC DISPARITY

See **regional inequality**

ECONOMIC REFORMS

See **Marković, Ante**

ECONOMIC SANCTIONS

See **sanctions**

ELECTIONS

One of the first signs of political change in the Yugoslav federation was the holding of multiparty elections in 1989–1990 for the republican assemblies. These were not the first occasions on which the population had been allowed to choose their political representatives. In municipal elections over several years, candidates other than nominees from the **League of Communists** (LC) or the Socialist Alliance (SA) had stood and been elected. **Janez Drnovšek**'s accession to the Slovene seat of the federal presidency had taken place by popular election. Nevertheless, the LC sustained its opposition to organized parties that could rival its authority. This was the basis of its attack on the Praxis Group of philosophers, as well as the disbanding of the Zagreb cultural organization Matica Hrvatska in 1972. The first breach in this policy was the registration of **political associations** in 1988.

The process of **democratization** cannot be measured entirely by the holding of elections. The democratic credentials of elections are dependent upon whether they can be considered to be "free and fair." In other words, can individuals and groups give free expression to their political views, put forward candidates, and make their choices as voters without incurring negative sanctions? Do those seeking election stand on a "level playing field" when it comes to the communication of their ideas to the electorate? It can be said that elections in Yugoslavia and its successor states have generally been *free* but rarely fully *fair.*

The freedom with which it has been possible for **political parties** or groups of citizens to present their candidates is indicated by the large numbers of candidates who appear on any ballot. In all republics, electoral law requires that parties register with the authorities, and individual citizens standing as candidates are required to secure a certain number of nominations. Clearly neither of these conditions is an effective deterrent against entering the electoral contest because in the first series of multiparty elections in Yugoslavia, more than 200 groups offered candidates.

There has also been little evidence of widespread direct harassment of political activists or voters, although there have been specific instances of this problem. Before the breakup of Yugoslavia this harassment was rare, and only the repeated attacks on the offices of the Serbian Democratic Party in Zagreb stand out as serious. Since the disintegration of the federation, however, political harassment has become more common. The arrest and beating of the Serbian opposition leader **Vukašin Drašković** and his wife in 1993 represent a case in point. The political life of **Mostar** since the war has been scarred by recurring acts of intimidation, and throughout **Bosnia-Hercegovina** the exercise of political freedom has been possible only because of the presence of the North Atlantic Treaty Organization's (NATO's) **Implementation/Stabilization Force** (I/SFOR). Nevertheless, infractions against the *freedom* of elections can be considered to be only localized and spasmodic rather than general and systematic. This is not the case, however, with respect to the *fairness* of elections.

The most conspicuous general difference between the fortunes of parties has been the fact that some entered the multiparty contest with resources inherited from the former LC or SA, including real estate, equipment, and funds, as well as relevant organizational skills and contacts. The Social Democratic Parties in **Macedonia, Montenegro**, and **Slovenia** all exemplify this point. It has been difficult for other parties to mount an effective challenge to the former Communists largely because of this discrepancy in resources, although in a few cases (notably the **Croatian Democratic Union** and Macedonia's Internal Macedonian Revolutionary Organization) the strength of their support among émigrés has contributed largely to such parties' success.

There have been significant differences in the extent to which parties have access to the communications **media.** The reasons for this situation vary considerably among the republics, ranging from attempts to control the media by ruling parties (as in **Croatia** and **Serbia**) to the absence of a diversity of voices in the media (as in Macedonia and Slovenia). An important part of the legacy of communism has been the inexperience of journalists in reporting electoral affairs, in particular their slowness to relinquish a habit of compliance with the wishes of the ruling party; journalists still tend to view such compliance as a potential or actual source of patronage or sanction.

As important as the context within which electoral politics takes place is the conduct of the electoral process itself. This process often works to undermine the fairness of elections, although these failures stem as much from unfamiliarity with electoral practice as from corruption.

The conduct of elections is generally determined in all of the successor states more by ad hoc legislation than by a permanent framework of law. This approach gives the governing party the opportunity to frame the rules shaping any electoral contest in ways that maximize its own advantage. Protracted controversy of this kind surrounded the creation of the Croatian Chamber of Districts. The detailed conduct of elections is typically in the hands of electoral commissions nominated by the parties. It has been alleged that this approach gives party activists an unjustifiable opportunity to influence management of the process.

The inadequacy of electoral lists has presented serious difficulties, especially in Bosnia-Hercegovina and Macedonia, stemming from the underdevelopment of municipal administration and partly from the failure to anticipate problems. For example, permitting voters to cast their vote upon presenting either a passport or an identity card offers the obvious opportunity to vote twice—using a different document on each occasion. The difficulties occasioned by the effects of war, especially the displacement of persons, in Bosnia-Hercegovina have been immense. Here attempts have been made to ensure that **refugees** have the opportunity to vote in the place of their temporary refuge, but perhaps even more difficulty has been experienced where they have been transported to their former homes in order to vote.

Details of electoral practice can undermine an atmosphere of fairness or challenge belief in the equity of the process. The absence of effective screens around polling booths, for example, can give the impression of surveillance and undermine the aim of secrecy, even where the voters are not actually overlooked.

Finally, there has been well-documented evidence for believing that the ballots might in some cases have been fraudulently handled—especially in **Kosovo**, where the crude arithmetic of the reported votes has been beyond credibility.

—J. B. A.

ENCLAVES

See **safe areas**

ENERGY RESOURCES

Energy resources and the associated infrastructure—key components of the economy of the former Yugoslavia—have been fought over fiercely during the Yugoslav wars. Formerly part of an integrated all-Yugoslav energy system, the federation's resources and infrastructure were damaged and fragmented after the constituent republics descended into civil war in 1991.

Croatia's main oil import pipeline from Omišalj, near Rijeka, to Sisak and **Slavonski Brod** was extensively damaged and was closed from 1991 to 1995 when large sections of it were controlled by the secessionist **Serb Republic of the Krajina** (SRK). Croatia's main oil-gas fields in **Slavonia** were operated by rebel Serbs until the fall of the SRK in 1995, and the resources of these fields were illegally exported to neighboring Serbia. As the producer of 25 percent of the annual oil-gas requirements of the former federation, these oil-gas fields were one of the main reasons the Serbs partitioned Croatia in 1991. The loss of these key assets resulted in severe shortages of power throughout government-controlled Croatia, particularly along the **Dalmatian** coastline. A measure of the importance of the energy company INA in Croatia was the appointment of its former chair, **Zlatko Mateša**, as Croatian premier in 1994.

In **Bosnia-Hercegovina**, where civil war began in April 1992, the main energy resources were a number of hydroelectric power generation facilities, which had earlier provided electricity as well for neighboring Croatia. The three main hydroelectricity generation stations at **Jablanica** were extensively fought over and damaged by **Bosnian Croats** and **Muslims** in 1993. Repaired and rendered operational after the creation of the **Muslim-Croat Federation** in 1994, these plants were then one of the key economic assets of **Herceg-Bosna**, giving Zagreb major leverage over the Muslim-led government in Sarajevo. Elsewhere in Bosnia, the progress of the war after 1992 resulted in life-threatening energy shortages. Coal output in the **Tuzla** Basin stopped, as did the import of oil at **Bosanski Brod**, a town with an oil refinery on the Bosnian side of the **Sava River**. Gas supplies previously imported along a pipeline connecting **Belgrade** to **Sarajevo** were also cut. During the **Bosnian Serb** siege of Sarajevo, control of gas, electricity, and water supplies was ruthlessly enforced, causing great human suffering in the city. The Bosnian Serb seizure of eastern Bosnia was partly motivated by energy issues, given the proximity of towns such as **Višegrad** and **Foča** to the hydroelectric power plants on the Serbian side of the **Drina River** at Bistrica (Serbia) and Piva (Montenegro), respectively.

A relatively large and well-developed electricity generation capacity based on coal, oil, and hydroelectric power enabled **Serbia** to remain a significant exporter of electricity and to weather the worst effects of the economic **sanctions** imposed by the United Nations (UN) from 1992 to 1995. At that time Serbian electricity was produced mainly from local coal deposits. Because of the sanctions, the large hydroelectricity plants at the Iron Gates on the **Danube River** border with nearby **Romania** were operated at below normal capacity for much of the 1990s. Oil was then illegally taken from Serb-occupied Croatia and also covertly imported from nearby **Greece** (via **Macedonia**) and **Bulgaria.** Mainly originating in **Russia,** this "sanctions-busting" flow of oil created a large **black market** in Serbia. Oil imports then also entered **Montenegro** from nearby **Albania.** Closed in 1992, Serbia's main gas import pipeline from **Hungary** was reopened in 1995. Carrying Russian gas, this pipeline had earlier supplied Serbia, Macedonia, and Bosnia. Bartering foodstuffs for Russian energy resources, Serbia is now in debt to Russia for the oil-gas supplies that have had to be imported following the reversion of Serb-occupied eastern Slavonia to Croatia in January 1998. Only **Slovenia** has remained unaffected by the wartime disruption of energy supplies, based on secure and undamaged oil-gas imports from Hungary and the Adriatic, plus well-developed domestic hydroelectric power.

—*M. M.*

See also: Krško Power Station; Peruča Dam

ENVIRONMENTAL FACTORS

By the end of the Federal Republic of Yugoslavia, the environment had moved from a peripheral issue to the center of the public agendas of several member republics and had assumed importance at the federal level. Although the country was not experiencing the catastrophic environmental misuse characteristic of parts of Eastern and Central Europe, there was general recognition among the scientific community that the country was fast approaching pollution problems on par with those of the Western industrialized nations. In 1978, a report on the Yugoslav environment published by the federal government produced the first comprehensive collection of data from all the member republics in the main areas of environmental concern. The report (updated in 1985) reflects Yugoslavia's decision to follow the Western path—industrialize first, clean up later.

The main industrial cities of Yugoslavia had air pollution conditions far exceeding international and domestic norms. During the winter months, **Zagreb** and **Belgrade** in particular registered days of excessive pollution. Where agriculture was modernized, as in **Slovenia** and the **Vojvodina,** soil erosion became a problem when elderly peasants were forced to abandon their protective hedgerows in favor of larger fields with less protection from the elements. Wherever there was heavy industry, wastewater disposal had become a problem. Most of the cities did not have adequate sewage treatment facilities, and waste runoff into the rivers contaminated streams.

The republics had made some attempt to cope with the situation, but organized, consistent, and priority-oriented environmental policymaking and management foundered at the federal level, in a constitution that gave strong residual powers to the republics, and where there was increasing tension and conflict between the republics and the federal constitution.

Transnational environmental **NGOs** (nongovernmental organizations) were hampered by the increasingly strident nationalism of the republican governments. As in most of the former communist countries, Yugoslavia knew two types of environmental NGOs: those authorized and supported by the republican governments and those operating in the gray, semilegal zone. The most active environmental groups were found in Slovenia, as well as in Zagreb and Belgrade. The Slovenian Greens operated under the aegis of the Communist Youth League, and after Chernobyl they worked for the closure of the reactor at **Krško.** Belgrade youth sparked a movement that united people from all segments of the population for a moratorium on nuclear power until the year 2000. The mass protests led the federal government to cut back on its plans to build four new nuclear power plants.

Slovenia was the one republic where the environmental movement gained real popular support. In 1989 the Slovenian environmentalists broke with the Communist Youth League to form their own party. At the first national **elections,** the Greens gained sufficient votes to win seats in the new parliament. However, upon the breakup of the federal republic, none of the new states had the legal and technical infrastructure capable of developing and enforcing national environmental regulations. The green groups that had been so active at the republican level seemed to fade away in the rising tide of war.

The total environmental cost of the Yugoslav wars has yet to be reckoned. One victim was the **Plitvice Lakes**, under the protection of the United Nations (UN) Man and the Biosphere Program. Another was the planting of more than six million **land mines** in **Bosnia-Hercegovina**, making the land impossible to use until these mines have been removed. One has only to look at the pictures of **Vukovar**, **Goražde**, and **Srebrenica** to realize the environmental desolation caused by the war. The flood of **refugees** has strained water and health facilities in Croatia and Slovenia.

Despite enormous difficulties, the new republics are making efforts to deal with environmental problems. One reason for the concern over the environment at the governmental level is the desire of the new states to eventually join the **European Union** (EU). To do so, they must develop environmental legislation compatible with European norms and create an infrastructure capable of enforcing these laws. Toward this end, Slovenia passed a comprehensive environmental law in 1994 and is beginning to develop environmental management plans utilizing market mechanisms. All the new states have established funds to finance environmental protection, although these funds are too small to be effective. With the lack of a tradition of public participation in decision making, these funds have tended to be considered part of the general budget, not independent of it. Air regulations are weak or nonexistent in all the countries but Slovenia, which alone uses the best available technology (BAT) as a requirement in its air emission regulations. The new states are only beginning to cope with regulations for toxic chemicals, industrial risks, and biotechnology. Nature conservation has the longest history of all aspects of environmental law, and the Yugoslav successor states have been able to build on previous legislation in this area. All maintain protected areas and designate protected species, but the adoption of new strategies of nature conservation (such as habitat conservation) is far less advanced. Progress has been made in writing national environmental action plans and in their regional coordination. The goal is to have a regionally integrated environmental management plan that can eventually be integrated into environmental management planning processes in the EU.

The drive to enter the EU has created the need for the formation of new legal professionals who specialize in the environment. Through programs developed by the EU, such as PHARE and TACIS, or USAID, a network of environmental professionals is slowly coming into being.

International aid is also re-creating environmental NGOs. The principal management agent for NGO activity is the Regional Environmental Center (REC) launched with grant aid by U.S. president Bush in 1990 and now a recognized international organization located in Hungary. The center has been active in promoting "East-East" environmental cooperation. The program has had some difficulty getting off the ground because of a lack of local funds, particularly in the former Yugoslav republics, where war has worsened the problems of **communication** breakdowns and where few people feel sufficiently secure or free from the cares of sheer survival to engage in NGO activity.

A new legal, economic, and administrative framework is slowly being built in each of the new states to replace the **workers' self-management** structures of the former Yugoslavia. International aid has been vital to this process. Japan has provided funding for training, education, and environmental impact assessment legislation. The World Bank and the European Bank for Reconstruction and Development (EBRD) have provided funding for energy efficiency and conservation projects (Bosnia, Slovenia); plant modernization (Slovenia); reform of health services (Bosnia and Macedonia); and reduction of particulate and sulfur dioxide emissions in polluted cities (Slovenia). One of the four projects approved by the Global Environmental Facility for the phasing out of ozone-depleting substances in the region was approved for Slovenia.

To date, Slovenia has been the major beneficiary of international funding and shows the greatest progress in restructuring its system of environmental management and regulation. The two major impediments to the reception of international aid for the new South Slav states are political instability and slow progress in economic restructuring. The ERBD, for example, has stressed that an important polluter, like the **energy** sector, needs "strong and independent institutions" to control environmental pollution and promote nuclear safety. The record to date indicates that the international lending institutions as well as international investors prefer a more secure economic environment before committing substantial resources to environmental remediation.

The paradox is that only through international commitment can these countries develop the political will and strength to tackle their substantial environmental problems.

—*B. J.-W.*

References: Jančar-Webster, Barbara (ed.), *Environmental Action in Eastern Europe: Responses to Crises.* Armonk, NY: M. E. Sharpe, 1991; Regional Environmental Center for Central and Eastern Europe. *Strategic Environmental Issues in Central and Eastern Europe,* vol. 2. Budapest: REC, August 1994.

ERDEMOVIĆ, DRAŽEN

Dražen Erdemović, born a Bosnian Croat in 1972, was the first to be sentenced (for a term of 10 years) by the United Nations (UN) **War Crimes Tribunal**, having admitted to being a member of the firing squad on 1,200 Muslims in **Srebrenica** following the **Bosnian Serbs**' capture of that enclave.

—*J. J. H.*

ETHNIC CLEANSING

The expression *ethnic cleansing* has come to stand for the policy of ridding an area of a national group regarded as undesirable in order to create an ethnically homogeneous region. There is some controversy over the term's origins, which have been attributed to the Serb historian **Vaso Čubrilović**. It has been documented as in use by royalist Serbian forces in December 1941. Only during the recent wars, however, has it acquired general currency.

Whatever the first use of the phrase may have been, however, the phenomenon has great antiquity on the Balkan peninsula. The folklore of **Montenegro** celebrates a massacre of **Muslims** in 1702, intended to rid the land of "the **Turk**"; and the establishment of an independent Serbian principality was accompanied by the deliberate expulsion of Muslims, especially after 1833.

Ethnic cleansing has come to be used with extreme looseness to refer to almost any act of violence perpetrated during the course of the conflict. In particular, there is a tendency to confuse (1) the spontaneous flight of civilian populations in the attempt to avoid direct involvement in war and (2) the deliberate terrorizing of these populations in order to acquire control over space. It is important to note that this phenomenon has generally been associated in practice with the struggle for land. It is a feature of predominantly rural areas, where agricultural land is the primary economic resource. In

Child victims of ethnic cleansing in northern Bosnia, 1994. (Stevan Filipović)

that respect **ethnicity** is secondary to economic importance.

The expression is interesting as a rhetorical device, the power of which derives from the ironic use of a word suggesting purity *(cleansing)* in order to identify actions that are inhuman.

—*J. B. A.*

See also: rural-urban differences

ETHNICITY

The term *ethnicity* refers to the identification of an individual or group with a "people," or *ethnie.* (Social scientists have come increasingly to take the French term *ethnie* as standard, although the word originates with the Greek *ethnos.*) The membership of an *ethnie* may be defined by **language**, **religion**, geographical location, the sharing of a common historical experience, or many other criteria. The defining characteristic is that people consciously identify themselves as belonging together. In the English language, *ethnicity* differs from **nationality** in that the latter term has come to indicate that the group in question shares certain political characteristics or aspirations-specifically the association between a nation of people and the state that governs them. Ethnicity is useful, therefore, as a means of referring to the existence of groups that have developed a distinct sense of their common identity but do not yet aspire to be a nation-state, or that exist as minorities within other states, possessing a sense of their own identity but not challenging the legitimacy of the state in which they live.

The terms *ethnic* and *ethnicity* are particularly problematic in relation to the analysis of society and culture in the former Yugoslavia in that the South Slav languages do not possess precise equivalents. They have received widespread currency during the Yugoslav wars, principally through the term *etničko čišćenje* (**ethnic cleansing**). Nevertheless, many dictionaries from the region do not carry *etnički*, or a derivative meaning "ethnicity," indicating that these terms are recent borrowings. There is a sense, therefore, in which to speak of "ethnicity" and "ethnic groups" in the **Balkans** is to impose an alien framework of ideas. Local discussion of these issues is much more likely to be framed in terms of "nation" (*narod*) and "nationality" (*narodnost*), although in the South Slav languages these terms carry rather different connotations from their apparent English equivalents.

—*J. B. A.*

EUROPEAN ACTION PLAN

The European Action Plan was a peace plan for **Bosnia-Hercegovina** proposed by the **European Union** in November 1993 and based on an initiative by the foreign minister of **Germany**, Klaus Kinkel, and his counterpart from **France**, Alain Juppé. Like the previous **Owen-Stoltenberg** peace plan, the European Action Plan implicitly accepted an internal partition of Bosnia along ethnic lines. However, it proposed that 3 percent more of Bosnia's territory be allocated to the Bosnian Muslims, that a modus vivendi be established between the government of **Croatia** and the **Krajina** Serbs, and that **sanctions** on the Federal Republic of **Yugoslavia** consequently be eased. The Bosnian government and the Clinton administration in the United States opposed the plan, which never made further progress. Like its predecessors, the plan failed because the parties to the conflict were unable to reach agreement and the main external actors were unable or unwilling to bring sufficient pressure to bear on them.

—*A. S. C.*

EUROPEAN COMMUNITY/ EUROPEAN UNION

The involvement of the European Community (EC) in the Yugoslav conflict marked the organization's emergence as a major actor in international security affairs in its own right, but it also highlighted the problems the EC members faced in pursuing their declared goal of establishing a "common foreign and security policy." (The EC formally became the European Union [EU] when the Maastricht Treaty on the European Union entered into force in November 1993). When the Yugoslav war broke out in June-July 1991, the EC rapidly took the leading role in managing the conflict, brokering an agreement on the island of **Brioni** whereby the **Yugoslav Peoples' Army** (JNA) would return to its barracks, **Slovenia** and **Croatia** would suspend their moves toward independence for three months, and a European Community **Monitoring** Mission (ECMM) would be deployed. Fighting, however, continued in Croatia. By September, there was debate over whether European Community members should intervene militarily to halt the conflict (using the framework of the EC's "defense arm," the **Western European Union**), but Britain vetoed this possibility. Instead, the EC appointed former British foreign secretary Lord **Carrington** as its peace negotiator, initiated peace talks in The Hague, and established the **Badinter Commission** to assess whether the various Yugoslav republics had met EC criteria for the **recognition** of their independence. The debate within the EC shifted to whether and when to recognize the independence of Slovenia, Croatia, and **Bosnia-Hercegovina. Germany** supported the early recognition of Slovene and Croatian independence. Britain and France opposed this step, arguing that it would undermine the peace process and risk spreading the conflict to Bosnia. In December, with Germany threatening to take unilateral action, EC foreign ministers agreed to recognize Slovene and Croatian independence in January. Attention now focused on Bosnia, where tensions were escalating. In February 1992, the EC proposed a settlement on the basis of a single Bosnian state that was divided into three ethnically based cantons—the premise of the Carrington-Cutiliero Plan (named after Carrington and Portuguese foreign minister José Cutiliero, since Portugal then held the EC presidency). The Bosnian government, however, rejected the plan and went ahead with an independence referendum; war broke out in the country. The EC recognized Bosnian independence in April. By this stage, international peace efforts were moving to the **United Nations** (UN), which had negotiated a **cease-fire** between Croatia and **Serbia** in November 1991 and deployed the **UNPROFOR** (UN Protection Force) to Croatia in February 1992.

In August 1992 Britain, then holding the EC presidency, convened an EC-UN conference on Yugoslavia in London. This subsequently became the **International Conference on the Former Yugoslavia** (ICFY), with politician **David Owen** appointed as Britain's EC cochair of the conference (alongside UN special envoy **Cyrus Vance**). The **London Conference** laid down the basis for a settlement, including a cessation of violence and the nonrecognition of any gains achieved by force. In January 1993, the ICFY produced a more detailed peace plan (the **Vance-Owen Plan**), based on the division of Bosnia-Hercegovina into 10 provinces. Although the EC was willing to support the Vance-Owen Plan, in the **United States** the new Clinton administration opposed it, arguing that it would be a victory for "**ethnic cleansing**." The Vance-Owen Plan failed, and fighting escalated in Bosnia. Divisions continued within the EC about the possible establishment of "**safe areas**" in Bosnia, the forces necessary to sustain them, and the basis for any peace settlement. In November 1993, a **Franco**-German initiative resulted in a new EU Joint [**European**] **Action Plan**, proposing a new internal division of Bosnia and an easing of **sanctions** on the Federal Republic of **Yugoslavia** (FRY), but this was again opposed by the United States. With the failure of the peacemaking efforts of the EC and ICFY, attention shifted first to the new **Contact Group**, which was established in April 1994, and later to U.S.-led diplomacy, which resulted in the **Dayton Agreements** in December 1995. It was notable that the EU was not represented in the Contact Group and that the United Kingdom, France, and Germany participated in the Contact Group and the Dayton negotiations in their own right rather than as EU representatives. The leading diplomatic role of the United States and the central military role of the **North Atlantic Treaty Organization** (NATO) in the events that led to the Dayton Agreements and in their implementation highlighted the extent to which political leadership of the international efforts to manage the Yugoslav conflict had shifted away from the EU.

Despite the failure of its peace initiatives, however, the EU did continue to play an important role in the Yugoslav conflict and the subsequent peace process. ECMMs remained in place in Bosnia and Croatia throughout the conflict, providing a valuable—and generally recognized as neutral—source of information (particularly on human rights abuses and local political developments). The EU also took over the administration of the divided Bosnian city of **Mostar** in 1994, launching a substantial effort to reunite the city. The effort was largely unsuccessful, however, and the EU's first administrator for Mostar, Hans Koschnick, accused EU member states of failing to support him or to put sufficient pressure on the **Bosnian Croats** and **Muslims** to support reunification. Swedish politician **Carl Bildt** replaced David Owen as the EU's special representative for the former Yugoslavia in June 1995 and subsequently became the international community's first high representative in charge of the Dayton peace process. In the context of the Dayton process, the EU and its individual members were among the largest aid donors to

Bosnia and Croatia. The EU also began to develop bilateral political and economic relationships with the former Yugoslav republics. The EU reached an agreement, known as the Association Agreement, with Slovenia, and the latter was among the first Central and Eastern European countries invited in 1997 to begin accession negotiations for EU membership. Political and economic cooperation agreements were arranged with Bosnia and the Former Yugoslav Republic of **Macedonia** (FYROM). Ties with Croatia and the FRY were limited by continuing disputes between the EU and these two countries over progress in implementing the Dayton Agreements, democracy, and human and minority rights. Although its growing ties with the former Yugoslav states gave the EU significant political leverage in the region, its involvement in the Yugoslav conflict had also sharply illustrated the problems it faced as an international actor and the difficulties of coordinating diplomacy among its members.

—A. S. C.

FEDERALISM

See **constitutional models**

FERAL TRIBUNE

The *Feral Tribune* is a weekly magazine, published in **Split**, that is satirical in purpose and the tribulations of which have been typical of several publications critical of the regime and style of the government in independent Croatia throughout the period of wider conflict. Originally a supplement to the daily *Slobodna Dalmacija,* it was disowned and subsequently harassed financially and otherwise by that paper after the latter came under state control in 1993. Despite further attention from the authorities, it continues to be printed, distributed, and read, regularly satirizing political figures in Croatia and in 1997 famously lampooning Croatia as "Tudjmanistan." The *Feral Tribune* remains the only "alternative" magazine nationally available in Croatia.

—J. J. H.

FILIPOVIĆ, MUHAMED TUNJO

Muhamed Filipović can be regarded as one of the architects of the idea of **Muslim** nationhood in Yugoslavia. During the period of the breakup of the Yugoslav federation, he emerged as one of the leading figures in opposition to the ruling **Party of Democratic Action** (SDA).

Born in **Banja Luka** in 1929, Filipović is a philosopher and academician, as well as a professor at the University of **Sarajevo.** During the period of liberalization signaled by the fall of Aleksandar Ranković (the Serb vice-president of Yugoslavia and head of the secret police) in 1966, Filipović began to argue that "Muslim" should be used as the designation of a nationality, and that it was illegitimate to attempt to pressure people to declare themselves to be either Serbs or Croats. Although he was expelled from the **League of Communists** for his efforts, his views soon became adopted as part of the official understanding of Muslim identity, along with the views of Atif Purivatra, a leading Muslim communist ideologist, and under the patronage of Džemal Bijedić, who until his death in 1977 was a close colleague of **Tito.**

When multiparty activity first became possible in 1990, Filipović was at first involved along with **Alija Izetbegović** in the creation of the SDA. It soon became evident, however, that they had radically differing appraisals of the relevance of Muslim identity for politics. Along with **Adil Zulfikarpăsić,** Filipović split from the SDA in September 1990 to found the Muslim Bosnian Organization (MBO), arguing no Islamic republic would be possible in Bosnia because religion could not be the basis of a constitution in a modern society. The SDA was accused of "clericalism," quite opposed to the modernizing and secular views that he held. Filipović was strongly critical of Izetbegović's attempts to negotiate a compromise with Bosnian Serb leader **Radovan Karadžić** in 1991, believing these to be naive in the extreme. In 1992 the MBO joined forces with the small Liberal Party to form the Liberal Bošnjak Party, which has become the outspoken voice of secular Bošnjak opinion. He served as ambassador of Bosnia-Hercegovina to London from 1995 to 1997.

—J. B. A.

See also: political parties

FILM

See **cinema**

FLAGS

See ***šahovnica;*** **Vergina, Sun of**

FOČA

A Bosnian town of around 40,000 inhabitants (52 percent Muslim and 42 percent Serb in 1991), Foča lies on the **Drina River** some 75 miles southeast of Sarajevo near the Montenegrin border. In April 1992, shortly after the Bosnian referendum on independence, it was occupied by Serb **paramilitary/irregular forces** in a particularly wild attack on Muslims and their property, with the apparent connivance of some local Serbs. Several hundred people, mostly women and children, were trapped in the local hospital. Foča was forcibly cleared of its non-Serb poulation. As *Guardian* journalist Ed Vulliamy poignantly points out, it was just 50 years since Foča had suffered a similar fate at the hands of the **Chetniks**.

—*J. J. H.*

Reference: Vulliamy, Ed. *Seasons in Hell: Understanding Bosnia's War.* New York and London: Simon and Schuster, 1994.

FRANCE

In the late 1980s and early 1990s, before the Yugoslav crisis became an armed conflict, France was like most other Western countries in that it was not much interested in Yugoslavia's evolution. With the end of both the Cold War and the need to stop the propagation of communism, Yugoslavia had lost its strategic importance. France, as most of the other countries, was more concerned about the unification of Germany or developments in the Persian Gulf.

When France finally got involved in the Yugoslav war, it mostly intervened hand in hand with the rest of the international community since it neither wished nor was able to act entirely by itself. Thus, France's participation in Yugoslavia was mostly through multilateral institutions such as the **United Nations** (UN), the **North Atlantic Treaty Organization** (NATO), the **Council for Security and Cooperation in Europe**, the **Contact Group**, and the **European Community**. Those institutions were often slow in their decision making since any action needed extensive negotiations before the different positions could be harmonized. Such procedures often led to delays and to actions that were too mild to be legitimately effective as a result of the need for a "middle road" between the different policies.

Nevertheless, in order to be considered as an important and independent actor on the international scene, on some occasions France tried to distinguish itself from the United States, Russia, and the multilateral institutions by proposing different initiatives. Thus, in May 1994, France suggested that the town of **Brčko**, held by Serbs, should be declared as a UN security zone in order to reduce the risk of a rupture of the cease-fire. This town, at the heart of a small corridor connecting two parts of the Serb territory, was one of the first objectives of the **Bosnian Serbs**, but the proposal was not accepted.

Under the presidency of François Mitterrand, French policy toward the Yugoslav conflict was rather pro-Serb. France opposed any kind of military action directed against the Serbs. France believed that an end to the conflict should be reached by diplomatic means and not through force; Mitterrand stated in August 1992 that "adding war to war will solve nothing." Thus, France tried to persuade the international community to employ its soldiers only for **humanitarian** aims, in order to protect the convoys from any kind of aggression.

Moreover, after a new division plan of Bosnia-Hercegovina was proposed by the **Contact Group** in July 1995 (a plan that included an ultimatum), France did its best to stop any kind of military intervention after the refusal by Bosnian Serb leader **Radovan Karadžić**. Along with **Russia** and the **United Kingdom**, France considered it better to try to solve the conflict peacefully and diplomatically by taking advantage of the disagreements existing between Karadžić and Serbian president **Slobodan Milošević** concerning this new proposal.

Over time, however, the French position has evolved for three main reasons. First, one must consider that France was very involved in the field; there were numerous French among the soldiers of the UN peacekeeping force **UNPROFOR** and among the volunteers in charge of the humanitarian convoys. Therefore, French nationals were directly exposed to aggressive actions in the former Yugoslavia but were not able to retaliate or even to defend themselves, since the UN did not allow the use of violence by its peacekeeping forces. The French government, which often hesitated to withdraw its soldiers, began finding it increasingly difficult to accept this situation.

Second, as the conflict went on, French **media** reported daily the **genocide** committed mostly by the Serbs, the movements of **refugees**, the suffering of people, and the devastation of entire towns under bombs, all of which had strong impact on opinion. The French people deeply resented the humiliation of French soldiers, who were unable to protect themselves and were used by Serbs as hostages and live shields at strategic sites. Images of these transgressions were widely relayed by humanitarian associations, artists, intellectuals, and celebrities, who agitated to end France's passivity in Bosnia since it seemed insufficient to deal with the conflict.

The last and most important reason explaining this change of policy was the presidential election of May 1995, which resulted in the designation of Jacques Chirac as the new president of the republic. Unlike Mitterrand, Chirac was not particularly pro-Serb and had no preconceived ideas concerning the Yugoslav conflict since he had not been in power during the earlier years. This opened new perspectives for French policy and intervention concerning Bosnia.

Therefore, mid-1995 can be considered as a turning point in France's Yugoslav policy; after this point, France became less pro-Serb and more ready for military intervention. On 2 June 1995, France, along with Britain and the Netherlands, sent more troops into Bosnia as part of the **Rapid Reaction Force**, which had the material and institutional capacity to retaliate against any attack on UN peacekeeping forces. Further proof of France's changing policy is that, a few months later, between 29 August and 20 September, France supported NATO's military intervention, including airstrikes against Serb strategic military sites, especially around the besieged city of **Sarajevo**.

—A. H.

See also: Janvier, Bernard; Morillon, Philippe

FYROM

See **Macedonia, Republic of (FYROM)**

G

GANIĆ, EJUP

Ejup Ganić is a powerful Bosnian **Muslim** (Bošnjak) politician associated with the Islamist wing of the ruling **Party of Democratic Action** (SDA) in **Sarajevo**, where he has also long been a close confidant of Bosnian president **Alija Izetbegović**. Born in 1946 at Novi Pazar, Ganić was educated at the University of Belgrade and the Massachusetts Institute of Technology. Later he worked as an academic researcher in the United States before returning to Sarajevo in 1982. An adviser on technology and development to the republican government during the 1980s, Ganić was a founding member of the SDA, becoming an elected member of the Bosnian presidency in November 1990.

A self-declared "Yugoslav" at that time, Ganić was appointed vice president of the presidency following the outbreak of **civil war** in **Bosnia-Hercegovina**. Second only to Izetbegović in the SDA and the presidency, he played a controversial role in the negotiations and violent events that secured the release of the kidnapped Izetbegović following his seizure by **Bosnian Serb** troops in April 1992.

Following the creation of the **Muslim-Croat Federation** in March 1994, Ganić was elected vice president of this new entity in the following May, but he continued his duties as republican vice president. Although the federation ended the brief Muslim-Croat civil war of 1993–1994, the creation of its common institutions was to prove difficult, and Ganić often found himself at odds with his **Bosnian Croat** superior, President **Kresimir Zubak**. Ganić was also strongly opposed to any formal recognition of either the Bosnian Croat statelet **Herceg-Bosna** or its Bosnian Serb equivalent, **Republika Srpska** (RS), although the latter was given a formal status by the **Dayton Agreements** of November 1995. Ganić reportedly opposed Izetbegović's acceptance of Dayton, which he regarded as leading to the final partition of Bosnia-Hercegovina. Upon the creation of a three-member collective Bosnian presidency under the Dayton provisions in 1996, Ganić lost his position as republican vice president but remained federation vice president.

Within the SDA, the unfolding of civil war in Bosnia resulted in a polarization between extreme nationalist currents and those favoring a multicultural Bosnia. Ganić has been associated with the former, although for essentially opportunistic reasons. His background before the war was secular and Yugoslav, quite unlike the Islamist stance adopted by Izetbegović. His seeming rejection of Bosnia's multicultural politics, as well as his role in the radicalization of the SDA, brought about increased conflict within the ruling party in Sarajevo, culminating in the forced removal from power of the more moderate **Haris Silajdžić** in 1995. By 1996–1997, when the SDA grip on Bosnian politics was more or less absolute, Ganić and other hard-liners in Sarajevo began openly to advocate the creation of a new Bošnjak state, as well as the liberation of the whole of Bosnia-Hercegovina through another war. Within the SDA, Ganić is now the most likely replacement for the ailing Izetbegović, who may already be little more than a figurehead, with power vested in the hands of his senior deputy and potential rival.

—*M. M.*

See also: Islam and the West

GENEVA CONFERENCE

See **International Conference on the Former Yugoslavia**

GENOCIDE

A legal understanding of the term *genocide* is based upon the **United Nations** (UN) Convention on the

Prevention and Punishment of the Crime of Genocide (1951). Article II defines genocide as acts committed "with intent to destroy, in whole or in part, a national, ethnical, racial or religious group as such." A large number of actions are identified by international humanitarian law as unacceptable—two characteristics distinguish acts of genocide. The emphasis is placed upon *mens rea,* a legal term signifying literally a "guilty mind"; in other words, there must be an *intention* to commit an action that is known to be wrong. The factor that distinguishes genocide from any other killing is that this intention is directed against the "national, ethnical, racial or religious" identity of the victims. This makes the crime of genocide different from similar offenses, such as the indiscriminate bombing of a city, in which case commission of the act itself is sufficient to count as a crime against humanity, regardless of any demonstrated intention.

Popular images of genocide are heavily influenced by the concept's most notorious modern instance: the attempted "final solution" to the "Jewish question" during the German Third Reich. Consequently, it is often assumed that in order to qualify as genocide, killing must take place on a very large scale, with perhaps thousands if not millions of victims. It is important to note, however, that within the terms of the UN convention, no account is taken of the number of victims. The execution of a handful of villagers for reasons of national, ethnical, racial, or religious identity might be legitimately regarded as an act of genocide.

Allegations of genocide have been leveled at all parties to the wars of Yugoslav succession, and many instances have been documented by international humanitarian organizations such as Helsinki Watch. Genocidal acts have been a recurring aspect of the process of "**ethnic cleansing,**" in which terrorists have used group killings as an incentive to cause other members of a particular ethnic group to flee from their homes and land. Although such acts were a significant feature of the war in **Croatia**, the greatest international concern has been aroused by the events in **Bosnia-Hercegovina**, where both Serb and Croat forces strove to eliminate **Muslim** populations. Several well-documented allegations of genocide relate to efforts to set up a separate Croat state of **Herceg-Bosna** in western Hercegovina and parts of central Bosnia. The most serious instances appear to have taken place in the **Drina River** Valley of eastern Bosnia, however—a region where Serb forces sought to eliminate the predominantly Muslim population. The extent of these atrocities has yet to be fully investigated, but several thousand persons are still missing and unaccounted for from this region, and there have been numerous discoveries of mass graves.

As with all **war crimes**, particular controversy surrounds the responsibility of political and military leaders for actions committed directly by their subordinates.

—J. B. A.

See also: Ahmići; Foča; Srebrenica; Višegrad

References: Cigar, Norman L. *Genocide in Bosnia: The Policy of "Ethnic Cleansing."* College Station: Texas A&M University Press, 1995; Sells, Michael A. *The Bridge Betrayed: Religion and Genocide in Bosnia.* Berkeley: University of California Press, 1996.

GENSCHER, HANS-DIETRICH

Hans-Dietrich Genscher (born 1927) was the German foreign minister during the start of the Yugoslav crisis. He was a dynamo in his tireless efforts to support the independence of **Croatia** and **Slovenia**. **David Owen** put it more strongly by saying that Genscher used "bulldozer tactics in the EC" (European Community) to get his own way. There was also a feeling that Genscher was aiming to make a final impact on history before his retirement.

Genscher's behavior is explained in part by his experience in helping lead **Germany** to reunification. This he accomplished according to the principles of the Helsinki Final Act: respect for human rights, self-determination, and the inviolability of borders. He strove to apply these principles to solve the Yugoslav crisis. However, as a member of the Free Democratic Party (the minority member of Germany's governing coalition), Genscher was particularly subject to practical political pressures. Initially committed to the preservation of the Yugoslav federation, he changed his mind during the summer of 1991 when he found himself confronted by a barrage of moral outrage and criticism from the media and politicians in his own nation. Since many of Germany's Croats were customary voters for Genscher's party, he was particularly responsive to the charges. As Timothy Garton Ash says, Genscher then "ran out ahead of his critics" and began his campaign for the recognition of the sovereignty of Slovenia and Croatia.

From late June 1991, Genscher advocated a series of initiatives that were all tailored to bring about conditions under which the states of the **European Union** would be obliged to recognize the two republics. On 28 June 1991, he called on the **Council for Security and Cooperation in Europe** (CSCE) to investigate the events in Yugoslavia. Soon thereafter he recommended that federal troops return to barracks if Croatia and Slovenia suspend their declarations of independence for three months. He proposed sending civilian observers to the conflict zones. On 5 August 1991, he called for economic sanctions against Serbia and warned of "tragedy and catastrophe" unless decisive action was taken to solve the ever-growing crisis. In September 1991 he renewed calls for the recognition of Slovenia and Croatia, as well as advocating that a peacekeeping force operating under CSCE jurisdiction be sent to the area. He expended considerable effort to ensure that **Bulgaria** did not press for **Macedonian** independence until **Greece** had accepted independence for Slovenia and Croatia. His final triumph, achieved in early December 1991, was to get the member states of the European Community to agree to **recognition** of Croatia's and Slovenia's independence on 15 January 1991 so long as certain conditions were met. With the conditions still somewhat undecided, he helped preside over Germany's precipitative decision for recognition.

In September 1990 Genscher had declared, "We want a European Germany, not a German Europe." On the basis of the evidence in this entry, it appears his actual goal was a Europe that would toe a German line.

—*M. H.*

References: Ash, Timothy Garton. *In Europe's Name: Germany and the Divided Continent.* London: Cape, 1993, p. 395, 386–387; Owen, David. *Balkan Odyssey.* London: Gollancz, 1995, p. 189.

GEORGIEVSKI, LJUBIŠA

Born in 1966, the youthful Ljubiša (Ljupčo) Georgievski is president of a Macedonian political party known as the Internal Macedonian Revolutionary Organization—Democratic Party for Macedonian National Unity (IMRO-DPMNU). His career as a poet was interrupted by his diversion into politics only when a plurality of **political parties** became possible in 1990. His brand of strident nationalism would have been totally unacceptable in the Communist period, although his authoritarian methods within his party are reminiscent of the **League of Communists.** In his opposition to mainstream nationalism in **Macedonia,** Georgievski represents one of its major contradictions, in that he is highly critical of the tradition of autonomism established after 1945 and looks back to the late nineteenth century, when the original IMRO was often openly pro-Bulgarian.

—*J. B. A.*

GERMANY

From an early point, German officials of state were outspoken champions for the recognition of Slovene and Croat independence. The stance earned them much criticism. As Timothy Garton Ash puts it, "Bonn behaved like a bull in a china shop, ramming its policy through the [European] Community at a particularly sensitive time when all Europe was assessing the implications of German unification."

As early as May 1991, the former chancellor and chair of Germany's Socialist Party, Willi Brandt, recommended the deployment of a "European intervention force" to secure peace in Yugoslavia. He was ignored. More significant was the statement by the current chancellor, Helmut Kohl, following the meeting of **Western European Union** Ministers at Vianden, Luxembourg, on 28 June 1991. Kohl emphasized the need to apply to Yugoslavia the principles of the **Council for Security and Cooperation in Europe** in terms of recognition of human rights, self-determination, and the protection of minorities. In the same speech he added, "We cannot go on supporting the federal government forever, no matter what." During the meeting Kohl had demanded that a $1 billion aid package to the federal authorities be suspended if violence continued.

Early the next month, Volker Rühe (then chair of the chancellor's own political party, the Christian Democratic Union) started appealing for international **recognition** of **Croatia** and **Slovenia.** Kohl lent his considerable weight to the rhetoric. He believed that the people of Yugoslavia must be free to choose their own path, and that the rest of Europe must be prepared to stand beside them. This issue was, in fact, a highly emotive one for the chancellor, who had steered Germany through reunification. He wanted self-determination extended to Croats and Slovenes because he felt that only through self-determination was Germany able to regain its unity. At The Hague on 6 August 1991, Germany advocated recognition to the other European states. A few days later, Bonn restored credits to Slovenia and Croatia. At the same time, it was demanding **sanctions** against **Serbia**. By mid-September Germany was stating openly that it would recognize the two breakaway republics if peace negotiations collapsed. The position was incorporated into a statement by the **European Community** that followed the Igalo Agreement of 17 September 1991. A clause acknowledged that since a new situation existed in Yugoslavia, there was a possibility of independence for Croatia and Slovenia. It was the first time an official EC communication mentioned the possibility.

German pressure to resolve the crisis in favor of the breakaway republics increased throughout November and December 1991. It provided the impetus behind the decision by EC nations to lift economic sanctions on Croatia, Slovenia, **Macedonia**, and **Bosnia** but to leave them in place for Serbia and **Montenegro**. When Croatia published a set of laws protecting ethnic minorities on 4 December and Slovenia issued a draft constitution a few days later, a Bonn spokesman pronounced these documents "satisfactory." Before Christmas 1991 the German Cabinet agreed to recognition. The decision was to come into force on 15 January 1992 so that the rest of the EC had an opportunity to get into line.

Germany's initiative was precipitative. It did not really pay sufficient attention to the position of Serbs in Croatia. It did not bother with the consequences for Bosnia-Hercegovina and Macedonia. German state officials were driven by complex motives. Deep and honest moral principles concerning the need to extend self-determination to Eastern Europe certainly played a role. There was a desire to atone for the past. Since Germany had been responsible for the war that had brought communism to the heart of Europe, it was now the conscious champion of liberation. Less admirable, however, was the feeling that the newly unified Germany was acting dramatically in order to make its presence felt in the international arena. Worse still, some felt the chancellor was trying to win the votes of Bavarian Catholics (since Croatia and Slovenia are Catholic countries) and Croats working in Germany.

In the short term, Germany's action only hardened the anti-Croat prejudices of Serbs. The reasons were historical. During World War II, Germany had invaded Yugoslavia and established a fascist state in Croatia under the **Ustaša**, which persecuted Serbs without mercy. This heritage was still alive in the minds of many. For example, the father of **Ratko Mladić** (commander of the **Bosnian Serb Army**) had been killed in fighting in Bosnia in 1945. People such as Mladić believed Germany's backing for Croatia and Slovenia signaled the establishment of a "Fourth Reich." The real mistake of Germany's involvement in the Yugoslav crisis was the failure to understand how such profound sensitivities had endured through the decades.

—*M. H.*

See also: Genscher, Hans-Dietrich

Reference: Ash, Tomothy Garton. *In Europe's Name: Germany and the Divided Continent.* London: Cape, 1993.

GHALI, BOUTROS

See **Boutros-Ghali, Boutros**

GLAVAŠ, BRANIMIR

Born in 1956, Branimir Glavaš rose to become commander of the Croatian National Guard in the **Osijek** region of eastern **Slavonia** in 1991. He led a paramilitary unit that took part in the "**ethnic cleansing**" of a number of Serb villages and was suspected of being implicated in the killing of the moderate chief of police in Osijek, **Josip Reihl-Kir**. Glavaš later became the regional party boss of the ruling **Croatian Democratic Union** (HDZ), president of the town council, and member of the Upper House of the Croatian Assembly. He resigned his positions on 7 September 1994 in what was rumored to be a purge of the right wing of the HDZ.

—*G. R. B.*

GLIGOROV, KIRIL

The first popularly elected president of the independent Republic of **Macedonia**, Kiril (Kiro) Gligorov was born on 3 May 1917 in Štip, completed his secondary education in **Skopje**, and graduated in law in Belgrade (1938). As a student he became involved in the communist movement. He worked as a lawyer in a bank until 1941, when he became a member of the Anti-Fascist Assembly of the National Liberation Movement of Macedonia (ASNOM) and the Anti-

Kiril Gligorov, the first popularly elected president of the independent Republic of Macedonia. (Tanjug)

Fascist Council of the National Liberation of Yugoslavia (AVNOJ). From 1945 he held several posts within the federal government service in relation to finance and the economy, becoming known as a leading advocate of movement toward a market economy during the 1960s. In 1974 he became a member of the Yugoslav Federal Presidency and speaker of the Federal Parliament. In 1978 he retired in order to write, but he returned to active politics in 1989 to take a position in the reforming government of **Ante Marković.** At this time also he promoted the idea of multiparty **elections** in Macedonia and successfully stood for election as president of the republic in January 1991. He played an energetic role in the final attempts to negotiate a new constitutional settlement for the federation. Gligorov presided over the peaceful transition of Macedonia to independence in November 1992. The victim of an assassination attempt by unknown assailants on 3 October 1995, he partially recovered his health and resumed his duties as president at the end of November 1995.

—*J. B. A.*

GLINA

A small town in the Banija region of **Croatia** approximately 30 miles south of the capital **Zagreb,** Glina was the site of clashes between police and residents on 29–30 September 1990. On 26 June 1991, the day after the declaration of Croatian independence, fighting broke out in the town as Serbs attempted to take control of the police station. The fighting lasted for several days, in which time four people were killed. More fighting took place there during August 1991, and by the end of the month the Croats in the town had been driven out.

On 9 February 1992, a breakaway session of the Serb rebel parliament—the assembly of the Republika Srpska Krajina (**Serb Republic of the Krajina,** the name used by the Serbs for the area of Croatia that they held from 1991 to 1995)—was held in Glina, at which the delegates accepted the **Vance Plan** for peacekeeping in Croatia.

In August 1995 Glina was the center of some of the fiercest resistance to the Croat offensive (**Operation Storm**), designed to secure control over the remaining Serb Krajina.

—*G. R. B.*

GORAŽDE

Goražde was one of the three Muslim enclaves in southeastern Bosnia. The Bosnian Serbs had attacked and besieged the other two, **Srebrenica** and **Žepa,** in 1993 as part of the general Serbianization process. Goražde, however, was of extra strategic importance not only as a remaining Muslim-held town in the **Drina River** Valley, but also as a Muslim link to the **Sandžak** and beyond. It was therefore as important for the Muslims to hold as for the Serbs to take, and it was not until April 1994 that the Serbs managed to occupy parts of the town, rendering the town's status as a United Nations (UN) "**safe area**" of doubtful meaning.

The local fate of Goražde and its citizens was disastrously overshadowed and to a great degree caused by the deep divisions among the international participants. There was an initial disagreement within the UN Protection Force (**UNPROFOR**) as to the likelihood of a Serb assault; a subsequent dispute between the **North Atlantic Treaty Organization** (NATO) and **Russia** over the use of airstrikes; and a final split between **Serbia** proper (which saw an opportunity of having **sanctions** lifted in return for a peace deal on Goražde) and the **Bosnian Serbs,** who refused to be deflected.

The main part of Goražde remained under Bosnian government control, athough some outlying

Houses destroyed during the fighting at Goražde, 1996. (UNHCR)

parts form a portion of the Bosnian Serbs' **Republika Srpska** (RS). Under the terms of the **Dayton Agreements** at the end of 1995, Goražde was linked to the territory of the **Muslim-Croat Federation** by a protected corridor through the RS.

—*J. J. H.*

GORNJI VAKUF

A town of 25,000 inhabitants (1991) in western Bosnia-Hercegovina, Gornji Vakuf lies on what was an important road for delivery of **humanitarian aid** and other supplies from south to north and was a staging point for convoys from the coast eastward across Bosnia. It was also the focal point of an area whose population was an equal mix of Croats and Muslims—the municipality itself was 56 percent Muslim and 43 percent Croat in 1991. These two factors combined to make Gornji Vakuf an epicenter of the Croat-versus-Muslim period of the Bosnian war. Through the summer, autumn, and winter of 1993, control of the town and its surroundings changed hands several times. Every building was destroyed or damaged, more than a thousand people were killed, and further atrocities were committed on both sides.

—*J. J. H.*

GOSPIĆ

A town on the southern arm of Croatia in the **Krajina,** Gospić (population 29,000) until 1991 housed barracks of the **Yugoslav Peoples' Army** (JNA). As the war between Serbs and Croats grew nearer after the Krajina Serbs' attack on **Kijevo** in August 1991, leading to the Croatian declaration of a war of liberation, the battle lines were firmly drawn. Gospić was behind the Croatian lines, and the JNA was effectively trapped. The JNA's attempt to break out through the surrounding Croatian National Guard resulted in the virtual destruction of the town, the capture of around 200 JNA soldiers, and the controversial death of the JNA's local commander. The loss of Gospić was significant for the local Serbs because it removed their base for establishing a corridor to the coast of **Dalmatia** only 40 miles to the west.

—*J. J. H.*

GRANIĆ, MATE

Mate Granić was born in 1947 at Baška Voda on the Dalmatian coast and was formerly a university professor of medicine in Zagreb. He served as vice-president of the first **Croatian Democratic Union** government in 1990, became foreign minister of

Croatia in 1993, and was responsible for the Croatian side of the negotiations in Washington over the **Muslim-Croat Federation.** He has been described as constructive and patient, and he has been involved in a great number of overseas journeys establishing relationships with other states on behalf of Croatia.

—*G. R. B.*

GRANIČARI

See **Military Frontier**

GREAT BRITAIN

See **United Kingdom**

GREATER CROATIA

The concept of Greater Croatia refers to the belief that the lands historically inhabited by Croats are much more extensive than the contemporary state of Croatia; this notion serves as the foundation for claims regarding the future enlargement of that state. It has its roots in the writings of Pavao Ritter Vitezović, who wrote in the aftermath of the Vienna War of 1699. During that war, the Venetian Republic and the **Habsburg Empire** were vying for control of the lands vacated by the **Ottoman Empire.** Vitezović's aim was to demonstrate that the Venetians had no claim upon Dalmatia by constructing an argument about the historical extent of Croatia; this argument was based on the belief that the appellation "Croat" applied to all Slavs. "Greater Croatia" thus encompassed a huge expanse of territory both in the Balkan Peninsula and north of the Danube River.

This argument owed almost nothing to cultural, linguistic, or religious factors, relying instead upon the tradition of "state right." This tradition, as developed by Eugene Kvaternik (1825–1871) and Ante Starčević (1823–1896), became one of the most powerful elements of political ideology during the Croatian Revival in the nineteenth century. The Croat people had state right in relation to the lands that they had occupied since their first migration into the Balkans in the sixth and seventh centuries. This right was indivisible, and therefore there could be only one political people in the state of Croatia—the Croats. This belief was conjoined with a territorial conception that encompassed all of the South Slav lands from the Alps to Bulgaria and from the Danube to Albania.

Starčević was extremely anti-Serb, seeing Serb political consciousness as a threat to Croats. Whereas he described the Slovenes as "Highland Croats," he labeled the Serbs as an unclean race, whose name derived from *servus,* the Latin for servant. He even claimed that the Nemanjić dynasty, Serbia's most important medieval rulers, were Croats. He also believed that Serbs could potentially become Croats if only the former could take on a Croatian political identity. Thus, he managed to provide for future Croatian nationalists a political ideology based on intolerance of difference, as well as a claim that Croatia should encompass the whole territory of the South Slavs.

When the political scene changed following the creation of the Kingdom of Serbs, Croats, and Slovenes in 1919, the concept of Greater Croatia changed as well. Previously the idea had been applied within the confines of the political struggles within the Habsburg Empire. Now Croat nationalism came directly into confrontation with a "**Greater Serbia**" program in the context of a unified South Slav state. During the 1930s the Frankovci (political descendents of Starčević through Josip Frank's Party of Pure Right) became more extreme in their nationalism. The concept of Greater Croatia—composed of **Croatia** proper, **Slavonia, Dalmatia,** and **Bosnia-Hercegovina**—came to represent an ethnically pure state, from which all Serbs had been cleansed. This vision found its expression in the **Ustaša** movement, created by **Ante Pavelić.**

In this form Greater Croatia became a reality following the German and Italian occupation of Yugoslavia in 1941. The Independent State of Croatia (Nezavisna Država Hrvatska—NDH) encompassed most of Bosnia as well as Croatia; the Ustaša thus had the opportunity to put into practice their ideology and to begin to "purify" the state of Serbs by killing them, deporting them, or converting them to Catholicism.

The concept was effectively corrupted by its connection with Ustaša atrocities. Following the communist victory in Yugoslavia and the creation of the Socialist Federal Republic, the borders of Croatia were confined once again to Croatia, Dalmatia, and Slavonia. The language of Croat nationalism became taboo within socialist Yugoslavia; during the **Croatian Spring** of 1971–1972, when Croatian nationalists began to argue for the attachment of western **Hercegovina** and parts of **Montenegro** to

Croatia, this argument proved to be the undoing of the movement.

"Greater Croatia" remained firmly off the political agenda for another 20 years, until the rise of Franjo Tudjman's Croatian Democratic Union (HDZ) after 1989. The fact that Tudjman's party was funded largely by the Croatian diaspora ensured the revival of the idea, aided by the fact that there were many Hercegovinan Croats in the top ranks of the HDZ. The project to create an autonomous Croat state of **Herceg-Bosna** based upon western Hercegovina was widely interpreted as the first stage in the realization of a plan to create a Greater Croatia. Only the combination of intense international pressure and the military inability to hold onto gains prevented this plan from being realized.

With the signing of the **Muslim-Croat Federation** agreement, as well as the agreements on military and political cooperation, which came about under the auspices of the **United States** in 1994, Croat nationalists were forced to relinquish their plans for a Greater Croatia. The difficulties that have attended the implementation of the **Dayton Agreements** in some predominantly Croat areas of Bosnia-Hercegovina, however, suggest that the idea is far from dead.

—G. R. B.

GREATER SERBIA

The controversial idea that all those who consider themselves Serbs should be united in one state has figured prominently in explanations of the possible causes of the Yugoslav wars of the 1990s. In particular, such explanations have alleged a conspiracy on the part of Serbian president **Slobodan Milošević** and his nationalist allies to create a "Greater Serbia." Following the disintegration of former **Yugoslavia** in 1990–1991, Greater Serbia was taken to mean the Republic of **Serbia, Montenegro**, the Serb-controlled territories in **Croatia** (known until August 1995 as the **Serb Republic of the Krajina**), and Serb-controlled **Bosnia-Hercegovina**, known as the Bosnian Serb Republic or **Republika Srpska.**

The allegation that Milošević was intent on creating a Greater Serbia on the ruins of the former Yugoslavia remains largely unproven. Where the idea has been politically significant, it has largely served as a negative pole in relation to which other national identities and states in the region have been constructed. Drawing on an older corpus of allegations about Serb aspirations for hegemony, **propaganda** about the supposed creation of a Greater Serbia during the 1990s was particularly strong among the **Slovenes**, Croats, and Bosnian **Muslims**, as well as their main foreign allies.

Similar to the Greek *Megali idea* (Grand Vision) but of far less antiquity, the idea of a Greater Serbia is highly problematic as an explanation of the confused historical evolution of the Serbian state and Serbian national identity. The first significant form of that state, the empire of the Nemanjić dynasty in the thirteenth and fourteenth centuries, excluded areas that later became associated with the idea of Greater Serbia, (notably Hercegovina, Bosnia, and the **Vojvodina**) and included territories such as mainland **Greece** and **Albania** that no Serb today imagines to be Serb. This medieval empire was centered on areas still focal for Serb identity, especially **Kosovo**, where in 1389 the golden age of Serb history came to an end. This long period of **Ottoman** domination became significant for the evolution of Serb national consciousness. The centuries of military struggle for the control of the **Balkan** Peninsula depopulated large tracts of former Serb lands, notably during the last decade of the seventeenth century, when a failed anti-Turkish uprising resulted in a major exodus of Serbs from Kosovo, Raška, and Bosnia northward toward those territories that later became known as the Krajina in Croatia, and the Vojvodina. Those territories abandoned by the migrating Serbs became inhabited by non-Slav peoples, foremost among which were the **Albanians** in Kosovo. The main effect of the Ottoman period on the Serbs was the crystallization of the link between Serb identity and the Serbian **Orthodox Church.** Focused on the Patriachate of Peč in Kosovo, until its abolition by the Turks in 1766, the Serbian Orthodox Church became ever more central to the evolution of Serb national identity, most notably in **Habsburg**-controlled Srem, in Croatia and in northern Serbia.

A product of the Ottoman *millet* system, whereby society was divided and administered along religious lines, the *knezovi* (local headmen) often led resistance against Ottoman oppression. In 1804 and again in 1815, major armed revolts led to the creation of a Serb principality. As Ottoman power waned and that of Russia increased, an independent Serbian state emerged by the end of the nineteenth century. During this period, when a distinct Serbian nation was being formed, the first coherent vision of what a Serbian state should become territorially also appeared. Written in 1844 by Ilija Garašanin, minister of the interior to the Karadjordjević dynasty, this document, known as the *Nacrtanje (Sketch* or *Outline)*, was later said to have been a blueprint for a new and aggressive Greater Serbia. Based on the assumption of declining Ottoman power in the Balkans and hostile to the pro-Austrian foreign policy of the deposed Obrenović dynasty, Garašanin's *Nacrtanje* was a piece of hard-headed realpolitik that argued for territorial expansion to the southwest primarily at the expense of the Ottoman Empire.

Following the Russo-Turkish War of 1877–1878 and the Congress of Berlin, the independent Serbian state (internationally recognized in 1856) was able to expand substantially southward for the first time. The seizure in 1878 of Bosnia-Hercegovina and the **Sandžak** by the powerful Austro-Hungarian empire, however, ruled out the possibility of Serb territorial expansion in that direction.

Serbia remained essentially weak and marginal well into the twentieth century. State authority was uncertain, as reflected in the continued rivalry of the Karadjordjević and Obrenović dynasties, as well as the rise of secret societies such as the Black Hand (Crna ruka). Serbian foreign policy remained essentially opportunistic and dependent on shifting factors over which it had little or no control. It was thus in 1903, at the time of the anti-Turkish Ilinden uprising, that **Macedonia** suddenly became a target of opportunity for Serb nationalists. Annexed by Austria-Hungary in 1908, Bosnia remained off-limits for Serb territorial expansion, although the Black Hand remained active there. During the Balkan Wars (1912–1913), when the Ottoman Empire lost most of its Balkan territories, Serbia nearly doubled its territory and population (from 18,650 square miles to 33,891 square miles, and from 2.9 million to 4.5 million inhabitants), taking in Kosovo and most of Macedonia and dividing the Sandžak with Montenegro. The main result of these Serbian successes was a further deterioration of relations with Austria-Hungary, culminating in the assassination of Archduke Franz-Ferdinand by a **Bosnian Serb** revolutionary organization known as Young Bosnia (Mlada Bosna), with the involvement of the Black Hand, in **Sarajevo** in 1914.

During World War I, and particularly after the Serbian army was driven out of Serbia into Albania and Greece in 1915, a highly mythologized Serb nationalism was given a boost, notably in relation to Kosovo. An important consequence of the war was the growth of solidarity among the South Slav peoples, culminating in the establishment in 1918 of the first Yugoslavia, formally known as the Kingdom of the Serbs, Croats, and Slovenes. Although dominated by Serbs during the interwar period, this was a new state and not just a Greater Serbia built upon artificial foundations, as its later detractors claimed. The existence of "Yugoslavia" (as it was called after 1929) changed the possible future for a purely Serbian state, as well as the manner in which a specifically Serbian national consciousness could be framed and expressed.

Far more so than the "First Yugoslavia," the "Second Yugoslavia" (communist Yugoslavia, from 1945) changed the nature of Serbian nationalism and identity. The wartime defeat and discrediting of the Serbian nationalist **Chetniks**, who had argued for the creation of a Greater Serbia on the ruins of the first Yugoslavia, was politically decisive. The communist **Partizan** forces who opposed them were extremely hostile to all forms of local nationalism. Consequently, in the federation that they erected after the war, support for Yugoslavia was at its strongest in Serbia and among Serbs more generally. Whatever its faults and problems, Yugoslavia had resolved the problem of uniting otherwise disparate and highly dispersed Serbs in one state.

Neither the first nor the second Yugoslav states, however, had resolved the problem of interethnic relations among these entities. The Serb-Croat conflict bedeviled the first Yugoslavia and weakened the second. During the early 1970s, a newly emergent Croatian nationalism posed the first major political challenge to the communist federation. Subsequently, a more assertive anti-Serbian Albanian nationalism focused on Kosovo had profound consequences for Serbian politics. Both sets of events called into question the nature of Serb identity and the place of Serbs in Yugoslavia.

One result of these developments was the publication of the controversial "Memorandum of the Serbian Academy of Sciences and Arts" (SANU) in 1986. Among other things, this document alleged a systemic denigration of Serbian culture in the second Yugoslavia and even **genocide** against the

Kosovar Serbs by the numerically dominant Albanians. Slobodan Milošević opportunistically seized upon this document to legitimate his own rise to power in Serbia and his attempt to create a more unitary Yugoslav federation. The memorandum was interpreted by many non-Serbs as another formulation of the idea of a Greater Serbia although in actuality it was far more about the past than any politically realistic vision of the evolution of Serbia and Serbdom. Its political influence on such questions has been marginal.

Following the violent disintegration of Yugoslavia during the 1990s, the dilemmas of Serb nationality, identity, and statehood became even more acute. An attempt has been made to form a "Third Yugoslavia" incorporating the two remaining components of the former federation—Serbia and Montenegro. Although internationally unrecognized and bitterly contested by the main Serbian nationalist parties, the use of this name and all that it implies politically remains the official policy of Milošević's Serbia and its ally, Montenegro. Milošević and his allies have never seriously attempted to unite this "rump" Yugoslavia with the separatist Serb-controlled entities that emerged during the Yugoslav wars of the 1990s. Although opportunistically supported at first by Milošević, these attempts to create an extended Serbian state have been shown to be unviable. A future Serbian state could be an extended one, most notably in relation to Bosnia. Based on Serbian experiences to date, however, such a scenario would probably come about as an essentially opportunistic exercise, not as the result of any belief in the idea of a Greater Serbia.

—*M. M.*

See also: Serbian Academy Memorandum

GREECE

Greece is the southernmost state in the Balkan Peninsula, bordering Albania and Bulgaria to the north, as well as the former Yugoslav federation. It has an area of 131,957 square kilometers and a population of around 10 million. Greek interest in the breakup of Yugoslavia has been centered upon two issues: (1) the conflict over the status of the former Yugoslav republic of **Macedonia** and (2) the possible destabilization of its own border with Albania as a consequence of a future attempt at secession by Albanians in **Kosovo**. Greece is the only Balkan country to become a member of the European Union, a fact that has given special importance to Greece's part in the international response to the Yugoslav crisis.

Along with the rest of the Balkan region, the area now known as Greece was incorporated into the **Ottoman Empire** during the fourteenth and fifteenth centuries. The Greeks were among the first people of the region to assert their independence from the Turks, creating a small state by 1829. Following the Congress of Berlin in 1878, when the Turkish presence was further reduced, the future of Ottoman power in Europe was called into question. Greece, Bulgaria, and Serbia entered into open competition for influence in Macedonia. This "Eastern question" was largely resolved after the Balkan Wars of 1912–1913, in which the Greeks united with Bulgaria, Serbia, and Montenegro, driving Turkish forces from the area and dividing Macedonia and Thrace among themselves. In spite of challenges to this territorial settlement during World Wars I and II, Greece acquired its current geographical boundaries at the end of the Balkan Wars.

The population acquired by Greece in 1913 was heterogeneous, although there have been divergent estimates of its ethnic composition. The Turkish census (1904–1905) of the three vilayets, or governorships (Salonika, Monastir [Bitola], and Kosovo), estimated the relative numbers of Greeks, Serbs, and Bulgarians as follows on the basis of religious affiliation rather than language or nationality:

Muslims	1,729,000
Greeks	648,962
Bulgarians	527,734
Serbs	167,601

One of the most detailed population assessments comes from Yugoslavia, based on Bulgarian and Greek sources just before the Balkan Wars of 1912–1913. According to this assessment, the composition of the population in Macedonia was as follows:

Slav Macedonians	326,426
Turks	289,973
Greeks	249,019
Vlachs	45,457
Jews	59,560

Following the disastrous war against Turkey, many thousands of Greeks were expelled in 1922 and resettled in Macedonia and Thrace. Large numbers of Slavs also left for Bulgaria. Consequently, the official Greek census of 1928 gave the following figures for Greek Macedonia:

Greeks	1,237,000
Slavophones	82,000
Others	93,000

The census of 1940, based upon language (and published in 1946 because of delays caused by the war), put the number of Slav-speaking Macedonians at 74,751 (4.24 percent of the population of Greek Macedonia).

During the Greek Civil War of 1946, a large number of Slav-Macedonians, having felt hostile toward the repressive Greek state, joined the Greek communist forces. After the defeat of the communist side, more than 35,000 fled to the Socialist Republic of Macedonia or to countries of the Warsaw Pact. During the 1950s a considerable number emigrated to Canada, the **United States**, or Australia. In 1992, the annual report of the U.S. Department of State put the Slavophone Orthodox population of Greece at between 20,000 and 50,000.

The onset of the Cold War stabilized Greek-Yugoslav relations—though the countries were in a state of mutual suspicion, largely as a result of the Macedonian issue. Yugoslav accusations of the suppression of a Slav Macedonian minority in Greece were countered by accusations of territorial ambition. For as long as the Republic of Macedonia remained locked into the Yugoslav federation, however, the stability of the **border** remained beyond question. This situation was undermined by the collapse of the Yugoslav federation in 1991, however, and the independence of a state calling itself "**Macedonia**."

Given that Greece is a member of the **European Union** (EU) and the **North Atlantic Treaty Organization** (NATO), successive Greek governments have had to take note of the views of their Western allies when formulating policy toward the former Yugoslavia, and toward **Serbia** in particular. Greece has thus acted both with and against the wishes of its major Western allies in the Yugoslav crisis. At the beginning of the violent disintegration of Yugoslavia in 1990–1991, under the New Democratic Party (NDP) government of **Konstantinos Mitsotakis**, Greece followed the policy set by the rest of the EU, which at that time was to argue for the preservation of Yugoslavia and (when this course of action was no longer viable) to recognize **Slovenia** and **Croatia** as independent states six months after their unilateral declarations of independence in June 1991. In April 1992, when the EU and the United States also recognized **Bosnia-Hercegovina**, Greece did the same. This policy toward the Yugoslav crisis was denounced by various pro-Serb and pro-Yugoslav forces, including the Pan-Hellenic Socialist Party (PASOK) of **Andreas Papandreou**, then in opposition. In Belgrade, Greece's decision to recognize three of Yugoslavia's secessionist republics was regarded with considerable disappointment. Greece has also been at one with the international community in not recognizing the "Third Yugoslavia" (Serbia and Montenegro) declared in Belgrade in April 1992 as the sole successor of the former Yugoslavia.

During the course of 1992, however, Greek policy toward the Serbs—and hence the international community's role in the former Yugoslavia—underwent a change. The reason for this shift was the vexing problem of international **recognition** of the Former Yugoslav Republic of Macedonia (FYROM). The problem of Macedonia, a key regional issue for Greek foreign policy after the Republic of Macedonia declared its independence from the former Yugoslavia in December 1991, pushed Greece closer to Serbia and away from its partners in the EU and NATO. In this context the decision of the EU and United States to recognize Macedonia under the provisional FYROM designation in April 1993 was a profound shock to Greek sensibilities.

Greece was unable to prevent the de facto international recognition of Macedonia, although Greek concerns were taken into account by the UN through the latter's decision to use a provisional designation for this former Yugoslav republic. Serbia, on the other hand, refused to recognize Macedonia under any name until 1996, when it granted full diplomatic recognition to the new state under its chosen name of the Republic of Macedonia. This created a common bond of interest between Belgrade and Athens that lasted for nearly five years. In addition to the issue of Macedonia, the shared heritage of **Orthodox** Christianity and a common hostility toward **Albania** and **Turkey** also bound Serbia and Greece together.

—N. M. G. and J. B. A.

GRUDE

The significance of Grude, a small town (population 16,000 in 1991) in western **Hercegovina**, is confined to the fact that it became the headquarters of the Croatian Union of **Herceg-Bosna**, whose leader (**Mate Boban**) was manager of the local supermarket and mayor of the town. Boban temporarily designated Grude as the capital of the Herceg-Bosna ministate pending his plans to transfer the capital to **Mostar**, 40 miles to the east.

—J. J. H.

H

HABSBURG EMPIRE

The Habsburg Empire was one of the great multinational empires that covered the Balkan Peninsula until World War I (the other being the **Ottoman Empire**). The history of the South Slav peoples in the western **Balkans** has been shaped in large measure by their experience under the Habsburgs, by the nature of the processes by which nations and independent states emerged in the region, and by the impact that Habsburg power had upon neighboring states. The division of the region between Ottoman and Habsburg spheres of influence has been one of the most influential factors shaping the view of the Balkans as permanently divided by a **cultural fault line.**

The origins of the Habsburg dynasty are to be found in the Frankish kingdoms of the early Middle Ages and subsequently the Holy Roman Empire. The Habsburg state began to take shape following the defeat of Ottokar by the Roman emperor at the battle of Marchfeld in 1278, when the Habsburg family acquired the March of Styria. Four years later the Habsburgs also acquired parts of modern Austria, and in 1335 the emperor bestowed upon them Carniola and Carinthia. It is one of the ironies of history that **Slovenia** should have constituted the heart of the Habsburg domains but subsequently came to be regarded as no more than part of the Slav periphery of an essentially Germanic empire. Croatian lands came to be incorporated into the Habsburg Empire in a variety of ways. In 1374 the county of **Istria** was added to the Habsburg lands. An independent Croatian kingdom emerged in the tenth century; however, on the death of King Zvonimir in 1089, following a dispute between rival claimants to the throne, appeal was made to King Ladislas I of Hungary (who was related to the Croatian dynasty) to take the throne, which he did in 1091, creating a personal union of the two crowns. The eastern area of modern Croatia (Srijem) was acquired separately by the Hungarian crown from the emperor of Byzantium in 1127. Consequently, when the Austrian and Hungarian kingdoms came together in 1526–1527, the Croatian lands were brought into the new union, although they had different constitutional statuses.

The campaigns of Sultan Suleiman the Magnificent, beginning with the defeat of the Habsburgs at Mohacs in 1526 but especially the campaign of 1532, devastated **Croatia** and reduced its capacity to operate as an independent state to a legal fiction. Ottoman advance was achieved in part through the fomenting of civil war within the empire, supporting Janos Zapolyai (a noble from **Slavonia**) against the Habsburg dynasty, which lasted until 1540. The frontier region between these two great rivals remained contested throughout the seventeenth century. (The Ottoman armies laid siege to Vienna in 1683.) Beginning in 1578 an attempt was made to stabilize and reinforce the frontier by the creation of a Militärgrenze (**military frontier**), which was an area of land of variable width extending the length of the Ottoman/Habsburg **border**, upon which were settled frontiersmen *(graničari)* who held land directly from the Austrian crown in return for regular military service. Large numbers of foreigners were welcomed as settlers in these largely depopulated areas. Particularly important were the many **Serbs** who moved into the frontier after the war of 1663–1664 and especially the war of 1683–1699. The permanent instability of this borderland is highlighted by the fact that further wars took place in 1704–1711, 1716–1718, and 1788–1791.

The Habsburg domains in the Balkans were further augmented by the collapse of Venetian power in the Adriatic and by the ceding of **Dalmatia** to Austria at the Treaty of Campo Formio in 1797. The rise of Napoleon had a permanent effect upon the political geography of the region. Dalmatia was acquired by France in 1805, as was the small Ragusan Republic (**Dubrovnik**), and until 1814 French possessions (including large parts of the Slovene and Croatian lands) were organized into the Illyrian Provinces as a part of the French Empire. Following the collapse of the Napoleonic enterprise, however, the former Venetian and Ragusan territories fell under Austrian control.

The patchwork of Austrian and Hungarian sovereignty and civil and military authority—as well as the legacies of Ottoman, Venetian, and Ragusan institutions—resulted in enormous economic, legal, and cultural diversity even within the Habsburg territories. Consequently, explanations of the complexities of Yugoslav history in terms of a simple contrast between the "Ottoman" and "Habsburg" legacies understate considerably the causes of this diversity.

In 1874 a revolt broke out among peasants in **Hercegovina** against their landlords; this revolt rapidly grew to become a wholesale uprising against Ottoman rule extending across large areas of the peninsula. In 1876 **Serbia** and **Montenegro** declared war against the Turks, and Russia followed suit a year later. The great European powers were drawn into the conflict in an attempt to enforce a solution. At the Congress of Berlin, which finally imposed a settlement upon the region in 1878, Austria was permitted to occupy **Bosnia-Hercegovina**. This protectorate was changed to outright annexation in 1908. These developments had far-reaching consequences for the entire region. The land-locked Serbian state was driven to look southward through **Macedonia** for a potential trading outlet to the sea; in pursuit of this policy, the Serbs participated in the Balkan Wars of 1912–1913. The wedge of Austrian control also threatened to undermine permanently any prospect of political union between the Serbs of Serbia and those of the two provinces. The direct collision of the aspirations of Austria and Serbia in Bosnia and Hercegovina was one of the primary causes of World War I—a war that destroyed Austria and propelled Serbia into a unified South Slav state in 1918. Going well beyond its significance as a historical factor underlying the formation of states and cultures in the region, the Habsburg Empire has acquired in **Yugoslavia** an added symbolic significance, which has been given exaggerated importance in the period of Yugoslavia's breakup. The historical confrontation between the Habsburg and Ottoman Empires has come to be represented as a permanent and essential cultural fault line that demarcates fundamentally incompatible cultures and provides foundation for believing in the "artificiality" of any unified South Slav state, as well as in the inevitability of the failure of any such enterprise. Slovenes and Croats have come to erect a heavily mythologized image of the contrast between "Habsburg" advancement and civilization, on the one hand, and "Ottoman" backwardness and barbarism on the other; these terms serve as short-hand summaries of the essentially alien nature of other Balkan peoples.

—J. B. A.

HADŽIĆ, GORAN

An ethnic Serb politician from **Croatia** and president of the secessionist **Serb Republic of the Krajina** (RSK) from 1992 to 1994, Goran Hadžić replaced the first RSK president, **Milan Babić**, in 1992. Hadžić was widely regarded as a loyalist of Serbian president **Slobodan Milošević**, who had secured Hadžić's position at the head of the RSK in 1992. In practice, however, all real power in the RSK at this time and thereafter resided with the republic's interior minister, **Milan Martić**, who himself replaced Hadžić as RSK president in 1994 (although the **election** that supposedly legitimated this change of leadership was actually won by Babić).

Following the military defeat of the RSK under the leadership of Martić in August 1995, Hadžić's Srem-Baranja region (eastern Slavonia) was the only remaining Serb-controlled area of Croatia. In November 1995, Hadžić publicly supported an international peace settlement for eastern **Slavonia** on the condition that the enclave's Serb population be allowed to remain there within a newly reunified Croatia. A less extreme nationalist than either Martić or Babić, Hadžić was subsequently elected to the presidency of the region of eastern Slavonia in April 1996. As the head of this region, he presided over its gradual reintegration into Croatia over a period of two years under the supervision of the United Nations Transitional Administration for Eastern Slavonia (**UNTAES**).

—M. M.

HADŽIMURATOVIĆ, IRMA

On 30 July 1993, a girl, only five years of age, suffered almost fatal injuries from a mortar bomb in **Sarajevo**. She became known to the wider world as

Irma. Although this was a tragic case, it was only one of scores in the capital during the Bosnian war, with the added poignancy that her mother was killed in the same attack. There were two reasons for the international highlighting of this case.

First, Edo Jaganjac, the Bosnian surgeon who treated Irma for the injuries to her abdomen, spine, and head but lacked essential equipment to save her life at the **Koševo hospital**, became frustrated at the delay in a decision on whether she qualified for treatment abroad. He enlisted the international **media** to publicize the urgency of this patient's case—and thereby many other cases. The delay resulted from the fact that the medical advisory committee set up by the United Nations High Commission for Refugees (**UNHCR**) met only monthly to consider cases for medical evacuation.

Second, the reception of the story in the press and on television in the United Kingdom was such that Prime Minister John Major and Foreign Secretary Douglas Hurd were moved to bypass the usual red tape and organize a special mercy flight. This decision itself caused controversy because it was open to the charge of being a public relations exercise, given the thousands of children known to be suffering in Bosnian hospitals and camps for whom no red tape had been cut. The publicity did, however, elicit charitable responses from hospitals to accommodate small numbers of similar additional cases.

Irma was flown out from Sarajevo and admitted to Great Ormond Street Children's Hospital in London on 9 August, where she remained recovering slowly for several months, though with no prospect of being able to walk again. She has not yet been able to return to Sarajevo with her father, Ramis Hadžimuratović. The story has gone quiet—the news value of suffering in Bosnia, as elsewhere, can be short-lived.

—*J. J. H.*

HDZ

See **Croatian Democratic Union**

HELSINKI PROCESS

See **Organization for Security and Cooperation in Europe**

HERCEG-BOSNA

With the outbreak of war in **Bosnia-Hercegovina**, several localities where there were predominantly Serb populations (such as the Romanija area east of **Sarajevo**) or where **Bosnian Serb** control would have given the Bosnian Serbs a strategic advantage (such as Semberija, in the area of **Bijeljina**) began to declare their status as autonomous *krajine* (regions). In March 1992, talks chaired by United Nations (UN) mediator **Cyrus Vance** produced a plan for the division of Bosnia-Hercegovina into 10 **cantons**, identified by their ethnic majorities, which reflected this principle. Although the agreement was signed on 18 March, it was repudiated by the Muslim **Party of Democratic Action** a week later. The proclamation of the plan gave an immediate stimulus, however, to "**ethnic cleansing**" in anticipation of the formal ceding of local control to ethnic factions. On 25 March the Bosnian Serbs declared the independence of a Serbian Republic of Bosnia-Hercegovina (later to be known as the **Republika Srpska**). Although an agreement regarding military cooperation had been signed on 15 June between Presidents **Franjo Tudjman** of Croatia and **Alija Izetbegović** of Bosnia-Hercegovina, both anxious to secure their positions in a deteriorating situation, Croats in western **Hercegovina** began to organize their own quasi-state, which was proclaimed on 5 July under the name Herceg-Bosna.

The aspiration of the new entity (led by **Mate Boban**) was eventual union with the independent state of **Croatia**. Herceg-Bosna was composed initially of the communes of Čitluk, Grude, Livno, Ljubuški, and Posušje. Extended for the most part over an agriculturally unproductive rural area, Herceg-Bosna's largest settlement was Livno (population 40,000 in 1991). The small town of **Grude** (population 16,000) became the entity's capital because of its safe distance from military activity. Herceg-Bosna has no historical identity; it was created as an ad hoc defensive formation, although all of the internationally brokered plans for the cantonal or other division of the republic have recognized in one way or another that Herceg-Bosna embodies an area of solidly Croat settlement—more ethnically homogeneous (even before the war) than most areas of the Croatian republic. By the summer of 1993, the defensive character of the project had been replaced by a more aggressive and expansionist stance, incorporating **Travnik**, **Prozor**, and Čapljina in June and Stolac in August. Herceg-Bosna's extension into central Bosnia has fluctuated considerably. With the collapse of the **Croatian**

Council of Defense's (HVO's) defense of Vareš in November 1993, however, and the growing power of the government forces in central Bosnia, Herceg-Bosna came under a serious threat that was averted only by the intervention of units of the **Croatian Army**.

Ethnic homogeneity, rural isolation, and apparent encouragement by outside interests have resulted in the dogged persistence of the political leadership of the region in their pursuit of a distinctively Croatian entity, separated from Bosnia. Long after the **Dayton Agreements** and the formal annulment of its existence, Herceg-Bosna continued to license its own cars, bestow insignia on its own police force, and use the Croatian currency *(kuna)* in preference to the Bosnian *dinar*. A new "government" of Herceg-Bosna was announced as late as June 1996.

This exclusive approach has been pursued via a mixture of noncooperation with the republican authorities and violence directed against outsiders. Among the greatest difficulties experienced by the office of the **United Nations** High Representative, as well as **European Union** commissioner Hans Koschnik during the post-Dayton period, has been the attempt to ensure that the writ of the federal government of Bosnia-Hercegovina ran effectively in **Mostar**. Although peripheral to Herceg-Bosna, Mostar has been coveted as a potential capital because of its significance as an economic and **communications** center. Consequently, west Mostar has been retained under vigorous informal Croat control, in spite of negotiated agreements and the active presence of the **Implentation/Stabilization Force** (I/SFOR). Following the signature of an agreement between the Croatian and Bosnian governments in Sarajevo on 15 August 1996, Herceg-Bosna was officially abolished. Nevertheless, effective federal control of Mostar had still not been established by the end of the year.

An important factor contributing to the difficulty of integrating Herceg-Bosna into the post-Dayton system has been the ambivalence of the Croatian government. Formally the **Tudjman** government assented to international agreements that recognized the integrity of Bosnia-Hercegovina, but in a variety of ways it has, to say the least, refrained from putting its weight behind the enforcement of these agreements and has actively connived at the secessionist aspirations of Grude. In part this behavior is understandable, in that the recovery by Croatia of control over its own Serb ***krajina*** could not have been achieved without the cooperation of the HVO in Herceg-Bosna. It has been widely claimed, however, that the compliance of **Zagreb** is based upon more than opportunistic reasons of this kind. The existence of a powerful "Hercegovina lobby" of political figures whose origin is in western Hercegovina is often cited as the primary factor in making for Croatian inconsistency. The most prominent supposed members of this lobby are **Gojko Šušak** and Borislav Škegro.

One of the most important points of international access to Bosnia-Hercegovina is the **Neretva River Valley**. This fact has made Mostar a key point in the control of the flow of goods, and the Neretva ports represent opportunities to tax that flow. Without resort to the conspiracy theory of a Hercegovina lobby, the continuing existence of a potential point of "strangulation" of this kind gives to Croatia a very powerful means through which to ensure the cooperation of the **Sarajevo** government. It is likely to be the case not that a Hercegovina lobby is in a position to ensure the continuing pliability of President Tudjman, but rather that Zagreb sees advantage in tolerating the "indiscipline" of Grude because of the leverage that this gives Tudjman in Sarajevo. Above all, the stability of the Dayton constitution remains in doubt; for as long as such doubt exists, a future return to war remains a possibility, and the question of the eventual division of Bosnia-Hercegovina must remain open. It will continue to be in the interests of Croatia to retain in this region, formally or informally, a potential base from which to extend its own claim to a part of the spoils in any such division.

—J. B. A.

HERCEGOVINA

The Yugoslav republic of Bosnia-Hercegovina was formed from two historic regions, the union of which is a consequence of their annexation under a common administration by **Austria-Hungary** in 1878. The cumbersome nature of this title has typically resulted in its abbreviation to "Bosnia" (prewar Yugoslavs were in the habit of abbreviating it to "BiH"!). Nevertheless, Hercegovina has always possessed a distinctive identity. Under the **Ottoman Empire**, Hercegovina had constituted a separate *eyalet* (province) of Hersek. The name Hercegovina derives from the assumption by Stefan Vukčić in 1448 of the title of "Herceg [from the German *herzog*, or duke] of Hum and the Coast," which he later changed to the "Herceg of St. Sava." The word *Hercegovina* therefore means simply "the Duke's lands." Along with other Slav princedoms, this minor Serb state was absorbed by the Ottomans during the fifteenth century.

Its boundaries are not exactly defined, but broadly speaking, Hercegovina is that part of Bosnia-Hercegovina that lies south of a line drawn east-west through **Jablanica** and Konjić. People from the region often have a strong sense of local identity, and both Serbs and Croats from Hercegovina regard it as of special historical significance for their own people. Vuk Karadžić based his attempt to standardize the Serb language (in the mid-nineteenth century) upon dialects of Hercegovina, on the grounds that they were the least corrupted by foreign influence. Serb settlement here is among the oldest in the Balkans. Franciscan missionary work resulted in the creation of some of the most ardently Roman **Catholic** communities in the Balkans, including the recently created international pilgrimage site of **Medjugorje**.

From an ethnic point of view, western Hercegovina has historically been predominantly Croat, and eastern Hercegovina has been mainly Serb. The 1991 census reported overwhelmingly Croat communes in **Grude** (99 percent), Posušje (99 percent), Čitluk (98 percent), and Ljubuški (92 percent). Similarly, there were mainly Serb communes in Ljubinje (89 percent), Bileća (80 percent), Nevesinje (74 percent), and **Trebinje** (69 percent). As a legacy of the Ottoman period, the principal towns and the major communications corridor of the **Neretva River Valley** had substantial proportions of **Muslims**—often as urban "islands" within a Slav rural "sea," such as Jablanica and Stolac (with Croat hinterlands) or Gacko (surrounded by largely Serb villages). The ethnic dispersion within Hercegovina, especially the economic and strategic significance of the Neretva Valley, made the region the focus of some of the fiercest fighting of the war and the locus of some of the most determined campaigns of "**ethnic cleansing**," as evidenced by the creation of **detention camps** at Rodoč, Ljubuški, Dretelj, and Čapljina.

—*J. B. A.*

See also: ethnicity; Herceg-Bosna; Mostar

HOLBROOKE, RICHARD

Richard Holbrooke, an American born in 1941, is a career diplomat who gained early experience in Vietnam in the 1960s. He continued his career by accepting various international assignments, including work for the Council on Foreign Relations and an appointment as assistant secretary of state for Asia with the Carter administration. After a break of nine years in industry, he returned to the foreign service with the Clinton administration in 1992 as assistant secretary of state for European affairs; in late 1994 he became U.S. special envoy to the former Yugoslavia. During the first part of his posting, the circumstances of the existing conflict deteriorated in many aspects, and Holbrooke robustly publicized his contempt for the lack of decisive action by the West concerning Bosnia. His concern to prevent a potential broadening of the war into a Balkan context led to his underrated success in calming the **Macedonian** question. However, with the fall of **Srebrenica**, he correctly gauged the tide of international opinion, and in the summer of 1995 he began a new diplomatic offensive backed by **North Atlantic Treaty Organization** (NATO) capabilities. By mid-September the Holbrooke plan for **Sarajevo** was drawn up, demanding the immediate withdrawal of Bosnian Serb heavy weapons, the cessation of Bosnian government hostilities, the reopening of the airport and roads for **humanitarian aid**, and a signed **cease-fire** in the presence of the United Nations Protection Force (**UNPROFOR**) commander, **Rupert Smith**; failure to comply would result in renewed and intensified action by NATO. The achievement of this cease-fire, coupled with talks in Geneva between the Serb and Croat representatives, provided the momentum for Holbrooke within three months to engineer the **Dayton Agreements**, which ended the Yugoslav war as such.

In the end Holbrooke's success was as swift as it was unexpected, and it has yet to be fully analyzed. Since Dayton, Holbrooke—as a proponent of a unified rather than partitioned Bosnia—has regaled the media with his frustrations over the lack of European commitment toward enforcing both political and civilian agendas relating to the terms of the agreement concerning Bosnia. At the time of writing Holbrooke was brokering a deal to end the violence against Albanians in **Kosovo**.

—*J. J. H.*

HOLLINGWORTH, LARRY

Larry Hollingworth spent 30 years in the British army; on "retirement" he became a field officer for **UNHCR** (United Nations High Commission for Refugees), assigned to Yugoslavia. A striking and media-friendly figure, he gained both grudging respect from officials and unusual affection from combatants and citizens for the way in which he carved out improbable supply routes for **humanitarian aid** in the Bosnian war. His experiences in **Bosnia-Hercegovina,** including **Sarajevo** and the "**safe areas,**" are vividly recounted in his book, *Merry Christmas, Mr Larry* (London, Heinemann, 1996).

—*J. J. H.*

HOS

See **Croatian Party of Rights**

HOSTAGE TAKING

Hostage taking is defined as a **war crime** under the terms of the Geneva Convention. Although the taking of hostages *between* the warring parties in the Yugoslav conflict was always an option (and was on occasion an occurrence), the very violence of the act either moved hostage taking onto another dimension in the form of **detention camps** or rendered it an unnecessary intermediate stage on the way to direct atrocities.

International attention, however, was focused on the hostages taken from among the **United Nations** (UN) peacekeeping forces. Although there were numerous cases of such hostage taking, it is surprising that these cases were not even more widespread, given the often **paramilitary** status of the combatants and the vulnerability of the peacekeepers, whose frontline positions and value as propaganda made them comparatively easy and desirable targets.

The hostage crisis came to a head beginning in late May 1995, when the **Bosnian Serbs**' refusal to reduce the intensity of their actions against the various "**safe areas**" in Bosnia led to the threat and then the activation of airstrikes by NATO (**North Atlantic Treaty Organization**) against Serb positions around **Sarajevo.** In **Žepa**, the helplessness of the peacekeepers was absurdly highlighted when the small troop of Ukrainians was effectively held hostage by both the defending Muslims and the besieging Serbs—the former demanding airstrikes, the latter demanding their suspension. Elsewhere, in **Tuzla** and **Goražde**, for example, the hostage taking was even more serious. In retaliation for airstrikes, the Bosnian Serbs took a total of more than 370 hostages from the peacekeeping forces, the great majority of these being French, with around 30 British and several others.

This move was an astute counter by the Serbs, who were proved right in their calculation that (1) the West's stated policy of refusing to deal with hostage takers would be put to the test and would fail and (2) public reaction in the home countries would lead to demands for the peacekeeping forces as a whole to be pulled out and brought home.

—*J. J. H.*

HUMAN RIGHTS

See **United Nations Commission on Human Rights**

HUMANITARIAN AID

Both during the war in the former Yugoslavia and after the relative peace arising from the **Dayton Agreements**, humanitarian aid arrived in many different forms. The groups providing aid have ranged extensively in size. The largest groups have been the United Nations High Commission for Refugees (**UNHCR**) and the International Committee of the **Red Cross** (ICRC). Medium-sized international nongovernmental organizations (NGOs) have included, for example, Caritas, Oxfam, and Médecins sans Frontières. There have also been smaller groups specifically focused on women and children, such as (from the United Kingdom) Women's Aid to Former Yugoslavia, who not only organized the collection of humanitarian aid but also delivered it to **women** in the camps in Croatia and Bosnia; and (from Croatia) Suncokret, who worked mainly with children. In addition, individuals from many places worldwide

A UNHCR humanitarian aid convoy in Bosnia-Hercegovina, 1993. (UNHCR)

often just turned up to help with their own technical or domestic skills where they could and to improvise on the spot.

The activities and programs with which this range of organizations and people were involved were many and varied. The work of UNHCR and ICRC is explained elsewhere in this volume. NGOs were involved in the practical tasks of providing food, clean water, heat, shelter, clothing, and medicines in many parts of the former Yugoslavia affected by the war, not only to those living in collective centers such as **refugee** camps, but also to people living in besieged towns, particularly in the hospitals.

The smaller groups provided assistance to the larger groups but were also involved in work of their own. Some came to see through a specific project, whereas for others the journey became an open-ended stay according to the type of work. This work ranged from rebuilding of houses, to clearing of land mines, to delivery of food and medicines to besieged towns, to educational projects, to counseling work related to the problems created by the war. Those who could not stay helped with the delivery of aid. Truck and car loads of assistance came from all over Europe. Small groups from, for example, Vaagenigen in Holland and Stroud in England would collect a variety of materials, load them, and make repeated runs to the former Yugoslavia.

Once in the conflict areas, these convoys were in considerable personal danger, particularly when confronted by **paramilitary** groups who had their own agenda for supplies. The drivers were extremely vulnerable: the United Kingdom's Overseas Development Agency employed over 60 drivers who took their vehicles through the front lines and suffered several fatalities. In general terms the humanitarian aid fell into three categories: relief of suffering, reconstruction, and self-help training. The huge influx of aid was not without problems of balance, however. There was too much delivery of clothes and toys when what refugees or displaced people really wanted was tools and other equipment for building or sanitary towels and other hygienic equipment. There were also cases when the counseling indirectly created damage by focusing on the immediate trauma without full understanding of the root causes—this was a war on European soil, but it had its own mental context. Humanitarian aid on this scale is a huge undertaking. Delivering such aid internationally and meeting the needs of its local recipients require proper planning and knowledge of the social and political issues in order to be wholly efficient. Given the nature of the conflict in Yugoslavia, there was a remarkable degree of coordination, and much of the aid was appropriate and well used. However, there was also much that was wasted. In Yugoslavia, as elsewhere, the decision to help requires obtaining confirmation of the best way to help.

—R. E.

See also: Red Cross; UNHCR

HUNGARY

As one of Yugoslavia's immediate neighbors, Hungary was inevitably affected by the Yugoslav conflict. Much of present-day **Croatia**, part of **Slovenia**, and the **Vojvodina** region of Serbia were part of Hungary before World War I, and Yugoslavia joined **Romania** and Czechoslovakia in the interwar Little Entente alliance against Hungary. There are now ethnic Hungarian minorities of 340,000–400,000 in **Serbia**/Federal Republic of **Yugoslavia**, 26,000–40,000 in Croatia, and 8,000–10,000 in Slovenia—although exact figures are contentious. Yugoslav/Serbian fears of Hungarian irredentism and the possibility that Hungary might be dragged into the conflict because of the Hungarian minorities formed the background for the country's involvement with the Yugoslav conflict. As the Yugoslav conflict emerged in 1990–1991, Hungarian sympathies lay with democratizing Slovenia and Croatia and against increasingly authoritarian Serbia. Early in 1991, relations with Serbia worsened when it was revealed that Hungary had sold 10,000 Kalashnikov assault rifles to Croatia in October 1990. The Hungarian community in the Vojvodina also became one of the victims of Serbian president **Slobodan Milošević**'s nationalist policies and began to press for guarantees of its rights. When war broke out in the summer and autumn of 1991, Yugoslav military aircraft violated Hungarian airspace during bombing raids on Croatia, culminating in the apparently accidental dropping of a small number of bombs on a Hungarian village. Hungary also received a significant number of **refugees** from Croatia and **Bosnia-Hercegovina**. With tensions growing in the Vojvodina, there were fears that Hungary might be dragged into the conflict. Hungary, however, sought to avoid this possibility and supported **European Community/European**

Union (EC/EU) and **United Nations** (UN) approaches to the conflict. Bilateral confidence-building measures (including a neutral airspace zone along the border and a hotline between air defense commands) were negotiated with the Yugoslav military, and violations of Hungarian airspace stopped. Hungary supported the international **recognition** of Slovenia, Croatia, and Bosnia-Hercegovina; the arms embargo on the former Yugoslavia; and the EC/EU- and UN-initiated peace negotiations. It rapidly developed good relations with Slovenia and Croatia, concluding bilateral cooperation treaties that included guarantees of the rights of the Hungarian minorities in these countries. In contrast, relations with Serbia/Federal Republic of Yugoslavia remained troubled by continuing tensions in the Vojvodina.

Support for international actions in the former Yugoslavia also allowed Hungary to develop closer relations with the West, particularly the **North Atlantic Treaty Organization** (NATO) and the **United States.** Hungary allowed NATO's Airborne Warning and Control System (AWACS) aircraft undertaking reconnaisance missions and U.S. aircraft dropping aid to Bosnia to use its airspace, and it let UN peacekeeping forces transit its territory. When NATO first authorized possible airstrikes in response to the war in Bosnia in 1994, however, Hungary did not permit its airspace to be used, fearing possible retaliation. When the NATO-led **Implementation Force** (IFOR) was deployed in 1996, Hungarian forces did not join the force because of the political sensitivities of deploying Hungarian forces in the former Yugoslavia. The southern Hungarian town of Kaposvar, however, became one of the main bases for the deployment of IFOR troops into Bosnia. Hungary's support for NATO-led actions and the IFOR thus helped to confirm the country's status as one of the primary Eastern European candidates for NATO membership. Hungary was invited to join the alliance in July 1997.

—A. S. C.

HVO

See **Croatian Council of Defense**

I

IFOR
See **Implementation/Stabilization Force**

IGMAN, MOUNT
Mount Igman, overlooking the Bosnian capital of **Sarajevo**, rises to a height of 1,500 meters. Its strategic importance during the recent conflict has been as a position from which to either protect or prevent the use of the route to the capital from the southwest for supplies and relief.

On 5 August 1993, less than a week after the latest cease-fire among the three armies in Bosnia (Bosnian Croats, Bosnian Serbs, Bosnian government), the **Bosnian Serbs** moved to take Igman to add to their recent acquisition of nearby Mount Bjelašnica. A consequence of this move was that more than 30,000 refugees fled from the numerous villages on the foothills of Igman into Sarajevo, which itself had been under siege by the Bosnian Serbs for the past year. The rest of the month was spent on international peace talks in an attempt to remove the Serbs from the mountain, including the threat of airstrikes by NATO. The eventual outcome was the designation of Igman as a demilitarized zone under Franco-British protection, with no presence permitted for either Bosnian government or Bosnian Serb forces. By mid-1994 the Bosnians, increasingly desperate over the lack of international progress on the fate of Sarajevo, directed forces of the **Bosnian army** to infiltrate the Igman zone.

—J. J. H.

ILLYRIAN MOVEMENT
See **Yugoslav idea**

IMF
See **International Monetary Fund**

IMPLEMENTATION/STABILIZATION FORCE (I/SFOR)
Under the **Dayton Agreements** of November 1995, the **North Atlantic Treaty Organization** (NATO) committed itself to deploy the Implementation Force (IFOR) to implement the peace process in **Bosnia-Hercegovina.** IFOR replaced the United Nations Protection Force (**UNPROFOR**) at the end of December 1995, had a maximum strength of 60,000 troops, and involved 35 countries (NATO's 16 members, plus forces from Central and Eastern Europe, **Russia**, and countries such as Malaysia and Egypt). The substantial involvement of ground forces from the **United States** was one of the central differences between IFOR and UNPROFOR. IFOR was mandated to maintain the cessation of hostilities, to separate the Bosnian **Muslim-Croat Federation** and **Republika Srpska** armed forces, to transfer territory between the two entities, to move the entities' forces and heavy weapons into approved sites, and to create a secure environment for the UN High Representative and other international organizations to implement the civilian elements of the Dayton Agreements. Unlike UNPROFOR, IFOR was mandated to use force to achieve these goals and had the troops and weapons necessary for this purpose. IFOR was highly successful in implementing the military components of the Dayton peace agreements.

IFOR's initial mandate was for a one-year mission only—largely because the U.S. Congress was reluctant to support a longer-term deployment of U.S. ground forces in Bosnia. It was widely feared, however, that the withdrawal of NATO forces would result in renewed fighting. The European allies were also highly reluctant to remain in Bosnia without a parallel U.S. commitment of ground forces. Thus, toward the end of 1996, IFOR's mandate was extended to June 1998, with the force to be reduced to 36,000 troops but still including U.S. ground forces.

I/SFOR troops and an armored vehicle in Bosnia-Hercegovina, 1996. (NATO photo)

The force was renamed the Stabilization Force (SFOR). Early in 1998, SFOR's mandate was further renewed, this time with no clear time limit. The issue of when and in what circumstances SFOR might withdraw from Bosnia remained controversial.

Although I/SFOR was successful in implementing the military components of the Dayton peace agreements, it faced serious problems in supporting the civilian elements of the agreements. Some within NATO (particularly its military leaders) feared that if NATO were asked to provide a safe environment for **refugees** to return to their homes, supervise **elections**, arrest war criminals, and counter nationalist propaganda, I/SFOR would be given goals it could not achieve, would become overstretched, and would neglect its core mission of maintaining the military peace—so-called mission creep. Others argued that if NATO did not undertake these tasks, it could not succeed in establishing a stable peace and would not create the circumstances in which it could withdraw without a renewed threat of war. Beginning in 1997, under pressure from some NATO states, I/SFOR gradually began to take a more proactive approach (for example, by arresting some war criminals and seizing television transmitters used to broadcast extreme nationalist propaganda). Nevertheless, there remained ambiguities and disputes about just what role SFOR should play in promoting peace in Bosnia.

—*A. S. C.*

See also: war crimes

Reference: Schulze, Carl. *IFOR: Allied Forces in Bosnia* (pictorial). *Europa Militaria,* no. 22. London: Windrow and Greene, 1996.

INFLATION

Both a cause and a consequence of the Yugoslav economic and political crises of the late 1980s and 1990s, high inflation and inflationary expectations have had a profound impact on all the successor states of the former Yugoslavia. Although it had risen steadily during the 1970s and 1980s, Yugoslav inflation did not reach critical hyperinflationary levels until the late 1980s. With high inflation at that time eroding real incomes throughout the federation, the political conflicts over scarce and dwindling economic resources intensified. Matters were made worse on this score by external pressure from the **International Monetary Fund** (IMF) for a strengthened federal government and real financial stabilization in return for IMF support. Although partly implemented by the federal government, led by Premier **Ante Marković** from 1989 to 1991, when Yugoslav inflation fell sharply, this IMF-approved package was to prove an ultimate failure. This failure was mainly due to the declining legitimacy of the federal institutions through which the package was to be implemented, as well as to opposition by the federation's constituent republics led by Serbia.

With the collapse of Marković's economic reform program and the Yugoslav federation as a whole in 1991, inflation reemerged in all the successor states of the former Yugoslavia. The major structural problems were (1) reckless fiscal and monetary expansionism at a time of declining output under conditions of war and (2) international isolation and the absence of external financial discipline by the IMF.

In the case of the Federal Republic of **Yugoslavia** (FRY), these structural problems took the most extreme form after the FRY was subjected to economic **sanctions** by the United Nations (UN) from 1992 to 1995. Unique in the former Yugoslavia in having retained the old and debased Yugoslav currency, the dinar, the FRY experienced the highest recorded hyperinflation of modern times in 1993: 1.3 trillion percent—even higher than the hyperinflation of the early 1920s in the German Weimar Republic. The result was to effectively demonetize the economies of **Serbia** and **Montenegro**. Because this hyperinflationary policy was so quickly reversed in 1994, when a new Yugoslav dinar was introduced, it came to be recognized in part as politically motivated, given that it actually strengthened the position of the Serbian government led by President **Slobodan Milošević**. Among other things, this economic disaster forced people to concentrate on personal survival rather than political opposition, and it economically wiped out the largely anti-Milošević middle class in **Belgrade** and other cities.

Elsewhere in the former Yugoslavia, high inflation was also the norm after 1991, although not to the same extent as in the FRY. Only **Slovenia** avoided hyperinflation (i.e., in excess of 50 percent per month). In **Croatia** hyperinflation grew from 1991 to 1993, mainly because of the republic's state of actual or potential war with Serbia at this time. The poorest of the Yugoslav republics prior to 1991, **Macedonia** suffered greatly from the withdrawal of fiscal and other subsidies from Belgrade; its government attempted to cover these losses with local fiscal and monetary expansionism. Even higher hyperinflation took place in war-ravaged **Bosnia-Hercegovina** at this time.

From 1994 onward, the introduction of new currencies, central banks, and **banking** systems in most of the former Yugoslav republics was followed by the introduction of deflationary financial stabilization throughout the region, often with the support and at the behest of the IMF. With the continuation of these policies and the end of the Yugoslav wars in 1995, inflation in most of the former Yugoslav republics was down to single digits. Low levels of inflation are an essential precondition for the restoration of economic confidence and real growth in the region after years of economic decline and the destructive results of war and sanctions.

—M. M.

INTELLIGENCE SERVICES

Operating at the covert level of politics and military conflict, the various intelligence services of the former Yugoslavia have played a key role in the region's crises of the 1990s. The new or post-Yugoslav intelligence services appeared during the demise of the former Yugoslav federation in 1990–1991; they originated in the former Yugoslav Intelligence and Security Community, in which the two main agencies were the State Security Service (SDB) and the Military Counter-Intelligence Service (KOS). At that time, the SDB came under the exclusive control of **Serbia**. Formerly part of the **Yugoslav Peoples' Army** (JNA), the KOS then also became an exclusively Serb agency. In April 1992, when the newly declared Federal Republic of **Yugoslavia**, consisting of Serbia and **Montenegro**, replaced the JNA with the new Army of Yugoslavia (VJ), a newly reorganized KOS became part of that army's general staff. The SDB was then nominally part of the federal interior ministry, but remained under the de facto control of the Serbian counterpart. Elsewhere in the former Yugoslavia, the rapid collapse left the other successor states without effective intelligence services of their own. In **Croatia**, the rise to power of the **Croatian Democratic Union** (HDZ) resulted in the creation in 1990 of the new National Security Office (UNS). Created by the former chief of the Croatian SDB, **Josip Manolić**, the UNS came under the control of Croatian president **Franjo Tudjman**'s son Miroslav in 1992. In the military sphere, the Intelligence Service of the Croatian Army (OSHV) was created in 1991 as part of the general staff of the new **Croatian Army** (HV).

In **Bosnia-Hercegovina**, which Serbian president **Slobodan Milošević** and Tudjman had secretly agreed to carve up as early as March 1991, the Serbian and Croatian intelligence services cooperated, helping to create allied political and military intelligence services among the **Bosnian Croats** and **Bosnian Serbs** in 1992. The least well prepared for civil war in 1992 was the Bosnian Muslim–dominated Sarajevo government, led by President **Alija Izetbegović**. Here the Bosnian Agency for Investigation and Documentation (BAID) was established. In addition, the **Bosnian army** established a military intelligence service in 1993.

In **Slovenia**, the defense ministry's Intelligence/Security Service (VOMO) was established as early as 1990. Related to VOMO operationally, the Slovene Defense Ministry also had a Reconnaissance and Intervention Service (MORIS) up to 1994. Collectively known as VOMO-MORIS, these military intelligence agencies were complemented by a smaller political intelligence service within the interior ministry. Similar intelligence services were also established in **Macedonia** in the early 1990s.

Then headed by a fanatical Milošević loyalist, Mihaj Kerteš, the SDB played a major role in encouraging and politically radicalizing the separatist Croatian and Bosnian Serbs in 1990–1991. In addition, the SDB and KOS also covertly supplied their paramilitary militias with arms, money, and tactical intelligence. In Serbia and Montenegro, the SDB organized the dispatch of **paramilitary/irregular forces** from the remaining Yugoslavia to Croatia and then Bosnia. One of these groups was led by **Željko Ražnjatović** ("Arkan"), a known SDB agent and professional assassin. In Croatia, and even more so in Bosnia, established SDB and KOS networks dating back to the communist Yugoslav period helped to give rebel Serbs the edge over their local enemies during the early stages of the Yugoslav wars. Thereafter, however, the strengthening of Croatian military and intelligence-gathering capabilities in particular resulted in a decisive shift in the regional balance of power against the Serbs by 1995–1996. In Croatia, the UNS and OSHV benefited from assistance and training from German and U.S. intelligence services. Croatia's intelligence services played a major role in the covert rearming of the HV.

In Bosnia, the creation of the **Muslim-Croat Federation** in March 1994 led to major strategic intelligence operations by the Central Intelligence Agency (CIA) and other U.S. agencies in this former Yugoslav republic; this involvement played a major role in the weakening of both the Croatian and Bosnian Serbs in 1995. Often the cause of tensions with the United States, BAID also established personnel training and other relations with the intelligence services of **Iran**. Following increased U.S. pressure on Izetbegovič in 1996, BAID was forced to curtail some of its joint intelligence and other operations with Iran.

Among the Bosnian Serbs, the covert influence of the Serbian government was reportedly at its most decisive in the intelligence sphere. The chief of the Bosnian Serbs' main intelligence service for most of the 1990s was a brother of Staniša Stanišić, chief of the Serbian SDB. Code-named "Typhoon," this intelligence service was based on older SDB and KOS networks in Bosnia and hence was almost certainly controlled from Belgrade. Following the final public split between Milošević and his former Bosnian Serb protégés in 1994, SDB infiltration of Typhoon posed a major threat to the Bosnian Serb leader, **Radovan Karadžić**. SDB agents were involved in the anti-Karadžić mutiny in **Banja Luka** in late 1994. Following the Bosnian Serb seizure of United Nations (UN) personnel as **hostages** in 1995, it was the Serbian SDB, in the person of Stanišić, who brought about their release.

More recently, the signing of the **Dayton Agreements** by Milošević in December 1995 reportedly resulted in increased SDB operations against the Bosnian Serbs, culminating in the forced removal of Karadžić from power in late 1996. A related move by Milošević at this time, possibly involving the KOS, was the forced removal of Gen. **Ratko Mladić** as commander of the Bosnian Serb Army. In the remaining Yugoslavia, the SDB has been used to curb the activities of various paramilitary groups and related mafia networks as part of a policy of cleaning up Serbia's international image.

Within all but one of the successor states of the former Yugoslavia (i.e., Slovenia), the powers given to political intelligence services have inevitably raised doubts about the states' democratic credentials. This was particularly the case with the SDB in the remaining Yugoslavia. In Serbia as well as in Croatia, criticism of the government has been equated with subversion and even treason, and UNS activities have often been more concerned with opponents of the HDZ than with genuine subversion of the Croatian state. The UNS has also been involved in high-level power struggles, such as Manolić's removal from his position in 1992, following alleged intrigues against his former mentor, Tudjman. Even in Slovenia, in 1994, a major arms-smuggling scandal involving VOMO-MORIS resulted in the removal from office of Defense Minister **Janez Janša**. In Bosnia, BAID has been implicated in serious criminality involving the local mafia. Intelligence service collusion with criminals has also been widespread in Serbia and Croatia.

There is little sign that such abuses of intelligence service powers are likely to be reformed. Powerful, corrupt, and largely unaccountable, these services continue to blight the prospects for genuine democratic politics throughout the former Yugoslavia. The involvement of foreign intelligence services in the crises of the former Yugoslavia has often been for selfish political and military reasons that have had little to do with the promotion of genuine democratic politics of the region in the future.

—M. M.

INTERMARRIAGE

Claims and counterclaims about the origins of the war in Yugoslavia have focused attention upon intermarriage as a sensitive indicator of interethnic toleration. The war was greeted with contradictory responses both within and outside the country. Assertions about the inevitable eruption of "age-old hatreds," as well as the boiling over of the seething pot of ethnic antagonism, were countered by equally emphatic claims about high levels of toleration

Young victims of a tragic war: children of mixed marriages in divided Sarajevo, 1993. (NATO photo)

among Yugoslavs and reports that Yugoslavs frequently were unaware of each other's ethnic identity. These diametrically opposed views have been cited anecdotally with approximately equal frequency. The propensity of the communications **media** to seize upon "human interest" stories has also served to heighten awareness of the problems of families that were created by ethnic intermarriage but that were either tragically divided by war or heroically rose above its horrors in familial solidarity.

The threat of the ultimate division of **Bosnia-Hercegovina** brought together a vocal and influential lobby of apologists for the historical continuity and integrity of a specifically Bosnian culture, of which mutual toleration has often been claimed to be an important characteristic. Sarajevo in particular has been held up as a symbol of multiculturalism and openness, and reportedly high rates of intermarriage have commonly been taken as confirming this picture.

Until the late 1970s, both Yugoslav government sources and social scientists concurred in the view that ethnic intermarriage in Yugoslavia was relatively frequent and becoming more so. More recent research, however, has challenged this view.

Accurate statistical analysis of changes in patterns of marriage over time is difficult in Yugoslavia for several reasons. In particular, the definitions of ethnic groups in the post-1945 censuses have changed (especially the definition of "**Muslims**"). There is considerable difficulty in interpreting the significance of individuals reporting their ethnicity simply as "Yugoslav." (Often this label has been taken as indicating that the respondent is of ethnically mixed parentage, but equally well it could be seen as an expression of socialist ideological orthodoxy.) Furthermore, it is not easy to disentangle the effect of **ethnicity** in shaping the choice of marriage partners from other related issues, such as level of education.

Historical rates of intermarriage in the Balkans were low. In traditional preindustrial communities, different ethnic groups were often characterized by different occupations, bearing different ranks in society and consequently subject to residential segregation; in addition, there were the more familiar barriers of **religion** or **language**. This was especially the case in the former **Ottoman** regions, where different confessional communities were given a substantial degree of self-government under the *millet* (religious administration unit) system and lived in separate *mehale*, or neighborhoods. Intermarriage is characteristic of rising levels of urbanization and education; hence, for the most part, it is a relatively recent phenomenon.

In general terms, the propensity to intermarriage has been higher among groups that share the Serbo-Croat language, although there are substantial regional variations in the patterns that characterize any particular ethnic group. Where groups constitute a small minority within a larger community, it is more difficult to find a partner from within one's own people. Consequently, rates of mixed marriage have been especially high in the **Vojvodina**, with its complex pattern of more than a dozen minority communities. Here the Croat population is exceptionally "open," although the most "closed" group is the Croat community in **Kosovo**. The Roma community remains a broadly stigmatized group (in spite of their enjoying a relatively better position in Yugoslavia than in other European countries), and this fact is reflected in their low rates of intermarriage. Where there are acute and long-standing local political antagonisms between groups (such as between Serbs and **Albanians** in Kosovo or between Macedonians and Albanians in **Macedonia**), both communities remain relatively closed to each other with respect to marriage.

Contrary to the widely reported claims, Bosnia-Hercegovina is not distinguished by particularly high rates of intermarriage, even in the capital, **Sarajevo**. The overall rate in the post-1945 period has moved irregularly between 10 and 12 percent, which is marginally below the average for the federation and markedly beneath that for **Croatia** (15–17 percent) or the Vojvodina (where rates rose steadily to more than 28 percent in the period 1987–1989). Sarajevo, with around 28 percent mixed marriages, is conspicuously behind several Croatian cities, such as **Pakrac** (35 percent) or **Vukovar** (34 percent). Studies of "ethnic distance" by Yugoslav social scientists have indicated persisting patterns in the degree of proximity or distance between the various ethnic groups, and generally speaking the degree of distance is greater between Muslim and non-Muslim groups than between different ethnic groups of the same religion.

—J. B. A.

See also: rural-urban differences

References: Bougarel, Xavier. *Bosnie: anatomie d'un conflit.* Paris: La Découverte, 1996; Mrdjen, Snježana. "La mixité en ex-Yougoslavie: integration ou ségrégation des nationalités?" *Revue d'Etudes Comparatives Est-Ouest* 27, no. 3 (September 1996):103–145.

INTERNATIONAL COMMITTEE OF THE RED CROSS

See **Red Cross**

INTERNATIONAL CONFERENCE ON THE FORMER YUGOSLAVIA

The joint International Conference on the Former Yugoslavia (ICFY) was established by the **London Conference** of August 1992. **David Owen** and **Cyrus Vance** were appointed, respectively, as the **European Community** (EC) and **United Nations** (UN) cochairs (Vance was replaced by **Thorvald Stoltenberg** in April 1993). The ICFY was convened in Geneva in September 1992, providing a framework for ongoing peace negotiations. It produced the **Vance-Owen Plan** of 1992–1993 and the Owen-Stoltenberg Plan of 1993, both of which envisaged internal divisions of **Bosnia-Hercegovina**, although along different lines. Both plans ultimately failed, and the ICFY was unable to promote a settlement of the Bosnian conflict. The failure of the ICFY reflected the inability of the parties to the conflict and the outside powers to agree on the nature of any possible peace settlement. The ICFY was superseded in April 1994 by the Contact Group, in which the **United States** and **Russia** played a greater role.

—*A. S. C.*

INTERNATIONAL COURT OF JUSTICE

The International Court of Justice (ICJ), which celebrated its fiftieth anniversary in 1996, may be considered to be the legal arm of the **United Nations** (UN); it constitutes the highest court of appeal in cases of international law. The ICJ was called upon to deal with three important cases relating to the Yugoslav conflict, and its decisions have been regarded on each occasion as making a significant affirmation of international **recognition** of the authority of the Bosnian government in Sarajevo.

In March 1993 an action was brought by the government of **Bosnia-Hercegovina** against the Federal Republic of **Yugoslavia** in which the former alleged violation of the 1948 **Genocide** Convention, asking the court to order Yugoslavia to cease from acts of genocide and to cease supporting **paramilitary/irregular forces** engaged in similar acts in Bosnia-Hercegovina. It also challenged the international arms embargo initiated by UN Security Council resolution 713 of September 1991, claiming that as a state it was entitled to seek support, including the necessary weapons, to defend itself. On 8 April the court declined to rule on the issue of the arms embargo, but it did make a provisional order regarding the protection of rights under the Genocide Convention, deferring a final decision on the matter. A second request for a protection order, filed in July, was heard on 25–26 August. The court ruled on 13 September that its order of 8 April should be "immediately and effectively implemented."

The court's response to the case was significant in that in recognizing the government of Bosnia-Hercegovina as lawfully constituted, it undermined the claim of the Federal Republic of Yugoslavia to be the sole legal successor to the former socialist federation. The order also drew attention to the wording of the Genocide Convention, which places signatories under obligation to "prevent and punish" genocide as well as to abstain from it.

In the following year, the Yugoslav government responded by bringing a case in which it claimed that the member states of the **North Atlantic Treaty Organization** (NATO), by their decision of 9 February to respond positively to the UN request for airstrikes in support of **Sarajevo**, were infringing the charter of the UN by threatening to use force without the direct sanction of the Security Council. The defendant states on this occasion did not consent to the court's jurisdiction, and the case was not heard. The outcome of these two cases indirectly paved the way for the use of air power by NATO forces later in the war.

Finally, in 1996 the ICJ returned to the case that had been brought by the government of Bosnia-Hercegovina against the Federal Republic of Yugoslavia and that alleged acts of genocide under the Genocide Convention; the court published its decision on 11 July. The defense had advanced the case that Bosnia was not a party to the convention at the relevant time and therefore was not entitled to bring the claim. Yugoslavia also argued that there was no international dispute between itself and Bosnia-Hercegovina—that the conflict in question was an internal one and should be considered as a **civil war** to which Yugoslavia was not a party in a territory over which Yugoslavia had no jurisdiction. The court ruled against Yugoslavia on both of these counts. By reaching this decision, the court laid the groundwork for a succession of trials on charges relating to the Genocide Convention to be brought before the International **War Crimes Tribunal** at The Hague.

—*J. B. A.*

INTERNATIONAL MONETARY FUND

When the Yugoslavs decided to abandon the Soviet version of a centrally planned economy in 1948 and opt for decentralization and **worker self-management**, the International Monetary Fund (IMF) began to be active in the former Yugoslavia. The early interventions by the IMF were mainly designed to assist the country in its struggle to survive after the immediate withdrawal of all forms of support from the Soviet Union in 1948, though there was also more than a hint of a U.S.-inspired push to get the Yugoslavs to move much closer ideologically toward capitalism. At this time the IMF wholeheartedly agreed with the Yugoslavs and their bold moves to radically decentralize the economy, since this implied a lesser role for the state and more scope for market mechanisms and nonstate sector activities. In the 1980s the IMF was again quick to come to the aid of the former Yugoslavia when the latter's economy went into rapid freefall after a series of major oil price hikes precipitated by wars in the Middle East.

The first major "shock therapy" economic reform program in Eastern Europe was also undertaken in the former Yugoslavia from 1988 onward, backed by the IMF through a standby financial agreement and through other forms of advice and support. The IMF was forced to recant some of its earlier advice concerning the wisdom of extensive decentralization, and it pushed hard for the Yugoslavs to recentralize the economic and political system in order to reinstate at least some degree of macroeconomic control. The lack of power of the center was a major problem for the Yugoslav economy. For instance, the federal government was unable to control the amount of foreign borrowings racked up by individual enterprises, mainly because each enterprise was supported by republican administrations keen on obtaining as much benefit for "their own" enterprises as possible. In spite of genuine attempts by the federal authorities to control the level of republican spending, the IMF made it clear that Yugoslavia nevertheless had to accept responsibility for repaying in full its huge foreign debt. The economic system was consequently given a strong push to restructure toward export industries and to cut back on imports, and the IMF also insisted on stringent cuts in government spending as part of the shock therapy approach.

Many believe that the severity and rapidity of the IMF measures contributed in no small way to the eventual breakup of the former Yugoslavia. The very rapid decline in living standards of the poorest sections of Yugoslav society, as well as the enormously widening gap between the richer northern republics and the poorer southern ones, proved to be very fertile soil for the hypernationalist outpourings of the leaders of Serbia and Croatia. Scapegoats were sought by all sides: if one republic was poor, it was because those in the richer republics were taking all the profits; if one republic was rich, it was because those in the poorer republics were lazy, incompetent, and unused to the needs of business. Belatedly, the promise of substantial IMF support was used during the conflict as an enticement to come to a political agreement, but it had little effect upon a generation of nationalist leaders intent on dividing up the former Yugoslavia at any cost.

—*M. B.*

INTERNATIONAL RECOGNITION

See **recognition**

INTERNATIONAL WAR CRIMES TRIBUNAL

See **War Crimes Tribunal**

INTERNMENT

See **detention camps**

IRAN

Among Muslim states, Iran was at the fore in trying to defend the beleaguered Muslim population of **Bosnia-Hercegovina** during the conflict from 1992 to 1995. It urged fellow Muslim countries to defend coreligionists, and there were persistent reports of Islamic guerrillas, or *mujaheddin*, operating in Bosnia on the government side. Serb nationalists exploited Iran's high profile to argue that they were engaged in a religious war against militant Islam.

Meanwhile, Western states were nervous that Iran was trying to import its brand of Islamic radicalism into Bosnia. Tehran's militant rhetoric was combined with energetic attempts by Iranian foreign minister Ali Akbar Velayati to improve links with **Croatia** and Central European states able to influence the outcome of the Bosnian conflict; Velayati was a frequent visitor to the region during the conflict.

Iran was able to channel weapons to the Bosnian government in 1994 via Croatia with the apparent collusion of the government of the **United States,** which was opposed to the arms embargo that other United Nations Security Council states had imposed on Bosnia and other combatant states. After the **Dayton Agreements** at the end of 1995, U.S. nervousness about the influence of Iranian advisers and *mujaheddin* in the Bosnian defense forces led to U.S. military aid being held up until the government in Sarajevo severed this link.

—*T. G.*

See also: arms transfers; Islam and the West; Muslim world and Yugoslav conflict; paramilitary/irregular forces

IRMA

See **Hadžimuratović, Irma**

ISLAM AND THE WEST

Among the attempts made to see the wider significance of the Yugoslav conflict has been an approach that identifies the **Balkans** as one locus of a global conflict between Islam and the West. This bears superficial similarities to the "**cultural fault lines**" approach, but in this case the relevant frontier lies between an Islamic East and the Christian West, rather than between the **Catholic** and **Orthodox** traditions of Christianity. Under this approach, Europe is depicted as facing anew the threat of an aggressive and expansionist Islamic world, much as it did between the fourteenth and sixteenth centuries. Consequently, the taproot of the conflict in **Yugoslavia** is presumed to be the existence of Muslim communities within an otherwise Christian Europe, which might prove to be the bridgehead for further expansion.

In part, this interpretation of the situation draws upon indigenous folk traditions that date from the **Ottoman** conquest; it can to some extent be read as an expression of a far more general intellectual tradition of "Orientalism," as identified in the work of Edward Said. It is cast in a different form—and seen as a more contemporary and more global phenomenon—in the writing of U.S. historian Samuel Huntington on the subject of the "clash of civilizations." Different points of emphasis can be identified within this broad approach to events.

Nationalistic Serbs see themselves as fighting a war on behalf of Europe as a whole, reviving the description of themselves popularized by British historian R. G. D. Laffan at the time of World War I as the "guardians of the gate." The continental importance of this mission has been taken as underwriting the practice of "**ethnic cleansing.**"

The notion of a global confrontation between Islam and the West also has wide currency among Yugoslavia's **Muslims.** The idea is used in order to explain the apparent indifference of the Western governments to the plight of Bosnia-Hercegovina; the ineffective implementation of the **no-fly zones;** the failure of the policy of creating "**safe areas**"; the inequity of the **arms** embargo; and the persistent attempts to dismember Bosnia into "**cantons**" or "entities" in a succession of internationally sponsored plans—in fact, the West's de facto connivance with **genocide.** All these can be represented as part of a general strategy of the West to rid Europe of Islam. Ironically, therefore, both **Bosnian Serbs** and Bošnjaci (Bosnian Muslims) often concur in their understanding of the script that is being enacted in Bosnia, although they cast themselves in starkly different roles within the drama.

—*J. B. A.*

See also: religion

References: Said, Edward. *Orientalism.* Harmondsworth, Middlesex: Penguin Books, 1985; Todorova, Maria. N. *Imagining the Balkans.* New York and Oxford: Oxford University Press, 1997.

ISLAMIC COMMUNITY

Although Islam lacks the tradition of hierarchical clerical authority found in both the Roman **Catholic** and the **Orthodox Churches,** the Yugoslav state sought to create a formal organizational structure through which it could communicate with the **Muslim** community and attempt to exert some control over the public manifestation of faith. For this reason the communist government established the Islamic Community (Islamska Zajednica), headed by the *reis al-ulema* (head of the community). The community was organized into four regions (**Sarajevo**, **Priština**, **Skopje**, and **Titograd**) corresponding to the four republics or autonomous provinces in which there were large Muslim communities. The seat of the *reis* was in Sarajevo. There were two *medresas* (colleges) and a theology faculty attached to the University of Sarajevo.

Successive Yugoslav constitutions guaranteed freedom of confession, although **religion** was identified principally in terms of *worship* and was expressly seen in terms of the sphere of private activity. Religion was to be clearly segregated from politics and indeed dissociated from any involvement in public affairs. The basic framework of religious life was laid down in the Law Concerning the Legal Status of Religious Communities (1953), although the activities of the Islamic Vakuf charitable foundations were already regulated by a statute of 1947. Unlike the prewar Yugoslavia, therefore, there was no public role envisaged for traditional *sharia* (canon) law.

Since the state did not acknowledge the public significance of religion, there have been no reliable and systematic attempts to assess religious allegiance in Yugoslavia. Estimates of the numbers of those with at least a nominal attachment to Islam indicate around 3.8 million (16 percent of the population) in 1981 and around 4.2 million (17.5 percent) in 1991. In addition to **Bosnia-Hercegovina**, where around 44 percent of the population declare themselves to be Muslims, and **Kosovo**, where about 70 percent of **Albanians** are believed to identify with Islam, there are significant numbers of Muslims in **Macedonia**, **Serbia** (especially the **Sandžak**), and **Montenegro**.

The position of Islam within Yugoslavia has been more complex and difficult than that of the other major religious groups. The history of the incorporation of large parts of the region into the **Ottoman Empire** has meant that the national mythologies of various ethnic groups have had a pronounced anti-Muslim color. In Slovenia and Croatia, it was possible to develop a working relationship between the Roman Catholic Church and the state after a period of mutual antagonism in the early postwar years. The same was also possible in Serbia, Montenegro, and Macedonia with the Orthodox Church—especially in Macedonia, where Communist Party support for the autonomy of the Macedonian Church served the overall purpose of building a sense of Macedonian national identity. The divided nature of society in Bosnia-Hercegovina, however, made it impossible to develop that kind of political accommodation. Consequently, the Islamic Community kept a very low profile and tended to take a very defensive position. In return, the state permitted the construction of around 400 mosques between 1945 and 1985, as well as the renovation of around 380 mosques.

The office of the *reis* remained a political appointment until 1991 and could be relied upon to be suitably critical of anything that (1) could be regarded as a manifestation of clericalism or (2) might feed the prejudices of non-Muslims about the potential role of Muslims in Yugoslavia as agents of fundamentalism. The position of the *reis* and of the Islamic Community has been rendered difficult, however, by the internal diversity of the Islamic faith, in ways that are not encountered in the other main religions in Yugoslavia. Islam is characterized by the significant influence of Sufism and by the presence of the Dervish orders (particularly in Kosovo). It is hard to gauge the weight of these influences because of their semiclandestine character. In 1974, however, a rival "community," the Zajednica islamskih derviša redova Alije (ZIDRA) was set up, interestingly appealing to the secular law relating to "self-managing" organizations in order to resist the orders of the official Islamic Community that it should disband. In 1986 it was reported to have about 540,000 adherents.

The Islamic Community has had to steer a delicate path between the highly secularized definition of "Muslims" fostered by the regime and an ability to reflect the undoubted revival of religious commitment and real piety among the faithful. Since the early 1970s, there have been repeated expressions of concern about the growth of Islamism in Yugoslavia, but in spite of the war this growth does not seem to have taken the radical form encountered in some other countries, such as Algeria or Egypt.

The accommodation between the **League of Communists** and the Islamic Community was put to the test, however, in 1983, with the trial of **Alija Izetbegović** and others, stemming from the publication of the ***Islamic Declaration***.

The breakup of the federation has presented the Muslim community in the region with some acute dilemmas. The designation of Muslims as a "nation" has resulted in a polarization of allegiance between (1) **political parties** that incline toward a traditionalist emphasis upon religious identity (increasingly the Party of Democratic Action—SDA) and (2) those that seek to interpret Bošnjak (Muslim) identity within a more modernizing and secular framework. The collapse of Yugoslavia into separate states has necessitated a reappraisal of the former structure of the Islamic Community, as well as a reconsideration of its political role in new states in which the actual situation of the Muslim faithful is quite varied, ranging from proximity to the governing party in Bosnia-Hercegovina to potential implication in an insurrectionary movement in Kosovo. The term of office of Reis Mustafa Cerić has been notable for the manner in which he has moved the office onto a much more public plane, engaging forcibly and articulately in debate about a variety of issues. The continuing fluidity of the political situation throughout the region plainly suggests that the Islamic Community (or more properly now, Communities) will continue to change for some time to come.

—*J. B. A.*

ISLAMIC DECLARATION

The *Islamic Declaration* is a plan for "Islamic renewal," written by **Alija Izetbegović**, that has come to provide a controversial focus for the discussion of **Muslim** identities in Yugoslavia. Written in 1970, the text was not publicly distributed until 1983. Together with his *Islam between East and West,* this pamphlet has made its author's reputation as one of the principal figures of political dissent in Yugoslavia. It bears curious comparison with the "Memorandum of the Serbian Academy of Sciences and Arts" in that it is widely cited as the foundation for different interpretations of events but evidently is rarely read with any care. Indeed, a Serbo-Croat edition was published only in 1988.

Following the serious civil disorder in **Kosovo** in 1981, the Yugoslav authorities were highly sensitive to challenges to the established basis of interethnic relations. The circulation of the *Declaration* resulted in the arrest, trial, and conviction of Izetbegović and his collaborators in 1983 on charges of "associating for the purpose of hostile activity and jeopardizing the constitutional order" and "acting from the standpoint of Islamic fundamentalism and Muslim nationalism." Sentenced to imprisonment, Izetbegović was released only on the eve of **Bosnia-Hercegovina**'s first multiparty elections in 1989, when he founded the **Party of Democratic Action**.

Although Izetbegović noted in his defense during his trial that the pamphlet never mentioned either Bosnia-Hercegovina or **Yugoslavia**, it is not hard to see the passages that would have identified it as subversive to Communist Party eyes. Its insistence upon the importance of the "supranational" *umma* (community of the faithful) implies a challenge to the supremacy of the state. Its characterization of Islam as essentially "anti-heroic" and rejecting the "immunity of public personalities" reads as a directly critical commentary on the place accorded to **Tito** in political life. Its references to Marxism as a "psychosis of historical necessity" and to "fossilized Marxist political economy" caused offense to the politically orthodox.

The interest and importance of the *Declaration* lies not in its possible role as an expression of conventional "dissent" but in its reflections upon Muslim identity. It defines its own aims in terms of a plea for "Muslim renewal" and the "Islamization of Muslims." It begins by addressing the poverty and weakness of the Muslim world and asking for an explanation of this inferiority. The second part investigates the attributes of "the Islamic order." Finally, it assesses the actual problems facing Islamic order in the contemporary world.

Central to the *Declaration* is the claim that Islam is not only a religion but a "demand for the conjunction of faith and knowledge, morals and politics, ideas and interests." Islamic order is a "unity of religion and law" and an "integrated way of life." Muslims find themselves misled by conservative theologians, in whose hands the Koran has "lost its active character while retaining what was irrational and mystic . . . lost its authority as law while gaining in sanctity as an object." Equally, the modernizing approach exemplified by Kemal Ataturk, the founder of the Turkish republic and president of Turkey from 1923–1938, reduces Islam to a religion, subordinating it in society to foreign models of thought, in relation to which Muslims have adopted a "vassal mentality."

The *Declaration* is a call to the "Islamization of Muslims" because only through renewal is it possible to establish an Islamic order in its completeness. This is possible only in countries where Islam is the faith of the majority; it cannot be imposed by force. "Islamic rebirth cannot begin without religious revolution, but it cannot be successfully continued and completed without a political one."

Although it is infused with a spirit of toleration toward other faiths and rejects the possibility of the violent imposition of Islamic order, the pamphlet clearly addresses a particular challenge to readers in multiconfessional Bosnia-Hercegovina. It has no place for the concept of Muslim identity "in the ethnic sense," detached from Islam. In a community where the demographic balance is moving in favor of Islam (and in which Muslims already form 44 percent of the population), it holds out the possibility of not only the "Islamization of Muslims" but also of the Islamization of *society.*

Although it must be remembered that the *Declaration* was written in 1970, it now hangs over the Party of Democratic Action as a huge ambiguity concerning the real nature of party's political program and, consequently, the kind of Bosnia that might be constructed that could also be acceptable to Serbs and Croats in collaboration with Muslims.

—J. B. A.

See also: Bošnjaci; Serbian Academy Memorandum

ISTRIA

Istria forms the northwestern peninsula of **Croatia** on its border with **Slovenia.** Istria saw relatively little fighting during the Yugoslav conflict, although the Yugoslav navy did bombard the town of Pula, which had been the Yugoslav navy's main base.

The region was a Roman territory; was conquered by Goths, Avars, and Byzantines; and from the thirteenth century was governed by the Venetian Republic until Napoleon brought the French Empire to the Balkans in the eighteenth century and incorporated Istria into the Illyrian Provinces. Austria became Istria's ruler in 1814. During the 500 years of Venetian influence, Istrian cities and towns had considerable powers of self-government. Through this history of continual change, the region has become ethnically mixed to a large extent, and many Istrians have developed a separate regional identity that has made them wary of Croatian nationalism. The strongest political forces in Istria since the defeat of the **League of Communists** have been Istrian regionalists. The majority of the Istrian political parties opposed **Franjo Tudjman**'s nationalist leadership of Croatia. They began to advocate separatism in response to the regime's suppression of difference and they favored regional identities over a jingoistic Croat nationalism. Tudjman attacked them for their opposition, especially during the political turmoil of early 1994, when the ruling party, the Croatian Democratic Union (HDZ), began to look increasingly embattled after having lost Stipe Mesić to the newly created Croatian Independent Democrats (HND). The Istrian Democratic Alliance (IDS), the main regional party, joined with six other opposition parties to contest the elections in October 1995 as a joint bloc; this move maintained the IDS's dominance by polling 18 percent of the vote.

—G. R. B.

ITALY

Relations between Italy and **Slovenia** have been bedeviled by territorial conflict concerning Trieste, property rights of Italians fleeing **Tito**'s regime, Slovenes living in Italy, and the problems of Slovenia's access to international waterways.

After World War I, Italy was given Slovene ethnic territory; it annexed ethnically mixed and purely Slovene-inhabited lands. At the end of World War II, Tito disputed the **border** between Yugoslavia and Italy. Eventually, in 1954, the Free Territory of Trieste was divided between Italy and Yugoslavia, with present-day Slovenia inheriting Yugoslavia's allocation. In 1974, the Osimo Agreements resolved the situation. In 1994, the Italian government under Berlusconi incorporated into its coalition the National Alliance, a descendant of the neofascist Italian Social Movement (MSI). The National Alliance demanded "irredenta" in **Istria** and **Dalmatia**, requiring abrogation of the Osimo Agreements and rectifications of the Italo-Slovene border. These demands, however, were not met. Since independence, Slovenia has sought an association agreement with the **European Union** (EU), but Italy has tried and successfully blocked negotiations to this end by demanding that Slovenia should first pay economic reparations to citizens who formerly owned land and property in Istria. In response, the Slovene government of **Janez Drnovšek** agreed to allow citizens who had resided in current Slovenia for three years to repossess their property. Furthermore, the Slovene constitution needed to be changed in order to allow both this and another demand forced upon Slovenia: to open up land for EU citizens. This successful Italian squeeze negates both the Osimo Agreements and a 1983 Rome Agreement. It is worth noting that Italy has not made reparations to its Slovene minority for the property, life, and rights lost mainly under fascist Italy. Hence, Italy has used its power in international bodies to extract gains bilaterally from Slovenia.

Berlusconi was succeeded by a more moderate government, which led to the unblocking of negotiations in March 1995 and the signing of an association agreement with the EU in June 1996.

Regarding minorities, the Slovene constitution guarantees special rights to Italians residing in Slovenia. The rights of Slovenes living in Italy are set forth in the 1954 London Memorandum and the Osimo Agreements. The Slovene minority in Italy possess a daily newspaper, radio stations, theater, and printing house. Likewise, the Italian minority in Slovenia operate a radio and television station. Cooperation between Slovenia and the Italian province of Friuli-Venezia Giula within the Alps-Adriatic working community has also eased tensions between the two peoples.

Finally, a 1968 agreement signed in Rome between Italy and Yugoslavia delimits the continental shelf in the Gulf of Trieste. As a consequence, Slovenia is now surrounded by **Croatian** and Italian territorial waters, and access to Slovene ports depends on right of "innocent passage" through foreign waters, posing potential prospects of diplomatic blackmail.

—I. R. B.

IZETBEGOVIĆ, ALIJA

Alija Izetbegović, president of **Bosnia-Hercegovina** since 1992, was the only president of the republics making up the defunct state of Yugoslavia who did not have a communist background. He entered politics in 1990, aged 65, as leader of the **Party of Democratic Action** (SDA), representing Bosnia's **Muslims.** He had a background of religious activism that earned him two years in prison from 1946 for organizing the Young Muslims, committed to defending Bosnia's Muslim Slav people. He later graduated in law from Sarajevo University and worked as a legal consultant to Bosnian firms. From 1983 to 1989 he served another jail sentence, his *Islamic Declaration* of 1970 being cited as evidence that he wished to proclaim a Muslim state in Yugoslavia. In the early 1990s his radical Serb opponents made constant references to that declaration, but until the end of the Bosnian war in 1995 they lacked stronger evidence that the "Islamization" of Bosnia was at hand.

Izetbegović has always identified with his party's "clerical" wing, which gradually became ascendant as the war in Bosnia caused intense suffering, particularly for rural Muslims. As the leader of the largest Bosnian party in 1990, he became president following the first contested **elections.** His solution for Yugoslavia's troubles was to turn the country into a loose confederation with most power devolved to republics and regions. Independence for Bosnia became his goal following the collapse of Yugoslavia in 1991. However, he misread the mood of Serb militants and placed too much trust in the idea that the West would intervene if Bosnia were to come under attack. The Serb onslaught began in April 1992 within days of the declaration of Bosnian independence. Lightly armed and ill-prepared government forces were driven from three-quarters of Bosnian territory.

Izetbegović himself was kidnapped in April 1992 by Serb fighters, his release being negotiated on Serbian television. In 1993 he reluctantly signed the **Vance-Owen Plan,** which effectively partitioned his state but which fell through because of rebel Serb opposition. He has appeared disorganized and indecisive, but his political skills have enabled him to isolate potential rivals and to appeal to Muslims as a symbol of their struggle for survival. In public he remained committed to a secular, Western-style democracy in Bosnia, but within the SDA Muslim nationalists were on the rise by 1994, and the war has helped to create the Muslim identity on nationalist lines hitherto absent from Bosnian politics.

In November 1995, Izetbegović was criticized for agreeing to the U.S.-brokered **Dayton Agreements,** which brought the war to an end. These agreements allowed for the retention of a separate **Bosnian Serb** entity within a theoretically united Bosnian federation, but they never explained how Muslim **refugees** could return to their homes, especially in the Serb "entity," from which over a million people were expelled after 1992.

A challenge to Izetbegović's leadership of the Muslim population from **Haris Silajdžić**, Bosnian foreign minister during most of the war, was repelled in 1996. In the elections held on 14 September 1996, under the terms of the Dayton Agreements, Izetbegović won overwhelming support from Muslims who feared that a Serb might occupy the federal presidency if they split their votes. However, he was only narrowly ahead of his Serb rival in elections that were widely criticized for numerous irregularities. Izetbegović's term of office runs for two years, and he is likely to remain the dominant figure in the politics of the Bosnian government territory as long as his health permits.

—*T. G.*

Alija Izetbegović, president of the Republic of Bosnia-Hercegovina and leader of the Party of Democratic Action. (Tanjug)

J

JABLANICA

Upriver from **Mostar** in the strategic **Neretva River Valley**, which divides **Hercegovina** and controls access to and from **Sarajevo** from the south, Jablanica is the location of the largest hydroelectric **energy** complex in **Bosnia-Hercegovina.** This complex supplied the Croatian coast with electricity during the Yugoslav period. Because of its strategic and economic importance, Jablanica was extensively fought over during the civil war between the Bosnian **Muslims** and **Bosnian Croats** in 1993.

Although it was a predominantly Bošnjak (Bosnian Muslim) town of 12,000 inhabitants before the war, Jablanica was awarded to the ministate **Herceg-Bosna** by the **Vance-Owen Plan** in 1993, thereby guaranteeing conflict between the Bošnjaks and Croats. Besieged by the **Croatian Council of Defense** (HVO) in league with the **Bosnian Serbs** in 1993, Jablanica's inhabitants, as well as a swollen population of **refugees,** were cut off from international **humanitarian aid** and food deliveries for long periods. As a result of a successful counteroffensive by the **Bosnian army** (Army of the Republic of Bosnia-Hercegovina—ARBH) later in 1993, Jablanica became a key position on the ARBH's new front line against the HVO on the Neretva River. Following the creation of the **Muslim-Croat Federation** in 1994, it was agreed to resume electricity generation at

IFOR troops at one of the power stations in Jablanica, 1996. (Army Public Relations, London)

Jablanica. This gave the Bosnian Croats major economic leverage over their Bošnjak partners in the federation. Since the **Dayton Agreements** of December 1995, Jablanica has been within the French zone of the **Implementation/Stabilization Force** (I/SFOR).

—*M. M.*

JAJCE

A town of 45,000 people before the Bosnian war, Jajce is one of the main urban settlements on the Vrbas River in west-central Bosnia. As well as being an important node of **communications** in the Vrbas Valley, Jajce, as one of the gateways to the **Krajina** in neighboring Croatia, is an industrialized town. Although inhabited mainly by Bosnian **Muslims** and **Bosnian Croats** before the war, Jajce fell to the **Bosnian Serbs** in October 1992 after a **siege** lasting five months, when the **Croatian Council of Defense** (HVO) abandoned the weaker **Bosnian army** (Army of the Republic of Bosnia-Hercegovina—ARBH). The town's civilian population fled before the advancing Serbs in one of the largest cases of "**ethnic cleansing**" during the Bosnian war.

The fall of Jajce caused great bitterness between Croats and Muslims. Jajce was awarded to the ministate **Herceg-Bosna** by the **Vance-Owen Plan** for Bosnia in 1993. It came under Bosnian-Croat control in the autumn of 1995 when large areas of western-central Bosnia fell to the HVO and the ARBH. As in 1992, this change of control was almost certainly the result of understandings between the Bosnian Serbs and Croats, given that the retreating HVO entered Jajce unopposed.

A key place in the history of communist Yugoslavia, Jajce was the location of the antifascist AVNOJ Congress in November 1943, when **Tito** proclaimed the creation of a new Yugoslav federation.

—*M. M.*

JANŠA, JANEZ

Janez Janša, born in Ljubljana in 1958, sprang to political prominence in **Slovenia** through the ***Mladina*** affair of 1988. As editor of that magazine, he criticized the privileged status of the **Yugoslav People's Army** and the use of soldiers to build a private villa for the defense minister of Yugoslavia. He and his colleagues were accused of and tried for stealing military secrets; the trial united Slovenes against authoritarian rule. Janša continued fostering an anti-Yugoslav youth culture, helping to foment the Slovene Spring, an uprising of nationalistic sentiment in 1988. He has been important as leader of the Social Democratic Party of Slovenia, and he served in the first postindependence government as minister of defense. He formed part of the Slovene delegation at the **Brioni** talks. Since the fall of the DEMOS (Democratic Opposition of Slovenia) coalition, he has been critical of Slovene foreign policy over the Bay of Piran and the Association Agreement with the **European Union**. Janša's personal account forms his book *The Making of the Slovenian State, 1988–1992: The Collapse of Yugoslavia* (Ljubljana: Mladinska knjiga, 1994).

—*I. R. B.*

See also: political parties

JANVIER, BERNARD

Lt.-Gen. Bernard Janvier, born in 1939 in Ardèches, France, was one of the commanders of the United Nations Protection Force (**UNPROFOR**) in Bosnia during the Yugoslav conflict. Nominated on 1 March 1995, Janvier replaced Gen. Bertrand de Lapresle. Four months after his assignment, when **Srebrenica** was attacked by the Bosnian Serbs, Janvier called off the airstrikes that had been launched by the North Atlantic Treaty Organization (**NATO**) because he was concerned about the life of the Dutch hostages held by the Serbs. UNPROFOR did not react and Srebrenica fell. United Nations (UN) officials later concluded that Janvier had deliberately allowed the city to fall to the Serbs; they noted that, in a briefing on 24 May 1995 in New York, he had argued for a withdrawal of UNPROFOR troops from the towns of Srebrenica and **Žepa** on the grounds that the towns were militarily indefensible. After an international conference in London on 21 July, it was decided that airstrikes should be used to protect the town of **Goražde** in case of Serb attack. The authority to decide to call for those punitive airstrikes was given to Janvier.

On 29 August, NATO launched airstrikes against strategic military Serb targets, especially around **Sarajevo**. The strikes were interrupted on 1 September for Janvier to negotiate with **Ratko Mladić**, the Bosnian Serb military commander. When those negotiations failed, the strikes were resumed for 15 days on 5 September.

—*A. H.*

JASENOVAC

Jasenovac lies some 70 miles southeast of the Croatian capital of Zagreb, near the confluence of the **Sava** and **Una Rivers,** and on the border with Bosnia. During World War II, it was the site of one of the **Ustaša** concentration camps where Serbs, Jews, and antifascists were imprisoned and thousands were killed. The camp has become a fundamentally ambiguous symbol in the Serb-Croat conflict, despite its undeniable status as a place of horror and death.

The numbers of victims from Jasenovac are fiercely disputed. Official Yugoslav statistics claim some 600,000 dead of all groups. Some Serb nationalist estimates claim 1,000,000 Serbs dead, whereas Croat nationalists have claimed far lower figures. **Franjo Tudjman**, the Croatian president and leader of the nationalist **Croatian Democratic Union** (HDZ), has claimed that only 60,000 Serbs died in all Ustaša concentration camps during the war.

These wartime atrocities, along with many smaller acts of violence committed in Serb villages in the **Krajina** and **Bosnia-Hercegovina** by the Ustaša, have returned as central elements of the contemporary political scene. Indeed, they have never been entirely absent because they were maintained as oral histories within families and villages during the socialist period when their public discussion was taboo. Serb nationalists have used these actions, whether as elements of objective or subjective history, to justify the retaliation in the face of the new Croatian nationalism of the HDZ, identifying this nationalism directly with the Ustaša movement. In this they were helped by the Croats themselves, who were stunningly insensitive in eagerly changing the state insignia to such symbols as the ***kuna*** (the new currency) and the ***šahovnica*** (an element of the flag) that were previously sported by the fascist Independent State of Croatia during World War II.

In the view of Croat nationalists, Jasenovac was a symbol of the socialist state's bias toward Serbs, implying that Croats were killers and others were victims. Croats who died at the hands of **Partizans** and Serb royalists, on the other hand, remained without a memorial.

The site of the camp, having been bulldozed immediately after the war, was turned into a memorial by the Communists in the 1960s. It was used to educate people about the evils of the fascist occupation of Yugoslavia; children went there on school trips. During the war in 1991, the museum was destroyed, partially through fighting and partially through deliberate vandalism. It is unclear who did the most damage. Books were ripped up, glass cases were smashed, files were scattered, furniture was broken, and graffiti from both Croats and Serbs defaced the walls.

Tudjman has caused additional offense to the Serb community by proposing that the camp should be redesignated as commemorating all victims of the war, including those Ustaša killed as war criminals and the recent dead from the war in 1991.

—G. R. B.

Reference: Djilas, Aleksa. *The Contested Country: Yugoslav Unity and Communist Revolution.* Cambridge, MA: Harvard University Press, 1991.

JEWISH QUESTION

Jews have made up a very small proportion of the population of Yugoslavia. However, there are three ways in which the Jewish presence in Yugoslavia has affected important issues.

The number of Jews in Yugoslavia fluctuated remarkably in post-1945 censuses, and many secularized Jews chose to declare themselves as ethnic "Yugoslavs." At the disintegration of Yugoslavia, Jews possibly numbered around 300,000. The growing historical importance of holocaust interpretation, i.e. the debate over the Holocaust, has provided a model in terms of which Serb nationalists have treated their own history. A great deal has been made in the past of the importance of the **Kosovo** stories as the basis for a "Christoslavic" mythology, in which Serbs have come to represent their own historical suffering as prefigured in the suffering of Christ, but recently the imagery of the Jewish Holocaust has also been appropriated as a model. In particular, **Ustaša** internment camps, such as the one at **Jasenovac**, have been presented very much as the equivalent for Serbs of Jewish experience in Dachau or Auschwitz. The poetic description of Serbs as a *nebeski narod* (heavenly people) has come to resonate not only with the religious imagery of Kosovo but almost equally with the description of the Jews as a "chosen people." Not surprisingly, Yugoslav Jews have tended to repudiate this kind of expropriation of their own historical symbolism in the service of Serb nationalism.

An additional ideological dimension of the conflict has been the tendency of Serbs (especially **Bosnian Serbs**) to depict themselves as engaged in a continuation of the historical struggle against "the Turk," taking up British historian R. G. D. Laffan's description of the Turks as the "guardians of the gate" of Europe against the incursion of **Islam.** This tendency to give excessive emphasis to the religious character of the war has been reflected in foreign policy. Serb politicians have drawn attention to the support given to Bosnia by the Islamic countries in a rather heavy-handed attempt to gain the diplomatic support of Israel. When Bosnian Serb leader **Radovan Karadžić** toured Britain at the time of the **London Conference,** he regularly shared a platform with a representative of the Serbian-Jewish Friendship Society.

These attempts to exploit the "Jewish question" to Serb advantage have contrasted dramatically with the stance generally taken during the conflict by Yugoslav Jews, who have been outspoken critics of nationalism. Slavko Goldstein, an active member of the former Croatian Liberal Movement, has been highly critical of nationalism. In **Sarajevo** the small Jewish community acquired during the siege a very high reputation for the disinterested work performed by its charity La Benevolencija, which has since been honored by the naming of a street.

The Israeli government intervened very actively in order to ensure that Yugoslav Jews who wished to leave the conflict areas could find shelter in Israel. As a result, the Jewish presence in the former Yugoslavia has been substantially reduced.

—J. B. A.

References: Friedenreich, Harriet Pass. *The Jews of Yugoslavia: A Quest for Community.* Philadelphia, PA: Jewish Publication Society of America, 1979; Sells, Michael A. *The Bridge Betrayed: Religion and Genocide in Bosnia.* Berkeley: University of California Press, 1996.

JNA

See **Yugoslav Peoples' Army**

JOVIĆ, BORISAV

Controversial politician Borisav Jović served as the member for **Serbia** on the collective federal presidency of Yugoslavia from 1989 to 1991. Born in 1928 in Batoćina, Serbia, Jović received his doctorate in economics from the University of Belgrade, where he joined the Communist Party (subsequently known as the **League of Communists**) of Yugoslavia in 1951. After holding several party, ministerial, and diplomatic posts, Jović became president of Serbia in 1988–1989, when he also became a close ally of rising Serbian leader **Slobodan Milošević.** Jović became Serbia's member on the federal presidency in 1989, and he was vice president of that body from May 1989 until May 1990, when he became president of the presidency. By that time, Milošević's elimination of the autonomy of Serbia's autonomous provinces (**Kosovo** and the **Vojvodina**) and his co-optation of **Montenegro** had given Belgrade four of the eight votes on the federal presidency, guaranteeing conflict with the non-Serb republics, especially **Slovenia** and **Croatia.** In January 1990 the League of Communists of Yugoslavia collapsed. In Serbia, this was followed by the formation of the **Socialist Party of Serbia** (SPS), of which Jović became president, leading the party to victory in Serbia's first postcommunist **elections** in December of that year.

A willing accomplice in Milošević's unconstitutional power games, Jović acted extremely provocatively on the federal presidency, at one point briefly resigning his position in a failed bid to paralyze the state body's functioning. Outmaneuvered by the Croatian representative, **Stipe Mesić,** who briefly became acting president of the presidency, Jović was forced to reassume his old position. When his term as president of the presidency expired in May 1991, Jović refused to step down in favor of Mesić, who should have succeeded him automatically.

Jović was a key figure in federal politics during Milošević's campaign to force the federal presidency to authorize a state of national emergency controlled by the **Yugoslav Peoples' Army** (JNA) in 1990–1991, although this attempt failed and further discredited Serbia's stance in the Yugoslav crisis. In Serbian politics Jović's actions were equally controversial. According to many observers, it was Jović who finally pressed then Federal Defense Minister Gen. **Veljko Kadijević** into authorizing the use of the JNA to suppress antigovernment demonstrations in **Belgrade** in March 1991.

With the progressive withdrawal of the non-Serbian members from the federal presidency during 1991, Jović continued to serve on a rump presidency consisting of Serbia and Montenegro. Following the promulgation of a new Federal

Republic of **Yugoslavia** in April 1992, he remained prominent in Serbian politics as president of the SPS and overseer of the party's second electoral victory in 1992. After Milošević's purge of government and the army in 1993, when the Serbian president was ridding himself of those who had served him during the late 1980s and early 1990s, Jović was increasingly sidelined. In 1995, Jović published a highly revealing and controversial diary from this period, thereby earning the permanent enmity of his former mentor.

—*M. M.*

Reference: Silber, Laura, and Alan Little. *The Death of Yugoslavia.* London: Penguin, 1995.

K

KAÇANIK, CONSTITUTION OF

In reaction to the new Serbian constitution of 1989, which did away with the autonomy of **Kosovo** for all practical purposes, the **Albanian** side (i.e. the Albanian members of the Kosovo parliament) proclaimed the existence of the "Republic of Kosovo" on 2 July 1990. Three days later, the parliament of **Serbia** declared the parliament of Kosovo to be illegal and threatened reprisals against parliamentarians in the capital, **Priština.** For this reason, Kosovo parliamentarians met on 7 September 1990 in the town of Kačanik ("Kaçanik" in Albanian), 35 miles south of Priština, and in an impromptu session promulgated the Constitution of the Republic of Kosovo. This constitution was confirmed in a Kosovo-wide referendum on 26 to 30 September 1991 by a majority vote of 87.5 percent. The republic was proclaimed but has not yet been internationally recognized.

—*R. E.*

KADIJEVIĆ, VELJKO

Veljko Kadijević was Yugoslav federal defense minister from 1988 to 1992 and hence political head of the **Yugoslav Peoples' Army** (JNA) at the beginning of the Yugoslav wars in 1990–1991. Born in 1925 at Glavin, near Split, Kadijević is of mixed Serb-Croat origin. He joined Tito's **Partizans** in 1943. After the war he was educated at the JNA Military Academy and at the Higher Military Academy in Belgrade. Kadijević was a protégé of Federal Defense Minister Adm. Branko Mamula during the 1980s. He served served as Mamula's immediate deputy from 1981 to 1988 and was appointed to Mamula's position upon the latter's retirement in 1988.

After initially supporting Federal Premier **Ante Marković**'s efforts to reform and preserve the Yugoslav federation in 1989–1990, Kadijević later attempted and failed to preserve that federation by force or to maintain the institutional autonomy of an army with no state to defend, becoming in the process a reluctant ally of the Serbian president, **Slobodan Milošević.** A key event in this attempt was Kadijević's involvement in the circumstances leading up to the JNA's suppression of antigovernment demonstrations in Belgrade in March 1991, after which Kadijević became increasingly estranged from Marković, who was later to demand the defense minister's resignation during the fighting in Croatia.

Although often charged with being in league with Milošević in pursuit of a "**Greater Serbia**," Kadijević was a relative moderate in the JNA leadership, where he always claimed to be legally defending the federation. He refused to be pushed by Serbia into declaring a national state of emergency without proper political authorization, which of course was not forthcoming from the hopelessly divided state presidency in 1991. This legalistic stance pitted him against his hard-line and increasingly uncontrollable deputy chief of staff, **Blagoje Adžić.** Toward the end of the first Serb-Croat war in Croatia in 1991, it became clear that Kadijević controlled neither the JNA hard-liners led by Adžić nor their ethnic Serb militia allies.

Kadijević's political confusion, as well as his inability or unwillingness to act at a critical time in the Yugoslav crisis, meant that he and Adžić were easily played against each other by Milošević for the latter's own purposes. With the end of the first Serb-Croat war and the deployment of the United Nations Protection Force (**UNPROFOR**) in Croatia in January 1992, Kadijević resigned as federal defense minister and was temporarily replaced by Adžić. Unique among the former leaders of the JNA during the early 1990s, he went on to publish his account of the events that overwhelmed him and the army he led. Entitled *Moje vidjenje raspada:*

vojska bez države (My memories of the break-up: army without a state) (Politika,1993), the book caused some controversy upon its publication in Belgrade.

—*M. M.*

KARADŽIĆ, RADOVAN

President of the **Republika Srpska** from 1992–1996, Radovan Karadžić is a poet, a musician, and by profession a psychiatrist. Born in **Montenegro** in 1945, Karadžić arrived in the Bosnian capital of Sarajevo in the 1950s, where he qualified and practiced as a psychiatrist. Imprisoned in the 1980s for offenses he claims were political in nature (and that others have alleged to be fraudulent), he rose to prominence after **elections** in **Bosnia-Hercegovina** at the end of 1990, in which his Serbian Democratic Party (SDS) gained around 30 percent of the vote. The SDS was included in a coalition government headed by Muslim leader **Alija Izetbegović**. From the outset, however, Karadžić expressed his support for the "**Greater Serbia**" project, which contributed to the breakup of Yugoslavia in 1991. Karadžić lacked commitment to Sarajevo's multicultural traditions and argued that the state **media** and government departments should be divided up on an ethnic basis, thereby calling for the ultimate partitioning of **Sarajevo** itself.

Radovan Karadžić, president of the Republika Srpska from 1992 to 1996. (Tanjug)

In November 1991, the SDS organized a referendum in majority Serbian areas, which overwhelmingly supported the notion of Bosnia staying in a Yugoslav or Serb state in the event of the federation disintegrating. A rival Serb parliament had already been established in **Pale**.

Beginning in 1992 Karadžić claimed that international **recognition** by outside powers had caused the war in Bosnia, but there was substantial evidence that a Serb takeover had been planned as far back as 1991, when the **Yugoslav Peoples' Army** had disarmed the republic's Territorial Defense Force. In September 1992, Secretary of State James Baker of the **United States** actually warned the **United Nations** (UN) Security Council of the aggression beginning to take shape in Bosnia.

Following the declaration of independence by the Bosnian government authorities, Karadžić and his supporters declared an independent Republika Srpska on 7 April 1992. Serb forces launched an assault on Sarajevo and began driving out Muslims from large areas of the republic with systematic ill treatment, detention, and murder. As a consequence, in 1994 Karadžić was placed under investigation by the **War Crimes Tribunal**.

On 21 April 1992, Karadžić told Warren Zimmerman, the last U.S. ambassador to Yugoslavia: "Today [Serbs] cannot live with other nations. They must have their own separate existence. They are a warrior race and they can trust only themselves to take by force what is their due." By mid-1994, the UN estimated that 9 out of every 10 Muslims and Croats living in territory controlled by Karadžić had been driven out or killed. Despite brutalities not witnessed in Europe since 1945, Karadžić became a highly visible figure on the European political stage, regularly attending international peace negotiations, receiving top Western emissaries, and being interviewed on television, where his good command of English and genial manner put a gloss on the atrocities of the brigands and gunmen who answered to him.

Karadžić's obsession with capturing Sarajevo, which he hoped would be the capital of a **Bosnian Serb** state, weakened his political and military capabilities. He neglected other parts of Serb Bosnia and underestimated the political and economic importance of **Banja Luka**. His star began to wane in 1993 when dissension broke out between the Serbs in Pale and those in Belgrade about whether to accept the **Vance-Owen** and **Owen-Stoltenberg** peace plans. The Bosnian Serbs proved obdurate, even though they would have been awarded 51 percent of Bosnian territory. After the collapse of the UN peace plans, the Belgrade media launched a **propaganda** offensive against Karadžić, accusing him of numerous irregularities. By 1994, he and his military commander, Gen. **Ratko Mladić**, were in dispute, and the much-vaunted Serb unity started to crumble.

The ability of Karadžić's family to escape the rigors of war earned him unpopularity among poorly paid soldiers trapped in a spiraling war. The collapse of the Serb-populated **Krajina** in Croatia in August 1995 and the massive **North Atlantic Treaty Organization** (NATO) bombardment of Bosnian Serb positions in September of that year were huge reverses for Karadžić. He and other Bosnian Serb leaders were excluded from the peace process of the **Dayton Agreements.**

On 27 June 1996, the UN War Crimes Tribunal formally indicted Karadžić with **genocide** and crimes against humanity, but on 29 June the SDS reelected him as leader for four more years by an almost unanimous vote. On 3 July he announced his candidacy for the presidency of the Republika Srpska in the elections of September 1996. Intense diplomatic pressures then built up to remove him from the political scene so as to prevent the Dayton settlement from being seen as a dead letter. U.S. diplomat **Richard Holbrooke**, the chief architect of the Dayton Agreements, claimed on 19 July that he had obtained the agreement of the Belgrade leadership to remove Karadžić from Bosnian Serb politics "immediately and permanently." Shortly afterward, Karadžić announced that he was stepping down from 11 political positions. Nevertheless, he remains at liberty owing to the reluctance of the **Implementation/Stabilization Force** (I/SFOR) military command to carry out the warrant for his arrest. He also retained the support of key elements in the **Orthodox Church**, and up until the end of 1996 it was widely thought that he continued to exercise political influence from behind the scenes.

—T. G.

Reference: Zimmerman, Warren. "Memoirs of the Last American Ambassador for Yugoslavia." *Foreign Affairs* 74, no. 2 (March–April 1995):20.

KARLOVAC

Karlovac (population 81,000 in 1991) lies approximately 35 miles southwest of the Croatian capital, **Zagreb.** It was founded in 1579 as a fortress that served as the headquarters of the Austrian **military frontier** (the **Krajina**). During much of its existence, it was the political and military center of Croatian life, whereas Zagreb was important as a cultural and religious center. Croatia, because of its unusual shape, is less than 35 miles wide in the vicinity of Karlovac; the capture of Karlovac by Serb forces would have cut the republic in two. The town's position on the border of the Krajina, with its large Serb population, meant that when war broke out in 1991, Karlovac was one of the first targets. It was shelled repeatedly from Serb positions farther into the Krajina, and the front line ran through the town for the next four years.

—G. R. B.

KARST

The Dinaric karst (from the Slovene word *kras*) is a geological formation, mainly limestone in character, that covers almost a third of the South Slav lands stretching the full length of the former Yugoslavia from the Julian Alps on the northwestern frontier of Slovenia south to the Albanian border and beyond. Its configurations of mountains, plateaus, and hydrological features were of great importance for guerrilla operations during the war of 1941–1945, and this importance has been echoed during the recent struggles in parts of western Croatia and Bosnia.

—J. J. H.

See also: terrain as a military factor

KASAGIĆ, RAJKO

Following the signing of the **Dayton Agreements** for **Bosnia-Hercegovina** in December 1995, Rajko Kasagić was endorsed as premier of the **Republika Srpska** (RS) by the **Bosnian Serb** parliament. A relatively moderate and pragmatic figure in the Serbian Democratic Party (SDS) and based in **Banja Luka**, Kasagić also enjoyed international support as a possible alternative to the former RS president, **Radovan Karadžić**. Willing to cooperate with the international community and with Serbian president **Slobodan Milošević** over Dayton, Kasagić was opposed by Karadžić from the start, culminating in Kasagić being forced out of office in May 1996.

Replaced by a more intransigent figure, **Gojko Kličković**, Kasagić remained politically active in Banja Luka, although he was not given high office after the rise to power of **Biljana Plavšić**, the new RS president after July 1996.

—*M. M.*

KIJEVO

Kijevo was a small village situated in the southern **Krajina** just 10 miles southeast of the region's "capital," **Knin**. The inhabitants of Kijevo were almost exclusively Croat. Entirely surrounded by Serb villages, it was always destined to be a thorn in the side of the leader of the Krajina Serbs, **Milan Martić**, and his proclaimed **Serb Republic of Krajina** because it potentially threatened the important road link between Knin and the Serb settlements to the south. On 18 August 1991, following the hostilities at **Plitvice** to the north, Martić issued an ultimatum to the Croatian police at Kijevo to leave the area within two days or risk an attack on the village. The Croatian refusal led eight days later to an all-out assault by Martić's men and the local force of the **Yugoslav Peoples' Army**, which flattened the village in 12 hours. Kijevo set a precedent for the rest of the Yugoslav conflict as the first example of territorial and **ethnic cleansing**.

—*J. J. H.*

KIR

See **Reihl-Kir, Josip**

KISELJAK

Located 15 miles west of **Sarajevo**, the town of Kiseljak controlled access to the capital of **Bosnia-Hercegovina** from the south and west when Sarajevo was besieged by the **Bosnian Serbs** from 1992 to 1995. A town of 24,000 people in 1991, Kiseljak's population was then predominantly Croat (52 percent) and Muslim (Bošnjak) (40 percent). Seized by the **Bosnian Croats** when the war broke out in 1992, Kiseljak thereafter remained a key stronghold of the **Croatian Council of Defense** (HVO). Despite being within artillery range of Sarajevo, Kiseljak's HVO forces did little to help lift the Bosnian Serb siege of the capital while at the same time restricting the flow of military and other supplies from Croatia to the mainly Bošnjak defenders. The fact that the HVO behaved in this manner at Kiseljak led to speculation that there was a secret understanding between the Bosnian Croat leadership and the Bosnian Serbs. Fought over during the Bosnian Croat–Bošnjak **civil war** in central Bosnia in 1993, Kiseljak remained under HVO control. Following the creation of the Implementation Force by the **Dayton Agreements** of December 1995, the town was placed within the French sector.

—*M. M.*

See also: Implementation/Stabilization Force (I/SFOR)

KLIČKOVIĆ, GOJKO

Premier of the **Republika Srpska** (RS) since May 1996, Gojko Kličković is a **Bosnian Serb** politician noted for his nationalist views. An economist by profession, he was always one of the more extreme elements in the Serbian Democratic Party (SDS). He was chosen by the president of the RS at the time, **Radovan Karadžić**, to supervise the evacuation of **Sarajevo**'s remaining Serb population after the reunification of the city in early 1996. Upon Karadžić's controversial dismissal of a relative moderate, **Rajko Kasagić**, as RS premier in May 1996, Kličković was appointed to this office. Unlike Kasagić, Kličković has never genuinely supported the idea of the sort of reunified Bosnian state as called for by the **Dayton Agreements** of 1995. With the subsequent unfolding of the power struggle between Karadžić and **Biljana Plavšić**, who replaced the former as RS president in July 1996, Kličković's position became more difficult in relation to the new Bosnian Serb leadership in **Banja Luka**.

—*M. M.*

KLJUIĆ, STJEPAN

A founding member of the Bosnian-Hercegovinian wing of the **Croatian Democratic Union** (HDZ), Stjepan Kljuić was elected to the seven-member Bosnian state presidency in December 1990. Although supportive of Bosnia's multicultural identity and politics in **Sarajevo**, he was compelled by events to lead his community into a closer alliance with the Bosnian **Muslims** (Bošnjaks) against the **Bosnian Serbs** after **Bosnia-Hercegovina** descended into civil war in April 1992. A relatively moderate Croatian nationalist from central Bosnia, Kljuić was opposed to the ethnic "cantonization" of Bosnia-Hercegovina as advocated by Croatian president **Franjo Tudjman** and the so-called "**Hercegovina Lobby**" centered on secessionist **Herceg-Bosna**. Because of his opposition to the Hercegovinian

Croats, then led by **Mate Boban**, Kljuić was forced to resign from the state presidency in November 1992, reportedly under pressure from Tudjman, in favor of a Croat separatist, Miro Lazić.

Although often reviled by the government-controlled **media** in Zagreb and the Hercegovina Lobby, Kljuić was reelected to the state presidency in October 1993, indicating that he remained popular in central Bosnia, the main area of **Bosnian Croat** settlement in Bosnia-Hercegovina prior to the Bošnjak-Croat conflict of 1993–1994. By this time Kljuić had split from the local HDZ, which he had come to regard as a negative political force that had led his community into disaster by the end of 1993. A member of the state presidency until that body was replaced by the institutions provided for by the **Dayton Agreements** of December 1995, Kljuić participated in the **elections** of September 1996 as leader of the integrationist Republican Party (part of the electoral alliance known as the Joint List for Bosnia-Hercegovina), finding his electoral base in central Bosnia and Sarajevo. Kljuić, now in semiretirement, remains the president of the National Olympic Committee of Bosnia-Hercegovina.

—*M. M.*

See also: cantons; political parties

KNIN

Knin is a town in the south of Croatia (population 43,000 in 1991) situated in the Dinaric Alps, about 50 miles east of **Zadar**. It is an important road and rail junction and a hub for connections between the Croatian capital of **Zagreb** and the **Dalmatian** coast. The town lies in an area of the Dalmatian hinterland that is between 75 percent and 90 percent Serb, and it was the center for the Serbian Democratic Party (SDS). On 17 August 1990, the Croatian Interior Ministry attempted to reimpose Croat control over Knin, where the police force, led by **Milan Martić**, had been defying the local commander of police based in Šibenik on the coast. **Milan Babić**, mayor of Knin, was leading the campaign for Serb autonomy. The town was also the center for the Knin corps of the **Yugoslav Peoples' Army** (JNA), which from early summer 1991 was led by Lt. Col. **Ratko Mladić.**

Knin was retaken by the **Croatian Army** in **Operation Storm** on 5 August 1995, after only one day of fighting. The vast majority of Serbs left for Bosnia and Serbia, and the political and military leadership disappeared before the Croatian Army reached Knin.

—*G. R. B.*

KOLJEVIĆ, NIKOLA (1936–1997)

A former vice president of the **Republika Srpska** (RS), Nikola Koljević remained an ally of Serbian president **Slobodan Milošević** at a time when most of the **Bosnian Serb** leadership had turned against their former mentor. Born in 1936 at Banja Luka, **Bosnia-Hercegovina**, Koljević read English literature at the University of Belgrade, becoming a respected academic and Shakespearean scholar by the 1970s. Following the accidental death of his eldest son, Djordje, in 1977, Koljević found solace in the **Orthodox** faith, becoming an extreme Serb nationalist in the process. At the time of Bosnia's first postcommunist **election** in 1990, he was elected as one of two ethnic Serbs on the Bosnian presidency, alongside his fellow academic at the University of Sarajevo, **Biljana Plavšić.** Along with the rest of the leadership of the Serbian Democratic Party (SDS), Koljević left the government in Sarajevo when Bosnia-Hercegovina descended into civil war in April 1992. At nearby **Pale**, the capital of the RS, Koljević became one of four top SDS lead-

Nikola Koljević, vice-president of the Republika Srpska from 1992 to 1996. (Tanjug)

ers, the others being Biljana Plavšić, **Radovan Karadžić**, and **Momčilo Krajišnik**. Although more urbane than some of his SDS colleagues, Koljević showed no sign of harboring any doubts about the barbaric methods used by his side throughout the Bosnian war.

During the early days of the siege of **Sarajevo** in 1992, it was reported that it was Koljević, the onetime scholar, who signed the order for the bombardment and destruction of the city's national library by the **Bosnian Serb Army** (BSA). Koljević was nevertheless able to maintain relatively cordial relations with the main representatives of the international community, with whom he could converse in fluent English. Unlike his superior, Karadžić, Koljević was thus never to be indicted as an alleged war criminal by the International **War Crimes Tribunal** in The Hague. Koljević was also the only one of the main Bosnian Serb leaders to stay on good terms with Milošević throughout the Bosnian war—loyalty that was to cost him a great deal once Karadžić and Milošević parted company in 1993.

A relative lightweight in the Bosnian Serb hierarchy, Koljević was dismissed as RS vice president by Karadžić just after the finalization of the **Dayton Agreements** in December 1995. Ironically, the relatively pragmatic Koljević then went into the political wilderness, just as his two more extreme colleagues, Plavšić and Krajišnik, went on to higher positions in post-Dayton Bosnia. At the time of Karadžić's removal from office in July 1996, Koljević was working as head of the Writers' Union in the RS, an insulting demotion that rankled him at a time when he also felt betrayed by Milošević. In January 1997, he committed suicide, although some observers claimed that he may have been murdered by Milošević's secret police to prevent him from revealing what he knew about the Serbian president's role in the war.

—*M. M.*

KONTIĆ, RADOJE

Radoje Kontić has served as prime minister of the Federal Republic of **Yugoslavia** (FRY) since March 1993. Born in Cetinje, **Montenegro**, in 1941, he was a member of the **League of Communists** (LC) of Montenegro and then the Party of Democratic Socialists of Montenegro (PDSM). He has been a close associate of Montenegrin president **Momir Bulatović** since the latter, with the support of **Serbia**, replaced the incumbent LC leadership in **Podgorica**. Kontić is also considered a Montenegrin ally of Serbian president **Slobodan Milošević**. Following the forced resignation of former Federal Premier **Milan Panić** in December 1992, Kontić was voted into his present office by the FRY assembly after more than two months of difficult negotiation over balancing Montenegrin interests within the federal government. In February 1993 he formed a government consisting of the **Socialist Party of Serbia** and the PDSM. On the key issue of the union between Serbia and Montenegro, Kontić has sought to balance the often conflicting interests of the two constituent republics of the federation, although not with great success in recent years. Kontić is one of the few remaining Montenegrins currently occupying leading positions in **Belgrade**.

—*M. M.*

KOPER (BAY OF PIRAN)

When **Croatia** and **Slovenia** became independent on 25 June 1991, they declared that no territorial claims existed between them, although several disputes emerged when the **borders** were demarcated. The most important set of these disputes involves the maritime border adjacent to the port of Koper, in the Bay of Piran, and relates to a land boundary, airspace, the extension of Slovenian territorial waters, fishing rights, and access to international waters. The land boundary dispute concerns Slovenian claims to four hamlets south of the Dragonja River, which empties into the Bay of Piran. In the past these hamlets have been administered by Croatia. The boundary was thought to have been settled in 1954, but there appears to be a difference between Slovene cadastral and Croatian administrative evidence.

Under the former Yugoslavia, the bay was an internal water in the terms of international law. Currently, each side controls up to the median line that splits the Bay of Piran, with the Slovenian police providing law enforcement over most of the bay as they did prior to independence. Ironically, even if Slovenia were to make good its claim to the whole Bay of Piran, Slovenian territorial waters would still be enclosed by Italian and Croatian waters, with no access via international waters to the open Adriatic Sea. This situation is a legacy of the Treaty of Osimo in 1975 between **Italy** and **Yugoslavia**, which delimited the two countries' maritime border in the Gulf of Trieste, and of a treaty signed in Rome in 1968 that demarcated Italian and Yugoslav continental shelves. Consequently, ships voyaging to Slovenia's major port of Koper must claim "innocent passage" through Croatian or Italian territorial waters. One suggestion to obviate this difficulty is for Slovenia to be given a sea corridor to international waters, but this would affect Croatian sovereignty.

The dispute is unlikely to escalate since Koper is beneficial to Croatia, although it competes with the Croatian port of Rijeka. Koper is also important to landlocked **Austria**, **Hungary**, Slovakia, and the Czech Republic. Croatia depends on transit routes through Slovenia to move its goods into Western and Central Europe.

An extra problem is that the Slovene airfield near Sečovlje is so close to the disputed boundary that airplanes normally use Croatian airspace to land and take off. If the border were shifted to include the four hamlets' area, then Slovene aircraft could remain in Slovene airspace.

Apart from these disputes over borders and **communications**, other minor disputes exist between the two countries. These include the ownership of forests near Mount Snežnik; the army barracks occupied by Slovene military units on Mount Zumberak and claimed by Croatia; a boundary on the Drava River; and a controversy over the delimitation of the village Raskrižje on the Mura River. A potential problem concerning the exploitation of the jointly built nuclear power station at Krško has recently been resolved.

The controversy has stirred political passions in Slovenia, with **Janez Janša**, erstwhile minister of defense and leader of the Social Democratic Party, wanting a more uncompromising attitude toward Croatia, whereas Zmago Jelinčič, leader of the right-wing Slovenian National Party, wants large-scale border changes.

Relevant to both the land and sea dispute are two papers specified in the references section.

—I. R. B.

References: International Boundaries Research Unit. "Croatia and Slovenia: The Four Hamlets Case." *IBRU Boundary and Security Bulletin* (January 1995); ———. "The Maritime Borders of the Adriatic Sea." *Maritime Briefing* 1, no. 8 (1996).

KOŠEVO HOSPITAL

One of the principal hospitals in the Bosnian capital of **Sarajevo**, Koševo is situated in the northeast of the city, close to the center. During the siege of Sarajevo, it became an important symbol of resistance as a result of extensive international press coverage given to the work of its (multiethnic) medical staff, who sustained their service uninterrupted in spite of the fact that the hospital regularly came under artillery fire. The symbolic importance of Koševo was heightened by the fact that the deliberate targeting of such locations as hospitals is in direct contravention of the Geneva Conventions. This enabled the Bosnian government both to underline its claim that the war was genocidal in character and to augment the **media** image of the inhumanity of the city's besiegers.

—J. B. A.

KOSOVO

Kosovo, also known as Kosova, is a region in the southern Balkans bordering on **Albania**, **Macedonia**, **Serbia** proper, and **Montenegro**. Its capital is **Priština** ("Prishtinë" in Albanian). Kosovo has a territory of 10,897 square kilometers and an estimated population of about two million. There are no reliable statistics as to the ethnic groups populating Kosovo, but it is generally accepted that speakers of the **Albanian** language make up 85–90 percent of the population, with Serbian speakers accounting for most of the rest (there are also small minorities of **Turks**, Romani, and Cirkassian speakers). After the collapse of the **Ottoman Empire** on the eve of World War I, Kosovo, which has been inhabited by Serbs and Albanians for centuries, was conquered by Serb forces. The inclusion of Kosovo in the new "Kingdom of Serbs, Croats, and Slovenes" left almost half the Albanian population in the Balkans outside their Albanian homeland, but it helped ensure the survival of Serbian culture in the "holy lands" of what was once known as Old Serbia. The Kosovo Albanians did not fare any better under their Serb rulers than they had under the Ottoman sultans. Denied all linguistic, cultural, and educational rights, they were forced to play the part of simple peasant farmers in a country that the South Slavs considered their exclusive property. Albanian-language schools remained as unlawful as they had been under the Turks, and even the possession of Albanian-language books was dangerous for the few people in Kosovo who could read at that time.

"**Ethnic cleansing**" was a keystone of Serbian policy toward Kosovo from the very start. In the

1920s and 1930s, indeed up to 1960, hundreds of thousands of Albanians were forcibly expelled from their homeland, mostly to Turkey, under the absurd pretext that they were Turks; Serbian colonists were more than willing to occupy and settle the newly vacated farmlands. Characteristic of the attitude taken by the Serbian authorities before World War II was a memorandum presented to the Belgrade government on 7 March 1937 by noted Serbian historian **Vaso Čubrilović** on the expulsion of the Albanians. As a consequence, Albanian loyalties to the royalist Yugoslav state were divided when Axis powers occupied Kosovo in 1941 and reunited the province with Albania, giving Kosovo Albanians schools and cultural facilities in their own language for the first time.

In early 1945, Kosovo was formally returned to Yugoslavia after President **Tito** persuaded communist leaders in Albania to give up the principle of self-determination and accept a "Marxist solution" for the region. Tito realized he would never receive Serbian support for a referendum on self-determination. On its reincorporation into Tito's Yugoslavia, Kosovo was nonetheless declared an autonomous region within the Republic of Serbia, not an integral part of Serbia.

The extreme political divergence between Yugoslavia and Albania that erupted in 1948 made it evident to Kosovo Albanians that they could not look to the Albanian capital of Tirana for anything more than moral support in the areas of culture and education. The Albanian **language** had finally been proclaimed one of the official languages of Kosovo, but the linguistic and educational rights that were theoretically enjoyed by the Albanian population in Kosovo long remained more abstract than concrete. Tito's would-be successor, Vice President Aleksandar Ranković, made active use of the secret police to repress and terrorize the Albanian population, whom he despised, in favor of a "**Greater Serbia**," until his fall from grace at the **Brioni** Plenum in July 1966.

The improvement of Yugoslav-Albanian relations in the wake of the Soviet invasion of Czechoslovakia in 1968, as well as the establishment of full diplomatic ties between the two countries in February 1971, brought about a political thaw for the Kosovo Albanians. In 1968, they won the right to fly their national flag, and in November 1969 the bilingual University of Priština was opened, facilitating higher education in Albania for the first time. Full cultural autonomy was first achieved after much delay under the Yugoslav Constitution of 1974, though only in Kosovo itself, not for the large Albanian community in Macedonia.

The spirit of Yugoslav brotherhood and unity and the semblance of autonomy and freedom that the Albanians enjoyed in the 1970s were brought to an abrupt end in 1981. The popular demand for republican status and equality with the other peoples of the Yugoslav federation (a demand supported by the vast majority of the population of Kosovo) was met with tanks and automatic rifles.

The suppression of the uprising of March–April 1981 signaled the end of peaceful coexistence in Kosovo and, at the same time, the beginning of the demise of Yugoslavia. Throughout the 1980s, the political and economic situation in the province deteriorated, and as a result intercommunal relations took a drastic turn for the worse—a harbinger of what was to come for all of Yugoslavia in the early 1990s. The mass rallies of 1989 held by Serb ultranationalists, under the leadership of **Slobodan Milošević**, to commemorate the six hundredth anniversary of the **Battle of Kosovo**, as well as the open Serbian military invasion of Kosovo in the summer of 1990, brought the province to the verge of civil war. The elected parliament and government of Kosovo were deposed, and the Albanian **media** were stifled; *Rilindja*, the only Albanian-language daily newspaper, was banned, and all Albanian-language radio and television broadcasting was shut down. Since then, "emergency legislation" has facilitated the direct takeover of all Kosovo industry and the firing not only of Albanian management but of all employees of Albanian nationality—literally hundreds of thousands of workers. In the autumn of 1991, teaching at the University of Priština was suspended, with the exception of courses reserved for students from the Serb minority, and all Albanian professors were expelled. Albanian-language elementary and secondary schools have been closed down. Nowhere in Europe, with the exception of **Bosnia-Hercegovina**, have human rights been so flagrantly and so systematically violated as in Kosovo.

The new Serbian constitution of 1989 did away with the autonomy of Kosovo for all practical purposes. The Albanians proclaimed the Republic of Kosovo on 2 July 1990. In an impromptu session held in Kačanik ("**Kaçanik**" in Albanian) on 7 September 1990, the "illegal" Parliament of Kosovo promulgated its own constitution. In a referendum held later that month, 87.5 percent of the population voted for Kosovo as an independent and sovereign state. The republic was proclaimed but has never been internationally recognized.

Since that time, Kosovo has been on the verge of **civil war**. Recognition of the tragedy of Bosnia is the only thing that has kept the two communities from total disaster. The ruling Serb minority continues to view Kosovo as an integral part of Serbia and ignores all claims of the Albanian majority for equal rights and national self-determination. The Albanians, for their part, who suffer from continuous human rights violations by the Serbian police, military, and legal system, have created a parallel state of their own in Kosovo under the auspices of a Kosovo government in exile. Alternative public institutions (schools, university, medical facilities, social assistance, tax system) have been put into place and function in a rudimentary manner.

By 1997, however, most Albanian political leaders in Kosovo and much of its population realized that the **Democratic League of Kosovo** (**LDK**) politics of passive resistance to Serb rule had achieved virtually nothing after seven years of heavy-handed occupation. The demands of the Kosovo Albanians were simply being ignored by Belgrade and by the international community. Increasing frustration resulted in increasing desire for more active forms of resistance. Among such alternatives has been the rise of an embryonic group calling itself the Kosovo Liberation Army (KLA, or "Ushtria Çlirimtare e Kosovës" [UÇK] in Albanian), which began isolated attacks on Serbian officials and on police and military installations, particularly around Skenderaj/Srbica in the Drenica region. By the end of 1997, the Serbian authorities had lost military control over the whole of the Drenica region, at least during nighttime. The economic, political, and social collapse of the Republic of Albania in March 1997, during which all the country's arsenals were plundered and huge amounts of weaponry dispersed among the population, resulted not only in increasing instability for the region as a whole, but also in a clandestine trade in arms. Paramilitary groups such as the KLA were, for the first time, in a position to extend operations in order, in their view, to defend the population from Serb attacks. The situation boiled over in March 1998 when a Serb military offensive in Drenica led to the slaying of dozens of Albanians, including women and children.

The only positive element of the current crisis is that the international community has finally been forced to take note of the oppression of the Kosovo Albanians and of the urgency of the situation. It remains to be seen whether the rest of the world will be any better at coming to terms with Kosovo than it was at dealing with Bosnia.

—*R. E.*

References: Elsie, Robert. *Kosovo: In the Heart of the Balkan Powderkeg.* Boulder, CO: East European Monographs, 1997; Malcolm, Noel. *Kosovo: A Short History.* London: Macmillan, 1998; Vickers, Miranda. *Between Serb and Albanian: A History of Kosovo.* London: Hurst, 1998.

KOSOVO, BATTLE OF

The Battle of Kosovo was fought on 28 June 1389 between **Ottoman** forces led by Sultan Murat and an alliance of Christian forces led by Serb prince Lazar. At the battle, the leaders of both armies perished and their troops withdrew from the field, neither side having won the day. Following the battle the Ottoman forces continued their advance into the Balkans, taking the last Serb fortress of Smederovo in 1459, after which **Bosnia-Hercegovina**, too, and then most of the coast of **Dalmatia** fell to the Turks. One of the immediate results of this advance was the migration of large numbers of Serbs in an attempt to escape domination by **Islam**. These early migrations account for the large numbers of Serb **Orthodox** communities found today in northern Bosnia and until recently in the **Krajina** region of **Croatia**.

The historical dimension of the Battle of Kosovo is in many ways less significant than its cultural meaning for Serb national consciousness; this meaning has been maintained by the cycle of epic ballads telling the story of the struggle against the Turks. The songs were composed according to the tradition of epic ballads that existed in all European cultures, except that these ballads lasted longer among the Serbs, since development of a literate public was stunted by the presence of the Turks. The purpose of such ballads is to endow the history of a national community with moments of both great heroism and great tragedy. Hence, there came to be three essential ingredients to the Serb story of Kosovo. First, Serb prince Lazar is offered a choice by the prophet Elijah between an earthly or a heavenly kingdom for himself and his people. His choice of the heavenly kingdom means that the Serbs will lose at Kosovo. Second, an important heroic part of the tale is that Serb hero Miloš Obilić kills the Turkish sultan. Third, the Serb defeat is guaranteed by the treachery of Vuk Branković, who flees the field instead of entering the battle with reinforcements. The element of betrayal is a late addition to the legend, probably invented during the sixteenth century.

The Kosovo story as told here bears little relationship to the actual events of the battle, although it has come to symbolize for many Serbs the disappearance of their empire and the beginning of their subordination under Ottoman rule. As a cultural icon, this Kosovo of folk memory has often been manipulated by nationalist politicians as a rallying call for solidarity and loyalty, as in the period of "national awakening" in the late 1980s, when the leaders of the different national groups all over the former Yugoslavia called on the population to stand firm against the perceived threats made by neighboring groups. The glory and tragedy expressed within the cycle of songs are simply a response to the generic demands of epic ballads. However, in an era in which those demands of artistic form are less well understood, the heroic elements of these ballads are open to interpretations that advocate violence and fear—an outcome at odds with the original purpose of the songs.

—D. A. N.

KOSOVO, DEMOCRATIC LEAGUE

See **Democratic League of Kosovo**

KRAGUJEVAC

Located 75 miles southeast of the Serbian capital of Belgrade in the Šumadija region, Kragujevac is a city with a population of nearly 200,000 whose prosperity had depended upon heavy industry. As the home of the giant enterprise Crvena Zastava (Red Flag), which focuses on domestic automobile manufacture, aircraft engineering, and munitions, it had been the main supplier to the **Yugoslav Peoples' Army** before and in the early stages of the Yugoslav conflict. Thus, Kragujevac indirectly supplied the Croatian and Bosnian forces who appropriated its products on their territory by force, circumstance, or connivance for military and related purposes. International **sanctions** hit particularly hard against the plant and its production of Zastava (Yugo) cars, which from 1986 to 1991 (following a complete modernization of the assembly lines) had been enjoying considerable success with quality-controlled exports to Western Europe and the United States. The economy of Kragujevac collapsed.

—J. J. H.

THE KRAJINA

"The Krajina" is the abbreviation used to represent the Republika Srpska Krajina (Republic of the Serbian Krajina—RSK), the name by which the secessionist Serb state set up within **Croatia** was known between 1991 and 1995. The name referred back to the former Habsburg **military frontier**, as local Serbs chose to emphasize their continuity with the culture of the free militias of the old imperial *Vojna krajina*. Whether the gun culture of these Serbs, remarked upon by many commentators, was linked to this centuries-old tradition of bearing arms or whether it had more to do with the Socialist Federal Republic of **Yugoslavia**'s institution of local territorial defense militias is difficult to say.

The presence of the Serbs in the Krajina presented the Socialist Republic of Croatia with certain demographic problems. Croatia, as with most modern states, was in no way nationally homogeneous. This situation was conducive to conflicts centered around national identity. Political discontent in Croatia frequently became focused upon the positions of Serbs in Croatia and of **Serbia** within Yugoslavia, most notably during the fascist **Ustaša** regime of 1941–1945. Croatian nationalism revived with some force during the **Croatian Spring** of 1971–1972, when the Croatian cultural society Matica Hrvatska became vocal in relation to a number of issues regarding **language**, the proportion of Serbs in government, and the economic position of the republic. The events of that year created a conflict between Serbs in Croatia and Croat nationalists over rights to cultural autonomy.

In 1990, as the newly elected government of the **Croatian Democratic Union** (Hrvatska Demokratska Zajednica—HDZ) began to introduce changes to the Croatian constitution and to the structure of Croatian society, Serbs interpreted the situation as a threat to their national rights and formed their own Serbian National Council to defend these rights. The referendum on Croatian independence of August 1990 was accompanied by serious disorder in several areas with mainly Serb populations, and by December these areas had declared their autonomy from Croatia. A vicious cycle of deteriorating community relations set in during 1991, with the creation of **paramilitary** formations on both sides. It is clear that there was a great deal of political manipulation by **Slobodan Milošević**, the leader of Serbia's ruling Serbian Socialist Party, and his political client, **Milan Babić**, but it was partly due to the precedents of the Ustaša terror and the Croatian Spring that such propaganda was able to take hold.

By mid-1991 there was widespead insurrection in the region, and by October three areas had been wrested from government control, declaring themselves to be autonomous regions: the area around and to the north of **Knin**, western **Slavonia**, and Baranja with western Srem. In December these areas declared themselves to be an autonomous state, the Republic of the Serbian Krajina. Milan Babić, the militant Serb political leader of the Knin region, was able to oppose the **Vance Plan** in December 1991 with the claim that disarming the Serbs of the Krajina was simply inconceivable; he knew that this position would be supported by many Serbs.

Elections were held for an 84-seat assembly in the RSK on 12 December 1993. The Serbian Democratic Party, led by Babić, emerged as the strongest party, although **Milan Martić** defeated Babić in the presidential race.

The project of creating a Serb state based in the Krajina collapsed under the impact of the **Croatian Army**'s **Operation Flash** and **Operation Storm** in May and August 1995.

—G. R. B. and J. B. A.

KRAJINA SERB ARMY

See **Serb Army of the Krajina**

KRAJIŠNIK, MOMČILO

Elected to the collective presidency of **Bosnia-Hercegovina** in September 1996, Momčilo Krajišnik was throughout the war the senior deputy to, and close associate of, **Radovan Karadžić**, the former leader of the **Republika Srpska** (RS); he also served a number of years in jail with Karadžić for alleged fraud in the 1980s. He first came to prominence when he was elected as a deputy of the nationalist Serbian Democratic Party (SDS) in December 1990. A founding member of the SDS alongside Karadžić, Krajišnik also became the parliamentary speaker of the Bosnian Republican Assembly in December 1990. In October 1991, in an attempt to prevent the **Bosnian Croats** and **Muslims** (Bošnjaks) from declaring the republic's sovereignty, he ended the parliamentary session at which this development was debated. In the same month, he became the speaker of the People's Assembly of the RS, which subsequently declared its adherence to the Yugoslav federation.

A committed supporter of the "**Greater Serbia**" project, Krajišnik remains a fervent Serb nationalist, but he was unlike the rest of the SDS leadership in being able to maintain cordial relations with the Bošnjaks and other opponents until Bosnia-Hercegovina finally descended into **civil war** in April 1992. These relatively civil relations often went back to the Yugoslav period, notably in relation to Bošnjak president **Alija Izetbegovič**.

Despite being closely associated with Karadžić throughout the three years of Bosnian civil war, Krajišnik seemed not to attract the international hostility that destroyed his superior, and he managed to retain relatively good relations with the main representatives of the international community. Although reportedly investigated for involvement in war crimes, Krajišnik has never been indicted for such offenses by the International **War Crimes Tribunal**. In July 1996, when Karadžić was removed from office and indicted as a war criminal by the Hague Tribunal, Krajišnik played an important mediatory role with the international community. He had played a similar role when Karadžić removed relatively moderate RS premier **Rajko Kasagić** from office two months earlier.

In September 1996, in the first post-**Dayton** general **elections** in Bosnia-Hercegovina, Krajišnik was elected to the three-member collective presidency, alongside Izetbegovič and Bosnian Croat leader **Kresimir Zubak**. During the poll, Krajišnik gained the second-largest number of votes after Izetbegovič, although the validity of his electoral performance was widely disputed owing to alleged irregularities at polling stations in the RS. During the power struggle between Karadžić and a rival, **Biljana Plavšić**, in 1996–1997, Krajišnik sided with his former mentor in **Pale**. Like Karadžić, Krajišnik is suspected of widespread corruption and is said to control a number of lucrative import monopolies.

In the event of Karadžić's final political demise, Krajišnik will almost certainly go down as well.

—*M. M.*

KRASNIQI, MARK

Mark Krasniqi was born in 1920 at Glavačica ("Gllavaçica" in Albanian) in Kosovo and graduated from high school at Prizren in 1941. From 1941 to 1943 he studied literature at the University of Padua (Italy), and from 1946 to 1950 he studied geography and ethnography at the University of Belgrade. From 1947 to 1949 he was also responsible for Albanian-language programs on Radio Belgrade. Having graduated in 1950, he worked from 1951 to 1961 for the Serbian Academy of Sciences and Arts of Sciences as assistant professor and later as a full professor. After finishing his doctorate at the University of Ljubljana in 1960, he returned to **Kosovo**, where he taught at the University of **Priština** from 1961 up until 1981, when he was expelled in the wake of the March/April uprising. Over the years Krasniqi has served as dean of the faculty of law and economics, as head of the Academy of Sciences and Art of Kosovo, and as head of the Kosovo Writers' Union (1970). His expulsion from the university in 1981 caused him to become increasingly involved in party politics in Kosovo, where, as head of the Albanian Christian Democratic Party of Kosovo, he is now a leading figure in public and political life. Krasniqi is also the author of works of literature, studies in ethnography, and lucid political essays on the question of Kosovo's autonomy.

—*R. E.*

KRIVA PALANKA

The settlement of Kriva Palanka (population of about 30,000) in northeast **Macedonia** lies close to the border with **Serbia**. In June 1994 tension in the region heightened when units of the **Yugoslav Peoples' Army** occupied high ground to the north of the town. It was suggested that the **border** between the Republic of Macedonia and Serbia should run along the watershed to the south of its previously accepted line. The road through Kriva Palanka is one of the primary **communication** routes between Macedonia and **Bulgaria**; this route would also be followed by the proposed new rail link between the two countries. The move was of considerable potential strategic significance to Macedonia, in that it created an enhanced travel and supply route east and west. Following mediation by representatives of the United Nations Preventive Deployment Force (**UNPREDEP**), the incursion ended the following month.

—*J. B. A.*

KRŠKO POWER STATION

Although Slovenia seceded early from Yugoslavia and from the war itself, it was not left without problems of property and territory. The only nuclear power plant built in the former Yugoslavia had been a joint project betwen **Slovenia** and **Croatia** at Krško on the **Sava River** between the capitals **Ljubljana** and **Zagreb**, only 15 miles into Slovenia from the border between the two republics. After independence there was serious disagreement between the two parties concerning distribution of the plant's debts and costs, as well as of the plant's power itself. Slovenia sought to close the plant because of financial and **environmental factors** (the Green Party, which had secured several seats in the election of 1992, was firmly involved); Croatia, less well provided with domestic sources of **energy**, urged a new reactor. Although by 1996 it had been agreed that the output should be distributed equally, the Slovenes saw a full settlement only as part of a broader agreement on property rights between the two states.

—*J. J. H.*

KUČAN, MILAN

On 23 November 1997, Milan Kučan, running as an independent candidate, won a second term as president of the independent Republic of **Slovenia.** Slovenes regard this mountaineer and erstwhile basketball player as embodying the spirit of the country that he led to independence from **Yugoslavia** in June 1991.

Kučan was born in 1941 at Križevci, Slovenia. After an early education in Murska Sobota, he joined the Communist Party at the age of 17. He studied law at the University of Ljubljana from 1959, simultaneously serving in various communist youth organizations. He graduated in 1963.

Kučan then held various political posts at republican and federal levels, and in 1971 he was involved in the preparation of Yugoslav constitutional amendments that helped decentralize the former Yugoslavia. From 1978 to 1982, he was president of

Milan Kučan, president of the Republic of Slovenia. (Tanjug)

the Slovene assembly, and in 1982 he became one of Slovenia's two representatives on the federal presidency. In 1986 he became president of the **League of Communists** of Slovenia (ZKS), turning this organization into a reformist, social, and democratic movement. Assuming leadership of the reformers, Kučan backed the "Slovene Spring," a renewed attitude of nationalistic spirit, increasingly coming into conflict with **Serbia**'s hard-line nationalist, communist leaders.

Kučan supported the idea of a multiparty system and **elections**, and the first freely contested, pluralist elections were held in 1990. Although his party lost overall to an anti-Communist coalition, DEMOS (Democratic Opposition of Slovenia), he was elected as Slovenia's first post-Communist president.

On 25 June 1991, Kučan proclaimed Slovenia's independence, which was internationally recognized in 1992. During the Ten Day War of independence, Kučan, in company with Defense Minister **Janez Janša**, sent out orders to Slovenian territorial defense units to resist the federal army (**Yugoslav People's Army**). During peace talks in July on the island of **Brioni**, Slovenian secession was formalized.

On 6 December 1992, Slovenia's first independent presidential and parliamentary elections were held. Kučan was elected president after obtaining 64 percent of the vote.

In 1993, Pope John Paul II dignified Kučan as a papal knight with the Medal of the Order of St. Pius.

—*I. R. B.*

See also: political parties

KUČAR

See **Dabčević-Kučar, Savka**

KUHARIĆ, FRANJO

Cardinal Kuharić (born 1919), head of the Roman **Catholic Church** in Croatia, began to speak out in support of Croat sovereignty in 1989 and on the issue of human rights in **Kosovo** in 1990. He and the church in general began to add their voices to the calls for multiparty **elections** and democracy in Croatia. Despite the **Croatian Democratic Union**'s attempts to claim the support of the clergy, and of Kuharić in particular, he refused to attend that party's founding convention, insisting that the church could not declare itself in support of any one party. Kuharić joined with Patriarch Pavle of the Serbian **Orthodox Church** to issue a series of three joint statements calling for peace in late 1992. After Pope John Paul II's visit to Zagreb in September 1994 (the first papal visit to Zagreb and only the second to Croatia since 1111) Kuharić attempted to ensure that the pope's message to the Croat faithful—to begin the process of reconciliation and to forgive their enemies—was promoted by the church at all levels. He came to believe that the **media** and nationalist politicians were deliberately failing to report this message, and he spoke out about this concern in *Glas Koncila*, a Catholic weekly.

—*G. R. B.*

KUMANOVO

Situated just over 20 miles to the northeast of **Skopje** and only 7 miles from the Macedonian **border** with Serbia, Kumanovo (population 71,853 in the 1994 census) commands the international north-south road and rail links along the Morava-Vardar corridor. Following the referendum on the sovereignty of the Republic of **Macedonia** of September 1991, the town was regularly troubled by demonstrations and other public expressions of opinion by its Serb minority. The commune has proportionately the largest Serb minority of any municipality in Macedonia. Several villages in the Skopska Crna Gora, to the west of the town, have largely Serb populations. Kumanovo was one of the centers of activity of the Democratic Party of Serbs, which in 1994 underwent an internal coup, during which the members of its leadership were replaced by figures sympathetic to Serbian president **Slobodan Milošević.**

—*J. B. A.*

KUNA

The *kuna* has been the unit of currency in **Croatia** since the latter gained independence from Yugoslavia The name is taken from the medieval Croatian state, where *kuna* (marten) skins were used as currency. Plans for the term's reintroduction were announced in July 1993 amid a storm of protest from the nonnationalist opposition and the Serbs. The *kuna* had last been used as a name for the currency of the Independent State of Croatia under the fascist regime of the **Ustaša.** Along with the ***šahovnica*** (an element of the new flag) and the renaming of streets in **Zagreb**, the *kuna* was seen as another example of the determination of the ruling **Croatian Democratic Union** to create a national state for Croatia seemingly without any regard for the opinions of the Serb minority.

The currency was officially introduced on 30 May 1994, replacing the Croatian *dinar* at a rate of 1,000 *dinar* to 1 *kuna.* It was nonconvertible, and many transactions in 1994 continued to be carried out using the German mark, which functioned as tender on the **black market.**

—*G. R. B.*

KUSTURICA, EMIR

See **cinema**

L

LAND MINES

Estimated at between five million and six million at the end of 1995, the large number of land mines deployed in the former Yugoslavia in recent years has made the area one of the most heavily mined on earth. A major land mine producer by the end of the 1980s, the Yugoslav federation had large quantities of such ordnance when it descended into civil war in 1991. During the Yugoslav wars, land mine production has continued in Serbia, Croatia, and Bosnia-Hercegovina. Of the mines produced and used in the former Yugoslavia, the most common have been antipersonnel devices made of virtually undetectable plastics.

Relatively cheap to produce and often laid without location maps, land mines have been extensively used by all sides in the Yugoslav wars of the 1990s. As effective area-denial weapons and force multipliers, land mines figured prominently in local military strategy based on fixed defenses and a prolonged war of attrition, rather than wars based on movement and brief pitched battles in open spaces.

The use of land mines has been concentrated in strategic **terrain**, i.e., border areas, front lines, transport/communications routes, and the approaches to major cities and towns. In the case of Croatia, the main high-risk mine areas have been in and around the former **Serb Republic of the Krajina** (SRK). Particularly dense minefields were laid in 1991 in and around **Knin**, **Osijek**, and **Vukovar** in eastern Slavonia, as well as **Dubrovnik** in southern

An unmapped minefield in Ilidža, Sarajevo. (UNHCR)

Dalmatia. In nearby Bosnia-Hercegovina, a three-way war took place over virtually the entire territory from 1992 to 1995. At the end of 1995, around 40 percent of Bosnian territory was designated as at high risk for mines, with particularly dense minefields along front lines, including the Bosnian capital, **Sarajevo**, as well as **Srebrenica**, **Goražde**, and **Tuzla** in eastern Bosnia; the **Posavina Corridor** in northeastern Bosnia; **Travnik** and a number of lesser towns in central Bosnia; the **Bihać** enclave in western Bosnia; and **Mostar** in Hercegovina. A further 40 percent of Bosnian territory was then designated as at medium risk for land mines.

With more land mines in place than people when its war ended in 1995, Bosnia became a high-priority area for costly and internationally funded land mine location and eradication conducted by the International Mine Eradication Program under the auspices of the **Implementation/Stabilization Force** (I/SFOR). Initially focused on urban areas and transport/communications routes, this process is now entering its most complicated stage: land mine clearance in rural areas. Pending the completion of local land mine eradication, local economic performance will remain less than optimal, particularly in terms of agriculture. Already responsible for around one-third of all wartime casualties in the former Yugoslavia, land mines will also continue killing and maiming people long into the future.

—*M. M.*

LANGUAGE QUESTION

During the disintegration of Yugoslavia, language has come to be significant as a mode of symbolic differentiation. Although linguistic differences cannot be counted among the causes of the war, conflicts about identity have often been expressed in terms of issues relating to language. Macedonian, Serbo-Croat, and Slovene (together with Bulgarian) came to be standardized during the nineteenth century as different "literary" languages, created from a closely related group of dialects within the family of Slavonic languages (the "south Slavonic languages"). Their linguistic similarities and differences are clouded by the use of different alphabets: Slovenes, Croats, and most Bosnians use the Latin script, while Bulgarians, Macedonians, Montenegrins, and Serbs (and some Bosnians) use the **Cyrillic** script. Before the nineteenth century, the Balkan Peninsula was divided between the **Habsburg Empire** and **Ottoman Empire**, so that the use of loanwords from German and Turkish has contributed to linguistic diversity, although some modern reformers have attempted to eliminate these borrowings. The process of standardizing modern languages involved everywhere the synthesizing of many local dialects and usually the selection of one of these as the core. (It has been said that the only difference between a dialect and a language is that a language is a dialect with an army!) These choices have often been political rather than linguistic.

Slovene was the first of the group to be standardized in literary form, beginning during the second half of the sixteenth century, a process accelerated by the Counter-Reformation. The linguistic renaissance in **Slovenia** was given an impetus by the work of Valentin Vodnik (1785–1819), who wrote a Slovene grammar and launched the first Slovene newspaper. The standardization and popularization of modern Slovene was largely the achievement of Jernej Kopitar (1780–1844). Several dialects of Slovene have close affinities with the *kajkavski* and *čakavski* dialects of **Croatia**.

In **Serbia** the process was begun by Dositej Obradović (1739–1811) and Vuk Karadžić (1787–1864), the latter publishing his dictionary in 1818. Vuk's reforms freed the written language from the archaism of ecclesiastical use. He took as the basis of standard Serbian the dialect of **Hercegovina**, considering it to be less contaminated than others by importations from Turkish and German. His work was developed by Djura Daničić (1825–1882). Subsequently, Serbian usage moved back toward the forms more familiar to people living in the Serbian state.

Early literacy among the Croats developed using *kajkavski* and *čakavski* dialects. Following the Napoleonic Wars, a Slav literary renaissance took place, moving in favor of the more widely used *štokavski* dialects (which also included Serbian). Under the influence of the Franciscan order, Croats also became aware of the need to develop the language in such a way as to embrace the speech of the **Catholic** population of **Bosnia-Hercegovina**; consequently, linguistic reformers such as Ljudevit Gaj (1809–1872), inspired also by the experience of Napoleon's Illyrian Provinces, sought to create a language that was as inclusive as possible.

These movements of linguistic convergence bore fruit in 1850 with the framing of the Vienna

Agreement between writers and scholars from Serbia and Croatia, which among other things approved a standard transliteration between the two versions of "Croato-Serbian," or (as it has since come to be more commonly termed by linguists) "Serbo-Croatian."

Bulgarian also came to be standardized during the second half of the nineteenth century, originally largely on the base of the dialect of northeastern **Bulgaria**, and was officially codified in 1899. The consequences were important for the subsequent development of Macedonian. The struggle for the future of **Macedonia** began in earnest after the Congress of Berlin (1878). There was intense competition, initially between **Greece** and Bulgaria but later including Serbia, to infuse the inhabitants of the region with an "appropriate" sense of national identity. The fact that the neighboring Slav states had already standardized their languages on models relatively remote from Macedonian usage created an opportunity for Macedonian autonomists such as Gorgi Pulevski (1838–1894) and Krste Misirkov (1874–1926) to argue for a distinctive Macedonian language that should not be made similar to either Bulgarian or Serbian. The division of Macedonia between Bulgaria, Greece, and Serbia in the Balkan Wars (1912–1913) interrupted any further development in this direction until the creation of a federal Yugoslav state in 1945. It then became opportune for the communist government to foster a sense of Macedonian linguistic identity within the federal system. The modern Macedonian literary language was standardized largely under the leadership of Blaže Koneski (1921–1993), taking as its principal base the dialects of Prilep-Bitola.

Montenegro entered modern literary culture largely dependent upon Serbian models. In spite of some evidence of linguistic difference in Bosnia-Hercegovina, the subordination of the region under **Turkey** and then **Austria** left the region's literary intelligentsia as satellites of Serbian or Croatian centers, although the powerful influence of the Franciscans inclined Bosnians toward the Latin script and Croatian forms.

After the reunification of the country in 1945, the government emphasized strongly the integrity of Serbo-Croat as one language in an attempt to bring about a measure of reconciliation after the mutual genocide of 1941–1945. In keeping with the federal principle, both Macedonian and Slovene were encouraged as separate languages (although with Serbo-Croat as the federal lingua franca). In 1954 the official cultural associations of the remaining federal units convened in Novi Sad and produced an agreement on the unification of the orthography of Serbo-Croatian (or Croato-Serbian) and made arrangements for the production of a standard dictionary. The appearance of the dictionary in 1967 resulted in great resentment in Croatia because of the volume's unbalanced treatment of the language, including the assumption that Serbian forms were to be taken as standard, whereas other forms were recognized only as dialect variations.

Neither Serbs nor Croats were happy with the way language use was developing. Some institutions attempted to find a balance between eastern and western variants. The armed forces tended to use Serbian spelling and vocabulary but to use the Latin script. The Communist Party daily *Borba* printed alternate pages in Cyrillic and Latin scripts. Nevertheless, Croats detected a movement toward Serbian linguistic domination through the influence of the federal administration, the **League of Communists**, and the army (in which Serbs and Montenegrins were numerically overrepresented). Serbs regretted the rapid disappearance of the Cyrillic script as a part of the general incorporation of Yugoslavia into Western culture. Consequently, the general growth of interrepublican economic and constitutional conflict during the 1970s saw the emergence of language as an important symbol of the continuing cultural integrity of different ethnic groups. Of particular importance in this process was the emergence of the Zagreb-based cultural organization Matica Hrvatska. The draft for a revised Croatian constitution produced in 1968 included reference to "Croatian" as the official language of the republic.

Language has also played its part in the drama of the recent disintegration of Yugoslavia. The "Memorandum of the Serbian Academy of Sciences and Arts" of 1986, in addition to indicting federal Yugoslavia for the economic and political damage to Serbian interests, castigated the regime for abetting the "disintegration" of Serb culture; in particular it noted the erosion of the public use of the Cyrillic script. Since independence, Croatia has moved strongly to emphasize language as a symbol of political autonomy; it has restored the notion of

"Croatian" as the official language of the country, and in 1995 it introduced the Law on the Croatian Language, which aimed at the "purification" of Croatian. It has been proposed that around 30,000 loanwords regarded as of foreign (including Serbian) origin should be purged and replaced with "authentically" Croatian terms; however, this type of goal is often accomplished only by the restitution of archaisms or by resort to neologisms. These linguistic reforms have aroused considerable controversy, and their durability in popular use has yet to be demonstrated.

In Bosnia-Hercegovina as well, attempts have been made to buttress the separateness of an independent state, free from Croatian and Serbian patronage, by the creation of a "Bosnian" language, the first dictionary of which was published in 1996.

The issue of language has been of special importance in Macedonia, where the coincidence of the same term to refer to the language, **ethnicity**, and **citizenship**, that is, "Makedonski" (Macedonian), has underlined the problem of the status and rights of minorities within the republic. A central political issue has been the attempt by the **Albanian**-speaking population of the republic to assert its right to education in its own language.

—*J. B. A.*

See also: Serbian Academy Memorandum

Reference: Nečak Luk, Albina. "The Linguistic Aspect of Ethnic Conflict in Yugoslavia." In Payam Akhavan and Robert Howse (eds.), *Yugoslavia, the Former and the Future: Reflections by Scholars from the Region.* Washington, DC: Brookings Institution, 1995.

LDK

See **Democratic League of Kosovo**

LEAGUE OF COMMUNISTS OF YUGOSLAVIA

The ruling party during the period of the Socialist Federal Republic of **Yugoslavia** (SFRY) from 1952 to 1990, the League of Communists of Yugoslavia (Savez Komunista Jugoslavije—SKJ) exercised a monopoly of power until 1990. The failure of the SKJ to relegitimate its decaying power and to find solutions to Yugoslavia's myriad problems of the 1980s resulted in its own demise and that of the communist Yugoslav federation that it had created.

In January 1990, at the time of its extraordinary fourteenth and final congress, the SKJ collapsed as a nationwide political force in Yugoslavia. In a related series of developments, the constituent leagues of the SKJ, together with the political "front organization," the Socialist Alliance of the Working People of Yugoslavia, were transformed into new political parties.

Between World Wars I and II, the predecessor of the SKJ, the Communist Party of Yugoslavia (Komunistička Partija Jugoslavije—KPJ), was an illegal organization under the control of the Soviet Comintern. It came to power after defeating its domestic rivals during World War II. Under the leadership of **Josip Broz Tito**, the KPJ was a highly centralized and hard-line Stalinist party during the 1940s and early 1950s. Following the historic split between Tito and Soviet leader Joseph Stalin in June 1948, the party experienced a major political and ideological crisis. Although the KPJ initially attempted to present itself as an orthodox Communist Party in response to the criticisms leveled by the Soviet leadership, it became clear that major political and ideological changes were required if the KPJ were to legitimate its break from a world communist movement. Tito ruthlessly purged the party of suspected Soviet agents and

A famous image of the communist past defaced on a wall in besieged Sarajevo, 1994. (Stevan Filipović)

sympathizers in 1948–1949 by using secret police terror to enforce party discipline and loyalty to himself alone.

The relegitimation of Yugoslavia's communist revolution involved the introduction of a system of **workers' self-management** and the adoption of a foreign policy based upon **nonalignment.** This necessitated the creation of a new Communist Party to guide and implement a distinctive Yugoslav form of socialism, which later came to be known as **Titoism.** The party was renamed the League of Communists of Yugoslavia at its fifth congress in November 1952. In January 1953 a new federal constitution was promulgated, introducing a measure of decentralization for the first time in postwar Yugoslav politics.

Although still a one-party state, Yugoslavia nevertheless experienced a measure of political liberalization after 1952, when the country also embarked upon radical socioeconomic change financed in part by Western aid. These changes once again posed a threat to party discipline. In 1954, one of Tito's closest associates, Montenegrin **Milovan Djilas,** demanded an end to the party's monopoly of power—a demand that was resolutely rejected by Tito and that resulted in Djilas's imprisonment.

The "Yugoslav road to socialism" experienced its first major crisis during the 1960s. The country's economic problems resulted in growing pressures for greater political diversity; these pressures were reflected in the promulgation of a new constitution in April 1963, when greater political decentralization was introduced into both the federation and the SKJ. These constitutional changes and the related economic reforms of 1965 led to the development of a renegotiated federalism, which allowed the open expression of republican, regional, and local political and other interests. This shift was to result in growing political conflict within and beyond the SKJ, with the leaderships of the more economically developed northern republics (Slovenia and Croatia) favoring more economic reform and further political decentralization. These views were opposed by the leaders of the less economically developed republics, led by Serbia. These conflicts came to a head in 1966, when Tito dismissed a conservative Serb associate, Aleksandar Ranković, as head of the country's security services for allegedly abusing his powers and opposing reform.

The fall of Ranković represented a major triumph for the country's reformers and for greater pluralism of thought, enabling more open debate on previously taboo subjects and problems within the SKJ itself. The continued monopoly of power of the SKJ, and even its legitimacy, were increasingly questioned in certain quarters—for example, by the Praxis group of philosophers, who argued for a "socialism with a human face."

The year 1968 witnessed antigovernment student demonstrations in **Belgrade** and the first serious disorders since 1945 in **Kosovo.** Protests were met by heavy police response and greater political reliance by Tito on the **Yugoslav Peoples' Army** (JNA). Having earlier sided with the reformers in the SKJ, Tito was not prepared to allow further political liberalization—and certainly not the granting of effective national independence to the federation's republics and autonomous provinces, nor the end of the political monopoly held by the SKJ and its subsidiary organizations.

The movement for radical political change became most significant in **Croatia** by 1971–1972, where a so-called *masovni pokret* (mass movement, or MASPOK) demanded national independence for Croatia. Although originating outside the League of Communists of Croatia (SKH), this mass movement was eventually supported by the SKH leadership, posing a serious threat to the SKJ and the SFRY itself. Alarmingly for Tito, similar tendencies manifested themselves in the Leagues of Communists of **Slovenia, Serbia,** and **Macedonia.** Supported by the JNA, Tito then implemented a repressive recentralization of power in the federation and the SKJ in 1972–1973. The league was purged of so-called nationalists and liberals at this time. According to critics of this policy, this action represented the retrenchment of Stalinism in Yugoslav politics. One important manifestation of this trend was the increased power and influence of the JNA within the SKJ.

The 1974 constitution appeared more or less to concede the Croatian case by further devolving real political power to the republics, autonomous provinces, regions, and local municipalities. The new constitution also introduced a delegate system to encourage greater popular participation at a time when the membership of the SKJ was overwhelmingly middle class and professional—far removed from its supposed orientation toward the working class. In 1976, the new Law of Associated Labor (Zakon o udruženom radu—ZUR) had the effect of further decentralizing economic decision making. These seemingly radical constitutional and legislative measures, however, masked two key political processes: there was a reaffirmation of control by the SKJ, albeit in new regionalized forms, and a repoliticization of the economy. At the federal level of both government and the SKJ, this de facto confederalization of political and economic power was to have serious and adverse consequences in due course.

Containable only as long as Tito was alive, Yugoslavia's endemic political and economic conflicts became increasingly unmanageable after his death in May 1980. Thereafter the country was governed by a collective state presidency of representatives of the constituent republics and autonomous provinces. This state presidency operated on the principle of unanimity and the regular rotation of its membership. In the related presidium of the SKJ (where the JNA was also represented), similar principles applied. These constitutional arrangements made effective decision making at the federal level of both government and the SKJ virtually impossible throughout the 1980s, leading to the demise of the federation and its ruling party by the end of the decade.

Communist Yugoslavia experienced its most serious economic crisis during the 1980s, beginning with an inability to service its foreign debt of over U.S.$18 billion and acceptance of a stabilization package from the **International Monetary Fund** (IMF) in 1983. The crisis resulted in the loss of economic security throughout the federation, further worsening political conflicts over ever scarcer resources. The urgent need to implement macroeconomic stabilization by the federal government in Belgrade presupposed a recentralization of power, which was unacceptable to the country's republics and autonomous provinces. There was institutional political deadlock, culminating in the resignation of the federal Yugoslav government in December 1988, when Federal Premier Branko Mikulić failed to secure acceptance of a budget based upon the economic reform package demanded by the IMF. His successor, **Ante Marković**, openly acknowledged that real economic reform based on macroeconomic stabilization and the introduction of free market mechanisms could be successfully implemented only in tandem with radical democratization and relegitimation of Yugoslavia's rigid and ineffective political system. This view was reinforced by the collapse of communism and the end of the Cold War elsewhere in Eastern Europe after 1989. The disappearance of the Soviet threat to Yugoslavia's security reduced the country's fragile internal cohesion. Simultaneously, the disappearance of the Soviet threat lessened Yugoslavia's geopolitical importance to the West. This rapidly changing external environment came just as the country's domestic crises began to pass the point of no return.

The major new factor toward the end of the 1980s was the rise to power in Serbia of **Slobodan Milošević**, who seized control of the League of Communists of Serbia (SKS) in 1987. Milošević's purge of the SKS, as well as the reimposition of centralized control by Belgrade over **Kosovo**, the **Vojvodina**, and **Montenegro** during the period 1988–1989, was experienced as deeply threatening to the other republics. An issue of particular importance for the other republics was Milošević's claim to speak for all Serbs, including the large ethnic Serb diasporas in Croatia and **Bosnia-Hercegovina.** Determined, as he saw it, to preserve Yugoslavia in the face of powerful fissiparous forces weakening the federation and the SKJ, Milošević could only worsen the conflicts between Serbia and the country's other republics. In Slovenia, the political trendsetter in Yugoslavia at this time, the League of Communists of Slovenia (SKS), under the leadership of **Milan Kučan**, allowed de facto political pluralism, with the first noncommunist parties of the postwar period emerging out of the Socialist Alliance as early as 1988.

Bitterly divided as they were by the end of the 1980s, Yugoslavia's republican political elites had a common interest in finishing off what remained of the federal government and the SKJ at this time. Marković's hopes of a politically reinvigorated federation were systematically sabotaged by the republics; the SKJ finally fell apart at its fourteenth congress in January 1990. By then, its Slovene and Croatian components had transformed themselves into new political parties to contest the multiparty parliamentary elections in spring 1990. The successors of the SKH in Croatia lost these first democratic elections, although neocommunist parties and personalities remained influential in Slovene politics. In Serbia, the neocommunist successor of the SKS, led by Milošević, retained power in the Serbian parliamentary elections of 1990. Neocommunists also remained in power in Montenegro and Macedonia. Only in Croatia and Bosnia-Hercegovina were neocommunist parties entirely supplanted by new nationalist forces.

—*M. M.*

LIBRARIES

All three of the combatants in this war have been responsible for destroying the culture, history, and national heritage of the people of the area—including churches, mosques, schools, other institutions of learning, cultural and historical monuments, libraries, and archives. Libraries were wantonly destroyed with very little thought as to the long-term consequences in terms of eradicating national heritage. The looting and destruction of libraries and archives were carried out in a deliberate, ruthless, and systematic way.

In Slavonia, in the areas where Serbs and Croats lived, cannons were used to attack the libraries at Vinkovci and **Vukovar**; the public libraries were burned to the ground. In all, 210 libraries have been seriously damaged, including 10 research libraries, 19 memorial libraries holding manuscripts dating from the sixteenth to nineteenth centuries, at least one monastery library, 13 special libraries, 33 public libraries, and 29 secondary schools with libraries containing at least 300 books each.

Casualties included the old Bishop's Library in **Pakrac** (Slavonia), established as the Pakrac Orthodox Diocesan Library and considered to be second only to the Library of the Matica Srpska in Novi Sad (Vojvodina). A number of important historical scripts, collections of poems dedicated to Serbian saints, 5,500 old books, and a considerable number of periodicals have been lost. The same thing happened in the Pakrac Seminary, Cathedral of the Holy Trinity, where books, manuscripts, and other church artifacts were destroyed.

The larger libraries in **Dubrovnik** were also destroyed. At the Dubrovnik Research Library—where before the war library holdings were 210,000 books, 1,286 periodical titles, 922 manuscripts, and 77 incunabula (13,490 items date from the period of the Dubrovnik republic)—old and new reference collections have been damaged. A similar fate befell the Institute for Historical Sciences of the Croatian Academy of Sciences and Arts.

One of the most publicized crimes against the library world was the destruction of the famous National and University Library of **Bosnia-Hercegovina** in **Sarajevo** (originally the parliament building—Vijećnica). A devastating fire gutted the building in August 1992 when 1.5 million books and documents, as well as 6,100 titles of periodicals and 350,000 copies of periodical publications, were destroyed. The most important rare books; original manuscripts; the archives of Bosnian, Croat, Serb, and **Jewish** writers; the entire catalog system; microfilms; computers; and photo laboratory were destroyed. Ninety percent of the collection was lost, and the salvaged 10 percent is housed in unsuitable conditions, not accessible to the public. Only 60 staff remain, housed in cramped and unsuitable accommodations.

Promises of international communities and banks to rebuild Sarajevo's library were slow to materialize after the signing of the **Dayton Agreements**. However, international funds are at last being made available for the reconstruction of the building, and the city has earmarked larger temporary accommodation for the library, although this needs substantial refurbishment. Representatives of publishing companies and of other libraries in Europe (e.g., the British Library) and the United States (e.g., the University of Michigan) have shown great interest in supporting projects connected with the restoration of the library and its collections. However, current estimates suggest that it may take 25 years to restore the collections and that a quarter of the collections are lost forever.

—*S. P.*

LILIĆ, ZORAN

In June 1993 Zoran Lilić was elected president of the Federal Republic of **Yugoslavia** (FRY). One of a number of younger Yugoslav politicians, he was born in Belgrade, Serbia, in 1953 and was educated at that city's university. He subsequently worked as a fashion model before entering politics. A member of the **League of Communists** of Serbia and then the **Socialist Party of Serbia**, Lilić became speaker of the National Assembly (Skupština) of Serbia in 1992–1993. He is considered to be very loyal to Serbian president **Slobodan Milošević** and was at first chosen to replace Milošević as president when the latter's final term of office expired in 1997. Failing to secure election in two rounds of voting, however, Lilić was compelled to give way to another candidate, Milan Milutinović.

—M. M.

LISBON AGREEMENT

The meeting of the Serb, Croat, and Bosnian leaders at Lisbon in February 1992 was expected (and turned out) to be the last chance for agreement before the Bosnian referendum on independence and the premature international **recognition** of an independent **Bosnia-Hercegovina.** The team of mediators from the **European Community** (EC) was desperate for compromise and initially managed to achieve two ostensible agreements among the three parties. The first agreement secured the parties' recognition of the current external borders of Bosnia, even though this implied the establishment of a Bosnian state, which, even with talk of "cantonization," was not the aim of either the Serbs or the Croats. The second agreement provided for the country to be divided into units based upon predominant **ethnicity**, a notion that had hitherto been opposed by the Bosnian **Muslims**, whose population was the most widely spread throughout Bosnia. However, the latter agreement was short-lived, as **Alija Izetbegović**, the Bosnian president, having returned to Sarajevo to report on his own compromise, changed his mind and rejected the division of Bosnia on ethnic lines in principle and in practice. The circumstances of the failure of the Lisbon Agreement served only to sharpen the rhetoric, tension, and resulting violence surrounding the referendum, and within a month Bosnia was at war.

—J. J. H.

LITERATURE AND WAR

See **Croatian writers; Serbian writers**

LJUBLJANA

As the chief city of **Slovenia,** Ljubljana became the capital and seat of government of the newly independent Republic of Slovenia in 1991. Situated on the Ljubjanica River, its current population totals about 275,000. It was the most prosperous city in the former Yugoslavia, and it retains the character of a central European city in outlook and general standard of living. During the 1980s it was a center for alternative expression, particularly on the artistic front. Immediately following Slovenia's declaration of independence on 25 June 1991, the **Yugoslav Peoples' Army** moved tanks from the city's barracks to Ljubljana's airport at Brnik and threatened airstrikes on the city itself. On 27 June, the shooting down by Slovene forces of a Yugoslav helicopter over central Ljubljana effectively marked the point of no return for Slovenia and its independence.

—J. J. H.

LONDON CONFERENCE

On 26–27 August 1992, a conference was held in London, hosted jointly by the British government (which held the presidency of the **European Union** [EU]) and by the **United Nations** (UN). The motivation behind this conference arose primarily from the reports of "**ethnic cleansing**" and **detention camps** in Bosnia; the conference itself provided the opportunity for representatives from over 20 countries to express individual and collective condemnation of Serb activities. The London Conference was also attended by leaders from the six former Yugoslav republics and the two former autonomous provinces, including **Dobrica Ćosić** and **Milan Panić** (the president and the prime minister of the as yet internationally unrecognized Republic of Yugoslavia), **Slobodan Milošević** (the Serbian president), **Alija Izetbegović** (the Bosnian president), and Bosnian Serb leader **Radovan Karadžić.** The conference issued a declaration covering matters such as **recognition** of **Bosnia-Hercegovina** by all former Yugoslav republics, guarantees for minorities, and rights of return for **refugees,** plus the establishment of an international peacekeeping force. The West's satisfaction at this display of unity and the seeming acquiescence of the Yugoslav delegation was almost simultaneously undermined by a row between Panić and Milošević. A subsequent serious problem concerned the fact that the Serbs came away with the text of a declaration, not the ultimatum that they had been expecting—Izetbegović's renewed appeal at the conference for military intervention or a lifting of the arms embargo had failed. It was at this conference as well that Lord **Carrington** handed over to Lord **Owen** the role as chair of the European Union's peace initiative.

—J. J. H.

M

MACEDONIA (GEOGRAPHICAL REGION)

The name Macedonia dates back to the ancient world, when a Hellenic empire of that name flourished in the fourth century B.C. The precise reference of the term has changed over time, but during the nineteenth century the term came to refer to a broad arc of territory extending clockwise from the Aliakmon River to the Strimion (Struma). Macedonia's western extremity is generally taken as marked by Prespa and Ohrid Lakes and by the Sar Mountains; its northern limit by the Skopska Crna Gora and Mount German; and its eastern edge by the Pirin Mountains. "Macedonia" is not understood to include the peninsula of Khalkidiki.

At the end of the Balkan Wars (1912–1913), the division of most remaining European territories of the **Ottoman Empire** among the victorious Balkan states left Macedonia divided among **Bulgaria**, **Greece**, and **Serbia**; the lines along which that division was agreed upon were broadly confirmed at the end of World War I and again after World War II. These borders had at the time no consistent geographic or ethnographic basis. The resulting subregions of Macedonia have come to be called "Pirin" Macedonia (Bulgaria), "Aegean" Macedonia (Greece), and "Vardar" Macedonia (Serbia and subsequently Yugoslavia). The formerly Yugoslav portion became the Republic of Macedonia upon the disintegration of Yugoslavia.

—J. B. A.

See also: Macedonia, Republic of

Reference: Poulton, Hugh. *Who Are the Macedonians?* Bloomington: Indiana University Press, 1994.

MACEDONIA, REPUBLIC OF

Macedonia is the southernmost of the six republics formerly united in the Socialist Federation of Republics of Yugoslavia; it is bordered to the north by **Serbia**, to the east by **Bulgaria**, to the south by **Greece**, and to the west by **Albania.** Its area is 9,925 square miles (25,713 square kilometers), and it has a population of 1,936,877 (1994 census). The capital city, **Skopje**, with a population approaching 500,000, is the home of every fourth Macedonian citizen.

The region was formerly settled by Illyrian and Hellenic tribes, but the end of the seventh century saw the arrival of Slav migrants—the ancestors of modern ethnic Macedonians, who make up roughly two-thirds of the population of the republic. The official language is Macedonian, which is closely related to Bulgarian. There are substantial minorities of Albanians (23 percent) and **Turks** (4 percent), as well as smaller groups of Roma, Serbs, and others. The majority religion is **Orthodox** Christianity, but perhaps as many as a quarter of the population identify themselves as **Muslims**.

During the time of the **Ottoman Empire**, there was no recognition of a Macedonian political or cultural identity. After the Congress of Berlin (1878), a small group of intellectuals began to discuss the possibility of an "autonomist" solution for the future of the region in the event of a breakup of the Ottoman state. There was heated controversy over the question of whether the Slavs of the region had a separate national identity (as "Macedonians") or should be assimilated as Bulgarians. Between 1878 and 1912, Bulgarians, Greeks, and Serbs contended for control over the Orthodox Church in the region and competed to open schools that would inculcate an "appropriate" national consciousness. These efforts were supplemented by armed terrorism. The problem was resolved in 1913, at the end of the Balkan Wars, by the division of geographical Macedonia among these three states, each of which adopted energetically assimilationist policies with respect to the Macedonians.

When the "First Yugoslavia" (created in 1918) was dissolved by the Axis powers in April 1941, the greater part of the former Macedonia was handed over to Bulgaria. Taking the approach that it was leading a "national liberation struggle" against the occupier, the Communist Party of Yugoslavia advocated, from 1943, a future federal Yugoslav state. The loyalty of all of the peoples of the region was sought on the basis that (unlike in the First Yugoslavia, which had been strongly centralist in its constitution) all nations would have a substantial degree of autonomy within a federation. The victory of the Communists in 1945 saw Macedonia recognized as one of the six Yugoslav republics. It was believed that strengthening the position of other nations, such as Montenegrins, Macedonians, and Slovenes, would provide a powerful third force minimizing the conflict between Serbs and Croats that had dominated interwar politics. The slogan "brotherhood and unity" emphasized the importance of mutual recognition and respect by all Yugoslavia's nations.

An important stimulus to the growth of a Macedonian national consciousness after 1945 was the formalization of a Macedonian language, which was then used in education, culture, and mass communication. An autocephalous Macedonian Orthodox Church declared its independence from the Serbian Church in 1967.

The creation of a Macedonian republic was met with varying degrees of resentment among the republic's neighbors. Bulgarians continued to maintain that Macedonian Slavs were really Bulgarians and that there was no basis for the recognition either of a separate language or of a state. Greeks feared that the fostering of a Macedonian state implied that the republic served as a front for Yugoslav territorial ambitions extending to the rest of geographical Macedonia, especially the port of **Thessaloniki**. Serbs maintained a title to "South Serbia" on the basis of the fact that Skopje had been the capital of a fourteenth-century Serb empire. Albanians feared that in a Macedonian republic their status as a mere national minority would reduce them in effect to second-class citizens.

The disintegration of Yugoslavia in 1991–1992 caused much anxiety within the Balkans and more widely; it seemed that the federation's breakup would again place on the agenda the question of Macedonia's future. Cut loose from its secure moorings within Yugoslavia, Macedonia would inevitably become the focus of irredentist ambitions on the part of its neighbors. Of particular concern was the situation of the large Albanian-speaking minority. Many observers anticipated that the collapse of Yugoslavia would result in the secession of the Albanian minority in **Kosovo** from Serbia, an event that might trigger a more general challenge to the definition of the borders. These fears were moderated by the outcome of the first multiparty **elections** in December 1990, in which the government was eventually formed by an alliance composed of the former Communists (Party of Democratic Change) and a moderate Albanian leadership in the Party of Democratic Prosperity (PPD).

The Macedonian government conducted a referendum on 8 September 1991. This referendum yielded a 95 percent majority (on a 75 percent turnout) for autonomy and independence "with the right to join an alliance of sovereign states"—keeping open the option of the reconstitution of Yugoslavia in a new form. Accordingly, the Sobranie (Assembly) declared the independence of the republic on 18 September. In December, when the **Badinter Commission** of the European Community (EC) canvassed the republics of Yugoslavia on the issue of their independence, the Macedonians applied for recognition. Although Badinter recommended recognition without preconditions, in response to Greek sensitivities the EC foreign ministers requested that recognition be dependent upon certain changes in the Macedonian constitution. That constitution was amended on 6 January 1992 to the effect that Macedonia had no claims on the territory of other states and would not interfere in the sovereign rights and internal affairs of other states.

The new state was immediately recognized by Bulgaria (although with the qualification that recognition of the state did not imply recognition of the language or nation). Protracted negotiations throughout 1992 failed to mollify the Greeks, however, and this failure brought down the Macedonian government in July. In April 1993 the matter was largely settled when Macedonia agreed to international **recognition** within the **United Nations** (UN) under the provisional title of the Former Yugoslav Republic of Macedonia (FYROM). General recognition then followed, although the use of the name of a Greek province to describe a former Yugoslav republic, and the use of a flag bearing a symbol based on a design found on a Greek archaeological site, still caused offense to the Greeks.

The UN-imposed economic **sanctions** against the Yugoslav federation produced acute difficulties for Macedonia. Although the severance from Yugoslavia passed without difficulty and the **Yugoslav Peoples' Army** withdrew peaceably from Macedonia in February and March 1992 (the only secession from Yugoslavia to be accomplished without violence), the Belgrade government withheld recognition in sympathy with Greece. The Yugoslavs relied heavily upon Greek support in order to evade sanctions, and they reciprocated with support on the Macedonian question. Macedonia was caught in a dilemma; it was under pressure to collaborate with those supporting the Yugoslav federation in the evasion of sanctions to sustain its own economic needs, but it was thereby necessarily denying itself the international support needed for its rehabilitation and development. Desperate attempts were made to explore the possibility of linking Macedonia to the Bulgarian rail network, thereby evading the Serb-Greek stranglehold.

In recognition of the increasing sensitivity of the area, the UN deployed a monitoring force (**UNPREDEP**) in the republic in June 1993. Anxiety reached its greatest level in the period leading to the Greek elections of 10 October, in which Macedonia was the most salient issue. The new Greek government imposed special trade sanctions against Macedonia on 16 February 1994. Mesmerized by the need to secure solidarity among member states, the European Union (EU) was unable to reach agreement on the issue, although loans by the **International Monetary Fund** and the World Bank served to ease the pressure.

In September 1994, UN mediator **Cyrus Vance** negotiated an agreement between the Macedonians and the Greeks by which the embargo was lifted in return for the withdrawal of the controversial "Sun of **Vergina**" flag endorsed by the Sobranie in October. The situation was ameliorated with the general stabilization of the region and the end of sanctions against Yugoslavia after the **Dayton Agreements**. The normalization of Macedonia's relations with its neighbors was largely completed with the recognition of Macedonia by the Yugoslav federation on 8 April 1996 (although the Greeks are not yet satisfied with respect to the issue of the name).

Although Macedonia has remained clear of the violent conflict that has engulfed other parts of the former Yugoslavia, confounding the early expectations of an uncontrolled conflagration affecting the entire Balkan peninsula, the region is still a source of anxiety. The success of the Macedonian parties in managing conflict between the Slav Macedonian and Albanian populations, through the incorporation of the PDP into a coalition government, cannot be relied upon as a permanent solution to the problems. The coalition could be undermined by continuing economic dissatisfaction. Macedonia remains vulnerable to destabilization in the event of an intensification of conflict surrounding the Albanian minority elsewhere in the former Yugoslavia, especially in Kosovo.

—J. B. A.

See also: Kriva Palanka; Kumanovo; Macedonia (geographical region); Macedonia, Republic of (FYROM); Tetovo

MACEDONIA, REPUBLIC OF (FYROM)

In the wake of the **European Community**'s failure to agree on **recognition** of the former Yugoslav Republic of **Macedonia** in January 1992 (in the face of persistent objections by the government of **Greece**), several lines have been pursued in the attempt to negotiate a compromise. Since one of the principal obstacles to Greek agreement was the use of the name "Macedonia" as the title of the new state, the **United Nations** (UN) admitted the Macedonian republic to membership in April 1993 under the provisional title of the "Former Yugoslav Republic of Macedonia," usually abbreviated to its acronym, FYROM. Aside from UN official documentation, consistent use of this title is largely limited to Greece and the Federal Republic of Yugoslavia; the great majority of states recognizing the new state have done so under its preferred title of the "Republic of Macedonia."

—J. B. A.

MACKENZIE, LEWIS

Maj.-Gen. Lewis MacKenzie was the Canadian army officer who served as the first chief of staff of the United Nations Protection Force (**UNPROFOR**) in the former Yugoslavia. As such, he was the key United Nations (UN) military figure on the ground in **Sarajevo** at the beginning of the Bosnian civil war in 1992. A graduate of the University of Manitoba,

MacKenzie joined the Canadian armed forces in 1960, serving with the North Atlantic Treaty Organization (NATO) in Germany and on eight UN peacekeeping tours in the Middle East, Cyprus, and Vietnam. Upon the deployment of UNPROFOR in Croatia and then Bosnia, he was appointed the force's chief of staff and deputy to the first UN forces commander in the former Yugoslavia, Gen. **Satish Nambiar**. Between March and August 1992, when the Bosnian civil war began in earnest, MacKenzie was primarily responsible for the creation of UN Sector Sarajevo and for making the 30-nation UNPROFOR operational.

In order to expedite the delivery of humanitarian aid from the UN High Commission for Refugees (**UNHCR**) and other agencies to the besieged Bosnian capital, MacKenzie negotiated the transfer of Sarajevo airport from the **Bosnian Serbs** to the UN. He was also involved in the evacuation of the **Yugoslav Peoples' Army** (JNA) garrison in Sarajevo, as well as the related release of kidnapped Bosnian president **Alija Izetbegović**.

An experienced UN peacekeeper but constrained by the limited resources at his disposal, MacKenzie skillfully used the foreign **media** to attain his objectives in Sarajevo, becoming an international celebrity in the process. A good example of such media manipulation took place when French president François Mitterand dramatically visited Sarajevo in June 1992, allowing MacKenzie to use the international publicity generated by Mitterand's presence to promote his own objectives, thereby placing the city at the forefront of international attention. MacKenzie was routinely criticized by all parties to the Bosnian conflict for his alleged biases. After leaving Sarajevo in August 1992, he retired from his country's armed forces in March 1993, subsequently published a lively memoir (*Peacekeeper: The Road to Sarajevo.* Vancouver: Douglas and McIntyre, 1993), and lectured internationally on his controversial and last tour of duty for the UN in the former Yugoslavia.

—*M. M.*

MAGLAJ/OZREN

The course of the war in northern Bosnia, although receiving relatively little international press attention, illustrates well the interweaving of several different general factors that shaped the course of the war. The ridge of Mount Ozren (Velika Ostrica, 918 meters above sea level) extends roughly 30 kilometers southeastward from **Doboj**, which stands at the junction of the valleys of the **Bosna** and Spreča Rivers. This ridge of high ground, which also came to be known as the "Maglaj finger," commands important lines of **communications**. Road and rail links run from north to south, from the key bridges on the **Sava River** at Šamac to **Sarajevo**, and east-west from **Tuzla** to **Banja Luka**. The city of Doboj itself (population 103,000 in 1991) is one of the main manufacturing centers of the republic. Control of the area was consequently a primary strategic objective for all sides in the war in Bosnia. Periodically the area saw fierce fighting, especially in May 1992, when it was subjected to intense "**ethnic cleansing**" of its **Muslim** population, and in the winter of 1993–1994, when the besieged population of Maglaj had to be supplied food via airdrops.

The ethnic dimension of the struggle was significant, both in terms of the claims that different groups advanced and as the basis for their claim on the economic resources of the area. The area includes parts of four municipalities with highly mixed ethnicities, primarily Serb/Muslim:

Ethnic composition of municipalities surrounding the Maglaj finger

	Croat	*Serb*	*Muslim*	*Other*
Doboj	3	39	40	8
Gračanica	—	23	72	5
Maglaj	9	31	45	5
Zavidovići	13	20	59	7

As in many parts of Bosnia, the Serb population tended to be disproportionately located in the villages, especially upon Mount Ozren itself. From the point of view of local people, this feature gave to the struggle a general strategic objective: defending their own historic homeland.

—*J. B. A.*

MAJEVICA

See **detention camps**

MANJAČA

See **detention camps**

MANOLIĆ, JOSIP

Born in 1922 at Kalinovac in the Podravina region of Croatia, Josip Manolić was one of **Franjo**

Tudjman's most trusted advisers between 1990 and May 1994, replacing **Stipe Mesić** as prime minister in 1991. He fought with the **Partizans** in the war of 1941–1945. He later became head of the prison service in Croatia, then a senior official in UDBa, the Yugoslav secret police. He was forced into retirement in 1972 in the purges following the nationalist upsurge of the **Croatian Spring**, but he returned to politics with the rise of the **Croatian Democratic Union** (HDZ), becoming a member of the presidential council, as well as president of the upper house of the assembly.

In 1994 he split from the HDZ to form the Croatian Independent Democratic Party (HNDS), together with Stipe Mesić. Eventually the two men took with them seven defectors from the HDZ. In the elections of November 1995, the HNDS joined in a coalition with four other small parties and the Croatian Peasant Party to challenge the HDZ, but they met with disappointing results.

—G. R. B.

MARJANOVIĆ, MIRKO

Mirko Marjanović has been prime minister of Serbia since 1994. A **Krajina** Serb, he was born in **Knin**, Croatia, in 1940. A professional economist by education, Marjanović occupied a number of lesser official positions in Croatia and then Serbia during the communist Yugoslav period. Prior to his appointment as Serbian premier in March 1994, he was director-general of Progress, a Belgrade-based company. Relatively unknown in Serbian politics until then, Marjanović is considered very loyal to President **Slobodan Milošević**. Although appointed to the Serbian premiership for his business experience, he has recently been implicated in a number of corruption scandals in Serbia. He reportedly sided with Milošević in a feud with the governor of the National Bank of Yugoslavia, **Dragoslav Avramović**, at the time of the latter's dismissal from office in May 1996.

—M. M.

MARKET ECONOMY

See **privatization**

MARKOVIĆ, ANTE (ECONOMIC REFORMS)

Ante Marković, a Croat from **Bosnia-Hercegovina** born at Konjić in 1924, was prime minister of Yugoslavia from 1989 to 1991 and is chiefly associated with attempts to reform his country's economy in the two years preceding its disintegration.

The Yugoslav economy experienced a continuous crisis throughout the 1980s, which worsened toward the end of the decade. In 1987 real output (gross social product) fell by 0.5 percent, and a further fall of 2 percent occurred in 1988, while the rate of **inflation** increased. Consumer prices rose by 120 percent in 1987 and 194 percent in 1988. Foreign debt peaked at U.S.$22 billion in 1987. The value of the dinar had depreciated throughout the 1980s, and massive debts had been built up to finance the persistent balance-of-payments deficits and to pay for imports of Western consumer goods. It is estimated that Yugoslav citizens had up to $13 billion in foreign banks. In 1987 the Yugoslav prime minister Branko Mikulić set up a government commission to prepare radical reforms, including the establishment of a stock exchange.

At the end of 1988 the first elements of the new economic reform were introduced. Amendments to the constitution were adopted in November, and new laws were enacted to encourage the development of privatization. A foreign investment law opened up Yugoslav enterprises to such investment, and a new law on enterprises, adopted in December, permitted the formation of joint stock and limited liability companies and other forms of private enterprise. Over the next two years more than 77,000 new small private enterprises were established, although probably fewer than half of them were economically active. The enterprise law also reduced the rights and responsibilities of workers' councils, while those of managers and shareholders were increased. A key institution of the **workers' self-management** system, the Basic Organisation of Associated Labour, was abolished.

However, these reforms were introduced in a rapidly deteriorating economic situation. Widespread demonstrations against the government took place in 1988, involving 400,000 workers in nearly 2,000 strikes, and demonstrators in **Vojvodina** forced the resignation of its provincial government in October 1988. In the face of this popular unrest, Branko Mikulić resigned in December 1988, but his resignation did not quell dissatisfaction with government policy. On 11 January 1989 the **Montenegro** government was driven out of office by demonstrations of 120,000 workers in Titograd and was replaced by a new government sympathetic to the Serbian leader **Slobodan Milošević**.

Ante Marković had been the leader of the Croatian **League of Communists of Yugoslavia** before becoming prime minister of Yugoslavia on 16 March 1989. He had previously worked as the general director of the electrical appliances firm Rade Končar, one of the largest enterprises in Croatia, in Zagreb. The economic situation that he encountered when he came into office was dismal, and he immediately declared that sweeping reforms were necessary to deregulate the economy and create free markets in goods, capital, and labor. By April 1989 inflation had reached an annual rate of 500 percent. Teachers went on strike, demanding that their wages be doubled, and more than 3,000 textile workers in Bosnia-Hercegovina took industrial action. The dinar had lost more than half its value against foreign currencies since the start of the year. By the end of the year inflation reached 2,600 percent. In 1989 industrial output fell by a tenth and living standards by a fifth. Marković declared that a solution to the crisis would not be possible without "a completely new economic and political system which would ensure economic efficiency and political democracy with full freedoms and human rights."

In December 1989 the official newspaper *Borba* published an article calling for the introduction of a multiparty system and free **elections**, following decisions in the same week by **Slovenia** and **Croatia** to adopt free elections and multiparty systems. At the same time, Marković announced further radical economic reforms. The dinar was revalued at a rate of 10,000 old dinars to 1 new dinar (ND) and was pegged to the deutschmark (DM) at a rate of 7 ND to 1 DM. Wages were to be frozen for six months. Prices would be allowed to rise except for energy, essential raw materials, and transport. A restrictive monetary policy was introduced that required strengthening the role of the National Bank of Yugoslavia and freeing it from political influence. The program was accepted by all the republics except **Serbia**, which at first rejected it and later never really fully committed to carrying it through, as the plan would have meant ending subsidies to Serbian enterprises and a consequent rise in unemployment. Crucially, however, the program was supported by the Western governments that rescheduled the Yugoslav foreign debt, and a standby arrangement was negotiated with the **International Monetary Fund** (IMF). Foreign currency reserves rose quickly to U.S.$10 billion, and inflation was initially brought under control, with prices actually beginning to fall by the middle of the year, reversing the experience of years of persistent and rapid inflation.

However, political disagreements between the republics quickly undermined the program. In April 1990 Slovenia and Croatia elected noncommunist governments that blocked the proposed increase in central control of taxation and banking. In addition, workers in Montenegro, Serbia, and **Macedonia** called a general strike in protest of the wage freeze. But the main problem was that no industrial restructuring took place, except to a certain extent in Slovenia, and loss-making enterprises continued to be subsidized. The Gulf crisis worsened the economic situation, as canceled oil deliveries from Iraq and canceled business contracts cost Yugoslavia $1.2 billion. In the second half of 1990 inflation reemerged, reaching 120 percent by the end of the year.

Further economic reforms and a privatization program were introduced in the second half of 1990. The law on social capital allowed enterprises, on the decision of the management board, to privatize their enterprises on the basis of internal shares, which were to be offered to workers at a discount of up to 70 percent, depending on length of service. The main difficulty was in the valuation of the social capital to be privatized. This valuation was to be done by the various privatization agencies established in each republic, but since there was no market for capital assets or for enterprises, the valuations were highly subjective and the process was open to abuse. Part of the share capital was also to be transferred to the republican pension funds. Internal shares could be distributed to workers in lieu of wages, although this provision was not adopted in Serbia. Shares could also be offered for sale at auctions, the proceeds of which were to go to Republican Funds for Development.

However, the privatization laws soon ran into difficulties, again resulting from differences in policy orientation between the republics. Slovenia and Croatia suspended the adoption of the federal privatization laws in October 1990. Slovenia did not adopt its own privatization law until several years later, while Croatia adopted its own privatization law in February 1991. The Croatian law envisioned a mix of limited employee shareholding and nationalization of enterprise assets. Serbian officials were reluctant to see the demise of the system of social property, but even there some progress was made. By March 1991 about 1,000 enterprises throughout Yugoslavia had begun the process of privatization and had offered internal shares to their workers. Mainly it was the more profitable enterprises that were privatized, since these were attractive to enterprise managers and employees, especially if it could be arranged that the assets would be undervalued and high discounts provided. Upon privatization, workers' councils were replaced by "assemblies of owners," and employee participation through the self-management system was eliminated in those enterprises. Deadlines were to be set for privatization, after which all nonprivatized assets would be transferred to the Republic Funds, i.e., nationalized. It was in each republic's interest to be in a position to design its own privatization law, as the gains to the ruling elite in each republic were potentially enormous. Since the privatization agencies and funds in each republic were effectively controlled by the respective republican governments, these bodies were in a powerful position to distribute favors to the members and associates of the politicians.

In January 1991 Serbia, flouting the monetary restrictions imposed by the reform program, took 18 billion dinars from the central bank to fund pay rises, pay pensions, and subsidize loss-making enterprises. The IMF had been supporting the Yugoslav economy on condition that it stick to the reform program. In response to the Serbian action it suspended its $1 billion standby arrangement, which in turn led to the suspension of a further $4 billion of Western credits. The Serbian action was also heavily criticized by **Franjo Tudjman,** the Croatian president, and both Croatia and Slovenia said they would retaliate by issuing their own currencies. However, this stance was not an indication of their support for the federal reform program. In moves equally disruptive of Marković's reformist policies, they challenged his federal budget for 1991, blocked his tax policies, and had already refused to deliver their budgetary contributions to the federation. Even by the end of 1990 Slovenia owed the federation 600 million dinars, and Croatia owed 578 million. In May 1991 Serbia blocked the candidacy of **Stipe Mesić** for the rotating presidency of Yugoslavia, effectively bringing the federation to an end.

On 19 May 1991 Croatia voted for independence. On 20 May the **United States of America** froze economic aid to Yugoslavia, ostensibly in protest at Serbian human rights violations in **Kosovo** (although such violations had been in evidence for several years) and urged other international lenders to do the same. While this U.S. action was undermining the federal government, **European Community** (EC) president Jacques Delors tried to mediate a resolution of the crisis and offered aid and closer relations with the EC in an effort to support Marković and the federal government, but with little success. At the end of May the United States rescinded its freeze on credits, but the damage was already done. Croatia announced it would declare independence on 30 June 1991. Slovenia announced 26 June as the date for its own independence. The war in Slovenia began on 27 June and ended ten days later with the withdrawal of the **Yugoslav Peoples' Army** from Slovenia. In the second half of 1991, war erupted in Croatia. Ante Marković resigned on 20 December 1991.

—*W. B.*

See also: banking; economic dimension; privatization

References: Bićanić, Ivo. "Fractured Economy." In Dennison Rusinow (ed.), *Yugoslavia: A Fractured Federalism.* Washington, DC: Wilson Center Press, 1988; Lydall, Harold. *Yugoslavia in Crisis.* Oxford: Clarendon Press, 1989; Secretariat for Information. *The Law on Economic Reform in Yugoslavia.* Belgrade: Yugoslav Survey, 1990.

MARKOVIĆ, MIHAILO

Mihailo Marković was vice president of the **Socialist Party of Serbia** (SPS) between 1990 and 1993. His career is of interest as a reflection of the history and weakening of political dissidence in Serbia.

Marković, born in Belgrade in 1923, took part in the "national liberation struggle" between 1941 and 1945. After the war against the Axis powers, he studied philosophy at the University of Belgrade and in London. Returning to Belgrade in 1955, he established a reputation as one of Yugoslavia's most eminent philosophers. In August 1963 the Korčula Summer School was launched, from which emerged the celebrated journal *Praxis,* in which Marković played an active role. Although careful to remain within the framework of Marxism, the *Praxis* group earned the opprobrium of the **League of Communists** (LC) because of a fear that the group aspired to constitute itself as a political alternative to the LC.

Marković supported the **student** protests in Belgrade in 1968. The LC organization within the faculty was dissolved following allegations that the young were being corrupted. The liberal leadership of the Serbian LC, under Marko Nikezić, resisted pressure to dismiss Marković and his colleagues; although the faculty were restricted in their access to the media, they still taught, published, met international colleagues, and traveled abroad. In 1972, following the events of the **Croatian Spring** and the ousting of Nikezić, eight professors from Belgrade, including Marković, were singled out for discipline. There was a hard-fought campaign within the university, supported by worldwide protest, against the LC's demands that the statutes of the faculty should be changed to permit greater involvement by outside political nominees. By the end of 1974, this campaign had failed, although Marković, as a full professor, could not legally be dismissed. The leading members of the *Praxis* group were prevented from teaching and were restricted in their access to publication within the country. The Center for Philosophy and Social Theory was set up in Belgrade to provide a legitimate framework for these arrangements. Although these restrictions remained in force formally until 1988, in practice they were eased after 1980.

After this long period of seclusion, Marković reemerged in July 1990 as a public figure when Serbian president **Slobodan Milošević** finally accepted the necessity for multiparty competition and redesignated the Serbian LC as the Socialist Party of Serbia (SPS). Marković was named vice president of the party as a public signal that the leopard really had changed its spots. In the intervening period, however, it seemed that Marković too had changed, his advocacy of socialist humanism giving way to a rather romantic, Hegelian nationalism. Along with several other prominent Serb intellectuals (such as Ljubo Tadić and Antonije Isaković), Marković appears to have been attracted by Milošević's platform of the need for an "antibureaucratic revolution" as well as by his espousal of nationalism.

Mihailo Marković's engagement with party politics was never more than as a respectable figurehead. With the dismissal from office of his old friend **Dobrica Ćosić** from the presidency of the Yugoslav federation in June 1993, Marković also found himself sidelined. He is interesting, however, as an illustration of Milošević's skill in building personal power through a very broad coalition within the SPS.

—J. B. A.

MARKOVIĆ (-MILOŠEVIĆ), MIRJANA

A Marxist sociologist at the University of Belgrade, writer, and politician, Mirjana Marković is also the influential spouse of former Serbian and later Yugoslav president **Slobodan Milošević**. The scion of a well-known **Partizan** family in Požarevac, Serbia, Marković married Milošević in 1964 and thereafter aided and exercised a strong influence over her husband. An inflexible and unreconstructed Marxist, Marković was one of the founding members of the **League of Communists—**Movement for Yugoslavia (SKJ-PJ) in 1990. To the political left of Milošević's **Socialist Party of Serbia** (SPS), the explicitly Yugoslav SKJ-PJ was strongly supported by a number of officers of the **Yugoslav Peoples' Army** (JNA) but fared very poorly in every **election** in which it competed in **Serbia** and **Montenegro** in the early 1990s. In 1994, in an effort to revitalize the flagging Marxist cause in Yugoslavia, Marković established the Yugoslav United Left (JUL), an alliance of socialist organizations closely allied to the ruling SPS. Although electorally insignificant, the JUL was and remains informally influential in Serbian politics, aided by Marković's position as Milošević's wife and political confidante. In June 1996, several prominent JUL members replaced SPS ministers in the federal and Serbian governments. In a manner closely related to her political activities, Marković is also a writer for the Belgrade-based magazine *Duga*, where her regular column has often provided a reliable guide to her husband's next political moves. Always hostile to the revival of Serb nationalism in the former Yugoslavia, Marković reportedly played a major role in convincing her husband to drop it altogether after 1994.

—M. M.

MARRIAGE

See **intermarriage**

MARTIĆ, MILAN

Milan Martić, a close political ally of Croatian Serb leader **Milan Babić**, was a police inspector in **Knin.**

In July 1990 he was the author of a letter to the federal interior ministry in Belgrade that expressed the refusal of the Knin police to wear the new Croatian uniforms with ***šahovnica*** badges. This letter sparked a visit by the Croatian interior minister, his deputy, and the Šibenik commander of police, responsible for the Knin municipality. Ostensibly there to defuse the crisis through dialogue, the delegation in fact simply provided Martić with an opportunity to humiliate the Croatian government. Trapped in the police station by an angry crowd, the three state officials had to turn to Martić to get them out safely. Martić installed himself as police chief and organized the distribution of arms from the police stores to the people of Knin when the Croats attempted to take back control of the town.

Following the failure of the Croatian government to reestablish control in Knin, Martić became the military leader of the Serbs in the Croatian **Krajina**. He organized the Serb militia (known as the Martićevci) in raids on **Pakrac** and the **Plitvice** national park in February and March 1991. Through July and August, he directed the Serb militia in a campaign of expansion that took in the municipalities of Kostajnica, Dalj, **Okučani**, and **Glina**. He planned the first major act of deliberate "**ethnic cleansing**" in Croatia, in the village of **Kijevo**, along with **Ratko Mladić**, the new chief of staff of the Knin Corps of the **Yugoslav Peoples' Army** (JNA). Martić and Mladić established a rapport very quickly, and Martić announced that the Martićevci were now acting in full cooperation with the JNA.

In 1992, when Milan Babić opposed **Slobodan Milošević's** orders to agree to the deployment of United Nations (UN) troops in Croatia, Martić broke with Babić and ordered the Serb militias to follow JNA orders in readiness for the UN's arrival. In January 1994 Martić was elected president of the so-called **Serb Republic of the Krajina,** directly defeating Babić. He remained in this position until the Croats retook the **United Nations protected areas** of western Slavonia and Krajina in May and August 1995.

—G. R. B.

MASLENICA BRIDGE

One of the most serious blows suffered by **Croatia** in the war was the destruction of the Maslenica Bridge in November 1991. This bridge spanned an inlet of the Adriatic Sea some 20 miles west of **Zadar**. With its destruction, the main road link was severed between Zadar, **Split** and all of southern **Dalmatia** (on one side of the bridge), and **Zagreb**, Rijeka, and the rest of the republic (on the other). The action by Croatian Serb forces was particularly effective since the rail link to Split via **Knin** had already been disrupted by the creation of the Serb **Krajina**. Overland **communication** between southern Dalmatia and the rest of Croatia consequently was reduced to minor roads along the island of Pag and ferry journeys to the mainland at Karlobag or Jablanac.

The bridge was replaced by a 270-meter pontoon constructed in July 1993, but the area was closed again by artillery fire the following month, having become a pawn in the negotiations over the implementation of **cease-fires** and the withdrawal of Serb heavy weapons. Such was the location's importance, however, that Croatian forces mounted a fierce assault during the period 9–15 September 1993, infringing all agreements brokered by the **United Nations;** this assault managed to drive Serb forces beyond artillery range. The heavy casualties sustained by Croatian forces and the international criticism earned by the move are indications of the enormous value placed upon Maslenica. A permanent replacement was opened in 1995.

—J. B. A.

MATEŠA, ZLATKO

Zlatko Mateša has been prime minister of **Croatia** since November 1995. Born in 1949 in Zagreb, Mateša was educated at that city's university and the Henley Management College in the United Kingdom. Having worked as a corporate lawyer and enterprise manager, he joined the **Croatian Democratic Union** (HDZ) in 1990. In 1992, Mateša was appointed director of the government's Agency for Reconstruction and Development, and in 1993 he became a member of the cabinet as minister without portfolio (one with general government responsibilities, but without responsibility for a particular department). As a technocrat with a business background, Mateša was given the premiership specifically in order to revive the ailing Croatian economy. As premier, Mateša has consequently striven to improve Croatia's standing internationally, notably through closer links with nearby **Bosnia-Hercegovina**, the latter's peaceful reunification as envisaged by the **Dayton Agreements**, and the implementation of the peace settlement for the formerly Serb-held enclave in eastern **Slavonia.**

Mateša has been strongly in favor of radical economic reform as demanded by the **International Monetary Fund.** Within the ruling HDZ, however, his relatively lightweight status has limited his room for action, dependent as he is on the uncertain patronage of President **Franjo Tudjman.** He is reported to have opposed the influence of the nationalist Hercegovina Lobby on Zagreb, although Tudjman's continuing support for Croat nationalist aspirations in **Hercegovina** has damaged Croatia's international rehabilitation and hampered economic reform. In the event of the death of the ailing Tudjman, Mateša will almost certainly be removed from office in Croatia.

—M. M.

MEDAK POCKET

The Medak pocket consisted of a collection of small rural villages and hamlets in United Nations (UN) Sector South, which formed a "finger" of Serb-controlled land protruding into Croatian territory. On 9 September 1993, Croatian forces mounted an attack in this area, overrunning it completely and killing or routing the few defenders. Possibly as a result of Serb attacks on **Zagreb** and **Karlovac,** within a few days the Croatians indicated a "willingness to withdraw" and turn over the territory to the peacekeeping force **UNPROFOR.**

As UN forces (consisting of troops from Canada and **France** under UN operational control) entered the area from 15 September, they found that every building in the area had been burned or demolished, livestock killed, and wells poisoned. According to the UN secretary-general, there was "evidence of mass murder that remains largely undocumented."

Sweep teams were organized to assess and record the extent of the damage, search for survivors, and collect bodies. The teams included civil police (CIVPOL) from the European Community (EC) for **monitoring,** UNPROFOR medical officers, and soldiers. A letter from the secretary-general to the UN Security Council reporting the incident noted that "there was a clear, obvious and overwhelming pattern of wanton destruction. . . . Devastation was total." Other UN reports on the incident note that the timing of the destruction was inconsistent with any legitimate military conduct and not of military necessity. Moreover, "the devastation was wrought in an unopposed withdrawal, not a contested advance or retreat."

Apart from the evidence of **ethnic cleansing,** the incidents at Medak are noteworthy for two other reasons. First, Canadian contingent reports stress that not only did the Canadian troops find themselves subject to Croatian-orchestrated delays in occupying the area, but that they were also involved in pitched battles with Croatian forces who began firing on them soon after occupation. It is possible that these Croatian soldiers had not received the **cease-fire** order, but it seems equally likely that these delays and attacks were intended to allow Croatian forces to complete their destruction of the area. There have also been allegations that much of the killing and destruction could have been prevented had UN troops been allowed to move into the area more quickly. UN orders that required soldiers to negotiate their way into the area, combined with Croatian delaying tactics, slowed the UN troops' movement.

Second, the United Nations has released the names of at least 10 individuals who acted as mercenaries for Croatian forces and who were involved in the Medak atrocities. Perhaps surprisingly, seven of these men were from the Netherlands, and a number of them had served in either **North Atlantic Treaty Organization** (NATO) or UN peacekeeping forces prior to their involvement the Yugoslav conflict. The remaining three named individuals were from Hungary, the United States, and Indonesia, respectively. Many of these men returned to their home countries after the war to their former lives. One is now reportedly a monk.

—J. D. D. S

See also: paramilitary/irregular forces; war crimes

MEDIA (DOMESTIC)

The mass communications media in Yugoslavia played an important role both in the genesis of conflict in the country and in the course of the conflict's development. In 1987 Yugoslavia boasted 2,825 newspapers with a total circulation of some 2.7 million copies. There were approximately 5 million radio receivers and 4 million TV sets, served by 202 radio stations, with TV centers in each of the republics and autonomous provinces. There were papers corresponding to the various **religions** and in the **languages** of the national minorities. The **Yugoslav Peoples' Army** alone published 22 titles.

A feature of the Yugoslav media was the lack of any federal network of communication. In 1990 only five papers had circulations exceeding 100,000. Fragmentation matched the process of political decentralization, with only the **League of Communists**' daily *Borba (Struggle)* appearing in both Latin and Cyrillic scripts, continuing a tradition established under King Aleksandar. The prestigious *Politika* (founded in 1903) was printed in **Cyrillic script** and remained a Belgrade-centered paper. The dominant characteristic of the Yugoslav communications media was their parochialism. A press law enacted in 1985 never managed to counter the wider decentralizing tendencies within Yugoslavia.

The long tradition of censorship in Yugoslavia antedates the communist period. The legal framework for the press was ambiguous. The 1974 constitution insisted that "the freedom and the rights of man and citizens are limited only by the equal freedom and rights of others, and by the constitutionally affirmed interests of the social community" (Basic Principles II, Article 153). Given the position of the League of Communists (LC) as the "organized leader of the ideal and political powers of the working class in the building of socialism" (Basic Principles VII) and hence, presumably, as the guardian of these "constitutionally affirmed interests," the point of balance between individual rights and collective discipline remained unclear. The criminal code gave the judiciary wide powers that could potentially be used against journalists, delineating offenses such as "counterrevolutionary activity" (Article 114), the commission of "hostile propaganda" (Article 118), and "verbal delicts" (Article 133). By law, publishers were required to lodge copies of galley proofs with the censor before publication, but the small size and inefficiency of the censor's office meant that this kind of intervention was infrequent. The major newspapers were published under the auspices of the Socialist Alliance, and the republican Associations of Journalists was also in a position to exercise control over its members. Ninety percent of accredited journalists in 1987 were members of the LC. Consequently, the burden of control was exercised largely through self-censorship. The vigilance of members of the LC in publishing houses occasionally resulted in "spontaneous" refusal to print material at the point of production. There were controversial cases of post-publication repression, the most frequent targets of which were the **student** papers such as *Mladina.* On rare occasions, as during the **Croatian Spring** of 1971, titles were closed as a direct result of political intervention. Even so, visitors to the country were often struck by the relative freedom of expression in Yugoslavia, which extended to religious controversy and soft pornography, as well as the diversity of political views.

During the 1980s the conflicts emerging in Yugoslavia found expression in the media. The edition of *Nova Revija* for February 1987 attracted enormous attention because it carried items on the nature and future of the Slovene republic, which was exhibiting on many fronts an increasingly independent attitude. The editor was fired—although the new editor and his executive council subsequently endorsed the *Review*'s policy. *Katedra* published an interview with political dissident **Milovan Djilas** in March 1987; and in April 1987 *Mladina* published allegations that the army was preparing a plan for the arrest of political undesirables in **Slovenia** in an attempt to suppress the growing movement toward democratization.

A new press law introduced in November 1990, as part of the reform program of **Ante Marković**, abolished the constitutional provisions for censorship and permitted private ownership of the press, including foreign participation. Soon new independent titles began to appear (e.g., *Vreme* in Belgrade, *Globus* in Zagreb).

The movement was not invariably toward greater openness and freedom. The situation of the press in **Serbia** became more difficult after the rise to power of **Slobodan Milošević**. The editors of *Duga, NIN, Intervju,* and *Svet* were all replaced within a year of taking office. In the summer of 1988, the editor of *Politika* was replaced by a Milošević nominee.

A key development in the struggle for communication took place in relation to the autonomy of **Kosovo** in 1987, when TV Belgrade installed its own team instead of accepting reports from TV **Priština.** The interrepublican rotation arrangements broke down in 1988, initiated by the withdrawal of TV Zagreb. This retreat from plurality was accelerated as disintegration approached.

Borba bucked the trend toward political clientship. A new editor took over in 1987 who switched the paper's role from being a pliable mouthpiece of the LC to offering critical and independent journalism. By 1989, however, the federation-wide media had been reduced to *Borba,* the agency Tanjug, and the short-lived *YUTEL* (the pan-Yugoslav TV station). In November 1990 the Zagreb government set up *HINA* (the Croatian State News Agency), to serve the interests of the **Tudjman** regime, undermining Tanjug's operations in Croatia. A pro-Milošević editor-in-chief was appointed to Tanjug in December 1991.

The post-Yugoslav republics have all adopted constitutions that affirm rights to the freedom of expression. In some cases these broad constitutional provisions are amplified in specific legislation. **Croatia,** for example, adopted a law on public communication in April 1992 that includes provision for a Council for the Protection of the Freedom of the Press. In spite of the existence of liberal **constitutional** frameworks for the operation of the communications media, all of these states have encountered problems in the creation of a free press.

The creation of new states has left intact the old media, staffed in the main by the same journalists, so that old habits of patronage and self-censorship fade slowly. This situation is not improved by the fact that the officials of ruling parties often tend to act much as did those of the old LC. Croatia has pleaded the exigencies of the war as a reason for failing to implement the provisions of its own press law in terms of creating the Council for the Protection of the Freedom of the Press. Croatian government officials have also interfered with the composition of management boards in the process of the **privatization** of former "social property." The ruling **Croatian Democratic Union** (HDZ) has made attempts to control the regional daily *Slobodna Dalmacija* and the current affairs weekly *Danas* in this way. The satirical weekly ***Feral Tribune*** has been the target of repeated legal harassment.

In Serbia, Belgrade effectively challenged the editorial independence of TV stations in Titograd (now **Podgorica**), Priština, and Novi Sad in 1989. The distribution of broadcasting frequencies and the technical specifications of transmitters have been used as means by which to control radio and TV stations critical of government. During the war, transmitters became important military objectives, especially in **Bosnia-Hercegovina,** in the effort to ensure the control of information and opinion as well as territory and the movement of people. The offices of ***Oslobodjenje*** were a prime target of the Serb besiegers of Sarajevo.

Control of TV and radio became particularly important during the war as the depressed economic situation of ordinary people throughout the former federation placed the print media beyond their reach. Efforts to control the flow of news through these means were to some extent limited by the relatively indiscriminate nature of broadcasting. Citizens of Zagreb could watch and listen without difficulty to Serb transmissions from **Banja Luka.** The attempts of the Serbian government to co-opt *Borba* came unstuck when the paper's former journalists launched a rival paper, *Naša Borba (Our Borba)* and drew attention to the heavy-handed oppressiveness of state interference. The result was similar everywhere: the spread of a general popular cynicism and distrust of all media.

International concern about the collapse of news reporting within Yugoslavia into a competition between extreme nationalist nominees of government prompted two remedial initiatives. The Soros Open Society Foundation has attempted to make the support of independent communication its first priority across the region. The activities of the foundation have met with determined political resistance and attempts to close its operations in both Zagreb and Belgrade. The lack of means to communicate freely was the main inspiration behind the creation of AIM (Alternativna informativna mreža) in October 1992, with international (especially French) assistance. This network of independent journalists in the former Yugoslavia and its neighboring states has done much to train a new generation of professionals and to promote their work. Such has been the grip of state-controlled media in the former Yugoslavia, however, that these journalists' main achievement has been to supplement communication on the international plane.

The ending of the war brought no sign of immediate improvement. Such was the disquiet of the Office of the United Nations High Representative in Bosnia just prior to **elections** in the **Republika Srpska** in 1997 that troops of the Stabilization Force (S-FOR) took over control of transmitters in order to ensure a more balanced flow of communication. In Serbia, journalists have regularly been the target of intimidation both by "heavies" employed by **political parties** and by economic racketeers. The harassment of *Feral Tribune* and other alternative voices in Croatia has continued. An attempt was made in Serbia to introduce a new and restrictive press law in 1997, though this law was defeated in the courts.

The obstacles to the creation of a free press have not all been of a political character, however; economic difficulties have perhaps been equally significant. The prevailing depression of living standards has meant that few citizens can afford the cost of a newspaper. The press remains dependent upon subsidy, which opens opportunity for political interference, or (as in Slovenia, with its very small potential readership) permanently on the verge of economic unviability. The press has failed everywhere to emerge as an element of civil society.

—*J. B. A.*

See also: Implementation/Stabilization Force (I/SFOR); propaganda

Reference: Thompson, Mark. *Forging War: The Media in Serbia, Croatia and Bosnia-Hercegovina.* London: International Centre against Censorship, 1994.

MEDIA (EXTERNAL)

The international press has played an important role in shaping perceptions of the Yugoslav conflict in the outside world and, consequently, in influencing the international response. Media professionals were relatively ignorant about Yugoslavia at the start of the conflict. Eastern European correspondents had been largely Moscow oriented or had recent experience reporting about Poland or East Germany or Czechoslovakia. Vienna was regarded in some quarters as a good base from which to cover the region. Correspondents such as Misha Glenny, who already knew the area, were rare. Journalists remained trapped in general frameworks of loose presupppositions about the Balkans or relied upon rather broad images of Eastern Europe

Journalists were caught between contradictory stereotypes. The fall of the Berlin Wall and the end of communism were to be applauded. Instability, however, was a bad thing. There was overemphasis on the supposed role of **Tito** as an authority figure making for unification and a good deal of mythology about "age-old hatreds." It was impossible to report events in Sarajevo without reference to the assassination of Archduke Ferdinand in 1914, however thinly relevant that occasion might have been to events there in 1992.

Several problems were caused by the way in which the various news media work. Members of the media are primed to look for *stories* that center upon *events,* not to explain processes. The long maturation of the Yugoslav crisis demanded a grasp of historical complexities that did not yield easily to packaging as news stories. The essential connectedness of events in different parts of Yugoslavia was lost. For example, reporters were unable to relate the role of **Kosovo** in the genesis of the conflict to the secession of **Slovenia**, which in turn could not be linked intelligibly to the civil war in **Bosnia-Hercegovina**, which appeared to have no discernable relation to the likely eruption of the question of **Macedonia**. This sequence of connections was essential to the Yugoslav problem. These questions, however, were defined as beyond the scope of journalism.

In democratic societies a good deal of the political response to international affairs is driven by media attention. Politicians and diplomats were seduced into concentrating upon a succession of disparate events (Slovenia, Croatia, Bosnia . . . or even **Zagreb, Dubrovnik, Vukovar**) without a mind to their location within a *pattern* of developments. The responses of political figures then became the objects of media attention, and politicians and the press fed on each other in a spiral of fragmentation. Because they rely upon briefings by politicians, journalists have been led to circulate the view that military intervention was inadvisable or impossible on military grounds, without questioning the fact that it was the lack of clear political objectives that made military intervention impossible.

The media tend to concentrate upon elite persons and places and events. The notion of a "Balkan strong man" to replace Tito was an attractive angle for journalists, so that **Slobodan Milošević** was given a misleading degree of importance. Early media coverage of the Yugoslav crisis almost conveyed the impression that he had masterminded the whole process, although actually he has achieved none of his primary goals. The characteristics of Serbian politics remained unexplored.

"**Sarajevo**" became an icon for the war in general, distorting coverage of the nature and course of the conflict. However, coverage of Sarajevo never asked why the Bosnian Croat army (the **Croatian Council of Defense**—HVO) did not attempt to relieve the largest threatened Croat community in Bosnia. The siege of Dubrovnik made headlines, but the equally important failure of Croat attempts to take **Trebinje** passed without comment. In spite of numerous small items about heavy fighting on the **Orašje-Brčko** front or mentions of the struggle in the **Bihać** enclave, no international team of journalists visited these key war zones.

The media are typically taken up by narratives of human interest, neglecting less glamorous developments. Personal dramas, such as the story of **Irma Hadžimuratović**, were treated as major stories. In this respect, the efforts of journalists were often subverted by the commercial priorities of their editors. By concentrating upon human interest stories and neglecting analysis, however, the press fueled the atmosphere of "something must be done" but undermined the understanding that might have made it clear what could have been done.

Journalists have contributed massively to the mystification of the war, although courageous and determined journalism has often ensured that we knew a great deal about the war's human costs. (The high death toll of journalists, reportedly around 30, in the course of the war should not be forgotten.) A sense of general helplessness in the face of an incomprehensible disaster was inadvertently created. This is not to blame journalists, however, as it is important that we understand that they operate within a framework that is not of their own making and that often subverts what we (and they) would like journalism to be. The line between news and entertainment has been heavily blurred, and sensationalism is often a response to what readers, listeners, and viewers have come to expect.

—J. B. A.

See also: propaganda

References: Bell, Martin. *In Harm's Way: Reflections of a War-Zone Thug,* rev. ed. London: Penguin, 1996; Gow, James, Richard Paterson, and Alison Preston. *Bosnia by Television.* London: British Film Institute, 1996; Thompson, Mark. *Forging War: The Media in Serbia, Croatia and Bosnia-Hercegovina.* London: International Centre against Censorship, 1994.

MEDIATION

See **conflict management and conflict resolution**

MEDJUGORJE

The small Hercegovinian village of Medjugorje came to world attention in 1981 following the experience of a vision of the Virgin Mary by a group of local children. It subsequently became a major international pilgrimage destination, creating great controversy because of the importance of this very public manifestation of religious piety in a state where the communist regime was determinedly secular.

The relevance of Medjugorje to the development of the Yugoslav conflict is twofold. This area of **Hercegovina** has a history of attachment to radical Croatian nationalism, reflected in its support for the **Ustaša** between 1941and 1945. In addition, the conflict between local Franciscans and the bishop of **Mostar** over recognizing the authenticity of the vision can be read as reflecting a strong sense of the distinctiveness of local and regional identity, as well as hostility toward metropolitan interference, which was also expressed in the attempt to create a ministate of **Herceg-Bosna**. The gap between popular religiosity and ecclesiastical authority illustrated in Medjugorje also underscores the importance of caution in generalizing about the significance of **religion** in Yugoslavia, including, in this case, the **Catholic Church**.

(There were also reports of international charitable donations to the cause of Medjugorje being diverted to the local Croat war effort.)

—J. B. A.

Reference: Markle, Gerald E., and Frances B. McCrea. "Medjugorje and the Crisis in Yugoslavia." In William H. Swatos (ed.), *Politics and Religion in Central and Eastern Europe.* Westport, CT: Praeger, 1994.

MEMORANDUM OF THE SERBIAN ACADEMY

See **Serbian Academy Memorandum**

MERCENARIES

See **paramilitary/irregular forces**

MESIĆ, STIPE

Born in 1934 at Slavonska Orahovica, Stijepan (Stipe) Mesić trained as a lawyer. He was jailed for two years in 1971 for his activities in the mass nationalist movement of the **Croatian Spring.** Following the victory of the **Croatian Democratic Union** (HDZ) in 1990, Mesić became president of the government (i.e., prime minister) of **Croatia.** When the Sabor (Assembly) recalled Communist Stipe Šuvar as Croatia's representative on the Yugoslav federal state presidency (FSP), Mesić was put forward as the new Croatian nominee. When **Borisav Jović** stepped down as vice president of the FSP in October 1990, Mesić was elected as the replacement. Mesić played a significant part during early 1991 when the Serbian, Montenegrin, and Vojvodinan representatives attempted to compel the FSP to authorize the **Yugoslav Peoples' Army** (JNA) to disarm Croatian police and the Slovenian Territorial Defense Forces.

Mesić's rotation to the post of president of the FSP was due on 15 May 1991, and he received assurances from the JNA that they would not oppose his accession in return for an agreement that the JNA could proceed with "peacekeeping" forces in the tense Serb regions of Croatia. The JNA would disarm all illegal forces and demobilize the police. Nevertheless, Mesić's rotation was blocked by the Serb members of the collective state presidency (CSP) and their allies, and the federal presidency ceased to function.

When Croatia declared independence on 25 June, the JNA was ordered by the federal government to intervene, despite the fact that Mesić had still not been installed as president of the CSP. (Consequently, there was no legitimate commander-in-chief of the JNA to ratify such an order.) Following the second visit of the **European Community**'s "troika"—a group comprised of the former, current, and next presidents of the European Community—to Yugoslavia, Mesić was finally declared president of the CSP on 30 June.

Mesić attempted to use his position to moderate the growing conflict, agreeing to a **cease-fire** with **Slovenia** on 2 July. His ambiguous position as a member of the party that had led Croatia to independence increasingly compromised the CSP. In September, Yugoslav defense secretary **Veljko Kadijević** refused to act on an order from Mesić (who accused the military of preparing a coup) to withdraw to barracks in Croatia. Mesić canvassed the **United Nations** (UN) for a peacekeeping force and pressed **Germany** to recognize Croatia. As fighting intensified he urged JNA conscripts to desert. Finally, on 5 July, he announced his resignation on the basis that Yugoslavia no longer existed.

In August 1992, after the second multiparty **elections** in Croatia, Mesić was elected president (speaker) of the House of Deputies. He held this position until April 1994, when he broke away from the HDZ with **Josip Manolić** to form the Croatian Independent Democratic Party (HNDS), disagreeing with **Franjo Tudjman**'s authoritarian leadership, the HDZ's support of the **Bosnian Croats**' war against the Bosnian government, and Tudjman's treatment of critics of the war.

—*G. R. B.*

See also: Dubrovnik

MILITARY FRONTIER

An important influence upon the development of patterns of ethnic settlement in **Croatia** and the **Vojvodina**, and consequently upon the genesis of the conflict in Yugoslavia, has been the historical legacy of the Military Frontier (Militärgrenze or Vojna *krajina*) established by the **Habsburg Empire**. As the **Ottoman Empire** was driven back from its occupation of Austrian and Hungarian lands during the late sixteenth and seventeenth centuries, the border zone was colonized by settlers whose right to land use exempt from feudal dues was linked to their willingness to offer permanent military service on behalf of the emperor. At its height the Military Frontier stretched from the Adriatic Sea, along the **Sava** and **Danube Rivers,** to Transylvania and Wallachia. Organized into military districts and regiments, the men of the region came to constitute a semistanding army. As the wars against the Ottoman occupier had left the area ravaged and depopulated, this force was constituted in large measure of immigrants, and by the end of the eighteenth century about half of the population were descendants of Orthodox refugees from south of the Sava. Sremski Karlovci became an important center of the Serbian **Orthodox Church**.

Although the Military Frontier was abolished in 1881, it retained its distinctive social composition, the former *graničari* (frontiersmen) being ancestors of the substantial Serb minority within Croatia. When over a century later armed conflict broke out between the Croatian government and its Serb minority in response to the republic's threatened secession from Yugoslavia, the boundaries of the autonomous **Krajina** proclaimed by the Serbs corresponded remarkably closely to that of the former Military Frontier.

—*J. B. A. and G. R. B.*

MILOŠEVIĆ, SLOBODAN

A highly controversial Yugoslav politician, Slobodan Milošević was president of **Serbia** throughout the greater part of the Yugoslav conflict and subsequently president of the Federal Republic of **Yugoslavia** (FRY). Of Montenegrin origins, he was born in Požarevac (Serbia) in 1941. Graduating in law from the University of Belgrade in 1964, Milošević subsequently married **Mirjana Marković**, from a prominent Serbian communist family.

Slobodan Milošević, president of the Federal Republic of Yugoslavia and leader of the Serbian Socialist Party. (Tanjug)

In 1968 Milošević gained his first important executive position at Technogas, a Serbian energy enterprise that he had first joined in 1964. Full membership in the ruling **League of Communists** of Serbia (SKS) followed in 1969, when **Ivan Stambolić** reportedly acted as Milošević's main sponsor. In 1973 Milošević became director-general of Technogas. In 1978 he became president of the powerful Beobanka (Belgrade Bank), a job that involved extensive travel abroad during the early 1980s, during which Milošević acquired a fluent command of English.

Sponsored throughout the 1960s and 1970s by his rising mentor Stambolić, Milošević was then an unremarkable official with unquestioned loyalties to **Tito** and **Titoism**. One of the beneficiaries of Tito's purge of a relatively liberal SKJ (League of Communists of Yugoslavia) leadership in the early 1970s, Milošević was typical of his political class in his opposition to Serbian nationalism. In 1984, when Stambolić became president of the SKJ central committee, Milošević became a full-time politician as head of the powerful SKJ committee in Belgrade; in 1986, when Stambolić was elevated to the presidency of Serbia, Milošević took over as head of the SKJ. This enabled Milošević to place his nominees throughout the SKJ apparatus in Serbia, a move that eventually gave him the means to destroy his mentor and friend in 1987.

In 1986 the influential **Serbian Academy** of Sciences and Arts (SANU) published a controversial memorandum that alleged a systematic anti-Serb bias in Yugoslav politics. Immediately seized upon as a rallying cry for a revived Serbian nationalism during the crises of the 1980s, Stambolić and other leaders of SKJ, including Milošević, initially condemned the memorandum. However, in April 1987, at a rowdy SKJ meeting in **Priština**, the capital of the predominantly Albanian-inhabited province of Kosovo, Milošević discovered the value of the rhetoric of Serbian nationalism for the first time, thereby becoming the most popular Serbian politician virtually overnight. Aided by the media in Serbia, Milošević's opportunistic co-optation of Serbian nationalism enabled him to outmaneuver Stambolić, culminating in the latter's removal from the Serbian presidency in December 1987. This stunning political and personal betrayal paved the way for Milošević's own elevation to the presidency in May 1989.

In 1988–1989, Milošević consolidated his power through an "antibureaucratic revolution." Aimed in the first instance against the incumbent SKJ leaderships in the autonomous provinces of the **Vojvodina** and **Kosovo**, the tactics of hysterical **media** propaganda and massive demonstrations quickly gave Milošević absolute power in Serbia. Following large demonstrations by Serbs in Kosovo during August 1988, the Kosovar Albanian SKJ leader, **Azem Vllasi**, was arrested. In October, the SKJ leadership in the Vojvodina were replaced by Milošević loyalists. In January 1989, Milošević supporters replaced the incumbent communist leadership in **Montenegro**. By March, Kosovo had been stripped of its autonomy, precipitating widespread ethnic **Albanian** demonstrations that resulted in loss of human life. In July 1989, the public celebrations attending the 600th anniversary of the **Battle of Kosovo** marked the peak of Milošević's popularity in Serbia.

Outside Serbia, however, Milošević's inflammatory nationalist rhetoric, unconstitutional appropriation of power, and opposition to any real political and socioeconomic reform led to the weakening and then the destruction of the Yugoslav federation.

Already strong in 1988–1989, Slovene and Croat opposition to Milošević's vision of a reunified

Yugoslavia under effective Serbian control culminated in the collapse of the SKJ at its congress in January 1990. Following the accession of new anti-Communist and anti-Serbian governments after the first multiparty **elections** in **Slovenia** and **Croatia** in April–May 1990, the Yugoslav crisis entered a decisive stage. Growing secessionist sentiments in the northern republics were met by refusal on the part of Milošević to discuss seriously the possibility of a new Yugoslav confederation. All the republican leaders continued to undermine what remained of the federal government and its laws in the disintegrating Yugoslav federation.

Serbia's first postwar multiparty elections took place in December 1990, when the renamed SKJ, the Socialist Party of Serbia (SPS), won a comfortable parliamentary majority, mainly because of Milošević's strength in rural and southern Serbia, tight government control of the media, and a badly divided opposition. The last of the Yugoslav republics to hold free (but not entirely fair) elections, Serbia remained an unreconstructed neocommunist dictatorship that had adopted the forms of Serbian nationalism in order to relegitimate its decaying power in the postcommunist era.

In March 1991, however, Milošević faced a major challenge to his power in Belgrade. Confronted with large opposition demonstrations against his rule, Milošević reportedly struck a secret deal with the powerful **Yugoslav Peoples' Army** (JNA), which was used to crush anticommunist unrest in Belgrade. This move reinforced an already widespread impression that the JNA was no longer a federal institution but rather a purely Serbian one under the control of Milošević.

During the subsequent descent into civil war in 1991, Milošević used the JNA to briefly contest Slovenia's unilateral declaration of independence in June of that year, as well as to assist an ethnic Serb rebellion in Croatia. Following the international **recognition** of Slovenia and Croatia by January 1992, Milošević suffered his first major setback. With the end of the first Serb-Croat war in late 1991, another and more serious ethnic Serb rebellion erupted into full-scale civil war in **Bosnia-Hercegovina** in April 1992, when the republic was internationally recognized as an independent state. Draconian economic **sanctions** were imposed by the United Nations (UN) against the recently proclaimed Federal Republic of Yugoslavia. Further strengthened in 1993, this sanctions regime and the international isolation of the FRY as a pariah state caused immense socioeconomic damage in Serbia and Montenegro. Paradoxically, this economic disaster strengthened Milošević and the SPS, which was reelected in December 1992 and again in December 1993. In a series of adept political moves, Milošević entered into a brief alliance with **Vojislav Šešelj**'s ultranationalist Serbian Radical Party (SRS), which was then used to rid of Federal President **Dobrica Ćosić** and Federal Premier **Milan Panić** after they had become too independent and a potential threat to Milošević's dictatorship.

Following the **Bosnian Serbs**' rejection of the **Vance-Owen Plan**, a far more potent threat to Milošević emerged during the course of 1993 in the form of the president of the Bosnian Serb Republic, **Radovan Karadžić**, and his military commander, **Ratko Mladić**. Their uncompromising Serbian nationalism was dangerous to Milošević because it conflicted with his changing political priorities. His foreign policy was no longer dominated by appeals to pan-Serb solidarity but by the need to get the UN sanctions against the FRY lifted as quickly as possible. Milošević's problems with the Bosnian Serbs led to a split with the influential Serbian **Orthodox Church**, which turned against him in 1993. In August 1993, Milošević purged the high command of the Army of Yugoslavia (VJ); he had never entirely trusted this Titoist institution, preferring instead to rely on the Serbian police as the main coercive instrument of his rule.

In January 1994 Milošević's position was strengthened by the introduction of a new Yugoslav dinar as currency and by the first macroeconomic stabilization program in Serbia since the communist period. In August 1994 he finally split with the Bosnian Serbs over their rejection of the **Contact Group**'s peace plan for Bosnia. This final abandonment of pan-Serb solidarity led to the first easing of the UN sanctions regime in September 1994. Thereafter, Milošević's basic political priority has been to stay in power by completing the international rehabilitation of the FRY, even if this has meant the abandonment of the Croatian and Bosnian Serbs in the process. Thus, he did not come to the aid of the Croatian Serbs in 1995; nor did he do anything to aid the Bosnian Serbs, who were forced to accept the **Dayton Agreements** in November 1995—the main result of which was the suspension of the UN economic sanctions against the FRY in December.

Following the more favorable political and economic circumstances of 1994–1995, the SPS was again reelected to power in the parliamentary elections of December 1996. Having served two terms as president of Serbia (the maximum allowed under the Serbian constitution), Milošević was compelled to accept the presidency of the FRY. It is indicative of the strength of his personal power base, however, that he has been able to continue to dominate the Serbian and Yugoslav political scene from a post that is constitutionally less significant than the one that he formerly held.

—M. M.

MINES

See **land mines; Trepča miners**

MITSOTAKIS, KONSTANTINOS

A native of Crete (born 1918), Konstantinos Mitsotakis became prime minister of Greece in April 1990, after his New Democratic Party (ND) won the general election. During his tenure of office, the disintegration of Yugoslavia took place, with far-reaching consequences for Greek foreign policy as well as for the unity of his own party.

Mitsotakis finished his education in law in Athens in 1940. In 1946 he became involved in politics in the Liberal Party. From 1951 he held several posts in various Greek governments in relation to finance and the economy, becoming known as a controversial political figure. In 1965, as a member of the cabinet of the Center Party government, he came into conflict with then-Prime Minister George Papandreou, resulting in the fall of the ruling Center Party. During the military takeover of the country in April 1967, he was arrested, but in 1968 he managed to escape abroad. He returned to Greece in 1974 after spending six years in Paris as a political refugee. In 1978 Mitsotakis returned to active politics as minister of finance in the ND government under the leadership of Kostantine Karamanlis. In 1987 he became president of the party and successfully ran for election as prime minister of Greece in 1990.

By that time the political situation in neighboring Yugoslavia was deteriorating rapidly. In general, **Greece**'s stance in relation to the Yugoslav crisis under the government of Mitsotakis could be described as supportive of **Serbia**, emphasizing the traditional and historical relations between the two countries; by contrast, the other members of the **European Community** (EC) held Serbia responsible for the spread of the Yugoslav wars. Although Greece stood for the preservation of the Yugoslav state, in December 1991 it went along with the rest of the EC members and recognized the independence of **Croatia** and **Slovenia.**

According to Mitsotakis's political opponents, this move was a grave political mistake because Mitsotakis had agreed to the recognition of Croatia and Slovenia without getting binding assurances from the EC that the "Republic of Macedonia" would not be recognized under this name ("Macedonia" is a Greek historical concept and nomenclature). Mitsotakis stated, on 19 October 1991, that although Greece on the international level had the diplomatic means to fight against Macedonia (known officially to the United Nations as "Former Yugoslav **Republic of Macedonia**" [**FYROM**]), it had no means to impose its will upon the people of the Macedonian republic as to how they would refer to their own country. His stance brought a strongly worded protest by his own foreign minister, Antonis Samaras, which resulted in the latter's resignation not only from the government post but also from the New Democratic Party itself.

—N. M. G.

MLADIĆ, RATKO

Gen. Ratko Mladić was the military leader of the **Republika Srpska** who masterminded the campaign resulting in the seizure of 70 percent of **Bosnia-Hercegovina** by **Bosnian Serb** forces in 1992–1993.

Mladić was born in eastern **Hercegovina** in 1943 in a mountainous area that has produced the most intractable of the nationalists who have emerged from the former Yugoslavia. His father, a **Partizan** fighter, was killed when Mladić was two. Mladić spent nearly 30 years in the **Yugoslav Peoples' Army** (JNA), where he was loyal to the communist ethos and known for his organizing abilities. When Yugoslavia collapsed in 1991, he was chief of staff of the army corps based in **Knin**, the seat of Serb insurgency in Croatia. In April 1992 Mladić was promoted to general "for extraordinary conduct in combat assignments of special importance for the armed forces and the defence of the country." In May he was appointed military commander of the **Bosnian Serb**

General Ratko Mladić, commander of the Bosnian Serb Army, 1992–1996. (Tanjug)

Army (BSA) at President **Slobodan Milošević**'s special insistence, according to diplomats.

Mladić was the chief strategist in the military campaign by insurgent Serbs in Bosnia. Given that much of the warfare was targeted against unarmed civilians, he earned a reputation for brutality. A former senior official of the United Nations (UN) who spent hours negotiating with Mladić described him as "highly intelligent and extremely violent," according to Ian Traynor of the *Guardian* newspaper of the UK (18 April 1994, p. 8). Mladić was instrumental in defeating the **Vance-Owen Plan** in 1993 by convincing the Bosnian Serb parliament that the plan would result in unacceptable territorial losses. He sought to deter Western military intervention by threatening to take the war to Washington, London, and Rome. In 1993–1994 his forces shot down **North Atlantic Treaty Organization** (NATO) planes over Bosnia and kidnapped hundreds of UN Protection Force (**UNPROFOR**) personnel. In 1994, relations with his political superior, **Radovan Karadžić**, deteriorated, but he retained close contact with, though autonomy from, President Milošević.

Mladić had already been made the subject of an investigation for alleged **war crimes** by the United Nations when he directed the slaughter of unarmed Bosnian men and boys after the fall of **Srebrenica** in July 1995. His bluff finally appeared to be called in August 1995 by the massive assault of NATO's Operation Deliberate Force, and the strategic advantage started to slip away from his side.

On 27 June 1996, Mladić was formally charged by the UN **War Crimes Tribunal** with **genocide** and crimes against humanity. He became a liability for the Bosnian Serb leadership as it sought to reposition itself after the **Dayton Agreements**. On 9 November 1996, he and 80 of his senior officers were cashiered from the BSA, but he remained at liberty owing to the reluctance of the NATO-led **Implementation Force** to secure his arrest.

—*T. G.*

MLADINA

Mladina (Youth) is a weekly magazine published in Ljubljana, capital of Slovenia, since 1943. In the mid-1970s it ventured to change from a general cultural magazine to one with a reputation for social and political criticism. It was often at odds with its sponsor, the League of Socialist Youth of Slovenia, attracting frequent censorship and therefore wider readership. Its increasing radicalism during the 1980s culminated in a political show trial of three of its staff, including **Janez Janša**, Franc Zavrl, and David Tasić, together with army officer Ivan Borštner, on charges involving military secrets. In 1990 it became independent, and although its circulation has now halved to under 30,000 copies (still a high figure given Slovenia's population of two million) because of the competition that its own activities had helped to free up, it remains influential and is still widely respected for its historic role in pluralizing perceptions of Slovene society and for contributing to the movement for self-determination and independence.

—*J. J. H.*

MONARCHY

The Karadjordjevič dynasty of **Serbia**, Europe's only native royal house as well as its youngest, was established in 1804. It reigned for a large part of the nineteenth century and early twentieth century, and it widened its territory after World War I with the creation of the Kingdom of Serbs, Croats, and Slovenes, which became the Kingdom of Yugoslavia in 1929. King Aleksandar I was assassinated at

Marseille in 1934, and a period of regency ensued under his brother Paul (Aleksandar's son Peter being only 11 years old at the time of his father's murder). Paul's collaboration with the Axis powers led to the coup and subsequent invasion of Yugoslavia in 1941, as well as to the exile of the Yugoslav royal house to London. After 1945 **Tito**'s new regime confiscated all royal property.

The current heir to the throne is Peter II's son Alexander Karadjordjevič, currently styled His Royal Highness Crown Prince. Born in London in 1945, he has of late argued for the restoration of a constitutional monarchy as the answer to the country's problems and has visited Belgrade on several occasions during the 1990s to enlist internal support. Although he appeals to what many Serbs see as their national tradition, his popular support is currently estimated at under 20 percent. He has declared himself to be free from allegiance to any political party, but to some extent he will be aided by the stance of the promonarchist Serbian Renewal Movement.

—*J. J. H.*

See also: Drašković, Vukašin

MONITORING

As one of the key mechanisms used to help the implementation of the various **United Nations** Security Council (UNSC) resolutions pertaining to the former Yugoslavia, monitoring activities have figured prominently in the Yugoslav wars. Monitoring by the United Nations (UN) and other international bodies involved in the struggles rarely prevented conflict, either military or civil. At best such activities produced well-documented reports on violations of UNSC resolutions or related agreements; at worst they were completely irrelevant. Monitors were deployed in either primarily civilian or primarily military roles.

In **Slovenia** and **Croatia** in 1991, the **European Union** (EU) provided unarmed civilian monitors. In the case of **Bosnia-Hercegovina**, unarmed UN monitors were also deployed for the first time along the **Drina River** to monitor the sanctions regime imposed by Belgrade against its former **Bosnian Serb** allies, following the rift between the **Serb Republic of the Krajina** and the Federal Republic of **Yugoslavia** (FRY) in 1994. In both Croatia and Bosnia, the UN High Commission for Refugees (**UNHCR**) and International Committee of the **Red Cross** (ICRC) used civilian monitors extensively for such matters as population exchanges, **humanitarian aid** distribution, and other services to **refugees** and displaced persons. More recently, civilian monitors of the **Organization for Security and Cooperation in Europe** (OSCE) have acted as observers during various **elections**. In the circumstances of a war zone, the successful operation of

A NATO/Western European Union naval force monitors actions in the Adriatic Sea in 1994 as part of Operation Sharp Guard. (NATO photo)

entirely civilian monitoring forces is largely dependent upon military protection, which, while increasing the forces' security, can compromise perception of them as neutral and limit their mobility.

In the military sphere, the UN Protection Force (**UNPROFOR**) deployments in Croatia (and subsequently Bosnia-Hercegovina) included large numbers of UN military observers (UNMOs), who were used mainly for the monitoring of **cease-fires**, aircraft movements, and other military matters.

The mandatory economic **sanctions** introduced against the FRY by UNSC Resolution 757 in May 1992 were followed by widespread "sanctions busting," which prompted a strengthening of the sanctions regime under UNSC Resolution 820 of April 1993. This led to the deployment in the **Adriatic** of a combined **North Atlantic Treaty Organization** (NATO)/**Western European Union** naval monitoring and embargo enforcement force, code-named Operation Sharp Guard. Focused on the coast of **Montenegro**, this operation had the power to stop and search vessels on the high seas, but its effectiveness was limited given that most sanctions busting by the FRY was land based. Along **Serbia**'s Danubian border with **Romania**, a combined UN/EU monitoring force was similarly of limited effectiveness given that it lacked credible enforcement mechanisms. However, despite the noncooperation of the FRY and, at times, of Romania, this UN/EU operation did manage to make local sanctions busting more difficult. Maritime-based violations of the UN **arms** embargo against the former Yugoslavia were never significant.

Macedonia became central to Serbian sanctions-busting activities in 1992–1993. As a result, UNSC Resolutions 795 (December 1992) and 842 (July 1993) extended and reinforced the UNPROFOR mandate to Macedonia. Named the UN Preventive Deployment Force (**UNPREDEP**), this UN/NATO operation was primarily intended to monitor possible military threats to Macedonia from Serbia, but it came to be used for embargo enforcement along the Serbian/Macedonian **border**.

Elsewhere, in more recent years, the successor to UNPROFOR in Croatia, the UN Confidence Restoration Operation (**UNCRO**), operated briefly prior to its curtailment in 1995 to a small presence in eastern **Slavonia.** Here its rump was redesignated the UN Transitional Administration in Eastern Slavonia (**UNTAES**), pending the reincorporation of the region into Croatia in January 1998.

In Bosnia-Hercegovina, the NATO operation that succeeded UNPROFOR—the UN **Implementation Force** (IFOR), renamed the Stabilization Force (SFOR)—enforced and monitored the military provisions of the **Dayton Agreements** of December 1995. More so than with UNPROFOR, which relied in general upon the physical presence of human observers, IFOR and SFOR have relied extensively used "nonhumint" (nonhuman intelligence) monitoring methods, foremost of which have been the surveillance and other satellite systems of the **United States.** Similarly, the UN-mandated air exclusion or **no-fly zone** of 1993, code-named Operation Deny Flight, also used sophisticated and relatively effective nonhumint monitoring and enforcement methods based on satellites and AWAC aircraft operating from NATO bases in Italy.

—*M. M.*

MONTENEGRO

Montenegro (Crna Gora) is the smallest of the constituent republics of the former Socialist Federal Republic of **Yugoslavia** (SFRY), with a population of 648,000 in 1991 and an area of 13,812 square kilometers. It is now the "junior partner" of **Serbia** in the current Federal Republic of Yugoslavia. Montenegro possesses little in the way of economic wealth, being a largely barren wasteland of mountainous limestone where the main economic activity is subsistence agriculture. The republic has small reserves of lead and silver. Montenegro boasts one of the most spectacular and unspoiled coastlines in the whole of Europe, and there is potential for winter sports in the Durmitor Mountain range. Its potential as a major foreign currency earner for the federation is therefore considerable. Its current importance within what remains of Yugoslavia is also due to its geographical position, providing the only direct access Serbia has to the Adriatic and Mediterranean Seas via the ports of Kotor and Bar. The latter is connected to **Belgrade** by a railway finished only in the mid-1970s via the Montenegrin capital of **Podgorica** (formerly Titograd). For these reasons the current debate over possible Montenegrin independence has a very sharp edge, with major implications for the future **communications** and economic status of Serbia.

Historically Montenegro has long retained its spiritual, if not actual, independence from foreign powers, and its inhabitants valued their role as the "keepers of the gate"—defenders of Christendom against the might of the **Ottoman Empire** and **Islam.** The veracity of these claims can be disputed, but they nevertheless exercise the mind of the population and thus bear relevance to the wars of Yugoslav succession.

The issue of Montenegrin independence, as well as the nature of the republic's relationship with Serbia, has been a vexing question since the late nineteenth century, when the pro-Serbian Whites *(bijelaši)* and the pro-Montenegrin Greens *(zelenaši)* clashed electorally and on occasions militarily. The former independent kingdom joined with Serbia at the end of World War I and was incorporated into the "First Yugoslavia." Montenegro was temporarily annexed by **Italy** during World War II, but its distinctiveness was again recognized by the creation of an autonomous republic within the SFRJ in 1945.

Since the breakup of the SFRJ, the issue of Serbian/Montenegrin relations has been very much at the fore in Montenegrin politics—although little discussed (at least publicly) in Serbia. Montenegrin support for Serbia during the wars of succession has been at best dilatory, although the role played by Montenegrin troops in the siege of **Dubrovnik** and the widespread looting that occurred south of that city might suggest otherwise. Subsequently, Montenegro has attempted to distance itself from these events and has taken a more conciliatory line over the **Prevlaka** question than has Serbia. Similarly, the treatment of **Albanians**, the **Sandžak,** and Bosnian **Muslims** has been considerably more liberal in Montenegro than in Serbia.

Serbia's response to the lack of Montenegrin support has been to exert what amounts to internal economic sanctions against the republic. At times this pressure has been quite overt, with food trucks being turned back at the internal border and frequent unexplained power cuts. To this must be added constant interference in Montenegrin politics—the most obvious example being the election of **Momir Bulatović** to the republican presidency. Montenegro, however, fared better in terms of the effects of United Nations (UN) economic **sanctions** than did Serbia. Prices, especially of gasoline, were lower and goods were in considerably greater supply as a consequence of widespread smuggling and "sanctions busting" through Italy and Albania. An oil pipeline was even laid between Montenegro and **Albania,** a fact of which the UN was aware.

An important part of the background to the disagreements with Serbia lies in the problem that Montenegrins have in establishing their identity and thus realizing where their interests lie. During the first few years of the independent Montenegrin state under the Njegoš dynasty, this question was never asked. With the expansion of Montenegro from its core around Cetinje into areas of Bosnia and Albania during the nineteenth century, numbers of non-Montenegrins were brought within the republic. (The current capital, Podgorica, was originally an Albanian town.) The incorporation of Montenegro within a unitary royalist state, later the Kingdom of Yugoslavia, did not help to settle matters. The present population is thus partly composed of elements who regard themselves as Bosnian, as Albanian, or as "true Serbs" who consider their primary allegiance to a "**Greater Serbia.**" What is left is a section of the population who consider themselves as quite different from the Serbs and regard possible Montenegrin independence as a restitution of their historic status as the guardians of freedom.

This last group are represented primarily by the Liberal Alliance of Montenegro (LSCG), whose primary support is rooted in the old heartland of the kingdom and within the urban, educated elite. The main thrust of the LSCG program is independence, a marketized capitalist economy, and integration with the West. In the runoff to the 1997 presidential elections, the LSCG advised its supporters to vote for **Milo Djukanović**. Djukanović duly won the election, and despite reservations in Belgrade, it seems his victory has been accepted by Serbia. Since his election, Djukanović has made much of such pro-Montenegrin sentiments by moving some governmental services to Cetinje and proposing a move of the capital to the old heartland town of Nikšič. This "upping the ante" would seem to be part of a bargaining process with Belgrade to win greater autonomy for the republic within a newly constituted federation, with the ultimate threat of total political independence, however dangerous this would be economically.

—R. J.

MORILLON, PHILIPPE

Lt.-Gen. Philippe Morillon of France (born in Morocco in 1935) played an important role during the Yugoslav conflict; he was twice designated a commander of troops in the former Yugoslavia.

After being second in command of the **United Nations** (UN) peacekeeping force **UNPROFOR**, he was nominated commander in **Bosnia-Hercegovina** on 30 September 1992. He negotiated with Serb, Croat, and Muslim military commanders in order to obtain a succession of **cease-fires**, which were never respected (such as those of 26 October and 26 November 1992).

Morillon became a focus for the international attention on **Srebrenica** in March and April 1993. On 11 March, while the city (held by Muslims) was besieged by the Serbs, Morillon went there with a few troops. He declared he would stay in the city to prevent it from being overrun by the Serbs, quoting his historical compatriot Marshal Marie MacMahon's declaration at the siege of Sevastopol in 1855, "J'y suis, j'y reste" (Here I am, here I stay). In April, Morillon left the city with his troops after having negotiated the evacuation of the Muslims from Srebrenica and Konjević Polje, subsequently designated "**safe areas**" by the United Nations.

After handing over his command of UNPROFOR to Lt.-Gen. Francis Briquemont of Belgium on 12 July 1993, Morillon continued to be active concerning the Yugoslav conflict. He continually warned his own government, as well as those of the countries participating in the conflict resolution, of the dangers of **ethnic cleansing** and of the inefficiency of the UN's protection of safe areas and **refugees.**

When France, the United Kingdom, and the Netherlands decided to create the **Rapid Reaction Force** on 2 June 1995, Philippe Morillon was given his second commanding post in Bosnia. This force of 5,000 soldiers had the military potential and political ability to decide armed interventions whenever UN peacekeeping forces were attacked. One of its main functions was its deployment around **Sarajevo** to deter any bombing by the **Bosnian Serbs** and to protect the **humanitarian** convoys.

—A. H.

MOSLEMS

See **Muslims in Yugoslavia**

MOSTAR

The fourth-largest city in **Bosnia-Hercegovina** and the largest in **Hercegovina** (population 126,000 in 1991), Mostar is strategically located toward the head of the **Neretva River Valley**, which controls the road/rail route between Sarajevo and the port of Ploče on the Adriatic coast. During the Yugoslav period, Mostar had a number of important industries, including the manufacture of military aircraft and helicopters.

As the site of a large **Yugoslav Peoples' Army** (JNA) garrison, Mostar experienced its first serious fighting in 1991 when the **Bosnian Serbs** and **Bosnian Croats** battled for control of the city. Although an ethnically mixed city before the war—when Bosnian Muslims, Serbs, and Croats accounted for 34, 33, and 19 percent of the city's population, respectively—Mostar became divided into a Croat western zone and a Serb eastern zone in April 1992. With the forced withdrawal of the JNA from Mostar (and subsequently Bosnia), the city fell to the **Croatian Council of Defense** (HVO) and various **paramilitary** militias in June 1992.

Having pushed the Serbs out to the east, local Croat leader **Mate Boban** declared Mostar to be the capital of **Herceg-Bosna**, thereby guaranteeing conflict with local **Muslims** (Bošnjaci) concentrated on the eastern bank of the river. On the western side of the city, the local **Croatian Democratic Union** (HDZ) set about the systematic "**ethnic cleansing**" of all remaining Bošnjaci. Subsequently besieged by the HVO and periodically bombarded by the Serbs to the east, the 50,000 Bošnjaci in eastern Mostar survived by organizing effective defenses and receiving periodic deliveries of **humanitarian aid** by the United Nations Protection Force (**UNPROFOR**).

During the siege in 1992–1993, large parts of eastern Mostar were destroyed. The fact that the **Vance-Owen Plan** awarded the city to the Bosnian Croats increased the latter's determination to drive out the city's Bošnjaci. In November 1993, the HVO finally destroyed the Stari Most (Old Bridge) over the Neretva River, the bridge which gave Mostar its name, in one of the worst acts of vandalism of the Bosnian war.

Although the subsequent creation of a **Muslim-Croat Federation** ended the fighting in 1994, the reunification provisions were never properly implemented, mainly because of HDZ opposition supported by the Croatian government. The local HDZ was particularly intransigent and obstructive on this issue.

Nominally under a **European Union** (EU) administration for two years to December 1996, as mandated by the terms of the **Washington Agreement** of April 1994 and the **Dayton Agreements** of December 1995, Mostar was never reunified in practice, particularly with respect to the free movement of persons. The success or failure of reunification was and remains central to the ultimate success or failure of the federation. Despite the signing of a 12-point agreement between the Sarajevo and Zagreb governments under external pressure in April 1996, all attempts to reverse the city's partition have run into (often violent) opposition from the HDZ, indicating the powerlessness of the Sarajevo government and the unwillingness of the Zagreb government to rein in its local agents. The former EU administration was ineffectual, mainly because it lacked any real support from UNPROFOR and the **Implementation/Stabilization Force.** In the end, the EU administration was driven out of Mostar by the Bosnian Croats, who went so far as to threaten the life of the administration's officials, including the EU commissioner, Hans Koshchnik. Following elections in Mostar in 1996–1997, a new municipal council was elected on the basis of prewar electoral rolls, although persistent HDZ sabotage has rendered this council meaningless in practice. Post-Dayton, Mostar has been in receipt of considerable international economic aid, although much of this has reportedly been misused by local gangsters. In the event of renewed conflict, Mostar is sure to figure prominently, with the possibility of its further destruction and permanent partition.

In 1997 Mostar was the center for an experiment in removal of geographical indicators from vehicle registration plates in a bid to deter ethnic attacks.

—M. M.

MOTORWAYS

See **communications and transport**

THE MUSLIM WORLD AND THE YUGOSLAV CONFLICT

Given the prevalence of explanations of the breakup of Yugoslavia as primarily a consequence of religious factors, it has often been remarked that the Islamic states have played a relatively unimportant part in international attempts to promote a solution to the problems of the region. This expectation has rested upon several misunderstandings. It presupposes a relatively undifferentiated "Muslim world" that might provide a response. It oversimplifies the Yugoslav situation, whereas different components of the configuration of conflicts in Yugoslavia have appeared very differently to observers in different Muslim countries. It neglects the complexity and even inconsistency on the part of representatives of diverse Muslim groups within Yugoslavia and its successors; these representatives have presented themselves in sometimes contrasting ways to the outside world, including Muslim audiences. Finally, it overlooks the fact that governments from Islamic countries have needed to orient themselves in relation to the conflict in ways that also take account of the often contradictory responses of other states, especially in the **European Community** (EC).

The concept of a "Muslim world," although encouraged by the Islamic concept of the *umma* (community of the faithful), is often a Western misperception of the actual degree of unity among Islamic states. These states vary considerably in relation to their economic strength (e.g., consider Saudi Arabia and Sudan), their religious homogeneity (**Iran** and Malaysia), their size (Pakistan and Qatar), and the potential direct impact upon them of the Yugoslav crisis (**Turkey** and Tadzhikistan). For various historical reasons, some countries in which Islam is clearly the dominant **religion** do not wish to emphasize an Islamic identity, as in the case of near neighbors **Albania** and Turkey. Others (such as Egypt or Algeria) are, for domestic reasons, concerned about the rise of radical Islamism and fear that the stimulation of Islamic solidarity might promote internal discord.

The Muslim world, dispersed across the globe, has not necessarily been any better informed about Yugoslav developments than has the West. Furthermore, those countries with a history of active cooperation with Yugoslavia, through the **Nonaligned Movement**, have not necessarily found that that experience promotes Islamic solidarity. The close links between Iraq and Yugoslavia, especially in relation to the trade in arms and oil, have tended to provide a basis for continuing support for **Serbia** rather than for **Bosnia-Hercegovina** or **Kosovo.**

There has been a degree of inhibition about the vigorous advocacy of international action to prevent **genocide** in Bosnia—on the part of Iraq and Turkey, for example, who would certainly not welcome action on a similar basis in support of Kurds living in their own territories. The expectation of a "Muslim" response to the Yugoslav war tends to underplay this real diversity.

Similarly, it is important to grasp the fact that the complexity of the Yugoslav situation is such that its relevance for **Muslims** more generally has not been uniform. For Turkey, the direct relevance of the situation in Bosnia-Hercegovina is quite different for that in **Macedonia**. The latter situation has an immediate bearing upon Turkey's relations with **Greece**, which is Turkey's overwhelming foreign policy priority; this effect is not present in Turkey's concern for Bosnia.

The Sarajevo government has been willing, at least on occasions, to "play the Muslim card." In July 1991 **Alija Izetbegović** visited Pakistan, Saudi Arabia, and Turkey, and envoys were sent to other states, after which Turkey and several other Islamic countries opened consulates in Sarajevo. At other times, however, the Bošnjaki (Bosnian Muslims) have taken to presenting themselves principally as *Europeans*, aware of the risk that too great an emphasis upon Islam might play into the hands of the Serbs, who have attempted to exploit fear of an expanded Islamic presence in Europe, which finds particular echoes in France. Leaders of Kosovo **Albanians**, too, have been generally reluctant to appeal to Islamic identity, aware of the confessional diversity of ethnic Albanians. They have emphasized instead the linguistic unity of their people, preferring to base their appeal to the international community upon the Western tradition of self-determination. The stance of nonviolent resistance adopted by the **Democratic League of Kosovo** appears strange to many from the Islamic tradition of political thought. In Macedonia the Albanian political movement has been divided in part by these choices.

The position of the Muslim world has sometimes been made difficult by the behavior of European governments and others, who have been inconsistent in their policies toward Muslim groups in Yugoslavia. The EC has tended to base its response to the situation in Kosovo on the inviolability of historic **borders**, although it has been prepared to countenance and even encourage the division of Bosnia-Hercegovina. The **Organization for Security and Cooperation in Europe** (OSCE) has tended more consistently to favor arguments based upon self-determination. The policy of the EC with respect to international **recognition**, following the report of the **Badinter Commission**, was inconsistent in the extreme. To the extent that Islamic governments have been prepared to accept the "Europeanization" of the Yugoslav crisis (and Iran has not)—i.e., European nations view it as a European crisis rather than a Muslim one—then they have experienced difficulty in following a "European" line.

The response of the Muslim world to the Yugoslav situation should not be underestimated. By the summer of 1992, the Organization of the Islamic Conference, an international forum which promotes Islamic solidarity among its member states, was becoming vociferous in its demands that something be done to address the plight of Bosnian Muslims. Egypt, Saudi Arabia, and Turkey were all outspoken in their demands for action. Different Islamic states have played an active role within the **United Nations** (UN) from time to time, organizing debates and formulating resolutions on the issues. The Turkish government promoted an international conference on Bosnia in July 1995

Assessment of the response of Muslims to the situation should also not be limited to official state action. Volunteer *mujaheddin* (paramilitary) units have played a small but significant role in the armed struggle in Bosnia. Islamic charitable organizations, such as Merhemet, have also played a part in the organization and supply of **humanitarian aid** that has been largely overlooked in the West.

—*J. B. A.*

See also: arms transfers; Islam and the West; paramilitary/irregular forces

MUSLIM-CROAT FEDERATION

The establishment of the federal state involving Muslim and Croat entities in Bosnia-Hercegovina in March 1994 was a somewhat surprising development in the context of preceding events in the Bosnian war.

During the first few months of the conflict in the spring of 1992, there had been a perceived if uneasy alliance of Croats and Muslims in the face of Serb advances. However, the emerging agenda in Zagreb and Belgrade for a division of Bosnia between Croats and Serbs led to several hostilities between Croat and Muslim forces later in the year. After the winter standoff in 1992–1993, full-scale conflict between them erupted in the following April, starting with the massacre at **Ahmići**. As Silber and Little, in their book *The Death of Yugoslavia* (London: Penguin Books, 1995), succinctly put it: "The Serbs had seized 75 percent of Bosnia, and the Croats and Muslims were killing each other for the rest." The prime mover, in this case, was the **United States**, which in the late summer of 1993 sensed an incipient interest among some leaders on both sides in coming to an arrangement. The advantages for the Bosnian government were more apparent, in terms of opening up routes from the coast and the West for relief supplies and potentially for arms (though this latter option was not official U.S. policy). What did suit the Americans, however, was the prospect of Bosnian government forces being freed from the Croatian fronts to concentrate on the Serbs. Although during the next six months there was no remission of hostilities on the ground, unofficial diplomatic maneuvers were proceeding. The Americans, in the persons of Charles Redman (President Clinton's special envoy) and Peter Galbraith (U.S. ambassador to Croatia) were impressing upon Croatian president **Franjo Tudjman** that he could not rely on political or economic support, or indeed immunity from **sanctions**, if he himself were to continue to sanction Bosnian Croat atrocities, whether instigatory or retaliatory.

The U.S. effort was importantly bolstered by the stance of Ivo Komšić, a **Bosnian Croat** politician, who had anticipated the creation of a Muslim-Croat federation as a more acceptable alternative to a Bosnian Croat ministate based on western **Hercegovina** (with its traditionally strong lobby led by **Mate Boban**) but containing only one-third of the Croat population of Bosnia. Komšić's plan also provided for a potential confederation with **Croatia** "proper," though short of the concept of a "**Greater Croatia.**"

These twin pressures, as well as the growth of international reaction to the continuing conflicts in Bosnia (especially the bombing of the marketplace in **Sarajevo**), led to an intensification of diplomatic activity in February and March 1994, talks in Vienna, and a series of meetings in Washington, D.C. These culminated in a signed agreement between the parties, subsequently known as the **Washington Agreement,** which was supposedly based upon Swiss-style **cantons**. Subsequent progress toward implementation was sporadic, but the armed hostilities between Croats and Muslims ceased. This scheme can be seen as preparing the ground for the Dayton Agreements, by which the Washington Agreement was superseded in the following year.

—*J. J. H.*

Reference: Silber, Laura, and Allan Little. *The Death of Yugoslavia.* Penguin Books: London, 1995, p. 354.

MUSLIMS IN YUGOSLAVIA

Ever since the formation of a united South Slav state, there has been controversy over the identity of indigenous, Serbo-Croat-speaking Muslims. Since the state did not acknowledge the public significance of religion, there have been no reliable and systematic attempts to assess religious allegiance in Yugoslavia. Estimates of the numbers of those with at least a nominal attachment to **Islam** report around 3.8 million (16 percent of the population) in 1981 and around 4.2 million (17.5 percent) in 1991. In addition to **Bosnia-Hercegovina**, with around 44 percent of the population declaring themselves to be Muslims, and **Kosovo**, where about 70 percent of **Albanians** are believed to identify with Islam, there are significant numbers of Muslims in **Macedonia**, **Serbia** (especially the **Sandžak**), and **Montenegro**.

In the "First Yugoslavia" (1918–1941), there was vigorous competition between Serb and Croat intellectuals and politicians for the allegiance of the country's Muslim population, each claiming that they were really Serbs/Croats whose ancestors had converted to Islam under the **Ottoman Empire** from the end of the fourteenth century. The wartime **Ustaša** regime in **Croatia** courted Muslim sympathy by declaring them to be the "flower of Croatia." A number of prominent postwar figures have adopted Serb identities, such as writer Meša Selimovič and (for a time) **Alija Izetbegović**. Nevertheless, the majority were unhappy with this solution. During the interwar period, specifically Muslim **political parties** flourished (the Yugoslav Muslim Organization and Çemijet) and depended upon their specifically Islamic appeal. Under the socialist regime, Muslims frequently declined to declare an ethnic identity in census returns, and the census officials were similarly puzzled as to how they could be identified. The first census of 1948 permitted Muslims to identify themselves as "uncategorized Muslims" (*neopredeljeni* Muslimani); the second in 1953 as "uncategorized Yugoslavs" (*neo-*

predeljeni Jugosloveni). In 1961 they were identified as "ethnic Muslims" (Muslimani-*etnička pripadnost*); in 1971 as "Muslims in the national sense" (Muslimani *u smislu narodnosti*); and finally in 1981 simply as "Muslims." The main determining factor here was the consolidation during the 1960s of the line within the **League of Communists** (associated with Atif Purivatra and Hamdija Pozderac) that distinguished clearly between the status of "nations" and "nationalities" within Yugoslavia and designated Muslims unambiguously as a nation.

Muslims have often been uncomfortable with the attempt of the former Yugoslav authorities to insist upon the use of the term *Muslim* in order to refer to a specifically national identity. In his ***Islamic Declaration,*** for example, Alija Izetbegović spells out clearly his opposition to this idea. Since the disintegration of socialist Yugoslavia, the proposal appears to have been gathering popular support that Muslims should be known as Bošnjaci (singular "Bošnjak"). The term appears to have some antiquity, but its modern revival has been associated particularly with a group of Sarajevo intellectuals, including **Muhamed Filipović**, Omer Ibrahimagić, Enes Karić, and Mustafa Imamović.

This solution, too, has its problems, in two respects. Whereas the term has the distinct advantage in the Bosnian context of strengthening the symbolic link (and hence the feeling of belonging and entitlement) to territory, in areas such as Macedonia or the Sandžak it might have the reverse effect. To identify oneself by a term that perhaps implies that one is a "Bosnian" could result in one's being identified as an outsider—even as a foreigner. Insistence by Bosnians upon describing Muslims in these areas as Bošnjaci might also be construed as Bosnian Muslims expressing territorial ambitions beyond the borders of Bosnia, resulting in the kind of problem that has afflicted Macedonia in its relations with **Greece.** A large internationally supported academic conference held in Sarajevo in May 1997 wrestled with these issues but did not reach a consensus.

The problem of Muslim identity is, in many ways, central to the future stability of Bosnia-Hercegovina in particular and the region more generally. It has figured as a central element in the **propaganda** war and lies at the heart of attempts to build a sense of general **citizenship** to which all residents of the territory are entitled. It is tied in with domestic and international fears about the implications of creating an avowedly Islamic state in Europe and the growth of "Islamic fundamentalism."

—*J. B. A.*

See also: ethnicity; nationality; religion

References: Allcock, John B., and Harry T. Norris. "The Bosnian Muslims and the Dilemma of Identity." In Frank Carter and David Turnock (eds.), *The States of Eastern Europe.* Dartmouth, England: Aldershot, 1998; Friedman, Francine. *The Bosnian Muslims: Denial of a Nation.* Boulder, CO: Westview Press, 1996; Pinson, Mark. *The Muslims of Bosnia-Herzegovina: Their Historic Development from the Middle Ages to the Dissolution of Yugoslavia.* Cambridge, MA: distributed for the Center for Middle Eastern Studies of Harvard University by Harvard University Press, 1993; Poulton, Hugh, and Suha Taji-Farouki, eds. *Muslim Identity and the Balkan State.* London: Hurst, for the Institute of Muslim Minority Affairs, 1997.

N

NAMBIAR, SATISH

After the experience of commanding the armed forces in his native India, Lt.-Gen. Satish Nambiar was the first in a succession of appointments by the United Nations (UN) to the command of its international peacekeeping force (**UNPROFOR**) in the former Yugoslavia.

The UN Security Council's resolution in February 1992 to send such forces was made in the context of deescalating the conflict between Serbs and Croats. Within one month up to 14,000 soldiers from 33 countries were deployed under the direction of Nambiar from his prophetically located headquarters in the Bosnian capital of Sarajevo, from where he later moved to the Croatian capital of Zagreb. It was only a further month before the war in Bosnia was to start. Nambiar was succeeded in March 1993 by Lt. Gen. Lars Eric Walgren (Sweden).

—*J. J. H.*

NATIONALITY

One of the persisting difficulties experienced by people from the English-speaking world in understanding Balkan politics is the problem of translating ideas, and the terms *nation* and *nationality* are potentially among the most confusing in this respect. The word that is translated as "nation" *(narod)* is also often translated either as "folk" or as "people's" (e.g., *narodna muzika* as "folk music," or Jugoslavenska Narodna Armija as "Yugoslav Peoples' Army"). Whereas the English term *nation* tends to set in motion a chain of associations of a primarily political character, linking it to the state (especially for North Americans), for South Slavs the associations are more likely to point toward a sense of belonging to a group with a shared past and culture.

The use of the terms *narod* and *narodnost* (nationality) were given very specific and to some extent novel connotations, however, by Communist political theory within socialist Yugoslavia. In the last predisintegration census (April 1991), 18 different groups were sufficiently numerous to be reported separately—not including those reported as "others" and those who declared themselves under a regional identity. The constitutional standing of these 18 specific groups has never been equal.

The history of Communist attempts to explain "nationality" is long and complex. The Communist Party of Yugoslavia (subsequently the **League of Communists of Yugoslavia**) before World War II was racked by acrimonious discussion on the issue. Influential attempts were made both by the former general secretary of the party, Sima Marković, and by **Tito**'s close associate and ideological mentor, Edvard Kardelj, to provide a coherent political framework for the treatment of the question. Only recently, by the time of the 1974 constitution, was a more or less standard way of handling the idea of nationality—one that could be acceptable within a Marxist ideological framework—developed in socialist Yugoslavia.

This approach hinged upon a difference between "nation" *(narod)* and "nationality" *(narodnost).* Republics were identified as the homelands of the South Slav nations who could be considered the "charter" groups of Yugoslavia (the word *Yugoslavia* means "land of the South Slavs," from *jug,* meaning "south"), even though group members might be found as minorities within other South Slav republics or elsewhere. There were six such republics: **Bosnia-Hercegovina**, **Croatia**, **Macedonia**, **Montenegro**, **Serbia**, and **Slovenia.** Nationalities, however, were those people whose "homeland" was found outside of Yugoslavia, regardless of how substantial their numbers were as a minority within the country. Thus, Serbs constituted a *narod,* whose homeland was Serbia, despite the existence of large numbers of Serbs in adjacent republics (particularly Bosnia-Hercegovina and Croatia). **Albanians** and Magyars, however, were *narodnosti* because their respective homelands were considered to be **Albania** and **Hungary** regardless of the antiquity of their settlement within the Yugoslav space. "Nationalities," in this sense, had no particular constitutional privilege, although the creation of two autonomous provinces within Serbia was linked rather ambiguously to the provinces' distinctive national composition (**Kosovo** and the **Vojvodina**).

Whereas the distinction between "nations" and "nationalities" provided a rule of thumb that could be used to justify the pattern of six republics and two autonomous provinces, linking each of these entities to a specific ethnic group, it created problems that were directly relevant to the subsequent breakup of the federation. On one hand, it created a sense of injustice on the part of Albanian-speaking persons, especially in Kosovo, where such persons constituted more than 80 percent of the population. These people thought that the concept of an autonomous province condemned them to second-class **citizenship** in Yugoslavia and that they should be entitled to **recognition** as a republic. On the other hand, the distinction also created an area of constitutional ambiguity within Serbia concerning the relationship between the republic and its autonomous provinces. It created further unease among Serbs because of the designation of a separate Montenegrin nation. Serb and Montenegrin identities have been closely intertwined in history, and some people believed that the designation of Montenegrins as a distinct nation was tacitly intended to divide and weaken this alliance.

In Bosnia-Hercegovina no nation had an overall numerical predominance, although the largest group were **Muslims**. The national consciousness of Muslims, who were distinguished historically from both Serbs and Croats by their religion, was unclear and undeveloped. Whereas the practice of identifying Muslims as a *narod* did create an effective balancing force to forestall a continuation of the earlier struggle between Serbs and Croats for domination within Bosnia-Hercegovina, it was also construed as implying a special association between Muslims and the republic—that Bosnia-Hercegovina was at least implicitly or potentially a Muslim republic.

—*J. B. A.*

See also: constitutional models; ethnicity; Muslims in Yugoslavia

NATO

See **North Atlantic Treaty Organization**

NAVAL POWER

The naval component of the **Yugoslav Peoples' Army** (JNA) played a very minor role when the former Yugoslavia descended into civil war in 1991. On Croatia's **Adriatic** coast, the main JNA naval bases at **Split**, Pula, Šibenik, and **Dubrovnik** then came under exclusive Croatian control. Of these naval facilities, only Dubrovnik was attacked (briefly) by the JNA. There was also military action around **Zadar**, the location of which—close to the **Serb Republic of the Krajina** (SRK)—meant that Croatian access to the town's main Adriatic ports and naval bases was impeded until the SRK fell in 1995.

Of around 100 major and minor naval vessels that made up the JNA navy in 1991, most were then seized by **Serbia** and **Montenegro** and moored in the Bay of Kotor, the sole naval facility available to the remaining Yugoslavia. The fact that Croatia's **Prevlaka** Peninsula controls access to the Bay of Kotor meant that the Yugoslav navy had to be confined there for most of the war.

The imposition of draconian economic **sanctions** by the United Nations against Serbia and Montenegro from 1992 to 1995 also resulted in the deployment of a combined **North Atlantic Treaty Organization/Western European Union** (NATO/WEU) naval monitoring and embargo enforcement on the Adriatic Sea beginning in 1993. Known as Operation Sharp Guard, this move prevented the operational deployment of the Yugoslav navy outside the Bay of Kotor. NATO's Operation Deny Flight over neighboring Bosnia after 1993 involved the periodic deployment of aircraft carriers and other major surface combat vessels from the **United States** in the Adriatic Sea. Although used mainly to project U.S. naval air power over Bosnia, these powerful forces also acted as a deterrent against the Yugoslav navy.

The Yugoslav navy has also suffered from deep cuts in spending during the 1990s, resulting in an

The British navy's aircraft carrier HMS Illustrious, *deployed in the Adriatic Sea as part of NATO's Operation Deny Flight and Operation Deliberate Force over nearby Bosnia-Hercegovina. (NATO photo)*

aging and increasingly obsolescent force. In Croatia, on the other hand, high expenditures on the **Croatian Army** in recent years have included major and ongoing expansion of naval forces. Croatia has established new naval facilities at Ploče, Lastovo, and Vis. In the longer term, this arrangement may well result in a new military and strategic situation in which Croatia supplants the remaining Yugoslavia as the foremost naval power in the area.

—M. M.

NERETVA RIVER VALLEY

The Neretva River, scene of an epic battle and **Partizan** victory that helped turn the tide of the war in the Balkans in 1943, rises near the Montenegrin border and flows in a steep arc of 150 miles through **Hercegovina** before reaching the Adriatic Sea in southern Dalmatia. After passing through **Jablanica**, it reaches **Mostar**, where it was crossed by the famous footbridge that was destroyed in the recent conflict. The lower reaches of the Neretva are strategically important for two reasons. First, the river is perceived as the dividing line between Serb territory to the east and Croat territory to the west; however, there are Croat communities on the eastern side, and this perception takes no account of the Muslim population—it also meant that cities like Mostar, which straddles the river, were to be the scenes of the most concentrated violence and barely imaginable destruction during the recent fighting. Second, for its last 15 miles the Neretva River flows from the old inland port of Metković, on the border of Bosnia-Hercegovina and Croatia, to the Adriatic coast at the important port of Ploče, constructed in 1966 in the context of Yugoslavia. In the context of the recent conflict, the river's strategic implications now concern access to the sea from Bosnia-Hercegovina.

—J. J. H.

NEUM

Neum, a small municipality in **Bosnia-Hercegovina** (population 4,268 in 1991), acquired a significance during the Yugoslav conflict quite out of proportion to its size. Located on the Adriatic coast south of the Neretva estuary, it was the site of the only coastline—12 kilometers long—in the republic of Bosnia-Hercegovina. During 1992 the settlement was occupied by Croatian troops, and although no international agreement has recorded the modification of the borders of the republic, it has remained under Croatian military control.

In spite of its ethnic Croat majority (82 percent in 1991), Neum has long historical links with Hercegovina. It fell within the medieval Bosnian kingdoms and remained attached to the See of Mostar after the incorporation of the area into the **Ottoman Empire** in the early sixteenth century. Under Ottoman rule it became part of the Sandžak of Hersek. After the occupation of the provinces by Austria in 1878, Neum remained part of Bosnia-Hercegovina until the unification of the South Slav state in 1918. Although these former territorial divisions were obliterated by the creation of a Croatian *banovina* (prefecture) in 1938, the creation of the "Second Yugoslavia" in 1945 restored Neum to the republic of Bosnia-Hercegovina.

The reason for Croatian interest in Neum is that the settlement formerly interrupted continuous Croatian control of the Adriatic coast and coastal communications. The economic significance of the place is otherwise trivial. Its worth as a tourist resort hardly merits regard. It has no value as a seaport, and it is linked by only a minor road to the rest of Bosnia-Hercegovina. The town has potential political significance, however, as a bargaining counter in any final settlement of the relationship between Croatia and its eastern neighbor.

The future of Neum is linked to the wider discussion of Bosnian access to the sea, in which the Sarajevo government itself might well prefer to surrender Neum in return for the other option discussed—guaranteed use of the **Neretva** port of Ploče. The Croatian government has an incentive to delay reaching a resolution of the problem, however, until the future of the other territorial bone of contention along the Adriatic coast—namely, the disputed border with Montenegro on the **Prevlaka** Peninsula—is determined.

—*J. B. A.*

See also: communications and transport

NGOS

See **nongovernmental organizations**

NO-FLY ZONES

First authorized in October 1992, when **United Nations** Security Council (UNSC) Resolution 781 banned all military flights in Bosnian airspace, no-fly zones in the former Yugoslavia have been breached more often than observed by local belligerents. Resolution 781 lacked credible enforcement mechanisms until March 1993, when repeated violations of its provisions by the air force of the **Bosnian Serb Army** (BSA) prompted the UNSC to authorize the shooting down of all unauthorized military aircraft detected over **Bosnia-Hercegovina.** Entrusted to **North Atlantic Treaty Organization** (NATO) forces operating under UN Protection Force (**UNPROFOR**) II command, this strengthened mandate reduced the number of Bosnian Serb flights but did not stop them entirely.

Known as Operation Deny Flight, this NATO operation used in Italy, aircraft carriers in the **Adriatic**, AWAC aircraft, and surveillance satellites operated by the **United States** to monitor the airspace of Bosnia-Hercegovina and nearby Serb-controlled territories in **Croatia** and **Serbia** proper.

Although it undoubtedly helped to keep the powerful Yugoslav air force out of the Bosnian war, over Bosnia itself Operation Deny Flight had more mixed results. Most violations by the BSA and other local belligerents were by low-flying military helicopters, which were hard to detect and were mainly used to transport troops and supplies over relatively short distances. Even when such flights were detected, very few were actually shot down. The offending parties were typically discreetly warned not to repeat their violations. The main worry was that shooting down such helicopters could lead to **hostage taking** of UNPROFOR troops by the **Bosnian Serbs.**

Only at the end of the war, in 1995, was NATO **air power** used in a sustained and credible manner to destroy Bosnian Serb air power and military

Bosnian Serb helicopters routinely violated the United Nations' no-fly zone over Bosnia-Hercegovina, a Security Council ruling enforced by NATO's Operation Deny Flight. (UNHCR)

airfields. Preceded by a minor NATO air attack against the main **Krajina** Serb military airfield at Udbina in Croatia, this bombing campaign in 1995 destroyed many BSA aircraft and helicopters on the ground. Following the end of the UNPROFOR II mandate in Bosnia-Hercegovina in 1995, enforcement of UNPROFOR's no-fly zone became the responsibility of NATO operations under the **Implementation/Stabilization Force** mandates.

—M. M.

NONALIGNED MOVEMENT

Nonalignment as an approach to foreign policy emerged in the period of the Cold War as an expression of the wish of a number of states to be independent of the two great power blocs. The movement was closely associated with President **Tito**; together with **workers' self-management**, nonalignment became a central plank of the distinctive Yugoslav approach to communism characterized as **Titoism**.

Following the conflict with the Soviet Union in 1948, which resulted in the expulsion of Yugoslavia from the Cominform, Yugoslavia's security and foreign policies had to be reconstructed. The first such attempt, in the form of the Balkan Pact with **Greece** and **Turkey** in 1954, was quickly undermined by the disagreement between Greece and Turkey over Cyprus.

The idea of a group of nonaligned states emerged from the Bandung Conference in 1955, which involved states of southern Asia. Tito quickly seized upon this idea as having a wider relevance, and much of the motivation for its development came from Presidents Tito, Nehru (of India), and Nasser (of Egypt). The first conference of nonaligned states took place in Belgrade in September 1961, at which 25 states were represented.

The movement grew steadily in the following two decades, addressing itself to a range of issues relating to colonialism, national independence, and social, cultural, and economic development. It is a moot point whether in this process nonalignment was more important to Yugoslavia than Yugoslav support was to the Nonaligned Movement (NAM). Although the countries of the NAM contributed a small share to Yugoslavia's trade, Yugoslavia's prominent part in the movement gave the country an international visibility that it would probably otherwise never have enjoyed.

Given this history of mutual involvement, many observers of the collapse of Yugoslavia have asked why the NAM played no role at all in the international intervention in Yugoslavia. The torch of international mediation was carried initially by the **Organization for Security and Cooperation in Europe** (OSCE), then the **European Community**, then the **United Nations** (UN), and finally the **United States**. In each case their efforts were hampered by their relative lack of familiarity with Yugoslav affairs. It seems natural to ask whether some of Yugoslavia's longstanding friends could not have been engaged to better effect.

Although the ninth conference of the NAM convened in Belgrade in September 1989, the movement was probably by then a spent force. Its raison d'être in the Cold War disappeared with the fall of the Berlin Wall and the collapse of Soviet hegemony in Europe. Furthermore, the banner of nonalignment united many countries with a diverse range of both economic and strategic interests. Yugoslavia had been unusual as a European member of an organization whose most solid support had always been among African and Asian countries with little real incentive to involve themselves in a European problem. Finally, the majority of the movement's members were relatively poor states without the capacity to project force beyond their own borders. Although expressing concern within forums such as the UN, therefore, the states of the NAM found themselves incapable of exercising any significant independent influence on events.

—J. B. A.

Reference: Singleton, Fred. "Yugoslavia's Defence and Foreign Policy in the Context of Non-Alignment." In M. Milivojević, J. B. Allcock, and P. Maurer (eds.), *Yugoslavia's Security Dilemmas.* Oxford: Berg, 1988.

NONGOVERNMENTAL ORGANIZATIONS

Nongovernmental organizations (NGOs) include a very wide range of bodies that are defined by the fact that they are neither private businesses run for profit nor public bodies controlled by government. For this reason, the same groups are often called nonprofit organizations or, particularly in the context of Central and Eastern Europe, the third sector. There is an important distinction between international NGOs—many of which operate in many different countries, usually in complex emergencies such as wars, famines, or earthquakes, undertaking a wide range of tasks—and local NGOs, which are registered and work in one country. Depending on the political and economic circumstances, local NGOs can play an important role in social development and have been seen, in Central and Eastern Europe particularly, as a vital component of civil society. Some local NGOs can also be called grassroots organizations, which are based in a specific area, community, or neighborhood and are often involved in campaigns on particular issues. Most international NGOs are primarily funded by governments from the northern and western countries and, in turn, often support local NGOs; hence, issues of independence are more complex than they may at first appear.

The role of different NGOs in post-Yugoslav countries during, as well as after, the conflicts has attracted much interest and has been the subject of considerable controversy. All the major international NGOs, much more experienced in working in the developing world than in Europe, also came to work in the countries in conflict, particularly in **Croatia** and later in **Bosnia-Hercegovina**. At times, it appeared that these NGOs were almost another army, having a highly visible presence with their white Jeeps and concerned that their logos be seen everywhere. The International Council for Voluntary Agencies suggests that, in August 1997, some 200 international NGOs were working in Bosnia-Hercegovina alone.

The reception of such NGOs by the general population was mixed: they performed a crucial role in delivering much needed food and other assistance, and many of their staff risked, and some lost, their lives in their efforts. However, in the absence of any diplomatic solution or agreement about use of force, such agencies became, often unwittingly or at least reluctantly, partners in a situation where people were kept alive only long enough to be shelled again. In short, they were part of an inadequate humanitarian answer to a political question. In addition, some agencies had a rather limited understanding of the causes of the conflict and were accused of a patronizing or even colonialist attitude.

In the field of social welfare, for example, instead of trying to rebuild established and (before the war) well-respected and highly professional existing local services, many organizations set up parallel services and also took the best staff away from the public sector by offering higher salaries. As the emergency ended, some of the larger organizations, such as CARE, Catholic Relief Services, and Oxford Committee for Famine Relief (OXFAM), tried to work more on developing local services, with some success.

The conflicts also saw the emergence of a wide range of smaller international NGOs, some of which were solidarity organizations associated with Western European and North American peace, **women**'s, and other social movements. In addition, many international NGOs provided volunteers to work on various aspects of the conflict through local NGOs and, in the case of the Balkan Peace Team, as human rights monitors and supporters of local activists. The organization Delphi/STAR, through its support for local women's organizations in all of the post-Yugoslav countries, also played a crucial role in maintaining and developing women's networks and projects.

All of these organizations, as well as agencies such as the **United Nations** and the **Organization for Security and Cooperation in Europe** (OSCE) and, indeed, the **Dayton Agreements** themselves, suggest that the development of local NGOs is the best hope for converting an uneasy peace into a true democracy based on civil society, human rights, and tolerance. Certainly, a number of activist organizations, perhaps better called "social movements," many of which have their origins in campaigns and protests in the 1980s, have been of immense importance in keeping alive alternative values. The best known are the organizations in the network of the Antiwar Campaign in Croatia (ARK), as well as the Center for Antiwar Action and Women in Black in Serbia; but there are many others undertaking equally important work with almost no funds and under considerable harassment from the authorities. The effectiveness of support for these groups has, however, been asserted rather than demonstrated. Some have argued that this kind of "politics from below" has marginalized formal political opposition parties, has turned social movements into project-based bureaucracies, and has appealed to only a narrow circle of intellectuals in the major urban centers. Others have suggested that the support has, in any case, been half-hearted at best, through lack of support from their governments,who have chosen to work with nationalist politicians on all sides.

What cannot be disputed is that the authorities in all of the conflict areas are very skeptical of, and sometimes openly hostile to, the actions of any NGOs that are not very close to their own nationalist positions. The Federation of Bosnia-Hercegovina and the Republic of Croatia both have new laws on NGOs that fall far short of international standards and imply an unreasonable opportunity for governmental control and sanction. In many ways, the situation in **Serbia** and the **Republika Srpska** in Bosnia is even worse. Commentators on Bosnia-Hercegovina have suggested that local NGOs are not having a real impact in civil society, at least partly because they are the artificial creation of international organizations in a hurry. However, a range of civil initiatives and alternative **media** organizations, such as Radio Zid and the Office for Human Rights in **Tuzla**, do represent an important, though small, countercurrent. The sense that any more positive role for local NGOs will take a very long time suggests that donors need to think about longer-term support for local organizations.

—P. S.

See also: humanitarian aid; peace movements

NORTH ATLANTIC TREATY ORGANIZATION

The involvement of the North Atlantic Treaty Organization (NATO) in the Yugoslav conflict was closely intertwined with the post–Cold War adaptation of NATO itself. Many observers suggested that if NATO could not play a role in a conflict on its doorstep, such as that in **Yugoslavia**, then the alliance had little future. NATO, it was argued, must go "out of area" or go out of business. The Yugoslav conflict also provoked bitter disputes within NATO and between the alliance and the other international organizations involved in the conflict.

Initially, NATO played relatively little role in international efforts toward **conflict management** in Yugoslavia. The **European Community** (EC) led the international mediation efforts, and the **United Nations** (UN) played the central role in military peacekeeping. The relative disengagement of the **United States** from the early stages of the conflict further weakened NATO's role in the former Yugoslavia.

Gradually, however, NATO came to play a growing role in the conflict. From July 1992, NATO **naval** forces monitored and enforced the UN **arms** embargo and economic **sanctions** against the former Yugoslavia in the **Adriatic** Sea as part of Operation Sharp Guard. From October 1992, NATO air forces monitored (and from March 1993 enforced) the UN-established **no-fly zone** over **Bosnia-Hercegovina**. In June 1993, the UN Security Council authorized "all necessary measures, through the use of air power" to support the **UNPROFOR** peacekeeping force in deterring attacks on the six UN-designated "**safe areas.**" This brought NATO air forces more directly into the Yugoslav conflict. There were disputes, however, among NATO's members and with the UN about the circumstances in and extent to which airstrikes should be used. Authorization for the use of air power was provide by a complex "dual-key" arrangement, requiring both NATO and UN agreement for any airstrikes. This arrangement, combined with the vulnerability of the UNPROFOR peacekeepers on the ground, limited the use and impact of NATO air power at this stage in the conflict.

Disputes over the use of NATO air power became intertwined with wider Western differences over policy toward the Yugoslav conflict, provoking some of the most bitter internal disputes in NATO's history. In 1993, the Clinton administration came to power advocating a policy of "lift and strike"—that is, lifting the arms embargo against the Bosnian **Muslims** in order to enable them to defend themselves and using airstrikes against any **Bosnian Serb** or **Bosnian Croat** aggression. The United States was unable to persuade its allies, particularly the **United Kingdom** and **France**, the largest contributors to UNPROFOR, to support this policy. The United States accused Western Europeans of appeasement in the face of Serbian aggression and "**ethnic cleansing.**" Western European states pointed out that the United States was unwilling to deploy ground forces of its own and that any airstrikes would make their own forces on the ground vulnerable targets for retaliation. The disagreements were so serious that observers suggested they threatened the very future of NATO itself. The overrunning of the safe areas of **Srebrenica** and **Žepa** by Bosnian Serb forces in July 1995 brought the issue to a head and paved the way for NATO to take a central role in managing the Yugoslav conflict. UNPROFOR was strengthened by the deployment of the **Rapid Reaction Force** and the withdrawal of UN peacekeepers from vulnerable positions; NATO began to plan for more widespread airstrikes, and the dual-key arrangement with the UN was abandoned.

In late August 1995, after a Bosnian Serb mortar attack on **Sarajevo**, NATO initiated a three-week campaign of airstrikes against Bosnian Serb forces—Operation Deliberate Force, which resulted in the Bosnian Serbs agreeing to a **cease-fire** and eventually led to the **Dayton Agreements.**

The Dayton peace agreements confirmed the central role of NATO in the Bosnian peace process. A 60,000-strong NATO **Implementation Force** (IFOR) was deployed in December 1995 to enforce the peace and implement the military components of the Dayton accords. In contrast to UNPROFOR, IFOR had the mandate, military means, and political backing necessary to maintain the fragile peace in Bosnia and for the first time included U.S. ground forces. In 1997 IFOR was renamed the Stabilization Force (SFOR) and its size was reduced to 36,000 troops. Early in 1998, NATO members agreed to a further extension of SFOR's mission with no clear time limit. The presence of the NATO force was widely believed to be essential to maintaining the fragile peace in Bosnia, whereas its withdrawal might well result in renewed fighting. The issue remained contentious within NATO. There remained strong pressures in the U.S. Congress for the withdrawal of U.S. forces from Bosnia at some point. The United States' European allies, however, were reluctant to remain in Bosnia without the involvement of U.S. ground forces. Additionally, should serious violence break out in **Kosovo** and/or **Macedonia,** NATO might be called upon to play a role in any military intervention—again raising difficult issues for the alliance's members. As of early 1998, therefore, the longer-term role of NATO in the former Yugoslavia remained uncertain.

NATO's involvement in the Yugoslav conflict also led the alliance to cooperate closely with states and international organizations with which it had not previously worked. In Operation Sharp Guard, NATO worked closely with the **Western European Union** (WEU). In supporting UNPROFOR, NATO worked closely with the UN, although the relationship was uneasy because of differences over the use of airstrikes. I/SFOR worked closely with the various civilian agencies involved in the Dayton peace process, particularly the UN's High Representative and the **Organization for Security and Cooperation in Europe** (OSCE). NATO also worked closely with a number of states outside the alliance. **Hungary** allowed NATO air surveillance operations to be undertaken from its airspace and the deployment of I/SFOR from its territory; **Albania** cooperated with NATO in enforcing the embargo in the Adriatic Sea; and 14 non-NATO countries (including **Russia**) participated in I/SFOR.

NATO's involvement in the Yugoslav conflict marked the organization's transition from a traditional defense alliance to a wider peacekeeping and peace enforcement body. The Yugoslav conflict, however, also highlighted the problems NATO would face in playing such a role.

—A. S. C.

References: Leurdijk, Dick A., and Auke P. Venema. *The United Nations and NATO in Former Yugoslavia, 1991–1996: Limits to Diplomacy and Force.* The Hague: Netherlands Atlantic Commission/Netherlands Institute of International Relations "Clingendael," 1996; Papacosma, S. Victor. "NATO and the Post–Cold War Balkans." *Journal of Political and Military Sociology.* Vol. 24 (1996) pp. 233–252.

NOVI SAD
See **Vojvodina**

NUCLEAR POWER
See **Krško Power Station**

O'GRADY, SCOTT

Scott O'Grady is a U.S. airman whose plane, an F-16 fighter jet, was struck by a Serb missile, causing him to parachute down in an especially hostile part of Bosnia in June 1995. He spent six days on the run or hiding from his **Bosnian Serb** pursuers. He was therefore the subject of a much publicized and remarkable story of personal survival and eventual rescue by **North Atlantic Treaty Organization** (NATO) military personnel. His experience is recounted in his book *Return with Honor,* New York: Harper, 1996.

—*J. J. H.*

O'KANE, MAGGIE

Maggie O'Kane is an Irish freelance journalist whose correspondence from war zones in the Middle East and the Balkans has won her several awards. Her reporting from Bosnia focused upon the human dimension, in places such as **Vitez,** Omarska (where she was first to expose conditions in the **detention camps**), and both **Goražde** and **Srebrenica** (whose perceived status as "**safe areas**" was graphically undermined by her firsthand accounts). She also brought international attention to the courageous work under siege of her professional colleagues on the Sarajevo daily ***Oslobodjenje.*** Her reports can be read particularly in British newspapers the *Guardian* and *Sunday Times.*

—*J. J. H.*

OKUČANI

Okučani is a small settlement in Croatia approximately 75 miles southeast of Zagreb and 20 miles south of **Pakrac,** lying on the **Zagreb**-to-**Belgrade** motorway (E-70, the Brotherhood and Unity Motorway). Its importance lay in its location on this international arterial **communications** route, which the Serbs were able to control. Following the incorporation by the United Nations of this part of western **Slavonia** into a **United Nations protected area** (UNPA), limited traffic was possible, although it could be interrupted at the will of the Serb forces. Military action against traffic on the road at Okučani in April 1995 provided the pretext for the Croatian government to launch **Operation Flash** in May, when the whole of the area was retaken.

—*G. R. B.*

OMARSKA

See **detention camps**

OPERATION DELIBERATE FORCE

See **North Atlantic Treaty Organization**

OPERATION FLASH

On 1–2 May 1995, Croatian armed forces mounted a surprise attack known as Operation Flash, directed at reclaiming for government control United Nations (UN) Sector West (western **Slavonia**)—part of the Serb-controlled **Krajina.** A pretext for armed intervention was offered by the persistent cutting off by Serb militias of the main highway in contravention of recently negotiated agreements. A heavily armed force estimated at 7,200 men captured some 1,500 Serb soldiers and drove many more across the **Sava River,** along with several thousand civilians, into **Bosnia-Hercegovina.** Fighting was particularly heavy around the towns of Lipik and **Pakrac.** Serb forces in Sector North responded by bombarding the Croatian capital of **Zagreb** with Orkan surface-to-surface rockets (commonly used in Eastern Europe, and manufactured under license in former Yugoslavia), killing 6 people and injuring 175. International condemnation of this attack on civilian targets blunted criticism of the fact that Croatian action disregarded the UN mandate. The action was, in effect, a dress rehearsal for the subsequent **Operation Storm**, which restored the authority of Zagreb over Sectors North and South.

—*J. B. A.*

OPERATION SHARP GUARD

See **naval power**

OPERATION STORM

Following a series of carefully prepared moves southward from the **Bihać** pocket and northward to secure the ridge of Mount **Dinara**, the Croatian government exploited the experience of **Operation Flash** in order to mount a major military offensive known as **Operation Storm.** This move was designed to secure control over the greater part of the remaining Serb **Krajina.**

On 4 August 1995, Croat formations estimated at 150,000 men launched a coordinated series of around 30 attacks into the former United Nations (UN) Sectors North and South along a 300-kilometer front. The operation lasted only five days. The capital of the Krajina, **Knin**, fell on the second day. Chief-of-Staff Gen. Ivan Tolj announced the success of the operation on the evening of 6 August, although the clearing of pockets of Serb resistance continued for two further days. The fiercest resistance appears to have been mounted in the area of **Glina**. Croatian forces suffered 174 dead and 1,430 wounded. No estimates have been issued for Serb casualties, either military or civilian. Around 5,000 Serb soldiers are believed to have surrendered.

There were two remarkable features of the Serb response to Operation Storm. Military resistance appears to have been in large measure symbolic, with artillery attacks on places such as **Karlovac** and **Dubrovnik**, which had no military relevance. The collapse of the Serb military went along with a massive withdrawal of the Serb civilian population. An estimated 150,000 civilians fled into Bosnia along with retreating Serb forces in a movement that was apparently not only coordinated but even impelled by the Serb command.

Unconfirmed reports suggest that **North Atlantic Treaty Organization** (NATO) air units were also engaged in attacks on Serb rocket batteries, although it is not clear whether this implied NATO complicity in the Croat action or simply a response to their use of rockets against civilian targets in settlements such as Karlovac.

—*J. B. A.*

Serb civilians fleeing the Croatian Army's Operation Storm in the Krajina, Croatia, 1995. (UNHCR)

ORAŠJE

The "Orašje pocket" is a strategically important territory lying to the south of the **Sava River** on the border between **Bosnia** and **Croatia** and to the immediate north of the **Posavina Corridor** centered on the **Bosnian Serb**–controlled town of **Brčko**.

With 28,300 people in 1991, Orašje was (and remains) an almost entirely **Bosnian Croat** settlement. One of four operational zone commands of the **Croatian Council of Defense** (HVO), Orašje and its surrounding pocket of territory have always been a key military position for the Bosnian Croats, and their only holding in northern Bosnia. Acting either alone or more often in concert with the Bosnian government's Army of the Republic of Bosnia-Hercegovina to the south, HVO forces in Orašje often attempted to sever the Bosnian Serb–controlled Posavina Corridor (at one time only two to three kilometers wide at Brčko). Although supported by the **Croatian Army** from across the Sava in Croatia proper, the HVO failed to cut this corridor. Nevertheless, the Bosnian Serbs' **Republika Srpska** remains at its most vulnerable in this part of Bosnia.

Since the **Dayton Agreements** Orašje has been within the U.S. sector of IFOR and then SFOR, both of whose logistics in northern Bosnia were highly dependent on a number of bridges across the Sava, including one at Orašje itself.

—*M. M.*

See also: Implementation/Stabilization Force (I/SFOR)

ORGANIZATION FOR SECURITY AND COOPERATION IN EUROPE

The Organization for Security and Cooperation in Europe (OSCE) is a pan-European body with 53 member states that acts as a framework for the promotion of democracy, respect for human rights, and security. The Conference on Security and Cooperation in Europe (CSCE) was established in 1975 (with Yugoslavia a founding member alongside almost all other European states) and became the OSCE at the end of 1994. When the Yugoslav conflict broke out in summer 1991, the CSCE discussed the issue, but its members were unable to agree on any action, and the focus of international efforts to end the conflict shifted to the **European Community** (EC) and the **United Nations** (UN). **Croatia** and **Slovenia** joined the CSCE in March 1992, followed by **Bosnia-Hercegovina** in April of that year. The Former Yugoslav Republic of **Macedonia** (FYROM) was granted observer status at the CSCE in April 1993, although its formal membership in the organization was delayed until 1995 by opposition from **Greece**. Participation of the Federal Republic of **Yugoslavia** (FRY, that is, **Serbia** and **Montenegro**) in the CSCE was suspended in July 1992. This suspension remained in place in 1998 and was likely to be lifted only once further progress had been made in resolving the Bosnian and **Kosovo** conflicts and in democratization within the FRY itself.

Although playing a lower-profile role than the European Union (EU), the United Nations, and the **North Atlantic Treaty Organization** (NATO), the OSCE has been directly involved in the Yugoslav conflict via a wide range of conflict prevention and peacebuilding activities. CSCE "missions of long duration" to the FRY regions of Kosovo, **Sandžak**, and the **Vojvodina** were established in September 1992, mandated to promote dialogue, collect information on human rights violations, establish contact points, and provide information on relevant legislation. These missions were withdrawn in June 1993 after the Yugoslav government suspended its cooperation and made the missions' return conditional on its own return to full participation in the OSCE. A "spillover monitor mission" to **Skopje** was established in September 1992 with the aim of preventing the Bosnian conflict from spilling over into FYROM. This mission monitored both the situation on FYROM's border with Serbia and developments within FYROM, particularly relations between the Macedonian majority and the **Albanian** minority. In order to support states in implementing the **arms** embargo against the former Yugoslavia and economic **sanctions** against FRY, the OSCE also established "sanctions assistance missions" in **Albania**, **Bulgaria**, Croatia, **Hungary**, FYROM, **Romania**, and Ukraine. An OSCE mission in Sarajevo was established in October 1994, and OSCE ombudsmen for Bosnia (representatives of the **Muslim**, Croat, and Serb communities) were appointed in December 1994. The ombudsmen were mandated to represent individual victims of human rights abuses (particularly "**ethnic cleansing**"), and the OSCE mission in the Bosnian capital of **Sarajevo** was assigned the task of supporting the ombudsmen and reporting to the OSCE on **humanitarian** matters.

The OSCE has also been involved in the Yugoslav conflict through the efforts of its high commissioner on national minorities (HCNM) and its Office for Democratic Institutions and Human Rights. The HCNM, Max van der Stoel, is mandated to support conflict prevention activities in relation to potential ethnic/national conflicts. He has made a number of visits to FYROM and Albania, examining developments in these countries (in particular the situation of the Albanian minority in FYROM and the Greek minority in Albania), relations between the two countries, and the situation in neighboring Kosovo. He has made various recommendations to governments on minority rights legislation and related issues (such as education) and has helped to manage tensions among the various ethnic groups. Alongside the OSCE mission to Skopje, the HCNM helped in particular to defuse tensions over the private Albanian university at **Tetovo** in FYROM in 1995. Van der Stoel was also appointed personal representative of the OSCE chairman-in-office for Kosovo in February 1997, with a mandate to examine the situation in Kosovo and explore ways of reducing tensions in the region. In 1997 he also began to visit Croatia, exploring relations between the Croatian government and the Serbian minority.

The OSCE Office for Democratic Institutions and Human Rights (ODIHR) is assigned the task of monitoring **elections** and promoting **democracy** and respect for human rights. Alongside the various OSCE missions, the ODIHR has been involved in monitoring and/or supporting a number of elections in the former Yugoslavia: the FRY republican, regional, and local elections of December 1992; the census in FYROM in June–July 1994; parliamentary elections in Croatia in October 1995; FYROM municipal elections in November 1996; FRY parliamentary and municipal elections in 1996; Bosnian municipal elections in September 1997; Serbian parliamentary and presidential elections in September, October, and December 1997; the Montenegrin presidential election in October 1997; and the **Republika Srpska** national assembly elections in November 1997.

The **Dayton Agreements** of November 1995 resulted in a major upgrading of the OSCE's role in Bosnia and Croatia, leading the organization to work closely with the UN High Representative and NATO's **Implementation/Stabilization Force.** In the context of the Bosnian peace process, the OSCE was charged with **monitoring** and supporting democratic elections, monitoring and promoting human and minority rights, promoting the development of free and fair **media**, and facilitating negotiations on the military confidence-building and arms control aspects of the Dayton Agreements. The Dayton Agreements thus led to a substantial expansion of the OSCE mission in Bosnia, which took on a wide range of peacebuilding tasks. At the beginning of 1998, a new OSCE mission to Croatia replaced the United Nations Transitional Administration for Eastern **Slavonia** (UNTAES). With a mandate to promote reconciliation and to support the return of **refugees** and the protection of human and minority rights, this was the largest OSCE mission to date; it made the OSCE the main international organization supporting the peace process in Croatia. Overall, the OSCE's involvement in the Yugoslav conflict highlighted both the organization's strengths and its weaknesses. The OSCE was a potentially usefully instrument for conflict prevention, democracy and human rights promotion, and peacebuilding. Its large membership, consensus decision making, limited resources, and lack of economic or military power, however, constrained its effectiveness.

—*A. S. C.*

ORIĆ, NASER

Naser Orić, a Bosnian Muslim who had previously been a bodyguard for Serbian president **Slobodan Milošević**, was still in his twenties when in April 1992 he used his position as a local policeman to assemble an armed troop in defense of **Srebrenica** and succeeded in driving out the Serb **paramilitary** forces occupying the enclave. Further bloody encounters ensued between Orić and the Serbs, and Orić was also responsible for detaining United Nations (UN) commander **Philippe Morillon** during the latter's visit to Srebrenica until Orić obtained assurances of protection and **humanitarian aid** for the town. Orić remained in charge of the local defense force until the final capture of Srebrenica by the Serbs in the summer of 1995.

—*J. J. H.*

See also: Bosnian army

ORTHODOX CHURCH

Central to Serbian identity and nationalism, Orthodoxy and the Orthodox Church have played an important and controversial political role in and beyond **Serbia** during the Yugoslav wars. An autocephalous church since the early twelfth century, the Serbian Orthodox Church was the principal institution that kept alive the idea of Serbdom, as well as the various national myths pertaining to it, after the defeat of the medieval Serb state by the Ottoman Turks at the **Battle of Kosovo** in 1389. Suppressed in 1459, the church's patriarchate at **Skopje** was restored at Peć in **Kosovo** in 1557. Paradoxically, the rule of the **Ottoman Empire** in Serbia thus strengthened the region's Orthodox Church. In 1689, however, a failed Serb revolt against the Turks resulted in the suppression of the Peć patriarchate in 1766. Thereafter, the new patriarchate at Sremski Karlovci became part of the influential Serb diaspora in the **Habsburg Empire**; from this patriarchate the Serbian Orthodox Church was to play a major role in the cultural revival and political emancipation of Serbia during the nineteenth century. The result was the creation of a national church inextricably bound up with Serbdom and the Serbian monarchy that emerged in the new Serbian kingdom after 1815.

With the rapid territorial expansion of Serbia during the Balkan Wars (1912–1913), when **Kosovo**-Metohija was returned to Serb control, and with the subsequent creation of the first Yugoslavia after World War I, the Serbian Orthodox Church came to wield immense social and political influence in Serbian politics and society. It was able during the interwar years to prevent a concordat between Yugoslavia and the Vatican. During World War II, the Serbian Orthodox Church was greatly weakened outside Serbia, especially in those areas then ruled by the **Ustaša.** Closely identified with the exiled Serb **monarchy** and the Serb nationalist **Chetnik** movement during World War II, the church suffered a second calamity when a new communist Yugoslavia came into being in 1945. Along with other ecclesiastical institutions, the Orthodox Church was repressed and strictly controlled during the postwar period, when widespread secularization also reduced the church's social influence.

The Serbian Orthodox Church, under its current patriarch, Pavle, experienced a marked revival in its fortunes during the 1980s, when the growth of a new Serb nationalism in Serbia and other Yugoslav republics was closely bound up with orthodoxy. Religious concerns figured prominently in the 1986 Memorandum of the **Serbian Academy** of Arts and Sciences. Pavle's support for the controversial policies of the new Serbian leader, **Slobodan Milošević**, who came to power on a tide of nationalist euphoria in 1987, was of considerable political importance. Church and state cooperated publicly and fully during the quasi-religious celebrations of the 600th anniversary of the Battle of Kosovo in 1989. Unconditional support by the church for a revived Serb nationalism proved highly controversial for Pavle, however; the patriarch was accused of being used by Milošević, who was a nonbeliever and arguably no more than an opportunist on the issue of the Serb national question.

Once Milošević had abandoned the Serb nationalist project by 1994–1995, the Serbian Orthodox Church openly turned against him, but by then the church's integrity and credibility had been badly damaged among many Serbs. Within the church itself, Pavle's authority came under attack from a number of younger bishops, both in Serbia and **Montenegro**, where a movement for an independent Montenegrin Orthodox Church has also gained ground in recent years.

In the wider Orthodox world, the Serbian Orthodox Church became more closely bound to its counterparts in **Russia** and **Greece** during the 1990s but remained hostile to the Macedonian Orthodox Church. Created in 1967 as a part of the Communist Party policy of building Macedonian national identity, the Macedonian Church also strengthened its links with the state during the disintegration of Yugoslavia and the emergence of an independent Macedonian republic. Ecumenism has never been a central concern of the Balkan Orthodox communities, and within the context of ethnic conflict throughout the former Yugoslavia, the Orthodox hierarchies have remained highly suspicious of any rapprochement with either the **Catholic Church** or **Islam**. Nevertheless, common opposition to the inhumanity of war has enabled Patriarch Pavle, as well as other senior Orthodox clergy, to issue joint statements calling for peace and reconciliation with Cardinal **Kuharić** and the Reis al-Ulema (the head of the **Islamic Community**).

—*M. M.*

See also: Macedonia, republic of; religion

OSCE
See **Organization for Security and Cooperation in Europe**

OSIJEK

Osijek (population 105,000 as of the 1991 census) is the capital city of **Slavonia**, the eastern region of **Croatia.** It lies some 125 miles east of the republic's capital, **Zagreb**, and is only 15 miles from the Serbian border. Eastern Slavonia is largely fertile farmland, part of the Pannonian plain that extends north into Hungary and east into the **Vojvodina.** There are also oil fields in the region.

In July 1991 Croatian Serbs, supported by the **Yugoslav Peoples' Army** (JNA), moved into villages around Osijek, bombarding them with tanks and driving Croats out. Fighting escalated through August and September, with Osijek itself coming under artillery fire from the JNA. With **Vukovar** destroyed on 17 November, even more forces were thrown against Osijek, and shelling continued into 1992. The front line moved up to and around the city, encircling it on three sides, so that access was possible only from the west.

Serbs in Osijek experienced considerable discrimination and human rights violations as a result of the conflict, and the Osijek Center for Peace, Nonviolence, and Human Rights was created as a response. The ruling **Croatian Democratic Union** (HDZ) had powerful local leaders in eastern Slavonia, such as **Branimir Glavaš**, who tended to be on the far right of the party, thus influencing and affecting the local populations—Serbs in particular.

—G. R. B.

See also: Croatia; peace movements

OSLOBODJENJE

The principal newspaper of the Bosnian capital of **Sarajevo**, *Oslobodjenje (Liberation)* was founded during World War II and published by the Socialist Alliance as a semiofficial daily. The *Oslobodjenje* building was one of the landmarks of entry into Sarajevo from the west. Situated close to the airport, it found itself very close to the front line between **Bosnian Serb** and Bosnian government forces. Although repeated artillery attacks devastated the building, production of the paper was moved to the basement and sustained throughout the war. The newspaper's regular appearance, in spite of the acute shortage of paper, made it an important symbol of resistance during the siege. Employing a multiethnic staff, *Oslobodjenje* also distinguished itself by its relative objectivity and detachment from party influence.

The deputy editor of the newspaper, Gordana Knezević, did much to emphasize these qualities and convey the spirit of the paper in her occasional participation on British television, suggesting that when Sarajevans couldn't find bread, they could find her newspaper. The paper's editor-in-chief, Kemal Kurspahić, is the author of an extraordinary account of publishing under fire in his book *As Long as Sarajevo Exists* (Stony Creek, Conn.: Pamphleteer's Press, 1997).

—J. B. A.

See also: media

Reference: Gjelten, Tom. *Sarajevo Daily: A City and Its Newspaper Under Siege.* New York: HarperCollins, 1995.

OTTOMAN EMPIRE

Between the middle of the fourteenth and the end of the sixteenth centuries, a Turkic empire under the Ottoman dynasty established itself over the **Balkans.** At its height, the empire extended across the greater part of the Middle East and North Africa and was able, on two occasions, to lay siege to Vienna, although by the end of the seventeenth century it began a slow but steady contraction. Caught between the expansionist ambitions of the **Habsburg Empire** and **Russia, Turkey** became the pivotal state in the nineteenth-century European balance of power. By the end of the century, the "Eastern question" (the issue of the future of Turkish possessions in Europe) became a major preoccupation of the great powers.

It was in the Ottoman possessions in the Balkans that revolutionary national movements had their early successes. The first Serbian uprising (1804) presaged a century of instability, and the creation of the Principality of Serbia in 1830 inspired the vision of the unification of all Serbs within a single state. In the long, dour struggle for full independence, **Serbia** found a willing ally in **Montenegro.** A shared religious confession, parallel histories, and common interests made union between them a natural objective both of policy and of sentiment.

Turbulence spread to **Bosnia-Hercegovina,** ruled by native Slav **Muslims** (Bošnjaci), whose remote ancestors had converted to **Islam.** The Bošnjak nobility rose in armed rebellion against modernizing reforms aimed at stabilizing Ottoman authority, provoking in turn a series of uprisings among the (mainly **Orthodox**) peasantry. In 1875 these uprisings spread throughout the province, giving the European powers the opportunity for intervention. The Treaty of Berlin (which concluded hostilities in 1878) set out to restore order by filling the vacuum left by weakening Ottoman authority. **Austria-Hungary** occupied Bosnia-Hercegovina, making the Bosnian Muslims strangers in their own land. Serbia and Montenegro, which had seen themselves as legatees of these provinces, were then forced to look southward for expansion and became embroiled in the struggle with **Greece** and **Bulgaria** for control of **Macedonia**. Like Serbia, Bulgaria had just won full independence, and its influence in the region was waxing strong. Numerous armed secret societies sprang up in Macedonia with the aim of ejecting the Turks; some aspired to union with Bulgaria, others wanted autonomy for Macedonia. Both tendencies were opposed by the Serbs and Greeks. Civil order, which collapsed in blood feuds and rapine, was never to be restored for as long as Ottoman rule lasted.

The year 1908 was a turning point in Balkan affairs. The "Young Turk" revolution in Istanbul deposed the sultan in an attempt to hang on to the remaining Ottoman possessions in Europe by creating a modern, centralized form of state. The response of Austria-Hungary was to formally annex Bosnia-Hercegovina, ushering in a new phase of its *Drang nach Osten* (a historical phrase meaning "push to the East," and referring to Austria-Hungary), backed by **Germany**. The threat of being disarmed and subjected to new taxation, combined with a ruthless policy of Ottomanization, sparked off rebellion among Turkey's **Albanian** subjects in 1909–1912. In order to preempt the creation of an Albanian state, Montenegro declared hostilities against Turkey on 12 October 1912 and within 10 days had been joined by other members of the Balkan League—Serbia, Bulgaria, and Greece. By May 1913, Turkish power in Europe had ceased to exist, its demise sealed by the victory of the league at Kirk Kilisse.

—L. B.

OWEN, (LORD) DAVID

Lord David Owen (born 1938 in Devon) is a British politician who was appointed to represent the **European Community** (EC) as the cochair of the **International Conference on the Former Yugoslavia**, set up after the **London Conference** of 26–27 August 1992. He served in this capacity between the end of August 1992 and June 1995, sharing the task until May 1993 with **Cyrus Vance** and subsequently with **Thorvald Stoltenberg**, both representing the **United Nations** (UN).

Having qualified as a neurologist, studying at Cambridge and St. Thomas' Hospital, Owen later made his career as a Labour Party politician, serving as Member of Parliament for Plymouth Sutton (1966–1974) and Plymouth Devonport (1974–1992). His posts in government included the following: parliamentary undersecretary for defense, with responsibility for the navy, 1968–1970; ministerial appointments in the Department of Health and Social Security, 1974–1976; and secretary of state in the Foreign and Commonwealth Office, 1976–1979. He retired from Parliament in 1992 and was elevated to the House of Lords as a life peer in 1992.

David Owen's public involvement with the war in Yugoslavia began with a letter to British prime minister John Major, also published in the London *Evening Standard* of 30 July 1992, in which he wrote: "I urge you not to accept the conventional wisdom that nothing can be done militarily to stop the escalation of fighting and the continuation of such grotesque abuses of human rights." Subsequently, in his published account of

Lord David Owen, European Union peace envoy and cochairman of the International Conference on the Former Yugoslavia, 1992–1995. (Central Office of Information)

his service as a negotiator, he cited a remark by Otto Bismarck ("The Balkans are not worth the healthy bones of a single Pomeranian grenadier") and then made the following observation: "I was to discover that it was this view which was held by all the key governments when it came to committing troops on the ground in **Bosnia-Hercegovina**, and which ensured that international diplomacy without military power was the hallmark of every attitude and action towards the former Yugoslavia" (*Balkan Odyssey*, p. 17).

His efforts to promote a negotiated settlement were reflected primarily in four draft schemes: the **Vance-Owen Plan** of January–February 1993; the Owen-Stoltenberg Plan of August 1993; the **European Action Plan** of December 1993–January 1994; and the **Contact Group** Plan of July 1994.

His painstaking personal account of his attempts to bring peace to the former Yugoslavia is presented in his substantial book *Balkan Odyssey* (London: Gollancz, 1995).

—*J. B. A.*

See also: United Kingdom

OZREN (MOUNT)
See **Maglaj/Ozren**

P

PAKRAC

Pakrac is a town in the western **Slavonia** region of **Croatia** (population 287,500 in 1991, 40 percent of whom were ethnic Serbs) approximately 70 miles southeast of the capital, **Zagreb.** During early 1991 Pakrac became one of the first flashpoints in the developing conflict between Serb and Croat nationalists. On 1 March, Serbian police reservists attempted to take formal control of the town on the basis of a decision on 22 February by the municipal authority. The Serbian reservists attempted to disarm their Croatian counterparts, and thousands of Serbs came out on the streets in support. Two hundred heavily armed Croatian riot police went in to oppose the Serbs. The following day, **Borisav Jović,** Serbian head of the Yugoslav federal collective presidency, approved intervention by the **Yugoslav Peoples' Army** (JNA), and troops forced the Croatian police to withdraw on 3 March, leaving Pakrac effectively under Serb control.

Fighting over the next year shifted the front line until it ran through the middle of the town. The **cease-fire** of January 1992 and the deployment of the United Nations (UN) peacekeepers (**UNPROFOR**) placed Pakrac in the western Slavonia **United Nations protected area** (UNPA), otherwise known as Sector West. This UNPA was the only one to encompass both Serb-held territory and territory still under Croat control. The area reaching from the front line to the north of Pakrac was open to Croats, as well as to international **nongovernmental organizations.** This accessibility meant that Pakrac became the site for a unique attempt to deal with the conflict—the Pakrac Social Reconstruction Workcamp. International volunteers worked under the supervision of Croat activists from the Anti-War Campaign of Croatia, with the aim of rebuilding the social and material infrastructure of the town. Croatian government control was reestablished by **Operation Flash** in May 1995.

—*G. R. B.*

See also: peace movements

PALE

Pale is a small town in an elevated and readily defendable location; it is only 12 miles southeast of the Bosnian capital of **Sarajevo** on the road to **Goražde.** The **Bosnian Serbs** strategically chose the town (1) as the capital of their **Republika Srpska** for the seat of their own parliament, (2) as a military center with ammunition stores to supplement their own army (whose headquarters were at Han Pijesak to the north), and (3) as the hub of their own television service. Virtually all negotiations with the Bosnian Serbs from the start of the war were initially routed through Pale, which was only rarely penetrated by outside officials or reporters.

—*J. J. H.*

PANIĆ, MILAN

Milan Panić served as prime minister of the Federal Republic of **Yugoslavia** (FRY) in 1992. Panić was born in Belgrade in 1942 but left his country for the United States in 1955, later acquiring U.S. citizenship. A professional and champion cyclist at the time of his defection from communist Yugoslavia, he later became a successful businessman as the director of a pharmaceuticals company in California. Never an active part of the anticommunist Serb émigré community in the United States, Panić was reportedly invited back to Belgrade by Serbian president **Slobodan Milošević** and the federal president at the time, **Dobrica Ćosić,** in an effort to improve the battered international image of the FRY in 1992. More controversially, Panić was allowed to purchase a controlling interest in the leading Serbian pharmaceuticals company, Galenika, at this time. In July 1992 he was appointed to the premiership of the FRY.

Initially perceived as a buffoonish figure beholden to Milošević, Panić gained political credibility locally when he attempted to act independently in office, publicly criticizing Serbian policies in **Croatia** and **Bosnia-Hercegovina.** At the time of the **London Conference** on the Former Yugoslavia in August 1992, Panić reportedly humiliated Milošević in public. In October 1992, he and Ćosić effected a limited rapprochement with Croatia over the disputed **Prevlaka** Peninsula, apparently without the consent of the presidents of Serbia and **Montenegro.** Even more significantly, Panić attempted a public dialogue with ethnic **Albanian** political leaders in the Serbian province of **Kosovo,** although this initiative came to nothing.

In December 1992, Panić unsuccessfully ran against Milošević in new **elections** for the powerful Serbian presidency. Already subjected to endless slanders in the government-controlled **media** in Serbia, Panić was forced from office by a no-confidence motion in the FRY assembly initiated by **Vojislav Šešelj**'s ultranationalist Serbian Radical Party. He subsequently left the FRY and returned to the United States.

—*M. M.*

PAPANDREOU, ANDREAS (1919–1995)

Andreas Papandreou was prime minister of **Greece** during the greater part of the Yugoslav war and leader of the socialist PASOK party (the Pan-Hellenic Socialist Movement). He was born on the Aegean island of Chios. A Trotskyite in his youth, he was forced to leave Greece for the United States in 1939. He was educated at Harvard University and taught at various universities, becoming known as a good economist. In 1964 he returned to Greece and became involved in politics, but in 1967 he was arrested by the Junta and incarcerated for eight months for socialist activities. In 1968 he left Greece again to spend six years in exile, returning in August 1974. In September of the same year, he proclaimed the formation of PASOK, which in 1981 won the national election. Papandreou thereby became prime minister of Greece.

The rapid political developments in Yugoslavia took place when PASOK was no longer in power (1990–1993). For Papandreou, the possible disintegration of Yugoslavia would lead not only to the independence of the Socialist Republic of **Macedonia** but also to the republic's recognition by **Bulgaria**, destroying the axis that had existed between Greece and Bulgaria. The leader of PASOK took an uncompromising stance over the recognition of the Former Yugoslav Republic of Macedonia (FYROM). He was strongly critical of Prime Minister **Konstantinos Mitsotakis**, and he considered the way the conservative government was handling its diplomatic contact with FYROM to be a total failure.

PASOK came to power again in October 1993. In February 1994, Papandreou closed the Greek consulate in **Skopje** and imposed on FYROM a trade embargo with the exception of **humanitarian aid** such as food and medicine. He accused the Skopje government of political intransigence, bad faith in negotiating a settlement over the issue of the name "Macedonia," and offensive irredentist **propaganda.** In September 1995, in New York, after long negotiations between the two sides mediated by **Cyrus Vance**, an interim accord was singed. Papandreou agreed to lift the embargo in exchange for **constitutional** amendments, the removal of the Star of **Vergina** from the Macedonian flag, and a treaty on the inviolability of the **borders** of Greece and Macedonia (FYROM).

—*N. M. G.*

See also: Macedonia, Republic of (FYROM)

PARAGA, DOBROSLAV

Dobroslav Paraga was a student leader during the **Croatian Spring** and was jailed in the 1970s for his part in the *maspok* (nationalist mass movement). He later created the extreme nationalist **Croatian Party of Rights** (HSP). In 1990 the HSP claimed to have 10,000 armed men in its own militia, the Croatian Defense Force (HOS), which wore black uniforms echoing the **Ustaša** of half a century earlier.

Although the HOS was responsible for a number of **paramilitary** actions in Croatia and **Bosnia-Hercegovina**, Paraga had few supporters. He was arrested in November 1991 on charges of misappropriation of funds and arms, and the rally called in his support was poorly attended. The arrest was allegedly an attempt to divert attention from Paraga's criticism of the government's handling of the siege of **Vukovar.**

During 1992 Paraga frequently and publicly accused President **Franjo Tudjman** of letting parts of eastern **Slavonia** go in the **Vance Plan**, and the HSP campaigned on a platform of restoring "historical" **Croatia**—a state encompassing all of the territory that medieval Croatia had incorporated at its largest extent. The HSP drew symbolically on the traditions of Ante Starčević's Party of Right, as well as the Frankist Croat Party of Right, which had inspired **Ante Pavelić** and the Ustaša.

In 1995, Paraga was thrown out of the HSP after internal feuding amongst the party's hierarchy. He then founded the Croatian Party of Rights (1861), which has taken a more moderate stance.

—G. R. B.

PARAMILITARY/IRREGULAR FORCES

Although they never exceeded a few thousand members each since the beginning of the Yugoslav wars of the 1990s, the various paramilitary/irregular forces active in Croatia, Bosnia-Hercegovina, and Serbia have been responsible for a disproportionate share of the killing, "**ethnic cleansing**," looting, and general mayhem. Used by all sides, these forces were of greatest significance during the conflict's early stages. More recently, however, they have become relatively marginal, being replaced by regular military forces and thereby expendable for wider political reasons.

A Serbian paramilitary/irregular soldier in Bosnia-Hercegovina, 1992. (Stevan Filipović)

In **Serbia**, a number of paramilitary units appeared as early as 1990, mainly in response to the rebellion of the **Krajina** Serbs in Croatia. Composed of ultranationalist volunteers, these forces loosely called themselves Četnici (**Chetniks**) after the followers of Gen. Draža Mihailović, the main anticommunist leader in Yugoslavia during World War II. Foremost among these forces were the units loyal to **Vojislav Šešelj**, the founder of the Serbian Radical Party (SRS). Lesser groups included the White Eagles led by Mirko Jović and the Serbian Guard associated with **Vukašin Drašković**'s Serbian Renewal Movement (SPO). Reportedly more criminal than patriotic in its membership and almost certainly a part of Serbian president **Slobodan Milošević**'s secret services, the Serbian Volunteer Guard (SDG), or Tigers, led by **Željko Ražnjatović** ("Arkan"), did not have royalist loyalties.

In **Croatia**, where the Krajina Serbs also organized their own irregular forces in 1990, the role of their allies from Serbia was to act as a reserve force for the **Yugoslav Peoples' Army** (JNA). Armed by Serbia's secret services and the JNA, these units typically moved in after the regular armed forces had taken key towns and other strategic targets. Only partly controlled by the JNA, these often undisciplined forces were responsible for much of the killing of unarmed civilians, ethnic cleansing, and looting in eastern **Slavonia** in 1991. In May 1991, an SRS Chetnik ambush of Croatian police in the eastern Slavonian village of **Borovo Selo** marked the real beginning of the Croatian civil war. In other military operations, such as the siege of **Vukovar**, SRS Chetniks and Tiger forces played a more important role, although always under JNA direction.

Elsewhere in the Krajina, a former Yugoslav-Australian soldier and mercenary known as Captain Dragan played a key role in organizing rebel Serb forces around Knin, from where he led special forces known as Kninjas against the Croatian National Guard. Subsequently, the Kninjas became the elite units of the more regularly organized armed forces of the **Serb Republic of the Krajina**, which were initially commanded by a JNA officer, Col.-Gen. **Ratko Mladić.**

Relatively poorly prepared for civil war in 1991, Croatia founded its National Guard (Zbor narodne garde) (ZNG) in April of that year. Initially little more than an amalgamation of local police and territorial defense forces, the ZNG also made extensive use of Croat émigré volunteers and foreign mercenaries. Despite being poorly organized and badly equipped, the ZNG played a key military role in several military operations, notably at Vukovar.

The other main Croatian irregular armed force was the Croatian Defense Force (HOS), the militia of the neofascist **Croatian Party of Rights** (HSP) led by **Dobroslav Paraga**. Active in both western Hercegovina, a traditional **Ustaša** stronghold, and eastern Slavonia, HOS was banned by the Croatian government in November 1991, when Vukovar finally fell to the Serbs. After the end of the first Serb-Croat civil war in late 1991, the ZNG was replaced by the regular **Croatian Army** (HV). In **Bosnia-Hercegovina**, the civil war began with a notorious Tiger ethnic cleansing of the predominantly Muslim town of **Bijeljina** in eastern Bosnia in April 1992. Loosely cooordinated by local JNA units, the Tigers and other Chetnik irregular forces then ethnically "cleansed" large areas of eastern and northern Bosnia throughout the rest of 1992. At this time local Bosnian Serbs also founded a paramilitary force that later became the **Bosnian Serb Army** (BSA). It was at this time that the worst atrocities and war crimes of the Yugoslav conflict took place.

Originating in the Croatian Union of **Herceg-Bosna** in western Hercegovina, the **Croatian Council of Defense** (HVO) was initially little more than a disorganized group of local militias aided by the ZNG and the HV in nearby Croatia. Unlike HOS, the HVO did not recruit among local Bosnian Muslims. Aided by the regular armed forces of Croatia, the HVO often also covertly colluded with the BSA, notably during the civil war between the **Bosnian Croats** and **Muslims** in 1992 and 1993.

Unprepared for civil war in 1992, the Muslims of Bosnia-Hercegovina did not have any armed forces to speak of when the JNA and Serb irregulars went on the attack. In **Sarajevo**, the besieged city's defense initially fell to a motley collection of police, territorial defense units, and criminal gangs. Later partly organized into official military units, such as the Green Berets, these forces were notoriously undisciplined and often a major security and political problem for the Sarajevo government. A recognizable **Bosnian army** (ARBH) did not appear in practice until 1993. In 1993–1994, the Sarajevo government stamped out a number of armed criminal gangs in the Bosnian capital.

Elsewhere in Bosnia, a number of other irregular forces emerged at this time, most notably in the **Bihać** enclave, a strategic territory in western Bosnia controlled by a local businessman and politician turned warlord, **Fikret Abdić**.

Focused on central Bosnia, the military operations of the ARBH during the 1990s were also aided by a number of Islamic *mujaheddin* units recruited and financed abroad. Based in and around the town of **Zenica**, these forces played an important military role during the Croat-Muslim civil war of 1992–1993. At various times, however, they have been a problem for the ARBH because of their political activities or military indiscipline. Their political significance has been considerable because of the growing influence of the clerical wing of the ruling **Party of Democratic Action** (SDA) in Sarajevo and that wing's international Islamic connections, most notably with **Iran** and Saudi Arabia, resulting in some concern in the West about a "fundamentalist bridgehead" in Bosnia.

Undoubtedly guilty of widespread atrocities and war crimes, many of the leaders of paramilitary groups have been charged with or indicted for war crimes. Foremost among these have been Šešelj, "Arkan," and Mladić, all of whom were indicted as war criminals by the United Nations International **War Crimes Tribunal** (IWCT) in 1994. More recently, the IWCT has also indicted a number of HVO commanders for alleged war crimes.

Looked at as a whole, the paramilitary/irregular forces of the Yugoslav wars have rarely played a central military role, even when they were at their most significant in 1991–1993. Even at that time the Chetniks, the Tigers, the HOS, the Green Berets, and other similar groups did not have more than 5,000 troops each. Of the Serb and Croat groups, all were armed and partly commanded by regular military forces and the governments that controlled them. By 1994–1995, when the Yugoslav wars entered a new stage in Croatia and Bosnia, regular military forces became the dominant players. Many of these forces had become politically expendable by 1994–1995, most notably on the Serbian side, where Milošević split with Šešelj and the Bosnian Serbs at this time. In the specific context of Bosnia, one of the key provisions of the **Dayton Agreements** was that all unauthorized or "foreign" military forces had to leave this former Yugoslav republic forthwith.

—*M. M.*

PARTIZANS

The name "Partizans" (from the Serbo-Croat "Partizani") or "Partisans" was given to guerrilla fighters for the communist cause during World War II. Controlled by the Comintern during the interwar period, the underground Communist Party of Yugoslavia (KPJ), under the leadership of Josip Broz **Tito**, organized a National Liberation Army (NLA) to resist the 1941 Axis invasion and dismemberment of the first incarnation of Yugoslavia. Of the 12,000 KPJ cadres that constituted the highly politicized operational core of the NLA in 1941, around two-thirds perished during a three-year war against the Axis occupiers and their domestic collaborators. Initially composed largely of ethnic Serbs but later representative of most of the rest of the Yugoslav peoples, the Partizans had essentially won the civil war by 1943, when the KPJ-directed Anti-Fascist Council for the National Liberation of Yugoslavia (AVNOJ) declared the creation of a second Yugoslavia and forbade the return of the former **monarchy**. Following the liberation of **Belgrade** in 1944, with Soviet assistance, the Partizans became the undisputed masters of a new communist Yugoslavia.

Having both won the civil war and successfully defied Stalin in 1948, Tito's Partizan generation exhibited great self-confidence and revolutionary élan in all fields. The wartime Partizan ethos was at its strongest in the **Yugoslav Peoples' Army** (JNA), the postwar successor to the NLA, and its various veterans' organizations. The grip on power exercised by this Partizan generation was not to be loosened until the late 1970s. With his death in 1980, Tito's legacy began to fade during the political and economic crises of the 1980s, when local nationalisms replaced an all-Yugoslav communism as the main legitimating motif of the elites and divided the decaying Communist Party.

During the Yugoslav crises and wars of the 1990s, a number of **political parties** espoused a kind of rehabilitated **Titoism**, appealing to the old Partizan myths, confined mainly to **Serbia**, **Montenegro**, and **Macedonia**. The most significant of these were the **Socialist Party of Serbia** (SPS) and its ultraleft ally, the Yugoslav United Left (JUL).

—M. M.

PARTY OF DEMOCRATIC ACTION

Founded on 26 May 1990 as a movement of "citizens belonging to **Muslim** cultural and historical traditions," the Party of Democratic Action (Stranka demokratske akcije—SDA) emerged as the largest party in the first competitive **elections** held in **Bosnia-Hercegovina** in November 1990. It held 43 of the 130 seats in the Chamber of Citizens and the same number of the 110 seats in the Chamber of Municipalities. In neither case did it have a controlling majority, and in order to forestall ethnic conflict an attempt was made to form a coalition government. Its leader, **Alija Izetbegović**, became head of the collective Bosnian presidency in November 1990, and head of state when Bosnia declared itself independent in March 1992.

During the warfare that ensued, the SDA tightened its hold on the territory remaining in Bosnian hands. Its influence increased particularly in the **media**, the economic sphere, and the armed forces. Clericalists, who wished to forge a national identity for Bosnia derived in large part from its traditions within **Islam**, became increasingly powerful in the party. Those emphasizing the multicultural heritage of Bosnia found a champion in **Haris Silajdžić**, foreign minister and later premier through the war years, but he quit his government posts in August 1995 and formed a new Liberal Party in March 1996, in readiness for the elections due six months later. The old emblems of multiculturalism disappeared during the election campaign, and SDA rallies were awash with Islamic symbols.

The SDA has extended its grip particularly over the armed forces and over sectors of the economy, giving rise to accusations of nepotism and outright corruption. President Izetbegović has not excluded liberal elements entirely from top positions, but it is clericalists who are rising fastest within the SDA. The growing nationalist and Islamic character of the party is encouraged by the increasing prominence of previously rural-based Muslims uprooted by the war, who today form a significant proportion of the population in **Sarajevo**, as well as **Zenica**, **Travnik**, and other urban centers controlled from the capital.

—T. G.

See also: Bosnian army; political parties; rural-urban differences

PAVELIĆ, ANTE (1889–1959)

Ante Pavelić was a lawyer in Zagreb and politician in the Croatian Party of Right (Hrvatska stranka prava—HSP). The party was created in 1919 by followers of Josip Frank, whose Party of Pure Right had split from Ante Starčević's original Party of Right. The Frankists had always been Croat nationalists, although they were generally staunch **Habsburg** loyalists, especially in relation to **Serbia**. By 1928 they were a confused and ineffective political force. Pavelić established links with Mussolini's government in Italy and left Croatia in 1929 after King Aleksandar declared a royal dictatorship in Yugoslavia. In Italy Pavelić founded the **Ustaša** (Insurgent) movement. Pavelić made links with the Internal Macedonian Revolutionary Organization (VRMO) and, with their help, organized the assassination of the king in Marseille on 9 October 1934.

Following the German and Italian defeat of Yugoslavia in 1941, Pavelić (with the sponsorship of the Axis powers) became the *poglavnik* (chief) of the Independent State of Croatia (Nezavisna Država Hrvatske—NDH), entering Zagreb on 15 April 1941. When the government's patrons were pushed out of Yugoslavia in 1944, Pavelić fled initially to Austria with remnants of the Ustaša and then to Argentina. He subsequently settled in Spain under General Franco's patronage.

—G. R. B.

PEACE MOVEMENTS (CROATIA)

From very early in the war in 1991, activists from various social movements were gathering together to oppose the violence. Many of the people involved in this antiwar work had known each other before, e.g., as students in the University of Zagreb or in groups that were part of the Socialist Alliance of Working People of Croatia—ecology groups and feminist groups among them. They also made links across republics, to **Slovenia**, to **Bosnia-Hercegovina**, and crucially to **Serbia**—where there were also antiwar activists opposed to the use of force to manage the conflict.

One group of people came together in **Osijek**, the capital of eastern **Slavonia**, where in 1991, during the military battles in and around Osijek, representatives of European peace movements visited a group of people who were searching for a nonviolent response to the fighting. Within a year approximately 20 peace education workshops took place on subjects like prejudice reduction, communication skills, mediation, nonviolent action, and human rights protection. The Center for Peace, Nonviolence, and Human Rights was created from the small group involved in these activities; it had approximately 30 members by October 1994. The center has educational and advisory programs, which are engaged in long-term, delicate, and persistent work situated within the context of a spiritual belief in the importance of reconciliation. Projects of the center include the following: training activists and volunteers for work in the protection of human rights; therapeutic work with war invalids; a reconciliation project with the displaced villagers of Laslovo; stimulating and supporting **refugees** and displaced **women** to become involved in a learning and working process focused on using tailoring skills, with the aim of providing a renewal of motivation, creating community, and developing practical skills; and workshops with teachers who had suffered the traumas of war, with the aim of helping them regain and strengthen self-confidence, develop positive attitudes toward the future, learn nonviolent communication, and reduce prejudice in order to overcome the difficulties they faced as displaced people, as well as to acquire new knowledge with which they could better respond to the needs of those children affected by the war. The teachers then worked with schools in the area on specific projects at nine primary schools in Osijek and nearby, involving 20 teachers, several volunteers, and between 800 and 1,000 children. The Osijek center collaborated with Friedensbrugg (Bridge for Peace) and the Helsinki Citizens Assembly on a project designed to enable people who used to be neighbors and friends in Baranja, but who had been divided by the events of the immediate prewar period and the war itself, to meet once more and break down the barriers of fear and prejudice that existed between them.

The Osijek Center for Peace was an affiliate of the Antiwar Campaign in Croatia (Anti Ratna Kampanja—ARK), perhaps the best-known of the Croatian peace groups internationally. ARK is in fact a network rather than a **nongovernmental organization** (NGO) in itself, and it works through its member projects and centers. Although many of its members are based in the capital, Zagreb, ARK's work is firmly focused on the ground level and the localities; its network stretches from Dubrovnik to Istria and from the Zagorje to Slavonia, as well as having links to Slovenia, Bosnia, the Vojvodina, and Serbia.

ARK was founded in Zagreb at the beginning of July 1991 by a group who believed that people in the

Yugoslav region would have to continue to live together; that these people would have convergent interests in economic, social, and ecological issues; and that war and violence would inflict pain and injury on all communities. The founders of ARK declared their rejection of violence and war, as well as their readiness to maintain communication and cooperation across nationalities and state borders in the face of political extremism and despite the fractures that war created.

From the start, ARK has realized that its work would not have quick results. Accordingly, they have chosen to develop long-term projects in the areas of human rights, peace education, and **conflict management and conflict resolution**. Their chosen strategy has involved fostering self-organized groups and creating a network of such groups and organizations. ARK aims to develop and apply nonviolent methods of conflict resolution in the context of the conflict in Croatia and to create the conditions for lasting peace. In October 1994 ARK was a network of about ten local and specialized organizations and was coordinating and planning new projects. These projects included the following: the Center for Peace, Nonviolence, and Human Rights—Zagreb, which ran the "Media and War" research project; the ZAMIR-ZG computer network, designed to facilitate up-to-date information transfer, and connected with ZAMIR-BG in Serbia and GreenNet; and *Arkzin,* an internal bulletin that from April 1993 appeared as a monthly (and from July 1994 fortnightly) newspaper promoting peace, human rights, and civil society.

ARK also hosted workshops on nonviolent communication and on education for nonviolence. In addition, it was involved in the first meeting of international conflict resolution trainers and trainees from the territories of the former Yugoslavia; this meeting was organized by the International Fellowhip of Reconciliation at Budapest in November 1993. ARK also found itself drawn into direct protection in cases of human rights abuse. Members have given legal advice, acted as advocates, lobbied, and engaged in nonviolent direct action.

One of ARK's best-known projects is the Social Reconstruction Workcamp in **Pakrac**. The physical rebuilding work that had to be done to restore the possibility of normal life was recognized to be only half of the story. ARK worked in cooperation with the Social Reconstruction Program of the United Nations Office in Vienna (UNOV—part of the United Nations Development Program, UNDP) to create a long-term project starting in July 1993. Beginning its work on the Croatian side of Pakrac, the project also started in January 1994 to work on the Serbian side of the **cease-fire** line. It aimed to reconstruct the town physically and socially. Teams of short-term volunteers from 14 different countries labored with local work brigades on rebuilding houses. The volunteers also organized social activities such as English lessons, sports, music, and discussion groups; made community visits to give help to the elderly and socially disadvantaged; carried out rebuilding work outside the official work brigades; ran a women's group; and ran a youth development program, including a youth club.

Political tensions stopped the international volunteers' work on the Serbian side in April 1994, but such work began again in October that year. In addition, the Pakrac project cooperated with the Belgrade organization Most (which means "bridge" in Serbo-Croat), sending volunteers to work on the Serbian side, although not continuously, after March 1994. The Pakrac project pointed toward the importance of physical and social reconstruction work as the foundations of reconciliation. Its work was stopped when the **Croatian Army** retook western **Slavonia** in May 1995, and the conditions in which it worked were transformed—almost no Serbs were left. Nevertheless, the Pakrac volunteer project continued to work after the military operation. It collaborated with the School of Social Work in Zagreb; took part in the reconstruction of a community center in a Serbian village; established a young women's group; and set up a Pakrac bulletin board system to extend the existing ZAMIR e-mail network, linking other centers of the network in Zagreb, Split, Sarajevo, and Belgrade.

ARK's work has by no means been reduced since the retaking of the **Krajina** and western Slavonia. Centers have been established in Gavrinica and Daruvar to serve the area of western Slavonia and in Petrinja, Vojnić, and **Knin** to serve the Krajina. There are also centers in Županja, **Karlovac**, Pula, Rijeka, and Poreč that have been working to build peace in many ways. Peacebuilding workshops are run by the Miramida Pakrac project both in Pakrac and in **Gornji Vakuf**, Bosnia-Hercegovina. The Small Step Center for a Culture of Peace and

Nonviolence published a book containing games and activities focused on cooperation and conflict resolution and gave workshops for children in the primary schools around Pakrac.

Given the continuing poor performance of the Croatian government in the fields of human rights, notwithstanding the moves toward closer institutional relationships with Western Europe, it is therefore all the more important that the peace groups remain vocal and active in the pursuit of an ethically justified transformation of the conflict and its effects. A recent optimistic note was sounded in late 1996 with the foundation of the Center for Peace Studies (Centar za mirovne studije) in Zagreb.

—*G. R. B.*

PEACE MOVEMENTS (GENERAL)

Although periodically significant in various former Yugoslav republics in recent years, the longer-term political impact of peace movements in the region has been fairly marginal. Dating back to 1985 in Slovenia, where what later became known as the Slovenian Movement for the Culture of Peace and Nonviolence (MCPN) became the first recognizable group of its type in communist Yugoslavia, local peace initiatives were part of a wider alternative politics throughout Eastern Europe during the 1980s. Broadly committed to peace, democracy, human rights, freedom of speech, and social justice, such groups also argued for the creation of a "civil society" independent of decaying communist state structures increasingly bereft of legitimacy.

The coming to power of reformist Communists in **Slovenia** in 1986 meant that groups like the MCPN were tolerated at the republican level of government in Ljubljana, if not in other Yugoslav republics or at the federal level of government. In this and other respects, Slovenia was unique in the twilight years of the former Yugoslav federation.

Even before the violent dissolution of Yugoslavia in 1990–1991, the MCPN and similar peace groups in **Croatia** and **Serbia** were divided as to whether their campaigns should have an all-Yugoslav character or be defined along national or republican lines. In any event, wider developments in Yugoslavia led to locally defined and organized peace movements emerging throughout the region, a circumstance that arguably lessened the movements' effectiveness.

Where all-Yugoslav peace initiatives did emerge, as with the Sarajevo meeting of the Yugoslav branch of the Helsinki Citizens Assembly (HCA) in May 1991, they tended to be prompted by outside influences, in this case the Helsinki process of the **Organization for Security and Cooperation in Europe** (OSCE). Another key foreign organization in this respect was War Resisters International (WRI), a longstanding network of antiwar activists and pacifists that has helped to coordinate various antiwar campaigns in the former Yugoslavia and that made their activities known to an international audience through publications such as *Peace News* (London).

A large number of other peace groups had emerged throughout the former Yugoslavia by 1991, including Citizens Action for Peace (GAMA, in Belgrade), AntiWar Campaign/Green Action (ARK, in Zagreb), Citizens' Forum (in Sarajevo), and League for Democracy (in Skopje).

With the outbreak of civil wars in Slovenia and Croatia in the summer of 1991, earlier disagreements within all-Yugoslav forums like the HCA became more pronounced, with the MCPN in particular taking the line of condemning these wars not in general, but rather only when the wars were waged by one side, namely Serbia. In this sense the activities of the main Slovenian and Croatian peace groups did not conflict with the policies of their respective governments. The Slovene peace movement's views, as expressed by the MCPN in particular, became dominant in the international peace movement. Already completely demonized by **propaganda** produced both locally and by the international **media**, Serbia became exclusively equated with aggressive warmongering, although the Belgrade-based peace movement was arguably more influential and principled in its antiwar stance than its counterparts in both Slovenia and Croatia.

In March 1991, Belgrade-based peace and **student** groups played a central role in antigovernment demonstrations that nearly toppled President **Slobodan Milošević**. In Slovenia and even more so in Croatia, on the other hand, local peace groups tended to be caught up in the mainstream or official consensus in favor of unilateral declarations of independence and statehood, as well as in incumbent governments playing the nationalist card to the point of civil war.

In terms of the practical mechanisms that could impede if not stop the Yugoslav wars of the 1990s, by far the most significant antiwar activities took place in Serbia in 1991–1992. As the seat of the Yugoslav branch of the HCA and the home of numerous peace and other groups in Belgrade, an alternative Serbia then existed to the one represented by Milošević and presented in the international media. Public support for desertion and draft dodging in 1991–1992 was widespread in Serbia, thereby limiting what Milošević could do in both Croatia and Bosnia. According to local (Anti-War Action, Belgrade) and foreign (WRI) sources, around 125,000 men of military age left Serbia to avoid conscription in 1991–1992. Including those mainly young men who also fled **Kosovo** for the same reason at this time, around 250,000 males fled Serbia by 1993. This left the JNA seriously short of conscripted manpower in Croatia and Bosnia, forcing it to rely more and more on unruly **paramilitary/irregular** volunteers and the indiscriminate use of heavy firepower to achieve its objectives. In the supercharged "patriotic" atmosphere in both Slovenia and Croatia at this time, on the other hand, desertion and illegal cross-border flight were relatively rare.

On a more negative note in Serbia, local peace groups in Belgrade and Novi Sad were limited in their influence to the issue of encouraging and helping to organize mass draft dodging. The growth of an extreme Serb nationalism precluded the possibility of Belgrade-based peace groups taking a principled stand on other controversial issues that presented a potential for war, foremost of which was the situation in Kosovo. This failing was to mark the entire Serbian opposition to Milošević during the 1990s, including those political parties that later emerged out of the Belgrade peace movement, such as Vesna Pešić's Civic Alliance.

The last of the former Yugoslav republics to descend into civil war in April 1992, **Bosnia-Hercegovina** experienced large and multiethnic antiwar demonstrations in **Sarajevo** and other cities immediately before its three years of conflict began. Here the Citizens' Forum was an important local influence. Others included the Center for Peace and the International Peace Center, both based in Sarajevo. Greatly influenced by older peace movements in Slovenia and Croatia, these Bosnian groups on the whole took a patriotic stance on Bosnian independence and statehood, even if this meant **civil war**. This stance became particularly strong for understandable reasons once the **siege** of Sarajevo began in earnest. The siege cut off Bosnian peace activists from the outside world and forced many of them to leave the Bosnian capital as the war in Bosnia became more severe and prolonged. During the Bosnian war, issues of **humanitarian aid** and activities by local and foreign **nongovernmental organizations** (NGOs) tended to overshadow all others, including those pertaining to peace, for self-evident reasons of survival. Only after the end of the Bosnian war in 1995 did local peace groups reemerge.

One of the most interesting projects created by peace movements anywhere in the former Yugoslavia since the end of the war has been the plan to convert the Metelkova barracks in **Ljubljana** to civilian uses. With the cooperation of the city authorities and the Slovene ministry of culture, this former military establishment is being converted to include a cultural center, a resource center for NGOs, and facilities for handicraft production and other cooperatives.

Elsewhere in the former Yugoslavia, the end of its wars in 1995 mainly had the effect of reinforcing the trend toward the merging of peace movements into more generalized antigovernment forces committed to removing from power those **political parties** and personalities who had led Yugoslavia and its peoples into war in the first place.

—M. M.

PEACEKEEPING
See **UNPROFOR**

PERIŠIĆ, MOMČILO

Col.-Gen. Momčilo Perišić was for a time chief of staff of the Army of Yugoslavia (VJ). Born in Gornji Milanovac, Serbia, in 1944, he was educated at the Military Academy for Ground Forces and the elite Higher Military-Political School of the **Yugoslav Peoples' Army** (JNA). Perišić commanded JNA units in **Croatia** and **Bosnia-Hercegovina**, where he became a corps commander at **Mostar**. He participated in the JNA siege of **Dubrovnik** and was later responsible for the evacuation of key JNA military production facilities from Bosnia to **Montenegro** and **Serbia**. Promoted to commander of the Third Army, at Niš in 1992, Perišić became chief of staff of the new VJ in August 1993. One of a number of younger military professionals, he replaced Gen. Zivota Panić, an older Titoist officer purged by

Serbian president **Slobodan Milošević**. Considered a Milošević loyalist, Perišić has since been concerned mainly with the reorganization of the VJ following that army's replacement of the multiethnic JNA.

—*M. M.*

PERUČA DAM

On 22 January 1993, Croatian forces mounted an offensive designed to strengthen their position in **United Nations** (UN) Sector South, especially to regain control over the strategic **Maslenica Bridge.** Retreating Serb forces mined the Peruča Dam, which holds back an artificial lake on the Cetina River, eight miles north of Sinj. The dam was seriously damaged, but the majority of the mines failed to detonate. Had they done so, several villages in the Sinjsko *polje* (plain) would have been destroyed, and **Croatia** would have been robbed of a vital source of hydroelectric **energy**. The UN assembled a joint civil and military mission of experts that was able to render the dam safe and eventually restore it to production.

—*J. B. A.*

PETERLE, LOJZE

Lojze Peterle is the leader of the Slovene Christian Democrats. In the **elections** of April 1990 his party attracted the largest number of votes within the Democratic Opposition of Slovenia (DEMOS) coalition. He was appointed prime minister at the age of 43, and his party was awarded the Ministries of Education and Culture. The DEMOS coalition lasted from May 1990 to April 1992, during which time it made important decisions concerning independence and the pluralist development of **Slovenia** and its civil society. DEMOS contained too many differing viewpoints, however, and was unified only by the desire to see an anticommunist transition to democracy. Eventually the Christian Democrats and the Slovene Democratic Alliance came into conflict over the issue of **privatization.** Peterle and his party are to the right of center and have a peculiarly religious slant on affairs reflected in Peterle's own view of Slovenia's future. Of his electoral success he said (quoted by Leonard J. Cohen), "All of my dreams are based on Christian foundations. In my dreams, the ecology and economy are linked with social responsibility. Neighbourhoods play an important role. Yugoslavia failed twice in this century because it failed to solve its nationalities' problems. In both cases it acted as a dictatorship. A third attempt, if successful, could be made only on the basis of democratic structures."

Peterle participated with **Milan Kučan, Igor Bavčar, Dimitrij Rupel,** and **Janez Drnovšek** in negotiating the **Brioni Accord** on 7–8 July 1991, which marked the end of the Ten Day War in Slovenia. Prior to this event, he was involved in the decision to continue payments of the Slovene portion of the Federal Fund for Underdeveloped Regions only if those payments were earmarked for Slovene enterprises in the less developed regions of Yugoslavia. When the Slovene legislature adopted its declaration of sovereignty, Peterle claimed that this declaration meant not secession but that he wanted a sovereign Slovenia within a Yugoslav confederation.

Since independence, the Christian Democrats have also participated in Drnovšek's new government formed after the elections of December 1992, and Peterle was made deputy prime minister for foreign affairs in January 1993. In the 1996 elections he and his party made controversial campaign promises to seek the restoration of land and property to the **Catholic Church**.

—*I. R. B.*

See also: political parties

Reference: Cohen, Leonard J. *Broken Bonds: The Disintegration of Yugoslavia.* Boulder, CO: Westview Press, 1993, p. 94

PINK ZONES

Following the signing of a cease-fire in **Croatia** on 3 January 1992, the **Vance Plan** provided for the setting up of United Nations protected areas (UNPAs), which were to be demilitarized as an aid to creating conditions for a negotiated resolution of the Serb-Croat conflict in these areas. These areas did not coincide precisely with the areas under the de facto control of Serb irregulars and the **Yugoslav Peoples' Army** (JNA). The Serb-controlled areas not projected as part of the UNPAs were designated as "pink zones," and it was expected that they would be returned quickly to the control of the Croatian authorities. This scheme was accepted on 9 February at a meeting of representatives of the Serb **Krajina** convoked by Serbian president **Slobodan Milošević** (against the opposition of Krajina Serb leader **Milan Babić**); it was scheduled for implementation on 21 February by a **United Nations** force set up by Security Council resolution. In any event, the withdrawal of Serb forces into the designated protected areas was never completely achieved until these Serb forces were overthrown in **Operation Flash** and **Operation Storm** in May and August 1995.

—*J. B. A.*

See also: UNPROFOR

PIRAN

See **Koper (Bay of Piran)**

PLAVŠIĆ, BILJANA

Biljana Plavšić became president of the **Republika Srpska** (RS) in 1997, having been acting president since July 1996, when **Radovan Karadžić** was formally indicted as an alleged war criminal and disqualified from holding any public office in **Bosnia-Hercegovina.** Born in 1931 in Sarajevo, Plavšić studied biochemistry locally and in the United States and then pursued an academic career at the University of Sarajevo. Her political career in the Serbian Democratic Party (SDS) began at the time of the party's formation and the first postcommunist elections in 1990. Then an ardent Serb nationalist in pursuit of the "**Greater Serbia**" project and an open advocate of the "**ethnic cleansing**" of Bosnian **Muslims** from all Serb-controlled territories, Plavšić was elected to the collective Bosnian presidency in November 1990. Along with the rest of the SDS leadership, Plavšić left the all-Bosnian government in Sarajevo when the republic descended into civil war in April 1992. Even more extreme in her nationalist politics than her mentor, Karadžić, Plavšić became known as the "Iron Lady" of the **Bosnian Serbs** and regarded herself as the epitome of the Velika Srpkinja (Great Serbian Woman). One of two RS vice presidents from 1992 to 1995, Plavšić bitterly opposed acceptance of the international peace plans for Bosnia in 1993 and 1994.

Unlike other leaders of the SDS, Plavšić has seldom hidden her loathing for **Slobodan Milošević** and his wife, **Mirjana Marković.** As a result, she was banned from entering Serbia in 1993 and thereafter vilified as a warmonger or worse by the government-controlled **media** in Belgrade.

Although her co-vice president, **Nikola Koljević,** was widely perceived as being an ally of Milošević, Plavšić soon became Karadžić's anointed heir. Granted some of his powers, including the right to negotiate internationally after the signing of the **Dayton Agreements** at the end of 1995, she became acting president the following July.

Unlike Karadžić, Plavšić has never been indicted as a war criminal. Despite her hostility to the idea of a reunified Bosnia-Hercegovina, as envisaged by Dayton, Plavšić nevertheless proved her willingness to cooperate with the international community post-Dayton. Based in **Banja Luka,** Plavšić has also strongly attacked Karadžić and his **Pale**-based clique as being highly corrupt at a time of serious socioeconomic collapse. The power struggle over these issues entered a decisive stage in 1997, when Plavšić won the open support of the international community and the **Stabilization Force** of the **North Atlantic Treaty Organization** (NATO). Within an increasingly divided RS, she abandoned the disintegrating SDS in 1997 and founded a new Bosnian Serb political party in Banja Luka. During new parliamentary **elections** in November 1997, her political strength in Banja Luka and western Bosnia did not translate into a definitive victory over Karadžić's SDS, although it did ensure her the presidency of the Serb entity.

—*M. M.*

PLITVICE LAKES

Plitvička jezera, or the lakes of Plitvice, form a national park that has long been of importance for domestic and foreign tourism and, consequently, a major source of income for Croatia. Located in the Lika region, a mainly Serb part of western Croatia, the area was of more than symbolic significance as a natural asset in the early hostilities involving the **Krajina.** In summer 1990, talks had been planned between the local Serbs and the Croat Party of Democratic Change (the reformed Communists, who were in opposition centrally but in power locally) concerning future development of the park; however, these talks were forestalled by **Milan Babić**'s SDS (Serbian Democratic Party). In February 1991 the central government in Zagreb, in response to the spreading rebellion of the Krajina Serbs, established a police station in the park; the Serb nationalists staged a forceful demonstration and replaced the managers of the park. A month later the Croatian police entered the park and regained control after a short exchange of fire that resulted in the first two killings of the war. The federal government in Belgrade drew up a plan whereby the **Yugoslav Peoples' Army**, rather than the Croatian police force, was to maintain a **cease-fire** in the area. This plan was rejected by the Croatian president, **Franjo Tudjman**, and the tensions throughout the Krajina were thus unsurprisingly heightened.

—J. J. H.

PLOČE

See **Neretva River Valley**

PODGORICA

Podgorica, with a population of 117,000 in 1991, is the current capital of the Republic of **Montenegro**, having been selected over the traditional capital, Cetinje, when the Socialist Federal Republic of Yugoslavia was created in 1945. The town is built on the Morača River and until the destruction during the War of Liberation (the Yugoslav term for World War II battles fought on Yugoslav soil) was composed of two main quarters (Turkish and Montenegrin) separated by a tributary of that river. It stands on a wide fertile plain (one of few in Montenegro) that stretches some 18 miles from Lake Skadar. It thus occupies an important position for what large-scale agriculture exists in the republic.

Podgorica was, until its acquisition from the **Ottoman Empire** in 1877, a predominantly Muslim town of considerable importance for the conduct of trade, straddling a lowland zone dividing the Prokletije (Accursed) Mountains of **Albania** from those of Montenegro. After the War of Liberation, little of the historic architecture of the town was left, and rebuilding became a potent symbol of pride in the new, socialist Yugoslavia. The town was then renamed Titograd and has only recently had its former name restored. Although Podgorica has historically had reasonable **communications** with the coast (by road and narrow-gauge railway) and Lake Skadar, it was not until 1976 that a standard-gauge railway was completed from the port of Bar to **Belgrade**, linking Podgorica to the Yugoslav interior.

Montenegrin nationalists frequently refuse to recognize Podgorica (formerly Titograd during the communist era) as the capital of the republic, and in the last two years there has been a campaign to restore that honor to the town of Cetinje, which stands at the center of Montenegro's old heartland. Certain government functions have already moved, creating confusion in a republic not known for its efficient bureaucracy.

—R. J.

POLITICAL ASSOCIATIONS

Under the Communist regime in Yugoslavia, **political parties** opposed to the **League of Communists** (LC) were not permitted. The LC justified the suppression of the *Praxis* group of philosophers in the early 1970s largely on the grounds that the group aspired to be a political party. The weakening hold of the LC upon Yugoslav politics in the 1980s, however, was marked by the creation of "political associations" that secured recognition within the framework of the Socialist Alliance of the Working People of Yugoslavia (SA).

The LC was the lineal descendant of the pre-1941 Popular Front, through which the Communists operated after the suppression of the party in 1920, and the United People's Liberation Front of the 1941–1945 war. It took its recent form at the fourth congress of the LC in 1953. As a "large-scale public tribune of socialist thought and politics," it functioned as a means of public information and mobilization on behalf of the regime, and it came into its own at periods when the way was being prepared for major political changes, such as the debate over the series of **constitutional** amendments in the late 1980s. At that time it acquired a surprising new role as the medium through which emerging political dissent could be channeled (and perhaps controlled) by creating political associations, which were explicitly intended as forums for the discussion of political issues but not as "parties."

The first such association, formed in May 1988, was the Slovenska kmečka zveza (Slovene Peasant League), organized by Ivan Oman. In January the following year, **Dimitrij Rupel** led the formation of the Slovenska demokratična zveza (Slovene Democratic League). This was followed in November 1989 by the Udruženje za Jugoslovensku demokratsku inicijativu, created by a group of academics from both Belgrade and Zagreb, anxious to promote the process of **democratization** generally in Yugoslavia.

Although this strategy became irrelevant after the collapse of the LC in January 1990, the political associations played an important role in loosening the LC's monopolistic hold on Yugoslav politics, eventually leading to the development of multiparty politics. The associations prefigured three quite different types of political parties: the representation of an economic interest group, a nationalistic mass movement, and a broad coalition of interests around a general ideological purpose.

—*J. B. A.*

POLITICAL PARTIES

The emergence of competing political parties in Yugoslavia to challenge the **League of Communists of Yugoslavia** (SKJ) was an important element in the general process of the disintegration of the former Yugoslav state. The diversity of parties appearing in 1989–1990 was symptomatic of the ills of the federation and contributed in some respects to the development of destructive conflict.

During the first round of multiparty **elections**, more than 200 parties competed for votes. The great majority of these parties stood no chance of making a longer-term impact upon the political scene. The more significant ones in each republic are treated in separate entries in this volume, and a survey of party formation is given below for each of the post-Yugoslav republics; however, it is useful to first record some systematic patterns and problems in connection with this aspect of the emerging conflict.

The majority of parties operated within a single republic. The process of political diversification was set in motion by *republican* political leaderships and was resisted by the federal presidency. The SKJ was able to obstruct the emergence of organized opposition at the level of the federation. For diverse local reasons, however, it was not possible to prevent **political associations** at first and then parties from emerging at republican level. Indeed, in **Slovenia** the LC was active in promoting this political diversification process as part of its own bid to relegitimate itself.

There have been noteworthy exceptions to this localization of politics. The Alliance of Reform Forces led by former premier **Ante Marković**, although formed too late to contest the first Slovene elections, set out to build a federation-wide force for economic modernization. The **Croatian Democratic Union**, in spite of formal separation, has always operated in a coordinated fashion in both Croatia and Bosnia-Hercegovina. The **Party of Democratic Action** (SDA), created as the main vehicle for the expression of **Muslim** political aspirations in **Bosnia-Hercegovina**, has maintained close links with the party of the same name in the **Sandžak**. Although it has often been commented that post-Communist politics in Yugoslavia took the form of *ethnic* politics, this remark must be qualified. Party formation cut across ethnic lines on *regional* principles. Whereas the main voice of Serbs in Serbia has been the **Socialist Party of Serbia**, in Bosnia-Hercegovina it has been the Serbian Democratic Party. In Croatia, the Serb voice was divided between the Zagreb-based Serbian National Party and the Serbian Democratic Party, centered on the **Krajina**. **Albanians** in Kosovo have mostly given their allegiance to the **Democratic League of Kosovo**; in **Macedonia** to the Party of Democratic Prosperity; and in **Montenegro** to the Democratic Coalition.

The importance of this *local* (or even parochial) element in politics is revealed by the numerous "microparties" and by the large number of independent candidates competing in every election. Some of these had conspicuous local success, especially in **Istria** and **Dalmatia**. It should be noted also that in Serbia the main opposition parties, such as the Serbian Party of Renewal, have been confined in their support largely to the industrial region surrounding the capital, **Belgrade**. This fragmentation of the political scene militated against the creation of any federation-wide consensus about the future for Yugoslavia.

It is necessary to keep in mind this local or regional refraction of issues, as well as the difficulty of generalizing across the federation about the nature of conflict and the causes of the disintegration of Yugoslavia. Nevertheless, it is possible to identify two broad, general axes of differentiation between parties. It is possible in all republics to contrast those parties that emerged from within the former Communist establishment (either the SKJ itself or its "popular front," the Socialist Alliance) and those that were set up outside this apparatus and in opposition to it. It is also useful to compare parties across all regions in terms of their relative commitment to either modernization or traditionalism. (Sometimes, but not always, this characteristic corresponds to the **rural-urban** character of the parties' support base.)

Three other general characteristics are worthy of comment in terms of the general pattern of party formation.

Although social scientists have generally linked **democratization** to the emergence of more individualistic values, there is little evidence of this phenomenon in any region of the former Yugoslavia. The new parties have not represented individualistic responses to Communist collectivism; rather, they have merely expressed different kinds of collectivism—predominantly nationalism. Those groups that founded their platforms in 1989–1990 on the defense of civil liberties or individual rights made little headway with the electorate. This was the case even in Slovenia, where the erroneously labeled "civil society" (a fringe of protest groups that emerged in the late 1980s primarily around the implementation of individual rights in politics, artistic expression, or sexual orientation) was obliterated when political dissent made the transition to *party* competition.

Although the disintegration of Yugoslavia has often been laid at the door of the religious dimension of social difference, the confessional element in party formation has been negligible. Only Slovenia has been different in this respect; the Slovene Christian Democrats have managed to secure a following on the basis of **religion**. Nationalism elsewhere sometimes does employ religious rhetoric, but as often as not attempts to do so have *divided* rather than united the ethnic group in question. This has been most notably the case with **Islam**. The SDA has always been identified as a "Muslim" party; however, the more the faction associated with **Alija Izetbegović** has made an issue of the specifically religious meaning of "Muslim" identity, as opposed to the diffusely ethnic meaning, the stronger other competitors for the Muslim vote (such as the Party for Bosnia-Hercegovina, led by **Haris Silajdžić**) have grown. Although Islam is the faith with the largest number of adherents among Albanians, *all* parties that have appealed to the Albanian constituency have done so on the basis of the *linguistic* unity of Albanians, using such issues as educational provision or access to the communications **media**.

Two difficulties attend any attempt by outsiders to understand party activity in the post-Yugoslav countries, particularly if the framework for comparison is Europe. The traditional "left/right" axis of division makes no sense at all in the Balkan setting in terms either of ideology or of the social base of party support. A party such as the Socialist Party of Serbia might be considered "left" from the point of its socialist heritage and habits of collectivism in economic policy, but its nationalism and its social base among petty officials, small-town society, and the peasantry place it closer to the traditional support for European fascist movements. Macedonia's VMRO-DPMNE (Internal Macedonian Revolutionary Organization—Democratic Party for Macedonian National Unity) has no discernable economic policy; its harking back to historical themes might be said to identify it as a "conservative" party, but its constitutional iconoclasm brands it as "radical."

A great difficulty faces anybody who sets out to study party life in the republics of the former Yugoslavia because the scene keeps changing. Parties merge, divide, and change their names. There is an absence of clear ideological forms or established loyalties. Parties are often in large measure the followings of individual leaders rather than the political expression of stable social formations. This gives a marked volatility to the situation, which suggests that the party politics of the region will remain fluid for some time to come.

—*J. B. A.*

Reference: Szajkowski, Bogdan (ed.), *Political Parties of Eastern Europe: Russia and the Successor States.* London: Longman, 1994

Political Parties in Bosnia-Hercegovina

In many respects the League of Communists in Bosnia-Hercegovina represented the nadir of the League of Communists in Yugoslavia as a whole during the last years of Federal Yugoslavia. Throughout the post-1945 period, the league had been controlled by a rather conservative and rigid element in the party, exemplified by the trials of **Alija Izetbegović** and others in 1983. Through the ordeal involving Agrokomerc (a food-processing company managed by **Fikret Abdić**), the LC had come to be branded as corrupt. The Yugoslav federal elite's attempt to deal with economic crisis had come to a head in the spectacular failure of the government led by Bosnian Branko Mikulić.

In the 1990 elections, it is not surprising that the republican LC—although it had reformed itself as the Party of Democratic Change (SDP)—fared less well than any of the former LCs, winning only 19 seats (out of 240) in the two houses of Bosnia-Hercegovina's assembly. Ante Marković's attempt to appeal to ethnic toleration and the continuation of a federal Yugoslavia, in the form of the Alliance of

Reform Forces, did better in Bosnia-Hercegovina than elsewhere, with 12 seats in the lower house. A small Social Democratic Party (DSS) sustained a token presence. Nevertheless, electoral support in 1990 split almost completely on ethnic lines.

The space vacated by the LC was occupied by the **Party of Democratic Action** (SDA); the Serbian Democratic Party (SDS), led by **Radovan Karadžić**, **Nikola Koljević**, and **Biljana Plavšić**; and the **Croatian Democratic Union** (HDZ), led locally by **Stjepan Kljuić** but generally regarded as a branch of the Zagreb organization. Only ethnic Muslim opinion showed any measure of diversity, with the emergence as well of the Muslim-Bošnjak Organization (MBO) under **Adil Zulfikarpašić** and **Muhamed Filipović**. Only 15 percent of the vote in Bosnia-Hercegovina in the 1990 elections went to parties that did not have an ethnic or religious base.

It is only with the incipient collapse of the Bosnian state into ethnic substates that these ethnic hegemonies have been challenged. For as long as war raged, there were strong pressures to create an army-party machine that controlled affairs in the Muslim, Serb and Croat areas. Since the **Dayton Agreements** and the return to electoral politics, the diversity of opinion within each ethnic bloc has reemerged. As in other parts of the former Yugoslavia, parties with a local basis have emerged to contest **elections** at all levels of politics. The situation is complicated further for the outside observer by the appearance of numerous local, regional, and entity-wide coalitions.

Among Muslims, the MBO has evolved into the Liberal-Bošnjak Organization (LBO), emphasizing the party's secular credentials in the face of the increasing influence of **Islam** in the SDA. The LBO was upstaged in the 1996 elections, however, by **Haris Silajdžić**'s Party for Bosnia-Hercegovina, which took 7 percent of the vote.

Croatian politics has its echoes in the challenge to the HDZ presented by the Croatian Peasant Party (HSS) and the **Croatian Party of Right**. **Stjepan Kljuić** left the HDZ (which he formerly headed locally) to found the Republican Party. In predominantly Croat areas, there has been significant electoral support for the Associated List (ZL) of groups, including Social Democrats, seeking to play down the ethnic factor.

Politics within the **Republika Srpska** (RS) is quite different from that in Serbia itself in that there is no equivalent of the Socialist Party of Serbia, although **Vojislav Šešelj**'s Radicals and a cluster of other basically Serbian parties are active. The elections of September 1996 in the RS saw two coalitions emerging to challenge the SDS: the Democratic Patriotic Bloc (DPB) and the Alliance for Peace and Progress (SMP). The SDS retained its dominance, with two-thirds of the popular vote. The subsequent open conflict between Radovan Karadžić and Biljana Plavšić has resulted in the splitting of the SDS, with Plavšić creating the Serbian National Party (SNS). There have been signs of the further strengthening of forces in favor of interethnic cooperation, as well as a return to wider policy issues than ethnic conflict, with the rapid emergence of Milorad Dodik as leader of the Party of Independent Social Democrats (SNSD) and his incorporation into the governing coalition of the RS as prime minister after the elections of 1997.

The fragmentation of the party scene is a common feature of political life in all of the former Yugoslav republics but nowhere more so than in Bosnia-Hercegovina. In the 1998 elections to the assembly of the Republika Srpska, the electorate in **Goražde**, for example, was offered a choice among no fewer than 48 parties!

—J. B. A.

Political Parties in Croatia

The remarkable feature about Croatian party politics is the fact that **Franjo Tudjman**'s **Croatian Democratic Union** (HDZ), although it has retained its dominant position since the first **elections** in April–May 1990, has never captured an absolute majority of the votes of the Croatian electorate. Tudjman himself, however, although chosen by the members of the Sabor (Assembly) under the former constitution, has—under the new constitution of December 1990—secured personal popular majorities, even while his party is the object of suspicion and even antagonism. Three important factors have assisted the HDZ cause: the vigor of regional loyalties, the impact of the war, and the general ineffectiveness of the party's principal rivals. These factors have made it difficult to put together a united and effective opposition.

The HDZ has fared poorly in eastern **Slavonia**, the northern parts of the Adriatic coast, and especially **Istria**, where the Istrian Democratic Assembly and the Rijeka Democratic League have trounced the HDZ in every contest. The HDZ also does relatively poorly in the bigger cities (controversially failing to secure the mayoralty of **Zagreb** but refusing to comply with the verdict of the electorate). Its most reliable support has come from the parts of the country that are ethnically most homogeneous, reflecting the party's general ethnic intolerance.

The war has been used to create a sense of national emergency in which challenge to the government has been branded as disloyalty. Successive military victories have been used to offset the government's conspicuous failings in economic policy. The war has also effectively placed the Serb minority outside the electoral system (whether isolated in the **Krajina** or driven out as **refugees**) or divided them. In the period of disintegration before the war, the Serb vote was divided between (1) parties that appealed to the continuing integrity of Yugoslavia and the socialist tradition, such as the reformed Communists of the Party of Democratic Change (SDP), led by **Ivica Račan**, or the Socialist Party of Croatia (SSH), or (2) those that flew the flag of Serb nationalism, such as **Jovan Rašković**'s Serbian Democratic Party (SDS) or the more accommodationist Serbian National Party (SNS), led by Milan Dukić. (The first contested elections took place too early to engage Ante Marković's short-lived Alliance of Reformed Forces). Occupying a rather broad and ill-defined territory, ideologically speaking, the HDZ has been able to drive a wedge between other opposition forces. The more extreme fringes of nationalism have been abandoned to **Dobroslav Paraga**'s **Croatian Party of Rights** (and its fractious heirs) or to the Croatian Democratic Party (HDS). The competition for the votes of those who would prefer to play down the national question and the war, as well as get on with economic modernization, has been acutely divided between (1) a kind of reformist "old guard" led by the venerable **Savka Dabčević-Kučar** and the Croatian National Party (HNS) and (2) a shifting coalition surrounding the Croatian Social-Liberal Party (HSLS), led by Dražen Budiša. An extraordinary feature of the Croatian party scene is the persistently strong showing of the Croatian Peasant Party (HSS), which led the national movement before 1941, survived the communist period in exile in Canada, and returned to the fray in 1990. The HSS could conceivably be seen as a more moderate version of the traditional romanticism that characterizes the HDZ but without the latter's authoritarianism and "cult of personality"; its success possibly partly accounts for the marginalization of attempts to found environmentally conscious Green Parties. The attempt made by **Stipe Mesić** and **Josip Manolić** to found a Croatian National Democratic Party (HNDS) was intended to pull together this rather amorphous middle ground in Croatian politics but seems only to have added complexity. Although half a dozen groups have regularly made a strong enough electoral showing to add convincing weight to a coalition, no concerted oppositional force has been able to coalesce, starting with the Coalition of National Agreement (KNS). They all lack leadership, critical force, and the capacity for pragmatic synthesis that could put together a movement to topple the HDZ, which like the **Socialist Party of Serbia** remains in power not because it is either capably led or popular but because the opposition is weak. As the dust of war settles, however, and issues of economic well-being, social justice, and freedom return to the political agenda, there are signs of a revival of the fortunes of the SDP.

During the brief existence of the Serb Krajina, a semblance of party life was created. This took place mainly along two axes: parties were either proxies of powerful interests in **Serbia** itself (particularly **Slobodan Milošević** and **Vojislav Šešelj**) or personal followings of local "bosses," such as **Milan Martić** and **Milan Babić**.

—J. B. A.

Political Parties in Macedonia

The emergence of a multiparty system has been characterized by some remarkable reversals of fortune. The collapse of the monopoly of the **League of Communists** was greeted in Macedonia by the meteoric rise of the Movement for Pan-Macedonian Action (MAAK) in the spring of 1990. Headed by poet Gane Todorovski, the MAAK fielded a glittering list of the great and good in the elections in December. To the astonishment of all, however, it failed to take a single seat in the 120-seat Sobranie (Assembly), completely upstaged by the more plebeian (and cumbersomely named) Internal Macedonian Revolutionary Organization–Democratic Party for Macedonian National Unity (VMRO-DPMNE). The latter borrowed its name from the autonomist revolutionary movement that flourished after 1878 and led the Ilinden Revolt in

1903, but it owes more in practice to post-1945 Macedonian migrant workers. Led by the charismatic **Ljubiša Georgievski** and having a solidly working-class following, this rather strident nationalist movement has always been the largest group in the Sobranie (38 seats in the first elections). Having little expertise or experience on which to build, it relied at first upon a nonparty "government of experts" before falling to a coalition formed around the former Communists.

Contesting the 1990 elections as the Party of Democratic Change, the League of Communists in Macedonia adopted the title Social Democratic League of Macedonia (SDSM) in 1991. Although it has retained **Kiril Gligorov** as a figurehead and elder statesman, its relegitimation owes a good deal to the early adoption of a youthful new leadership group under **Branko Crvenkovski.** It has occupied the middle ground on most issues and has been sufficiently moderate in its nationalism to reach an eventual settlement with **Greece**, as well as to keep (for most of the time) moderate **Albanian** representation within a governing coalition. The success of the SDSM in this respect has been partly responsible for the division of ethnic Albanian political allegiance in Macedonia among (1) the more pragmatic and accommodationist Party of Democratic Prosperity (PDP), led by Dzeladin Murati, (2) a more radically nationalist faction inspired initially by Menduh Thaçi, and (3) the National Democratic Party (PDP), led by Iljaz Halili.

Because no party has been able to govern without a coalition, the balance of power was held for a time by the Liberal Party, led by Stojan Andov. Although its pragmatism, modernism, and moderate nationalism made this possible, the persistent failure of the SDSM to address economic issues undermined the coalition, driving the SDSM back into unstable collaboration with the PPD. The wild card in the Macedonian pack is the Democratic Party, which split from the former Communists in 1993, with a small following of former federal presidency member Petar Gošev. It is doubtful that the SDSM would ever accept Gošev as a partner; and until elections revise the balance of party representation in the Sobranie, the Liberals are not in a strong enough position to work with him, in spite of their ideological similarities. A relatively long trail of minor party/independent representation, as well as a pattern of unstable allegiances, make the future of Macedonian politics rather unpredictable, although the key to stability in the republic will be some form of coalition between the moderate nationalism of one of the Macedonian parties and the Albanian PPD.

—*J. B. A.*

Political Parties in Montenegro

Montenegro launched into multiparty politics in December 1990 looking very much like a scaled-down version of **Serbia.** This similarity was due to the dominant position held by Montenegro's Democratic Party of Socialists (DSS), composed of former Communists and led by **Momir Bulatović,** the protégé of **Slobodan Milošević.** With 83 of the 125 seats in the first assembly, the DSS seemed likely to retain a fairly firm hold, and Bulatović was apparently able to keep moderate autonomist opinion on board by his occasional displays of distance from the Serbs. Economic **sanctions** imposed by the UN against the new Federal Republic of **Yugoslavia,** however, drove a wedge into this arrangement, polarizing opinion in relation to cooperation with Serbia and opening up the historic split between *bjelaši* and *zelenaši* (Whites and Greens, or proponents of closer union with Serbia or greater independence from it, respectively).

The issue was made more serious by the insensitive treatment of the federal relationship by the dominant Serb partners in Belgrade, as well as by the prospects of more favorable treatment held out to Montenegrins by European and U.S. diplomats. The ruling party split between supporters of Bulatović and those of **Milo Djukanović,** with the latter winning the presidential elections in December 1997. The balance of other parties falls along the same axis, with the Liberals and the group of minor ethnic parties operating as the Democratic Coalition in support of greater autonomy and with Novak Kilibarda's National Party inclining toward solidarity with the Serbs.

—*J. B. A.*

Political Parties in Serbia

As in Croatia (with the dominant position of the Croatian Democratic Union, HDZ), **Slobodan Milošević's Socialist Party of Serbia** (SPS) holds a dominant place that enables it to divide and rule all other contenders for power. Even before the **League of Communists** in Serbia was compelled to accept the inevitability of multiparty **elections,** the SPS had begun the task of relegitimation, transforming itself into a populist and moderately nationalist party. Milošević skillfully used the anxieties of the population at large about the impending economic transformation, and he played upon the insecurity generated by the demographic situation of Serbs both in Serbia and in the federation more generally. Exploitation of the concerns of the Serb diaspora in this way enabled Milošević to preempt other appeals to defend the integrity of Yugoslavia (for example, **Ante Marković's** Alliance of Reform Forces).

With the SPS continuing to fly the banner of socialism, no serious socialist alternative could appear, leaving the "left" to the nostalgic "Party of Generals," i.e., the League of Communists-Movement for Yugoslavia (SK-PJ). Under the leadership of Milošević's wife, **Mirjana Marković**, the SK-PJ subsequently renamed itself the Yugoslav United Left (JUL). Otherwise the attempt to create a political force that does not rely principally upon the rhetoric of nationalism has been limited to a small Civic Alliance (GS), led by sociology professor Vesna Pešić, and the Democratic Party (DS), founded by another academic sociologist, Dragoljub Mićunović, but subsequently led rather more dynamically by Zoran Djindjić. Although these groups have been able to cooperate to some extent with representatives of the ethnic minorities (such as the Democratic Party of Magyars from the **Vojvodina** and the Party of Democratic Action from the **Sandžak**), it has been impossible to break out of politics defined by the nationalist agenda.

This situation has been a consequence partly of the wars elsewhere in Yugoslavia, but also of the way in which the problem of **Kosovo** has cast its shadow over the future of the region. An important feature of the SPS has been its solid base of support in small-town and rural communities. This has meant that attempts to create a force for opposition based upon economic interest, such as the now defunct Alliance of Peasants of Serbia (SSS), have had difficulty in defining and keeping an electoral constituency.

The other available alternatives have been other varieties of nationalism. There have been three principal contenders in this area: the Serbian Renewal Movement (SPO), associated with writer **Vukašin Drašković**; the fascistic **Serbian Radical Party**, complete with its *Vojvoda*, or *Führer*, **Vojislav Šešelj**; and the Party of Serbian Unity (SSJ) of the confectioner-cum-mobster **Željko Ražnjatović**, known as "Arkan." The first has striven hard to modify its appeal in the light of international preferences for democratic politics and has tried unsuccessfully to put together a succession of moderate opposition coalitions (DEPOS and Zajedno) with groups such as the DS and the GS. Irreconcilable differences between the leaders have quickly undermined each such project. The other two contenders have strong similarities in their concentration upon a leader rather than an ideology (beyond aggressive nationalism), their close links with **paramilitary** forces, and their links with the criminal underworld. Deprived of majorities in the Skupština (Assembly) from time to time, Milošević and the SPS have been able to create and break alliances with both the Serbian Radical Party and the SSJ in a spirit of cynical opportunism on both sides.

It is necessary to comment briefly also on the party situation in **Kosovo**, although the **Albanian** Kosovars have consistently boycotted official electoral politics at all levels while electing representatives to their own shadow assembly. International attention has always centered upon the **Democratic League of Kosovo** (LDK), led by **Ibrahim Rugova** and **Bujar Bukoshi**. This focus is understandable, if only because in the 130-seat alternative assembly the LDK secured 96 seats. Kosovar political opinion is diverse, however, and has become more diverse as the policy of nonviolent resistance advocated by Rugova came under increasing strain during 1997. There are also the active and well-organized Parliamentary Party of Kosova, led by Veton Surroi; the Social Democratic Party (PSD), led by internationally respected journalist Shkëlzen Maliqi; the Peasant Party of Kosova (PFK); and an Albanian Demo-Christian Party (PDS).

—*J. B. A.*

Political Parties in Slovenia

Slovenia led the rest of the former federation in 1988 during the creation of the Slovene Peasant League and Democratic League as **political associations**, led respectively by Ivan Oman and **Dimitrij Rupel**; both associations subsequently acquired the status of parties. Both participated in an electoral coalition of six anticommunist parties that fought the **elections** in April 1990 under the title DEMOS (Demokratska opozicija Slovenije) and won seats in the assembly. Rupel's group merged in 1992 with a small group of Social Democrats to create the Democratic Party, which secured six seats in the elections of that year. Their platform combines a strong emphasis on modernization with vociferous separatism.

The Peasant League was subsequently absorbed by the Slovene Christian Democrats (SKD), led by **Lojze Peterle.** The SKD stands in the broad traditions of European Christian democracy, strongly anticommunist and committed to the implementation of **Catholic** social doctrines. Formerly involved in the ruling coalitions and the leading partner of DEMOS, the SKD has had difficulty in sustaining cooperation with other groups on both of those grounds. Other nationalist and anticommunist groups, such as Zmago Jelinčič's Slovene National Party (SNS), have been too small to provide valuable coalition partners, and the dominant groups that provide the obvious cores of possible coalitions (the Associated List and the Liberal Democratic Party) have been too close to the former **League of Communists** (LC).

The Associated List is a coalition of four parties that came together initially as an electoral convenience in 1992 and merged the following year. Its core is provided by the former LC, which has survived post-Yugoslav politics in Slovenia fairly well. It distinguished itself during the late 1980s by its clear call for a radical reform of the one-party system, and its withdrawal from the final fourteenth congress of the League of Communists of Yugoslavia (which precipitated that league's collapse) was centered on this issue. Changing its title to the Party of Democratic Reform in order to campaign in the elections in 1990, the former LC actually emerged as the largest party in the assembly, but it was excluded from government by the formation of DEMOS. Its candidate for the presidency, **Milan Kučan**, has sustained the popularity he acquired during the period of secession.

The success story of Slovene politics has been the creation of the Liberal Democratic Party, which emerged initially from the Communist youth movement, became the second party in the elections of 1991, and took 22 of the 90 seats in the assembly in 1992. It owes its success partly to the leadership of **Janez Drnovšek**, partly to its energetic and youthful core of workers, and partly to its pragmatic and nonideological approach to politics that has enabled it to occupy the middle ground on all key issues.

The Greens have managed to hold on to representation in the assembly, although weakened by a history of internal division. The Slovene People's Party (SLS), led by Marijan Podobnik, gained 11 seats in 1992 and has played a significant role as a coalition partner with the Liberals. It owes its survival to a combination of presenting itself as a less dogmatic version of the SKD, its incorporation of some dissident sections of the environmentalist Green movement, and the ability of its leader. The SLS mixes well—unlike the Social Democratic Party of Slovenia, which is the personal following of **Janez Janša.** An idiosyncratic success in Slovene politics has been the Democratic Party of Pensioners of Slovenia (DeSUS).

The Slovene constitution allows for protected representation in the assembly of the country's 2,000-strong Italian and 8,000-strong Magyar minorities—but not the 63,000 Croats, 52,000 Serbs, or 19,000 Muslims. Slovene politics has a closed and insular feel about it, which results partly from the very small size of its "political class." Having lit the fuse that ignited explosion elsewhere in Yugoslavia, Slovenes scarcely let the war figure as an issue—certainly less so than the divisive matter of the foreign ownership of economic assets, where it was necessary to alter the constitution in order to meet the requirements of association with the **European Union.**

—J. B. A.

POPULATION

In several respects population questions can be seen to have importance in the genesis of the Yugoslav conflict. Population is a vital resource in any state; the state's people provide the labor force that creates the state's wealth, the incomes from which it generates its taxation, the youth from which it recruits its soldiers. The composition of that population determines some of the central priorities and problems of the state. A youthful population concentrates demands in the field of education, whereas an aging population will focus expenditure more on health care and pensions.

Differential rates of population growth were the source of political problems during the disintegration of Yugoslavia in two respects. Before World War II, the Balkans were distinguished by very high rates of population growth, and rural overpopulation was regarded as a problem throughout the region.

In common with the rest of Europe, however, most parts of the Yugoslav federation experienced falling rates of fertility after 1945. The movement of population into towns meant that children were no longer regarded as an essential asset for contributing labor to the family farm. The restriction of family size helped to raise living standards, partly through releasing women to become wage earners outside the home. The lack of living space in urban apartments, as well as the shortage of accommodation for new families, also imposed pressure upon couples to limit the size of their families.

These processes did not operate uniformly, however, and in communities that remained tied to the land traditional values tended to prevail, which encouraged high rates of fertility. In the more economically backward rural areas, the lack of education and poverty inhibited the spread of contraceptive methods. Consequently, some rural communities continued to exhibit very high rates of population growth.

The issue became of acute political relevance because of the way in which these differences mapped onto patterns of ethnic settlement. In a pattern familiar across the world, urban, industrial settlements that were failing to reproduce their populations drew in a workforce from rural areas. Hence, **Ljubljana**, Maribor, and **Zagreb** became attractive poles for rural Bosnians; **Skopje** and **Belgrade** had growing populations of **Albanians**. Exactly as elsewhere, these migrant laborers came to be the focus of ethnic intolerance. In the climate of economic recession of the late 1980s, they came to be accused of "taking our jobs" and being a burden on the public purse. The hostility to *južnjaci* (southerners) has been a feature of the campaigns of the Slovene nationalists led by Zmago Jelinčič.

The situation came to be especially difficult in relation to Albanians in **Serbia** and **Macedonia**. Urbanization in the post-1945 period has been particularly rapid in Macedonia. In 1991 more than 58 percent of Macedonians lived in towns, and approximately one in every four lived in the capital, Skopje. The Albanian minority, located mainly in rural areas and especially in the west of the republic, exhibited a very high birth rate, growing from 11 percent of the population in 1948 to 21 percent in 1991. Macedonians came to fear that the steady "Albanianization" of western Macedonia, as Albanians occupied farms deserted by Slav Macedonians, might eventually create a situation in which there was pressure to cede this region to neighboring Albania. At the same time, as they grew in significance as a minority within the republic, Albanians began articulating wider demands for more explicit formal recognition within the state.

Similar processes in the former autonomous province of **Kosovo** have seen the Albanian population of the region grow from 68 percent in 1948 to 80 percent in 1991. Relationships between Serbs and **Albanians** were intermittently troubled throughout the post-1945 years, but in the period leading up to the breakup of Yugoslavia, nationalist politicians in Serbia utilized the fear of the ultimate loss of this symbolically important area for Serbs as a means of mobilizing the population. Their level of fertility came to be the principal element in the negative stereotype of Albanians. Fears of national extinction and the loss of control over historical territories have also been manipulated among Serbs in **Bosnia-Hercegovina**, whose share of the population of the republic fell from 44 percent in 1948 to 31 percent in 1991.

—*J. B. A.*

See also: rural-urban differences; women's status

POSAVINA CORRIDOR

The Posavina Corridor is a strategic territory in northeastern Bosnia. Held by the **Bosnian Serbs** since the Bosnian conflict began in April 1992, the 100-kilometer-long corridor runs along the **Sava River** valley (hence its name) and connects the western and eastern territories of the Bosnian Serb Republic (BSR, subsequently the **Republika Srpska**), which would be unviable without it. Heavily defended by the **Bosnian Serb Army** (BSA) concentrated around the town of **Brčko**, the Posavina Corridor has been repeatedly fought over since 1992. To the north of the corridor is the **Orašje** pocket, the only area of northern Bosnia controlled by the **Bosnian Croats** and the **Croatian Army** (HV). To the south are territories controlled by the Bosnian government in Sarajevo and the **Bosnian army** (Army of the Republic of Bosnia-Hercegovina—ARBH). No more than two to three kilometers wide at its narrowest point around Brčko, the corridor is considered vulnerable to the HV and the ARBH in due course. Successive HV-ARBH offensives against the BSA in the area, however, have failed to breach its defenses.

U.S. I/SFOR troops at Brčko, the main Serb-held town in the Posavina Corridor, in 1996. (NATO photo)

The political status and extent of the Posavina Corridor have always been highly contentious for all three sides in the conflict. The area was populated before 1992 mainly by Croats and Muslims. Subjected to "**ethnic cleansing**" by Bosnian Serbs in 1992, this territory will remain Serb-controlled only as long as the BSA can defend it. According to the Bosnian **Muslims** and Croats, it is a territory that should revert to their joint control in due course. The Bosnian Serbs, on the other hand, have not only refused to discuss this demand but have also insisted that the corridor should be widened to take account of their vital interests. The result has been a continued political impasse.

In 1993–1994, the problem of the Posavina Corridor was one of the major reasons the Bosnian Serbs rejected the **Vance-Owen** and **Contact Group** peace plans for Bosnia-Hercegovina. During the negotiations leading to the **Dayton Agreements** for Bosnia in November 1995, the Posavina Corridor was once again a major sticking point and very nearly aborted the deal that was finally struck among the Bosnian, Croatian, and Serbian presidents. Consequently, it was mutually agreed that the problem should be determined by independent international arbitration. As things stand, it is difficult to envisage how any international ruling on this problem could be acceptable to all the parties to the dispute. The final status and extent of the Posavina Corridor is likely to be decided in the same way it was originally created: by force of arms.

—M. M.

THE PRESS

See **media**

PREVLAKA

The Prevlaka Peninsula, because of its strategic location, remains one of the intractable problems resulting from the division of Yugoslavia. The peninsula is located at the mouth of Boka kotorska (Kotor Bay) on the borders of **Montenegro** and **Croatia** and is currently a demilitarized zone under the auspices of UNMOP (United Nations Mission on Prevlaka).

Kotor Bay is a strategic asset in the **Adriatic Sea**, and its control has been sought by various naval powers. Currently the bulk of Yugoslav **naval power** is moored within the bay at Tivat, and there are major submarine facilities. The entrance to this bay, which is 35 miles in circumference, is only 1 mile wide, with the Prevlaka Peninsula overlooking the narrow Otranto straits. The bay is also one of the most scenic parts of the coastline of former Yugoslavia and possesses enormous tourist potential.

Since the creation of socialist Yugoslavia, Prevlaka has been located within the Socialist Republic of Croatia; Croatia, when it declared independence in 1991, stated that the internal borders of the former republic were now its international **borders**. Croatian **paramilitary** forces attempted to seize the peninsula from the **Yugoslav Peoples' Army** (JNA) in September 1991 but failed. A temporary peace was negotiated by Croatian president **Franjo Tudjman** and the federal Yugoslav president at the time, **Dobrica Ćosić**. In line with a **United Nations** (UN) resolution, the peninsula was placed under control of a UN peacekeeping force and effectively demilitarized.

An uneasy peace has been kept, with violations on both sides. The work of UNMOP has been hampered especially by the Croatian authorities, who have steadfastly refused access to parts of the demilitarized zone by UN observers, probably because of the construction of military facilities.

A settlement of the dispute is essential for both parties. Prevlaka is only a few miles from **Dubrovnik**, and the restitution of the **tourism** industry will require the removal of tension in this area. The Montenegrin coast is perhaps more attractive than that of Croatia, yet no major airport facilities exist there for foreign tourists; access is dependent upon Dubrovnik's Čilipi airport. At present there seems to be little prospect of a permanent solution, although the election of **Milo Djukanović** to the Montenegrin presidency may well change this. As of this writing, the UN Security Council has authorized a continuation of UNMOP until 15 July 1998.

—R. J.

PRIJEDOR

An important town on the Sana River in northeastern Bosnia, Prijedor had a population in 1991 of 112,000, of which 44 percent was Muslim. However, in early summer 1992, as with many such towns and villages in the Bosnian **Krajina**, it was attacked, overrun, and effectively subjected to "**ethnic cleansing**" by the **Bosnian Serbs**. Many of the Muslims and some Croats were simply driven out or fled, but there is evidence of systematic capturing by social category and the targeting of the local elite, both political and economic. Those captured were taken to the local **detention camp** set up by the Serbs in a ceramic factory on the edge of the town, where one month later there was a mass killing, estimated at over 100, with others left badly wounded. Prijedor became and remained a Bosnian Serb town.

In July 1997 two Serbs from Prijedor widely suspected of the war crimes—Simo Drljača and Milan Kovačević—were tracked down by SAS troops from the **Stabilization Force** (SFOR) of the North Atlantic Treaty Organization (NATO). Drljača, the former chief of police in Prijedor who organized several camps in the area, was killed in return fire on the road to Omarska; Kovačević, director of the hospital at Prijedor and the town's deputy mayor, was arrested at the hospital to face trial at the International **War Crimes Tribunal**. While facing the charges, he died of a heart attack in his cell at The Hague on 1 August 1998.

—J. J. H.

PRIŠTINA

Capital of the Serbian region of **Kosovo** (population 155,000 in 1991) and capital of medieval **Serbia**, Priština (Prishtina or Prishtinë in Albanian) is situated close to the site of the historically significant **Battle of Kosovo** (1389). It is a center for communications, administration, education, and culture; it is also the center for Kosovar **Albanian** political and cultural life. The town's lavish offices of the **League of Communists**, as well as its monumental public architecture of the 1970s and 1980s, contrast with the shantytown poverty of the residential areas. Priština has textile, metal, and electrical industries and is central to the surrounding mining region as well. Its university, founded in 1970, accommodated approximately 37,000 students. In 1990, when the use of the Albanian language in secondary and university education was forbidden, Albanian faculty were fired and students were refused entry to all such educational institutions. Since that time Priština has been the center for the oppressive Serbian military administration of the region. Regular nonviolent **student** demonstrations that are centered on the university, demanding the right to education, have earned violent response from the

Serbian regime but have also gained increasing international recognition.

—*A. T. Y. and N. J. Y.*

PRIVATIZATION

The former Yugoslavia was one of the first of the Eastern European countries to commence a program of privatization in late 1988, in the final days of the federal government of Branko Mikulić. The Law on Enterprises adopted in December 1988 and Law on Social Capital Circulation and Management adopted in December 1989 were the key pieces of legislation that made it possible to transform socially owned property into private property. The initial focus in the plan for privatization was to convert social property into a form of individual worker ownership through "internal shareholdings." Each worker in an enterprise was to be given a package of shares in that enterprise and was invited to purchase more if he or she so wished. This would transform the enterprise into a worker-owned enterprise. These plans were abandoned in the face of the growing economic and political crisis in the former Yugoslavia.

Because of the conflict, the process of privatization was largely suspended in most republics, and the political will to dispose of social property primarily to the employees was henceforth lost. Although there were some minor sell-offs to private-sector interests during the conflict, the process more or less remained frozen during the fighting. The government's promise to offer preferential access to the privatization process once the fighting was over was widely used throughout the conflict as a form of deferred payment to loyal supporters. In return for military, financial, and other forms of support during the conflict, individuals, organizations, and even particular countries were promised first chance to purchase choice state assets to be sold off after the conflict. In Croatia, for example, the government nationalized socially owned assets very early on in the conflict, and this move provided a sellable asset base with which to reward the government's key supporters once the conflict began to reach a conclusion. Many members of the Croatian diaspora, who were especially supportive of Croatian president **Franjo Tudjman** both during the conflict and in the years before when he was struggling to gain power, were given especially preferential access in the sell-offs that followed.

In addition, the many demands of the immediate postconflict period further distorted the privatization process and led some governments to maximize the short-term benefits at the expense of vital longer-term efficiency and equity considerations. In Serbia the privatization process remained on hold for many years on account of the sanctions that were imposed by the United Nations (UN), which barred foreign interests from participating. However, once the main set of sanctions (the so-called inner wall) were removed, the Serbian government very quickly used the sale of state assets to provide an urgent cash injection with which it was able to pay off pension and state-sector wage arrears. President **Milošević** undertook the sale of the Serbian Telecommunications Company to Greek and Italian investors in order to placate the population shortly before a key election. In Bosnia the main interest in the program of privatization is coming from foreign investors wishing to buy into the region's traditionally rich raw material resources. Most manufacturing capacity has been wiped out and consequently is attracting very little interest.

Slovenia and Macedonia are probably the main upholders of the old tradition of worker participation. In Slovenia the privatization program was deliberately structured to result in a significant worker-owned sector that would benefit from the higher levels of motivation and investment of "sweat equity" thought possible when employees have a substantial individual stake in their own workplace. It would also satisfy those Slovenes wary of selling off the most profitable parts of their small industrial base to rich foreigners. Most small and medium-sized enterprises were sold off to their employees, with the result that the economy is now estimated to be composed of more than half worker-owned companies. In Macedonia worker ownership came about by default rather than by design: since so few people or organizations in Macedonia had the financial resources to actually purchase state assets and invest in their future operation, the only realistic possibility of changing ownership was simply to give enterprises to their employees for free or at hugely discounted prices. The hope was that employees would be willing to generate at least some of the desperately needed investment resources through their own savings or, more realistically, through even further reductions in their own wages.

—*M. B.*

PROPAGANDA

Based upon false and fearful images of demonic "others," propaganda has played a major and insidious role on all sides of the Yugoslav wars. So central has been its role in the former Yugoslavia that we can say that the country might not have descended into civil war without it. Propaganda can be considered at two levels: that intended for local consumption and that circulating in the international media.

During the period of rule of the **League of Communists of Yugoslavia** (SKJ), propaganda in Yugoslavia had a number of themes. Particularly significant in this context were the denial of some aspects of the reality of the Yugoslav civil war of 1941–1945 and uncritical acceptance of the **Partizan** myth of the "brotherhood and unity" *(bratstvo i jedinstvo)* of the Yugoslav peoples. The lack of an honest appraisal of the experience of 1941–1945 left this period in an intellectual twilight zone, in which it was possible for countermythologies to flourish unchecked by historical scholarship. In the period of the collapse of Communist legitimacy, these countermythologies were all the more readily accepted because they could be presented as hitherto suppressed "truth." Communist propaganda thus often served inadvertently to perpetuate the ideological and political divisions of the wartime years, reducing serious discussion of alternative accounts of history (especially where these touched upon national cultural differences) to the status of threats to brotherhood and unity.

With the decline of the Yugoslav socialist project during the crisis of the 1980s, Communist propaganda was gradually undermined by mutually antagonistic nationalist propaganda themes at the behest of the bitterly divided republican elites in search of new legitimating historical myths. In the case of **Serbia**, this shift took place almost immediately after **Slobodan Milošević** came to power in Belgrade in 1987. A crude process of national stereotyping turned all Croats into "**Ustaša**" (fascists) and all Bosnian **Muslims** into "Mujaheddin" (guerrillas). Similarly in **Croatia**, after **Franjo Tudjman** came to power in 1990, all Serbs became "**Chetniks**"—a theme later taken up by Bosnian Muslims. Soon it was almost impossible to engage in public debate about contemporary political issues without framing them in relation to these references to a mythologized past. In both Croatia and **Slovenia**, all-Yugoslav themes and institutions were systematically denigrated and denied, so as to suggest that a common Yugoslav life was impossible and that the breakup of the country was both necessary and inevitable. Anybody who challenged this view was to be branded as guilty of "**Yugonostalgia**" at best and as a traitor to the evident interests of the nation at worst. Political opposition everywhere has experienced the greatest difficulty in redefining the terms of debate.

Preceded by the domestic media war of the 1980s, the wars of the 1990s in Slovenia, Bosnia-Hercegovina, and Croatia took on a further propaganda dimension through the international media. In many respects this coverage became merely an extension of the internal propaganda campaigns, directed at the demonization of others. This was especially the case in relation to the competition to establish blame for starting the war. By the time the conflict had escalated to the point at which it merited international attention, demonizing stereotypes had become such an entrenched feature of the domestic political scene that they were taken up uncritically by foreign journalists as providing a factual basis for describing and explaining the war, rather than as symptoms of the problems that caused it. The parties to the war have been differentially successful in their attempts to secure the ear of the world.

The Slovenes achieved remarkable success in removing almost entirely from scrutiny their own part in the political genesis of the war and in defining the issues entirely and simply in terms of external aggression. Television images of columns of tanks readily triggered a range of associations in the West, ranging from Hungary in 1956 to Tiananmen Square in China over three decades later, in which communist states were depicted in terms of the naked exercise of brutal force.

The Croats were much less successful in putting over their view of the war. Their initial approach dwelt almost entirely upon their role as *victims* of a brutal foe. Carried away by the task of portraying Serbs as barbarians who were spiritually alien to Europe, they at first deployed images of atrocity. A special issue of the *Croatian Medical Journal* gave wide circulation to numerous detailed photographs of injuries sustained by civilian victims. European media were not only unused to publishing this kind of material, but in many cases were legally prevented from doing so. The images of **Dubrovnik**, a city internationally known as one of historical significance and beauty, under siege and shelling by the Serbs and Montenegrins, turned the tide of the propaganda war in favor of the defending Croats. In many respects the Bosnian campaign was damaged by a similar overuse of the depiction of Bosnians as defenseless victims; although this approach stimulated public sympathy in the West, it produced a sense of frustration in that it offered no clear sense of positive possibilities. A propagandist approach that rests centrally upon the suffering of unarmed civilian victims in war sits uneasily with demands to lift the arms embargo—because lifting the embargo would presumably make it easier to multiply the number of such victims.

The Serbs have, generally speaking, suffered in the propaganda war from the success of others parties in communicating the view that the Serbs were to blame. Even academic commentators have fallen for oversimplified explanations in terms of the ambitions of a demonic Milošević. The Serbs were also poorly served by their external advisers, who were too closely linked with émigré circles to have a clear view of Western media priorities and practices; these advisers tended to recycle abroad imagery originally created for domestic consumption. These early propaganda failures reinforced the stance, into which Serbs had stooped in the domestic context, of embattled isolation. So widespread did the view that they were misunderstood or misrepresented become that two notable Serb propaganda victories have generally passed without comment.

First, by accident rather than design, the Serb reliance upon their role as the defenders of Christian Europe against the threat of expansionist **Islamic** "fundamentalism" did resonate with anti-Islamic prejudices already entrenched within Western public opinion. This resonance was effective in triggering responses particularly at the level of "opinion leadership," sensitized already to such ideas in relation to the Gulf War. Oddly, this kind of propaganda was more likely to be effective in political circles, where the theories of Samuel P. Huntington on a "clash of civilizations" had come to be taken seriously, especially in the **United States**.

Second, Serbian politicians were also able to take advantage of the legacy of the Cold War and to develop a mythology of the history of Pan-Slav solidarity, which used every threat of military action against Serbia as an occasion upon which to raise the specter of intervention by Russia. The fact that Russian politicians, apart from extreme nationalists such as Zhirinovsky, never proposed Russian military engagement in the Balkan crisis does not seem to have diminished the idea's effectiveness as a propaganda image.

Consideration of the Yugoslav war suggests an important generalization about the use of propaganda. To be effective, propaganda must be sown in soil that is already receptive to it. The addressees of propaganda (whether domestic or foreign) must be already predisposed to accept it, even if for reasons entirely unrelated to the situation in question.

—M. M. and J. B. A.

See also: cinema; media (domestic); media (external); religion

PROZOR

A town in northern **Hercegovina** with around 20,000 inhabitants—one-third Muslim, two-thirds Croat—Prozor lay on the route of the supply line to Muslim towns under threat from Serb attack in central Bosnia. At the end of October 1992, Prozor was the scene of an argument between local entrepreneurs of the **Bosnian army** and **Croatian Army** concerning receipt of a supply truck carrying gasoline. Although the two sides had for several months been fighting together against the Serbs, this incident immediately escalated into an ethnic battle, resulting in the sacking of all Muslim property in the town, a total exodus of the Muslim inhabitants, and reports of massacre.

—J. J. H.

PUČNIK, JOŽE

A Slovene dissident who had been a lecturer in West Germany, Jože Pučnik (born 1932) was a candidate for the presidency of Slovenia in September 1989. The election was effectively about the republic's potential withdrawal from the Yugoslav federation. His candidacy was on the ticket of the DEMOS coalition of seven **political parties**; DEMOS took over half of the popular vote, but Pučnik was defeated for the presidency by the Communist president, **Milan Kučan**.

—J. J. H.

PULA

See **naval power**

Q

QOSJA, REXHEP

Rexhep Qosja (born 1936) is a Kosovo **Albanian** scholar, writer, and literary critic and a leading political figure in **Kosovo**. He studied Albanian language and literature in **Priština** and Belgrade and is now a member of the Kosovo Academy of Sciences and Art. He is the author of many works on Albanian literature and on the present political situation. Among these are *Dialogje me shkrimtarët (Dialogues with Writers),* Priština, 1968; *Panteoni i rralluar (A Rarified Pantheon),* Priština, 1973; *Morfologia e një fushate (Morphology of a Campaign),* Priština, 1980; *Historia e letërsisë shqipe: romantizimi (History of Albanian Literature: Romanticism),* Priština, 3 vols., 1984–1986; *Populli i ndaluar (The Banned People),* Priština, 1990; *Strategia e bashkimit shqipta (Strategy of Albanian Unification),* Priština, 1992; and *Çëstja shqiptare: historia dhe politika (The Albanian Question: History and Politics),* Priština, 1994, which has been translated into French and is currently being published in English. His novel *Vdekja më vjen prej syve të tillë (Death Comes with Such Eyes),* Priština, 1974, has also been translated into French and German. As a public figure in Kosovo, Rexhep Qosja has become somewhat of a father figure for the nation. In the political spectrum, he is considered the proponent of a course of more active than that of the **Democratic League of Kosovo** (LDK) under **Ibrahim Rugova** in its opposition to the Belgrade regime.

—R. E.

R

RAČAN, IVICA

Ivica Račan (born 1944) was leader of the League of Communists in Croatia until 1990 and was thereby also a leading member of the **League of Communists of Yugoslavia** (SKJ). His distrust of the Serb Communist leadership had been sown in 1987 following demonstrations in Belgrade by Serbs from **Kosovo**. He sided with the Slovenes in 1989 during the SKJ central committee's discussions of the Slovene amendments to the Yugoslav **constitution**, and in January 1990 he broke with **Slobodan Milošević** by walking out of the party congress along with the delegation from **Slovenia**, declaring that "the League of Communists of Yugoslavia no longer exists."

As the Croatian nationalist cause grew apace, harnessed by **Franjo Tudjman**, Račan's dilemma was between feelings for an independent, even pluralistic Croatia, on one hand, and a loyalty to the Communist cause on the other. Withstanding pressures from the **Yugoslav Peoples' Army**, Račan renamed and partly reformed his party as the Party of Democratic Change. At the Croatian **elections** in May 1990, he received wide support from Serbs in Croatia and did well to gather five-sixths of the total votes gained by Tudjman's **Croatian Democratic Union**, though the system gave Tudjman three times the number of seats.

Račan ceded the presidency at that point but remained active in Croatian politics on his own terms and in seeking coalitions.

—J. J. H.

RAPE

It has frequently been alleged that a particular feature of the recent Balkan conflicts has been the frequency of rape. Indeed, there have been widely reported claims that such sexual assault has taken an organized form and that rape on a massive scale has been adopted as a part of a deliberate policy of intimidation. Whereas rape is a regrettably regular feature of human communities throughout the world and across history, particularly during times of war, these claims about its scale, organization, and status as an item of policy have marked out the recent experience of Yugoslavia as highly unusual if not unique.

Statistics of the incidence of rape are notoriously unreliable if for no other reason than the fact that its victims have powerful disincentives not to report it. These disincentives may be presumed to be particularly strong in societies such as those of the Balkan peninsula, which are characterized by high value placed upon the "honor" of women and the shame attached to their violation. Measured by official criminal statistics, rape has been a relatively uncommon crime in the former Yugoslavia. Nevertheless, there have been repeated claims about the high frequency of this crime during war, with estimates ranging up to 50,000 rapes.

It is hard to assess arguments in this area, not only because of the inherent difficulty of obtaining reliable information but also because of the tendency of press coverage to sensationalize the issue, which in sections of the British press has created a kind of legitimated pornography. The problem is compounded by the propaganda value that attaches to such stories as components of a campaign of demonizing the enemy. For these reasons, stories of "rape camps" are to be distrusted. A briefing document from the United Nations High Commission for Refugees (**UNHCR**) reported that no human rights organization or NGO (nongovernmental organization) had been able to corroborate the existence of special camps, and suggested that numerical estimates of any aspect of the issue be treated with caution. There have been well-substantiated reports of the creation of ad hoc military bordellos on a relatively small scale. The sexual abuse of women held in detention has been widespread;

however, to designate these as "rape camps" carries an additional symbolic significance, with obvious rhetorical echoes of concentration camps, that might account for the use of the phrase in spite of its evident liability to distort the truth.

Three points should be made in approaching interpretation of the incidence of rape during the Yugoslav conflict. In the first place, it does not appear to be true that the frequency of this crime has been uniquely high during the course of the Yugoslav conflict. A French study notes that in Japan in 1937, after the sack of Nankin, where thousands of Chinese women were violated, the Japanese government decided to provide "girls" for the soldiers in order to avoid the worsening of anti-Japanese feeling in China. Consequently, around 200,000 Asian women (mainly from Korea) were enclosed in military brothels. It was South Korean feminists who lifted the veil over this occurrence in 1980. Thousands of women were raped by the Russians in Germany in 1944, in Vietnam by U.S. forces, and during the Algerian civil war. Yugoslav historians Vladimir Dedijer and Antun Miletić have observed "in the Balkans, rape was always a part of military campaigns" (*Genocid nad Muslimanima*). For these reasons, therefore, claims about the uniqueness of recent Yugoslav experience should be regarded with suspicion.

A second point to note in this context is the characteristic "normal" pattern of sexual violence in Yugoslavia. The low rates of reported rape in prewar Yugoslavia contrast with relatively high rates of domestic violence. The seriousness of this latter problem is also reported to have increased during the course of the war. Rape cannot be understood as a phenomenon in isolation; rather, it must be considered in relation to other aspects of gender relations in society and to other forms of aggression.

There are few reliable data concerning the ethnicity of either rapists or their victims in Yugoslavia. Nevertheless, a study commissioned by the Forum for Human Rights in 1990, following a period of growth of particular concern about allegations of rape in **Kosovo** between 1986 and 1988, concluded that interethnic rape was relatively rare and that its incidence was heavily overrepresented. In spite of the widespread moral panic about alleged rapes of Serb women by Albanians, "the proportion of Albanians who perpetrate rape is less than their proportion in the total Yugoslav population." There are good reasons for being cautious about generalizing to the whole of Yugoslavia results of a study that relate to highly specific conditions in Kosovo.

In **Bosnia-Hercegovina**, the available evidence suggests that the majority of cases involved Muslim women raped by Serbian men. Most documented cases of rape occurred between the autumn of 1991 and the end of 1993, with the highest reported incidence between April and November 1992. The perpetrators came predominantly from the military, **paramilitary** groups, and the local police.

Even if the phenomenon of rape in Yugoslavia has not been particularly unusual, what is remarkable is the prominent part played by the "discourse of rape" during the period of the disintegration of the federation. Atrocities such as rape emerge as having a particularly significant symbolic role. There is a wide range of theoretical approaches available that seek to conceptualize the nature of the symbolic processes at work. Many of these approaches have a recurring theme, however, that can be summed up in the words of Ruth Seifert: "The rape of women . . . communicates from man to man" (*Mass Rape*, p. 54–72). Seifert insists that rapes are part of the "rules" of war and have to do with the manner in which war engages masculinity in a variety of projects, including diminishing the masculinity of other males, denigrating those males' culture, and even living out the "culturally rooted contempt for women" (*Mass Rape*, p. 54–72) that characterizes their own culture. In addition, because of the symbolic power of allegations of rape, these allegations tend to become a particularly effective element of **propaganda** against an enemy, especially when they are given the additionally aberrant twist of "rape camps" and rape as systematic policy.

Over 40 alleged perpetrators of rape have been named defendants before the **War Crimes Tribunal**, but the first successful prosecution did not take place until March 1998.

—*J. B. A.*

See also: women's status

References: Dedijer, Vladimir, and Antun Miletić. *Genocid nad Muslimanima 1941–1945.* Sarajevo: Svjetlost, 1990; Niarchos, Catherine N. "Women, War, and Rape: Challenges Facing the International Tribunal for the Former Yugoslavia." *Human Rights Quarterly,* vol. 17, no. 4 (November 1995):649–690; Stiglmayer, Alexandra (ed.). *Mass Rape: The War against Women in Bosnia-Hercegovina.* Lincoln: University of Nebraska Press, 1994.

RAPID REACTION FORCE

The Rapid Reaction Force (RRF) was the first force deployed in **Bosnia-Hercegovina** that was exclusively commanded by the **North Atlantic Treaty Organization** (NATO). It was the precursor of the Atlantic alliance's **Implementation/Stabilization Force** operations after 1995. Under command of the United Nations Protection Force (**UNPROFOR**) II during most of the Bosnian conflict, NATO forces in Bosnia were hampered from taking on a more offensive role against the **Bosnian Serbs.** Although opposed by France and not specifically requested by the United Nations (UN), the RRF was created by NATO in March 1993; however, this 14,000-strong force was not fully operational until well into 1994 and was not actually used until 1995. Immediately bedeviled by arguments between the United Kingdom and France (the two main contributors of troops to UNPROFOR II) over who should command the largely Anglo-French force, the RRF also suffered from conflicts with the UN and UNPROFOR commanders. Here the main problems were the limited nature of the UNPROFOR mandate and fears of **hostage taking** of its troops by the Bosnian Serbs if the RRF were used in an offensive mode.

As a purely NATO operation, the RRF was well equipped with armor, artillery, and close air support capabilities. The deployment of the RRF around **Sarajevo** in 1994–1995 helped to lift the siege of the city. With the replacement of UNPROFOR II by the Implementation Force in 1995, the RDF was subsumed in this new NATO operation.

—*M. M.*

RAŠKOVIĆ, JOVAN

Jovan Rašković was a leader of the Croatian Serbs and founder of the Serbian Democratic Party (SDS) in Croatia. He was born in **Knin** in the Dalmatian hinterland of Croatia. A close friend of **Dobrica Ćosić**, Rašković became leader of the Croatian Serbs in January 1990 with the support of Ćosić and in collaboration with Jovan Opačić, who was one of the first Croatian Serbs publicly to espouse Serb national interests. Opačić was imprisoned in Šibenik on the Dalmatian coast in the summer of 1989; after his release he met Ćosić in Belgrade and was encouraged to meet Rašković, who was working as a consultant psychiatrist in the local hospital. Rašković was a charismatic man, with bushy hair and beard, who held moderate nationalist views and wanted to create a "Democratic Party" without a specific Serb nationalist program; Opačić, however, insisted on naming the new party the Serbian Democratic Party and making it the vehicle of Serb national interests in Croatia. The party was founded in Knin on 17 February 1990. Under Rašković the SDS demanded cultural autonomy for the Croatian Serbs within Croatia and full national rights of the kind that they had possessed as a constituent nation of Yugoslavia; there was no territorial dimension to the demand for autonomy. Rašković met **Franjo Tudjman**, the Croatian president, a number of times in May 1990 to discuss possible ways around the conflict. However, the rejection of any form of Serb autonomy in the draft Croatian constitution of June 1990 radicalized the Serb political leadership and marginalized Rašković, who was supplanted by **Milan Babić**.

—*G. R. B.*

RAŽNJATOVIĆ, ŽELJKO

An alleged criminal, Serbian **paramilitary** militia leader, and businessman, Željko Ražnjatović (usually known by his nom de guerre of "Arkan") also has political ambitions on the ultranationalist wing of politics in **Serbia.** Born in Belgrade in 1952, his

Željko "Arkan" Ražnjatović, Serbian warlord and commander of the "Tiger" militia during the Yugoslav wars of the 1990s. (Tanjug)

origins are obscure, but he was reportedly a professional criminal and agent of the Yugoslav secret services during the 1970s and 1980s; he is said to have assassinated a number of prominent anticommunist Croatian émigrés in Western Europe and North America. Ražnjatović is named in a number of Interpol (International Criminal Police Organization) arrest warrants for serious crimes committed in Sweden and other countries.

In 1990 he became sporting president of the Belgrade Red Star Supporters Club. Following the outbreak of civil war in Croatia in 1991, he was one of the cofounders, and later the leader, of the Serbian Volunteer Guard (SDG), one of a number of **paramilitary/irregular forces** that appeared in Serbia at that time. Also known as the Tigers and the Arkanovci, the SDG was reportedly supported by the Serbian secret services.

During the siege of **Vukovar** in eastern Slavonia in 1991, the Tigers were accused of widespread atrocities against Croats and other non-Serbs. In April 1992, the Bosnian civil war began with the Tigers conducting a notorious **ethnic cleansing** of the predominantly Muslim town of **Bijeljina** in eastern Bosnia.

In 1993 Arkan founded the Serbian Unity Party (SUS), an ultranationalist group that served as a political platform for his controversial election as a member of Parliament for a constituency in the province of **Kosovo** at the parliamentary elections in Serbia in December. Then regarded as little more than a political diversion devised by **Slobodan Milošević** after he had split with **Vojislav Šešelj**'s Serbian Radical Party (SRS), the SUS has never been a serious force outside Kosovo.

Accused of extensive looting of property in Croatia and Bosnia, Ražnjatović reportedly became one of the richest businessmen in Serbia after the imposition of United Nations (UN) economic **sanctions** against the Federal Republic of **Yugoslavia** in 1992. Mainly derived from "sanctions-busting" trade in oil and from arms smuggling, this illicit wealth explained the lavish funding of the SUS. Access to large sums of money also explained why the Tigers were the best armed of the Serb paramilitary groups.

One of the first Serbian militia leaders to be charged with war crimes, Ražnjatović was formally indicted as a war criminal by the International **War Crimes Tribunal** for the Former Yugoslavia in 1994. Never as much of a political threat to Milošević as Šešelj, Ražnjatović became a growing liability to the Serbian president by the time of the latter's partial international rehabilitation in 1995 and may thus be eliminated by his former mentor in due course. At the popular level, Arkan continues to cultivate the image of a heroic warlord in Serbia, but how seriously people take this idea is hard to say.

—*M. M.*

RECOGNITION

Under international law the criteria governing the mutual recognition of states are straightforward in principle. A state has a defined territory and a permanent population. This territory and population are under the effective control of the government of that state, which has the capacity to engage in formal relations with other such states. In short, recognition involves the acknowledgement by other states that the state in question is able to act as a state. In theory, recognition does not imply the moral or political approval of any specific actions or policies of a government, although in practice it is not uncommon for recognition to be withheld for these kinds of reasons. Under these circumstances the refusal to recognize the state can be used as a sanction, albeit often of more rhetorical than practical significance. The disintegration of the Yugoslav federation was accompanied by some remarkable inconsistencies in the theory and practice of international recognition. The issues are somewhat different in relation to the various emergent republics.

The criteria drawn up by the **Badinter Commission** for the recognition of **Bosnia-Hercegovina** included the requirement that the government demonstrate that recognition as an independent state would have popular support; this requirement was taken as implying the holding of a referendum, which took place in February 1992. Paradoxically, if the holding of a referendum is to be interpreted as an extension of the requirement that the government has effective control over the territory and population of the state, this very requirement triggered the breakdown of relations between the Bosnian government and its Serb population, which was to lead to armed conflict following the declaration of independence. This unusual request for a demonstration of popular support is believed to have resulted from awareness in **Germany** of the need for popular legitimation in relation to its own recent experience of unification.

The requests to the **European Community** (EC) for recognition by **Slovenia** and **Croatia** were accorded equal status. At the point at which they were considered by the EC, however, in the winter of 1991, the Slovene case can be considered to have been unproblematic, whereas the Croatian government was already embroiled in civil war with its Serb minority, which at the time (with the assistance of units of the **Yugoslav Peoples' Army**) controlled an estimated one-third of the territory. Recognition therefore took place in spite of the conspicuous failure of the country to meet the criteria of effective control over territory or population. In this case recognition took place not as an acknowledgment of the de facto situation but as an attempt to bring about a political change. Several influential figures in the EC believed that recognition would signal to the Yugoslav government that the international community would not tolerate any attempt to destabilize the Croatian state; they hoped that recognition would serve to bring about stability.

The government of **Macedonia** met all of the criteria laid down by Badinter for recognition of its independence, including (as in the case of Bosnia-Hercegovina) the holding of a referendum. Recognition by the states of the EC was withheld, however, because of the opposition of **Greece**, which objected to the use of the name "Macedonia." The sole reason for not granting recognition on this occasion appears to have had nothing to do with the normal criteria; rather, the goal appears to have been to promote the continued appearance of a united front among the states of the EC in relation to the Yugoslav crisis.

The treatment of Macedonia resembles in some respects that of the Federal Republic of **Yugoslavia**, from which recognition has been withheld by a large number of states in spite of the fact that the government meets all of the criteria regarded in theory as "normal." This situation has arisen for two main reasons. First, the other states emerging from the Socialist Federation of Yugoslavia have sought to use nonrecognition as a negotiating counter to be traded in relation to various issues connected with the breakup of Yugoslavia, such as the bargaining over dividing the international debt of the former federation. Other countries have seen nonrecognition as an extension of the wider policy of **sanctions** adopted by the **United Nations.**

Whereas the theoretical considerations governing recognition would appear to have dictated a relatively straightforward course of action in each of these cases, in practice a wide range of other factors also intervened. These factors have led to according or withholding recognition on the basis of the other states' political goals, rather than on the political conditions prevailing within the state seeking recognition.

—J. B. A.

RED CROSS

The International Committee of the Red Cross (ICRC) is the founder and coordinating body of the Red Cross and Red Crescent movement operating in virtually every country. It is probably the most instantly recognizable and reputable **humanitarian aid** organization in the world. It was founded in the last century as a strictly nonpolitical humanitarian aid agency to bring care and respite to the casualties of armed conflict and other humanitarian disasters. The ICRC's unparalleled reputation was founded on the willingness of its staff to work in areas of conflict in order to bring comfort and dignity to those most affected by the consequences of war, particularly the noncombatant population.

During the conflict in the former Yugoslavia, the ICRC operated a large network of delegations and subdelegations throughout **Bosnia-Hercegovina** and the United Nations (UN) protected areas in **Croatia.** These offices were charged with implementing and overseeing ICRC operations, which included prison visits, prisoner exchanges, reuniting of families separated by the war, message exchange services,

An International Committee of the Red Cross aid convoy in Bosnia-Hercegovina. (CICR)

and a range of general relief activities. The ICRC coordinated many of these activities with local Red Cross offices, which were also struggling to provide humanitarian relief and other services. It also worked with many local and international **nongovernmental organizations** (NGOs) to achieve its humanitarian goals. The ICRC was instrumental in mediating between the warring parties whenever called upon to do so. It acted as a guarantor of evenhandedness in activities that involved the warring parties meeting to discuss humanitarian and related issues, to exchange prisoners, or to transport **refugees** across military boundaries. Through its high-level contacts in the political world and in international organizations, the ICRC was one of the main parties impressing upon all sides of the conflict the need to respect the articles of the Geneva Conventions, the international treaty that the ICRC had been directly instrumental in establishing; this treaty lays down a set of "acceptable" rules of conflict. Unfortunately, the war in the former Yugoslavia was to see many breaches of the conventions of "acceptable" conflict, particularly on the issue of "**ethnic cleansing**" and the rights of noncombatant populations to remain in their homes.

As with the work of other organizations, the ICRC's work in one region often became a bargaining chip with which to secure access to ICRC benefits for other less deserving cases in other regions. For instance, reasonable access to prisoners on one side was effectively possible only by instituting an aid program that would deliver benefits to the local population on the other side. This was obviously frustrating for those wishing to assist the most needy, but it was a largely unavoidable part of the conflict and a price that had to be paid if the rights and survival of those most affected by the conflict were to be addressed. It was, for example, the ICRCs insistence and ability to visit every prison camp in the region that largely led to the uncovering of the terrible conditions meted out to inmates in some of the **detention camps** located in the Bosnian Serb sector in the north, such as at Omarska. On several occasions the ICRC was charged with assisting in the ethnic cleansing process being carried out by each of the warring parties. When local populations decided that they had "had enough," they were permitted to leave their homes (usually for a fee) and go to the region where their particular ethnic group was in the majority, or to a third country. The ICRC was called in to ensure that these people remained safe and were not mistreated on their journey. However, this situation presented a real problem for the ICRC: it could either refuse to assist, and therefore abandon whole populations to their fate within contested regions; or else it could help these people relocate to new areas (with the provision that these moves were temporary and the people could return at the end of the conflict) but thereby be seen to be assisting in the ethnic cleansing process. Most of these dilemmas were handled with patience and diplomacy and the ICRC was able to emerge from the conflict with its reputation for neutrality and impartiality intact. But the Yugoslav conflict certainly presented one of its most problematic fields of operation since the World War II.

—M. B.

REFUGEES (EXTERNAL)

Estimating the numbers of persons displaced involuntarily by the wars (i.e., refugees) in the former Yugoslavia is difficult for a variety of reasons. The main source of systematic information is the United Nations High Commission for Refugees (**UNHCR**). This commission has been represented in Belgrade since 1976, but in response to the war it opened an additional office in Zagreb in December 1991. For a variety of reasons, it is unable to record all movements of those who might be considered as refugees. There is a gray area between economic migration and flight from war. At the outbreak of war, an estimated 750,000 Yugoslav workers and their families were already registered as working abroad as migrant workers. The migrant tradition extends back at least a century, so that many Yugoslavs were aware of kin living in other countries. Contacts of this kind were often resorted to in the early days of the conflict, in the expectation that they might provide temporary relief until the trouble blew over. It is known that large numbers of young men, for various reasons, left Yugoslavia in order to avoid military conscription. There is no reliable way of estimating the numbers involved in these movements, who never registered with UNHCR.

The brief war in **Slovenia** occasioned very little refugee displacement. It was not until November 1991 that conflict involving the Serb minority living in **Croatia** reached sufficient intensity to result in large-scale **population** movement, and the greater

Croatian refugees from Davor, Bosnia-Hercegovina, victims of ethnic cleansing, arrive in Croatia in 1995. (UNHCR)

part of this movement was handled within the territory of the former Yugoslavia. The greatest displacement of refugees began after the outbreak of major violence in **Bosnia-Hercegovina** in March–April 1992. Within three weeks more than 200,000 people were recorded as refugees by UNHCR. Although some European states took the view, voiced by the British government, that refugees were best received in areas as close as possible both spatially and culturally to their own homes, local resources very rapidly reached the point at which such areas were unable to manage additional numbers. Following is a list of numbers of Yugoslav refugees recorded by UNHCR. (Note that many of these figures are unconfirmed or estimates.)

Country	*February 1993*	*June/July 1996*
Albania	3,000	5,000
Austria	73,000	80,000
Belgium	3,371	6,000
Czechoslovakia (Czech and Slovak Republics combined)	10,000	3,900
Denmark	7,323	22,449
France	4,200	15,000
Germany	250,000	330,000
Hungary	40,000	8,500
Italy	16,500	8,200
Netherlands	5,995	23,000
Norway	3,674	12,000
Spain	4,654	2,500
Sweden	62,202	122,119
Switzerland	80,000	20,000
Turkey	18,060	8,000
United Kingdom	5,900	13,000
Others	32,429	6,865

The figures for several neighboring countries are high partly because of historical connections, including the presence of ethnic minorities from these countries in Yugoslavia (**Italy**, **Hungary**, **Turkey**). Other states are traditionally noted for their high levels of support to humanitarian causes (Switzerland and the Scandinavian countries). The extremely heavy involvement of **Germany** fits neither of these patterns.

The return of refugees to their homes began to feature as a political issue in the summer of 1996. Following the successful reclaiming of the former Serb **Krajina** by the **Croatian Army**, as well as implementation of the military provisions of the **Dayton Agreements**, expectations of the continuing stabilization of conditions in the former Yugoslavia rose. Also, in several states (notably Germany), the economic and social costs of sustaining large numbers of refugees began to become an internal political issue. Repatriation has proved to be difficult to achieve, however, in spite of the repeated statements by the Croatian government that Serbs are welcome to return to their homes, as well as the provisions of the Dayton accords emphasizing the freedom of movement and right to resettlement. Undoubtedly there has been considerable resistance on the part of refugees to pressures that they should return to a country that they still regard as unsafe (especially where agricultural land is unusable because of the widespread danger from **land mines**). These concerns have been enhanced by a succession of incidents in which parties of refugees attempting to return have met with harassment from the local authorities and, on occasion, have experienced intimidation and violence. Organized returns from countries outside the former Yugoslavia, as recorded by UNHCR, amounted to only 21,361 persons by 3 December 1996.

—*J. B. A.*

REFUGEES (INTERNAL)

The general problems of identifying who is to be counted as a "refugee" are discussed in the preceding entry. These problems are doubly difficult in relation to the displacement of **population** between and within the republics of the former Yugoslavia. Many individuals attempted to resolve their problems on a personal level by finding accommodation with kin. Those evading military service (for example, large numbers of young Serbs from Bosnia moving into Serbia proper) avoided any registration of their movements. Students of Serb ethnicity from Dalmatia electing to study in Belgrade or Novi Sad instead of Split or Zagreb blur the edges of discussion considerably. The United Nations (UN) estimated in February 1993 that perhaps a further 93,000 persons were unregistered, in addition to the more than 2 million of whom they had records, and the UN criteria exclude several varieties of involuntary displacement. At this time **UNHCR** (United Nations High Commission for Refugees) reported that it was "assisting" approximately 1 million other individuals not formally counted as refugees.

In the case of internal movement, certainly in the early stages of the war, a high proportion of those displaced were accommodated with local families, resulting in the spread of the burden of care over a wide segment of the population, especially in Croatia.

Although the cessation of hostilities following **Operation Flash** and **Operation Storm** in **Croatia**, as well as the conclusion of the **Dayton Agreements**, created conditions of greater stability, and although the Croatian government began to fund a large program of reconstruction in the former **Krajina**, the return of refugees and other displaced persons has been far from complete. In the first quarter of 1996, UNHCR still reported more than 1.75 million people within the republics of the former Yugoslavia in its care.

—*J. B. A.*

Table 1 Estimates of Displaced Persons/Refugees within Former Yugoslavia (as of 25 February 1993)

Present Location	*From Croatia*	*From Bosnia-Hercegovina*	*Total*
Croatia	246,000	283,000	561,000* R
UN protected areas	87,000	—	87,000 E
Serbia	164,000	294,000	458,000 R
Bosnia-Hercegovina	70,000	740,000	810,000 E
Montenegro	7,000	58,000	65,000 R
Slovenia	N/A	N/A	40,000 R
Macedonia	3,000	29,000	32,000 R
Total	577,000	1,404,000	2,053,000**

*Includes 32,000 registered refugees from other republics of former Yugoslavia but not an estimated 93,000 unregistered refugees
**Does not include some 1,000,000 persons also assisted by UNHCR
R—Registered
E—Estimated
N/A—Not available

Table 2 Beneficiaries in the Region

Republic	*Refugees*	*Internally Displaced Persons*	*War Affected (Vulnerable Cases)*	*Total*
Bosnia and Hercegovina	N/A	1,000,000	1,400,000*	2,400,000
Croatia	170,000	180,000*		350,000
Sector East	—	60,000		60,000
Subtotal: Croatia	170,000	240,000		410,000
FYROM	6,300	—		6,300
Slovenia	16,500	—		16,500
Federal Republic of Yugoslavia	330,000	—		330,000
Grand total	522,800	1,240,000	1,400,000	3,162,800

*Receiving partial assistance
N/A—Not available
It is underlined that all figures quoted for beneficiaries are for operational and budgetary planning purposes only and have no geopolitical implications.

Reference: Mertus, Julie, Jasmina Tešanović, Habiba Metikos, Rada Borić, eds. *The Suitcase: Refugee Voices from Bosnia and Croatia.* Berkeley: University of California Press, 1997.

REGIONAL INEQUALITY

Regional inequalities have bedeviled Yugoslavia since its foundation as a nation-state in 1918. A persistent north-south division was inherited from the historical experience of subjugation under the **Austro-Hungarian Empire** in the north and the **Ottoman Empire** in the south. The more developed northern republics of **Slovenia** and **Croatia** and the province of **Vojvodina** had formed part of the Austro-Hungarian Empire, and the southern republics of **Serbia**, **Montenegro**, and **Macedonia** and the province of **Kosovo** had formed part of the Ottoman Empire. **Bosnia-Hercegovina** passed from the Ottoman Empire to a protectorate of Austria-Hungary in the nineteenth century. In the post–World War II period between 1945 and 1990, economic policy was framed by this historical legacy.

At the end of World War II, Yugoslavia was a largely agricultural economy, and what little industrial infrastructure existed had been badly damaged in the war. Under the political hegemony of the Communist Party, broad national support existed for a program of rapid industrialization under state ownership and central planning. Throughout the postwar period a variety of different approaches toward economic policy were pursued, including central planning between 1947 and 1952, administered self-management between 1953 and 1964, market self-management between 1965 and 1973, and so-called self-management planning between 1974 and 1989.

Central planning was abandoned in the early 1950s with the introduction of the system of **workers' self-management,** which had two effects: first, it gave greater autonomy to enterprise managers; second, it introduced some basic elements of a market economy. In the early years of the new economic system, however, central control over the allocation of investment funds was retained by the planners. The Federal Investment Fund directed investment resources between the various republics. In the mid-1960s, the centralized system of investment allocation was abandoned and the reforms of 1965 deepened the market elements of the self-management system. Enterprises were able to keep and reinvest their own profits, and the share of investment financed by enterprises increased from 32 percent in 1964 to 46 percent in 1966 following the reforms. The development of self-management was closely connected with a decentralization of political power. These two processes were rooted in the ideological concern with the "withering away of the state," but they merely resulted in a transfer of economic powers from the federal state to six new republican mini-states. In an attempt to restore its power, the federal state sought to reintroduce planning in the mid-1970s and to reduce market freedoms. The solution was found by introducing a system of "self-management planning" combining some market and planning elements in a complicated system of bargaining among the various levels of political and economic power. Policy conflict during this period, up to the

Levels of Social Product per Capita (Yugoslavia = 100, current prices)

	1955	*1965*	*1975*	*1989*
Slovenia	175	184	204	200
Croatia	122	121	125	126
Vojvodina	94	112	115	119
Serbia	91	96	96	94
Bosnia	83	72	66	67
Macedonia	71	67	69	66
Montenegro	77	76	68	74
Kosovo	43	36	33	26

Source: Razvoj Republike Prethodne SFR Jugoslavije 1947–1990. Savezni zavod za statistiku, Beograd, 1996.

end of the 1980s, centered on the distribution of foreign exchange earnings. A new foreign exchange law introduced in 1977 created republican "self-managed communities for foreign trade," which were responsible for allocating above-quota foreign exchange among regional importers at a premium above the official exchange rate, effectively bringing about a regionalization of foreign exchange earnings. These policy conflicts among the republics became more and more acrimonious over time.

Regional inequalities increased between 1955 and 1990. The ratio of social product per capita between the most developed republic, Slovenia, and the least developed, Macedonia, increased from 2.5 to 3.0 during these years. The position of Kosovo, an autonomous province from 1974 to 1989, was even worse, with a continuous relative decline throughout the entire period.

During the period of administrative self-management up to 1964, the relative positions of Slovenia, Vojvodina, and Serbia improved while those of other regions worsened. In the period of market self-management up to 1974, only the northern republics (Slovenia, Croatia, and Vojvodina) experienced relative improvement. The southern republics fell further behind (with the exception of Macedonia, which recorded a small improvement). After the introduction of self-management planning in 1975 the relative improvement in Slovenia came to a halt, and the differentials between the regions were virtually frozen throughout the late 1970s and 1980s. The main changes occurred in Montenegro, which improved its relative position while Kosovo continued to fall further behind.

Over the whole postwar period it is remarkable how the pattern of regional inequality persisted despite various experiments with planning and market self-management systems. In the mid-1960s a special development fund called the Federal Fund for the Development of the Less-Developed Regions was established, financed by a 1.56 percent tax on incomes of the more developed regions, but this program seems to have had little impact. Only Vojvodina managed to cross the threshold from relative underdevelopment to above-average levels of output per capita, and that region was not a main beneficiary of the fund. Kosovo, which was a main beneficiary, experienced a continuous worsening of its economic performance, probably resulting in part from the relatively high birth rates among **Albanians** in the region. What little change there was in the pattern of inequality throughout the postwar period favored the northern republics.

An important element of economic development in the 1980s was the onset of the international debt crisis, which hit Yugoslavia particularly hard. Having already decentralized economic policy-making powers, the federal government was weakened and unable to respond effectively to the debt crisis. As the costs of repaying foreign loans rose, many of which had been entered into independently by the republican authorities, it proved necessary to restrict further borrowing and restrain consumption through restrictive macroeconomic measures. This policy brought about a fall in levels of output and incomes throughout the 1980s. Each republic tried to resist the impact of the recession by promoting its own economic interests at the federal level. It was not a worsening of economic inequalities among the republics, therefore, that led to interrepublican tensions so much as the onset of economic crisis in the context of preexisting and persistent economic inequalities. In 1986 there was an attempt to restore federal power in the area of foreign exchange distribution—a key policy issue in the context of balance-of-payments deficits. The retention quota system was replaced by "free market" for foreign exchange, which in effect meant a centralized system for the allocation of foreign exchange, since the ability to import was controlled by a system of import quotas and licenses determined according to a system of federal priority sectors. The Slovenes objected to this system and called for a return to the system of retention ratios. The unwillingness of the Slovenes to accept a reduction in their relatively favorable economic position fueled the secessionary movement. The republic's economy was already well integrated into Western markets, and it had little to fear from the breakup of Yugoslavia. In October 1990, in an attempt to protect its own industries from Slovenian competition, Serbia imposed import duties on Slovenian goods, ushering in the breakup of the single Yugoslav market. Political breakup followed soon afterward.

—*W. B.*

See also: economic dimension

References: Bookman, Milica Žarković. "The Economic Basis of Regional Autarchy in Yugoslavia." *Soviet Studies* 42, no. 1 (1990):93–109. Flakierski, Henryk. *The Economic System and Income Distribution in Yugoslavia.* Armonk, NY: M. E. Sharpe, 1989; Pleština, Dijana. *Regional Development in Communist Yugoslavia: Success, Failure and Consequences.* Boulder, CO: Westview Press, 1988.

REIHL-KIR, JOSIP

An adopted Croatian of German-Slovene descent, Josip Reihl-Kir was a tragic figure in the Croat-Serb conflict. As the regional chief of the Croatian police force based at **Osijek** in eastern Slavonia, he saw his role as that of a moderator in the escalating conflict in the first half of 1991. However, in trying to defuse the hardening confrontation in the village of **Borovo Selo**, he was overtaken by events. The police force was being increasingly taken over by the **Croatian Democratic Union** (HDZ); Kir's bridge-building approach became increasingly futile, and his request to be transferred to Zagreb for personal safety proved justified but in vain: on the day before his approved transfer on 1 July 1991, he was assassinated by a gang of HDZ extremists.

—*J. J. H.*

RELIGION

Other entries in this volume deal with the history and character of particular religious communities in Yugoslavia. The focus here is upon the general significance of religion as a factor in the development of the Yugoslav conflict. The war in Yugoslavia has been depicted not infrequently as an "ethnoreligious" struggle—in other words, as a conflict between peoples who are primarily constituted as confessional groups. This case has been made with particular vigor by Paul Mojzes and by Michael Sells. Such a depiction is also implicit in the interpretative framework advanced by Samuel P. Huntington in terms of a "clash of civilizations"; his "civilizations" (which supposedly come into collision in the **Balkans**) are defined by reference to the religious cores of their historical cultures.

There is a very important distinction to be made at the heart of this discussion—a distinction that is often confused. It is one thing to claim that conflict is caused by religious divisions, but it is quite another matter to argue that a conflict is expressed symbolically in a religious form. The latter position is argued here.

Three main religious communities have claimed adherents in Yugoslavia: the Roman **Catholic** Church, **Orthodox** Christianity, and the Sunni tradition of **Islam**. (There have been relatively small numbers of others, such as Uniates, various churches in the Protestant tradition, relatively recent sects [such as Adventism], Jews, and Shiite Muslims. Their numbers have been, with local exceptions, too small to merit discussion here.)

As in other parts of the world, claims of religious adherence have to be distinguished from religious behavior—particularly from attendance. Measures of active involvement indicate a picture substantially different from those suggested by figures for confessional identity. The proportion of "believers" in Yugoslavia fell from 87 percent in 1953 to between 45 and 50 percent as measured in subsequent surveys, the decline being most marked among the Orthodox. Measures of regular and consistent practice vary, but as in many Western European countries, those with a strongly religious orientation make up around 5–10 percent of the adult population. Figures of this kind cannot be taken as evidence that religion is unimportant, however, and U.S. political scientist Sabrina Ramet has listed four senses in which religion can be seen as a constitutive part of the identities of peoples in the region. First, religion provides the historical core of the culture of most groups. Second, it acts as a badge of identity, distinguishing "us" from "them." Third, religious figures have been at the forefront of the development of the national languages and literatures of the region. Fourth, the clergy have often played leadership roles historically, as among the most educated and articulate members of the group, in explicitly nationalist and other political movements.

In the post-1945 period, the **League of Communists** (LC) adopted a generally hostile attitude toward religion. Religion was denied any place in public life; although the constitution proclaimed freedom of religious belief, the expression of such beliefs was confined to the private sphere. Nevertheless, the Communists recognized the historical and cultural importance of religion and were prepared to countenance and even encourage certain of its aspects. Three of these aspects have been of particular importance:

The first is the creation of a Macedonian church. The task of winning the "national liberation struggle" imposed upon the Communists an early commitment to a federal structure. There are competing theories as to the intentions that lay behind the particular pattern that emerged. One view sees the task in terms of the need to ensure adequate representation for Serbs; another emphasizes the supposed need to contain the Serbs. Whichever interpretation one chooses, there was a need to consolidate the balance among different republics within the federation. The official institutionalization of the "Macedonian literary **language**" as a way of clearly differentiating Macedonians from Serbs was supplemented by the sponsorship of an autonomous Macedonian Orthodox Church, separated from the Serbian hierarchy. (Similar, although so far unconsummated developments have made their appearance in **Montenegro** since the breakup of Yugoslavia.)

Second, in a similar manner, the LC can be seen to have actually sponsored Muslim ethnogenesisas a means of regulating the competition between Serbs and Croats in **Bosnia-Hercegovina**. There seems to have been little if any serious consideration given to the possible alternative, i.e., attempting to build a purely regional identity for the Bosnian Muslims; in the absence of any realistic possibility of designating Bosnians as a special linguistic community, religion once again was identified as providing the appropriate symbolic core of an identity.

Third, a relatively neglected but nevertheless influential factor that has served to bring to the foreground the religious element of ethnic identities in the post-1945 period has been **tourism**. In the search for visible evidence of local heritage that could be developed as tourist sights, religious monuments have been given great prominence. The definition of Yugoslav identities to outsiders has largely taken place through the medium of the great monastery or church. Huge sums of money have been expended by the state, therefore, in the preservation of the religious heritage of the Yugoslav peoples, ironically by an avowedly atheist regime, in pursuit of the entirely secular goal of earning foreign exchange.

Consequently, while the link between national identity and religion was feared and actively discouraged in relation to Serb and Croat identity, there were ways in which the actions of the regime operated to entrench this link and others. It has often been remarked that communism acted in Yugoslavia to contain the seething potage of ethnicity. In this respect, as in many others, however, the actual effect of state policy with respect to religion has been to emphasize the specifically religious lineaments of national identity, ensuring that the eruption of conflict in an ethnic framework would also have a religious coloring.

—J. B. A.

References: Davis, G. Scott. *Religion and Justice in the War over Bosnia.* London: Routledge, 1996; Huntington, Samuel P. *The Clash of Civilizations and the Re-making of World Order.* New York and London: Simon and Schuster, 1997; Mojzes, Paul. *Yugoslavian Inferno: Ethnoreligious War in the Balkans.* New York: Continuum, 1994; Ramet, Sabrina Petra. *Balkan Babel: Politics, Culture, and Religion in Yugoslavia.* Boulder, CO: Westview Press, 1992; Sells, Michael A. *The Bridge Betrayed: Religion and Genocide in Bosnia.* Berkeley: University of California Press, 1996.

REPUBLIC OF MACEDONIA

See **Macedonia, Republic of**

REPUBLIKA SRPSKA

Since the Dayton Agreements of 1995, the Republic of **Hercegovina** consists of two entities: (1) the Federation of Bosnia and Hercegovina (effectively Muslim-Croat) and (2) Republika Srpska (RS) (effectively Serb). The title Republika Srpska is normally used in order to distinguish the entity from

Bosnian Serb soldiers, Republika Srpska, 1992. (Stevan Filipović)

the Republic of Serbia, which forms part of the Federal Republic of **Yugoslavia.** Although gaining international **recognition** only under the Dayton accords, the Republika Srpska was first proclaimed in March 1992. Earlier, during 1991, the ruling Serbian Democratic Party (SDS)—the Bosnian offshoot of the party of the same name in the **Serb Republic of the Krajina** (SRK)—established four "Serb autonomous provinces" (SARs) in those municipalities where ethnic Serbs were numerically preponderant. Through the later union of these SARs (Eastern and Old **Hercegovina,** Bosanska Krajina, Romanija, and Semberia), the RS was formed in a move that was immediately declared illegal by the state presidency.

The four SARs had rejected a resolution in the Bosnian assembly in favor of the sovereignty of Bosnia-Hercegovina and the inviolability of its **borders** in October 1991. The SDS leadership, under **Radovan Karadžić,** organized a referendum throughout the SARs in November 1991; the Bosnian Serbs overwhelmingly voted to remain in a common state with neighboring Serbia and **Montenegro.** Nevertheless, the government of Bosnia-Hercegovina organized its own referendum on the subject of the republic's independence; this referendum was boycotted by the **Bosnian Serb** community. Although a majority of those who voted (Bosnian **Muslims** and **Bosnian Croats**) supported the referendum, and an independent Bosnia-Hercegovina was proclaimed (internationally recognized in April 1992), the Bosnian Serbs refused to accept the result. Karadžić and the leaders of the SDS left Sarajevo and declared a Serb Republic, which came to be known as Republika Srpska with its capital in nearby **Pale.**

Supported by Serbian president **Slobodan Milošević** since its emergence as the principal Serb party in the Bosnian **elections** of December 1990, the SDS hoped to continue the integration of predominantly Serb areas of Bosnia-Hercegovina into a common state with Serbia and Montenegro, in effect creating a "**Greater Serbia**" on the ruins of the former Yugoslavia. In the context of an ethnically mixed Bosnia-Hercegovina, this goal could be realized only through **civil war.** Beginning with a well-planned siege of **Sarajevo** that was to last nearly three years, Karadžić's government in Pale initiated the Bosnian civil war, using the locally deployed **Yugoslav Peoples' Army** (JNA), a new **Bosnian Serb Army** (BSA) that emerged from its ranks once the JNA left Bosnia-Hercegovina in May 1992, and various **paramilitary/irregular forces** from Serbia to accomplish its territorial objectives.

In a ruthless blitzkrieg in the spring and summer of 1992, the RS was forcibly expanded to cover around 70 percent of the territory of Bosnia-Hercegovina—far in excess of what could be legitimately claimed by the Bosnian Serbs, who then numbered around 1.5 million people, or only 33 percent of the total population. This landgrab involved widespread "**ethnic cleansing**" of non-Serbs. Spread over eastern Bosnia (the **Drina** valley), northeastern Bosnia (the **Posavina Corridor**), north and western Bosnia (around the city of **Banja Luka**), and eastern Hercegovina (to the east of the **Neretva River**), the RS came almost to encircle the remainder of Muslim-controlled territory in central Bosnia.

The RS greatly benefited from the brief civil war between Muslims and Croats in Hercegovina and central Bosnia precipitated by the **Vance-Owen Plan** in May 1993—which led to worsening relations between Milošević and Karadžić thereafter. The first public splits between Pale and the other major center of Bosnian Serb influence, Banja Luka, also appeared in 1993. It was not until 1994, however, that a major strategic shift against the Bosnian Serbs and the RS took place. Created under the auspices of the **United States**, the **Muslim-Croat Federation** of March 1994 enabled both the **Bosnian army** (Army of the Republic of Bosnia-Hercegovina—ARBH) and the **Croatian Council of Defense** (HVO) to stop fighting each other and concentrate on the overextended Bosnian Serb Army. These two forces were then far stronger than they had been in 1992, mainly because of the provision of armaments from abroad. The Bosnian Serbs' intransigent rejection of the **Contact Group** peace plan for Bosnia finally led to an open split between Karadžić and Milošević in August 1994, as well as the economic isolation of the RS from Yugoslavia. This blockade resulted in RS's virtual collapse and the emigration of a large proportion of its population to Serbia by 1995, one result of which was a severe shortage of manpower for the BSA.

Although on the defensive since its territorial gains of 1992, the RS and the BSA overextended themselves in a series of offensives in western Bosnia in late 1994, prompting a major ARBH-HVO counteroffensive and the increased use of **North Atlantic Treaty Organization** (NATO) air power in 1994–1995, following which the RS suffered a series of major military defeats. This resulted in the rapid contraction of the RS from 70 percent of the territory of Bosnia-Hercegovina to 49 percent (the figure set out for the Bosnian Serb entity in the Contact Group peace plan of 1994). In December 1995, the Dayton Agreements formally recognized the RS as an entity on the basis of this territorial dispensation.

Indicted as alleged war criminals by the International **War Crimes Tribunal** in The Hague, both Karadžić and his military counterpart **Ratko Mladić** were forced to relinquish their offices in July 1996. Karadžić's political demise then benefited Banja Luka-based **Biljana Plavšić**. Aided by NATO forces in Bosnia, Plavšić became the new RS president in 1997. Under her more pragmatic leadership, the RS has been moved to cooperate with the international community in Bosnia, although many doubts remain about its longer-term political and economic prospects.

—M. M.

REPUBLIKA SRPSKA KRAJINA

See **Serb Republic of the Krajina**

ROMAN CATHOLICISM

See **Catholic Church**

ROMANIA

Relations between Romania and Yugoslavia (and **Serbia** before it) have traditionally been close. In 1992 a Bucharest newspaper stated, "Whoever knows the history of this European region knows that Serbia is the only neighbor that has never launched an attack on us."

Romania discreetly preserved its links with the remaining Yugoslavia while the latter became an international pariah. Like his Serbian counterpart **Slobodan Milošević**, Romanian president Ion Iliescu was an old aparatchik (member of the former communist bureaucracies) who used nationalism to defame the opposition and prevent an orderly change of government. On 5 April 1994, when Bucharest was one of the few capitals to which Milošević was able to pay an official visit, Iliescu said, "Our relations are positive from every point of view." Such remarks fueled speculation that Romania was allowing food and energy supplies to flow across its porous border into Serbia after reluctantly agreeing on paper to international economic **sanctions** in 1992. Nothing was done in 1993 to prevent Romanian territorial waters from being used to transport hijacked oil-laden ships to Serbia.

After the victory of reformers in the Romanian elections of 1996, President Emil Constantinescu sent a personal emissary to meet opposition leaders in Serbia, thus abandoning his predecessor's stance of identifying with the hard-line Milošević. Romania's contribution to the peacekeeping force led by the **North Atlantic Treaty Organization** (NATO) in **Bosnia-Hercegovina** was stepped up, and Romania is a firm supporter of efforts by the **United States** to stabilize southeastern Europe and deter nationalist and neocommunist influence.

—T. G.

General Sir Michael Rose, commander of the United Nations Protection Force in Yugoslavia (UNPROFOR) in Bosnia-Hercegovina from 1994 to 1995. (Army Public Relations, London)

ROSE, MICHAEL

Gen. Sir Hugh Michael Rose (born 1940) gave service as a professional soldier in many areas of the world, including the Falklands and the Gulf States, before succeeding **Philippe Morillon** as commander of the United Nations Protection Force (**UNPROFOR**) in **Bosnia-Hercegovina** from 1994 to 1995. His term started with his attempts to engineer a form of settlement that would prevent the use of **North Atlantic Treaty Organization** (NATO) airstrikes following the mortar bomb dropped on **Sarajevo**'s marketplace on 5 February 1994, which killed 69 civilian shoppers. Rose's four-point plan was designed to produce a cease-fire, a withdrawal of heavy weaponry on both sides to 20 kilometers from Sarajevo, the stationing of UNPROFOR troops between the lines, and the establishment of a joint committee for implementation. The plan was to be the subject of a meeting on 9 February at Sarajevo airport arranged by Rose. The **Bosnian Serb** side was skeptical but turned up at the appointed time; the Bosnian government, however, despite assurances from colorful Deputy Commander Jovan Divjak (himself a Serb in the **Bosnian army**), initially did not. Not for the only time during his term did Rose display anger; he interrupted a television interview being conducted with Bosnian president **Alija Izetbegović** and forced the latter to attend the meeting. Rose was also having to work against a simultaneously issued deadline from NATO threatening airstrikes if the Serbs did not withdraw. The last-minute outcome of the subsequent maneuverings (including interventions by **Russia**) was Rose's "green line" across Sarajevo patrolled by UNPROFOR; this did afford Sarajevo a breathing space from the violence, as well as a partial restoration of everyday activity, but at the same time it effectively aided the Serb aim of permanently partitioning the city.

General Rose's other major involvement came two months later in the struggle for the eastern enclave of **Goražde**, designated as one of the "**safe areas**" under UN protection. Here his mission was virtually impossible. The nature of the Serb advance and the divisions among the international community could only compromise Rose's preferred profile as a peacekeeper rather than peace enforcer, and it was Rose himself (with UN approval) who on 10 April was provoked by Bosnian Serb Gen. **Ratko Mladić**'s refusal to halt the attacks into ordering NATO intervention from the air. These limited strikes, as Rose probably suspected, had little effect other than to identify his own men as an opposing force, and within a week he had to request air cover to enable evacuation of personnel. Rose was a believer in the essential neutrality of UNPROFOR—Goražde was a severe test of such belief. His one-year term of office expired in January 1995 and he was succeeded by **Rupert Smith**.

—J. J. H.

ROYALTY
See **monarchy**

RUGOVA, IBRAHIM

In the multiparty parliamentary elections of 24 May 1992 (boycotted by the Serb minority and ignored by the Belgrade authorities), Ibrahim Rugova was elected with 97 percent of the votes as president of the self-proclaimed Republic of **Kosovo**. He was born on 2 December 1944 near Istok in Kosovo. His father and grandfather were executed by the Communists on 10 January 1945. Rugova finished his undergraduate studies of Albanian language and literature at the University of Priština in 1971. From 1976 to 1977, he studied at the École Pratique des Hautes Études in Paris under the internationally eminent French writer and literary critic Roland Barthes. It was in the late 1960s that Rugova began writing and specializing in literary criticism. In 1972 he worked as a research scholar and professor of literature at the Albanological Institute in Priština, where he was responsible for the academic periodical *Gjurmime Albanologjike (Albanological Research)*. Among his major publications are *Vepra e Bogdanit, 1675–1685 (The Works of Bogdani, 1675–1685)*, Priština, 1982; *Kahe dhe premisa të kritkës letrare shqiptare, 1504–1983 (Directions and Premises of Albanian Literary Criticism, 1504–1983)*, Priština, 1986; and *Refuzimi estetik (Aesthetic Rejection)*, Priština, 1987.

On 23 December 1989, Ibrahim Rugova was elected as chair of the **Democratic League of Kosovo** (Lidhja Demokratike e Kosovës—LDK), the political party called into being to defend the rights of the **Albanian** community in Kosovo. His views, his policy of passive resistance, and his particular approach to maintaining peace and calm in an explosive region have been well put forward in the French-language volume *La question du Kosovo: entretiens avec Marie-Françoise Allain et Xavier Galmiche (The Kosovo Question: Conversations with Marie-Françoise Allain and Xavier Galmiche)*, Paris: Fayard, 1994. Ibrahim Rugova lives surprisingly in **Priština**.

—R. E.

RUPEL, DIMITRIJ

Dimitrij Rupel (born 1946) studied at the Universities of Ljubljana (Slovenia) and Essex (England), graduating in 1976 with a doctorate in sociology from Brandeis University in the United States. He taught in Canada and the United States before becoming a full professor in 1992 at Ljubljana University. In 1982 Rupel helped create the monthly review *Nova Revija (New Review)*, which became a forum for the Slovene opposition, especially in the face of the nationalist views emanating from the Serbian Academy of Arts and Sciences. In 1987 he became the editor of *Nova Revija* and published issue 57, famous for containing the article "Contributions for the Slovene National Program." The review regularly criticized the Slovene political establishment and analyzed the crisis in Yugoslav affairs. **Milan Kučan**, leader of the central committee of the League of Communists of Slovenia (LCS), made sure the writers were not prosecuted, steering a fine line between party hardliners and moderates. *Nova Revija*, together with the Communist Youth Organization's journal ***Mladina***, helped to form political debate in Slovenia, particularly by promoting the idea of "civil society."

In 1989 Rupel founded the Slovene Democratic Union, the first opposition party to openly challenge the one-party system. In 1990 the Slovene Democratic Union joined an opposition coalition, DEMOS (Democratic Opposition of Slovenia). After the DEMOS electoral victory, Rupel became minister of foreign affairs, holding the post from April 1990 to January 1993.

After **Slovenia**'s declaration of independence, Rupel lobbied intensively for international **recognition**, pointing out that Slovenia was willing to negotiate with any Yugoslav republic about common concerns. During the Ten Day War, Rupel and Kučan met German foreign minister **Hans-Dietrich Genscher** at Klagenfurt, informing him of the military situation. Rupel believes that Genscher's contribution was vital in establishing the meeting brokered by the **European Community** (EC) on the island of **Brioni** at which the Slovene delegation, which included Rupel, exerted the effective pressure that brought about Slovenia's international recognition.

After giving up his post as foreign minister, Rupel has continued as a member of parliament and has been mayor of **Ljubljana**. In September 1997 he was appointed plenipotentiary ambassador to the United States and Mexico. He has attracted attention in other ways, stimulating debate over the finer points of developing the democracy that he was so important in building. In the issue of *Mladina* dated 28 February 1995, journalist Bernard Nezmah published an article critical of Rupel, who filed a defamation suit, won, and saw Nezmah subjected to a prison sentence of one month. Journalists are now assessing the weaknesses of legislative and constitutional guarantees of freedom of the press and the confidentiality of sources.

Rupel's views are represented by his chapter "Slovenia's Shift from the Balkans to Central Europe," in *Independent Slovenia: Origins, Movements, Prospects.*

—*I. R. B.*

Reference: Rupel, Dimitrij. "Slovenia's Shift from the Balkans to Central Europe." In Jill Benderly and Evan Kraft (eds.), *Independent Slovenia: Origins, Movements, Prospects.* New York: Macmillan, 1994.

RURAL-URBAN DIFFERENCES

A great deal of attention has been paid to **ethnicity** as a focus of the problems that led to the breakup of Yugoslavia, and this topic has been discussed in relation to the emergence of regionalism. One important axis of social and economic conflict that has a bearing upon both **ethnicity** and regionalism has been largely overlooked, however: the relationship between the city and the countryside.

Yugoslavia became urbanized only recently. In 1921 there were only two cities with populations greater than 100,000 and six greater than 50,000. In 1948 these figures were 5 cities and 10 cities, respectively. In 1921 nearly 80 percent of the population lived directly from agriculture, and by the end of World War II this figure had declined only to 75 percent. Under the communist regime, which was committed to industrialization, that picture changed dramatically: by 1991 two-thirds of the population were town dwellers. Nevertheless, their recent rural heritage has continued to have an effect upon people's lives and the way they think.

A substantial part of national tradition is rooted in village life, and the appeal to images drawn from this past has made up an important strain in the creation of contemporary nationalist mythologies. A Serbian politician has coined the phrase the "folklorization of politics" to describe the changes in political culture that have taken place with the collapse of communism. The ideological void created by the discrediting of communism has been filled by an amalgam of images drawn from the rural past. The most prominent of these is the use of the **Kosovo** legends within Serb nationalism.

There has always been a strong sense of the opposition between town and country, dating back to the days when towns were centers of trade and government dominated by foreigners (**Ottoman**, Austro-Hungarian [**Habsburg**], or perhaps Venetian). For those living in the villages, this sense of cultural distance has not been completely eroded by the spread of modern styles of living. This sense of hostility was entrenched by the opposition of the communist authorities to the private ownership of farmland. One of the important features of political change in all of the post-Yugoslav republics has been the emergence of a contrast between the political expression of urban and rural populations, often expressed in support for different **political parties.**

In Slovenia, for example, the Christian Democrats are a largely rural party. Croatia has its Croatian Peasant Party. Among Bosnian Croats **Stjepan Kljuić**, the voice of sophisticated **Sarajevo,** was ousted by the "redneck" support of **Mate Boban.** Among the Bosnian Serbs, former Zagreb professor **Biljana Plavšić**, who finds her main base of support in the city of **Banja Luka**, has been a major rival to **Radovan Karadžić**, who hails from largely rural Montenegro. In Serbia, **Slobodan Milošević** (from Pozarevac) has been able to draw his electoral support very largely from the small-town and village electorate, while opposition leaders such as **Vukasin Drašković** and Vesna Pešić have not been able to break out of the bigger cities to create a genuinely nationwide opposition. Politics in the post-Yugoslav states is often about the conflict between urban and rural perspectives.

This dimension is particularly significant in **Bosnia-Hercegovina**, where as a legacy of the Ottoman influence **Muslims** were overrepresented in the larger cities (with the sole exception of Banja Luka). The **Bosnian Serb** population, however, is heavily overrepresented in smaller settlements. Of the 19 Bosnian communes outside Sarajevo with populations in 1991 of fewer than 15,000, 16 had substantial Serb majorities (the exceptions being **Jablanica**, Kreševo, and **Neum**). **Nationalism** among Bosnian Serbs is in appreciable measure an expression of traditional hostility to "the big smoke" (i.e. the urban industrial centers). This has led to real difficulties for the Bosnian Serbs militarily, in that their capacity to put together a mobile infantry force was hampered by the reluctance of recruits to see military service in terms wider than the defense of their own homes. It is possible that at least one factor contributing to the disproportionate share of Bosnian Serbs in the committing of atrocities during the war has been the extent to which they have been compelled to rely upon semicriminal **paramilitary/irregular forces** recruited in **Serbia** itself.

—*J. B. A.*

See also: ethnic cleansing

RUSSIA

The collapse of the Soviet empire in Central and Eastern Europe, the breakup of the Soviet Union, and the economic and military weakness of Russia severely reduced the country's influence in the former Yugoslavia. Russia, however, remained important because of its continuing status as a great power, its permanent membership of the United Nations (UN) Security Council, and political and economic ties with **Serbia** and the **Bosnian Serbs.**

When the Yugoslav conflict erupted in summer 1991, the primary concern of the Soviet government at the time was the precedent that the breakup of Yugoslavia (and any international intervention in the conflict) might set for the Soviet Union itself. The Soviet government repeatedly argued that developments in Yugoslavia were an internal issue for that country. In July and August 1991, the Soviet Union opposed possible military intervention when the issue was discussed in the UN Security Council.

After the breakup of the Soviet Union in the early 1990s, Russian policy remained caught between two currents: (1) support for the prevalent Western policy of putting political and economic pressure on the Serbian leadership and (2) support for the Serbs. Russian support for Serbia and the Bosnian Serbs was motivated by a variety of factors: sympathy for the Serbs as Slavic kin; obvious parallels between the situations of post-Soviet Russia and post-Yugoslav Serbia; potential economic benefits from trade with Serbia/FRY (Federal Republic of **Yugoslavia**); and a desire to counterbalance Western influence in the region and more generally. At the same time, Russia had obvious interests in maintaining cooperation with the West and would not necessarily be willing to sacrifice that cooperation in order to support the Serbs.

In May 1992, Russian foreign minister Andrei Kozyrev visited the former Yugoslavia, brokering a **cease-fire** in **Bosnia-Hercegovina.** The Bosnian Serbs immediately violated this cease-fire, however, prompting significant shifts in Russian policy. Russia lifted its previous veto on economic **sanctions** against Serbia and **Montenegro** and accepted the suspension of Yugoslavia's membership of the Conference on Security and Cooperation in Europe (CSCE). These steps also reflected the generally pro-Western foreign policy of Kozyrev and Russian president Boris Yeltsin. These shifts in policy provoked the Russian parliament (where support for the Serbs was significant) to demand a moratorium on UN sanctions against the remaining Yugoslavia. Strong parliamentary support for Yugoslavia and the Bosnian Serbs, as well as disagreements between the Yeltsin administration and the parliament, characterized Russian policy throughout the Yugoslav conflict.

Beginning in late 1992, Russian foreign policy shifted away from its earlier pro-Western direction, and this change was reflected in attitudes toward the Yugoslav conflict. Russian officials and parliamentarians called for the lifting or easing of **sanctions** on the FRY, called for the imposition of sanctions on **Croatia,** and opposed proposals for international military intervention in Bosnia or the lifting of the arms embargo on the Bosnian **Muslims.** Russian parliamentarians visited Serbia, and there were reports of Russian weapons supplies to the Serbs and of Russian mercenaries fighting with the Serbs. Russia also sought to enhance its diplomatic role in relation to the conflict with various proposals for a peace settlement. Despite these developments, however, there was no fundamental break with the West over the Yugoslav conflict, and Russia largely accepted the diplomacy of the **International Conference on the Former Yugoslavia** (ICFY) and the deployment of the **UNPROFOR** peacekeeping force.

The failure of the various mediation efforts in the former Yugoslavia, as well as Russia's ties with the Serbs, provided a means for Russia to assert diplomatic influence. In spring 1993, with diplomacy faltering, Kozyrev joined ICFY cochair **David Owen** in proposing the progressive implementation of the **Vance-Owen Plan.** Similarly, in February 1994, Russian diplomacy and the deployment of Russian peacekeepers achieved a (short-lived) cease-fire around the Bosnian capital of Sarajevo.

The establishment of the **Contact Group** (United States, Russia, Great Britain, France, and Germany) in April 1994 formalized Russia's enhanced diplomatic role. During this period, Russian deputy foreign minister **Vitalii Churkin** emerged as a significant figure, working as the Russian representative to the ICFY and the Contact Group and as an interlocutor with the Bosnian Serbs. The limits of Russian influence, however, became clear from 1994 onward as the **North Atlantic Treaty Organization** (NATO) used airstrikes against the Bosnian Serbs—despite Russian arguments that Russia should be consulted before any use of **air power**. The failure of Russian efforts to persuade the Bosnian Serbs to stop shelling **Goražde** in April 1994 also highlighted the limits of Russian influence over the Serbs.

As the United States and NATO took the lead in international efforts to end the Bosnian conflict in 1995, the Russian role became increasingly marginal. Russia had little influence over the decisive developments that lead to the **Dayton Agreements** and effectively had to accept the NATO airstrikes of August–September 1995 as a fait accompli. Russia's continuing great power status and ties with the Serbs, however, did give it a role. The United States wished to retain Russian support as far as possible and used the NATO **Implementation/Stabilization Force** (I/SFOR) operation as a means of intensifying military cooperation with Russia. Thus, Russia is a member of the Dayton Peace Implementation Council; Russian troops joined the I/SFOR; and special U.S./Russian military command arrangements were established. Russian forces were deployed to the sensitive **Brčko** corridor area in order to assuage Bosnian Serb concerns.

Overall, Russia's involvement in the Yugoslav conflict illustrated the drastic decline in the country's influence in Central and Eastern Europe. However, Russia's continuing status as a major European power, its permanent membership of the UN Security Council, and its role as a sometime ally of Serbia and the Bosnian Serbs assured it a role in the conflict.

—A. S. C.

See also: Organization for Security and Cooperation in Europe

S

SACIRBEY, MUHAMED

Muhamed Sacirbey (born 1956) was Bosnian ambassador to the **United Nations** (UN) from 1992 to 1995 and subsequently foreign minister of **Bosnia-Hercegovina.** From a prominent **Sarajevo** Muslim family that left communist Yugoslavia in his childhood, Sacirbey grew up in Ohio after 1967 and became a U.S. citizen in 1973. Acquiring numerous academic laurels, including a doctorate in law, he had a meteoric career as a corporate lawyer on Wall Street, becoming senior vice president of the merchant bankers Security Pacific.

In May 1992 Sacirbey became Bosnia-Hercegovina's first ambassador to the United Nations. In television studios across the world, he proved a formidable advocate of what, at many points, seemed the lost Bosnian cause. His familiarity with life in the United States made him effective in Washington, D.C., while his religious orientation enabled him to mobilize the Islamic world with the help of Bosnian prime minister **Haris Silajdžić.** His mastery of media sound bites and his clean-cut, moderate image (the antithesis of the customary political image of Islam in the West) were vital in what became a media-based as well as territorial war. In June 1995 he became foreign minister after the helicopter of his predecessor, Irfan Ljubijanović, was shot down by **Bosnian Serbs.** He returned to the post of Bosnian ambassador to the UN in 1996. He is close to President **Alija Izetbegović** and has been supported by confessional **Muslims** opposed to secularists inside the ruling **Party of Democratic Action** (SDS).

—*T. G.*

See also: Islam and the West; media (external)

SAFE AREAS

Immediately following the virtual surrender of **Srebrenica** to the **Bosnian Serbs,** in mid- April 1993 the Security Council of the **United Nations** (UN) passed Resolution 819, which designated Srebrenica as a "safe area." Just over one month later, this status was extended to five other Bosnian **Muslim** areas: the Bosnian capital of **Sarajevo** itself; **Goražde** and **Žepa** (like Srebrenica, in the southeast); **Tuzla** in the northeast, and **Bihać** in the northwest.

Often mistakenly referred to as "safe havens" (a term that the UN itself rejected because of its specific meaning in international law), these safe areas were almost as mistakenly named. There was little or no prospect of making them safe without the UN taking sides, which hitherto it had resolutely not been pre-

An anxious displaced woman, victim of ethnic cleansing policies, in a UN safe area of Srebrenica, 1995. (UNHCR)

pared to do; instead, the UN had emphasized its role as **humanitarian** and diplomatic. Resolution 819, therefore, served only to show irresolution: the UN could not be keeper of the peace without being its enforcer, and to enforce the peace meant abandoning the very neutrality necessary to keep the peace, thus adding to the inherent weakness of the concept the acute difficulty of implementing it.

The UN secretary-general at the time, **Boutros Boutros-Ghali**, backed the plan for safe areas by calling for 35,000 troops to patrol them; as it turned out, the member nations supplied only one-fifth of that number. By the time of the **Dayton Agreements**, the three safe areas in the southeast had been taken by the Bosnian Serbs, while the other three remained as far from being safe as could be imagined.

The plan for safe areas, however well meant, was hurried, impractical, and consequently a failure, even though it was that failure that eventually precipitated the direct armed intervention by the international community that brought the Bosnian war to an end.

—*J. J. H.*

ŠAHOVNICA

The *šahovnica* (meaning chessboard) is part of the national flag of **Croatia**, consisting of a shield covered by a red and white checkered pattern and taken from a coat of arms of the medieval Croatian Kingdom. One of the first changes made by the nationalist government led by **Franjo Tudjman** and the **Croatian Democratic Union** (HDZ) in 1990 was to replace the Communist flag of the republic with a new national flag incorporating the *šahovnica.* This move antagonized the Serbs in Croatia because the former Croatian fascist **Ustaša** movement had used this symbol for the Independent State of Croatia during World War II.

The controversy highlights the symbolic dimension to the conflict between Serbs and Croats. Serbs claimed that use of the *šahovnica* showed that the HDZ sympathized with the Ustaša regime and its record of atrocities. Croats claimed that they were restoring the insignia of their medieval state suppressed by the socialists. There were elements of political manipulation on both sides, but these arguments also have roots in the group memories of the two communities.

—*G. R. B.*

SALONIKA

See **Thessaloniki**

SANCTIONS

Although of doubtful effectiveness in earlier contexts, such as South Africa, economic sanctions were the least politically contentious option available to the members of the United Nations Security Council (UNSC) when the wars in Croatia and then Bosnia unfolded in 1991–1992. In the absence of any international consensus on the use of military force by **United Nations** (UN) member states to stop or ameliorate the effects of these conflicts, sanctions became the principal means to influence the ultimate outcomes.

Despite the high political hopes the sanctions engendered, the effects of the sanctions used in the former Yugoslavia during the 1990s were rarely those intended. Even so, the longer-term consequences of sanctions were often profound, helping to change the balance of forces in **Bosnia-Hercegovina** in particular and hence helping to bring about an end to the Yugoslav wars in 1995.

In the case of the state against which they were exclusively aimed (the Federal Republic of **Yugoslavia** [FRY], composed of **Serbia** and **Montenegro**), the international community's economic and other sanctions were certainly a major factor in changing FRY policies toward the Bosnian conflict even before the conflict ended in 1995. Elsewhere in the former Yugoslavia, the economic blockade of **Macedonia** by **Greece** over the former's chosen name failed to secure the outcome sought by the Greek government.

Economic sanctions were first unilaterally introduced by the **European Union** (EU) against Serbia and Montenegro as part of a failed diplomatic effort to end the first Serb-Croat war in October 1991. They had no effect on that conflict. This phase was ended by the first UN peacekeeping deployment in the former Yugoslavia. In May 1992 UNSC Resolution 757 was introduced against the FRY for the latter's role in bringing about the Bosnian civil war. By far the most draconian mandatory sanctions ever imposed against any state in modern times (including Iraq before and after the Gulf War of 1990), Resolution 757 banned all trading and financial links with the FRY, froze all the republic's overseas assets, forbade all types of cooperation, and imposed a ban on all commercial flights and mar-

A Roma beggar in Serbia under economic sanctions, 1994. (Stevan Filipović)

itime links to and from that country. Subsequently further reinforced by Resolution 821 in April 1993, when all transshipment of goods by third parties across the territory of the FRY was also banned, this comprehensive economic embargo remained in place for over three years. Following the signing of the **Dayton Agreements** in December 1995, all its provisions were lifted except for a number of financial limitations pertaining to the unresolved problems of the Yugoslav succession. Concomitantly, the unilateral Greek economic blockade of Macedonia dating back to March 1994 was also lifted. Pending the lifting of the so-called outer wall of financial sanctions, the future economic prospects and international standing of the FRY remain problematic.

In terms of their purely economic effects, the trade and other sanctions imposed against the FRY from 1992 to 1995 were highly damaging. During this period, the combined gross domestic product (GDP) of Serbia and Montenegro fell by half, and their combined foreign trade declined by two-thirds. Politically, however, the sanctions-induced disaster paradoxically strengthened the position of the Yugoslav government. In relation to the Bosnian conflict (the issue that had led to sanctions in the first place), the split between Serbian president **Slobodan Milošević** and the **Bosnian Serbs** did not come about until 1994; the sanctions issue was only one of a number of factors that led to this change of policy in Belgrade. Similarly, the diplomatic success scored at Dayton, as well as Milošević's participation in the process, resulted from military changes in Bosnia rather than economic sanctions, although the Serbian president obviously wanted to expedite the lifting of sanctions against the FRY at that time.

By then it was also clear that widespread regional "sanctions busting" had undermined the effectiveness of the economic embargo against the FRY. Greece's economic blockade of Macedonia had also caused economic chaos locally and had completely failed to induce Macedonian government compliance on the central issue of the republic's chosen name. Greek economic blackmail had the effect of strengthening Macedonian nationalism, ruling out any possibility of a political settlement favorable to Greece.

UN economic sanctions of the sort used against the FRY were also seriously threatened against **Croatia** in 1993 for the latter's role in the Bosnian conflict, helping to pave the way to the creation of the **Muslim-Croat Federation** in March 1994. Also in 1994, the FRY began to enforce economic sanctions against the Bosnian Serbs. Croatia also used economic sanctions against its secessionist ethnic Serbs in the **Krajina**, thereby weakening the Serbs' ability to resist a Croatian military onslaught in 1995.

—*M. M.*

See also: economic dimension

SANDŽAK

The name *Sandžak* has come to be applied principally to an area of southeastern Serbia comprising the communes of Nova Varoš, Novi Pazar, Priboj, Prijepolje, Sjenica, and Tutin. The term originally designated units of regional military organization within the **Ottoman Empire**. Only during the late nineteenth century did it come to be used to refer to one specific area.

After the Congress of Berlin in 1878, Serbia and Montenegro both acquired territory at the expense of the government, or Porte, of the Empire, but in response to Austrian insistence they were precluded from having a common frontier. The Sandžak of Novi Pazar that separated them remained within the Ottoman Empire, thus preventing the potential formation of a strong and independent Slav state to rival Austrian-Hungarian (**Habsburg**) power in the Balkans. This area was more extensive than that to which the term is usually applied now, and it included the modern Montenegrin communes of Bijelo Polje, Ivangrad, Plav, Pljevlja, and Rožaj. The Sandžak was divided between **Serbia** and **Montenegro** at the end of the Balkan Wars in 1913, after which time the term has tended (erroneously) to be used to refer only to the Serbian part of the area.

As a consequence of its status as a residual Ottoman possession between 1878 and 1913, the Sandžak retained its Islamic population. Indeed, there is some evidence that the Muslim population of the region was augmented in this period by refugees moving in from the territories occupied by Serbia after 1878. The effects of this movement continue to be seen today, in spite of attempts to encourage the emigration of Muslims to Turkey both between 1918 and 1936 and after the reunification of Yugoslavia in 1945.

Although the existence of an indigenous, Serbo-Croat-speaking, Muslim population has come to be widely recognized as a distinctive feature of society in Bosnia-Hercegovina, partly as a consequence of the recent war, this group is equally important within the demographic structure of the Sandžak as well. In the 1991 census, 45 percent of the population of the 11 communes in Serbia and Montenegro that today make up this region were **Muslims**, who formed a majority of the population in Novi Pazar, Plav, Rožaj, Sjenica, and Tutin. This distinctive pattern of ethnic settlement has come to be significant during the period of the disintegration of Yugoslavia.

When a plurality of **political parties** began to emerge after 1989, the **Party of Democratic Action**, the principal political voice of Muslims in Bosnia-Hercegovina, also began to organize in both the Serbian and Montenegrin areas of the Sandžak. In Montenegro, where the party worked within the framework of the Democratic Coalition (a group of parties representing ethnic minorities), the party's activity was centered upon Rožaj. The party's main strength lay in the Serb part of the Sandžak, centered upon Novi Pazar, where it was led by Sulejman Ugljanin.

The war in Yugoslavia has impinged upon the Sandžak in several ways. Sandwiched between **Bosnia-Hercegovina** and **Kosovo**, the Sandžak has felt itself to be permanently on the brink of being engulfed by an extension of the war. This sense of threat has been enhanced by the growth of tension between local Muslims and Serbs; these groups have been under the bombardment of **propaganda** from Serbian political parties endeavoring to represent the war primarily as a struggle for the defense of **Orthodox** Christianity in the face of militant Islam. Although the dangers in the Sandžak fall well short of the state of affairs in Kosovo, there has been a rise in the level of physical threat experienced by Muslims, exemplified by the detention of Muslim political activists and damage to mosques. The Sandžak has also been the recipient of large numbers of **refugees** from Bosnia-Hercegovina, displaced from areas such as **Foča** and **Goražde**.

The prospect of the territorial division of Bosnia-Hercegovina, leaving a specifically Muslim statelet, has been on the agenda of various internationally sponsored negotiations since 1992; it has placed a question mark over the future of the Sandžak. Some have feared that such a statelet would provide the occasion for further "**ethnic cleansing**," with local Muslims forced to emigrate to some Islamic "Bantustan" (or South African homeland) in central Bosnia. As the war moved steadily in favor of the government forces in its later stages, however, more militant factions began to entertain the idea of creating a Muslim state that would encompass the Sandžak. Whereas there seems little possibility for the redrawing of international boundaries in this way, the proposal is an indication of the depths to which Serb-Muslim relations have sunk during the course of the war. It also suggests the reality of fears that a breakdown of the constitutional terms of the **Dayton Agreements** in Bosnia-Hercegovina, as well as a return to war or some future eruption of conflict in Kosovo, could well see the Sandžak drawn directly into the fighting, which it has so far managed to escape.

—*J. B. A.*

SARAJEVO

The capital city of the Yugoslav republic of **Bosnia-Hercegovina**, Sarajevo in 1991 had a population of 527,000, making it the fourth-largest city of the federation. Following the war it has become the capital of the new Federation of Bosnia-Hercegovina. The population of greater Sarajevo in 1991 was 49 percent Muslim, 30 percent Serb, and 7 percent Croat, with a further 11 percent declaring themselves to be "Yugoslavs." Composed of 10 municipalities, the city had a diverse character, with the center and Stari Grad (Old Town) predominantly Muslim and the suburbs more ethnically diverse. Its strategic and symbolic significance during the conflict can be summarized at a number of levels.

Located at the junction of valleys, Sarajevo has always been important as a center of **communications**. A major airport has recently been added to complement historic road and rail links.

As the historic capital of Bosnia-Hercegovina, Sarajevo had come to contain many of the symbols of Bosnia's identity. The struggle for Bosnia has largely been conducted in terms of claims to identity. The destruction of symbolic monuments elsewhere in Bosnia (most notably in **Banja Luka** and **Mostar**) suggests what the fate of the city might have been had it fallen, as exemplified by the targeting by Serbian artillery of cultural objects such as the National **Library** of Bosnia-Hercegovina in Sarajevo. The siege of the city, lasting from May 1992 to December 1995, became the prism through which the world looked at the war. This preoccupation with Sarajevo was broken only intermittently by attention to events elsewhere, such as the discovery of **detention camps** or the destruction of the bridge in Mostar. Bosnian Serb politician **Nikola Koljević** remarked that with the world's gaze fixed on Sarajevo, it was possible for the Serbs to do what they wanted in northern Bosnia.

This somewhat sensational focus on Sarajevo is reflected in the fact that at least one foreign charity

Children play on a car by ruined buildings in Sarajevo New Town. (NATO photo)

(Harmonie Internationale of France) directed its attention solely to the city. In 1997 the city was the location for a British feature film based upon the war *(Welcome to Sarajevo).*

As a strategic objective, Sarajevo was relatively unimportant for Croat forces, taking second place in that respect to Banja Luka. For the Bosnian government, it retained a preeminent role as a symbol of effective and continuing political presence. Conversely, for the besieging Serbs, its capture would have been read as signaling the end, to all intents and purposes, of any realistic claims to the existence of a Bosnian state—the eclipse of a specifically Bosnian identity.

The symbolic importance of Sarajevo was very ambiguous. On the one hand, it received unrivaled attention because of its heroic resistance under siege conditions; it was, in that role, of incalculable political and psychological value to the government side. On the other hand, it could be said that overattention to Sarajevo, at the expense of a balanced reporting of events elsewhere, created an image of Bosnians as perpetual victims, undermining the Bosnians' claims to be accepted as a state in their own right. In that respect, the Bosnian government found itself in a position similar to that of the Croatians during the early stages of the war. It appears that in each case a decision was made to focus on securing international sympathy for the suffering of Bosnians, who were portrayed as being at the hands of an aggressive outside force that was willing and able to perpetrate all kinds of horrors. In each case, however, the tactic came close to backfiring because international opinion, while responding charitably to suffering, was reluctant to become involved in the support of a state that appeared to be incapable of mounting the basics of its own defense.

The first armed conflicts in the area of the city began on 5 April 1992, when a peace march came under fire from Serb **paramilitary** forces. The following day a demonstration on behalf of peace, in which 60,000–100,000 people gathered in front of the republican assembly, came under fire from Serb snipers installed in the Holiday Inn. Although it marked the **European Community**'s announcement of **recognition** of an independent Bosnia-Hercegovina, that day may also be taken as signifying the start of the siege of the city. Units of the

Yugoslav Peoples' Army (JNA) seized the airport, and artillery bombardment began.

The most critical moment of that siege occurred close to its beginning. On 2 May 1992, Serb forces attempted to cut the city into sections, moving one armored column toward the city center through the southern suburb of Grbavica and a second column from the western suburb of Ilidža through Dobrinja. Although lightly armed, the hastily formed units of the Patriotic League (also known as the Green Berets), which defended the city, beat back both offensives. The first was stopped when armored vehicles became jammed in the city's narrow streets. A persisting weakness of the Serb military effort was revealed in that their massive superiority in hardware was not backed by either effective leadership or adequate infantry. Although defeated, the attack laid the foundation for a continuing important feature of the subsequent siege. The limited Serb gains gave the Serbs control of several positions from which it was possible to offer snipers effective cover of large areas of the city, making daily movement difficult and dangerous for the inhabitants.

Under siege conditions, obtaining supplies remained highly problematic for the city for the next four years. The exposed situation of the airport, as well as its proximity to an active front line, meant that the airport was at best a tenuous link with the outside world, even when periodic negotiations rendered it officially "open" (as following the remarkable lightning visit by French president François Mitterand on 28 June 1992). For the greater part, **humanitarian aid** depended upon overland convoys, which were subject to stringent control (and exploitation) by Serb and Croat checkpoints.

Three factors, in different ways, eased the supply problem. The United Nations Protection Force (**UNPROFOR**) was able to open an all-weather route in addition to the heavily fought-over **Neretva River Valley**, linking Sarajevo to **Split** via Kupres and **Vitez**. A highly risky route into the city over Mount **Igman** was secured, although this route remained exposed to intermittent Serb gunfire. Most remarkably, **Bosnian army** engineers dug a tunnel under the airport. Carrying a light rail track, this tunnel remained a vital route for both goods and personnel.

Sarajevo was declared a "**safe area**" by the United Nations (UN) in May 1993, although its continuing exposure to attack after that date stood as a permanent challenge to both the ideals behind and reality of that UN policy. An explosion in one of the city's marketplaces on 5 February 1994 killed 49 (eventually 69) and injured more than 200. UNPROFOR ballistics experts confirmed that the explosion was caused by a 120-millimeter mortar bomb, but they were unable to identify with any certainty the location from which it had been launched. This made for controversy, although there remains some doubt as to whether this uncertainly was real or simply a form of leverage used by UNPROFOR commander Gen. **Michael Rose** to reverse Bosnian government refusal to take part in negotiations over demilitarization of the city, scheduled for 8 February. The event was especially important in mobilizing public opinion in **France**, however, and the response of Foreign Minister Alain Juppé was to demand the demilitarization of Sarajevo.

A second such incident, on 28 August 1995, killing 37 people and injuring many others, was less ambiguous in its interpretation and was one of the events that led to **North Atlantic Treaty Organization** (NATO) military intervention in the form of Operation Deliberate Force two days later.

—J. B. A.

See also: media (external); *Oslobodjenje;* siege warfare

References: Gjelten, Tom. *Sarajevo Daily: A City and Its Paper under Siege.* New York: HarperCollins, 1995; Karahsan, Dzevad, and Slobodan Drakulić. *Sarajevo: Exodus of a City.* New York: Kodansha International, 1994; Kurspahić, Kemal. *As Long as Sarajevo Exists.* Stony Creek, CT: Pamphleteer's Press, 1997.

ŠARINIĆ, HRVOJE

Born at Šušak in 1935 and trained as an electrical engineer, Hrvoje Šarinić worked in Zagreb for the Electricity Board before emigrating to France to work as an expert in atomic energy; he amassed considerable wealth as a result of this work. He returned to Zagreb in 1980 representing the French nuclear lobby. In 1990 he was appointed to the post of presidential chief of staff following the election victory of the **Croatian Democratic Union** (HDZ), and he was made prime minister after the 1992 **elections.** Šarinić has a reputation as a technocrat and a political intriguer. He acted as the chief negotiator for Croatia during the talks on a renewed **cease-fire** after the **Maslenica** offensive against the local Serbs in January 1993. In 1995 he was presidential chief of staff once more, but in the October elections he failed to secure reelection.

—*G. R. B.*

SAVA RIVER

In terms of its economic and political geography, the Sava River is the most important river wholly within the territory of the former Yugoslavia. It is also the longest; rising in the Julian Alps of the extreme northwest, it flows southeastward for some 600 miles (945 kilometers) through three republics—Slovenia, Croatia and Serbia—linking their capital cities of **Ljubljana**, **Zagreb**, and **Belgrade** where it joins the **Danube River.** Its lower part, along with the Drava River and the Danube, has helped to form the southern half of the wide Pannonian Plain, a fertile and well-populated region; in the earlier stages of the Serb-Croat conflict (1991–1992), this lower part witnessed destruction, conflict, or tensions along most of its course. For one-third of its course, the Sava also forms the northern border between **Croatia** and **Bosnia.**

—*J. J. H.*

SDA

See **Party of Democratic Action**

ŠEKS, VLADIMIR

Vladimir Šeks (born 1943), a lawyer from **Osijek** in the eastern Slavonia region of Croatia, was a member of the far-right nationalist wing of the **Croatian Democratic Union** (HDZ). He served as deputy president (speaker) of the Sabor (Assembly) from 1990 to 1992 and as deputy prime minister of Croatia from 1992 to 1994. He was an outspoken populist, aligned with **Gojko Šušak,** Sime Djodan (who was minister of defense for a time), and Antun Vrdoljak (head of Croatian Radio and Television), among others. This wing of the HDZ favored a militaristic, authoritarian, and **Catholic** Croatia that would include as much of the territory of **Bosnia-Hercegovina** as could be taken and held. They opposed the technocratic faction of the HDZ, which included **Hrvoje Šarinić, Nikica Valentić,** and Franjo Gregurić. Šeks resigned from his post in September 1994 in what was seen as a purge of the HDZ's right wing. He was deputy speaker of the Croatian parliament in 1995.

—*G. R. B.*

SELF-MANAGEMENT

See **workers' self-management**

SERB ARMY OF THE KRAJINA

The Serb Army of the Krajina (SAK) was the armed force of the **Serb Republic of the Krajina** (SRK) that existed in Croatia from 1990 to 1995. Created in the summer of 1990, the SAK emerged from an ad hoc mixture of former Territorial Defense Force reservists, police, and paramilitaries in the Serbian **Krajina** in northern **Dalmatia** and **Slavonia.** The new SAK was initially little more than a glorified police force, consisting of hard-line Serb nationalists known as Martićevci, named after the interior minister at the time, **Milan Martić.** Although nominally subordinate to the SRK president, **Milan Babić** (and his successor after 1992, **Goran Hadžić**), Martić was always the real power in the SRK because of his control of the Martićevci (and later the SAK) long before he formally assumed the presidency in 1994. The Martićevci at the core of the SAK in 1990–1991 were joined by a number of **paramilitary/irregular forces.** Here the key group was commanded by a Serbian émigré mercenary from Australia known as Captain Dragan.

The locally deployed **Yugoslav Peoples' Army** (JNA) turned the SAK into a well-armed and properly organized military force by the time of **Croatia**'s declaration of independence in June 1991. Here, the key figure who aided the SAK—and openly supported the ruling Serbian Democratic Party (SDS) leadership in **Knin**—was the commander of the JNA corps headquarters (HQ), Gen. **Ratko Mladić.** Well connected in the general staff in Belgrade, Mladić, together with local operatives of the military counterintelligence service KOS, authorized the covert arming of the Krajina Serbs long before the SAK and the SRK were formally constituted. This secret assistance, as well as the de facto support of the JNA that the SAK enjoyed in 1990–1991, placed the SAK at an advantage in relation to the poorly equipped Croatian National Guard (HNS) when Croatia descended into full-scale civil war in 1991.

The first armed clashes of the Yugoslav wars took place in the SRK in the summer of 1990, when the SAK cut off Knin and other towns in the Krajina from the rest of Croatia. Known as the "log revolution" (after the wooden blockades used in this action), this move deprived the government of **Franjo Tudjman** of unimpeded access to its Adriatic

Krajina Serb soldier in Eastern Slavonia, 1991. (Stevan Filipović)

coastline. Knin's strategic importance derived from its being the main road and rail junction on the route from **Zagreb** to **Split**. Similarly, the occupation of territories in Slavonia by the SRK deprived Zagreb of the area's considerable economic resources and use of the motorway to the border with **Serbia**.

Consisting of somewhere between 40,000 and 50,000 troops at the time of the SRK's secession from Croatia in March 1991, the SAK undertook its first major operation in the **Plitvice** National Park. After Croatia's declaration of independence in June 1991, coordinated SAK-JNA actions took place throughout Croatia, including the seizure of **Glina** and other towns in western Slavonia and territorial gains in a triangle bounded by **Osijek**, Vinkovci, and **Vukovar** in eastern Slavonia.

The JNA general staff had envisaged a strategy of dismemberment and partition in its contingency plans for the secession of **Slovenia** and Croatia; these plans were code-named Ram-1 and Ram-2. In all the major operations planned for in Ram-2 (Croatia), the heavy firepower of the JNA was decisive, with the SAK and the paramilitary militias essentially acting as reserve forces. Culminating in the fall of Vukovar in November 1991, these operations resulted in a situation where the SAK controlled a third of the territory of Croatia. This military and political disaster for Croatia was frozen by the deployment of the United Nations Protection Force (**UNPROFOR**) I in Croatia from 1992 to 1995, although this extended pause in the Serb-Croat conflict in Croatia allowed Tudjman's government to strengthen the **Croatian Army** (HV) and prepare it for a showdown with the SAK in 1995.

Under immense domestic political pressure to resolve the problem of the SRK, Tudjman had the HV initiate a number of probing actions against the **pink zones** of UN Sectors North and South in 1992, followed by a major attack against the **Medak pocket** in 1993. Hostilities ended with a **cease-fire** sponsored by the **United States** in March 1994. Later the same year, in a move coordinated with the **Bosnian Serb Army** (BSA), the SAK overextended itself by participating in a major Bosnian Serb offensive in western Bosnia. Including SAK air attacks against Bosnian **Muslim** (Bošnjak) positions from the air base at Udbina in the Krajina, this offensive led to a disaster for the Krajina and Bosnian Serbs alike. It gave Tudjman the pretext he needed to order the HV into western Bosnia in order to encircle the Krajina heartland in 1994–1995, when the Bosnian Croats and their Bošnjak allies also went on to the offensive in western Bosnia. Worst of all, the **North Atlantic Treaty Organization** (NATO) subjected the BSA and its SAK allies to the heaviest air attacks of the Bosnian war, decisively tipping the balance of power against the Serbs in Bosnia.

Within the SRK the coming to power of Martić, as well as his alliance with the Bosnian Serbs, resulted in serious problems with President **Slobodan Milošević** in Serbia. The Serbian president was to use his leverage over the SRK to foist a new commander on the SAK, Gen. Mile Mrkšić, a regular Yugoslav army officer whose only loyalties were to Milošević, not to the Martić leadership in Knin.

The collapse of the Serb position in western Bosnia in 1994–1995 was accompanied by two major and connected offensives against the SRK: **Operation Flash** against western Slavonia in May 1995 and the larger **Operation Storm** against the Krajina proper in August 1995. The second of these eliminated the SRK in only five days, resulting in the forced flight of the SRK's 150,000 civilian population into nearby Bosnia in the single largest **ethnic cleansing** of the Yugoslav wars of the 1990s. The military weaknesses of the SAK were then cruelly exposed. Overextended along very long front lines, the SAK was chronically short of manpower. Its static and traditional strategy inherited from the former JNA proved no match for the modern war of movement, combined arms, and high-grade tactical intelligence waged by the U.S.-trained HV.

It has been suggested that Milošević ordered Mrkšić to give up the SRK without a real fight—speculation that was given credence by the fact that the SAK retreated in relatively good order, leaving behind large stores of military equipment and the elaborate defenses of Knin intact. Most of the resistance that did take place at this time was localized and uncoordinated. The SAK mounted an ineffective attack against Zagreb using ex-JNA Orkan surface-to-surface missiles. This move was a purely revenge attack against civilians, resulting in the indictment of Martić as a war criminal by the International **War Crimes Tribunal** at The Hague in 1996.

The SAK was still a relatively significant force as late as early 1995. Then manned by around 40,000 troops commanded by six corps HQs in northern Dalmatia, Lika, Kordun, Banija, western Slavonia, and Baranja/eastern Slavonia, the SAK was subdivided into 27 infantry brigades, 3 mechanized brigades, 1 artillery brigade, 1 antitank regiment, and 1 special forces brigade. Its equipment inventory consisted of around 240 main battle tanks, 100 armored personnel carriers, 500 pieces of artillery, a number of surface-to-surface missiles (SSMs), various types of antitank and antiaircraft missiles, some 50 air defense guns, 12 fixed-wing combat aircraft, and 5 armed helicopters. Although deployed mainly in the SRK, the SAK also played a major role in the Bosnian civil war, notably in and around the strategic **Posavina Corridor**.

Even more than was the case with the BSA, however, the SAK was dependent on Serbia for military materials, fuel, finance, and even some of its commanders throughout the entire period of its existence. This dependency and weakness gave Milošević far more leverage over the Krajina Serbs than over their Bosnian Serb counterparts. This weakness cost the SRK its very survival when Milošević decided it was indefensible and expendable from 1994 onward.

Following the fall of the Krajina and western Slavonia in 1995, a "rump" SRK remained in eastern Slavonia (the former UN Sector East). Under the terms of the Erdut Agreement, this territory was to be peacefully reintegrated into Croatia proper by 1998. This arrangement could not be avoided given Milošević's unwillingness to use the Army of Yugoslavia to defend the last remaining Serb enclave in Croatia in the event of a major attack by the HV. The defenses of this exposed eastern Slavonian rump of the former SRK lacked real credibility, consisting of only one corps, commanded by Gen. Budimir Lončar. This pathetic remnant of a once significant armed force disappeared altogether in 1998.

—M. M.

SERB REPUBLIC OF THE KRAJINA

The Serb Republic of the **Krajina** (SRK) was the former Serb-controlled entity that existed in Croatia from 1990 to 1995. In response to the coming to power of the **Croatian Democratic Union** (HDZ) in May 1990, the Serb Autonomous Region (SAR) of the Krajina was declared at **Knin** in October 1990. In February 1991, under the leadership of **Milan Babić** and the Serbian Democratic Party (SDS), this entity declared its separation from Croatia. This move was followed by the creation of similar SARs in western and eastern **Slavonia** in August 1991. During the subsequent Serb-Croat civil war, the **Yugoslav Peoples' Army** (JNA) and the **Serb Army of the Krajina** (SAK) seized around one-third of the territory of the Republic of **Croatia**.

Through a union of the three SARs, the SRK was formally proclaimed in December 1991. Centered on northern **Dalmatia**, the SRK was able to impede **Zagreb**'s access to the **Adriatic Sea** via the main rail route from the Croatian capital to **Split**. Similarly, the proximity of the SRK to **Karlovac** and Zagreb threatened to cut Croatia in half. In western and eastern Slavonia, the SRK cut the main motorway to the east and deprived Zagreb of the economic resources of this part of Croatia.

With the end of the first Serbo-Croat war in late 1991, the United Nations Protection Force (**UNPROFOR**) was deployed in the former Yugoslavia in and around the SRK. By freezing and policing the front lines between the SAK and the **Croatian Army** (HV), UNPROFOR I effectively aided the survival of the SRK and consolidated a Serbian sphere of influence in Croatia. Babić, the SRK's first president, opposed UNPROFOR deployment and was removed from power by pressure from **Serbia**. Led by **Goran Hadžić** from 1992 to 1994, the SRK was completely dependent on Serbia and its proxies in neighboring **Bosnia-Hercegovina** for its survival. Real power in the SRK was wielded by the SRK interior minister, **Milan Martić** (a protégé of Serbian president **Slobodan Milošević**), who replaced Hadžić in 1994.

Cut off from the rest of Croatia, the SRK experienced a serious economic collapse. The population of the SRK never numbered more than 250,000 people—a figure that was further reduced by widespread emigration to Serbia after 1992. The SRK's extended shape without natural means of **communication**, as well as the absence of either natural or industrial resources, undermined the economic and military viability of the republic from the outset. Without the possibility of permanent association with the Serb-controlled regions of Bosnia-Hercegovina, the SRK's long-term existence as a state was impracticable.

An unstable and unsustainable situation of neither peace nor war persisted from 1992 to 1995, during which time the HV regularly conducted probing actions in the **pink zones** around UN Sectors North and South. These limited military operations were ended by a **cease-fire** between the HV and the SAK in March 1994 following the creation of a new **Muslim-Croat Federation** in Bosnia. Following an SAK offensive in aid of the Bosnian Serbs in western Bosnia later in 1994, however, the HV counterattacked and surrounded the Krajina heartland. In Serbia, Milošević had by then decided to abandon the isolated and indefensible SRK in return for a rapprochement with Croatia and rehabilitation by the international community. In May 1995, the HV's **Operation Flash** eliminated the SRK in western Slavonia. In August 1995, the much larger **Operation Storm** eliminated the Krajina core in UN Sectors North and South. In neither case was the SAK able to mount an effective resistance, nor was help forthcoming from either the Bosnian Serbs or Serbia. The SDS leadership fled, and with the forced flight of 150,000 Serb civilians, Croatia divested itself of a large part of its ethnic Serb minority.

The only remaining SRK territory in eastern Slavonia (UN Sector East) was peacefully reintegrated into Croatia in 1998 under the UN Transitional Administration in Eastern Slavonia (**UNTAES**), an interim body that replaced UNPROFOR I in Croatia after the fall of most of the SRK in 1995.

—*M. M.*

SERBIA

The largest and most powerful of the former Yugoslav republics, Serbia has played a pivotal and controversial role in the Yugoslav wars of the 1990s. Formerly known as the Socialist Republic of Serbia, a constituent partner of the former Socialist Federal Republic of **Yugoslavia** (SFRY), Serbia was renamed the Republic of Serbia under the new Serbian constitution promulgated in 1990. Under the 1974 SFRY constitution, Serbia formerly included two autonomous provinces, **Kosovo** and the **Vojvodina**. Under the new constitution of 1990, the autonomy of both the Vojvodina and the renamed province of

Kosovo-Metohija was revoked, thereby creating a highly centralized system of governance.

In April 1992, in response to the final international recognition of the demise of the SFRY, Serbia and the former Yugoslav republic of **Montenegro** declared a Federal Republic of **Yugoslavia** (FRY), a nominally federative state wherein Serbia was the dominant partner. The FRY claimed to be the sole successor of the former SFRY, although this claim has never been recognized either internationally or in the rest of the former Yugoslavia.

Located along a strategic east-west **communications** route in the eastern Balkans, Serbia has international borders with **Croatia** and **Bosnia-Hercegovina** (along the **Danube** and **Drina** Rivers, respectively), **Hungary**, **Romania** (with which Serbia also shares a Danubian boundary), **Bulgaria**, and **Macedonia**. Connected to the Black Sea along the Danube, Serbia's only access to the Adriatic and Mediterranean Seas is through Montenegro. The FRY covers 102,173 square kilometers; Serbia itself accounts for 88,361 square kilometers and is divided into the Pannonian plains of the Vojvodina (about one-quarter), central-southern Serbia (or Inner Serbia, about one-half), and Kosovo-Metohija (about one-eighth). Inner Serbia includes most of Serbia's major cities, including the capital of **Belgrade** as well as **Kragujevac**, and encompasses the strategic province of the **Sandžak**, which connects Inner Serbia to Montenegro. Inner Serbia also contains the **Sava River**, which joins the Danube at Belgrade, and the Morava River, which flows southward to Macedonia. The Morava and Vardar Valleys form an important natural corridor carrying international as well as national communication routes.

In 1991 Serbia and Montenegro had a combined population of around 9.9 million, accounting for around 40 percent of the former Yugoslavia's total population of around 25 million; 5.7 million lived in Inner Serbia. Belgrade, with a population of 1.1 million in 1991 and in excess of 1.5 million more recently (because of an influx of Serbian **refugees** from elsewhere in the former Yugoslavia), is by far the largest city in Serbia, followed by Novi Sad, Niš, and Kragujevac in Inner Serbia, as well as **Priština**, the capital of Kosovo-Metohija. Serbia's two formerly autonomous provinces, the Vojvodina and Kosovo-Metohija, each had a population of around 2 million people in 1991. Within Serbia, birth rates are at their highest in Kosovo-Metohija and the Sandžak and at their lowest in the Vojvodina.

In 1991 Serbia was the least ethnically homogeneous of the former Yugoslav republics; only 63 percent of its population were ethnic Serbs, although Inner Serbia, where 85 percent of the population were ethnic Serbs, had one of the most homogeneous populations of the federation. One in four of all Serbs lived outside the republic. This large diaspora of around 2.5 million people was formerly concentrated mainly in Bosnia-Hercegovina and Croatia. It has been greatly reduced by the **population** movements arising from the Yugoslav wars of the 1990s. In Serbia itself, the Kosovar Albanians, who accounted for 17 percent of the republic's population in 1991, are the largest non-Slavic ethnic minority. Accounting for around 90 percent of the population of Kosovo-Metohija, ethnic **Albanians** are also to be found in Inner Serbia and Montenegro. The numerically predominant Slav **Muslims** of the Sandžak are the other significant ethnic minority. In the Vojvodina a large non-Slavic ethnic minority of Hungarians accounted for around 20 percent of the former province's total population in 1991. Other important minority communities in Serbia include Roma, Vlachs, and Bulgarians.

Religious affiliation among the Serbs is overwhelmingly to the Serbian **Orthodox Church**. Dating back to the sixth century in the Balkans, the Serbs largely converted to Orthodox Christianity by the twelfth century, when an autocephalous Orthodox Church was established in "Old Serbia." By the fourteenth century, a Serbian empire had been created around what is now southern Inner Serbia. Following the defeat of this empire by the invading Ottoman Turks at the **Battle of Kosovo** in 1389, Serbia became a vassal state of the **Ottoman Empire** for over 400 years. During this period Serbian national identity and its key myths were preserved by the Serbian Orthodox Church.

Following an unsuccessful Serb rebellion against the Turks in 1689, the demographic and geopolitical core of Serbdom moved northward to northern Inner Serbia and the Vojvodina (then part of the **Habsburg Empire**). During the course of the nineteenth century, the independent Serbian Kingdom gradually emerged in northern Inner Serbia, or the so-called Šumadija (Land of Forests). The kingdom did not include Old Serbia, the Sandžak, or Kosovo-Metohija until the Balkan Wars (1912–1913), and it acquired the Vojvodina only in 1918.

Following the creation of the Kingdom of Serbs, Croats, and Slovenes in 1918 (renamed Yugoslavia in 1929), Serbia essentially expanded its military and political power into the whole of this new South Slav state. Dominated by Serbia and the Serbs during the interwar period, the first Yugoslavia experienced chronic political instability because of its failure to address the national concerns of its non-Serb peoples. Invaded and dismembered by the Axis powers in 1941, the former Yugoslavia became the scene of a three-way civil war among the Serbian nationalist **Chetniks**, the communist **Partizans**, and the Croatian fascist **Ustaša.** Under direct German military occupation during the wartime period, with a puppet government under Gen. Milan Nedić owing nominal allegiance to the former king, Serbia was liberated by the largely diaspora-Serb communist Partizans, led by Josip Broz **Tito**, in 1944–1945. As the strongest support base of the royalist Chetniks led by Draža Mihailović (1892–1946), Serbia proper was subjected to severe treatment upon the creation of a new communist Yugoslav federation in 1946.

Uniquely in the SFRY, Serbia was thus subdivided through the creation of the autonomous provinces of the Vojvodina and Kosovo. Based on a Titoist policy of a weakened Serbia as the essential precondition of a strong Yugoslavia, this weakening of Serbia and Serbdom more generally in the second Yugoslavia meant that Serb nationalism then became a taboo subject in this and other Yugoslav republics. Politically, postwar Yugoslav communism was at its strongest in Serbia and within institutions where Serbs were disproportionately represented, such as the **Yugoslav Peoples' Army** (JNA). With the de facto confederalization of the Yugoslav federation in the 1960s and 1970s, a particularly hard-line form of communist rule became more entrenched in Serbia, notably after a group of more liberal Serbian communists were purged by Tito during the early 1970s.

—*M. M.*

Reference: Judah, Tim. *The Serbs: History, Myth and the Destruction of Yugoslavia.* New Haven, CT: Yale University Press, 1997.

SERBIA (GREATER)

See **Greater Serbia**

SERBIAN ACADEMY MEMORANDUM

This document has been extremely influential as a focus for perceptions of the character and direction of Serbian political thinking in the period leading to the breakup of the Yugoslav federation. It bears comparison with the ***Islamic Declaration*** in that its influence has been based upon the circulation of incomplete and mythologized versions rather than actual contents of the document itself. Hence, the memorandum has come to play a part in the demonization through **propaganda** of one group in the Yugoslav conflict. As with the *Islamic Declaration,* the controversial views of a particular minority have, in distorted form, been circulated as evidence of a systematic, generalized, and conspiratorial plan with which an entire ethnic group has been identified by its opponents.

The memorandum began life as a confidential paper by a number of scholars attached to the Serbian Academy of Sciences and Arts (SANU). It was never an official publication of the academy, although the title by which it came to be known was evidently chosen to convey an impression of official status. Parts of the document were leaked to a Belgrade evening paper in November 1986, and a variety of incomplete (often highly selective) versions was published over the next few years. The full text did not appear in Serbo-Croat until 1993, and the greater part of critical comment on it was based upon either incomplete texts or secondary sources. A brief summary of its contents will be appropriate before discussing its significance.

The memorandum falls into two halves, the first a general critique of the Yugoslav political and economic system and diagnosis of its problems, the second a consideration of the "position of **Serbia** and the Serb people" within **Yugoslavia.**

The crisis in Yugoslav society is claimed to be economic and political at root. The economic crisis is the heart of the matter, going back to the failure of the economic reforms of the 1960s. The Yugoslav economy had been characterized by low productivity, inappropriate and unproductive investment, and lack of economic discipline. Decentralization took the place of a needed diminution of bureaucratization of the economy and only reproduced bureaucracy at the republican level. In this process the state abdicated its proper function in providing economic coordination.

The malaise is particularly attributable to the constitutional and structural reforms of the 1970s, which were based upon ideological rather than economic foundations. The program of economic stabilization introduced in the late 1970s failed to address the key areas of institutional failure, leaving intact a constitutional structure that was "contradictory, dysfunctional and expensive . . . a text-book example of ineffectiveness." In particular, the confederalization of government led to a permanent situation of mutual veto by republics on all significant proposals for change.

At the political level, **workers' self-management** led to a "disintegration of the working class" and a return to the "inheritance of Stalinism and the Comintern," including methods of "democratic centralism." Its authors paint a damning picture of a political system based upon the authoritarianism of a self-serving, inflexible, and dogmatic elite, which is strongly reminiscent of the diagnosis of **Milovan Djilas**. "The entire system is constituted upon the principle of the activity of the summit of the political hierarchy, and the hopeless passivity of the people." This "summit" is staffed by "loyal but incompetent cadres."

In moving toward a remedy for this state of affairs, the authors cite "four principles of civilisation which are indispensable conditions for the growth of society." These are the sovereignty of the people; the self-determination of nations; the institutionalization of human rights; and the primacy of rationality, including respect for expertise.

The second half of the document switches dramatically to what are believed to be the current problems of Serbia and the Serb people within the Yugoslav federation. This section is the one that has been most widely and controversially reproduced. The key to the problems of Serbia is located in the interwar Comintern line, which explained the problems of the "First Yugoslavia" in terms of "Serbian oppression." Consequently it is alleged that the "Second Yugoslavia" was constructed, at a stage during World War II when it was not possible to ensure proper representation of Serb interests, in such a way as to limit and contain Serbia. The course of postwar development has been dictated by the most economically powerful republics (**Slovenia** and **Croatia**) in a manner that ensured that Serbia remained relatively underdeveloped economically.

The greater part of this section spells out the claim that Serbs who find themselves in the position of national minorities have suffered as a result of the constitutional "confusion" that has prevailed. In particular it laments the "physical, political, legal and cultural **genocide** of the Serb population of **Kosovo**-Metohija," although it affirms that to a lesser extent the Serb minority in Croatia has suffered similar discrimination. "In less than ten years, if things do not change essentially, there will be no Serbs in Kosovo; it will have been 'ethnically cleansed.'"

Without specifying the constitutional or other changes that might be necessary, the document closes with a demand that "the equality of all the peoples of Yugoslavia" be restored as a precondition for the resolution of the political and economic crises that the country faces. It states that this resolution can be brought about by a "democratic mobilisation of the entire moral and intellectual forces of the nation."

Alleged to have been a blueprint for the creation of a "**Greater Serbia**," this often miscited or unread document in fact has more to do with past Serb grievances than with any politically realistic vision of the future of Serbia and Serbdom. The authorship of the memorandum remains uncertain, although the writers are said to have included **Dobrica Ćosić**, **Mihailo Marković**, and several other philosophical and literary figures. All the people with whose names it has been linked were born between 1911 and 1932, and the majority of them were identified closely with the Partizan struggle. The memorandum's lack of internal coherence, far from indicating a firmly conceived plan for the future role of Serbia in Yugoslavia, highlights the lack among Serbs of a shared diagnosis of their problems as well as a lack of clear vision as to how those problems might be addressed. The secrecy of the original project has been explained in terms of its role within a nationalistic conspiracy. Its open attack upon the constitutional order in Yugoslavia (in particular the conduct of the "leading role" of the **League of Communists**) and upon **workers' self-management** points toward an explanation in terms of simple self-preservation.

Alleging a systematic anti-Serb bias in the second Yugoslavia, in particular in the Serb province of Kosovo, the document lists many Serb grievances and for that reason was taken up by the **media** and a number of leading politicians in Serbia. Although he was initially critical of the document, the Serbian president **Slobodan Milošević** opportunistically seized upon some of its ideas when he came to power in 1987. Using a revived Serb nationalism (in which he never believed) to legitimize his rise to power, the neocommunist Milošević was later to abandon all the memorandum's central tenets. In 1993 Milošević and the federal president Ćosić parted company politically, by which time the SANU memorandum was effectively dead in Belgrade.

—*M. M. and J. B. A.*

SERBIAN RENEWAL MOVEMENT

See **Drašković, Vukašin**

SERBIAN WRITERS

A number of authors from Belgrade have turned their artistic talents to the events of the war. Their novels tell the story from the perspective of how the war was experienced in their cities and encapsulate and express the fears and anxieties of ordinary people whose lives are intimately influenced by events taking place at a distance. At home, everyday life is molded by international economic **sanctions** that have cut off **Serbia** from the rest of the world, giving these novels a feeling of claustrophobia. Reality is dominated by the possibility of military call-up or the news of a relative's or friend's death at the front. The social environment cannot escape the sudden return to extreme poverty, and individuals cannot entirely avoid the intrusive presence of the mass media bombarding the population with relentless images of war and with messages that do not reflect the full horror of those images.

Slobodan Selenić's novel *Ubistvo s predumišljajem* (1993) (translated into English as *Premeditated Murder* [New York: HarperCollins, 1996]) is the story of a young Belgrade student, Jelena Panić, who falls in love with a soldier from Croatia, Bogdan Bilogorac. The two of them research the life of Jelena's maternal grandmother, who is educated and sophisticated and comes from a rich Belgrade family. They examine the period of 1944, when the communist **Partizans** arrived in Belgrade and took control of the government, set on destroying everything cultured that Jelena's grandmother represents and replacing it with their own boorish peasant ways. At the same time, the grandmother has some kind of relationship with a Partizan officer. In the end her half-brother shoots the officer and then turns the gun on himself. For Selenić, there are many similarities and overlaps between 1944 and 1993. Belgrade is threatened with a new barbarism, and a civilized and cosmopolitan way of life is hemmed in by growing parochialism. Bogdan eventually returns to the front, where he is killed. Jelena travels to Croatia to bring his body back to Belgrade for burial, after which she emigrates to New Zealand. Selenić's novel expresses pessimism for the younger generation, for whom there seems little hope for the future.

Vladimir Arsenijević is a younger writer than Selenić, and his novel *U potpalublju* (1995) (translated into English as *In the Hold* [New York: Random House, 1996]) also concerns the younger generation. Arsenijević's narrator is a young man who lives with his wife, Andjela, in their Belgrade flat. He traces the events of the last three months of 1991 as the Serb-Croat war begins to unfold. His narrative concerns everyday life in the city, where he and everyone else are aware of what is happening but behave as if it cannot be. There is an air of unreality about events that gives them a dreamlike quality but often suddenly turns into a nightmarish vision of destruction and menace. The country where these people grew up, the former **Yugoslavia**, is disappearing before their eyes. They are told that people whom they previously regarded as friends are now enemies. Whoever can get away emigrates to the West, where they can barely exist as refugees. They have lost all sense of proportion, and there is no escape. In this environment the narrator and his wife retreat from the world and pursue their private goals, expecting their first baby. They live as if "in the hold" of a ship—hence the novel's title. There is no longer a life on the streets and in public places for ordinary people; they must survive in a new space below ground, out of sight, as if they do not exist anymore.

Other writers have taken different perspectives on the war. David Albahari has written two novels concerned with this period: *Snežni čovek* (1995) and *Mamac* (1997). The first concerns an unnamed narrator, a writer who manages to leave Belgrade with the aid of a scholarship from a Canadian university to spend a period as writer in residence. Little is actually said about the war, or even about Belgrade, but all the narrator's thoughts and actions are dominated by the extremity of the experience he leaves behind. The novel contains many episodes that reveal the psychological and emotional strain the war has wrought. At one point, for example, the narrator finds a collection of maps in the cellar of the house he is renting. They are maps of Europe, with the borders and frontiers of a world that no longer exists. He puts them on the walls in the kitchen as if surrounding himself with the knowledge that the world has not always been in chaos. The second book, *Mamac,* is a continuation of the same narrator's story, except that he links what is happening now with World War II. Some years before, the narrator persuaded his Jewish mother to record her memories of those years on tape. Now, again in Canada, he decides to transcribe her memories onto paper. The narrative jumps between his mother's memories and his conversations with Canadian friends about current events. The momentous nature of war even for the noncombatant population is constantly underlined.

Other novels set in these years, such as Miroslav Josić Višnjić's *Svetovno trojstvo* (1996), express a varied reaction to the war as experienced by ordinary people in Serbia. They frequently show attempts to make sense of current events by linking them to the past, although the attempt always fails, and history is revealed as just another narrative with no more real existence than these stories of individual lives. Belgrade hovers on the brink of unreality. The characters are portrayed not as participants in a war but as individuals seeing their lives, their past, everything they have ever believed in being torn apart, while they are powerless to prevent the horror. The literature of war that has been produced in Belgrade represents a very peculiar war. Everything that happens appears in television news bulletins every night. It is impossible to equate the flickering pictures of burned-out houses with memories of those same towns. The characters in these fictional works are not fighting; on the contrary, most are actively trying to avoid the front. They are lost in circumstances beyond their comprehension, isolated from the larger world and from one another. Nothing makes sense anymore, and there are no explanations.

—*D. A. N.*

See also: Croatian writers

ŠEŠELJ, VOJISLAV

Vojislav Šešelj is a controversial Serbian politician, militia leader, and alleged war criminal known for his extreme nationalist views and public advocacy of violence against non-Serbs during the Yugoslav wars. A **Bosnian Serb**, he was born in Sarajevo in 1941, educated at the Universities of Sarajevo and Belgrade, and later became a revisionist historian and writer. He has been imprisoned a number of times for his anticommunist views by the authorities in his home republic, **Bosnia-Hercegovina.** Later active in nationalist and anticommunist politics in **Serbia**, Šešelj cofounded the Serbian Renewal Movement (SPO) with **Vukašin Drašković** in 1990. Following a split with Drašković after the first multiparty parliamentary **elections** in December 1990, he founded the ultranationalist Serbian Radical Party (SRS), modeled on the pre-Serb-Croat war party of the same name.

Following the outbreak of civil war in **Croatia** in 1991, the SRS established a **Chetnik** paramilitary force, of which Šešelj began to style himself "*vojvoda,*" or warlord. Šešelj's Chetniks allegedly committed numerous atrocities against ethnic Croats and other non-Serbs in eastern **Slavonia.** Estimated to number over 5,000 troops at the time, the SRS militia was also implicated during 1992 in **war crimes** in eastern Bosnia. In Serbia proper, SRS Chetniks then also attempted a number of "**ethnic**

Vojislav Šešelj, leader of the Serbian Radical Party and self-declared Chetnik warlord. (Tanjug)

cleansings" of non-Serb ethnic minorities in the **Vojvodina**, notably in the village of Hrtkovci. Similar incidents later took place in **Montenegro**, where the SRS established a force strongly supportive of union with Serbia. SRS Chetniks were also periodically based in the predominantly **Albanian** province of **Kosovo**.

As a political ally of **Slobodan Milošević's Socialist Party of Serbia** (SPS) government in 1991–1992, Šešelj's SRS was instrumental in forcing the resignations of Federal premier **Milan Panić** and Federal president **Dobrica Ćosić**. Šešelj's party gained 73 seats in the parliamentary elections in Serbia in December 1992. Following a brief period of coalition government, Šešelj and Milošević split, mainly over Serbia's changing policy toward the Bosnian Serbs when the latter rejected the **Vance-Owen Plan** for Bosnia.

Subsequently denounced as a war criminal and an unbalanced extremist by the SPS-controlled **media** in Serbia, Šešelj has since been in the political wilderness. In 1994 he was publicly accused of war crimes by the government of the **United States** and formally indicted as a war criminal by the UN International **War Crimes Tribunal**. It remains unclear how much popular support exists for Šešelj and the SRS in Serbia and Montenegro now that they have been deprived of the backing of the SPS.

—*M. M.*

SFOR

See **Implementation/Stabilization Force**

SIEGE WARFARE

A characteristic of the war in Yugoslavia that has been of particular military interest, as well as providing the focus for a good deal of the **media** coverage, has been the role of siege warfare conducted against cities. Three events of this kind have been particularly significant, namely the sieges of **Dubrovnik**, **Sarajevo**, and **Vukovar**.

The besieging of cities has been a regular feature of war, ranging from Troy to Stalingrad. However, its prominence has perhaps been regarded with surprise in Yugoslavia, where expectations were framed partly by the guerrilla tactics of the **Partizan** struggle of 1941–1945 (reinforced by experience of the Vietnam War) and partly by general awareness of the high technology and mobility of modern weapons systems (illustrated in the Falklands War). The resort to the siege as a tactic is nonetheless understandable in the Yugoslav context. In a highly urbanized environment, there may well be a temptation to use concentrations of the civilian population as points of pressure—notwithstanding the Geneva Conventions.

In spite of their standing as an important manufacturer and exporter of armaments, the Yugoslav armed forces were not at the forefront of military technology. Military preparedness had been based upon the doctrine of "total people's defense," involving the widespread dissemination of basic military skills instead of a highly trained army of professional specialists. Under conditions of **civil war**, or something close to it, morale was often a problem, particularly on the part of the conscript-based **Yugoslav Peoples' Army** (JNA) and the forces of the Bosnian Serbs' **Republika Srpska**. The capture of a substantial modern city, particularly where it is defended with determination, is a difficult proposition in the best of circumstances. The task is rendered much more difficult where disciplined and well-trained infantry are in short supply.

Against the apparent attractions of the siege as a tactical device, however, it is necessary to set off a

A child amputee, victim of indiscriminate shelling of populated areas during the siege of Sarajevo. (UNHCR)

siege's clear political and **propaganda** drawbacks. The besieging of any city, even with the most scrupulous attention to the discrimination between military and nonmilitary targets, is likely to lay the attacker open to accusations of committing **war crimes**—of the deliberate targeting of noncombatant populations and the wanton destruction of cultural monuments. The propensity of the **media** to focus upon the human-interest dimension of stories or on the role of elite persons, groups, and places makes it likely that cities under siege will earn a high degree of media exposure, with a focus upon the plight of the besieged rather than upon the besiegers. The selection of high-profile targets such as Dubrovnik (prewar Yugoslavia's primary center of **tourism**) and Sarajevo (host to a Winter Olympics) was the recipe for a public relations disaster of massive proportions from the Serb point of view, to which the alienation of public and governmental sympathy worldwide may in large measure be attributed.

In light of the Yugoslav experience, therefore (as well as that of the Russians in Chechnya), it is questionable whether, in the contemporary world, any military gains to be realized from the employment of siege tactics are likely to offset the political and propaganda losses that will be incurred.

—J. B. A.

SILAJDŽIĆ, HARIS

As foreign minister and prime minister of **Bosnia-Hercegovina** during the course of the Bosnian war, Haris Silajdžić became well known throughout the world as an eloquent defender of the cause of an undivided, multiethnic Bosnia. Born in 1945, Silajdžić is a professional historian by training who is fluent in both English and Arabic; his ability to find common ground between the Western and **Islamic** worlds made him a highly effective lobbyist for financial and military aid during the war. Silajdžić became foreign minister when the governing **Party of Democratic Action** (SDA, drawn from the **Muslim** population), along with its Croat allies, declared Bosnia-Hercegovina independent from the rest of Yugoslavia in April 1992. He played a key role in enabling the poorly armed and weak Bosnians to win the diplomatic and **propaganda** battle against their nationalist Serb opponents.

On 25 October 1993, Silajdžić was asked to form a government, and he chose ministers from the civic parties as well as his own party, the SDA. Shortly afterward, he ordered the **Bosnian army** to crack down on powerful mafia groups that had been terrorizing the civilian population of **Sarajevo**, particularly non-Muslims. The government successfully asserted its authority, and the army emerged from the operation stronger and more respected abroad.

Silajdžić grew increasingly concerned with the rise of elements within the SDA committed to a gradual "Islamicization" of the state. In early 1995 he blamed military reverses on promotions in the army based on loyalty to the SDA rather than professionalism, and it is clear that he had a poor working relationship with President **Alija Izetbegović**. Silajdžić resigned on 21 January 1996, having offered to do so the previous August. He accused the SDA of turning its back on a multicultural, secular state, and he formed a party to defend liberal ideals; this party took part in the September 1996 **elections** supervised by the international community. He was physically attacked on the campaign trail by SDA militants, and in a poll that saw the triumph of nationalists in each of the three Bosnian communities, his party made little impact. However, Silajdžić remains active in politics, and in recognition of his popularity abroad and among moderate Bosnians, Izetbegović has appointed him a member of the presidential council.

—T. G.

SKOPJE

In 1945 Skopje became the capital city and administrative center of the newly created Socialist Republic of **Macedonia** within Yugoslavia; since 1992, it has played the same role for an independent Macedonian state. Founded as a Slavic settlement at the end of the seventh century, Skopje (population of about 550,000) lies astride the Vardar River, on historically important trade routes between Central Europe, the Adriatic coast, and the Orient. In the fourteenth century, it was the capital of the great Serb empire of the Nemanjić dynasty.

On 26 July 1963, Skopje was struck by an earthquake that killed over 1,600 of its citizens and devastated the city. The spirit of reconstruction that the postearthquake period brought may in small part explain why ethnic tensions between the Slav majority and the large minorities of **Albanians** and **Turks** have, in the recent period of uncertainty, been less damaging than might otherwise have been expected.

—*J. J. H.*

SLAVONIA

Slavonia is the eastern region of **Croatia**, stretching between the **Sava River** to the south, the Drava River to the north, and bordering **Serbia** and the **Vojvodina** to the east. Eastern Slavonia is flatter than the western part of the region, being part of the large Pannonian Plain. No municipality in Slavonia was settled entirely by Croats. The Croat population in some areas is less than 50 percent, especially in the northeastern district of Baranja, where **Osijek** is situated; the finger of land that extends along the south bank of the **Danube River** from Vinkovci and **Vukovar** toward Novi Sad; and the area around **Pakrac**. These areas contained large numbers of Serbs who migrated into the region during the wars against the **Ottoman Empire**. Given these demographic facts, it is unsurprising that these areas were the scenes of fierce fighting during the early 1990s. Eastern Slavonia is of particular economic importance because it contains oil fields and fertile agricultural land.

Western Slavonia was in many ways the initial flashpoint of the war in 1991. In March, Serb police reservists attempted to take over the police station in Pakrac, precipitating several days of fighting; as a result, the **Yugoslav People's Army** (JNA) moved in to act as "peacekeepers." The same process then occurred in May at **Borovo Selo** in eastern Slavonia. Fighting spread throughout Croatia and had become particularly intense in Slavonia by July. On 22 July, 21 people died in battles in Slavonia, causing the new Croatian president, **Franjo Tudjman**, to return from talks in Macedonia on the future of the federation and to call a crisis meeting of the war cabinet in Zagreb. By now the JNA had abandoned its peacekeeping cover and was in open conflict with the Croatian National Guard.

On 25 July, nine Croatian national guardsmen were killed when the JNA attacked their barracks in Erdut, on the east Slavonian border. Further violence on 26–27 July left scores dead. Thousands of **refugees** converged upon the capital, **Zagreb**, in response to advances made by the Serbs and supported by JNA bombardments. A number of villages near Osijek were lost, with about 80 people dying in the tank bombardment. A Serbian autonomous region (SAR) was proclaimed in western Slavonia during July.

During August, Osijek, Vukovar, and Vinkovci all experienced heavy fighting and bombardments. By September 1991 the Serbs controlled a stretch of the Zagreb-Belgrade motorway in western Slavonia as well as most of eastern Slavonia, with only the major cities holding out. Through most of this fighting, the Croats were hampered by lack of heavy weapons and matériel, but the Croat blockades of JNA bases that had been ongoing through the summer were beginning to provide caches to the Croats.

Croat forces took advantage of a **cease-fire** on 23 September to move their forces into positions around Vukovar and Novska, near the blocked motorway. The JNA and Serb militias maintained the extreme pressure on Vukovar, which by now was in dire straits, and by 17 November 1991 the town had fallen to the JNA, who then switched attention to Osijek.

After the cease-fire agreement of January 1992 paved the way for the deployment of United Nations peacekeepers (**UNPROFOR**), the Serb-held areas in eastern and western Slavonia became United Nations protected areas (UNPAs) and were designated Sector East and Sector West, respectively. The latter was the only UNPA to be divided into a Serb-controlled section and a Croat-controlled section—the dividing line ran through Pakrac, with the Serbs maintaining control of **Okučani**, **Jasenovac**, and the E-70 highway. Sector East was wholly Serb controlled. For the next three years, Croats were unable to reenter these areas, despite the UNPROFOR mandate to enable refugees to return home. These constituencies proved to be powerful political tools for the Croat nationalists, who were able to use them as living examples of the Serbs' wrongdoing and the iniquity of the UN agreement that effectively divided a sovereign state.

Through 1993 attention was focused on Sector South, where Croat offensives were launched in an attempt to regain the **Maslenica Bridge**. After the cease-fire agreement of March 1994, as well as ongoing mediation between the Croatian Serb leaders and the Croatian government, agreement was reached over the reopening of the motorway in December 1994. Over the next four months, the motorway was the site of a number of incidents between Serbs and Croats that gave the Croat leadership their excuse to undertake **Operation Flash** on

1–2 May. By 18 May, only 1,800 Serbs were left in the area. After retaking the rest of the **Krajina** in August 1995, and despite frequent threatening statements, Tudjman proved wise enough not to attempt a military retaking of eastern Slavonia. Serbian president **Slobodan Milošević** gave no support at all to the other UNPAs, but a conspicuous column of tanks moved up to the border with eastern Slavonia during **Operation Storm** in August 1995. It appeared for a while that Croatia might have to accept the loss of this portion of the country. However, as the international community began to step up pressure all around just prior to the **Dayton Agreements**, a negotiated agreement emerged on the peaceful reintegration of Eastern Slavonia (the Basic Agreement, signed on 12 November 1995 between the Croatian government and the local Serb authorities). The **United Nations** (UN) agreed to set up the UN Transitional Administration in Eastern Slavonia (**UNTAES**) to oversee the process. The new peacekeeping operation was established beginning in January 1996 by UN Security Council Resolution 1037. UNTAES was created for an initial period of one year, and its 5,000 troops were headquartered at Vukovar.

UNTAES had a broad mandate. Its most immediate task was to supervise the demilitarization of the region; this process took place successfully in the first month after the full deployment of the force. The ongoing tasks of UNTAES also included overseeing the return of refugees and displaced persons; establishing and training a transitional police force; monitoring the treatment of prisoners; organizing local **elections**; monitoring the international **borders** of the region; monitoring the parties' commitment to human rights; cooperating with the International Tribunal for the Former Yugoslavia in investigating and prosecuting **war crimes**; and ensuring the maintenance of peace and security in the region.

UNPROFOR had begun with a mandate to demilitarize the UNPAs in 1992; UNTAES provided a sharp contrast with the difficulties experienced by that first peacekeeping mission to Croatia. The demilitarization of the region was completed on 20 June 1996, with both Serbs and Croats having proved willing to abide by the Basic Agreement. Heavy weapons were withdrawn or handed over to UNTAES for destruction. From March 1996 to 26 June, 93 tanks, 11 armored personnel carriers, 35 antitank systems, 107 artillery pieces, 123 mortars, and 42 anti-aircraft guns were removed from the region. Also, between October 1996 and February 1997, over 15,000 weapons and 435,000 rounds of ammunition were collected in the weapons buyback program financed by the government of Croatia and organized by UNTAES. The transitional period officially ended on 16 January 1998, with the ceremonial withdrawal of the UN authorities.

—G. R. B.

SLAVONSKI BROD

Slavonski Brod is a large Croatian town (population 114,000 in 1991) in the **Slavonia** region, lying on the northern bank of the **Sava River** opposite the Bosnian town of **Bosanski Brod.** Halfway along the Brotherhood and Unity Motorway between the Croatian and Serbian capitals of **Zagreb** and **Belgrade**, it is also an important railway town between the two cities, with a further line to the Bosnian capital of **Sarajevo.** (It is often referred to as just "Brod," and its station has been featured in more than one international adventure film.) Its pivotal location for communications made it the home of one of the largest barracks of the **Yugoslav Peoples' Army** (JNA); these barracks were eventually taken by the Croats. The town and its supply route south across the bridgehead had been fiercely attacked by the Federal army and Serb snipers, which hampered the exodus of **refugees.** Conversely, the town later received many refugees from the conflict in northern Bosnia.

—J. J. H.

See also: communications and transport

SLOVENIA

The Slovenes were among the Slav peoples to filter into the Balkans, settling the **Sava River** Valley in the middle of the sixth century. They owed allegiance at first to the Avars, but when the Avars were defeated by Heraclius the Slovenes created a state under Franko Samo (who ruled from about 627 to 658) that extended from the Sava to Lake Balaton and to Leipzig. In 748, these lands were acquired by Charlemagne, whereafter the aristocracy was germanized, the teachings of the **Catholic Church** introduced, and the peasants reduced to serfdom. The germanization process accelerated after the Carolingian Empire was partitioned and the Slovene area gained by the German state. During the tenth century, under Holy Roman Emperor Otto II, the Slovene area became the Duchy of Karantania. This helped the Slovenes preserve some sense of identity while under German control, probably through the actions of native Roman Catholic priests. During the thirteenth century, the lands fell under the sway of Ottokar II, whose imperium covered Bohemia, Styria, Carinthia, Carniola, and Istria. The Habsburgs determined to regain their lost lands, and by 1335 they had regained Styria, Carinthia, and Carniola and by 1382 had added Istria and Trieste. Except for a brief period during the Napoleonic Wars, the Slovenes made up part of the **Habsburg Empire** until 1918.

Despite their subject status, glimmerings of a Slovene national consciousness can be discerned. In 1584, Dalmatin completed a translation of the Bible into Slovene and Bohorič finished a Slovene grammar using the Latin alphabet. In 1768, a monk, Marko Pohlin, wrote a Carniolan grammar (the Carniola region being the center of Slovene settlement). Under Napoleonic rule, Slovenes became part of the Illyrian Provinces and were introduced to enlightened ideas and more efficient administrative methods. The Slovene language was used in schools, law courts, the press, and textbooks; the French believed such usage served as a method of combating Habsburg germanization. After the restoration of the Habsburg system, the Slovenes had to wait until 1843 to see the publication of a Slovene-language newspaper in **Ljubljana**.

In 1848, a Slovene political program was formulated demanding a unified Slovene province within the Austrian Empire. The 1848 revolutions saw the destruction of the remaining elements of feudalism. By the end of the century, peasants started to form cooperatives, literacy reached levels of over 80 percent, and the population movement into towns facilitated political development. By 1914, three Slovene political parties existed (liberals, clericals, and socialists). Together they sought to combat germanization. Because their demographic numbers were so small, they realized that cooperation with a South Slav movement was essential to secure autonomy within Austria-Hungary.

At the end of World War I, the Slovene territories were joined to the Kingdom of the Serbs, Croats, and Slovenes (although portions of Slovene land passed to Italy and Austria). In spite of the centralized constitution adopted in 1921, the Slovene People's Party continued to represent Slovene aspirations for a degree of political autonomy. (The kingdom was renamed the Kingdom of Yugoslavia in 1929.)

During World War II, Slovenia was partitioned among **Italy**, **Germany**, and **Hungary**. Various resistance movements sprang up. The father of current president **Milan Kučan** was a resistance officer and was killed by the Nazis. After the Allied victory in 1945, Slovenia became a constituent republic of the Federal People's Republic of **Yugoslavia**. Italy was forced to return some territory in **Istria**, and in 1954 part of the free territory of Trieste was awarded to Slovenia, but many Slovenes still live in Italy and in Austrian south Carinthia.

Beginning in 1945, Slovenia established a measure of cultural and economic independence, becoming the most economically developed area of Yugoslavia. In 1963 and 1974, new federal constitutions introduced increasing measures of decentralization. When **Tito** died in 1980, however, his successors gradually moved toward a more centralizing political stance. Amendments were proposed to the 1974 constitution with the intention of clamping down on anti-Communist and secessionist groups, and Slovene intellectual circles became convinced that these amendments were calculated to destroy the autonomy of the various republics.

Although Slovenes debated these issues, it became apparent that contemporary institutions were incapable of addressing Yugoslavia's dire economic situation. Between 1983 and 1988, governments failed to design and implement economic reforms desired by the **International Monetary Fund**. Additionally, the military trial in Ljubljana of **Janez Janša** and two other journalists during the ***Mladina*** affair unified Slovenes of all political persuasions and helped force Slovenia's split from Yugoslavia.

The decay of communist power throughout Eastern Europe indicated that the old order could be challenged. Accordingly, in September 1989, the Slovene assembly voted for constitutional amendments that included the right "as an independent sovereign and autonomous state to secede from Yugoslavia." In April 1990 Slovenia held its first multiparty **elections**; Milan Kučan, leader of the Party of Democratic Renewal (former Communists) was elected president, while a coalition of center-right opposition parties, DEMOS, won a parliamentary majority. On 2 July, the assembly declared its sovereignty by a majority of 187 to 3 and assumed control over the Territorial Defense Force. On 23 December, 88.5 percent of voters supported a referendum for an independent Slovenia. Independence was declared on 25 June 1991, resulting in the Ten Day War, in which the **Yugoslav Peoples' Army** (JNA) was defeated by the **Slovenian Army.** On 7 July, the **Brioni Accord** terminated JNA military involvement in Slovenia; a three-month moratorium on independence was agreed upon. When this time ran out, Slovenia declared independence on 8 October, took control over its own **borders**, introduced the *tolar* as its currency, and adopted a new constitution. On 15 January 1992, the **European Union** (EU) recognized Slovenia, which joined the **United Nations** (UN) in May 1992.

Slovenia has since joined many international organizations, signed the Association Agreement with the European Union, run further free elections, and looked after **refugees** from the regional conflict; it will be supplying four noncombat aircraft to the Stabilization Force of the **North Atlantic Treaty Organization** (NATO) in **Bosnia-Hercegovina.**

—I. R. B.

See also: economic dimension; political parties; recognition

SLOVENIAN ARMY

A well-organized and effective force based on territorial defense principles, the Slovene Army (SA) successfully made a reality of Slovenia's declaration of independence from Yugoslavia in June 1991. Formed from the Slovenian Territorial Defense Force (STDF), which the **Yugoslav Peoples' Army** (JNA) failed to disarm in 1989–1990, the SA was formally constituted in June 1991. Unlike the territorial defense forces of other Yugoslav republics, which the JNA managed to disarm before the beginning of the war, the STDF was well prepared for confronting the JNA, largely because of the foresight of President **Milan Kučan** and Slovenia's first defense minister, **Janez Janša.**

It was Janša who reorganized and strengthened the STDF in the year before independence, through the covert acquisition of modern armaments in **Austria** and elsewhere. By mid-1991, the STDF was capable of mobilizing 60,000–70,000 troops. A small cadre of professionals headed by a general staff within the defense ministry deployed modern infantry weapons, including portable antitank and air defense armaments. This force outnumbered the locally deployed JNA by a factor of around three to one. The JNA forces under the command of the Ljubljana Army Corps headquarters at that time totaled around 20,000 troops, plus large quantities of heavy weaponry, including **air power.**

Upon Slovenia's declaration of independence, the Yugoslav state presidency in Belgrade controversially authorized the use of the JNA to counter what it claimed was an illegal act of secession by the Slovenes. Although Kučan may have earlier struck a secret deal with Serbian president **Slobodan Milošević** over Slovenia's exit from the federation, the JNA saw its constitutional role as the defender of that federation. In the case of **Slovenia** and **Croatia** the JNA had contingency plans in place, code-named Ram-1 and Ram-2, to deal with possible secessionism. Like the disintegrating state it was constitutionally mandated to defend, however, the JNA high command was divided as to what it should do to preserve **Yugoslavia.** The chief of staff, Col.-Gen. **Blagoje Adžić** , advocated a hard-line policy, set out in Ram-1. His political superior, Defense Minister Col.-Gen. **Veljko Kadijević**, on the other hand, was more cautious, insisting upon the course of action that was finally implemented— namely, a limited military operation to secure Yugoslavia's main international border-crossing points and customs facilities, Ljubljana's Brnik airport, and a number of other strategic objectives. This strategy seemed to imply that Kadijević and the federal government in Belgrade thought that a show of force would be enough to intimidate the Slovenian government into backing down. This fatal miscalculation resulted in the JNA's defeat in Slovenia and its forced withdrawal in humiliating circumstances. Ironically, it was the JNA's intervention in Slovenia that finally convinced the international community that the country's bid for independent statehood was worthy of diplomatic **recognition** by January 1992.

Using only 2,000 of its troops in Slovenia, the JNA Ljubljana Army Corps headquarters launched what later became known as the Ten Day War on the day following Slovenia's 26 June 1991 declaration of independence. It employed long, slow, and exposed convoys of tanks and other vehicles, raw conscripts who had been told they were about to stop a foreign invasion of Slovenia, and seemingly uncoordinated air attacks by the air force. This approach made it easy for Janša's STDF to intercept, isolate, and then destroy most of the federal forces. The main JNA forces not committed to battle during the Ten Day War were easily trapped in largely urban-based garrisons, ruling out any possibility of their use to help trapped convoys then on the road. Using territorial defense principles and modern portable antitank and air defense armaments, the flexible and highly mobile STDF stopped the JNA in its tracks after only a few days of fighting.

Dramatic **media** images of the Ten Day War, widely interpreted as a "David and Goliath" struggle, quickly changed the attitudes of the international community toward Slovenia and, hence, what remained of the Yugoslav federation. Within the **European Union** (EU), this media triumph by the Slovenes forced a period of intense peacemaking diplomacy, culminating in the **Brioni Accord** of July, which formally ended hostilities and stipulated that all JNA forces should leave Slovenia. To add to the problems of the departing JNA, Janša's STDF refused to allow the JNA to evacuate much of its heavy weaponry and equipment, which was later either deployed locally or sold to other former Yugoslav republics.

The JNA in Slovenia had been shown to be far from invincible—indeed, ineffective and poorly led. Had Kadijević chosen to use all the firepower at his disposal, things might have turned out very differently for the STDF. In his memoirs Kadijević acknowledges that Adžić 's Ram-1 option was available to him but that he decided not to use it for fear of the large civilian casualties and international uproar that these would have entailed. On the Slovene side, there was always an acute realization that entering into a war with the JNA was a considerable gamble, although the risks involved were carefully evaluated and judged to be worth taking—a view cogently expressed in Janša's book on the war.

Although freed of the JNA and independent of the Yugoslav federation (in fact as well as in word) in 1991, Slovenia was far from fully secure as the war unfolded close to its borders in **Croatia** and then in **Bosnia-Hercegovina**. For this reason, the SA has continued to modernize, necessitating relatively high defense expenditures in a country where such outlays have traditionally been unpopular. Janša's ambitions and his enmity toward the neocommunist Kučan were also to embroil the army in controversies of various sorts. The reported sale of SA military materials to the **Muslim** (Bošnjak) side in the Bosnian war, involving both Kučan and Janša, led to a major political scandal, culminating in the forced resignation of Janša as defence minister in 1993, although Kučan himself emerged unscathed from the affair.

The two main objectives of Slovenian foreign policy during the 1990s have been to secure full membership in both the **North Atlantic Treaty Organization** (NATO) and the EU. In March 1994, Slovenia became the first of the former Yugoslav republics to be admitted into the Atlantic alliance's "Partnership for Peace" program, subsequently providing SA troops for joint exercises with NATO forces and participating in NATO operations in Bosnia and **Albania**. Although full EU membership is increasingly probable for Slovenia by around 2000, full NATO membership is some way off, mainly because of a veto by the **United States** against Slovenian membership. The United States has justified this stance on the grounds of cost and the incompatibility and inferiority of the SA with respect to NATO norms; this viewpoint has been opposed by a number of EU states. Given its military weaknesses, Slovenia will have to increase its spending on modernization if it is ever to be admitted into NATO, where it is now regarded as being of little strategic importance.

A mainly conscript force with a small cadre of professionals, the active SA consisted in 1996–1997 of 8,000 troops, plus 70,000 reservists, deployed over 7 military districts divided into 27 regions. The active SA consisted of 7 infantry brigades, 1 surface-to-air missile (SAM) brigade, 1 helicopter brigade, and 3 independent mechanized brigades. Under wartime mobilization, the reserve would also contribute 1 special forces brigade, 2 independent mechanized brigades, 1 artillery battalion, 1 coastal defense detachment, and 1 antitank detachment. Wartime mobilization would place Slovenia's 5,000-strong paramilitary police forces under military command.

In 1996–1997, the SA ground forces inventory consisted of 30 main battle tanks; around 50 armored fighting vehicles; a larger number of artillery pieces, mortars, and air defense guns; 9 SA-9 SAMs; and various portable antitank and air defense missile systems. This inventory is being upgraded to give the SA more firepower and mechanized mobility. The greatest military weakness of the SA is the weakness of its air force, which in 1996–1997 consisted of 2 armed helicopters, 4 fixed-wing training aircraft, and 50 Strela SAMs. Based at **Koper**, the SA navy consisted of only 2 coastal defense craft. Without an air force or navy, the SA is incapable of properly defending Slovenia's airspace and contested territorial waters, notably in relation to Croatia's growing military power. Although the costs of acquiring such air and naval power would be very high and politically controversial, Slovenia seems set on doing just that, partly to meet the preconditions for future NATO membership.

—*M. M.*

References: Janša, Janez. *The Making of the Slovenian State, 1988–1992: The Collapse of Yugoslavia.* Ljubljana: Mladinska knjiga, 1994.

SMITH, RUPERT

Lt.-Gen. Sir Rupert Smith, commander of the United Nations Protection Force in Yugoslavia (UNPROFOR) in Bosnia-Hercegovina in 1995. (Army Public Relations, London)

Lt.-Gen. Sir Rupert Smith (born 1943) was the British soldier appointed to succeed Sir **Michael Rose** as commander of the United Nations Protection Force (**UNPROFOR**) in Bosnia in 1995. His was the last such appointment before UNPROFOR handed over operations to the **North Atlantic Treaty Organization** (NATO) in December of that year. This transfer could be said to have been indirectly influenced by Smith's term of command. By no means a figure who sought publicity, Smith nevertheless from the start possessed the determination to act upon his realization that, in the circumstances at hand, UNPROFOR could no longer retain its solely peacekeeping role via either evenhandedness or appeasement; instead, UNPROFOR was now in the business of peace enforcement. Like his predecessors he was faced with **Bosnian Serb** refusal to comply with return of heavy weaponry to United Nations (UN) supervision; he also encountered the fall and massacre of a protected enclave—**Srebrenica**—on 11 July 1995, as well as a further attack on a marketplace in **Sarajevo** (this time killing 37 civilians). Although he had inherited a seeming **cease-fire**, it was only seasonal; notwithstanding his expectation that force would result in **hostage taking** of peacekeepers, he ordered airstrikes by NATO in May and the destruction of a Bosnian Serb arsenal close to their headquarters at **Pale**. The United Nations' civilian response through **Yasushi Akashi** was a demand that there be an immediate return to UNPROFOR's peacekeeping role, but Smith—by now supported by the Franco-British **Rapid Reaction Force** of 12,000—was in a strong position to either confront the Serbs or evacuate safely. In any event the Serb attack on Srebrenica and its immediate aftermath heralded the end of international opposition to peace enforcement, which effectively gave Rupert Smith and his NATO counterpart, Adm. Leighton Smith, the authority to react to any new event. This they did in August 1995 following the Serb attack on the marketplace in Sarajevo; without reference to the overall authority of French general **Bernard Janvier**, Smith and Smith launched a combined territorial and aerial attack on Bosnian Serb positions that lasted two months. This combined attack exposed the divisions within the UN between its official establishment personnel at New York headquarters, who were appalled at the risks, and the UN representatives (both military and civilian) in Bosnia, who were largely supportive. The Bosnian Serbs, for whom this action effectively marked the end of their ability to dictate matters, themselves hinted at a certain respect for Rupert Smith; his status among the

Bosnian people and their government (who offered him honorary citizenship at the end of his term in December 1995) approached that of national hero.

Rupert Smith will remain a controversial figure in the annals of the Bosnian conflict, but it could be said that, without taking sides (in the moral sense of the phrase), he used decisive means to achieve an end that forced the Bosnian Serbs back to the negotiating table with the Bosnian government and the Croatian forces, no longer as Bosnian Serbs in their own right but through the Serbian Presidency. Thus, he indirectly paved the way toward the **Dayton Agreements** in December 1995 and a more lasting period of relative peace.

—*J. J. H.*

SOCIAL CHARACTER

The theory of social character is one of the forms taken by that view of the **Balkans** that sees the region as divided by a permanent "**cultural fault line**." This approach is associated with the work of Croatian-American anthropologist Dinko Tomašić (*Personality and Culture in Eastern European Politics,* Stewart, New York, 1948). Tomašić argued that there are continuities in society and politics in Eastern European societies; these continuities extend across the period of the rise of communism and are rooted in the "dominant personality types" of the region. He identifies two major types of social character, rooted in quite different forms of ecology and family organization. The first of these he calls the "*zadruga* type" (after the Serbo-Croat name for a type of extended family found in the region). This type is associated with the farming folk of the plains and is to be contrasted with the "dinaric type," which derives from the culture of the seminomadic pastoralists who invaded Europe during the early Middle Ages.

Tomašić's theory states that different types of ecology (settled agriculture and pastoralism) give rise to quite different forms of family organization, and that these in turn make for contrasting types of dominant personality (or social character). Among the *zadruga* farmers, "the wide diffusion of political power, personal freedom and economic security, combined with exposure to happy family life and mild discipline, favoured an optimistic, peaceful, just and well-ordered conception of the world, an emotionally well-balanced, nonviolent and power-indifferent personality." The dinaric warrior-herdsmen, on the other hand, are characterized by "insecurity of life and property, despotic local and state organization, exposure to hostile and arbitrary family backgrounds, and to family discipline constantly alternating between the extremes of harshness and indulgence." These conditions favor "an emotionally unbalanced, violent, rebellious and power-seeking personality, together with tense interpersonal and cultural relationships, and extreme political instability." The history of the Balkans is seen as a succession of episodes in which the "dinaric" mountaineers descend upon the plains and seize power. The rise of communist elites after World War II was interpreted in these terms.

Tomašić's ideas have been taken up recently by another Croat émigré to the United States, Stjepan Meštrović, who uses them in order to provide an interpretation of the reasons for the disintegration of **Yugoslavia**. This version of history has come to command growing interest among Croatian intellectuals. Although it has some superficial attractions for Croatian nationalists (who see the Serb inhabitants of the former **Krajina** as modern instances of the dinaric warrior-herdsman), this use of Tomašić breaks down in the face of the evidence. As with other versions of the "cultural fault line" explanations for the breakup of Yugoslavia, the attempt to apply Tomašić's theory of social character is of interest principally as an illustration of the way in which the parties to the Yugoslav conflict have come to represent their differences in terms of inescapable historical necessity.

—*J. B. A.*

See also: ethnicity; nationalism

SOCIAL POLICY

The failures of Yugoslav social policy belong high on the list of factors that have promoted the disintegration of Yugoslavia. Although explanations of the breakup of the country have tended to concentrate on the area of **ethnicity** and ethnic conflict, other factors deserve greater attention—in particular the **economic dimension** to events. Closely related is the inability of successive Yugoslav governments to grasp the significance of growing social and economic inequalities and their failure to devise and implement policy measures that could remedy the disruptive effects of social and economic deprivation.

Although Yugoslavia was a socialist country (and as such a good deal of outward deference was paid to the notion of equality among citizens), social policy operated in arbitrary and sometimes controversial ways to promote a sense of relative deprivation on the part of particular groups. Throughout most of the life of the Socialist Federation, for example, the self-employed (primarily individual cultivators but also artisans, traders, and increasingly those engaged in providing services) were excluded from social security. Whereas some people working in the private sector (especially following the liberalization of the law relating to private enterprise in 1989) were among the best-off members of the population, many others (especially in rural locations) were not only very poor but were kept outside the net of social security provision.

Access to a wide range of benefits in Yugoslavia before the collapse of the Socialist Federation could be had only through one's place of employment and participation in the system of **workers' self-management.** For example, collective provision through an enterprise was the avenue through which a large section of the population gained access to housing. Housing was in very short supply as a consequence of the rapidity of the urbanization process. Studies have indicated, however, that this scarce resource was made disproportionately available to managerial and professional workers and those with higher levels of skill. Those with positions in social-political organizations (especially functionaries of the **League of Communists**) were especially well provided for.

In comparison with other industrialized countries with developed "welfare state" systems, there were important gaps in Yugoslav provision. The attention of health professionals was free to all, but it was necessary to pay for medicines. Not all of the costs of education (especially higher education) were met by the public purse.

Fiscal policies tended to be regressive in their effects. Individual incomes were not generally taxed, as public revenues were drawn from employing enterprises rather than as deductions from personal wages or salaries. The recovery of income tax from the small section of the better off who qualified to pay income tax was inefficient and incomplete. On the other hand, the largest source of public income was through sales taxes, which applied equally across the board and proportionally bore more heavily on the poorer citizens.

A study of the pattern of social transfers in 1988 concluded, "The distribution of social transfers among social groups is more unequal than the distribution of original revenue." In other words, social policy actually operated in former Yugoslavia to augment rather than diminish the degree of social disadvantage. What is more, inequalities of provision and access tended to accumulate systematically to the disadvantage of the rural population. The same study also concluded that "social transfers are oriented towards the urban population, and the more one moves from urban to rural the less important they become."

Two things follow from this consideration of the limitations of Yugoslav social policy. It is important to recognize the weight of resentment and economic insecurity that had accumulated across the federation by the end of the 1980s. It was possible for demagogic politicians to exploit this situation, finding particularly in other republics and other ethnic groups those who could be held to blame for deprivation and distress. Furthermore, the operation of social policy in deepening **rural-urban differences** was reflected in the tendency of rural areas to give electoral support to nationalist parties. The most vigorous support for the **Croatian Democratic Union**, for example, is found in the "backwoods" of the Croatian Zagorje and in **Herceg-Bosna.** Similarly, economic deprivation has a great deal to do with the rise and continuing strength of the Internal Macedonian Revolutionary Organisation in **Macedonia.**

—*J. B. A.*

See also: political parties

SOCIALIST PARTY OF SERBIA

The Socialist Party of Serbia (SPS) was the successor to the former League of Communists of Serbia (Savez komunista Srbije—SKS) and the league's main political front organization, the Socialist Alliance of the Working People of Serbia (SAWPS). It was founded in its current form on 16–17 July 1990 to contest Serbia's first postwar multiparty parliamentary **elections** in December of the same year. The SPS thereafter remained in power in **Serbia** and the Federal Republic of **Yugoslavia** (FRY) throughout the 1990s. A neocommunist political organization representing the old SKS nomenklatura (a list of names from which posts under a communist system could only be filled) and presiding over a de facto one-party state, the SPS also initially espoused Serb nationalism under the leadership of **Slobodan Milošević**. More recently, however, the SPS has reverted to its SKS roots—namely, a rehabilitated **Titoism**. Since 1994, it has thus closely allied itself with the Yugoslav United Left (JUL), a coalition of left-wing organizations led by Milošević's spouse, **Mirjana Marković**.

Effectively organized and financed throughout **Serbia**, where it has also always exercised a tight control over the **media**, the SPS is thought to have had a membership of around 400,000–500,000 during the 1990s. Genuinely popular just prior to the elections in December 1990, the SPS gained 194 of the 250 seats. In **Belgrade**, however, the SPS was much less popular. In March 1991, Milošević's party was confronted with major and violent antigovernment demonstrations. Its main electoral constituencies have been **rural** and provincial Serbia. During the elections for new federal and Serbian assemblies in December 1992, the SPS suffered a decline in its electoral support, gaining 47 of the 138 seats in the federal assembly; in the all-important Serbian assembly, only 101 of the 250 seats then went to the SPS, and as a result the party was forced into a brief coalition with the ultranationalist Serbian Radical Party (SRS), led by **Vojislav Šešelj**. In the concomitant poll for the Serbian presidency, Milošević gained 56 percent of the votes cast, compared to 34 percent for **Milan Panić**. One year later, in December 1993, a snap poll for a new Serbian assembly gave the SPS 123 seats, with 37 percent of votes cast. Always accused of blatant electoral malpractice by the opposition parties, the SPS claimed to have won federal and local elections in November 1996, but these results were widely contested in Serbia and internationally. In December 1997, the elections for the new Serbian assembly resulted in the SPS, even together with the JUL and New Democracy, gaining only 110 of the 250 seats and thereby becoming a minority government.

Under Milošević's controversial leadership, the SKS and then the SPS partially relegitimated decaying Communist power through an alliance of convenience with Serb nationalism during the late 1980s and early 1990s. In so doing, Milošević precipitated the end of the **League of Communists of Yugoslavia** (SKJ) in January 1990 and then the Yugoslav federation itself in 1991. Within Serbia and the FRY, the SPS thereafter retained an effective hold on power as a result of its espousal of Serb nationalism, the weaknesses of the opposition, economic collapse, tightly controlled media, and the power of the police, although the party's electoral support has steadily declined. Essentially opportunistic, Milošević and the SPS abandoned nationalism by 1994, by which time it was clear that the earlier pursuit of a "**Greater Serbia**" had come to nothing. Thereafter, the SPS-JUL alliance went for a rehabilitated Titoism, with Milošević presenting himself internationally as a regional peacemaker. Following the effective end of the Croatian and Bosnian civil wars in 1995, Milošević and the SPS made much of the partial international rehabilitation of the FRY in 1996. Fortified by international support, Milošević and the SPS thereafter expected to remain in power indefinitely, but the regime nevertheless began to fall apart.

—M. M.

ŠPEGELJ, MARTIN

Martin Špegelj was a senior general in the **Yugoslav Peoples' Army** (JNA), commanding the Fifth Army District (**Slovenia** and most of Croatia) before he retired. In April 1990 he criticized the JNA for disarming the Territorial Defense Force in Croatia. After the **Croatian Democratic Union** (HDZ) took power in May, he was given the post of defense minister. Špegelj spent the next year organizing Croat officers in the JNA who were to defect to the new national army when independence was declared; he also armed groups of Croat citizens. He began to smuggle arms into the country to reequip the newly recruited police reserves. Having secured recorded video and audio evidence of him discussing covert operations to secure arms (broadcast on Serbian television), the JNA attempted unsuccessfully to arrest him.

Špegelj argued that for Croatia to secede safely, the most effective military strategy would be to besiege JNA barracks in Croatia, cutting them off from their logistics bases and forcing them to capitulate, thereby delivering large amounts of weapons to the Croats. President **Franjo Tudjman** and the rest of the defense council rejected the plan, arguing that its political and diplomatic drawbacks were too large. Tudjman and Špegelj continued to disagree, with Špegelj considering that Tudjman was to blame for Croatia's lack of preparedness for war when it came. When the JNA attacked Slovenia and Tudjman reneged on his understanding with

Slovene president **Milan Kučan** that Croatia would support Slovenia, Špegelj resigned.

—G. R. B.

SPLIT

Croatia's second-largest city (population 267,000 as of the 1991 census), Split is a major seaport on the coast of **Dalmatia,** approximately 250 miles south of the capital, Zagreb. Split is an ancient city built on a peninsula around the ruins of the palace of Roman emperor Diocletian, who was born just inland in the capital of Roman Dalmatia, Salona (now Solin).

Split and its **communications** were first affected by the growing conflict between Serbs and Croats in October 1990 when the railway lines and roads were blocked around **Knin**, cutting off direct traffic to southern Dalmatia. The city was further isolated by the destruction of the vital road bridge at **Maslenica** in September 1991. On 15 September 1991, the Yugoslav navy began a blockade of Split, along with six other ports, during which the city was extensively damaged by bombardments.

—G. R. B.

See also: naval power

SPORTS

National expression through sports was a strong and unifying feature of identity in the former Yugoslavia. The successor states, particularly Croatia, have since exploited it just as fully.

Of those sports with the highest international profile, it has been soccer (in which the former Yugoslavia was for long regarded as of world class in skill) that has aroused the greatest expression. Indeed, shortly after the Croatian elections in May 1990, it was an incident during a Yugoslav league match between the two leading teams from Zagreb and Belgrade (Dinamo and Red Star) when a Croatian player made inciting gestures to the visiting Serb fans that caused unprecedented violence among spectators and became an early symbol of the wider conflict to come. The breakup of Yugoslavia led to an exodus of many top players to the rich teams of Western Europe; interestingly, two leading players (Davor Šuker from Croatia and Predrag Mijatović from Serbia) joined the same Spanish team, Real Madrid, and together helped the team win the Spanish championship in 1996. Sporting sanctions hampered several international careers until Croatia was admitted to the European Nations Cup in 1996 (where it reached the quarterfinals). The qualifying rounds for the World Cup in 1998 were opened to Slovenia, Croatia, Bosnia-Hercegovina, Macedonia, and the Republic of Yugoslavia, but the draw more than coincidentally placed the first three of these teams in the same qualifying group, from which only one team could progress. Croatia exceeded all expectations by achieving third place in the World Cup Finals held in France in 1998, beating the powerful German team in the quarterfinals. Croatian president Franjo Tudjman's attendance as a spectator at the last stage was an indication of the political capital which was to be made from this sporting success. An interesting sidelight in the context of the aftermath of the conflict when the Slovene magazine ***Mladina*** commissioned a public opinion poll following the earlier match between Germany and Yugoslavia: the poll showed that 31 percent of Slovene fans were supporting the German team, but 45 percent the Yugoslav team.

Tennis, too, has made an impact: the former number one women's player in the world, Monica Seleš from the Vojvodina, exchanged her Yugoslav nationality to become a citizen of the United States, and Goran Ivanišević and Iva Majoli from Croatia have reached the world's top four in the men's and women's rankings. Ivanišević has been the losing finalist at the Wimbledon championships three times in the last six years.

International sanctions excluded the Yugoslav nations from the Olympic Games of 1992 (only eight years after the Bosnian capital Sarajevo had itself hosted the Winter Olympics), but all were readmitted at Atlanta in 1996.

—J. J. H.

SPS

See **Socialist Party of Serbia**

SREBRENICA

Located close to the **Drina River** bordering Serbia in eastern Bosnia, Srebrenica was one of three Bosnian **Muslim** (Bošnjak) enclaves in a region otherwise controlled by Serbs from 1992 to 1995. A predominantly Bošnjak town before the war, Srebrenica (along with nearby **Žepa** and **Goražde**) was able to defend itself successfully when a Bosnian Serb blitzkrieg swept through eastern Bosnia in the spring of 1992. As a result of the "**ethnic cleansing**" of nearby territories, Srebrenica's prewar population of 37,000 increased to over 60,000. Besieged by the **Bosnian Serb Army** (BSA), the city was isolated from Bošnjak-controlled territories to the west, and **humanitarian aid** deliveries by the United Nations Protection Force (**UNPROFOR**) were irregular and entirely dependent on the cooperation of the Serbs.

Srebrenica's well-organized defenses, led by **Naser Orić**, resulted in a number of stunning victories against the BSA in late 1992 and early 1993. In order to avert a full-scale BSA attack, the UNPROFOR commander in Bosnia, Gen. **Philippe Morillon**, dramatically visited and promised to protect the enclave without the permission of his political superiors in March 1993.

The following month, Morillon's action prompted **United Nations** (UN) Security Council Resolution 819, which authorized the creation of the UN "**safe areas**." Subsequently one of six safe areas in **Bosnia-Hercegovina**, the Srebrenica enclave was never properly defended by UNPROFOR. Of the 34,000 troops requested for these six enclaves in Bosnia, only 7,600 were forthcoming, of which 750 Dutch troops were deployed at Srebrenica. Unable credibly to deter the BSA, these lightly armed troops were also powerless to enforce the demilitarization of the area and to disarm the 5,000 Bošnjak defenders. As a result, Orić's troops were used to raid nearby Serb territories, provoking counterattacks that could be used to the political advantage of the Bosnian government in Sarajevo.

Although of great political and symbolic significance, Srebrenica was in state of military stalemate from 1993 to 1995. In July 1995, at a time when the tide of war was beginning to turn against the Bosnian Serbs, local BSA forces under the command of Gen. **Ratko Mladić** attacked and overran the enclave. Immediately before the fall of the town, Orić and many of his troops were evacuated, giving credence to rumors that the enclave was "traded" for Serb-held suburbs in Sarajevo. Local UNPROFOR troops failed to stop the BSA offensive, largely because of a lack of support further up the UN chain of command. Despite Mladić's promises that no captured civilians or troops would be harmed if they surrendered, the BSA massacred around 7,000 people, notably on what became known as the "March of Death" toward **Tuzla**. This massacre made Srebrenica the worst single war crime of the entire Bosnian conflict and resulted in the indictment of Mladić as a war criminal by the International **War Crimes Tribunal** at The Hague in June 1996.

Looked at in relation to the wider progress of the war, Srebrenica now appears to have been part of a chaotic and cynical "endgame," wherein the town was sacrificed and left to a horrific fate both by its leaders in Sarajevo and by its supposed protectors from abroad. Since 1995 the Srebrenica story has been the subject of a number of books, foremost of which are the following: Jan-Willem Honig and Norbert Both, *Srebrenica: Record of a War Crime.* (London: Penguin, 1996) and David Rohde, *A Safe Area—Srebrenica: Europe's Worst Massacre since the Second World War* (London: Pilot, 1997).

—M. M.

STABILIZATION FORCE

See **Implementation/Stabilization Force**

STAMBOLIĆ, IVAN

Ivan Stambolić (born 1936) was president of the presidency of the **League of Communists** (LC) in **Serbia**, as well as a friend and patron of **Slobodan Milošević**. His deposition at the hands of his former protégé, however, signaled the start of major changes in Serbian politics in 1987.

Educated at the Faculty of Law in Belgrade, where he met and befriended Milošević, Stambolić made his career at first in industry and subsequently as a professional politician. He became a representative in the republic's assembly, a member of the central committee (CC) of the Serbian LC, and subsequently the LC's president. He was able to use his position to assist Milošević's career within the LC, both of them occupying the rather technocratic and undogmatic "liberal" wing of the party.

These interests and inclinations led him to underestimate the explosive political potential of the intensifying conflict between Serbs and **Albanians** in **Kosovo** during the 1980s. In the summer of 1987, Dragiša Pavlović, the head of the LC in Belgrade, was arraigned by the Serbian CC for allegedly disregarding the party line in relation to Kosovo by his public criticism of nationalistic articles that had been appearing in the Belgrade press. The move against him was reputedly engineered by Milošević. Matters came to a head on 26 September 1987, when, following a heated 20 hours of debate, the CC voted to strip Pavlović of his responsibilities. Stambolić misjudged the situation badly, and by apparently minimizing the seriousness of the issues, he antagonized the more nationalistically minded factions in the party, thus preparing the ground for his own political disgrace. He was compelled to resign his post on 15 December 1987.

Milošević, who replaced Pavlović, is regarded as having used the occasion as a means of judging the change of mood within the LC, and in Serbia more generally, as an opportunity to frame his own populist appeal in what was later known as the "antibureaucratic revolution." The occasion was also a means for Milošević to advance his own career by presenting himself as the "firm hand" needed to replace vagueness and vacillation.

Ironically, after retiring from politics, Stambolić moved into banking—the career that Milošević had previously followed.

—J. B. A.

STAR OF VERGINA
See **Vergina, Sun of**

STEPINAC, ALOJZIJE (1898–1960)
Born in Krašić, west of Zagreb, Alojzije Stepinac fought in World War I, joined the priesthood in 1924, and became archbishop of **Zagreb** in 1937. Stepinac was known for his extreme piety and believed that the Serbs should "return" to the Roman **Catholic Church**. Stepinac praised the creation of the Independent State of Croatia by the **Ustaša** in 1941 and appears to have been extremely naive in his understanding of the true nature of the regime that was taking power. His attitude toward the Ustaša and its leader, **Ante Pavelić**, has been the subject of strong emotions and political controversy ever since World War II; to a large extent, the reality of the case is less important than its symbolic effects. Stepinac appears to have realized sometime in early 1942 that the rumors of mass killings among the Serbs, Jews, and Gypsies (Roma) were true, and from then on he spoke out in sermons against these actions. He also maintained his approval of Ustaša measures against swearing and indecency, however, and would not break his links with the regime.

In 1945 **Tito** met Stepinac and attempted to persuade him to break with Rome and form a national Catholic Church loyal to the Communist regime. Always an anticommunist both in relation to the Soviet Union and the Yugoslav party, Stepinac refused. Tito then had Stepinac tried for his alleged responsibility in the mass forced conversions of Serbs during the war, as well as for his links to the Ustaša. Stepinac was found guilty as a war criminal in 1946 and sentenced to 16 years of hard labor. He served five years in solitary confinement, after which he was exiled to his home village. Stepinac was elevated to the rank of cardinal in 1952 in recognition of his services to the Catholic Church. He died in 1960 and was buried in Zagreb Cathedral behind the altar. His grave then became a shrine for Croatian Catholics as well as nationalists. Stepinac posthumously became controversial once more in the 1980s, when Pope John Paul II refused to visit Yugoslavia unless he were allowed to pray publicly at Stepinac's tomb.

—G. R. B.

References: Alexander, Stella. *The Triple Myth: A Life of Archbishop Alojzije Stepinac.* Boulder, CO: East European Monographs (dist. by Columbia University Press), 1987.

STEWART, BOB
Lt. Col. Bob Stewart, DSO (Distinguished Service Order), was appointed commander of the First Battalion, the Cheshire Regiment, in 1991. After service in Northern Ireland, he transferred with his regiment to Bosnia for a tour of **humanitarian** duty for the United Nations (UN) from October 1992 to April 1993. His activities in central Bosnia, particularly **Gornji Vakuf** and **Vitez,** including his discovery of the **Ahmići** massacre, are the subject of his book *Broken Lives: A Personal View of the Bosnian Conflict* (London: HarperCollins, 1993).

—J. J. H.

STOLTENBERG, THORVALD
Born in Norway in 1931, Thorvald Stoltenberg is a politician and diplomat whose career has embraced ministerial service at home and ambassadorial service abroad. His first contact with Yugoslavia was as a member of the Norwegian Foreign Service in Belgrade from 1961 to 1964; he was minister of foreign affairs for two periods between 1987 and 1993, in between which he spent two years as ambassador to the United States. He also headed the Norwegian team that had some success in brokering a deal for peace in the Middle East in 1993.

Following the resignation of **Cyrus Vance**, Stoltenberg was appointed by the secretary-general of the United Nations (UN) as special envoy to the former Yugoslavia in 1993 (he had formerly served as UN high commissioner for refugees) and thus became the cochair of the **International Conference on the Former Yugoslavia** (ICFY) with his **European Union** counterpart **David Owen.** He was involved in all the negotiated developments concerning **Bosnia-Hercegovina** over the next two years, including, with Owen, the meetings on the British aircraft carrier HMS *Invincible;* on this ship, in the wake of the demise of the Vance-Owen Plan, Owen and Stoltenberg mediated the Serbian proposal for a "Union of Three Republics" (Serb, Muslim, and Croat), which would have allowed the Serbs a virtually contiguous area for their republic in a union of Bosnia-Hercegovina. This plan is unofficially and somewhat inaccurately referred to as the Owen-Stoltenberg Plan. Stoltenberg held the special envoy post until 1996.

—*J. J. H.*

STRATEGIC BALANCE

By the end of the Yugoslav wars in 1995, the regional strategic balance of military, political, and economic power was very different than what it had been when the former **Yugoslavia** collapsed in 1991. The main change in this balance has been the decline of the Serb position in relation to that of the Croats and Bosnian **Muslims** (Bošnjaks). At the beginning of the conflict in 1991–1992, **Serbia,** its Croatian Serb and **Bosnian Serb** proxies, and the effectively Serb-controlled **Yugoslav Peoples' Army** (JNA) were in a position of clear military superiority over their declared enemies in the former Yugoslavia. This military advantage was indirectly aided by the imposition of the **United Nations** (UN) arms embargo against the whole of the former Yugoslavia in October 1991. During the first Serbo-Croat war in **Croatia** in 1991, the Zagreb government had only a weak national guard to defend its contested independence. The government of **Bosnia-Hercegovina** lacked any recognizable military force when civil war began in Bosnia in April 1992. Only in **Slovenia,** where the Yugoslav wars began in the summer of 1991, was a credible military force—the **Slovenian Army** (SA)—deployed against the JNA.

Using superior JNA firepower and **paramilitary/irregular** proxy forces, Serbia was able to seize around 30 percent of the territory of Croatia by the end of 1991, followed by around 70 percent of the territory of Bosnia-Hercegovina by the summer of 1992, creating a large Serbian sphere of influence, or a "**Greater Serbia.**" In the case of Slovenia, however, the lack of a significant ethnic Serb minority meant that the Ten Day War fought between the SA and the JNA in the summer of 1991 was of greater significance politically than militarily. Hampered by internal divisions and a Serb willingness to see Slovenia go, the JNA was defeated and humiliated in

Powerful NATO military forces played a decisive role in ending the Bosnian war in 1995 and guaranteeing its post-Dayton peace thereafter. (Army Public Relations, London)

Slovenia. The primary strategic lesson of the conflict in Slovenia was that, notwithstanding superior firepower, the poorly led and demoralized JNA could be defeated if confronted by an effective opponent. In Croatia, and even more so in Bosnia, on the other hand, the JNA and its local proxies in 1991–1992 did not face any such opponents.

The widespread reluctance in the West to intervene militarily during the early stages of the Yugoslav wars meant that the myth of Serb military invincibility was given an unjustified credence for essentially political reasons. The Serb military position in the former Yugoslavia, and Bosnia in particular, was aided by such attitudes, by the lack of military preparedness among the Croats and Bošnjaks, and by the brief **civil war** between the **Bosnian Croats** and the Bošnjaks in 1993. First deployed in Croatia and then Bosnia, the UN Protection Force (**UNPROFOR**) also indirectly strengthened the Serb position by effectively freezing the front lines created by the earlier, largely unopposed Serb blitzkrieg.

The dominant position of the Serbs began to unravel almost at the same time as it reached its peak in 1992. The UN imposed draconian economic **sanctions** against Serbia and **Montenegro** for their role in the Bosnian war in May 1992. One of the results of this major setback for the Serbs was the split between the Bosnian Serbs and Serbian president **Slobodan Milošević** in 1993–1994. Widening splits in the Serb camp took place just as the covert external supply of **arms** to the **Croatian Army** (HV), the **Croatian Council of Defense** (HVO), and the **Bosnian army** (Army of the Republic of Bosnia-Hercegovina—ARBH) made these military forces far stronger than they had previously been. No less significantly, in both the political and military spheres, the creation of the **United States**–sponsored **Muslim-Croat Federation** in Bosnia in 1994 fundamentally changed the strategic balance in the former Yugoslavia. Increased determination on the part of the **North Atlantic Treaty Organization** (NATO) to curb the Bosnian Serbs in 1994–1995 also led to a serious weakening of the Serb position in 1995. By then internally divided, economically exhausted, and internationally isolated, the Serbs experienced a series of major military defeats in 1995, beginning with the loss of virtually all the Croatian territories seized in 1991 and ending with the reduction of the Bosnian Serb entity to less than 50 percent of the territory of Bosnia-Hercegovina.

This new strategic balance in the region was confirmed by the **Dayton Agreements** in December 1995. Post-Dayton, the decay of Serbian military, political, and economic power has continued unabated. Meanwhile, Croatia has become the major new regional force under U.S. auspices.

—*M. M.*

STUDENT ACTION

Although student action was initially significant in parts of the former Yugoslavia, the longer-term political impact of such action in the region has been fairly marginal during the 1990s. In line with the rest of Europe, Yugoslavia experienced a major student revolt in 1968. Students were also prominent in the Croatian mass nationalist movement known as *maspok* (the **Croatian Spring**) in 1970–1971. With the decay of Communist power during the 1980s, student movements in favor of greater democratization and openness emerged in a number of Yugoslav republics. Foremost of these was **Slovenia**, where some of the activists of 1968 reentered political life. Younger student journalists then played a major role in the influential Slovene magazine ***Mladina.***

Although later often subsumed in nationalist drives for independence in Slovenia and Croatia, distinctive student involvement in **peace movements** continued when the Yugoslav crisis descended into civil war in 1991. These movements became particularly significant in **Croatia**, **Bosnia-Hercegovina**, and **Serbia**, although their ultimate political impact was to prove limited owing to the fact that their members were largely limited to the urban middle classes in cities like **Belgrade**, **Sarajevo**, and **Zagreb**. In the case of Serbia, student action against the drift toward war and in favor of democratic alternatives to nationalism was particularly strong in Belgrade, where major antigovernment demonstrations involving students took place in March 1991. During the first Serb-Croat war in Croatia later in 1991, organized draft dodging against conscription into the **Yugoslav Peoples' Army** (JNA) became endemic; large numbers of university students and other young people subsequently fled to Western Europe. In Croatia, student action in favor of more open **media** did not become significant politically until later in the 1990s. In both republics, however, student action and dissent were regarded as treason by the republics' ruling parties.

In 1996–1997, large antigovernment demonstrations in which students were prominent took place in both Serbia and Croatia. On a more negative note, the political fragmentation of the former Yugoslavia during the 1990s inevitably had an adverse effect upon the ability of students to act in a coordinated manner in the region. In Bosnia-Hercegovina, the most "Yugoslav" of the former Yugoslav republics, alternative student movements also campaigned for peace and against local ethnic divisions, although their impact was limited and essentially confined to Sarajevo and **Tuzla.**

—M. M.

SUN OF VERGINA
See **Vergina, Sun of**

ŠUŠAK, GOJKO (1945–1998)
Gojko Šušak acted as minister for the émigré community in the first postindependence Croatian government and, after the resignation of **Martin Špegelj,** became minister of defense.

Born in 1945 at Široki Brijeg in Hercegovina, Šušak emigrated to Canada and began to work with telecommunications and computers, subsequently making money in the pizza business. He became an influential figure among the Croat community in Canada, and he played an important part in the financing of the **Croatian Democratic Union** (HDZ) in the party's early period. It is reported that he was involved in covert acquisitions of arms for Croatia during 1990 and 1991, funding these acquisitions with some of his own wealth.

In April 1991 Šušak apparently forced **Josip Reihl-Kir,** a moderate chief of police in **Slavonia,** to guide him and others to the outskirts of **Borovo Selo,** where three shoulder-launched rockets were fired at the town. There were no casualties, and one rocket that failed to explode was taken by Interior Minister Petar Gračanin to the federal presidency, where Gračanin confronted **Stipe Mesić** with the evidence of a Croatian attack against Serbs.

Šušak was known as an influential member of the "Hercegovina Lobby," who were instrumental in the support of the **Herceg-Bosna** ministate.

He died of cancer in May 1998.

—G. R. B.

ŠUŠTAR, ALOJZIJ
Although the profile of the **Catholic Church** in **Slovenia** in relation to the independence movement was not as pronounced as its counterpart in Croatia, the role of Archbishop Alojzij Šuštar was significant. Born in 1920, Šuštar spent nearly 40 years abroad, initially in Italy and mostly in Switzerland, combining an academic career in philosophy and theology with pastoral work and high ecclesiastical office. In 1977 he returned to his native Slovenia, becoming archbishop of **Ljubljana** and Slovene Metropolitan (a position between archbishop and patriarch) in 1980. Because his moderate approach to the integration of the church into the political fabric of Slovene society was highly successful when Slovenia was part of Yugoslavia, his influence as an archbishop was significant in the formation of the new independent Slovenia a decade later.

—J. J. H.

SYMBOLS
See **Chetniks; Ustaša**

T

TADIĆ, DUŠAN

Dušan Tadič (born 1955) is a **Bosnian Serb** from the **Prijedor** region. A former café owner and police reservist, he joined the Bosnian Serb militia in northwestern Bosnia in 1992. He underwent the first full trial by the International **War Crimes Tribunal** at The Hague in 1997 on charges of various atrocities, including murder and **rape** of Bosnian **Muslims** in **detention camps**, particularly Omarska, in the summer of 1992. On 7 May 1997, he was convicted on 11 of 31 charges but only under the general headings of persecution and crimes against humanity. A combination of lack of physical evidence and conflicting testimonies of over 100 witnesses restricted the court's specificity of judgment, as did the dispute surrounding the definition of the Bosnian war as "international" under the Geneva Conventions. On 14 July Tadič was sentenced to 20 years imprisonment.

—*J. J. H.*

See also: Erdemović, Dražen

TEN DAY WAR

See **Slovenian Army**

TERRAIN AS A MILITARY FACTOR

Covering 255,804 square kilometers in southeastern Europe, the former Yugoslavia's varied terrain has figured prominently as a military factor in the region's recent wars. The wars of the 1990s have directly or indirectly impinged upon the security of the seven neighboring states with which Yugoslavia shared international **borders**.

In the case of Slovenia, **Italy** and **Austria** were closely affected by the fighting, given that the conflict took place largely over a number of international border-crossing points and the roads leading to them. During the Ten Day War, **Slovenia**'s small size and largely moutainous terrain were major factors in the quick defeat of the **Yugoslav Peoples' Army** (JNA) by the **Slovenian Army** (SA).

Croatia's crescent-shaped territory was difficult to defend against JNA and local rebel Serb attacks during the first Serb-Croat war of 1991. Aimed at truncating and partitioning Croatia, Serb military strategy was aided by the republic's odd shape and varied terrain. In the self-declared **Serb Republic of the Krajina**, centered on the Dinaric Mountains of northern **Dalmatia**, the natural defenses were not overrun until 1995. In southern Dalmatia, Serb control of the mountainous hinterland still poses a potential threat to Zagreb's control of this isolated area of Croatia. The Serbs easily seized part of the Danubian plain to the north, as well as large areas of western and eastern Slavonia, in 1991. Here the flat lands aided conventional military operations by the JNA. The **Croatian Army** quickly retook western Slavonia in May 1995 for similar reasons.

The central geopolitical position and complicated **ethnic** mix in **Bosnia-Hercegovina** made the region the focus of the imperialist ambitions of both **Serbia** and Croatia when the area descended into war in 1992. Dominated by mountainous terrain and bounded by two major rivers to the north (**Sava**) and east (**Drina**), with the **Neretva River** dividing **Hercegovina** to the south, Bosnia-Hercegovina became a three-way battleground in which the main military factors on the ground were basically struggles for the control of valleys with their **communications and transport** routes, as well as for surrounding mountain- and river-crossing points.

Terrain more or less decided the type of war that could be fought: one of prolonged **sieges** of cities, attrition rather than rapid battles based on movement, and unconventional warfare using terrorist

Bosnia's mountainous terrain, river valleys, and associated transportation routes largely determined the course of the war. (Tanjug)

paramilitaries to promote "**ethnic cleansing**." In the case of **Sarajevo**, the Bosnian capital, the **Bosnian Serbs** controlled the surrounding mountains, of which the most strategically important was **Mount Igman**. Similar sieges took place at **Mostar**, **Tuzla**, and **Bihać**.

The decisive factor ending the Bosnian war in 1995, however, was not the character of the ground; rather, it was the use of sustained **air power** by the **North Atlantic Treaty Organization** (NATO) against the Bosnian Serbs—notwithstanding the operational difficulties arising out of Bosnia's mountainous terrain and its difficult weather conditions.

During the negotiations that preceded the **Dayton Agreements** in late 1995, the **United States** used sophisticated computer-generated terrain-mapping techniques to help secure a final agreement on the key issue of territory. These techniques demonstrated the viability or nonviability of different versions of the "Inter-Entity Border Line."

—*M. M.*

TERRITORIAL WATERS

See **Koper (Bay of Piran); Neum; Prevlaka**

TETOVO

The city of Tetovo (population 51,000 as of the 1991 census) is located in the Vardar Valley 20 miles west of **Skopje**. With more than 70 percent of its population of **Albanian** ethnicity (the highest proportion of any municipality in the Republic of **Macedonia**), Tetovo has become an informal capital of the predominantly Albanian region, which extends in an arc across western Macedonia from Skopje to Ohrid. It is the center of the more radically nationalistic wing of Albanian politics, represented by the National Democratic Party.

In the early 1990s, Albanians in the republic expressed growing impatience with the response of the Macedonian government to demands for equal representation of the Albanian **language** in the education system. As a consequence, on 17 December 1994, an attempt was made at Mala Rečica (a village near Tetovo) to launch an independent, Albanian-language university. At first suppressed violently, the new university was opened on 15 February 1995 and was subsequently tolerated by the authorities in spite of their unwillingness to grant the institution legal status. The suppression of the former Albanian-language facilities at the University of **Priština** by the Serbian government, at the time of the abrogation of **Kosovo**'s status as an autonomous province, deprived Macedonian Albanians of an important opportunity for higher study in their own language. The Macedonian government has been torn between (1) a sense of the importance of insisting upon the primacy of the Macedonian language and (2) a concern that Albanians forced to seek higher education elsewhere might be weakened still further in their attachment to the Macedonian state. Tetovo has consequently continued to be the focus of concern that ethnic tension could draw Macedonia into a wider Balkan conflict should the troubled issue of Albanian political autonomy in **Serbia** develop into armed conflict.

—J. B. A.

THESSALONIKI

Thessaloniki is the second-largest city in **Greece** (population 378,000 in 1991), a meeting point for different peoples and civilizations, and an old Balkan metropolis built on a key geographical location. Its value as an international port has placed it at the center of attention in relation to the future of **Macedonia** during the Yugoslav crisis.

Throughout the centuries the city has been a melting pot of contrasting ideas and cultures. Founded by Cassandros (the brother-in-law of Alexander the Great) in 316 B.C., it has always been a city of vital interest for the entire Balkan Peninsula; it has had a significant meaning for the Slavs of the region as well as for Greeks. The Slavs first appeared in the Balkans in the sixth century and gave to the city the name Solun (Salt). In other words, Thessaloniki was for the South Slavs the "city of salt," a substance that symbolized civilization. The brothers Cyril and Methodius, who preached in the Slav vernacular and brought Christianity to the Slavs, came from Thessaloniki.

The city's position was exalted when, in the ninth century, Antioch and Alexandria both fell to the Arabs; Thessaloniki became the second-most important city in the eastern Byzantine empire. Although it fell to the **Ottoman** armies in the fourteenth century, Thessaloniki remained a major center of administration, and its location at the mouth of the Axios/Vardar ensured its supremacy as a trading outlet for the entire peninsula. Following the trade war between Austria and Serbia in 1906, the port became an objective of Serb expansionist ambitions into Macedonia. A primary reason for continuing Greek opposition to the creation of a Slav state of "Macedonia" has been concern that this process might become the first step in the revival of that hope.

—N. M. G. and J. B. A.

See also: Greater Serbia

TITO, JOSIP BROZ (1892–1980)

Josip Broz, known generally by the Communist Party code name "Tito," which he adopted during World War II, was president of **Yugoslavia** between 1945 and 1980. Under his leadership, the distinctive combination of the system of "**workers' self-management**," a foreign policy stance based upon nonalignment, and the complex balance of nations and nationalities in the federation came to be known as **Titoism**.

Tito was born to mixed Croat-Slovene parents in the village of Kumrovec. Following a period as an engineering worker, he joined the Austro-Hungarian (**Habsburg**) army. In 1915 he was captured in Russia, where he joined the Communist Party. Returning to the newly unified Kingdom of Serbs, Croats, and Slovenes in 1920, he took a variety of manual labor jobs, becoming secretary of the Metal Workers' Union of Croatia in 1927. Arrested in 1928 for his activity in the illegal Communist Party of Yugoslavia (CPY), he was sentenced to five years' imprisonment. He was freed in 1934 and shortly afterward was co-opted by the Comintern to work for its Balkan secretariat in Moscow. In 1937–1938 he took over as secretary of the Yugoslav party with the remit of reviving a small, fragmented, and demoralized organization; by 1941 he had built the party up to 8,000 members. He was aided in this effort by a core of committed and able comrades, including **Milovan Djilas**, Edvard Kardelj, Moše Pijade, and Aleksandar Ranković. Following the Axis invasion of Yugoslavia in April 1941, the CPY found itself embarrassed by the Soviet Union's indecision as to whether the partitioning of Yugoslavia was acceptable. When Hitler threw aside his alliance with the Soviets and invaded Russia in June 1941, however, the CPY launched itself upon the path of insurgency.

In the struggle that followed, three broad strands were intertwined. Insurgent forces were pitted against the invaders—the former Yugoslavia was divided between German and Italian military zones of responsibility, within which some areas were occupied by Bulgarian or Hungarian troops. The division of Yugoslavia into puppet states meant that each of these states organized local defense forces. Furthermore, the Communist **Partizans** were not the only resistance movement in the field. The partizans also faced units of the royalist army, led by Col. Draža Mihailović and known as **Chetniks.** This internecine struggle is estimated to have killed more Yugoslavs than the fight against the Axis. Finally, although the CPY set out to create a broad popular uprising (a "national liberation struggle"), it also hoped to steer this movement eventually toward a socialist revolution.

In this extraordinarily difficult set of circumstances, Tito managed to lead his Partizan units to victory in 1945. Historians are still divided over the issue of whether his greater strength in this process lay in his political or military abilities. He was undoubtedly aided by a number of developments beyond his control: the Italian capitulation of 1943; the political and military ineptitude of the **monarchy**'s government in exile and their forces in Yugoslavia; the extreme oppressiveness of the indigenous fascist **Ustaša** regime in Croatia; and the assistance of the armed forces of the Allies. These considerations should not be allowed to detract, however, from the fact that Tito did emerge from the struggle as the successful and highly charismatic leader of a broadly popular movement.

Victory in 1945 was followed by a ruthless process of ensuring the political supremacy of the CPY; a nominal coalition government was brushed aside after a few months. Programs of land reform and the nationalization of productive resources and infrastructure were undertaken. The new regime signaled its toughness on the international stage by its obdurate attempt to secure Yugoslav control of the Adriatic port of Trieste, as well as by its support for the communist forces in the civil war in Greece. It was equally uncompromising against domestic opposition, rooting out the last areas of royalist resistance and suppressing harshly an **Albanian** nationalist uprising in **Kosovo**.

All of these events have continued to have their repercussions in the period of the collapse of the Yugoslav federation. Sensitivities on the part of **Italy** have raised problems in relation to the territorial definition of the newly independent **Croatia** and **Slovenia**; the aspirations of the Kosovar Albanians are still not addressed; the stability of the region has been affected by concerns on the part of **Greece** about the creation of an independent **Macedonia**; and the wartime fight against both Croat and Serb nationalist movements has provided an ample fund of symbols in which to clothe contemporary issues.

Among the most significant elements of the legacy that Tito left, dating from this wartime period, was the enormous self-confidence of the **League of Communists of Yugoslavia**. This assurance perhaps prevented the league's leaders from realizing the severity of their country's problems and led them to overestimate their own ability to tackle the issues that arose.

Surviving a dispute with the Soviet leadership in 1948, which resulted in the imposition of an economic blockade by the socialist countries, Tito went on to create a somewhat idiosyncratic version of what Eastern European political scientists often refer to as "really existing socialism." His synthesis of workers' self-management at home and a stance of nonalignment in international relations became the foundation stones of a system that came to be known as Titoism. To this might be added a third element: the complex structure of checks and balances among the numerous "nations" and "nationalities" that made up the Yugoslav peoples.

Perhaps it is a consequence of Tito's ubiquitous and energetic presence on the international stage that his importance for the development of Yugoslavia has been misunderstood. The process of disintegration that culminated in the wars of 1991–1996 has often been represented as a result of his death in 1980 and the country's failure to find a successor to his strong leadership. (It is a curious irony that this hankering after authoritarian leadership is heard most often in democratic states.) Nevertheless, the system that he bequeathed was in large measure of his design. The problems that brought Yugoslavia to its end (problems of the creation of political consensus in a multiethnic state; of the management of economic modernization in a communist framework, which denies a place to key components of modernity; of the creation of a secure and stable state within an international context in which the relationships among the major players are themselves changing) can be seen to have been present at the birth of that system. Tito must be seen, at least in part, as the architect of Yugoslavia's problems in the 1990s. Even so, many of those who have suffered in the recent wars would probably agree with the graffiti seen on a Zagreb wall: "Bravar je bio bolje!" (The locksmith was better!); which referred to Tito's modest beginnings as a locksmith and metal worker.

—*J. B. A.*

References: Auty, Phyllis. *Tito: A Biography,* rev. ed. Harmondsworth: Penguin, 1974; Guikovaty, Emile. *Tito.* Paris: Hachette, 1979; Pavlowitch, Stevan K. *Tito, Yugoslavia's Great Dictator: A Reassessment.* London: Hurst, 1992.

TITOGRAD

See **Podgorica**

TITOISM

Titoism was the strategy of exploiting Yugoslavia's unique geopolitical position at the intersection of two superpower blocs in order to maintain independence from both. The result was an unstable equilibrium that finally succumbed to the contradictions inherent in the notion of "market socialism." Following the break between Yugoslavia and the Soviet Union in 1947, the Communist Party of Yugoslavia (commanded by Josip Broz [**Tito**], Edvard Kardelj, **Milovan Djilas**, and Aleksandar Ranković) embarked upon a revision of Marxism-Leninism that both justified the independent "Yugoslav road" to socialism and tried to legitimate Communist power through a new version of Marxism. As Kardelj explained in 1952, the role of the party was not to exercise power on behalf of the working class, but instead to nurture the forms of "direct democracy" appropriate to a self-governing society *(društveno samoupravljenje),* based on the management of industry by workers' councils. (The party's fifth Congress also adopted the name "**League of Communists**" in deference to the authority of Marx and Engels.) Meanwhile, Yugoslav diplomacy was moving closer to the West and to the **Nonaligned Movement**, in which Tito played an international role. This process of ideological repositioning culminated in the historic Program of the Seventh Congress (1958), which was an assertion of independence in the face of Soviet imperialism and a presentation of the party's liberal communist credentials to the world.

Within Yugoslavia the impetus to change was halted by the shocking defection of Djilas and the death of Stalin. The party and the state security service (UDBa) maintained a tight political grip, and the main economic reforms embodied in the 1953 constitution were abandoned within months. Soviet Army tanks in Budapest in 1956 put the steam back into reformism, but the surface unity of the Seventh Congress concealed a split within the political bureaucracy; this split hardened as decentralization began to falter around 1960. Led by Ranković, the hard-liners opposed reforms that gave more control to enterprises, fearing that such reforms would increase the power of **Croatia** and **Slovenia** within the federation and open up Yugoslavia to penetration by capitalism. The reformers favored a polycentric distribution of power between the republics and drew their support from the Communist technocracy.

Ranković controlled the UDBa and the party machine, but he could not prevent the passing of a more liberal constitution. The following year, the Eighth Congress endorsed economic reforms that came into force during 1965, and in July 1966 Ranković fell from power.

The aim of the reform program was to broaden the composition of the federal elite by incorporating the leaders of the republican party organizations, which won greater autonomy. This move was combined with a series of constitutional amendments giving the republics an effective veto on all matters except defense, security, and foreign affairs. The effect was to create a counterweight to **Serbia**, the bastion of centralism. Serbs dominated the military and security forces and occupied key strategic networks in the party-state apparatus. The unintended consequence was to institutionalize interrepublican rivalries. Bitter disputes sprang up about the proper limits of federal authority, opening up a political space for nationalism as a mass movement. Meanwhile, economic reform had flung Yugoslavia into deep recession, revealing the unmistakable contours of a class-divided society, with poverty, unemployment, and emigration figuring as major social problems.

By the Ninth Congress (1969), the tide of reformism was already on the turn. Tito called for the strengthening of the party leadership to counter deviationism, and Kardelj chimed in with an attack on "technocracy," arguing that economic reform had produced conditions conducive to "capitalist relations." Voices silenced by the fall of Ranković were heard again, calling for a return to the communist virtues of equality and self-denial and the restoration of party discipline, which they pointedly linked with the growth of "dinar nationalism." Croatia and Slovenia repeatedly complained that "their" economies were being milked to sustain the federation, and these quarrels were allowed to surface in the press. What began as a policy of controlled mobilization of public support quickly got out of control. In November 1971, the extreme nationalist-led student body at Zagreb University went on strike in defiance of the Croatian party leaders, who were immediately forced to resign.

A rolling purge was set in motion to eliminate "national-chauvinist deviations" from the republican party organizations, beginning with the dismissal of 1,000 functionaries in Croatia. The rule of democratic centralism was reasserted, and the classic communist "cell" structure was revived in the state administration. The party's Tenth Congress (1974) and another constitution in the same year were supposed to redress the balance in favor of centralism, but the result was a fudge. The congress rejected both a centralized "supranational" organization and a "federal coalition" of republican party organizations, while the constitution confirmed the economic and social jurisdictions of the republics. Meanwhile, the economy continued to fare poorly. One-third of enterprises were operating at a loss but survived through political intervention, including simply falsifying the books. Moreover, the fate of a system driven neither by markets nor by centralized planning was the "feudalization" of the economy; the republics found it easier to trade abroad than with each other, inciting separatism and nationalism.

The Eleventh Congress (1978) was held against a background clamor of renewed demands for economic reform. An aging core elite grouped around Tito as the president for life continued to monopolize the apex of the party-state machine, but the substance of their power was dissolving. The congress was decisive in entrenching the power of the republican party organizations, and for the first time the doctrine of democratic centralism was diluted. A "Tito initiative" was launched to cope with the succession problem, which effectively gave each republic control of the levers of power in a short-term rotational system, but this approach resulted only in political paralysis.

By Tito's death in May 1980, the system to which he gave his name was moribund. As he went to his grave, with his funeral procession followed by hundreds of foreign dignitaries, cynics in the cafés remarked that they had come to collect foreign debts owed to them: the rocketing costs of servicing foreign debts brought a catastrophic drop in living standards and the beginning of hyper**inflation**. When it came to formulating policies for economic recovery, the republics could not reach consensus and refused to implement majority decisions that did not suit them. The party did not exactly wither away, but it was reduced to its repressive function, awakening fears of a "Yugoslav Stalin" and igniting nationalist animosities that exploded in 1989. After 40 years, the Yugoslav experiment in socialist democracy was over.

—L. B.

See also: constitutional models; economic dimension; workers' self-management

TOURISM

In assessing the **economic dimension** and impact of the war in Yugoslavia, tourism merits special attention, both as an illustration of the general economic disruption caused by war and as a mark of the peculiar vulnerability of the Croatian economy.

The foundations of Yugoslav tourism were laid in the late nineteenth century, and by the 1930s the **Adriatic** coast had emerged as a significant economic asset for the "First Yugoslavia" (created in 1918). Although the postwar communist regime at first discouraged international tourism, the economic problems of the country—recognized in the reforms of the mid-1960s—resulted in a vigorous attempt to develop the tourist trade. Between 1968 and 1988, arrivals of foreign tourists grew from 3.9 million to more than 9 million (a 232 percent increase), and their overnight stays grew from 17 million to more than 52 million (304 percent). The rising standard of living of Yugoslavs also stimulated the domestic market, so that foreign visitors never exceeded 40 percent of total demand. By 1988 Yugoslavia's annual income from tourism in convertible currencies had reached U.S.$1.5 billion. With a recurring problem of a negative balance of payments from the trade in goods, the receipts from tourism (along with the remittances of Yugoslav workers abroad) were a vital factor in ensuring the economic viability of the country and above all in assuring Yugoslavia's international creditworthiness.

Tourism is both highly price sensitive and extremely susceptible to the threat of disturbance. The rise in international oil prices in 1978–1979 resulted in a sudden drop of 7 percent in the demand for Yugoslav tourism, and negative press stories about Yugoslav resorts in 1980–1981 saw a drop of 10 percent. Consequently, the outbreak of war in Yugoslavia brought about an almost total collapse of this sector.

With its long Adriatic coastline, **Croatia** provided by far the greater part of Yugoslavia's tourist facilities. The unsettled state of the country resulted in a decline in foreign demand between 1987 and 1990 from 59.8 million to 45.8 million overnight stays (a drop of 23 percent). When Croatia became directly involved in war in 1991, this figure fell to 6.8 million, from which level it has never fully recovered. The damage to the tourism industry itself was magnified by the fact that the creation of the Serb **Krajina** prevented even domestic tourists from visiting the **Plitvice** area; these domestic tourists were also hampered in their access to southern **Dalmatia** by the destruction of the **Maslenica Bridge**. Fighting in some coastal areas resulted in huge damage to accommodations that will take many years to rectify; indeed, because of the depopulation of some areas, the accommodations may never be fully replaced. The economic consequences for Croatia have been catastrophic.

Demand for Croatian tourism was dominated by three countries in particular (**Austria**, **Italy**, and **Germany**), which together accounted for more than half of Croatia's foreign demand before the war. These countries have also been among the most loyal customers since 1992. Given the level of popular contact with Croatia in these countries, it is not altogether surprising that they should have been the most active in supporting Croatia's demand for international **recognition**.

—J. B. A.

See also: Dubrovnik; war costs

TRANSPORT

See **communications and transport**

TRAVNIK

Lying on the Lašva River, Travnik (a former Turkish capital of Bosnia) is at the geographical center of **Bosnia-Hercegovina**. Before the outbreak of hostilities, it comprised a mixed population of Serbs (11 percent), Croats (37 percent), and Muslims (45 percent), totaling around 75,000 including its industrial suburb of Novi Travnik.

Travnik was at the heart of the two main phases of the war in central Bosnia. In the first phase, under constant bombardment itself, Travnik became the destination for thousands of **refugees** and deportees from the Serb offensive in northern Bosnia during the summer of 1992; reports suggest that it received most of the Muslim population of **Jajce**, some 25 miles to the northwest. In the second phase, after the winter, the alliance between the **Bosnian army** and the **Croatian Council of Defense** (HVO), which had seemed capable of holding the town, broke down violently. The **Vance-Owen Plan** assigned Travnik to the Croats, and in his expansionist aims **Mate Boban** envisaged Travnik as part of his ministate of **Herceg-Bosna**.

Travnik became headquarters of the Seventeenth Brigade of the Bosnian army, known as the Krajina Brigade, which comprised mainly refugees from Muslim areas subjected to "**ethnic cleansing**" by the Serbs. These troops were motivated to the extreme by their refusal to submit to a second such experience at the hands of the Croats. After some of the bloodiest action of the war, Travnik became effectively a Muslim town.

—J. J. H.

TREBINJE

The principal town in eastern **Hercegovina** (with a population of 31,000 in 1991) in a predominantly Serb-inhabited area southeast of **Mostar**, Trebinje is strategically located close to the border with **Montenegro** and in the hinterland of the southernmost tip of Croatia's Dalmatian coastline. During the first Serb-Croat war in 1991, the route to Dubrovnik from Montenegro passed through Trebinje. After the outbreak of civil war in Bosnia-Hercegovina in April 1992, when the Croats and the Serbs moved to divide Hercegovina between themselves, Trebinje was the scene of fierce fighting and "**ethnic cleansing**." Seventy percent Serb before the war, Trebinje became the capital of Serb-held eastern Hercegovina. Ruled by a Serbian Democratic Party (SDS) nationalist warlord, Božidar Vukarević, Trebinje was also the headquarters of the Hercegovina Corps of the **Bosnian Serb Army** (BSA). Although one of the most isolated regions of the **Republika Srpska**, Trebinje was important because of its proximity to those areas of southern **Dalmatia** that the **Bosnian Serbs** hoped to annex so as to secure access to the Adriatic Sea. At various points in the Croatian and Bosnian wars, proposals were made that the Croats regain the hinterlands of **Dubrovnik** in return for the granting to Serbs maritime access on the **Prevlaka** Peninsula to the south, although nothing ever came of these considerations. Since the **Dayton Agreements** of December 1995, Trebinje has been within the French sector of the **Implementation/Stabilization Force.**

—*M. M.*

TREPČA MINERS

The strike of miners at the Trepča complex near Kosovska Mitrovica in February 1989 was one of the key events that both promoted and demonstrated the collapsing legitimacy of the **League of Communists of Yugoslavia** (SKJ). The lead and zinc mines were first developed in the 1930s and became one of Yugoslavia's largest industrial assets.

A central element of the strategy of **Slobodan Milošević** following his rise to power in 1987 was to revise the constitution of the Republic of **Serbia** so as to reduce the autonomy of the republic's provinces. In October 1988 the central committee (CC) of the SKJ agreed to these changes in principle. To implement them, however, it was necessary to engineer the compliance of the leadership of the League of Communists (LC) in the provinces. An attempt was made to force the resignations of Kaqusha Jashari, **Azem Vllasi**, and Svetislav Dolašević from the CC of the LC in **Kosovo** and to replace them with compliant nominees of Belgrade: Rahman Morina, Husamedin Azemi, and Ali Shukria.

This move provoked a strong reaction in the province. On 17 November 1988, miners from the Trepča complex marched to the capital, **Priština**, where they were joined by students and others in demonstrations that lasted over five days. The demonstrators combined an expression of dissatisfaction over falling living standards with demands to defend the 1974 constitution. There were vociferous counterdemonstrations in several Serbian cities.

The leadership changes Milošević sought were forced through, but dissatisfaction continued to grow. In February 1989 the Trepča miners once again moved to the forefront of the political stage, commencing a strike underground, with many of them announcing that if necessary they would fast to death in order to compel the restoration of provincial autonomy. A list of 10 demands was published, including the abandonment of the forced leadership changes. The strike attracted immense sympathy across Kosovo, with many solidarity meetings in other parts of Yugoslavia and internationally. The Croatian head of the SKJ, Stipe Šuvar, traveled to Trepča to ask the miners to call off their action.

Milošević responded with a series of "meetings" (rallies) designed to demonstrate support for the changes he was pursuing. International **media** attention was intense, with reporters moved by the impassioned determination of the miners in conditions of desperate poverty. In Kosovo the event rapidly escalated into a general strike. By 28 February 1989, after eight days underground, it seemed that the miners had won when the three forced resignations were "suspended." The strike was called off.

The contested constitutional amendments were nevertheless forced through in March, in the face of serious rioting in Kosovo that resulted in the deaths of 29 people. In October, Vllasi and the director of the mine were arrested with others on charges of "counterrevolutionary activity" (it was alleged that the general strike was to have been the prelude to an armed uprising).

The events surrounding the strike polarized opinion across Yugoslavia. Slovenes and Croats in particular tended to support the miners; Slovene president **Milan Kučan**, addressing a rally, called the miners' action a defense of AVNOJ (antifascist) Yugoslavia. The willingness of the northern republics to involve themselves actively in the events in Kosovo was muted, however, by these republics' realization that such involvement would weaken their own economic case—that they should not be required to subsidize the Kosovar economy. As the security situation deteriorated in Kosovo, militia units from Slovenia and Croatia were withdrawn, and the political disengagement of the secessionist republics can be seen to have begun.

—*J. B. A.*

TRNOPOLJE

See **detention camps**

TUDJMAN, FRANJO

Franjo Tudjman is founder of the **Croatian Democratic Union** (HDZ), which since 1990 has

Franjo Tudjman, president of the Republic of Croatia and leader of the Croatian Democratic Union. (Tanjug)

been the ruling party in **Croatia**, and he has been president of the republic since its independence from **Yugoslavia** in 1992.

Born in 1922 in Veliko Trgovišće in the Croatian Zagorje, north of Zagreb, Tudjman joined the **Partizans** during World War II. He remained in the **Yugoslav Peoples' Army** (JNA) after the war, rising to the rank of major general in 1960, the youngest of the generals. For the thesis that he was required to write before promotion to the rank of general, Tudjman selected a historical subject; on retiring from the army in 1961, allegedly disenchanted with its Serb-dominated elite and the downplaying of Croat achievements, he began to work as an academic historian on aspects of Croatian national history.

In his historical work, he examined the evidence relating to the numbers of Serbs, Jews, and Gypsies (Roma) killed by the **Ustaša** (particularly at **Jasenovac**). He argued that numbers had been drastically inflated by the Communists, concluding that only 30,000–35,000 had been killed—only one-tenth the number given in "official" estimates.

Tudjman became involved in the **Croatian Spring**, having signed the "Declaration Concerning the Name and Position of the Croatian Language," which was issued by the Croatian Writers' Club on 7 April 1967. This followed publication of a new Serbo-Croat dictionary, which the declaration attacked as condoning a semi-official language which showed Serbian bias. For his part in the mass movement *(maspok)*, he was expelled from the **League of Communists** and jailed in the 1970s and 1980s. After his release he still had the use of a passport (something many other dissidents were denied), enabling him to travel abroad, where he made links with Croat émigré communities. These communities were later to stand him in good stead, providing support and money to pay for the election campaign in 1990.

The HDZ was founded in June 1989, and under the leadership of Tudjman it won the **elections** for the government of Croatia in April 1990. Tudjman was duly elected president of the republic. He has directed the development of a constitution that gives great power to Croatia's president, permitting the creation of an authoritarian political system. The inner core of his advisers and cabinet have frequently been changed when they have opposed his views, although throughout most of his tenure he has been identified with the "Hercegovina Lobby," a group of Croatian political figures of western Hercegovina origin. Through his support for **Mate Boban** in **Hercegovina** and the creation of the Croat ministate of **Herceg-Bosna**, Tudjman alienated some of his own closest allies, such as **Stipe Mesić** and **Josip Manolić**, who split from the HDZ in 1994.

Although Tudjman has been successful in leading Croatia to independence and restoring its **borders** in the face of the secessionist struggle of the Serb **Krajina**, his leadership has attracted great controversy. He has been criticized for failing to understand the depths of Serb distrust of the movement to independence, and he has been blamed for failing to prepare Croatia adequately for war in 1991, allowing the JNA to support the Serbs in their expansion of the Serbian autonomous provinces. It has been alleged that he allowed **Vukovar** to fall, despite having some capability to relieve the siege, in the hope that the city's loss would provide the spur for international intervention. Most controversial has been his proposal to replace the memorial at Jasenovac (erected to victims of fascism) with a memorial for all Croatian victims of war, including communist oppression.

Tudjman has been intolerant of such criticism, responding by curtailing freedom of speech and exacting repressive measures on the independent **media**, including replacement of editorial boards and attempts to close papers down. A new press law was passed in May 1996 reestablishing some aspects of the former communist penal code, which had been abolished in 1991; this law included provision to make "slander" against the state leadership illegal.

Nevertheless, Tudjman secured reelection as president in 1995. It has been widely said that he wants to be remembered as the president of an independent Croatia and as the man who led Croatia to reunification. After the military victories of May and August 1995, he was able to claim plausibly that he had succeeded in his ambition. Unfortunately, he will also be remembered as the man who presided over the "**ethnic cleansing**" from Croatia of approximately 450,000 of its 582,000 Serbs. The HDZ and Tudjman now face the more complex task of setting Croatia on a course for economic prosperity, social stability, justice, and peace among the still considerable national minorities.

—G. R. B.

TUPURKOVSKI, VASIL

Vasil Tupurkovski pursued a career as an academic, being a professor at the Faculty of Law in Skopje, but he was also active in the **League of Communists**. He rose to being elected to the league's central committee and eventually represented **Macedonia** on the presidency of the Socialist Federal Republic of **Yugoslavia** on the eve of its breakup. Tupurkovski played a very active role in support of **Kiril Gligorov** in the final attempts to broker a negotiated solution to the constitutional problems of Yugoslavia, as well as in resisting the militarization of the political crisis in 1991–1992. His reputation rested not only on the great rapidity of his rise to political leadership, but also on the extreme informality of his manner of dress!

—J. B. A.

TURKEY

The disturbances in what was once **Yugoslavia** have raised the question of Turkey's reaction. The stability that followed the end of World War II has been wrecked, and the region has returned to the instability for which it was traditionally known. Turkey could not avoid veering its attention back to the **Balkans**.

Between the end of the fourteenth century and the beginning of the eighteenth century, the **Ottoman Empire** dominated the Balkans. For the next two centuries, this empire was steadily pushed back until its European territory was restricted to a small area in Thrace. The Yugoslav events have revived the memory of Turkey's cultural and historical ties with the **Muslims** of Bosnia, **Albania**, **Macedonia**, and various areas of **Serbia** (**Kosovo** and the **Sandžak** of Novi Pazar) and have compounded the problems faced by Turkish foreign policymakers seeking to adapt to the new realities.

Despite its secularism Turkey remains an Islamic country that feels an affinity with some Muslim communities, especially those once ruled by the Ottoman Empire; **Bosnia-Hercegovina** fits that picture because the bulk of its 43 percent Muslim population had been converted by the Ottomans. The Turkish public has been aroused by the atrocities perpetrated against Bosnian Muslims, and Turkey was at the forefront of calls for Western military intervention.

Turkey's concern about the disintegration of Yugoslavia became apparent before the violence in **Croatia** spilled over into Bosnia-Hercegovina. Turkish fears were growing in 1991, but the situation in the Balkans was still far from being one of Ankara's priorities until mid-1992. The Turkish government was heavily occupied with the war between Azerbaijan and Armenia, as well as the intensifying Kurdish revolt in eastern Anatolia. Also, Turkey's growing relations with the newly independent Turkic-Muslim republics in Central Asia were a major interest for Turkish policymakers.

As the fighting in Bosnia-Hercegovina intensified, Turkish feelings of concern increased, and yet the Turkish reaction was relatively silent because there was hope that the **sanctions** might work and that the efforts of the **United Nations** (UN) or the **European Union** (EU) would succeed. Very soon, however, with the fighting in Yugoslavia entering a new phase and taking on a potentially more explosive international dimension, Turkey became increasingly involved in the Balkan conflagration. The result was feverish Turkish diplomatic activity in the summer of 1992 to try to strengthen Western response to the crisis. Turkey offered to place 1,000 troops at the disposal of a combined expeditionary force.

The violent disintegration of Yugoslavia, the war in Bosnia-Hercegovina, and the plight of Muslims moved Ankara's relations with other Balkan capitals to a new level. Relations between Turkey and **Greece**, which traditionally had a stabilizing role in the Balkans, have been strained by Turkey's recognition of (in February 1992) and diplomatic and economic support for the Republic of **Macedonia** (**FYROM**). At the same time, Turkish support for Macedonia has contributed to the ongoing improvement in the formerly very tense diplomatic and military relations between Turkey and **Bulgaria**. With a population of some 65 million and a geographic position on the Anatolian Peninsula as well as the Balkan Peninsula, Turkey has a definite political advantage over all its Balkan neighbors. Because Turkey has no apparent territorial ambitions in the Balkan Peninsula and has no strong military ties to any country in the region, it does have a degree of flexibility and freedom of action. Turkey may play a significant role in the seething Balkans, where new hostilities and new political alliances are emerging, and a large Muslim population looks to Turkey as a potential ally.

—B. G.

TURKS

A relatively small but significant element in the ethnic composition of the former Yugoslavia has been the area's Turkish minority. These individuals numbered about 119,000 in the 1991 census (0.5 percent of the total) but formed a strong local minority in **Macedonia**—102,000, or 4.15 percent of that population (86 percent of Yugoslav Turks). They are concentrated to the east of the Vardar River. Other notable local concentrations are found in **Kosovo** (especially Prizren and Priština) and to a lesser extent in the **Sandžak**.

Turkish settlement in Yugoslavia dates from the conquest of the region by the **Ottoman Empire** between the fourteenth and sixteenth centuries. Turkish speakers distinguish themselves from Serbo-Croat-speaking or Macedonian-speaking Slavs and Albanians, whose ancestors converted to **Islam** during the Ottoman period.

Turkish numbers have declined appreciably with the contraction of the Ottoman state, largely as a result of an earlier experience of "**ethnic cleansing**." After the Balkan Wars, especially after the creation of the "First Yugoslavia" (1918–1941) in 1918, an estimated 150,000 people left the Kosovo region alone, and in 1925 **Turkey** refused to admit more refugees from Yugoslavia. The 1921 Yugoslav census recorded more than 150,000 Turks, roughly in their contemporary distribution.

Turks in Yugoslavia benefited greatly from the Communist policy of ethnic toleration. During the period of the breakup of the federation, however, they have once again been used, especially by Serb nationalists, as a symbol of past imperial domination. The presence of a significant Turkish minority in Yugoslavia and the presence of numerous descendants of former inhabitants of the region in Turkey have been factors that have stimulated the engagement of Turkey's government with the fate of Yugoslavia.

—J. B. A.

TUS, ANTUN

Antun Tus, a Croatian general in the armed forces, is widely credited as the man who founded and "professionalized" the **Croatian Army**. He was formerly the commander of the Yugoslav federal air force, from which he had been ousted as a non-Serb in a key role. In the summer of 1991, he was appointed by **Franjo Tudjman**, the Croatian president, to lead the armed forces of Croatia, which had hitherto consisted of volunteers, reservists, police, and other disparate groups. By the end of 1991, Tus had organized a force of up to 250,000 soldiers, divided into brigades that gave Croatia the formidable potential to attack or defend with confidence from virtually any part of its territory.

—J. J. H.

TUZLA

The third-largest city (population 131,000 in 1991) in **Bosnia-Hercegovina** after **Sarajevo** and **Banja Luka**, Tuzla is the principal urban settlement in northeastern Bosnia. Part of the rich farming areas of Podrinje and Posavina to the north, Tuzla is also an important road-rail junction and the site of one of the largest airports in the former Yugoslavia. It also has its own university. During the Yugoslav period, Tuzla was an important lignite mining center and industrial zone. The city's coal-fired power station also produced most of the electricity used in northeastern Bosnia.

After the descent of Bosnia-Hercegovina into civil war in April 1992, the city's population quadrupled following a large influx of displaced persons from other parts of Bosnia. These mainly Bosnian

Muslim (Bošnjak) **refugees** were almost entirely dependent on deliveries of **humanitarian aid** for their survival from 1992 to 1995. The **United Nations** (UN) declared Tuzla to be one of its six "**safe areas**" in 1993, although this status did not prevent artillery bombardments and other attacks by the besieging **Bosnian Serb Army** (BSA).

A highly ethnically mixed and cosmopolitan city before the war, Tuzla was of too great a strategic importance to be allowed to fall to the Bosnian Serbs. Following the forced evacuation of the **Yugoslav Peoples' Army** (JNA) garrison in the spring of 1992, Tuzla has been under the military control of the **Bosnian army** (Army of the Republic of Bosnia-Hercegovina—ARBH), whose Second Corps operates from the city. Throughout the Bosnian war, the Second Corps attempted to sever the strategic **Posavina Corridor**, focused on the town of **Brčko** to the north, so as to cut the Bosnian Serb entity in half. Although the ARBH failed to achieve this goal, the **Republika Srpska** remains at its most vulnerable here.

In May 1995, in one of the worst atrocities of the Bosnian war, the BSA bombarded Tuzla, killing 72 mainly young people and wounding a further 150 in a single mortar attack. This attack (and similar Bosnian Serb outrages in Sarajevo) created a new climate of international opinion that was to eventually lead to **North Atlantic Treaty Organization** (NATO) airstrikes against the BSA later in 1995.

A major base for the peacekeeping force **UNPROFOR** from 1992 to 1995, Tuzla thereafter became the headquarters of the **United States**' contingent to NATO's **Implementation/Stabilization Force**. Although reportedly used for secret arms deliveries for the ARBH earlier in the Bosnian war, Tuzla's airport was not fully reopened until 1996, when the city's economy also began to revive.

Although nominally controlled by the Sarajevo government led by President **Alija Izetbegovič** throughout the war, Tuzla has always been unique in Bošnjak-controlled Bosnia. Municipal government has been in the hands of a coalition of civic and nonnationalist parties opposed to all attempts to partition the city and country along ethnic lines, including those efforts emanating from the **Party of Democratic Action** (SDA) in Sarajevo. For this reason, the city's Civic Forum coalition, led by Mayor Selim Beslagić, has often openly opposed the government in Sarajevo. With the rise to power of an ultranationalist faction in the SDA during the Bosnian war, Beslagić's coalition came under pressure from Sarajevo, culminating in a failed attempt to remove the coalition from office in 1995. In March 1996, the largest gathering of the Democratic Alternative—a nationwide grouping of civic and nonnationalist parties—took place in Tuzla. Although such an alternative did not pose a serious threat to the SDA in subsequent elections in Bosnia, it did remain dominant in Tuzla, showing once again that this city was still as much a bastion of multiethnic and civic politics and tolerance as it had ever been.

—M. M.

U

UNA RIVER

The Una River was a significant natural feature in the Bosnian war. During its course of 135 miles, it closely follows the northwestern border between Bosnia and the **Krajina** tract in Croatia, except where it cuts across the "**Bihać** pocket" via **Bosanska Krupa**. The river's crossings were of tactical importance at the numerous points of conflict between Bosnians and Serbs along its course.

—J. J. H.

UNCRO

As part of the general restructuring of its peacekeeping forces in the former Yugoslavia, the Security Council of the United Nations (UN) resolved on 31 March 1995 to replace its protection force (**UNPROFOR**) with three separate peacekeeping operations. In **Croatia** it established the UN Confidence Restoration Operation; the corresponding acronym, UNCRO, served also to identify the United Nations specifically in Croatia. UNCRO was established in response to the Croatian government's objections to a continuation of UNPROFOR's role, balanced by the need for the UN to maintain a profile in Croatia in case of renewed hostilities. To reflect this need for balance, UNCRO was provided with both a military commander and a civilian chief of mission.

—J. J. H.

UNHCR

The United Nations High Commission for Refugees (UNHCR), together with its affiliated United Nations (UN) agencies (World Food Program and Food and Agriculture Organization), is a major provider of emergency food relief to noncombatant populations in conflict areas. It was especially active in the former Yugoslavia throughout the conflict, managing a highly organized convoy system to deliver food aid under the protection of UN troops. It operated, for the most part, in cooperation and agreement with the military authorities on all sides.

Given Bosnia's past history as an agricultural region, with a heavy percentage of the population working their own land, in many parts of the country the food aid was useful though not critical to survival. However, in the various enclaves that existed in Bosnia and Croatia for much of the war, the situation was radically different, and food assistance from the UNHCR was vital to the survival of besieged populations. Without such aid it was clear that these people would either have succumbed to starvation or would have had to leave the region and seek refuge elsewhere. The possibility of deliberately engineering the latter outcome—a "voluntary" **ethnic cleansing** of a local population—led

Sadako Ogata, United Nations High Commissioner for Refugees during the Yugoslav wars of the 1990s. (UNHCR)

the military and political authorities on all sides in the former Yugoslavia to use food as a major strategic weapon throughout the war.

Although the UNHCR attempted to maintain a steadfastly nonpolitical approach throughout the conflict, the use of food as a military weapon meant that the commission was often dragged into the political arena and charged with aiding one party to the conflict more than the others. By insisting on fulfilling its mandate to support any beleaguered population by delivering needed food aid, the UNHCR naturally frustrated the wishes of those military and political leaders who were working toward the forcible relocation of people in order to create an ethnically pure region for themselves. The commission came into disagreement with the military authorities on many occasions, and there were many instances of aggression and antagonism shown toward it. UNHCR convoys were sometimes hijacked, food deliveries were routinely turned back by the military authorities on some spurious pretext, bribes were necessary in the form of a certain percentage of the total load being taken, and local populations were regularly stirred up to block convoys going to "the other side." Permission for UNHCR food assistance to be delivered to the enclaves became an unavoidable bargaining chip with which all sides in the conflict attempted to secure food aid for their own populations much less in need of direct support, or more generally for supporting the war effort of one side against the other(s).

—*M. B.*

Reference: Minear, Larry, et al. *Humanitarian Action in the Former Yugoslavia: The U.N.'s Role 1991–1993.* Providence, RI: Thomas J. Watson Institute for International Studies, 1994.

UNITED KINGDOM

The United Kingdom (UK) has been a major diplomatic and military player in the Yugoslav wars. British involvement may be considered from the point of view of its historical background, its international context, and its domestic political context.

Successive British governments reflect a long history of involvement in the Balkan region dating back to the late-nineteenth-century "Eastern Question," in which the primary consideration was the protection of communications between Britain and its empire in the East and vital economic interests such as the stabilization of energy supplies. Allied to **Serbia** in World War I and to those allied powers with the closest involvement in Yugoslavia in World War II, the British government developed very good relations with **Yugoslavia** after 1945. Consequently the UK approached the recent Yugoslav crisis with a positive commitment to the desirability of preserving Yugoslavia and with a tendency to define the nature of the state and its problems by previous wartime experiences.

When the collapse of Yugoslavia attracted international attention in 1991, the British Foreign Office was already deeply preoccupied with the implications for European security of the demise of Soviet hegemony in Eastern and Central Europe, and of German reunification in particular. In December 1991 the Foreign Affairs Committee of the House of Commons began a series of hearings on the Yugoslav situation, and it is significant that committee members titled their report *Central and Eastern Europe: Problems of the Post-Communist Era.* The Yugoslav problem was set within a frame of the general problems of the redefinition of European security structures. The primary problem was the need for a new continent-wide security system, in relation to which the disturbances in the Balkans were seen as dependent and relatively peripheral.

Yugoslavia was nevertheless deemed to be important because in a situation in which the general outlines of a new configuration of international relations were ill defined, British officials recognized that there was a real danger of localized conflicts within Yugoslavia "spilling over" the entire Balkan region. In the early stages of the conflict, the central objective of British policy in the region might be termed "containment." An important problem of the new security pattern in the region concerned the relative roles of the **United States** and European powers. Since World War II a key component of British foreign policy, especially under Conservative administrations, had been support for the Atlantic alliance. The Yugoslav crisis coincided with a shift within Europe from the earlier concept of a common market toward a more ambitious understanding of regional institutions, including the possible development of a common foreign policy. The change was indicated at the time by the redefinition of the European Community as a European Union.

Prime Minister John Major visits British military forces and local civilians, Bosnia-Hercegovina, 1995. (Army Public Relations, London)

Although the UK was heavily committed to making European institutions such as the Council for Security and Cooperation in Europe (CSCE), there was still a measure of ambivalence in its policy as well as uncertainty about Europe's ability to handle the Yugoslav situation alone. Consequently, although British diplomats (Lord **Carrington** and Lord **Owen**) played vital roles as representatives of collective European involvement in the crisis, Britain has also been one of the leading supporters of an extension of responsibility to include the **United Nations** and the **North Atlantic Treaty Organization** (NATO) and has been actively involved as one of the permanent members of the UN Security Council.

Like all the principal international actors in Yugoslavia, British political figures tended to see the situation to some extent through a prism of domestic issues. U.S. perceptions of military involvement were clouded by the memory of the Vietnam War. German perceptions were influenced by issues of unification and the heavy criticism it had received for its lack of active involvement in the Gulf War. British concerns about the Yugoslav problem were overshadowed by anxieties about devolution in Scotland and the conflict in Northern Ireland, where what had begun as an attempt to secure a temporary respite for politicians in 1968 turned into three decades of costly commitment for the British army. This experience provided the basis for British insistence, as expressed by Lord Carrington, that "there is no point in having a peacekeeping force if there is no peace to keep." Military engagement made sense only within a context of clearly defined political objectives. Since a divided international community could not agree readily upon such objectives, UK leaders remained cautious about military involvement, though when such involvement was deemed necessary the British army consistently provided a mjor contribution to the international effort. However, military intervention was always seen as subsidiary to the twin tracks of mediation and diplomacy.

The involvement of the UK in the Yugoslav crisis has had both positive and negative aspects. The commitment to agreed-upon international action has resulted in a slowness to respond that critics have sometimes interpreted as obstructive. At the start of the crisis, however, no one understood how cumbersome the hitherto untested "unusual military activities" mechanism of the CSCE would prove to be. The understandable caution about military engagement resulted in widespread accusations that the UK was simply pro-Serb, but these critics failed to recognize the difference between British intentions and the unsought effects of policy.

The Foreign Office preference that "boundaries should not be disturbed save by agreement" has also been criticized as adherence to legalism in defiance of the realities on the ground. Nevertheless, British reluctance to recognize the independence of **Slovenia** and **Croatia** because such **recognition** would lead to greater difficulties in resolving the situation in **Bosnia-Hercegovina,** and related skepticism about the effectiveness of the **Badinter Commission,** turned out to be justified.

British officials were generally realistic in their assessment of the Macedonian problem, although, while understanding Greek concerns about irredentism, British utilitarianism failed to grasp the symbolic dimension of the issue.

The principled position of the UK with respect to the change of **borders** broke down once Yugoslavia had disintegrated irretrievably. At this point the UK government hovered unpredictably between support for self-determination (in **Macedonia** and Bosnia-Hercegovina) and legalism (in Croatia and **Kosovo**); this indecisiveness again tended to fuel accusations of pro-Serb bias.

In general, far too much emphasis was placed upon the ethnic dimension of the conflict to the exclusion of other aspects of its causes—especially economic factors, which were never seriously considered. Even in the area of **ethnicity,** policy was clouded by oversimplified and mythological definitions of the situation, which resulted partly from the inability of policymakers in the Foreign Office to listen with sufficient patience to experts in their own research and analysis department.

In spite of early British reluctance to commit troops to the former Yugoslavia, once military forces were engaged, the British contribution was significant, effective, and consistently carried out. Of the maximum deployment of 17,000 troops in **UNPROFOR** (1993), the British contingent reached 6,000, making it the largest national contribution. UNPROFOR II was headed by two British generals at different times: **Michael Rose** and **Rupert Smith.** In the **Implementation/Stabilization Force (I/SFOR)** deployment of more than 60,000 troops, the UK has provided the second-largest (after the United States) contingent, about 13,000. In spite of its problems, the British participation in the **Rapid Reaction Force** is regarded as marking an important development in NATO practice.

M. M. and J. B. A.

See also: European Community/European Union; Germany; Organization for Security and Cooperation in Europe

Reference: House of Commons, Foreign Affairs Committee. *Central and Eastern Europe: Problems of the Post-Communist Era.* 2 vols. London: HMSO, 1992.

UNITED NATIONS

The United Nations (UN) was one of the main organizational frameworks for the international community's efforts to contain and end the Yugoslav conflict. Under the UN Charter, the UN Security Council has primary responsibility for matters relating to "international peace and security." The Security Council quickly became a key forum for international deliberations on the Yugoslav conflict, providing authorization and legitimacy for most international actions. UN Security Council Resolution (UNSCR) 713 of September 1991 imposed an **arms** embargo on the whole of the former Yugoslavia. UNSCRs 721 and 743 of November 1991 and February 1992 mandated the deployment of the peacekeeping force **UNPROFOR** (UN Protection Force) to **UN protected areas** (UNPAs) in the **Krajina** region of **Croatia.** UNSCR 757 of May 1992 imposed political and economic **sanctions** on **Serbia.** UNSCR 776 of September 1992 extended UNPROFOR's mandate to **Bosnia-Hercegovina.** UNSCR 781 of October 1992 established a **no-fly zone** in Bosnian airspace. UNSCRs 819 and 834 of April and May 1993 established **Srebrenica, Tuzla, Goražde, Bihać, Sarajevo,** and **Žepa** as "**safe areas.**" UNSCR 827 of May 1993 established the International **War Crimes Tribunal** for the former Yugoslavia. UNSCR 836 of June 1993 authorized UNPROFOR to protect the six safe areas. UNSCR 998 of June 1995 authorized the deployment of the **Rapid Reaction Force** to reinforce UNPROFOR.

The UN was also heavily involved in many of the operational aspects of international efforts to manage the Yugoslav conflict. Alongside the **European Community** (EC), the UN jointly managed the **International Conference on the Former Yugoslavia** (ICFY) from August 1992 until it was superseded by the **Contact Group** in 1994. Successive UN special representatives to the former Yugoslavia played a central role in international mediation efforts: **Cyrus Vance** from October 1991 to May 1993; **Thorvald Stoltenberg** from May to December 1993; **Yasushi Akashi** from December 1993 to October 1995; and Kofi Annan from October 1995. The UN also organized, commanded, and controlled key peacekeeping efforts: the UNPROFOR, **UNPREDEP** (UN Preventive Deployment), and **UNTAES** (UN Transitional Administration for Eastern Slavonia) forces. The UN secretary-general (Javier Perez de Cuellar until January 1992, **Boutros Boutros-Ghali** after that date) also played an important role in international mediation efforts and as ultimate commander of UN peacekeeping forces. Individual UN commanders also played an important role in shaping the responses of the UN peacekeeping forces to the conflict. Other UN agencies, such as the UN High Commission for Refugees (**UNHCR**), contributed to international efforts to ameliorate the suffering caused by the Yugoslav conflict.

The UN's role in the Yugoslav wars proved highly controversial. The inability of the UN to end the conflict, the repeated violation of UN Security Council resolutions by the various Yugoslav factions, and the inability of UN peacekeepers to prevent ongoing fighting starkly illustrated the limitations of the organization. This humiliation of the UN, and especially its peacekeepers, was most brutally emphasized when the **Bosnian Serbs** overran the UN-designated safe areas of Srebrenica and Žepa in July 1995. UN special envoy on human rights Tadeusz Mazowiecki resigned in protest at the organization's failure to protect the safe areas. Critics charged that the UN had utterly failed in the former Yugoslavia. Key officials of the UN, particularly Secretary-General Boutros-Ghali and Special Representative Akashi, were criticized for their reluctance to authorize the use of force (particularly airstrikes) against the Bosnian Serbs and for their concern for the security of UN peacekeepers (as opposed to the victims of the Bosnian conflict). Although there may have been some validity to these criticisms, many people pointed out that the responsibility for the UN's failures in the former Yugoslavia lies at least as much—and probably much more—with the member states of the organization (especially the major powers). The permanent members of the UN Security Council repeatedly voted for Security Council resolutions that they did not have the will to enforce. Thus, they authorized the UN-designated safe areas but then failed to provide the military forces that the UN secretary-general argued were necessary to defend these areas. Supporters of the UN's role in the former Yugoslavia argued that, for all its failures, the UN had at least helped to ameliorate or limit the human suffering caused by the conflict and that it could not have done much more unless its members were willing to commit greater resources to support its efforts.

The "failures" of the UN led to its gradual displacement as a central actor in the former Yugoslavia. In 1995, controversial "dual-key" arrangements between the UN and the North Atlantic Treaty Organization (NATO), requiring the approval of both organizations for the authorization of airstrikes, were removed; this move allowed NATO to undertake airstrikes without specific UN approval in each case. U.S.-led diplomacy, NATO's sustained airstrikes against the Bosnian Serbs in August-September 1995 (Operation Deliberate Force), and the **Dayton Agreements** of November 1995 established the United States and NATO as the key international actors. The Dayton peace agreement has been policed not by the UN, but rather by NATO's **Implementation/Stabilization Force** (I/SFOR). Nevertheless, the UN Security Council seems likely to remain an important framework for international discussions of the Yugoslav conflict, and various UN agencies are likely to have a continuing role in international efforts to build a lasting peace in the area.

—*A. S. C.*

See also: conflict management and conflict resolution; UNCRO; UNHCR; United Nations Commission on Human Rights; United Nations Protected Areas; UNPREDEP; UNPROFOR; UNTAES

References: Akashi, Yasushi. "The Limits of UN Diplomacy and the Future of Conflict Mediation." *Survival* 37, no. 4 (Winter 1995–1996): 83–98; Leurdijk, Dick A., and Auke P. Venema. *The United Nations and NATO in Former Yugoslavia, 1991–1996: Limits to Diplomacy and Force.* The Hague: Netherlands Atlantic Commission/Netherlands Institute of International Relations "Clingendael," 1996.

UNITED NATIONS COMMISSION ON HUMAN RIGHTS

The United Nations Commission on Human Rights (UNCHR) has been in existence since 1946 but has rarely come into prominence. For most of the period of the Yugoslav wars, the figure most publicly associated with the organization was Tadeusz Mazowiecki.

Mazowiecki was first noted internationally for his spell as prime minister of his native Poland during 1989–1990. A former Communist Party official and journalist, he became a dissident in the 1970s and a leading member of Solidarity (the Polish workers' trades union movement). In August 1992 an extraordinary session of the UNCHR in Geneva appointed him as "special rapporteur" for Yugoslavia, with the broad brief of investigating allegations of human rights abuses.

Mazowiecki was an energetic investigator who gave voice to many thousands of people who found themselves caught in a war not of their own making. Although the numerous reports that the UNCHR produced under his leadership focused primarily on **Bosnia-Hercegovina**, especially the role of the **Bosnian Serbs**, they contained many criticisms of all sides in the conflict. The reports covering the actions of, for example, the **Croatian Army** in the **Krajina** (where that army was accused of operating a "scorched earth" policy) were largely overlooked by the international press and interested foreign parties.

Throughout his term within the UNCHR, Mazowiecki frequently complained of a lack of support from other arms of the United Nations (UN) and maintained that the lack of power of the organization gave rise to frequent misunderstandings "on the ground." His two main criticisms were centered on the role of the UN Protection Force (**UNPROFOR**) and the position of the UNCHR within the UN hierarchy. Within a month of his appointment, he recommended that UNPROFOR's mandate be extended to cover human rights abuses; he consistently argued for this change throughout his tenure. In particular he maintained that UNPROFOR and UNCHR workers on the ground had much evidence of abuse that was not passed on to the commission itself—and could not be ordered to do so. This stems from the relatively junior position of the commission within the UN structure, as it reports to the Economic and Social Council, which is subordinate in status to the Security Council.

Much has been made of Mazowiecki's resignation, particularly that it was a protest against "**ethnic cleansing**" by the Bosnian Serbs. This much is correct, although there were reasons that lay beyond this explanation. In his resignation statement on 27 July 1995, he made pointed references to the failure of the UN and other bodies to provide support for victims of the war, especially the fall of the supposed "**safe area**" of **Srebrenica**. He suggested that it was not possible to speak about the protection of human rights with credibility when one is confronted with the lack of consistency and courage displayed by the international community and its leaders. Undoubtedly his own experience as a political prisoner in Poland during 1981–1982 enabled him to empathize with victims of war and abuse (especially those effectively imprisoned within the safe areas), and this manifested itself as disillusionment with the international community. This was especially apparent in his disappointment over what he saw as the downgrading of human rights considerations in any of the proposed and actual settlements to the conflict.

Ultimately it can be said that Mazowiecki and UNCHR drew the world's attention to human rights abuses in the region and thus added fuel to the **media** war, but they were able to do little in practical terms.

—R. J.

UNITED NATIONS PROTECTED AREAS

In February 1992, the Security Council of the United Nations (UN) authorized the deployment of the UN Protection Force (**UNPROFOR**) to three United Nations protected areas (UNPAs) in the **Krajina** region of Croatia. The UNPAs were to be demilitarized to help create the circumstances for a peaceful, negotiated resolution of the Krajina conflict between Croats and Serbs. UNPROFOR (and its successor, the United Nations Confidence Restoration Operation in Croatia—**UNCRO**) was mandated to control access to the UNPAs, ensure their demilitarization, and monitor the functioning of local police forces. UNPROFOR/UNCRO was only partially successful in implementing its mandate, and the UNPAs were never fully demilitarized. Croatia recaptured the Krajina and western **Slavonia** regions from the Serbs in August 1995, rendering the concept of the UNPAs irrelevant. The fate of the UNPAs illustrates the mismatch between UN Security Council mandates and the military resources and political support provided for UN forces throughout the Yugoslav conflict.

—A. S. C.

UNITED STATES OF AMERICA

The United States of America did not play a major role in the early years of the Yugoslav conflict, but from 1994 it gradually came to play a central part in international efforts to end the conflict. During 1990–1991, the Bush administration's attention was focused on a number of other major international issues: President Mikhail Gorbachev's reforms in the Soviet Union, the process of German unification, the Gulf War, and the Soviet coup attempt with subsequent disintegration of the Soviet Union. Having been a supporter of **Yugoslavia** (against the Soviet Union) during the Cold War and fearing the precedent that the breakup of Yugoslavia might set for the Soviet Union, the United States supported the maintenance of the Yugoslav federation. In June 1991 Secretary of State James Baker made the United States' continued support for Yugoslavia clear in a speech in Belgrade. Many analysts suggest that this effectively gave a "green light" for **Serbia** to attack **Croatia** the following week. Seeking to reduce its Cold War commitment to Europe, the Bush administration then encouraged the **European Community** (EC) to take the lead in diplomatic efforts to end the conflict and signaled that it would not deploy ground forces for any peacekeeping or peace enforcement operation. This relative disengagement from the conflict formed the basis of U.S. policy for the next two years.

Within the United States, however, criticism gradually emerged of both the Bush administration and European efforts to end the conflict. Within the U.S. Congress, there was little support for the deployment of U.S. ground forces to the former Yugoslavia. There was support, however, for the use of U.S. airpower against the **Bosnian Serbs** and for the lifting of the **arms** embargo against the Bosnian **Muslims** (in order for the latter to defend themselves). Candidate Bill Clinton also criticized the Bush administration for its policy toward the Yugoslav conflict in the 1992 U.S. presidential elections. When the Clinton administration came to power in 1993, it undertook a major review of policy toward the Yugoslav conflict, committing itself to a more active role and to a policy of "lift and strike" (i.e., lifting the arms embargo against the Bosnian Muslims and supporting them with airstrikes against the Bosnian Serbs). In May 1993 U.S. secretary of state Warren Christopher toured European capitals seeking support for this new policy. The United States' European allies (particularly Britain and France, the largest contributors to the **UNPROFOR** peacekeeping force) rejected the U.S. policy. They argued that airstrikes would make their

The United States has been the premier military power involved in peacekeeping in the former Yugoslavia in recent years. (NATO photo)

troops on the ground targets of retaliation, that lifting the arms embargo would only intensify the bloodshed, and that the United States should also provide ground forces. The dispute created real bitterness between the United States and its European allies and seriously undermined the unity of NATO.

Despite the apparent defeat of its proposed lift-and-strike policy, the United States gradually began to play a greater diplomatic and military role in the former Yugoslavia. In March 1994, U.S.-led diplomacy resulted in the establishment within **Bosnia-Hercegovina** of the **Muslim-Croat Federation**, itself to be confederated with Croatia. In the spring of 1994, the **Contact Group** (the United States, **Russia**, **United Kingdom**, **France**, and **Germany**) replaced the joint EC-UN **International Conference on the Former Yugoslavia** (ICFY) as the main diplomatic forum for the Yugoslav conflict. From this point on, the United States began to play a greater role in international diplomacy toward the conflict, shaping the Contact Group's proposals. As discussions emerged on the possible withdrawal of UNPROFOR, the United States agreed for the first time that it would be willing to deploy ground forces in the former Yugoslavia in a possible NATO-led operation to evacuate European forces. The United States also deployed 300 ground troops as part of the **UNPREDEP** peacekeeping force in Macedonia.

There remained strong support within the United States for the ideas underlying the proposed policy of lift and strike. In November 1994, the U.S. Congress voted to forbid U.S. participation in enforcing the arms embargo (although this was a largely symbolic step, since the U.S. government did not actually start supplying arms). From 1994 on, the Clinton administration "turned a blind eye" to (and perhaps actively encouraged) the building up of the military strength of Croatia and the Bosnian Muslim-Croat Federation, enabling the latter forces in summer and autumn 1995 to reverse earlier Bosnian Serb military advances. Fears for the unity of NATO, the risk of a chaotic withdrawal of UNPROFOR (with U.S. forces involved), and the massacre in **Srebrenica** in July 1995 prompted more active U.S. engagement. The deployment of the **Rapid Reaction Force** to support UNPROFOR, as well as the withdrawal of peacekeepers from vulnerable positions, paved the way for the NATO-led airstrikes against the Bosnian Serbs in August–September 1995, in which the United States played a central military role. U.S. diplomat **Richard Holbrooke** emerged as a central actor at this point, brokering what were to become the **Dayton Agreements**. In essence, the Dayton accord was a U.S.-designed agreement—reflecting the extent to which the United States had now come to play the central diplomatic and military role in the international response to the Yugoslav conflict.

Under the Dayton Agreements, furthermore, the United States agreed for the first time to deploy ground forces in Bosnia, providing 20,000 of the 60,000 troops in NATO's **Implementation Force** (IFOR). The U.S. Congress, however, remained wary of any long-term commitment of forces to Bosnia. Thus, IFOR's initial mandate was for one year only (to the end of 1996). Toward the end of 1996, the United States agreed to an extension of the mandate of IFOR (now renamed the Stabilization Force—SFOR) to mid-1998, including a continued U.S. commitment. Early in 1998, the United States agreed to a further (and this time largely open-ended) extension of SFOR's mandate, again including a large U.S. component. The United States also continued to play an important diplomatic role in the Bosnian peace process, in bringing pressure to bear on the Serbian and Croatian governments, and in international efforts to prevent conflict in **Kosovo** and **Macedonia**. There remained, however, doubts about the extent of U.S. domestic support (especially in Congress) for a long-term military commitment to support peace in the former Yugoslavia.

—*A. S. C.*

Reference: Kyrou, Alexandros K. "Castle-building in the Balkans: American Aspirations in Southeastern Europe Since the Dissolution of Yugoslavia." *Journal of Political and Military Sociology* 24 (1996): 253–284.

UNPREDEP

The United Nations Preventive Deployment Force (UNPREDEP) was created under United Nations (UN) Security Council Resolution 983 of 31 March 1995, as part of a general restructuring of UN peacekeeping forces in the former Yugoslavia. It was constituted as a separate peacekeeping force with headquarters in **Skopje**, the capital of Macedonia. The joint theater headquarters for all the peacekeeping operations, based in **Zagreb**, was known as the United Nations Peace Forces Headquarters (UNPF-HQ), which existed until the end of January 1996.

From March 1995 to January 1996, overall command and control of UNPREDEP were the responsibility of Special Representative of the Secretary-General (SRSG) **Yasushi Akashi**, based in UNPF-HQ Zagreb; his successor, Kofi Annan; and Theater Force Commander Lt. Gen. **Bernard Janvier** (of France). From February 1996 the SRSG was Henryk Sokalski (of Poland). The military commander from March 1995 to February 1996 was Brig. Gen. Juha Engstrom (of Finland), and the force commander from March 1996 was Brig. Gen. Bo Lennart Wranker (of Sweden).

The total strength of the mission by late 1995 was 1,000 military personnel, plus 26 civilian police monitors and 168 civilian peacekeepers. The tasks of UNPREDEP in Macedonia remained the same as they had been for **UNPROFOR** (UN Protection Force) III between 1992 and 1995: (1) **monitoring** the **borders** of **Macedonia** with the Federal Republic of **Yugoslavia** (FRY) and **Albania**, and (2) working with other agencies to provide **humanitarian aid** while promoting reconciliation among ethnic and political groups within Macedonia. Although Macedonia was never directly involved in the Yugoslav wars, the political situation there remained tense, especially with respect to relations between the republic's Macedonian Slav majority and the large Albanian minority. Although the ruling coalition under President **Kiril Gligorov** has passed a number of reforms supporting democratization, the substantial demands of the **Albanian** community have not been met.

When the government of Macedonia requested the continuation of UNPREDEP following the termination of the missions in **Bosnia** and **Croatia**, it explained this need primarily in terms of external security concerns. These concerns included the need for the normalization of relations with FRY; the need for stability and sustainability around the peace process in **Bosnia-Hercegovina**; and the need for Macedonia to build up its own indigenous defense capabilities. Beginning on 1 February 1996, UNPREDEP became an independent mission reporting directly to UN headquarters in New York, and the mandate was renewed.

Although the internal situation has not been resolved, it is generally agreed that this experiment in preventive deployment has been successful and that UNPREDEP has made a significant contribution to stability in the region, as well as to the security of Macedonia. Some of the factors that are said to have contributed to this success are the presence of a battalion from the **United States** in the mission, signaling a U.S. military and political interest; the balancing of these troops with Nordic troops, with their long experience of peacekeeping; and the continuing monitoring of the military, political, economic, and social situation, providing an objective knowledge of events. This monitoring enabled a good knowledge of risk and risk assessment to be built up, helping to counter rumors and the potential for conflict escalation that such rumors may have generated. For example, in 1994 the assessment of the U.S. State Department was that there was a significant risk of the conflict spreading if there were a mass exodus of ethnic Albanians from the **Kosovo** region of Serbia through Macedonia and on to the Greek border. Such a move would threaten conflict between **Greece** and **Turkey**, but regular monitoring by UNPREDEP suggested that the risk was in fact low. Similarly, some observers believed in March 1995 that military tension in the southern Balkans was high and that a number of Serb units were massed along the border with Macedonia. UNPREDEP was able authoritatively to deny this and thus contributed to deescalation. UNPREDEP's border identification and verification also contributed significantly to confidence building. The force's use in connection with the monitoring of economic **sanctions** against the FRY, however, is generally agreed to have been less effective.

Macedonia's border with Serbia was the subject of long-standing dispute. The UN commander proposed an administrative UN boundary, initially called the Northern Limit of the Area of Operations (NLAOO) but generally referred to as the UN Line. By July 1994 both Serbian and Macedonian patrols had come to respect this boundary, which had become a buffer zone between potentially conflicting parties.

Full costs for UNPREDEP have not been determined, but costs for the six months from January to June 1996 were estimated at U.S.$25 million.

—O. P. R. and T. W.

UNPROFOR

The conflicts that erupted in the former Yugoslavia beginning in 1991 presented **United Nations** (UN) peacekeepers with unparalleled challenges. As the military conflict intensified and spread from

The United Nations Protection Force base in Bosnia-Hercegovina, 1993. (UNHCR)

Slovenia and **Croatia** into **Bosnia-Hercegovina**, the humanitarian problems increased, manifested in the form of large numbers of **refugees** and displaced people, as well as extensive violations of human rights, particularly associated with "**ethnic cleansing.**" The response of the UN took a number of forms.

In August 1992 the **United Nations Commission on Human Rights** (UNCHR) convened a special session on the human rights situation in the former Yugoslavia. The commission appointed a special rapporteur to investigate violations, and from March 1993 the Centre for Human Rights, the practical arm of the UNCHR, set up field offices in Zagreb and Skopje, as well as later in Sarajevo and Mostar.

In October 1992 the UN Security Council established a commission of experts to examine the evidence of grave breaches of the 1949 Geneva Conventions. This move was followed in May 1993 by the decision to establish an International **War Crimes Tribunal** to prosecute those persons responsible for breaches of international humanitarian law in the former Yugoslavia.

In the face of widespread violations of human rights, the number of refugees rose dramatically. Twelve funding appeals for humanitarian assistance were launched between 1991 and 1995 under the auspices of the UN High Commission for Refugees (**UNHCR**). The first appeal anticipated that 500,000 people would need help; by September 1995 it was estimated that humanitarian assistance was needed for 3.5 million people, with a funding need of U.S.$823 million.

Provision was made in September 1992 for the establishment of a limited military force, the UN Protection Force (UNPROFOR), with a mandate to intervene in support of the provision of **humanitarian aid**; this force was authorized to provide protection for UNHCR convoys.

Serious conflict in Yugoslavia first broke out in Croatia. It was initially regarded as an internal affair. The Security Council did not take any formal action on the Yugoslav crisis until September 1991, when it passed UN Security Council Resolution (UNSCR) 713, imposing an embargo on the delivery of arms and other military equipment to the area. On 9 November 1991, the Yugoslav federal presidency asked the Security Council to consider the situation in Croatia and requested the deployment of UN troops to the area. UNPROFOR was established initially for one year and headquartered in **Sarajevo**, the capital of neighboring Bosnia-Hercegovina; it was later moved to the Croatian capital, **Zagreb**. From March 1992 until April 1993, UNPROFOR was headed by its force commander. In May 1993 **Thorvald Stoltenberg** was appointed as special representative of the secretary-general for the former Yugoslavia and became the first civilian head of UNPROFOR. He was succeeded by **Yasushi Akashi** in January 1994. Between March 1992 and March 1995, there were five military officers who served as force commanders: Lt. Gen. **Satish Nambiar** (of India) from March 1992 to March 1993; Lt. Gen. Lars-Eric Wahlgren (of Sweden) from March 1993 to June 1993; Lt. Gen. Jean Cot (of France) from June 1993 to March 1994; Gen. Bertrand de Lapresle (of France) from March 1994 to March 1995; and Gen. **Bernard Janvier** (of France), who took up the post from March 1995. UNPROFOR had three operational commands: UNPROFOR in Croatia (usually referred to as UNPROFOR I), with force commander Maj. Gen. Eid Kamel Al-Rodan of Jordan in March 1995; UNPROFOR in Bosnia-Hercegovina (usually referred to as UNPROFOR II), with force commander Lt. Gen. **Rupert Smith** of the United Kingdom in March 1995; and UNPROFOR in the **Republic of Macedonia** (referred to as UNPROFOR III), with force commander Brig. Gen. Juha Engstrom of Finland in March 1995.

The estimated UN expenditure on the peacekeeping force in the former Yugoslavia between January 1992 and March 1996 was almost U.S.$4.7 billion. This figure includes the costs of UNPROFOR from February 1992 to March 1995, as well as the costs of the UN Confidence Restoration Operation (**UNCRO**), the UN Preventive Deployment Force (**UNPREDEP**), and UN Peace Forces Headquarters (UNPF-HQ). As of March 1995, total deployed force strength stood at 38,599 military personnel, including 684 military observers, with contingents from 39 different countries. The force also included 803 civilian police, 2,017 international civilian staff, and 2,615 local staff.

UNPROFOR was the largest and most expensive peacekeeping mission ever deployed by the UN. By 1994, because of experiences in the former Yugoslavia, as well as in Somalia, peacekeeping was the most controversial activity in which the UN was involved. A series of criticisms was made. Some accounts argued that the whole peacekeeping intervention in Bosnia especially was misconstrued and that not only was the peacekeeping force ineffective but more seriously that it made matters worse. The criticism is partly directed against third-party intervention in **civil war** in general, on the grounds that such interventions cannot be impartial and that their effect is simply to prolong the conflict and thereby, possibly, the suffering. From this kind of argument flows the idea that peacekeeping is an inadequate tool for intervention in active **civil wars** and that its use should be limited to those conflicts that have been terminated. In these circumstances, where a primarily **monitoring** presence—based on consent—is required, the tested principles of classical peacekeeping can be applied. The alternative argument is that peacekeeping forces in former Yugoslavia were inadequately equipped to carry out the demanding mandates that they were given. Consequently, peacekeeping should not be scaled back but significantly strengthened in order to secure the humanitarian and political objectives that it has acquired, in addition to its military roles. Thus, the need for new doctrines and concepts of peacekeeping has been argued, embodied in terms such as "peace support operations" and "second-generation peacekeeping."

UNPROFOR I (Croatia)

In November 1991 a **cease-fire** agreement was reached among Croats and Serbs that included a proposal for a peacekeeping operation. UNPROFOR was eventually established under UNSCR 743 of 21 February 1992. The plan initially called for the deployment of 13,000 troops (12 battalions), civilian personnel, and civilian police. Its main function was to stabilize the situation in Croatia, creating conditions of peace and security within which negotiations for an overall solution could take place. By 23 March advanced deployments of infantry were under way. UNPROFOR was deployed into four sectors within three **United Nations protected areas** (UNPAs): Sectors North and South covered the **Krajina** region of Croatia, while Sector West was in western **Slavonia** and Sector East in eastern Slavonia on the border of the Serb region of the **Vojvodina**. These UNPAs were areas in Croatia occupied by armed Serb militias, where fighting had been most intense and where there were large proportions of Serbs in the civilian populations.

Within each UNPA the UN force was mandated to stabilize the situation (including the maintenance of "interim" existing arrangements for local administration and public order), demilitarize or effect the withdrawal of armed forces, protect the local population, authorize traffic in and out of the UNPAs, monitor local police forces, and assist in the voluntary return of displaced persons and refugees.

The full deployment of UNPROFOR was delayed by several months, and the force was not fully operational until late June 1992. The late arrival of some elements of UNPROFOR was due to financial wrangling in New York as well as complications created by the outbreak of war in Bosnia. One result of this delay was that "ethnic cleansing" continued virtually unchecked, so that by the time UNPROFOR was operational, most of the area's non-Serb population had already been expelled from the UNPAs. Although UNPROFOR battalions reported continued violations of the cease-fire and were often restricted in their freedom of movement, they did manage to set up regular patrols, checkpoints, and observation posts, and they began the crucial process of establishing liaison networks.

UN military observers (UNMOs) reported that although elements of the **Yugoslav Peoples' Army** (JNA) were withdrawing from the UNPAs, as called for in the cease-fire agreement, they were leaving behind arms and equipment for local Serb militias. This problem became significantly worse when, on 27 April 1992, Serbia and **Montenegro** formed the Federal Republic of **Yugoslavia** (FRY). In an attempt to establish its credentials and to counter mounting international pressure, the FRY announced the withdrawal of all Serbs and Montenegrins who were serving in the JNA in other republics. This move stranded large numbers of well-armed troops in both Croatia and Bosnia and led to an influx of soldiers into existing militias. In Croatia this meant that UNPROFOR was faced with a far more militarized situation than had been anticipated and would now be responsible for demobilizing a much larger number of militiamen.

During this initial period of UN activity, another unexpected problem arose that would do much to undermine the effectiveness of the operation in Croatia and to increase the complexity of the task. Areas adjacent to the UNPAs (later called **pink zones**) were held by the JNA but did not come under the UN's mandate (which was restricted to the UNPAs) or the cease-fire agreement. UNPROFOR again found itself in a position of having to mediate in a tense and difficult situation.

The increasing complexity of the situation meant that UNPROFOR's mandate was constantly expanding as experience on the ground brought to light further complexities in implementing the original mandate. UNPROFOR became involved in interviewing individuals who had been forced from their homes, organizing patrols to protect such homes, and compiling data on those groups believed to be responsible for the expulsions. Based on a laboriously negotiated agreement over the **pink zones,** UNPROFOR began monitoring both the withdrawal of the JNA and the activities of local police. UNPROFOR's tasks were enlarged again when the force was authorized to carry out immigration and customs functions at the international borders of the UNPAs. The mandate of UNPROFOR was further extended in October 1992 when the force was given the responsibility of monitoring the demilitarization of the **Prevlaka** Peninsula.

At the beginning of 1993, growing frustration on the part of the Croatian government, particularly over the pink zones but also over the return of displaced persons to the UNPAs, led to a major offensive by the **Croatian Army** (HV) in the southern part of the Krajina (Sector South). A cease-fire agreement based on an earlier Security Council resolution was signed on 6 April 1993. The agreement called for the end of hostilities and the withdrawal of the HV to positions held prior to the incursion of 22 January. Over the following nine months, there were two more major offensives by the HV, and the situation in the pink zones and the UNPAs continued to deteriorate. UNPROFOR continued its efforts to mediate between the two sides and to carry out its mandate.

Violations of negotiated cease-fires continued through 1994 and 1995, and in March 1995 the UN secretary-general recognized that it would not be possible to keep UNPROFOR in its present role because of objections by the Croatian government. However, it was also clear that the withdrawal of UNPROFOR from Croatia might have led the war there to escalate; furthermore, the operation in Bosnia could not have been properly supported without the UN support facilities in Zagreb. These concerns were the basis for the restructuring UNPROFOR at the end of March 1995.

On 31 March 1995, the Security Council decided to replace UNPROFOR with three separate peacekeeping operations: in Bosnia-Hercegovina the mandate and name of UNPROFOR was retained; in Croatia UNPROFOR was replaced by the UN Confidence Restoration Operation; and within Macedonia UNPROFOR III was renamed the UN Preventive Deployment Force. The joint headquarters, based in Zagreb, became known as the United Nations Peace Forces headquarters. Each component was headed by a civilian chief-of-mission and a military force commander.

UNPROFOR II (Bosnia-Hercegovina)
Over the months following the deployment of peacekeepers in Croatia, the attention of the Security Council and the international **media** shifted from Croatia toward the troubles of **Sarajevo** and Bosnia. In response to international pressure and the obvious threat to regional peace and security posed by the conflict, the Security Council progressively stretched UNPROFOR's mandate, which was originally confined to certain areas of Croatia, to include Sarajevo and eventually to include a large-scale humanitarian relief effort throughout Bosnia. Continued fighting, as well as reports of **ethnic cleansing** and other atrocities in Bosnia, led the Security Council to pass Resolution 757 on 30 May 1992 under the enforcement provisions of Chapter VII of the UN's charter (the peacekeeping force in Croatia was not authorized under enforcement provisions). The UN imposed economic **sanctions** against Serbia and Montenegro and demanded that a security zone be formed around the Sarajevo airport. At the same time, the council began considering a report from Secretary-General **Boutros Boutros-Ghali** that detailed possible alternatives for the protection of **humanitarian aid** convoys. The concern was that the use of force could compromise not only the peacekeeping operation but also the position of relief agencies operating in the area. Moreover, setting clear and attainable political aims for such enforcement was considered virtually impossible. Boutros-Ghali suggested that negotiating agreements for the transport and delivery of aid would be the preferable option and recommended a more limited operation focused on opening Sarajevo's airport to relief flights.

Foreshadowing what later would evolve into UNPROFOR II, UNPROFOR's mandate was extended on 8 June 1992 under UNSCR 758. The Security Council voted to deploy military observers in Sarajevo to supervise the withdrawal of heavy weapons from the city and the surrounding area. This was considered the necessary first step in a process that would eventually see the UN take over control of the Sarajevo airport and secure it for the delivery of humanitarian aid. Progress toward implementation of the new mandate was slow, largely owing to lack of cooperation from the parties and the fragility of the cease-fire. Nevertheless, after tough negotiations, the UN took control of the Sarajevo airport from the Serb militias, whereupon the Security Council passed a resolution authorizing the deployment of more peacekeepers to the area. Despite the arrival of more troops in Sarajevo, the war and the humanitarian crisis continued unabated.

The European peace efforts under Lord **Peter Carrington** were characterized by a series of brokered and then broken **cease-fire** agreements, and his tenure as the European Community's main negotiator ended amid some controversy. In the middle of off-and-on peace talks, Carrington negotiated an agreement with the Bosnian factions that called for supervision of heavy weaponry in and around Sarajevo by UN forces. The Security Council quickly agreed to the plan. Boutros-Ghali complained, however, that the new mandate was not only close to impossible to carry out but had been "thrust" upon UNPROFOR without adequate consultation and without financial and other material commitments. He argued that the UN was already desperately overstretched and needed to pay more attention to crises elsewhere in the world. Eventually the dispute was resolved, but it had contributed to a growing feeling in the European Community and elsewhere that an internationalization of peacemaking efforts and a new negotiating framework were necessary; this feeling led to the establishment of the **International Conference on the Former Yugoslavia** (ICFY) based in Geneva.

Between March and July 1992, the humanitarian crisis in Bosnia had worsened considerably. Reports of atrocities in **detention camps** and widespread ethnic cleansing led to an even greater stream of **refugees** seeking to escape the war. The work of the international aid agencies became increasingly difficult and dangerous. In one case a UNHCR convoy had to negotiate its way through 90 roadblocks between Zagreb and Sarajevo, many of them manned by undisciplined militias. In view of these difficulties, on 12 May, following a report by Under Sec. Gen. Marrack Golding, Boutros-Ghali argued in a recommendation to the UN Security Council that Bosnia "in its present phase was not susceptible to the United Nations peacekeeping treatment." An attack on a UN aid convoy heading for the besieged town of **Goražde** at the end of July 1992, however, shifted international opinion toward taking more concerted action in Bosnia. The stalemated peacemaking process served to fan the flames of increasingly adamant demands for enforcement.

Under growing international pressure, the Security Council adopted two resolutions on 13 August 1992 under the enforcement provisions of Chapter VII of the UN's charter. The first resolution (UNSCR 770) called upon all states to take "all measures necessary" to facilitate the delivery of humanitarian aid to Sarajevo and other parts of Bosnia. It further stated that all detention camps in the former Yugoslavia must be immediately opened for international inspection. A second resolution (UNSCR 771) demanded unimpeded and continued access to all camps, prisons, and detention centers within the territory of the former Yugoslavia.

International response was sluggish, however, even after an Italian transport plane bringing humanitarian supplies into Sarajevo was shot down on 3 September 1992, killing the four crew members. It was not until 10 September that the Secretariat presented its report on a "concept of operations" for Bosnia based on UNSCR 770. The proposal suggested that UNPROFOR's mandate be extended and the military personnel sent to fulfill UNSCR 770 under the overall direction of the force commander. The Bosnia Command, headquartered just outside Sarajevo in **Kiseljak**, was subsequently responsible for Sector Sarajevo and four new zones, each with an infantry battalion. Each battalion was responsible for providing protective support to UNHCR-organized convoys inside its own zone.

The Security Council approved the plan on 14 September 1992. Although the operation was authorized under Chapter VII of the UN's charter, it did not (through to the end of 1993) use force to carry out its mandate. In this situation, peacekeepers were expected to negotiate local agreements and talk their way through the roadblocks that dotted the Bosnian countryside. Eight European countries agreed to contribute to and pay for the new force. By early November 1992, UNPROFOR II comprised 7,000 troops from eight European countries plus an infantry battalion from Canada and a field hospital from the United States. However, the full deployment of peacekeepers was hampered by lack of cooperation from the warring parties and the need to negotiate locally the specific terms of their deployment.

At the beginning of October 1992, the Security Council passed yet another extension of UNPROFOR's mandate. It authorized the imposition of a ban on military flights in Bosnian airspace and authorized the UNPROFOR to monitor compliance with this resolution (UNSCR 781). The ban lacked the power of enforcement, and by December 1992 the United States confirmed that Serbian planes had flown more than 200 unauthorized flights; by April 1993 the number of flight violations had risen to 500. The UN finally authorized the shooting down of unauthorized aircraft in the **no-fly zone**. This order was interpreted as a measure of "last resort" and had little impact on the situation.

From the beginning of the civil war in **Bosnia-Hercegovina, Muslims** were slowly forced back into enclaves and both the UN and the aid agencies were regularly denied access to these areas. In one of the worst cases, in the eastern Bosnian town of **Srebrenica**, no aid convoys had been allowed through for months. The crisis prompted the Security Council on 16 April 1993 to declare Srebrenica a "**safe area**" and demand access to the town (UNSCR 819). Canadian troops were allowed into the town two days later, but they were then subject to the same **siege**, and Serb forces refused to allow either convoys or troop supplies and reinforcements through.

On 6 May 1993, the Security Council voted to add Sarajevo, **Tuzla**, **Žepa**, **Goražde**, and **Bihać** to the list of safe areas. Continued noncompliance by Serb militias led the Security Council to pass a resolution under Chapter VII to "ensure full respect for the safe areas" (UNSCRs 824 and 836). The secretary-general, responding to the request of the Security Council, presented a report detailing the new requirements for troop reinforcements and redeployments based on the new mandate. The report suggested that a troop level of 34,000 would be needed to ensure "deterrence through strength" but that the mandate could be implemented, at least initially, with 7,600 new peacekeepers. In establishing and securing the safe areas, UNPROFOR II was given the task of deterring attacks, monitoring a cease-fire, occupying key points in and around the safe areas, and protecting the delivery and distribution of humanitarian relief. In the end the safe areas mandate was not enforced, and by December 1993 only a few thousand troops had arrived—far short of the minimum level needed to do the job. By the end of July 1993, the "safe areas" were so unsafe that a UN special rapporteur on human rights reported that Goražde had been bombarded by **Bosnian Serb** militia artillery for 18 consecutive days in June, leaving half of the city's houses destroyed. To complicate matters further, in May 1993 intense fighting broke out between **Bosnian Croat** forces and the **Bosnian army** in southern and central Bosnia.

Peacekeepers were increasingly targeted by Bosnian factions, particularly Serb **paramilitary** groups. By the end of 1993, the ICFY was no closer to reaching agreement in either Croatia or Bosnia, where, according to UN mediator **Thorvald Stoltenberg**, 69 separate cease-fires had been negotiated and broken.

On 5 February 1994, 69 civilians were killed and nearly 200 injured when the central market in Sarajevo was shelled. In response, the secretary-general requested that the **North Atlantic Treaty Organization** (NATO) be authorized to conduct airstrikes against artillery or mortar positions around Sarajevo that might be responsible for attacks on civilians. A "weapons exclusion zone" of 20 kilometers from the center of Sarajevo was declared, enforced by NATO and monitored by UNPROFOR. However, by the end of March 1994 Bosnian Serb forces launched an attack against the safe area of Goražde, involving indiscriminate shelling of the city and outlying villages. On 22 April, following a request from the secretary-general, NATO declared a military exclusion zone around Goražde and threatened airstrikes against Bosnian Serbs if they did not withdraw before the deadline of 20 April. Similar zones were declared around the other four safe areas. However, the conflict escalated again in the summer and autumn of 1994 when Sarajevo was repeatedly attacked by snipers, and UNPROFOR called in NATO warplanes to attack Bosnian Serb positions violating the exclusion zone around Sarajevo.

A cease-fire in Bosnia-Hercegovina negotiated by former U.S. president Carter, which had come into force on 1 January 1995, failed to last, with violations committed by both Bosnian Serb and Bosnian government forces. Following a military agreement on February 20 between Bosnian and Croatian Serbs, combined Serb forces tightened their blockade of the Bihać enclave in northwestern Bosnia, one of the UN-designated safe areas. Early in March 1995, the governments of Croatia and **Bosnia-Hercegovina** concluded a military alliance, and Bosnian government forces started successful offensives against Serb positions on Mount Vlašić near **Travnik** in central Bosnia, as well as north and east of Tuzla.

Serb forces resumed heavy shelling of Sarajevo in April 1995, and an assault by Bosnian government forces in May aimed at breaking the siege of Sarajevo failed after heavy losses. Late in May, the UNPROFOR force commander in Bosnia, Lt. Gen. **Rupert Smith**, issued an ultimatum to the Bosnian Serbs and to the Bosnian government to withdraw their heavy weapons from a 32-kilometer exclusion zone around Sarajevo. The next day Smith ordered bombing raids by NATO aircraft against Serb weapons stores near their headquarters at **Pale**, whereupon in retaliation the Serbs initiated **hostage taking** of over 300 UN soldiers. The last of the hostages were all released by June 18 following mediation by President **Slobodan Milošević** of Serbia.

With mounting pressure for more decisive and forceful action against Serb attacks, in early June 1995 defense ministers from NATO and other countries decided to create a 14,000-strong **Rapid Reaction Force** consisting of British, French, and Dutch troops to support UN units and to protect the remaining safe areas. However, the Serbs captured the safe area of Srebrenica in July, having previously disarmed the Dutch battalion stationed there. The safe area of Žepa fell to the Serbs in the same month.

In August 1995, Serb forces suffered a series of military defeats at the hands of Croatian and Bosnian government forces in western and central Bosnia, losing a significant amount of territory. Most significantly, the U.S. government began to pressure parties to the conflict in Bosnia to agree to peace talks and on 5 October secured a general cease-fire agreement. On 1 November 1995, under the auspices of the U.S. government, negotiations began in **Dayton**, Ohio, that were to end the conflict in Bosnia. UNPROFOR ceased to exist on 20 December 1995 when authority was transferred to the **Implementation Force**.

UNPROFOR III (Macedonia)
See under **UNPREDEP**

—*O. P. R. and T. W.*

UNTAES

Under the **Dayton Agreements** of November 1995, the eastern **Slavonia** region of Croatia (which had been seized from Croatian control by the Serbs in the autumn of 1991) was to be peacefully reintegrated with Croatia but administered by a UN force for an interim 12–24 months. The United Nations Transitional Administration for Eastern Slavonia, Baranja, and Western Sirmium (UNTAES) was established in January 1996. The force, with a strength of 3,200, was mandated to facilitate the demilitarization of the region, monitor the return of **refugees**, contribute to peace and security in the region, and assist in the implementation of the peace agreement. During its period of deployment, UNTAES was relatively successful in implementing its mandate. The force was, however, withdrawn and replaced by a smaller mission from the **Organization for Security and Cooperation in Europe** (OSCE) in January 1998, when the region came fully under Croatian control. Shortly before this time, most of the region's remaining Serb population fled, fearing for their prospects in a nationalist Croatian state.

—*A. S. C.*

URBAN CHARACTER

See **rural-urban differences**

USTAŠA

Memories of the pre-1945 Ustaša-Hrvatska Revolucionarna Organizacija (UHRO, Insurgency-Croatian Revolutionary Organisation), usually referred to simply as Ustaša, have exercised a powerful influence as a weapon in the **propaganda** war between **Croatia** and **Serbia**.

The fact that there has been little contemporary research into the Ustaša reveals Yugoslavs' reluctance to address the subject objectively. The Ustaša was founded in 1929 by the Zagreb lawyer **Ante Pavelić**, a former leader of the Croatian Party of Rights. It acted as a small terrorist organization between 1929 and 1941 and was responsible for several terrorist attacks in Yugoslavia. The Yugoslav dictatorship under King Aleksandar repressed the group and sought to murder its agents abroad, many of whom were being funded by and operating from Hungary and Fascist Italy. The Ustaša gained wider notoriety in October 1934, when its agents, in collaboration with the Macedonian terrorist group IMRO, assassinated King Aleksandar and the French foreign minister in Marseilles, possibly to aid the disintegration of Yugoslavia and provide an opportunity to found an independent Croatia.

Ustaša ideology was rooted in nineteenth-century concepts of nationalism in which the goal was the re-creation of "Greater Croatia" based upon the boundaries of King Tomislav's medieval Croatia, which had included Croatia, **Dalmatia**, **Slavonia**, and much of **Bosnia-Hercegovina**, to be achieved through an Ustaša-directed insurgency. Ustaša ideology was anti-Serb, anticommunist, antidemocratic, and antimodern in that it focused upon peasant forms of socioeconomic organization. Roman Catholic identity was central to Ustaša ideology, **Catholic** Croatia being seen as the historic bulwark of the Christian West against a series of Eastern invaders, including Slavs and communists. The claim of descent from the Goths meant that those of Croatian ethnic origins were considered to be distinct from their "inferior" Serb neighbors. **Bosnian Muslims**, however, were considered part of the Croatian nation, indeed the purest of all Croats, and more than 12 percent of NDH officials and Ustaša members were Muslims.

The Ustaša achieved power after the Nazi invasion of Yugoslavia in April 1941 when Pavelić was invited to become *poglavnik* (leader) of the newly created puppet Independent State of Croatia (Nezavisna Država Hrvatska—NDH) after Vladko Maček, the German choice for the office, refused the appointment. Occupied by Axis forces, the NDH was nominally ruled as a kingdom by the Duke of Spoleto under the title Tomislav II, although he never set foot in Croatia. The NDH gradually became a cipher, increasingly subject to Nazi political influence and economic exploitation.

Within weeks of coming to power, Ustaša units began the forced conversion, expulsion, or extermination of the **Orthodox** Serb population, which comprised approximately 20 percent of the population of the NDH, occasionally with the blessing and, in some cases, the participation of individual members of the clergy. Serbs were forced to wear armbands featuring a letter P, symbolising *pravoslavac* (Orthodox). The NDH operated 24 concentration camps, the main extermination center being at **Jasenovac**. Special courts handed down death sentences to be carried out within three hours, although many Serbs were executed in village massacres. The chaos caused by the massacres and forced conversions resulted in the creation of a Croatian Orthodox Church, under a White Russian prelate, to provide an acceptable identity for Croatian Serbs.

Despite the fact that the Ustaša stressed their religious affinities, the NDH was not recognized by the Vatican, owing to its extremism. Although the Croatian Catholic Church did initially endorse the Ustaša regime, Christian voices were raised in protest at certain aspects of Ustaša policy, especially that of Cardinal **Alojzije Stepinac**, who, although he described the NDH as "the hand of God in action," objected to the persecution of non-Catholics.

Croat nationalism was tarred with the brush of fascism in postwar Yugoslavia in order to discredit and undermine the nationalist movement. Memories of Ustaša atrocities were resurrected in 1946 during the trial on charges of collaboration of Stepinac, who symbolized, in Croatian eyes, the spirit of the Croatian nation and defiance of Serb hegemony. The suppression of Croat nationalism in **Tito**'s Yugoslavia was also aided, Croats feel, by exaggerations of the scale of Ustaša atrocities by his regime. This issue was addressed by **Franjo Tudjman** in his book (*Bespuća povijesne zbiljnost;* originally published in Zagreb in 1989) in which he revised downward the estimate of the numbers killed at Jasenovac.

The revival of Ustaša imagery and claims, by Serbs, of "Ustashoid" behavior in Tudjman's Croatia were important to the Serb insurrection in Croatia in 1991. German **recognition** of Croatian independence presented Serbs with uncomfortable parallels with 1941, as did the decision to reintroduce the ***kuna*** as the unit of currency and the ***šahovnica*** (chessboard) as the national flag. Ustaša persecution shaped Serb **propaganda** designed to portray themselves to the West as victims, including parallels with the Holocaust intended to enlist the sympathy of Israel and of Jews, who were also Ustaša targets. Such propaganda informed much of the West's response to the crisis in the early years of the war. This strategy was effective in the **Krajina** when the Serb **media** exploited the Croatian policy of replacing **Cyrillic** signs with Latin in mixed areas, the dismissal of Serbs from their posts, and the reintroduction of perceived Ustaša symbols to claim that the new Croatian state was fascist.

The one party in Croatia to embrace the Ustaša legacy is **Dobroslav Paraga**'s extremist **Croatian Party of Rights** (Hrvatska Stranka Prava—HSP). Its activists wear the Ustaša black shirt and a U on their caps. The HSP's paramilitary wing, the HOS (Hrvatske Obrambene Snage, or Croatian Defence Forces), included several thousand fighters who partially compensated for the **Croatian Army**'s shortage of soldiers and proved to be the most effective force in the field, holding out in **Vukovar** for three months. Television and poster images of the HOS featured black-shirted young men raising their arms in the Nazi salute with the Ustaša U carved on their rifle stocks and using the old Ustaša slogan "Ready for the Homeland." Tudjman's aim to circumvent the HSP and appeal directly to nationalists led him to portray the NDH in a more favorable light, introduce NDH symbols, and honor former Ustaša leaders. It has been claimed that the absorption of Croatia into postwar Yugoslavia denied it the opportunity to come to terms with its Ustaša past and present its former enemies with the opportunity to "absolve" Croatia of war-guilt.

—*M. J. W.*

See also: Jewish question; Language question; Religious dimension

References: Irvine, Jill A. "Nationalism and the Extreme Right in the Former Yugoslavia." In L. Cheles, R. Ferguson, and M. Vaughan (eds.), *The Far Right in Western and Eastern Europe,* 2nd ed. Longman: London, 1995; Tudjman, Franjo. *Horrors of War: Historical Reality and Philosophy.* New York: M. Evans, 1997.

V

VALENTIĆ, NIKICA

Nikica Valentić (born 1950) was president of the government (prime minister) of Croatia in 1993, succeeding **Hrvoje Šarinić**. He was a member (along with Šarinić, Franjo Gregurić, and Mladen Vedriš) of the technocratic, moderate wing of the **Croatian Democratic Union** (HDZ). This group wanted to pursue economic reform and integration with Western markets; they eschewed the ideologically based program of the hard-line **Hercegovinan** faction, who wanted to maintain the war in Bosnia. Rumors that Valentić and his group were seeking to ensure their own material gain from their positions caused problems for them among their opponents.

When **Stipe Mesić** and **Josip Manolić** split from the HDZ to form the HNDS (Croatian Independent Democratic Party), many people saw Valentić as a natural political ally. However, although Vedriš (Valentić's close friend and colleague) did join them, Valentić and Gregurić did not. Valentić, through his threat to resign, was instrumental in lifting the blockade of the **United Nations protected areas** (UNPAs) by displaced Croats in August 1994. Had he resigned, Croatia would have probably lost the **International Monetary Fund** (IMF) loan of U.S.$246 million needed to shore up the ***kuna*** (Croatia's new currency).

—G. R. B.

VANCE, CYRUS

Cyrus Roberts Vance (born 1917) is a lawyer and former government official of the United States who was appointed to represent the **United Nations** (UN) as cochair of the **International Conference on the Former Yugoslavia** (ICFY), set up after the **London Conference** of 26–27 August 1992. He served in this capacity until May 1993. Vance qualified as a lawyer at Yale Law School and initially made his career with a New York firm, becoming president of the New York Bar Association from 1974 to 1976. In 1961 he also began an intermittent career in public service that included posts as secretary of the army (1962–1964) and deputy secretary of defense (1964–1967). He was appointed as President Johnson's special envoy on the Cyprus situation in 1967 and on the Korean situation in 1968, as negotiator at the Paris talks on Vietnam in 1968–1969, and as a member of the Independent Commission on Disarmament and Security in 1980.

Vance's personal acquaintance with **David Owen** antedates by a long time their cooperation in the ICFY, and Vance is believed to have been an important influence securing Owen's involvement. Although his engagement with Yugoslavia is primarily associated with the **Vance Plan** and the **Vance-Owen Plan**, Vance also brokered the agreement in September 1995 normalizing relations between **Greece** and **Macedonia**.

He has held a wide range of other functions in connection with the law, business, and public service, including a stint as chair of the board of the Rockefeller Foundation (1975–1977). He holds several honorary degrees, was awarded the Congressional Medal of Freedom in 1969, and became an honorary Knight of the British Empire in 1994 in recognition of his work in Yugoslavia.

—J. B. A.

VANCE PLAN

Cyrus Vance arrived in Yugoslavia in the autumn of 1991 as the peacemaker sponsored by the **United Nations** (UN), to some extent complementing if not superseding the initiatives of Lord **Carrington** sponsored by the **European Community** (EC). The Vance Plan, however, was centered on **Croatia**. It involved the creation of four **UN protected areas** (UNPAs)—East, West, North, and South—covering the three parts of Croatia (the **Krajina,** western **Posavina,** and the eastern end of **Slavonia**) that were in Serb hands. It provided for the following: the deployment of 12,000–15,000 UN troops (which became the UN Protection Force, or **UNPROFOR**); the demilitarization of the areas through the withdrawal of the **Yugoslav Peoples' Army**, the **Croatian Army**, and Serb **paramilitary** forces; a general **cease-fire** in Croatia; and the return of **refugees.**

—J. J. H.

VANCE-OWEN PLAN

The Vance-Owen peace plan was devised by **Cyrus Vance**, the **United Nations** (UN) peace envoy, and Lord **David Owen**, the **European Union** (EU) mediator. It was presented in January 1993, some nine months after the start of the conflict in Bosnia. The plan was guided by a desire to preserve **Bosnia-Hercegovina** as a multiethnic unitary state by formalizing the internal distribution of territories on the basis of **ethnicity** with regard to both the geographical and the historical contexts.

This goal was to be achieved by instituting 10 provinces (usually referred to as "**cantons**"), each with substantially devolved powers. This geographical solution could hardly be described as neat, given the historically diverse and intermingled distribution of the three communities: Serb, Croat, and Muslim. Three of these provinces were to be mainly Muslim, three mainly Serb, and two mainly Croat; in the center-west it proved difficult to characterize the proposed tenth province as other than mixed Muslim-Croat, and in the case of **Sarajevo** itself (province 7) all three of the ethnic groups were to share power. Sarajevo was also to be the seat of a weakened central government for Bosnia-Hercegovina.

Of the parties to be convinced, only the Croats could accept the cartography with readiness, as it offered them scarcely less than their highest expectation. The mainly Muslim Bosnian government could not support a diminution of their central powers, nor what in their eyes involved ethnic manipulation, but they eventually accepted it under international pressure in their expectation that the Serbs would not agree to it in any case. This left the Serbian government in Belgrade to be persuaded to put pressure upon the **Bosnian Serbs** to accept. Serbian president **Slobodan Milošević** was himself under pressure from a new round of proposed international economic **sanctions**, but he was prepared to put the plan to the Bosnian Serbs in return for certain clarifying assurances. These assurances related to (1) the potentially Croat-controlled **Posavina Corridor** that linked the Serbs of **Banja Luka** and the northwest with **Serbia** "proper"; (2) the control of territories already taken and "Serbianized" by the Bosnian Serbs but that would now be returned to Croat/Muslim administration; and (3) the question of whether the collective presidency proposed under the Vance-Owen Plan would operate on the basis of majority voting or consensus. Having been assured of the role of the UN forces in relation to the first two points and of the principle of consensus (which could effectively imply a veto) in relation to the last, Milošević felt able to sell the plan to the Bosnian Serbs as one that they could manipulate toward the formation of a unified Serb state on Bosnian territory. After protracted pressure, Bosnian Serb leader **Radovan Karadžić** was persuaded in an environment of ultimatum at Athens on 2 May 1993 to agree to the plan, with his proviso that it be ratified by the Bosnian Serb parliament in **Pale.**

This was the closest that the Vance-Owen Plan came to fruition. Cyrus Vance himself felt able at this point to effect his previous indication that he would retire, and David Owen affirmed his faith in Milošević to prevail at Pale; in fact, however, the Bosnian Serb parliament voted by almost 5 to 1 in favor of a referendum, and the plan was effectively dead, as a referendum would undoubtedly have resulted in the plan's rejection.

Owen himself was later to complain of the change in, and lack of, support that he received from the new administration of the **United States.** The Vance-Owen Plan had been well intended in the context of a search for a multiethnic solution, but the price of failure was bound to be high in leaving a potentially worse situation than had previously been in place; the plan had now firmly implanted on all sides the notion of territoriality and preemptive gain. Furthermore, if only temporarily, it reopened the conflict between Croats and Muslims and undermined the influence that the Belgrade government had hitherto held over the Bosnian Serbs. A plan designed for peace had (unintentionally) escalated the war.

—J. J. H.

VARAŽDIN

A historic fortified town on the Drava River in northern Croatia, Varaždin was formerly home to a large garrison of the **Yugoslav Peoples' Army** (JNA). In September 1991, during the Serb-Croat conflict, Varaždin was one of the first JNA bases to surrender to the Croats; its commander, Vlado Trifunović, was subsequently tried and sentenced in Belgrade for treason on grounds of no resistance. The newly formed **Croatian Army** took full possession of the barracks and armory for its own use.

—J. J. H.

VERGINA, SUN OF

One of the primary obstacles to Greek **recognition** of the **Republic of Macedonia** was the use of the Sun of Vergina (referred to by Greeks as the Star of Vergina) as the Macedonian state symbol. Following the declaration of independence of the Republic of Macedonia in January 1992, there was considerable debate about the adoption of a national symbol. The golden lion on a scarlet background favored by many was rejected as too provocative with respect to opinion in **Bulgaria** in that it had heraldic associations with medieval Bulgarian emperors. A deputy in the Sobranie (Assembly) from Gevgelija proposed a sun design found in several historical and archeological sites in Macedonia, and the 16-pointed golden sun on a scarlet background was adopted.

The proposal immediately met with a hostile reception in **Greece** because the best-known instance of this symbol was an archeological discovery at Vergina, near Mount Olympus. Its adoption by the Macedonian Republic was seen as implying territorial ambitions to the whole of geographical Macedonia and as claiming an illegitimate connection between the modern Macedonian state and the ancient Macedonian Empire of Alexander.

On 13 September 1995, an agreement was signed in New York, brokered by United Nations mediator **Cyrus Vance**, that resulted in the lifting of the Greek trade embargo against Macedonia in return for the abandonment of the use of this symbol. The agreement was ratified by the Sobranie on 13 October, and the offending symbol was replaced by another design—also featuring a 16-rayed golden sun on a scarlet background.

—J. B. A.

See also: Macedonia (geographical region)

VIŠEGRAD

A predominantly Bosnian **Muslim** (Bošnjak) town of 21,000 inhabitants (as of 1991), Višegrad lies on the **Drina River** along the border with **Serbia**, some 70 miles east of the Bosnian capital of **Sarajevo**. Like **Zvornik** to the north and **Foča** to the south, Višegrad's strategic location has long made it central to Serbian nationalists intent on creating a **Greater Serbia** in the region. For this reason the town was ruthlessly subjected to "**ethnic cleansing**" by **paramilitary/irregular forces** from Serbia in April 1992. During these atrocities, Bošnjak civilians were murdered and then, in a symbolic gesture, thrown off the famous sixteenth-century bridge immortalized in Ivo Andrić's novel *The Bridge on the Drina* (Belgrade: Prosveta, 1945). At the height of the killing, the large number of bodies floating in the Drina clogged the hydroelectric **energy** generation station on the Serb side of the river at Bistrica. (An isolated but potentially significant incident was the earlier action of a local Muslim soldier, Murad Sabanović, who had temporarily taken control of the dam and bluffed the Serbs into believing he was on the verge of blowing it up.)

Thereafter a purely Serb town in the **Republika Srpska** (RS), Višegrad is now one of a number of crossing points between Serbia and the **Bosnian Serb** entity. Previously far removed from the United Nations Protection Force (**UNPROFOR**), Višegrad came into the French sector of the **Implementation/Stabilization Force** after the signing of the Dayton Agreements in December 1995. Politically, Višegrad became a bastion of hard-line Serb nationalists supportive of former RS president **Radovan Karadžić** in his power struggle against RS president **Biljana Plavšić**. Economically, Višegrad has suffered through its isolation from the rest of Bosnia, particularly Sarajevo.

—M. M.

VITEZ

A small town of 27,000 people before the war, lying between **Travnik** and **Zenica** in north-central Bosnia, Vitez is strategically placed in the Lašva Valley, the major supply route to besieged **Sarajevo** from Croatia during the Bosnian war of 1992–1995. The scene of major fighting between the Bosnian **Muslims** and **Bosnian Croats** in 1993, Vitez then became part of the ministate **Herceg-Bosna**—but just barely. Since the first United Nations Protection Force (**UNPROFOR**) deployments in Bosnia in 1992, Vitez and nearby **Gornji Vakuf** have been the operational headquarters of all British military forces in Bosnia. In 1995 Vitez was also the headquarters of the Anglo-French **Rapid Reaction Force.**

In the event of renewed hostilities in Bosnia, the Travnik-Zenica-Vitez triangle is sure to figure prominently as a war zone. More or less evenly divided between Muslims and Croats before the war, the "**ethnic cleansing**" of the former by the latter, as well as subsequent atrocities in the area, have left Vitez bitterly contested. The **Vance-Owen Plan** for Bosnia in 1993 inexplicably awarded Vitez to the Croats, guaranteeing conflict in and around the town later the same year.

—M. M.

VLLASI, AZEM

Azem Vllasi, an ethnic **Albanian,** was head of the youth organization of the **League of Communists of Yugoslavia** and was at one time known as "**Tito**'s pet." His trial in 1989 became a cause célèbre marking the deterioration of Kosovar-Serb relations. Following the strikes of the **Trepča miners** in 1981, Vllasi was put in charge of the Kosovo League of Communists. His stand against Serb leader **Slobodan Milošević**'s policy toward **Kosovo** stems from his discussions and disagreements following Milošević's provocative speech to the Serbs of Kosovo on 24 April 1987. After demonstrations in November 1988, in reaction to proposed Serbian constitutional changes, Vllasi was expelled from the central committee of the League of Communists. He was taken into custody in February 1989, although massive protests delayed his trial until August, when he was accused of counterrevolutionary activity. Although Vllasi was in prison at the time of a further miners' strike in March 1989, when 24 Albanians were killed, he and 14 other "organizers" were held responsible. The farcical trial of Vllasi and his codefendants, which began in October, was eventually abandoned, partly as a result of international pressure. He was released from prison in April 1990 at the same time as **Adem Demaçi.**

—A. T. Y.

VOJVODINA

The Vojvodina forms the northern part of **Serbia,** bordered by **Hungary** to the north. It is a fertile region of 8,300 square miles (21,000 square kilometers) bisected by the **Danube** and Tisa Rivers. Its population totals just over 2 million, including a significant minority of Hungarians. The capital city is Novi Sad, whose population of nearly 200,000 makes it the second-largest city in Serbia after the capital, **Belgrade.** After 1945 the Vojvodina enjoyed political status as an autonomous province, as did **Kosovo** in the south of Serbia, and through the Yugoslav constitution of 1974 was granted extended powers similar to those granted to the six main republics of the Yugoslav federation. After the death of President **Tito** in 1980, the Vojvodina was made eligible for the rotating presidency. These developments were seen by many Serbs as a weakening of the Serb sphere of influence, and following the events surrounding the **Albanian** majority in Kosovo during the 1980s, Serbian president **Slobodan Milošević** turned his attention to curbing the powers of autonomy in the Vojvodina. His orchestrations during the summer of 1988 culminated in the so-called "yogurt revolution" in October when tens of thousands of Serb demonstrators gathered in Novi Sad, with full cartons of yogurt as missiles to humiliate and to drive out the presidency and party leadership of the Vojvodina. Despite the previous conciliatory interventions by Boško Krunić of the local party, the linking of the Vojvodina with the problems of the Serbs in Kosovo was a winning card that Milošević laid before the Serbs of the Vojvodina. The Vojvodina remained a province, but its new leaders were chosen to bring it firmly under the control of Belgrade.

—J. J. H.

VUKOVAR

Vukovar is a town in the eastern **Slavonia** region of **Croatia.** Because of the **siege** that ended in the destruction and capture of the city in the autumn of 1991, Vukovar became an international symbol for the war in general. Prior to the war, the town had a population of 84,000, 43.7 percent of whom were Croat and 37.4 percent Serb.

Vukovar was first shelled in July 1991 but came under sustained attack toward the end of August, by which time most of the more nationalistic Serbs had left, although many Serbs remained, refusing to identify with radical nationalism. The towns of Vinkovci and Vukovar stood in the way of Serb con-

A 1992 street scene in Vukovar. (Nikomoy Faynia)

trol of the region, which is rich in oil, with fertile agricultural land.

Because Vukovar is situated at the start of the spur of Slavonia that reaches toward Novi Sad in the Vojvodina, the **Yugoslav Peoples' Army** (JNA) and Serb militia found it easy to maintain pressure against the city. In September 1991 Vukovar became the scene of fierce fighting, with Zagreb radio reporting 80 dead on 14 September; hospital records state that between 16 and 80 wounded came into the hospital daily for the next fortnight. Fighting in eastern Slavonia became more intense when a column of around 100 tanks, numerous artillery pieces, and armored personnel carriers was sent to the region on 19 September.

By October, people were living in communal shelters and the whole city was being regularly bombarded by mortars, artillery, and aircraft. Despite the overwhelming superiority of the JNA and Serb militia in both hardware and numbers, and although the city was encircled, the Croatian defenders prevented substantial territorial gains. The conscripts of the JNA had no sense of purpose, and the officers of the different regional forces were unable to sustain a single chain of command. Following reorganization of the army and militia by Gen. Života Panić, however, the final push to take the town began on 3 November.

Over the next two weeks, the JNA, supported by **paramilitary** units, took district after district of the city, forcing the remaining inhabitants into the hospital complex. By 18 November, after a siege of 89 days, Vukovar had fallen. Convoys of displaced people left the city for other parts of Croatia, but many of the men who were still in the town when the JNA took it disappeared and are believed to have been killed. Vukovar was almost completely destroyed in the fighting, and despite its reoccupation by Serbs very little has been done to rebuild it. Outside the **United Nations** headquarters in Zagreb, a wall stretches the length of two sides of the Borongaj barracks, each brick inscribed with the name of someone who disappeared in Vukovar.

Vukovar became for Croats one of the most powerful symbols of the Serb aggression, partly through the exceptional organization and determination of the city's displaced population, who continued to elect a city council in exile and sustained pressure on the Croatian government for action on a number of issues relating to the war.

—G. R. B.

WAR COSTS

Undoubtedly the costs inflicted by the war in terms of the breakup of Yugoslavia have been enormous; the difficulty lies, however, in making any kind of accurate assessment of their scale. If there have been problems in assessing the human **casualties** resulting from war, the difficulties of calculating material and financial costs are even greater for several reasons.

The prewar inventory of any region affected by war is not accurately known. The assets of a region or state are not constant and in some cases are highly variable. The trade in **tourism** coming to the **Adriatic** coast has varied from year to year, for example, so that it is not possible to say with certainty just how many foreign visitors would have come to **Croatia** (and how much they might have spent) had there not been war. The yields of agriculture vary enormously with such factors as the weather, and the prices of commodities fluctuate on the world markets. Consequently it is not easy to say how much Yugoslav farmers might have made from the sale abroad of, say, maize if not for the war. Above all, it is hard to make any firm estimate of the loss to the state caused by the death or incapacity of a productive worker. With the best of intentions, therefore, assessments of war damage must contain an element of guesswork.

Two additional and special difficulties lie in the way of accurately estimating the costs of war in Yugoslavia. A substantial part of the military costs of the war stemmed from breaking the **arms trans-**

An improvised burial ground in Sarajevo. (UNHCR)

fer embargo imposed by the **United Nations** (UN) in 1992, and consequently a high degree of secrecy surrounds the military expenditure of parties to the conflict. Furthermore, the states that have emerged from the former Yugoslav federation did not exist as separate states before the war. For this reason it is not possible to measure an increase in their military expenditure as a result of the war because this type of expense was not accounted for on a republican basis before the war.

The problem is compounded by the high incentives to overestimate the value of damage. The temptation to inflate the cost of an individual's insurance claim would be tempered to some extent by the knowledge that one's premium in subsequent years would be higher. There is no such disincentive to inflated claims about war damage. Where states expect to be able to claim reparations from other states, there will be an incentive to magnify the figures, although that is a minor aspect of the Yugoslav conflict. When those who have suffered in war are presenting their case to international bodies that administer aid, there is certainly a temptation to overstate their needs and to use "aid" as a means of augmenting investment. Not surprisingly, therefore, there has been a systematic discrepancy between (1) the accounts of the scale of war damage prepared by various parties to the Yugoslav conflict and (2) the estimates of the scale of such costs prepared by outside bodies. The World Bank, for example, has estimated the costs of direct war damage in **Bosnia-Hercegovina** at U.S.$15 billion, although the government of the federation has calculated that the figure should be U.S.$150–200 billion. It is not easy to reconcile discrepancies of this order.

Finally, it is important to make conceptual distinctions between the costs of waging war, the costs of remedying damage caused by the conduct of war (reconstruction), and the costs of the wider consequences of war. The third category, while perhaps the hardest to estimate, is in many respects likely to be the most important in the long run. A high proportion of the population that has left the region as a result of war will not return. Within this group it is likely that the higher levels of skill and training are overrepresented. The indirect loss to the economy therefore has to be reckoned in terms of a deterioration of the country's economic potential. Of course, more direct costs relating to the labor force, such as the health costs occasioned by injury, disease, and poor living standards caused directly by war, as well as the impact of war upon the requirements for providing pensions, must also be considered.

It is impossible to give firm figures for the costs of the Yugoslav conflict in any of the senses just mentioned. Nevertheless, an illustration of the order of comparison is appropriate. The **population** of Yugoslavia before the war was one-tenth that of the United States (24 million), yet it is not unlikely that all combined aspects of the costs of war in Yugoslavia might eventually equal the annual budgetary receipts of the U.S. government (U.S.$1,257 billion in 1994).

—*J. B. A.*

WAR CRIMES

Actions that are generally known as "war crimes" are precisely specified in international humanitarian law, particularly in the four Geneva Conventions of 1949; the Convention on the Prevention and Punishment of the Crime of **Genocide** (1951); and the two Protocols Additional to the Geneva Conventions (1977). These instruments draw a distinction between international and noninternational conflicts (the latter is often called "**civil war**"), and the conditions governing these types of conflict differ significantly. This distinction is important in relation to the Yugolav conflict for several reasons. Numerous states agreed to the **recognition** of both **Slovenia** and **Croatia** following the lead set by the **European Community** (EC) in January 1992. After 6 April 1992, several states recognized the independence of **Bosnia-Hercegovina**, which was admitted as a member of the **United Nations** (UN) on 22 May. The newly formed federation of **Serbia** and **Montenegro** as the Federal Republic of **Yugoslavia** was declared on 27 April 1992, after which it too was recognized by a number of states, especially members of the **Nonaligned Movement**. From the early summer of 1992 onward, it seems appropriate to treat the Yugoslav conflict as primarily international, although prior to that there is justification in regarding it as civil war.

This view lends a different aspect to the brief war in Slovenia, as well as the initial occupation of the Croatian **Krajina**, relative to the struggle in Bosnia-Hercegovina, for both occurred while Yugoslavia was still one country, just before Slovene and Croatian independence. Although this perspective is problematic for a number of reasons, its broad utility is strengthened by the facts that (1) Croatia became a "High Contracting Party" to the Geneva Conventions on 11 May 1992 and (2) representatives of Croatia and Yugoslavia had already met in Geneva on 26–27 November and 19–20 December 1991 and signed agreements to comply with all provisions of international humanitarian law. The government of Bosnia-Hercegovina has also repeatedly committed itself to abide by these provisions, initially in its statement announcing a state of war on 22 July 1992. The government of the Yugoslav federation has insisted upon its status as the legal successor to the former Socialist Federal Republic of Yugoslavia, which was a signatory to all of the relevant conventions and protocols and can therefore also be considered to be bound by them.

The Geneva Conventions and related instruments lay down rules for the conduct of military activity in a wide range of circumstances: treatment of prisoners; immunity of civilian populations, including the prohibition of terror attacks designed to damage morale; designation of appropriate military objectives and exclusion of civilian objects—especially those of cultural significance; and treatment of journalists. Several actions are specifically forbidden, including torture and other outrages against human dignity; **hostage taking** and the use of human shields; attacks upon the sick and wounded and those caring for them; and the forced displacement of civilian populations.

According to evidence collected by Helsinki Watch, it appears that hardly any article of international humanitarian law has not been contravened during the course of the Yugoslav conflict. Some of these violations became major items of international **media** attention, giving to the war its defining characteristics, especially the artillery bombardments of **Dubrovnik**, **Vukovar**, and **Sarajevo**; the humiliating treatment and mass execution of prisoners in **detention camps**; the wholesale forced displacement of civilians that came to be known as "**ethnic cleansing**"; and the capture of UN personnel as hostages and their deployment as human shields in order to deter attack.

It was as a result of concern about the scale and seriousness of infractions against international humanitarian law in the course of the conflict that the **War Crimes Tribunal** was established at The Hague in 1993.

—*J. B. A.*

Reference: Helsinki Watch. *War Crimes in Bosnia-Hercegovina; A Helsinki Watch Report.* London and New York: Human Rights Watch, 1992.

WAR CRIMES TRIBUNAL

In May 1993, responding to increasing evidence of atrocities in **Bosnia-Hercegovina**, the **United Nations** (UN) established the International **War Crimes** Tribunal for the Former Yugoslavia (the first such organized international initiative since the Nuremberg trials of Nazi personnel half a century earlier). Its internationally structured status is important, as there was general reluctance to echo the form of the Yugoslav trials of **Chetnik** leader Draža Mihailović, Archbishop **Stepinac**, and others in 1946.

The War Crimes Tribunal sits in The Hague (Netherlands) and is presided over by an international lawyer from Italy, Antonio Cassese. Its terms of reference include **genocide**, crimes against humanity, and violations of the laws of war (especially with respect to **rape**), including the Geneva Conventions. It has the power to investigate allegations, assess evidence, indict suspects, issue warrants for arrest, and (only since implementation of the **Dayton Agreements**) conduct trials. The tribunal also has its own detention center at nearby Scheveningen, where those indicted are held pending trial. Its first trial was that of **Dušan Tadić**, a **Bosnian Serb** in 1996, and his successful prosecution one year later partly boosted the morale of both the tribunal and the dispossessed in the former Yugoslavia, as did the voluntary coming to trial of **Bosnian Croat** commander Tihomir Blakšić. On 9 March 1998, the first prosecution for rape was successful when Dragoljub Kunarac, a 37-year-old Bosnian Serb, who a few days earlier had given himself up to French forces in Bosnia, admitted to organizing rapes of **Muslim** women in the town of **Foča**. However, frustration has remained high. One reason is that there has been a limited budget both for traditional methods and for newer initiatives such as DNA "fingerprinting." However, the main source of frustration has been the lack of positive action by **North Atlantic Treaty Organization** (NATO) forces and others in seeking out those whom the tribunal has indicted, in particular Bosnian Serb leaders **Radovan Karadžić** and **Ratko Mladić**. Out of 75 persons indicted by the summer of 1997, only 10 were in the hands of the tribunal. The recent introduction of "sealed" (as opposed to public) indictments does show signs of bringing greater numbers to trial. The tribunal publishes regular bulletins on its activities through its information office.

—*J. J. H.*

WAR REPORTING

In addition to the general issues that have confronted the media in covering the unfolding events in Yugoslavia, several specific difficulties were attached to the coverage of developments there by specialist war reporters.

A recurring problem for war reporters (who typically describe themselves as "foreign correspondents") is that the nature of the conflict is usually already defined in the minds of editors and the public. Hence, these reporters come to their task with a framework of inferences already in place about the nature of the conflict and its causes. Regular coverage by specialist correspondents on the ground of the fighting in Yugoslavia seems to have begun in November 1991. By this time the conflict had been defined as an interethnic struggle, which tended to limit investigative reporting about, for example, the nature and significance of action by the **Yugoslav Peoples' Army** in **Croatia** and imposed upon reporters the definition of government forces in **Bosnia-Hercegovina** as "Muslim," despite evidence to the contrary.

It has been said that generals are always fighting the previous war. Some specialist commentators on warfare (for example, Christopher Bellamy) have suggested that a feature of the current historical period is that the nature of war is changing, confronting armed forces with a range of unfamiliar situations. To the extent that this situation is true, it also poses problems for the professional war reporter. The Yugoslav war was in significant respects unlike the major conflicts that preceded it and that would have provided the background experience for reporters covering it—the Gulf War, the Falklands War, and the wars in Vietnam and Afghanistan. Consequently, it was hard for war reporters to interpret a form of warfare played according to unfamiliar rules.

One important feature of the Yugoslav war, for example, was its diffuseness. It was rarely possible to "go to the front." Front lines, insofar as they could be defined, sometimes extended as far as 1,000 kilometers and shifted all the time. Lines tended to change in small increments as the result of local actions on a very small scale, but small changes (such as the capture of a crossroads in mountainous territory) could produce significant shifts of the military balance. There were few obvious "battles" but a multiplicity of struggles for control over pockets of settlement. Ed Vulliamy has written, "There were two wars, really: the phenomenon and torture of the **Sarajevo** siege, and the war of '**ethnic cleansing**' in the rural hinterland. Oddly, they rarely overlapped." Alliances and enmities also switched in a disconcerting way so that **Bosnian Serbs** collaborated with **Bosnian Croats** in the **Neretva River Valley** but resisted them bitterly in the **Posavina Corridor. Fikret Abdić**'s "Muslim" army cooperated in the **Bihać** pocket with the army of the **Republika Srpska**, which was simultaneously besieging "Muslims" in Sarajevo.

The task of journalists, particularly with respect to this "second war," was made difficult by the nature of the information sources available to them. War reporters are typically heavily dependent upon the professional military for briefings and for protection, and here two important characteristics of the conflict had major consequences for their work. External military forces were primarily involved through the **United Nations** in a **humanitarian aid** role, not as primary combatants. These humanitarian activities became the focus of the briefings officials of such forces were willing and able to give journalists, rather than the progress of the main conflict. UN activities were generally confined to the cities, using limited and well-defined communication routes, to which and along which foreign journalists typically moved. Any attempt to move independently outside this framework of support entailed extraordinary risks, which journalists were understandably reluctant to take. Reliance upon the UN meant that areas not covered by this relief network were underreported in spite of their evident military significance—for example, the struggle for **Trebinje**, the sustained conflict around **Doboj**, and the Croat advance in western Bosnia that preceded **Operation Storm.**

On the other hand, the flow of information from the actual combatants was very uneven, and the support and protection offered by them to foreign correspondents was very limited. The Serb side developed a reputation for downright obstruction (especially the Bosnian Serbs) and in some cases open hostility to foreign reporters. The Bosnian government side was possibly the most cooperative. All sides, however, lacked professionalism in communicating with the media. An illustration is the extraordinary insensitivity of the Serb forces following the fall of **Vukovar**, when the victors hosted a reception for journalists in the ruins of the city, evidently oblivious of the way in which the siege of the city had been covered in the foreign press.

The Yugoslav war was very unlike the Gulf or the Falklands Wars, in which news was heavily managed by the military to the point at which military officials were criticised for undue censorship. In Yugoslavia, in some respects, the opposite appears to have been the case in that often members of the press were left to their own devices with respect to the specifically *military* aspects of developments.

Not all war reporters in Yugoslavia were foreign reporters. The domestic media faced the problem of a lack of experienced war reporters. The relative poverty of the Yugoslav media before the war meant that they had largely relied on agency sources in covering military conflicts elsewhere. In any case, the general bias of the Yugoslav media had been toward the priority of *political* events. A professional journalist with a knowledge of military affairs, such as Miloš Vasić of Belgrade's *Vreme*, was a rare commodity, and even his expertise tended toward the coverage of the armed forces as domestic political actors.

The market within which the communications media operate, especially in the richer Western countries, also imposes particular pressures upon reporters in situations such as the Yugoslav war. The commercial payoffs from more immediate coverage of actual conflict, especially where the images contain matter of dramatic human interest, increasingly drive journalists to take risks that in the past would have been regarded as unjustifiable. This situation is illustrated by the fact that it is now taken for granted that journalists covering conflicts such as the one in Yugoslavia will be equipped with body armor and will travel in armored vehicles. Their readers, listeners, and viewers are often unaware of the considerable danger to which reporters are exposed in delivering material that the public now takes for granted as "news," especially where the professionalism of the journalist plays down the degree of exposure to risk. The foregoing comments on the difficulties faced by reporters in providing a balanced and complete coverage of the war, and the limitations of their endeavors, must be placed within the context of acknowledgment of their courage and professional dedication in delivering the information we do have.

J. B. A.

See also: Media; Propaganda

References: Bell, Martin. *In Harm's Way: Reflections of a War-Zone Thug,* rev. ed. London: Penguin, 1996; Bellamy, Christopher. *Knights in White Armour: New Art of War and Peace.* London: Hutchinson, 1996; Gutman, Roy. *A Witness to Genocide: The First Inside Account of the Horrors of "Ethnic Cleansing" in Bosnia.* Shaftsbury: Element Books, 1993; Vulliamy, Ed. *Seasons in Hell: Understanding Bosnia's War.* New York and London: Simon and Schuster, 1994.

WAR RESISTANCE

See **peace movements (general)**

WASHINGTON AGREEMENT

On 18 March 1994, following the cease-fire between Croat and Muslim forces in **Bosnia-Hercegovina** on 23 February and progress on other fronts, leaders of both sides signed the Washington Agreement in Washington, D.C., at a ceremony hosted by President Clinton. In its aim of ending the conflict between Croats and Muslims, the agreement—which was engineered in great part by the United States—was largely successful, but it effectively heightened the war with the Serbs through the opening up of arms supply routes and the redeployment of joint forces.

The Washington Agreement was an accord on the creation of a **Muslim-Croat Federation** within Bosnia-Hercegovina, with a further preliminary agreement for a confederation of this new federation with Croatia itself. The Muslim-Croat Federation's power was to be shared between the two ethnic groups, with provision for the rotation of the posts of president and prime minister between Muslims and Croats. By the end of the month, the accord had been ratified by the assemblies of both Bosnia-Hercegovina in Sarajevo and the Bosnian Croats in **Mostar**.

The confederation agreement, a portion of the Washington Agreement, which was signed by Presidents **Franjo Tudjman** of Croatia and **Alija Izetbegović** of Bosnia-Hercegovina, provided for a Confederal Council with a rotating chair, as well as for moves toward economic and cultural cooperation and coordination of defense policies.

—J. J. H.

WESTERN EUROPEAN UNION

The Western European Union (WEU) is the putative "defense arm" of the **European Union** (EU). Its 10 members are members of both the European Union and the **North Atlantic Treaty Organization** (NATO). When debate emerged over whether Western European states should intervene militarily to halt the Yugoslav conflict, the WEU was the most likely vehicle for any such intervention. In September 1991, the Netherlands proposed four possible options at a meeting of WEU ministers: logistical and technical support for European Community (EC) observers; armed bodyguards for EC observers; a light peacekeeping force of 5,000–6,000 troops; and a larger intervention force of 25,000–30,000 troops. The **United Kingdom**, however, vetoed any use of force by the WEU, while the **United States** was also unwilling to deploy forces alongside its Western European allies. As a consequence, when the UN Protection Force (**UNPROFOR**) was deployed in 1992, its mandate was limited to peacekeeping, rather than including military intervention to halt the war. Some critics argue that had the WEU been willing to intervene militarily in 1991 or early 1992, the Yugoslav conflict could have been ended at that point. Others argue that without U.S. support the WEU members lacked both the military means and the political will to undertake such an intervention.

A NATO warship on embargo enforcement duties in the Adriatic Sea as part of joint Atlantic Alliance–Western European Union Operation Sharp Guard, 1994. (NATO photo)

The WEU was involved in the Yugoslav conflict in a number of other ways. Beginning in 1992, under Operation Sharpguard, WEU **naval** forces (working in a complex parallel arrangement with NATO forces) helped to enforce the economic **sanctions** against the Federal Republic of **Yugoslavia** (FRY) and the **arms** embargo against all the former Yugoslav states from the **Adriatic** Sea. The WEU supported **Hungary**, **Bulgaria**, and **Romania** in enforcing the economic sanctions and the arms embargo along the **Danube River** by providing civilian customs and police officials to reinforce these countries' own operations. From 1994 on, the WEU also supported EU efforts to reunite the divided Bosnian city of **Mostar**, in particular by providing a police force from WEU countries to help establish a unified Croatian-Muslim police force in the city. The effectiveness of EU/WEU efforts to reunite Mostar, however, was at best limited.

The 1995 **Dayton Agreements** gave the central military role in implementing the Bosnian peace process to NATO, thus sidelining the WEU. This transition was confirmed when NATO's **Implementation Force** (IFOR) was deployed, with the United States playing the leading role. With doubts over the willingness of the United States to continue to deploy forces in **Bosnia-Hercegovina** over the longer term, debate emerged over the possibility of a European-only force under WEU command as IFOR's successor. Western European states, however, were reluctant to stay in Bosnia without the United States, and IFOR's successor, the Stabilization Force (SFOR), remained a NATO force with substantial U.S. involvement. Nevertheless, should the United States withdraw its military forces from Bosnia, a European-only successor force under WEU control remains a possibility. WEU's involvement in the Yugoslav conflict, however, clearly illustrated the problems Western European states faced in undertaking military operations without U.S. participation and leadership.

—*A. S. C.*

WOMEN'S STATUS

Women in all the Yugoslav successor states are worse off today than they were when the breakup of the federal republic occurred in 1991. To understand the impact of the breakup on women, it is necessary to look at the history of women's liberation within the territories of the former Yugoslav republics and then to briefly examine what happened to women in the course of the breakup and the transition to market economy and **privatization**. The Kingdom of Serbs, Croats, and Slovenes, which came into being in 1918, was far from a unified state. Within the territorial boundaries, there were three principal gender cultures that structured behavior patterns between men and women: **Catholic**, Serbian **Orthodox**, and **Islam**. These cultures were rooted in the traditional **Balkan** culture of patriarchy and enforced through the dominant institutions of **religion**. In the interwar period, the cultural values transmitted through these cultures were challenged. Since cities provided more opportunity for women and greater exposure to new values of modernity, urban women, particularly women with education, provided the backbone of the interwar women's movement. In the countryside, on the other hand, gender relations remained virtually unchanged until World War II.

Woman's urban culture goes back to the beginning of the nineteenth century and the rise of South Slav nationalism. The cultivation of a sense of national identity demanded the development of intellectual skill to research past history and to recover or discover the national language. Educated women who possessed these skills were attracted to the movement and soon predominated as schoolteachers all over the Balkans. In addition to the growth of a women's nationalist culture, women developed economic and civil rights cultures that carried over to the interwar period. Because of their greater degree of economic development and greater contact with European intellectual movements, Slovenia and Croatia experienced a fuller growth of these two cultures prior to World War I.

During the interwar period, these cultures spread throughout Yugoslavia until women's participation in economic, humanitarian, and civil rights movements reached substantial proportions. The most important women's organizations were the Alliance of the Women's Movement and the Yugoslav Association of University-Educated Women. The two main instruments of Communist Party penetration into the women's movement were these legal women's organizations and the youth movement. The Communists also formed their own youth group, the Union of Communist Youth of Yugoslavia (SKOJ), whose members infiltrated many local women's groups, gradually assuming leading positions. The culmination of the economic and civil right activities of the women's movement was a massive turnout of women in demonstrations against the high cost of living, peace marches, and right-to-vote campaigns during the late 1930s. Women's participation in the "national liberation struggle" (the war against the Axis powers in Yugoslavia) of 1941–1945 was a critical factor in the extension of their rights. The official figure for women's participation on the **Partizan** side was 2 million. Some 100,000 were soldiers in the Partizan forces, a quarter of whom were killed; approximately 2,000 women achieved officer's rank. An estimated 282,000 women are believed to have died or been killed in the concentration camps. From 1942 to 1944, the Communist-organized and -led Anti-Fascist Front of Women (AFZ) was successful in managing a network of medical, procurement, supply, and administrative agencies in the liberated areas. The AFZ's very success led to its downfall. In 1944, the Communist leadership subordinated the local AFZ groups to the emerging institutions of local government, and in 1950 these groups were formally absorbed into the National Front, the mass organization through which the Communist Party sought to mobilize support of all citizens (later renamed Socialist Alliance of the Working People of Yugoslavia), as the "Women's Section."

The postwar Yugoslav constitution confirmed and legitimated the civil and economic rights awarded to women during the conflict, but there was virtually no further improvement in Yugoslav women's status after 1945. In all six republics, women experienced the feminization of jobs and job categories typical of the industrialization process. By 1970, half of all women were employed in industrial or socialized work areas. In the political and administrative sphere, Yugoslav women were most visible at the local level. Female membership in the **League of Communists of Yugoslavia** peaked at around 27 percent in 1984, with highest membership in **Slovenia**, while women's representation in the central committees of the various republican Communist Parties ranged around 20 percent. Perhaps, the most lasting legacy of the communist period lay in the educational opportunities offered to women. By the 1970s, women constituted almost half of those attending institutions of higher education. As was the case in other industrializing countries, their better education was accompanied by the feminization of academic disciplines, with women predominating in the humanities, education, and nursing.

In the late 1970s, a new women's movement emerged, with complementary groups in **Zagreb** and **Ljubljana.** Those in Zagreb were not associated with any other organization and were oriented almost exclusively toward feminist issues. The group in Ljubljana remained under the aegis of the Communist Youth League and was active in the antinuclear and peace movements. In 1978 the movement held its own unauthorized international conference on women's emancipation. During the 1980s, the movement became involved in antinuclear protests over Chernobyl and contributed to the formation of a protest that spread across republican boundaries to demand the end of nuclear power. The revival of a women's movement in Yugoslavia held out a faint hope of being able to rise above the noise of patriarchal nationalists, forcing the clashing republican governments to settle their differences peacefully.

The breakup of the federal republic led to the supremacy of nationalist ideologies and a resurgence of the three traditional gender cultures. The relative prosperity of **Slovenia** enabled the new democratic, elected government to take a less harsh stance on social issues. In **Croatia**, however, the **Catholic Church** tried to use its newly found leverage to demand an end to legal abortion. In Serbia, **Slobodan Milošević** stifled women's organizations, as he did with all attempts to form a civil society. Childless married couples were threatened with huge taxes, and women's groups were forced to narrow their activities to *Kinder, Kirche and Küche* (Children, Church and Kitchen) and the problem of battered wives.

In the political sphere, women welcomed the freer environment of the 1990s with the formation of women's parties (in Zagreb, the Croatian League of Women was formed in March 1990; in Belgrade, the Women's Party of Belgrade and the Democratic Movement of Women arose in November 1990). However, with the onset of national independence and the first national **elections**, women's representation in the new national parliaments fell. War further contributed to the deterioration of women's political status. In Serbia and Croatia, feminists have been demonized as the authoritarian regimes have forced the traditional female roles upon their populations. In all the new states, women have borne the brunt of the deteriorating economic situation. They are the first to lose their jobs and tend to find new jobs at the lowest levels of the wage scale. The social safety net of kindergartens, paid maternity leave, and other amenities has all but disappeared as the new governments struggle with the economic downturn and the devastating impact of **refugees.**

It is in **Bosnia-Hercegovina** where women have suffered the most in the 1990s. During the 1980s, a resurgent **Islam** had adopted a progressive attitude toward women. In 1981 the first woman graduated from the Islamic Theological Faculty in **Sarajevo.** In 1986 the first female imams completed their course of study in **Skopje.** In 1989 a group of **Albanian** women organized an unauthorized protest over social conditions in **Kosovo.** The self-confidence that accompanied these achievements was shattered by the appalling history of **rape** and "**ethnic cleansing**" in Bosnia.

Women and children make up the majority of refugees. Humanitarian organizations and women's groups have worked alongside local groups to help women cope with the trauma of war. One of the best known of these groups is the Center for Women War Victims, located in Zagreb. One of the problems with these well-intentioned efforts is that Western women have brought to the rape and refugee centers their own cultural values and have found it difficult to empathize with the gender culture of the women victims.

The situation of women in the former Yugoslavia will remain critical as long as the new national leaders insist on ascribing national identify to a narrow, dogmatic worldview based on traditional religious patriarchy. Essential to any improvement in women's situation is a durable and lasting peace based on recognition by all parties of the existence of an essential and unchangeable cultural diversity in all the Yugoslav communist successor states.

—*B. J.-W.*

See also: rural-urban differences

References: Jancar-Webster, Barbara. *Women and Revolution in Yugoslavia 1941–1945.* Boulder, CO: Arden Press, 1991; Niarchos, Catherine N. "Women, War and Rape: Challenges Facing the International Tribunal for the Former Yugoslavia." *Human Rights*

Quarterly 17, no. 4 (November 1995):649–690; Ramet, Sabrina Petra. "Feminism in Yugoslavia." In Ramet, Sabrina Petra (ed.), *Social Currents in Eastern Europe,* 2nd ed. Boulder, CO: Westview Press, 1995; Stiglmayer, Alexandra, ed. *Mass Rape: The War against Women in Bosnia-Hercegovina.* Lincoln: University of Nebraska Press, 1994; Tomšić, Vida. *Women in the Development of Socialist Self-Managing Yugoslavia.* Belgrade: Radnička štampa, 1980.

WORKERS' SELF-MANAGEMENT

The feature for which the former Yugoslav federation was most widely known was its distinctive system of political and economic organization known as *radničko samoupravljenje* (workers' self-management—WSM). There is an irony in the fact that a system that was associated throughout most of the post-1945 period with Yugoslavia's success in sustaining its independence from Moscow should have turned into one of the causes of the federation's demise. The dispute between Yugoslavia and the Cominform in 1948, which resulted in Yugoslavia's expulsion from the socialist bloc and led to a rigorous economic blockade, left the country in an extremely difficult situation. The **Tito** regime was now shunned by its former socialist partners, and its commitment to the revolutionary transformation of capitalism also prevented its ready acceptance by Western governments. The idea of workers' self-management was conceived at the moment of the greatest international isolation of the country, when the regime was also engaged in a bitter struggle with Yugoslav Communists who adhered to the Cominform line. It is generally acknowledged as the brainchild of Edvard Kardelj.

Launched tentatively in 1950, the scheme allowed for factories to be governed by councils of their workers. Its success led to its general adoption in 1953. The new system permitted the Yugoslav Communist Party (later known as the **League of Communists of Yugoslavia**—SKJ) to reaffirm its Marxist-Leninist credentials in the face of hostility from the Cominform while presenting itself to the West as independent of Soviet influence, boosting domestic morale and international prestige. The system underwent a succession of major revisions, particularly in the constitutional reform of 1963 and again in 1976, expanding its scope well beyond the original factory councils in three important respects.

All work organizations were ultimately included within its remit, including areas of public service such as educational institutions, hospitals, and government bureaucracy. Its operation was generalized into an overarching structure of "delegation," whereby representatives were elected not only from work organizations but also from units of neighborhood government, which combined into a pyramid of "delegated" bodies at the municipal, republican, and ultimately federal level. Arrangements for the provision of a variety of services, both to the public and between industrial and commercial enterprises, took the form of an elaborate edifice of self-managing agreements *(samoupravni dogovori)* and self-managing communities of interest (*samoupravne interesne zajednice*—SIZovi).

The bewildering complexity of this system reached its fullest development after the introduction of the Law on Associated Labor (Zakon o udruženom radu—ZUR) in 1976. This law disaggregated enterprises and larger organizations into their component "basic organizations of associated labor" (*osnovne organizacije udruženog rada*—OOUR), so that any organization might be composed of several such semiautonomous units. (A large motor manufacturing plant in Slovenia, for example, had no fewer than 31 of these units.) The process of *oourizacija* (OOURization) broke down university faculties into separate self-managing departments. These basic organizations could then be recombined, through self-managing agreements, into complex organizations of associated labor (*složene organizacije udruženog rada*—SOUR).

The ideological purpose behind these developments was to maximize participation; indeed, impressive numbers of Yugoslavs were involved in positions of one kind or another within the structure (649,525 of these positions in 1986). A disadvantageous feature of the system, however, was the burden of participation in many meetings within a structure that many people did not understand. This tended to concentrate participation in the hands of better-educated management and supervisory personnel, as well as active members of the SKJ who were highly motivated to make it work. (It also operated to discourage equal participation by **women**, who in a society characterized by conservative, peasant family values continued to bear the greater burden of domestic responsibilities.)

WSM had a number of drawbacks in addition to its complexity. There were no safeguards to prevent the multiple occupancy of functions. Consequently, a system presented as primarily directed toward maximizing participation ended up becoming a means of ensuring effective control by the SKJ. Of primary relevance with respect to the disintegration of Yugoslavia, however, are four other features. The commitment to self-management made for inflexibility of response in relation to the developing economic problems of the country. The need for *economic* reform was characteristically met by *political* change thorough refinement of WSM. Yugoslavia's move away from reliance upon the system of central planning, originally copied from the Soviet Union, has often been interpreted in terms of "market socialism." This description shows a misunderstanding of the process in that the creation of nominally independent enterprises operating within a framework of "indicative planning" did not, in fact, result in the creation of a true market for goods and services. Price formation remained subject to a good deal of administrative interference. Enterprises also tended to avoid genuine competition with each other, operating very often as local or republican monopolies. There was no effective capital market; rather, investment was negotiated between firms and the banks according to basically social and political criteria. The extremely soft budgetary constraints under which firms operated also meant that wage levels were not always determined by the market situation of the enterprise; sometimes these levels were artificially sustained by credit. These features contributed directly to some of the problems of Yugoslavia's economic adjustment by creating built-in pressures toward **inflation** and low labor productivity.

In part these tendencies have been linked to the distinctive understanding of the nature of property that characterized the Yugoslav system. Assets were not owned by the state, as in other socialist countries; nor were they the private property of individual workers in enterprises. (Workers were not entitled to sell their "share" in the organization to which they were attached.) Ownership of economic assets was described as "social property"; in other words, rights were diffusely resident in society as a whole. The system has been criticized as creating a sense of irresponsibility, in that workers were said to develop a view of the organization that emphasized their rights within it (especially rights to employment and remuneration) but without developing an equally strong sense of obligation.

An equally important consequence of WSM was that the system created a structure of vertical segmentation, which obstructed the formation of patterns of cooperation across the federation. The logic of *oourizacija*, as well as the pyramid of delegation based upon local "communities of interest," made for a pervasive parochialism of outlook and action. The growth of nationalism in Yugoslavia can be regarded in part not as the upwelling of sentiment from some deep substratum of culture, but as a consequence of the way in which the system encouraged the adoption of criteria of *local* self-interest as the fundamental standard by which choices should be made, rather than economic rationality or some wider notion of **citizenship**.

In spite of the fact that events in Yugoslavia have often been subsumed under some general notion of a transition to "postcommunist" economies in Eastern Europe, across the former federation it is possible to see the continuing influence of WSM. Where the former system based upon "social property" has undergone a process of **privatization**, there has been a tendency to prefer strategies that (1) endow the employees in work organizations with preferential access to stock in the newly privatized firm and (2) invest a large proportion of the equity in funds that service the employees' pensions. In other words, it is still regarded as appropriate that a firm should be run by and in the interests of its workforce.

—*J. B. A.*

See also: economic dimension; Titoism

Y

YUGONOSTALGIA

The term *Yugonostalgia* is used, usually in a derogatory fashion, to refer to any tendency to look back upon life in the Yugoslav federation and compare that past favorably with the present. Used in this sense, it carries connotations of disloyalty to the contemporary, newly independent states, and it suggests that "Yugonostalgics" are people who live in a world of fantasy. Yugonostalgia is possibly best illustrated by the graffiti reportedly seen on a wall in Zagreb: "*Bravar je bio bolje!*" ("The locksmith was better!"—in reference to **Tito**, who was apprenticed to the engineering trade in his youth).

—*J. B. A.*

YUGOSLAV IDEA

The belief that the South Slav peoples share a common identity that should be expressed in their unification in a common state is known as the Yugoslav Idea. For many centuries common political identities have been imposed on the peoples of the region via incorporation into Byzantine, **Ottoman**, and **Habsburg** Empires. The **Balkan** peoples have passed much more of their history in multiethnic states than in national states. It should not be surprising, therefore, that the modern period has seen the simultaneous rise of movements of ideas that have dwelled upon aspects of this common history, along with nationalism.

The Yugoslav Idea is a creation of the nineteenth century and primarily the work of Croat thinkers. Roman **Catholic** speakers of the South Slav languages who eventually came to identify themselves as Croats have faced a persistent problem in terms of their dispersion among several states. In each of these states, they were mingled with people of different identities. At the end of the eighteenth century, they were divided among Austrian crown lands; the Kingdom of Croatia; the Kingdom of Hungary and the **Military Frontier** administration in the Habsburg Empire; the Republics of Venice and Ragusa; and the provinces of **Bosnia-Hercegovina** within the Ottoman Empire.

The Napoleonic conquest of the Eastern Adriatic and the creation of the Illyrian Provinces there in 1809 gave an important stimulus toward a common Croatian identity. This experience inspired Ljudevit Gaj (1809–1872) to publish the first Croat vernacular newspaper *(Danica)* in 1835. With Austrian encouragement, his "Illyrian movement" (which promoted the linguistic and cultural unity of the South Slavs) was directed against the growth of Magyar nationalism. Its most significant achievement was the establishment of the more widely used *štokavski* dialects in place of the *kajkavski* of the Zagreb region. This launched Croat literary culture on a path that facilitated readier communication with Serbs and Bosnians as well as among the more narrowly defined Croat lands.

The "year of revolutions," 1848, saw a radical challenge to the Habsburg constitutional order from Magyar nationalism. The intervention of the Croatian *ban* (governor), Josip Jelačić, with an army of Croat and Serb units, restored the authority of the emperor and left a legacy of South Slav cooperation.

After a period of constitutional instability, a new *Nagodba* (Compromise) was negotiated between Austrian and Magyar interests in 1868, tilting the balance in favor of the influence of Budapest in the Croat kingdom. In the face of intense pressure toward the "Magyarization" of cultural life, a movement to defend Slav culture emerged, associated with the ideas of Bishop Josip Strossmayer of Djakovo (1815–1905). Strossmayer founded the Yugoslav Academy of Science and Art in Zagreb (a significant name in that it contained the word

Yugoslav, meaning "South Slav") in 1867 and the University of Zagreb in 1874; he saw both institutions as contributing to South Slav unity. With the dismantling of the Military Frontier (abolished in 1881), the proportion of Serbs within the Croatian state grew markedly, and the Hungarian authorities attempted to sustain their own position by tactics of "divide and rule." This approach also characterized the Austrian administration in Bosnia-Hercegovina after the occupation of the provinces by Austria in 1878. Consequently, until the outbreak of World War I, the idea of South Slav cooperation was weakened. If anything it tended to be overlaid by appeals to wider Slav solidarity within the empire, as a "Trialist" solution to its constitutional problems was debated. (This notion envisaged a reconstruction of the Habsburg state around three entities—Austrian, Hungarian, and Slav.) The low point was reached in the anti-Serb riots in **Zagreb** in 1902 and the manipulated show trial of Serbs on charges of treason in 1908.

In spite of these difficulties, the Yugoslav Idea had its advocates. During the constitutional crisis of 1904–1905, an assembly of the Croat deputies in the *Reichsrat* from Croatia, **Istria**, and **Dalmatia** formulated a set of reforming proposals that came to be known as the Fiume Resolution in October 1905. These proposals received the support of Serb deputies assembled in Zara very shortly afterward. The possibilities for effective cooperation between different South Slav groups were indicated in 1913, when the controversial Railways Act was repealed, bringing an end to Magyar attempts to impose their own linguistic privilege in public settings.

The destruction of Austria-Hungary during World War I saw the creation of the first unified South Slav state—the Kingdom of Serbs, Croats, and Slovenes. This state drew together not only the South Slav regions of Austria-Hungary, but also former independent kingdoms of **Serbia** and **Montenegro**, together with the former Ottoman lands that the former kingdoms had acquired as a result of the Balkan Wars (1912–1913). Ironically, this state was in many respects quite unlike the kind of state sought by any of its components before the war. Serbia had hoped at best to further the process of unifying in one country the scattered Serb settlements of the Balkans. The former Habsburg peoples had perhaps anticipated a movement toward a "trialist" structure within the empire. The wider course of the war, however, left the South Slavs in a series of situations in which their interests faced the threat of being set aside by the greater powers pursuing their own aims. As a consequence, the Yugoslav Committee (which represented the South Slavs within the Habsburg Empire) and the Serbian government in exile came together in July 1917 to issue the Corfu Declaration, affirming their common aspiration to set up a "constitutional, democratic, and parliamentary **monarchy**" that would unite both their territories in any postwar settlement.

The creation of a unified state (known as **Yugoslavia** after 1929) redefined the Yugoslav Idea. It shifted the focus of debate from the question of the place of South Slavs within multinational empires to the question of which **constitutional model** might provide an appropriate form in which to accommodate the cultural and historical diversity of the South Slav peoples. Furthermore, by bringing into one country other peoples—not only other Slavs such as the **Macedonians** but sizable non-Slav minorities such as **Albanians**—this unified state raised issues relating to common identity and citizenship that had never previously been addressed. By the outbreak of war in April 1941, the idea of "Yugoslavia" had come to appear as a problem rather than the solution to one, and under the impact of invasion by the Axis powers the country fell apart.

The idea of a united Yugoslavia was revived in a new form by the Communist Party during the course of World War II. None of the South Slav peoples separately were strong enough to present effective resistance to fascism and foreign occupation. Furthermore, the pursuit of nationalist solutions to the question of the future form of the state served only to set different nations against each other, actively undermining the possibilities for liberation. In the summer of 1942, therefore, when **Tito** and his **Partizan** movement organized the first meeting of the Anti-Fascist Council for the National Liberation of Yugoslavia (usually known as AVNOJ), the leadership were already committed to the creation of a new Yugoslavia, with the aim of drawing all South Slavs into a common patriotic struggle against the enemy. By then it had also become clear than any such enterprise would have to take the form of a federation that recognized the peoples' diversity, in place of the highly centralized structure of the first (royal) Yugoslavia.

Although the experiment of the Socialist Federation of Republics of **Yugoslavia** also fell apart in 1992, the South Slav peoples find themselves in a situation in which the idea of Yugoslavia may well return, although undoubtedly in a different form. To a group of small nations—typically dispersed along with other ethnic groups, sharing a substantial proportion of their cultural heritage, and surrounded by unfriendly states—the ideal of South Slav unity is and will continue to be available in a variety of guises, which from time to time will seem more attractive than insistence upon their diversity.

—*J. B. A.*

See also: language question; religion

YUGOSLAV PEOPLES' ARMY

The most powerful military force during the Yugoslav wars of the 1990s and formerly one of the power centers within the ruling **League of Communists of Yugoslavia** (SKJ), the Yugoslav Peoples' Army (Jugoslovenska narodna armija—JNA) was strongly identified with Communist Yugoslavia throughout its existence. Upon the demise of the former Yugoslav federation and the descent into civil war in 1990–1991, the JNA high command attempted to preserve the federation by force and maintain its own institutional autonomy, but it failed in both endeavors, becoming an exclusively ethnic Serb military force subordinated to the **Serbian** state. Following the Bosnian Serb victories in Bosnia-Hercegovina in April 1992, the JNA was formally disestablished and divided into two separate but related entities, the **Bosnian Serb Army** (BSA) and the Army of Yugoslavia (Vojska Jugoslavije—VJ).

Originating in World War II (1941–1944) when the Communist Party of Yugoslavia organized the National Liberation Army (NLA) to fight a **Partizan** struggle, the Army of Yugoslavia was formally created on 5 March 1945. Thereafter, Yugoslavia's military alliance with the Soviet Union turned the force into a virtual carbon copy of the Red Army. Following the historic split between Yugoslav leader **Tito** and Soviet leader Stalin in June 1948, the

Yugoslav Peoples' Army (JNA) tanks crossing the "Brotherhood and Unity" bridge connecting Croatia and Bosnia-Hercegovina, 1992. (Stevan Filipović)

Yugoslav army was reorganized as the JNA. By 1951, when the danger of a Soviet invasion of Yugoslavia was at its most acute, the JNA consisted of around 300,000 troops, organized into four army areas, with staffs in **Belgrade, Zagreb, Ljubljana,** and **Sarajevo** each commanding two corps. Tito ruthlessly purged the high command of suspected Soviet agents and sympathizers in 1948–1949, after which the army was to remain his most politically reliable constituency.

The Tito-Stalin split forced Yugoslavia into a brief military alliance with the **United States,** and in 1954 Yugoslavia entered into a U.S.-sponsored Balkan Pact with **Greece** and **Turkey**—two anti-Soviet **North Atlantic Treaty Organization** (NATO) states in the Balkans. During this period, when a state of military emergency existed in Yugoslavia, the JNA was expanded to 500,000 troops and defense expenditures reached a high 22 percent of gross domestic product (GDP). With the arrival of large quantities of U.S. military aid, the JNA was able to upgrade its hitherto relatively limited order of battle. By 1955 it was able to field 29 fully equipped divisions (with heavy armaments) and 15 lightly equipped divisions (mainly rifle infantry). U.S. military aid during the early 1950s enabled the JNA to establish a modern air force and the beginnings of a navy. At this time Yugoslavia also began to establish its own military industries to lessen its dependence on foreign suppliers of military materials.

Following the Soviet-Yugoslav rapprochement of 1955, Tito's government concluded that the Soviet threat to Yugoslavia's security had abated enough to justify a major demobilization. By 1968 the JNA consisted of only 200,000 troops, with federal defense expenditures down to 6 percent of GDP. During the 1960s, the JNA was extensively modernized, notably through the import of heavier Soviet armaments and the deployment of more sophisticated domestically produced military materials.

The JNA held a politically subordinate position within the SKJ from 1948 to 1966. During 1966, however, the JNA high command, in particular its counterintelligence service (KOS), played a key role in the removal from power of Alexander Ranković, head of the country's State Security Service (SDS) and a close associate of Tito. One result of this removal was the predominance of military intelligence over the SDS thereafter.

The Soviet invasion of Czechoslovakia in 1968 brought about major changes within the Yugoslav armed forces. A system of "total national defense" (TND) was created, combining the JNA and new Territorial Defense Forces (TDFs), which were modeled on the wartime NLA and the Partizan ethos of irregular revolutionary warfare in the face of invading forces. As a result of the creation of TDFs in each of the federation's six republics, the JNA was reduced in size still further during the 1970s and 1980s. By the late 1980s, its order of battle consisted of around 180,000 troops in three major services (ground, air, and naval forces) equipped with 1,500 main battle tanks, 2,500 artillery pieces, 3,000 antiaircraft guns, 350 combat aircraft, and 30 major warships and submarines. By the late 1980s, the TDFs had increased to around one million part-time troops. The growth of relatively cheap TDFs, however, did not lead to lower defense expenditures. In fact, these expenditures increased, mainly because modernization of the JNA implied an emphasis on firepower rather than manpower. One result of this development was that Yugoslavia became one of the world's top 10 armaments producers and exporters by the end of the 1980s.

The system of TND created a nationwide network of armaments storage facilities centered on Bosnia. Universal conscription for the JNA and later service in the TDFs meant that virtually all male Yugoslav citizens had some military experience, and private ownership of firearms became very high during the 1970s and 1980s. By the end of the 1980s, Yugoslavia was a highly militarized society in which firearms were plentifully available.

The fact that the JNA was no longer the federation's only armed force after 1968 had many significant outcomes, notably at the time of the **Croatian Spring** of 1970–1971. At that time certain Croatian nationalists demanded that Croatia's TDF be turned into a so-called Croatian Army. More than any other development, this demand led Tito to purge the Croatian nationalists in 1971–1972. Many of the centrifugal tendencies that manifested themselves in Croatia during the early 1970s, however, were later partly institutionalized in the 1974 federal constitution, which increased the powers of the republics at the expense of the federal government. Only in the military sphere did power remain centralized, with the JNA securing full control over the TDFs by the early 1980s. Within the increasingly confederalized SKJ, the strongly pro-Yugoslav JNA was increasingly represented on the SKJ's top ruling bodies during the 1970s and 1980s. Following the death of Tito in 1980, the JNA high command perceived itself to be the ultimate guardian of his political legacy.

Within the post-Tito collective state presidency, however, the crises of the 1980s and 1990s revealed that the power and influence of the JNA were limited and always subordinate to that of the ruling SKJ. With the violent and chaotic demise of the federation in 1990–1991, the JNA's position became very difficult, if not impossible. Its high command attempted to preserve the federation, but their ability to achieve this goal this proved very limited in practice. The JNA's claim to be an all-Yugoslav force above the fray of the nationalist politics was undermined by the fact that, although officially a multiethnic conscript force, its professional core was composed predominately of ethnic Serbs by the late 1980s. By that time, 40 percent of the JNA's manpower and 60 percent of its officer corps were ethnic Serbs. During the beginnings of the Yugoslav wars, the number of non-Serbs in the JNA fell dramatically, reaching no more than 3 percent of manpower by early 1992.

The hard-line communism and pro-Yugoslav loyalties of a mainly Serb high command and officer corps were unacceptable to many non-Serbs, particularly after new anticommunist and separatist governments were elected in Slovenia and Croatia. The army drifted into alliance with the government of **Slobodan Milošević**. Ostensibly committed to preserving Yugoslavia, Milošević also promised to continue financing the JNA at a time of great uncertainty in the disintegrating Yugoslav federation.

The major political challenges of the early 1990s proved too much for the JNA's often politically inept and divided commanders. Federal Defence Minister Gen. **Veljko Kadijević** and Chief of Staff Gen. **Blagoje Adžić** refused to impose a national state of emergency without proper political authorization, which could not be forthcoming from a hopelessly divided state presidency. Confronted with a rising tide of hostility toward the army, as well as war throughout the non-Serb areas of the former Yugoslavia, Kadijević and Adžić were easily manipulated by Milošević. In 1989 and 1991, the JNA allowed itself to be used for internal security purposes in the Serbian province of **Kosovo**. In March 1991 it openly allied itself with Milošević when it agreed to be used to help suppress antigovernment demonstrations in Belgrade. In June 1991, when **Slovenia** and **Croatia** unilaterally declared their independence from the imploding federation, the JNA mounted an inept invasion of Slovenia, from which it was forced to withdraw by Slovene TDFs.

In Croatia, Milošević's policy in the second half of 1991 was to use the formidable firepower of the JNA to partition the republic by the end of that year, with the JNA openly allied with local Serb separatists.

Having previously managed to disarm the Bosnian TDF, the JNA and its local Bosnian Serb allies were able to forcibly seize 70 percent of **Bosnia-Hercegovina** during the spring of 1992. The siege of Sarajevo in particular resulted in the imposition of United Nations economic **sanctions** against Serbia and **Montenegro** in May 1992. In a bid to avert international isolation, the remaining Yugoslavia then declared that the JNA would be withdrawn from Bosnia. In fact, the Bosnian Serbs within the JNA became the BSA—a well-armed force of around 50,000 troops. Of the 180,000 troops in the JNA prior to this supposed split, 130,000 henceforth became the new VJ, but few JNA troops actually left Bosnia in May 1992. Command of the BSA was also entrusted to a veteran JNA officer, Gen. **Ratko Mladić**.

Subsequently, Milošević has striven to retain close links with the Army of Yugoslavia, displacing the older Partizan clique around Gen. Života Panić and installing as chief of staff Gen. **Momčilo Perišić**, a veteran of the Bosnian war, in August 1993. Within the remaining Yugoslavia, the VJ has mainly been used for internal security purposes in the **Sandžak** and Kosovo in recent years. It has also been adversely affected by the serious economic crisis of the 1990s in Serbia.

—M. M.

YUGOSLAVIA (FORMER)

The breakup of Yugoslavia after 70 years (if not the manner in which it took place) came as little surprise either to those who were pleased with the split or to those who viewed it with regret. This lack of surprise can be attributed to a shared perception of Yugoslavia as a failure. Perhaps this perception was accurate, but in that case the surprise is that

Yugoslavia survived as long as it did, and there are lessons to be learned from that achievement. Created as an independent state only this century, Yugoslavia (or "the land of the South Slavs") could never throw off the effects of more than a thousand years of history since the Slavs became fully established on that geographically but naturally under-resourced territory. The collapse of the medieval kingdoms under the twin yoke of **Ottoman** assault from the east and **Habsburg** incorporation from the west condemned the individual peoples of the South Slavs to centuries of economic domination and cultural repression by one or the other of two occupying and opposing forces. The national awakenings of the late eighteenth and the nineteenth centuries were accompanied by the growth of the "**Yugoslav Idea**," though from then until now the idea has never been entirely separated from suspicions of individual hegemony in one form or another. World War I (which had been sparked by an event on South Slav soil) ended with the somewhat artificial realization of that idea in the creation of a union of all southern Slavs (except Bulgarians) as a Yugoslav state, i.e., the Kingdom of Serbs, Croats, and Slovenes (the Macedonian Slavs did not gain official recognition until 1945). For the Kingdom of Yugoslavia (so renamed in 1929), the interwar period was one of largely undistinguished government that did little to provide a sound base for whatever was to befall Yugoslavia after World War II. It was this war (the Yugoslav contribution to which became officially known as the War of Liberation) that determined the future course of Yugoslav history despite a significant contradiction. On the one hand, the Yugoslav Idea lay in tatters as a result of the fratricidal struggle among rival national groups within Yugoslavia; on the other hand, the struggle of the **Partizans** (who eventually gained international recognition over the **Chetniks** as the movement to support against the occupying German forces) became a Yugoslav movement in the sense of drawing its internal support from all parts of Yugoslavia and from many strata of its society. As the socialization and politicization of the movement began to develop alongside the military exploits of the resistance, there was some sense of a natural party of government to take power and responsibility for the rebuilding of Yugoslavia in the aftermath of war. The force of **Tito**'s personality was strong enough to ensure that the Yugoslav Idea would be put into practice; the longer he was around, the stronger the chances of national unity were, whatever the conflicting pressures.

In 1948 Yugoslavia achieved its independence from the Communist bloc when Tito broke with Stalin. The decision to "go it alone" and pursue an individual brand of communism, while by no means universally supported in Yugoslavia at the time, can still be seen as a unifying factor in itself. The "Yugoslav experiment" had begun, and at times of trouble (international or domestic, political or economic) it was skillfully reheralded to renew a feeling of national independence and unity, particularly within the context of a **nonaligned** foreign policy and "total national defense." This experiment, based upon the principle and practice of **workers' self-management**, was characterized by alternating periods of inflexibility and genuine reforms—most notably, individual national expression, political and economic decentralization, and the adoption of "market socialism" (for lack of a better term).

What the system achieved was a degree of social cohesion at the local level, a comparatively open political structure for a one-party state, and above all an educational system that within 30 years had transformed an overwhelmingly **rural** and underskilled base into a rapidly developing industrial economy with a high level of technical competence. What it clearly failed to achieve, however, as many Yugoslavs freely admitted, was a sufficiently flexible decision-making process, a stable economy, and a regional balance of prospects for its nationalities.

Tito's death in 1980 was never going to be compensated for through the ensuing approach of choosing a president from each of the republics in sequence. Internal nationalist aspirations were sparked in various ways, and the collapse of communism elsewhere in Eastern Europe served only to fan the flames. It is Yugoslavia's final irony that the most liberal of the communist regimes should have suffered the bloodiest transition of all.

—J. J. H.

See also: Titoism

YUGOSLAVIA (FEDERAL REPUBLIC)

The present Federal Republic of Yugoslavia (now often referred to in the West—at worst disparagingly and at best unhelpfully—as the "rump" Yugoslavia) is what remains of the former Socialist Federal Republic of Yugoslavia following the inde-

Old Town Sarajevo: capital of the most Yugoslav of the former Yugoslav Republics, Bosnia-Hercegovina. This city suffered the most in the urgent dissolution of the former Yugoslav Federation in the 1990s. (NATO photo)

pendence of its former constituent republics of **Slovenia**, **Croatia**, **Bosnia-Hercegovina**, and **Macedonia**. It has to date not been internationally recognized as the successor state to the former socialist federal republic, although United Nations **sanctions** were lifted in November 1995 immediately following the signing of the **Dayton Agreements**. Today it comprises two of the former republics: **Serbia** (including the **Vojvodina** in the north and **Kosovo** in the south) and **Montenegro**. The current estimated population is over 11 million (less than half the total of the former Yugoslavia), of which around two-thirds are Serb/Montenegrin, one-fifth **Albanian** (mainly in Kosovo), one-tenth **Muslim**, and one-twentieth Hungarian (mainly in the Vojvodina). The constitution of the new federal republic provides for a bicameral parliament: the lower chamber allocates 108 seats to Serbia and 30 to Montenegro; the upper chamber, however, is equally shared between the two republics with 20 members each. The federal president since 15 July 1997 has been **Slobodan Milošević** (previously president of Serbia), and the prime minister is **Momir Bulatović**. Milošević's **Socialist Party of Serbia** (the former Communists) is the largest party in the federal legislature and governs in coalition with the Yugoslav United Left and New Democracy.

—*J. J. H.*

Z

ZADAR

Zadar (population 137,000 in 1991) is a town on the Dalmatian coast of **Croatia**, approximately 200 miles south of the capital, **Zagreb**, and 100 miles northwest of Split. It is the nearest town to **Maslenica**, where the main bridge linking **Dalmatia** with the rest of Croatia was destroyed by Serb shelling. Zadar was blockaded by the Yugoslav **naval power** in 1991 and came under frequent artillery attack by Serbs from the hinterland toward **Knin**, which is about 60 miles to the east.

—*G. R. B.*

ZAGREB

Zagreb is the capital city of **Croatia** and the political, cultural, and religious center of the state. One million people live in and around the city, making it the largest population center in Croatia. It is located in the north-central region of the country, only 12 miles from the border with **Slovenia**. Zagreb networks with a number of **communications** routes: the **Sava River** runs through the city; the motorway to **Belgrade** passes it; and the international airport lies six miles to the southeast.

Zagreb's size and importance acted to limit the horizons of **Franjo Tudjman** and the **Croatian Democratic Union** (HDZ) when they took power in 1990 as the first noncommunist government of Croatia since 1945. Tudjman appears to have based his assessment of Serb nationalist feeling on his knowledge of the more moderate, urban Serbs living in Zagreb. Constituting only a tenth of Croatia's Serb population, however, they proved to have little or no influence on the outbreak of war.

Immediately following independence, Zagreb was the focus of much nationalist symbolic change. Streets and squares were renamed, involving removal of the socialist names and either reinstatement of old names from the Austro-Hungarian period or invention of new ones. Particularly insensitive changes included renaming the Square of the Victims of Fascism as the Square of Great Croats. The Croatian flag and the ***šahovnica*** (a red and white checked shield) replaced the old socialist insignia, and new rituals, such as the changing of the guard at the Sabor (Assembly), were invented to underscore the sovereign ambitions of the new state.

On 14 September 1991, the Croatian national guard began a siege of **Yugoslav Peoples' Army** (JNA) barracks all across Croatia, including the large "Marshal Tito" barracks in the Borongaj district. During this time Zagreb experienced light attacks from the Yugoslav air force and rocket batteries. The blockade continued until 28 November, when Tudjman bowed to international pressure to allow the JNA to leave. Although the atmosphere was extremely tense, there was little damage to the city. Zagreb was shelled on 2–3 May by Orkan surface-to-surface rockets in retaliation for the retaking of western **Slavonia.** Eleven rockets killed five people on 2 May, and six rockets killed one person on 3 May; 175 people were injured. Zagreb was never subject to ground-based attack.

When the United Nations Protection Force for Yugoslavia (**UNPROFOR**) first arrived in Yugoslavia, it was based in **Sarajevo**, but when it became clear that **Bosnia** was descending into violence, UNPROFOR took over the former JNA barracks in Zagreb as its center of operations. The European Community **Monitoring** Mission (ECMM) was also based in Zagreb. The city thus had a large complement of international residents, with the effect that many hotels were full of soldiers and diplomats, and the local economy was distorted by the amount of convertible currency available.

Zagreb also became the center of the **peace movement**, with many international **nongovern-**

mental organizations (NGOs) having offices there, as well as the Croatian Anti-War Campaign, many **women's** groups, and **refugee** aid organizations.

The city's importance as the religious and cultural center of the state was underscored when Pope John Paul II visited the city, addressing a crowd of 500,000 on 11 September 1994. Although he welcomed Croatian independence, his message to Croats was to promote reconciliation with Serbs, to seek forgiveness for their own actions, and to forgive the actions of those who had fought against them. The nationalist state and **media** effectively prevented this message from being spread across the rest of Croatia.

—G. R. B.

ZENICA

A steel-making town (population 146,000 in 1991) in north-central Bosnia, Zenica is a **Muslim** stronghold in a predominantly Muslim heartland, although the city itself had a more mixed population of 55 percent Muslim, 15 percent Croat, 15 percent Serb, and 11 percent self-declared "Yugoslav." During 1992 it received droves of Muslim refugees from areas of Bosnia being cleared by the **Bosnian Serbs**, making the city increasingly reliant on the security of the supply route northward from **Prozor**. Although subjected to assaults both by Serbs and later by the Bosnian Croat Army (**Croatian Council of Defense**) (**HVO**) during the latter's offensive in the spring of 1993, Zenica was never going to be an easy target. Apart from the presence of the Bosnian government forces under Enver Hasanović, the city was also a strong base for the more strident Muslim Armed Force (MOS), which was notionally under the command of the **Bosnian army** but which favored full-blown action for a Muslim state rather than negotiations with the West based on multiethnic principles. A third presence was that of more than 200 imported Muslim fighters from the Middle East; these fighters were akin to the *mujaheddin*, an extremist and unpredictable gang who acted like loose cannons around the town, feared by the Croats in surrounding areas and receiving little support from the Muslims of Zenica themselves. As the tide began to turn against the HVO in this area, the Muslim response was little short of the atrocities committed against them by the Croats; Zenica became a scene of internal "**ethnic cleansing**" of people and buildings on a wave of fundamentalist **Islamic** sentiment.

Zenica was also the location of a center dedicated to collecting reports and evidence of **genocide**, **rape**, and other atrocities against Muslim communities, as well as to providing a counseling service to surviving victims.

—J. J. H.

See also: paramilitary/irregular forces

ŽEPA

Žepa, located in a valley district off the **Drina River** in southeastern Bosnia, was a Muslim enclave in a traditionally Serb-dominated region. It lies halfway between **Srebrenica** and **Goražde**, and like those two cities it was one of the six enclaves designated as so-called **safe areas** by the **United Nations** (UN) in the spring of 1993. For almost a year before that, Žepa had endured almost continual siege by the **Bosnian Serbs**. In the 10 days at the start of May between the announcement of its protected status and the arrival of the United Nations to establish the safe area, Žepa had become a virtual ghost town, most of whose up to 10,000 inhabitants had finally been forced to flee—a "safe area" had been subjected to "**ethnic cleansing**." The Serbs finally took the town on 25 July 1995.

—J. J. H.

ZUBAK, KRESIMIR

Kresimir Zubak was elected to the collective presidency of **Bosnia-Hercegovina** in September 1996. A relatively moderate member of the **Croatian Democratic Union** (HDZ) from the **Doboj** area of central Bosnia, Zubak replaced the ferociously nationalist Mate Boban as leader of the secessionist Croat region of **Herceg-Bosna** in February 1994; at this time the strident nationalism of Croatian president **Franjo Tudjman**'s "**Hercegovina** Lobby" allies was causing increasing embarrassment internationally. Like his fellow central Bosnian **Stjepan Kljuić**, Zubak was of the opinion that Boban had disastrously led the **Bosnian Croats** into a brief **civil war** with the Bosnian **Muslims** (Bošnjaci) in 1993–1994. Appointed by Tudjman under pressure from the **United States** to improve relations with the Bošnjaks, Zubak became president of the newly created **Muslim-Croat Federation** in May 1994. Zubak did little to advance the reunification that the new federation was formed for, however, leading to numerous conflicts with its Bošnjak vice president, **Ejup Ganić**. On issues considered vital by the Hercogovinian Croats, such as the status of **Mostar**, Zubak was to prove as obdurate as Boban. For this and other reasons, Tudjman eventually replaced him as federation president with the more accommodating Vladimir Šoljić.

Along with Bošnjak leader **Alija Izetbegović** and Serbian president **Slobodan Milošević**, Zubak helped to negotiate the **Dayton Agreements** for Bosnia-Hercegovina in October–November 1995, signing them for the Bosnian Croats in the following December. Zubak's commitment to the reunified Bosnian state envisaged by Dayton was lukewarm at best. His role in attempts to create functioning federal institutions was neither prominent nor effective. Unlike the Bošnjaks, Zubak did not want to see the **Bosnian Serbs** completely defeated, thus staying in line with a wider policy set by Tudjman and the United States during the joint Muslim-Croat offensive against the **Republika Srpska** in 1995. Despite his forced resignation in 1996, Zubak remained politically dominant in Bosnian Croat politics. In September 1996 he easily defeated a more moderate Bosnian Croat candidate in the poll for a new Bosnian state presidency to share power with Izetbegović and Bosnian Serb leader **Momčilo Krajišnik.**

Zubak reportedly continues to doubt the survival of the Bosnian state envisaged by Dayton and to fear another war between the Croats and their supposed Bošnjak allies—a stance that places him in the same political bracket as Krajišnik and separates him from his nominal ally Izetbegović.

—*M. M.*

ZULFIKARPAŠIĆ, ADIL

Adil Zulfikarpašić is a Bosnian Muslim who in 1990 returned to his home country after spending 30 years in Switzerland, where he had become a successful businessman. He initially put much of his own money into supporting **Alija Izetbegović**'s Muslim **Party of Democratic Action** (Stranka demokratske akcije—SDA), but his more secular and less nationalistic profile led him to part company with that party a few weeks before the Bosnian **elections** and to cofound with **Muhamed Filipovič** the moderate group called the Muslim Bošnjak Organization (MBO). Within Bosnia his own influence, as well as that of his party, was comparatively slight, but it momentarily increased in summer 1991 when Serbian president **Slobodan Milošević** enlisted Zulfikarpašić's support for the idea of Bosnia remaining within Yugoslavia through a signing of the **Belgrade Initiative.**

Zulfikarpašić is also founder of the Bosnien Institut (Bosnian Institute) based in Zürich, which operates a charitable foundation dedicated to the study of Bosnian affairs and the cause of an independent **Bosnia-Hercegovina.**

—*J. J. H.*

See also: political parties

ZVORNIK

Located in northeastern Bosnia on the **Drina River**, which forms the border between Bosnia and Serbia, the town of Zvornik in 1991 had a population of 81,000, of whom around three-fifths were Muslims and two-fifths were Serbs. The town was effectively the opening scene of the war in Bosnia, to which **Bijeljina** had been the prologue. On 6 April 1992, the **European Community** (EC) had bestowed official **recognition** upon **Bosnia-Hercegovina** as an independent state. This move was the cue for which Serb troops from both the **Yugoslav Peoples' Army** and the **paramilitary** forces had been waiting: already assembled on the Serbian side of the river, they started shelling the town on 8 April. On the next day paramilitary leader **Željko Ražnjatović** ("Arkan") ordered the surrender of the **Muslim** citizens; their refusal to comply brought Arkan and his so-called Tigers into the town, which was taken on 10 April. Several thousand Muslims had managed to flee westward, but eyewitness acounts suggest an equal number were massacred—women, children, and the old included. **Ethnic cleansing** had come to Bosnia, and a vital bridgehead had been established between the eastern Serbs and the western Serbs in **Banja Luka** and the **Krajina.**

—*J. J. H.*

Bibliography

Of the more recently published bibliographies on Yugoslavia, the following may be useful for students needing to locate further background reading:

Friedman, Francine. *Yugoslavia: A Comprehensive English-Language Bibliography.* Wilmington, DE: Scholarly Resources, 1993.

Horton, John J. *Yugoslavia,* rev. ed. World Bibliographical Series, vol. 1. Oxford, England: Clio Press; Santa Barbara, CA, and Denver, CO: ABC-CLIO, 1990.

Peić, Sava, and Magda Szkuta. *The Balkan Crisis, 1990– : Catalogue, Part 1.* London: British Library, Slavonic and East European Collections, 1997.

Terry, Garth M. *Yugoslav History: A Bibliographic Index to English-Language Articles,* 2nd rev. ed. Nottingham, England: Astra Press, 1990.

The following is a selective list, mainly of books and monographs relating to general and specific aspects of the conflict in former Yugoslavia. Most of these have been written since the start of the conflict, but some earlier items have been included that remain helpful in providing background. The bibliography also incorporates those items that appear as end-of-entry references in the main text.

Adam, Frane, and Gregor Tomc. *Small Societies in Transition: The Case of Slovenia: Transformation Processes in a Small Post-Socialist Society.* Ljubljana: University of Ljubljana, 1994.

Akashi, Yasushi. "The Limits of UN Diplomacy and the Future of Conflict Mediation." *Survival* 37, no. 4 (Winter 1995–1996):83–98.

Akhavan, Payam, and Robert Howse (eds). *Yugoslavia: The Former and the Future: Reflections by Scholars from the Region.* Washington: Brookings Institution, and United Nations Research Institute for Social Development, Geneva, 1995.

Alexander, Stella. *The Triple Myth: A Life of Archbishop Alojzije Stepinac.* Boulder, CO: East European Monographs (dist. by Columbia University Press), 1987.

———. *Church and State in Yugoslavia since 1945.* Cambridge: Cambridge University Press, 1979.

Ali, Rabia, and Lawrence Lifschultz (eds.). *Why Bosnia? Writings on the Balkan War.* Stony Creek, CT: Pamphleteer's Press, 1993.

Allcock, John B. "In Praise of Chauvinism: Rhetorics of Nationalism in Yugoslav Politics." *Third World Quarterly* 11, no. 4 (October 1989):208–222.

Allcock, John B., et al. *Border and Territorial Disputes,* 3rd ed. London: Longman, 1992.

Allcock, John B., John J. Horton, and Marko Milivojević (eds.). *Yugoslavia in Transition: Choices and Constraints; Essays in Honour of Fred Singleton.* Oxford: Berg, 1992.

Allcock, John B., Anton Nikiforov, and Robert H. Frowick. "Bosnia: Prospects for Reconciliation" (three articles). *Cambridge Review of International Relations* 11, no. 1 (1997):65–104.

Allcock, John B., and Harry T. Norris. "The Bosnian Muslims and the Dilemma of Identity." In Frank Carter and David Turnock (eds.), *The States of Eastern Europe.* Aldershot, England: Dartmouth, 1998.

Almond, Mark. *Europe's Backyard War: The War in the Balkans.* London: Heinemann, 1992.

Andrić, Ivo. *Bridge on the Drina,* transl. L. F. Edwards. London: Allen and Unwin, 1959. Reprint, Chicago: University of Chicago Press, 1977.

Ash, Tomothy Garton. *In Europe's Name: Germany and the Divided Continent.* London: Cape, 1993.

Auty, Phyllis. *Tito: A Biography,* rev. ed. Harmondsworth: Penguin, 1974.

Banac, Ivo. *The National Question in Yugoslavia: Origins, History, Politics.* Ithaca, NY: Cornell University Press, 1984.

Bell, Martin. *In Harm's Way: Reflections of a War-Zone Thug,* rev. ed. London: Penguin, 1996.

Bellamy, Christopher. *Knights in White Armour: New Art of War and Peace.* London: Hutchinson, 1996.

Benderly, Jill, and Evan Kraft (eds.), *Independent Slovenia: Origins, Movements, Prospects.* New York: St. Martin's Press; London: Macmillan, 1994.

Bennett, Christopher. *Yugoslavia's Bloody Collapse: Causes, Course and Consequences.* New York: University Press; London: Hurst, 1995.

Bert, Wayne. *The Reluctant Superpower: The United States' Policy in Bosnia, 1991–1995.* London: Macmillan; New York: St. Martin's Press, 1997.

Bićanić, Ivo. "Fractured Economy." In Dennison Rusinow (ed.), *Yugoslavia: A Fractured Federalism.* Washington, DC: Wilson Center Press, 1988.

Biserko, Sonja (ed). *Yugoslavia: Collapse, War, Crimes.* Belgrade: Centre for Anti-War Action, 1993.

Bokovoy, Melissa K., Jill A. Irvine, and Carol. S. Lilly (eds.). *State-Society Relations in Yugoslavia, 1945–1992.* London: Macmillan, 1997.

Bookman, Milica Žarković. "The Economic Basis of Regional Autarchy in Yugoslavia." *Soviet Studies* 42, no. 1 (1990):93–109.

Borden, Anthony, Ben Cohen, Marisa Crevatin, and David Zmijarević (eds.). *Breakdown: War and Reconstruction in Yugoslavia.* London: Yugofax, Institute for War and Peace Reporting, in association with Helsinki Citizens' Assembly, Prague, 1992.

Bougarel, Xavier. *Bosnie: anatomie d'un conflit.* Paris: La Découverte, 1996.

Bowman, Glenn (ed.). *Antagonism and Identity in Former Yugoslavia.* Special issue of *Journal of Area Studies* (UK) no. 3 (1993).

Bringa, Tone. *Being Muslim the Bosnian Way: Identity and Community in a Central Bosnian Village.* Princeton, NJ: Princeton University Press, 1995.

Burg, Steven L. "Why Yugoslavia Fell Apart." *Current History* 92 (1993):357–363.

Burg, Steven L., and Paul Shoup. *Ethnic Conflict and International Intervention: The Crisis in Bosnia-Herzegovina, 1990–1993.* Armonk, NY: M. E. Sharpe, 1994.

Carter, Francis W, and Harold T. Norris (eds.). *The Changing Shape of the Balkans.* London: UCL Press, 1996.

Cigar, Norman L. *Genocide in Bosnia: The Policy of "Ethnic Cleansing."* College Station: Texas A&M University Press, 1995.

Cohen, Leonard J. *Broken Bonds: The Disintegration of Yugoslavia.* 2nd ed. Boulder, CO: Westview Press, 1995.

———. *Serbia's Secret War: Propaganda and the Deceit of History.* College Station: Texas A&M University Press, 1996.

———. *The Socialist Pyramid: Elites and Power in Yugoslavia.* Oakville, Ontario: Mosaic Press; London: Tri-Service Press, 1989.

Conversi, Daniele. *German-Bashing and the Breakup of Yugoslavia.* Seattle: University of Washington (Donald W. Treadgold Papers), 1992.

Ćosić, Dobrica. *Far Away Is the Sun,* transl. M. Heppell and M. Mihajlović. Belgrade: Jugoslavia Publishing House, 1963.

———. *A Time of Death,* transl. M. Heppell. New York: Harcourt Brace Jovanovich, 1983.

Crampton, Richard, and Ben Crampton. *Atlas of Eastern Europe in the Twentieth Century.* London: Routledge, 1996.

Crnobrnja, Mihailo. *The Yugoslav Drama,* rev. ed. London: I. B. Tauris, 1997.

Cushman, Thomas. *Critical Theory and the War in Croatia and Bosnia.* Seattle: University of Washington (Donald W. Treadgold Papers), 1992.

Čuvalo, Ante. *Historical Dictionary of Bosnia and Herzegovina.* Lanham, MD: Scarecrow Press, 1997.

Cviic, Christopher. *Remaking the Balkans.* London: Royal Institute of International Affairs/Pinter Publishers, 1991.

Danchev, Alex, and Thomas E. Halverson (eds.). *International Perspectives on the Yugoslav Conflict.* Basingstoke, England: Macmillan in association with St. Anthony's College, Oxford, 1996.

Danforth, Loring M. *The Macedonian Conflict: Ethnic Nationalism in a Transnational World.* Princeton, NJ: Princeton University Press, 1995.

Davis, G. Scott. *Religion and Justice in the War over Bosnia.* London: Routledge, 1996.

Dawisha, Karen, and Bruce Parrott (eds.). *Politics and Power in the Struggle for Southeast Europe.* Cambridge: Cambridge University Press, 1997.

Dedijer, Vladimir, and Antun Miletić. *Genocid nad Muslimanim 1941–1945.* Sarajevo: Svjetlost, 1990.

Denitch, Bogdan. *Ethnic Nationalism: The Tragic Death of Yugoslavia.* Minneapolis: University of Minnesota Press, 1994.

———. *Limits and Possibilities: The Crisis of Yugoslav Socialism and State Socialist Systems.* Minneapolis: University of Minnesota Press, 1990.

Dimitrijević, Vojin. "The 1974 Constitution and Constitutional Process as a Factor in the Collapse of Yugoslavia." In Payam Akhavan and Robert Howse (eds.), *Yugoslavia, the Former and the Future: Reflections by Scholars from the Region.* Washington, DC: Brookings Institution, 1995.

Djilas, Aleksa. *The Contested Country: Yugoslav Unity and Communist Revolution.* Cambridge, MA: Harvard University Press, 1991.

Djilas, Milovan. *Anatomy of a Moral.* New York: Praeger, 1959.

———. *The New Class.* New York: Praeger, 1959.

Djunić, Danko, et al. *Privatisation in Yugoslavia: Regulations and Application.* Belgrade: Yugoslav Survey, 1997.

Donia, Robert J., and John V. A. Fine. *Bosnia and Hercegovina: A Tradition Betrayed.* New York: Columbia University Press; London: Hurst, 1994.

Drakulić, Slavenka. *How We Survived Communism and Even Laughed.* London: Hutchinson, 1992.

———. *Balkan Express.* London: Hutchinson, 1993.

Drašković, Vukašin. *Nož.* Belgrade: Zapis, 1982.

Dyker, David, A. *Yugoslavia: Socialism, Development and Debt.* London: Routledge, 1990.

Dyker, David A., and Ivan Vejvoda (eds.). *Yugoslavia and After: A Study in Fragmentation, Despair and Rebirth.* London : Longman, 1996.

Elsie, Robert. *Kosovo: In the Heart of the Balkan Powderkeg.* Boulder, CO: East European Monographs, 1997.

Filipović, Zlata. *Zlata's Diary.* London: Viking, 1994.

Flakierski, Henryk. *The Economic System and Income Distribution in Yugoslavia.* Armonk, NY: M. E. Sharpe, 1989.

Friedenreich, Harriet Pass. *The Jews of Yugoslavia: A Quest for Community.* Philadelphia, PA: Jewish Publication Society of America, 1979.

Friedman, Francine. *The Bosnian Muslims: Denial of a Nation.* Boulder, CO: Westview Press, 1996.

Georgieva, Valentina, and Sasha Konechni. *Historical Dictionary of Macedonia.* Lanham, MD: Scarecrow Press, 1998.

Giovanni, Janine di. *The Quick and the Dead: Under Siege in Sarajevo.* London: Phoenix, 1994.

Gjelten, Tom. *Sarajevo Daily: A City and Its Paper under Siege.* New York: HarperCollins, 1995.

Glenny, Misha. *The Fall of Yugoslavia: The Third Balkan War*, 3rd rev. ed. London: Penguin, 1996.

Gow, James. *Legitimacy and the Military: The Yugoslav Crisis.* London: Pinter, 1992.

———. *Triumph of the Lack of Will: International Diplomacy and the Yugoslav War.* London: Hurst, 1997.

Gow, James, Richard Paterson, and Alison Preston. *Bosnia by Television.* London: British Film Institute, 1996.

Guikovaty, Emile. *Tito.* Paris: Hachette, 1979.

Gutman, Roy. *A Witness to Genocide: The First Inside Account of the Horrors of "Ethnic Cleansing" in Bosnia.* Shaftesbury: Element Books, 1993.

Hall, Brian. *The Impossible Country : A Journey through the Last Days of Yugoslavia.* London: Secker and Warburg, 1994.

Harris, Paul. *Cry Bosnia.* Edinburgh: Canongate, 1995.

———. *Somebody Else's War: Frontline Reports from the Balkan Wars 1991–92.* Stevenage: Spa Books, 1992.

Hastie, Rachel. *Disabled Children in a Society at War: Casebook from Bosnia.* Oxford: Oxfam, 1997.

Helsinki Watch. *War Crimes in Bosnia-Hercegovina: A Helsinki Watch Report.* London and New York: Human Rights Watch, 1992.

Hollingworth, Larry. *Merry Christmas, Mr Larry.* London: Heinemann, 1996.

Honig, Jan Willem, and Norbert Both. *Srebrenica: Record of a War Crime.* London: Penguin, 1996.

House of Commons, Foreign Affairs Committee. *Central and Eastern Europe: Problems of the Post-Communist Era.* 2 vols. London: HMSO, 1992.

Huntington, Samuel P. *The Clash of Civilizations and the Re-making of World Order.* New York and London: Simon and Schuster, 1997.

———. *The Third Wave: Democratizations in the Late Twentieth Century.* Norman: University of Oklahoma Press, 1991.

Ignatieff, Michael. *Blood & Belonging: Journeys Into the New Nationalism.* London: BBC Books/Chatto and Windus, 1993.

International Boundaries Research Unit. "Croatia and Slovenia: The Four Hamlets Case." *IBRU Boundary and Security Bulletin* (January). Durham, England: International Boundaries Research Unit, University of Durham, 1995.

———. "The Maritime Borders of the Adriatic Sea." *Maritime Briefing* 1, no. 8. Durham, England: International Boundaries Research Unit, University of Durham, 1996.

Irvine, Jill A. "Nationalism and the Extreme Right in the Former Yugoslavia." In L. Cheles, R. Ferguson, and M. Vaughan (eds.), *The Far Right in Western and Eastern Europe*, 2nd ed. London: Longman, 1995.

———. *The Croat Question: Partisan Politics in the Formation of the Yugoslav Socialist State.* Boulder, CO: Westview Press, 1993.

Iveković, R., B. Joanović, M. Krese, and R. Lazić. *Briefe von Frauen über Krieg und Nationalismus.* Frankfurt-am-Main: Suhrkamp, 1993.

Jambrešić Kirin, Renata, and Maja Povrzanović (eds.). *War, Exile, Everyday Life: Cultural Perspectives.* Zagreb: Institute of Ethnology and Folklore Research, 1996.

Jancar-Webster, Barbara. *Women and Revolution in Yugoslavia 1941–1945.* Boulder, CO: Arden Press, 1991.

Jancar-Webster, Barbara (ed.). *Environmental Action in Eastern Europe: Responses to Crises.* Armonk, NY: M. E. Sharpe, 1991.

Janša, Janez. *The Making of the Slovenian State, 1988–1992: The Collapse of Yugoslavia.* Ljubljana: Mladinska knjiga, 1994.

Jeffries, Ian. *Problems of Economic and Political Transformation in the Balkans.* London: Pinter, 1996.

Jelavich, Barbara. *History of the Balkans.* 2 vols. Cambridge University Press, 1983.

Jelavich, Charles. *South Slav Nationalisms: Textbooks and Yugoslav Union Before 1914.* Columbus: Ohio State University Press, 1990.

Judah, Tim. *The Serbs: History, Myth and the Destruction of Yugoslavia.* New Haven, CT: Yale University Press, 1997.

Kadijević, Veljko. *Moje vidjenje raspada: vojska bez države.* Belgrade: Politika, 1993.

Kaplan, Robert D. *Balkan Ghosts: A Journey through History.* New York: St. Martin's Press, 1993.

Karahsan, Dzevad, and Slobodan Drakulić. *Sarajevo: Exodus of a City.* New York: Kodansha International, 1994.

Kristo, Jure. "Catholicism among Croats and Its Critique by Marxists." In Dennis J. Dunn (ed.), *Religion and Nationalism in Eastern Europe and the Soviet Union.* Boulder, CO, and London: Lynne Rienner Publishers, 1987.

Kurspahić, Kemal. *As Long as Sarajevo Exists.* Stony Creek, CT: Pamphleteer's Press, 1997.

Kyrou, Alexandros K. "Castle-building in the Balkans: American Aspirations in Southeastern Europe since the Dissolution of Yugoslavia." *Journal of Political and Military Sociology* 24 (1996):253–284.

Lampe, John R. *Yugoslavia as History: Twice There Was a Country.* Cambridge: Cambridge University Press, 1996.

Lazić, Mladen (ed.). *Society in Crisis: Yugoslavia in the Early '90s.* Belgrade: Filip Visnjić, 1995.

Lešić, Zdenko (ed.). *Children of Atlantis: Voices from the Former Yugoslavia.* Budapest: Central European University Press, 1995.

Leurdijk, Dick A., and Auke P. Venema. *The United Nations and NATO in Former Yugoslavia, 1991–1996: Limits to Diplomacy and Force.* The Hague: Netherlands Atlantic Commission/Netherlands Institute of International Relations "Clingendael," 1996.

Lydall, Harold. *Yugoslavia in Crisis.* Oxford: Clarendon Press, 1989.

MacKenzie, Lewis. *Peacekeeper: The Road to Sarajevo.* Vancouver: Douglas and McIntyre, 1993.

Magaš, Branka. *The Destruction of Yugoslavia: Tracking the Break-up 1980–92.* London: Verso, 1993.

Malcolm, Noel. *Bosnia: A Short History,* new ed. London: Macmillan, 1996.

———. *Kosovo: A Short History.* London: Macmillan, 1998.

Markle, Gerald E., and Frances B. McCrea. "Medjugorje and the Crisis in Yugoslavia." In William H. Swatos (ed.), *Politics and Religion in Central and Eastern Europe.* Westport, CT: Praeger, 1994.

Marshall, T. H. *Citizenship and Social Class.* London: Pluto Press, 1992.

Mertus, Julie, Jasmina Tešanović, Habiba Metikos, and Rada Borić (eds.). *The Suitcase: Refugee Voices from Bosnia and Croatia.* Berkeley: University of California Press, 1997.

Meštrović, Stjepan G. *The Balkanization of the West: The Confluence of Postmodernism and Postcommunism.* London: Routledge, 1994.

Meštrović, Stjepan G., Slaven Letica, and Miroslav Goreta. *Habits of the Balkan Heart: Social Character and the Fall of Communism.* College Station: Texas A&M University Press, 1993.

Milivojević, Marko, John B. Allcock, and Pierre Maurer (eds.). *Yugoslavia's Security Dilemmas: Armed Forces, National Defence and Foreign Policy.* Oxford: Berg, 1988.

Minear, Larry, et al. *Humanitarian Action in the Former Yugoslavia: The U.N.'s Role 1991–1993.* Providence, RI: Thomas J. Watson Jr. Institute for International Studies, 1994.

Mojzes, Paul. *Yugoslavian Inferno: Ethnoreligious War in the Balkans.* New York: Continuum, 1994.

Morgan, Peter. *Barrel of Stones: In Search of Serbia.* Aberystwyth: Planet, 1997.

Mostov, Julie. "Democracy and the Politics of National Identity." *Studies in East European Thought* 46, no. 1–2 (1994):9–31.

Mrdjen, Snježana. "La mixité en ex-Yougoslavie: integration ou ségrégation des nationalités?" *Revue d'Etudes Comparatives Est-Ouest* 27, no. 3 (September 1996): 103–145.

Nečak Luk, Albina. "The Linguistic Aspect of Ethnic Conflict in Yugoslavia." In Payam Akhavan and Robert Howse (eds.), *Yugoslavia, the Former and the Future: Reflections by Scholars from the Region.* Washington, DC: Brookings Institution, 1995.

Niarchos, Catherine N. "Women, War and Rape: Challenges Facing the International Tribunal for the Former Yugoslavia." *Human Rights Quarterly* 17, no. 4 (November 1995):649–690.

O'Ballance, Edgar. *Civil War in Bosnia, 1992–94.* Basingstoke: Macmillan; 1995.

Okey, Robin. "The Historical Background to the Yugoslav Crisis." *Journal of Area Studies* 4 (1994):124–138.

Owen, David. *Balkan Odyssey.* London: Gollancz, 1995.

Papacosma, S. Victor. "NATO and the Post–Cold War Balkans." *Journal of Political and Military Sociology* 24 (1996):233–252.

Pavkovic, Aleksandar. *The Fragmentation of Yugoslavia: Nationalism in a Multinational State.* Basingstoke: Macmillan, 1996.

Pavkovic, Aleksandar (ed.). *The Disintegration of Yugoslavia: Inevitable or Avoidable?* Special issue of

The Nationalities Papers (UK) 25, no. 3 (September 1997).

Pavlowitch, Stevan K. *The Improbable Survivor: Yugoslavia and its Problems, 1918–1988.* London: Hurst, 1988.

———. *Tito, Yugoslavia's Great Dictator: A Reassessment.* London: Hurst, 1992.

Peress, Gilles, and Eric Stover. *Graves: The Forensic Efforts at Srebrenica and Vukovar.* Zurich: Scalo Verlag, 1998.

Pinson, Mark. *The Muslims of Bosnia-Herzegovina: Their Historic Development from the Middle Ages to the Dissolution of Yugoslavia.* Cambridge, MA: distributed for the Center for Middle Eastern Studies of Harvard University by Harvard University Press, 1993.

Pleština, Dijana. *Regional Development in Communist Yugoslavia: Success, Failure and Consequences.* Boulder, CO: Westview Press, 1988.

Plut-Pregelj, Leopoldina, and Carole Rogel. *Historical Dictionary of Slovenia.* Lanham, MD: Scarecrow Press, 1996.

Poulton, Hugh. *The Balkans: Minorities and States in Conflict,* new ed. London: Minority Rights Publications, 1993.

———. *Who Are the Macedonians?* Bloomington: Indiana University Press, 1994.

Poulton, Hugh, and Suha Taji-Farouki (eds.). *Muslim Identity and the Balkan State.* London: Hurst, for the Institute of Muslim Minority Affairs, 1997.

Pribichevich, Stoyan. *Macedonia: Its People and History.* University Park: Pennsylvania State University Press, 1982.

Prkačin, Nada. *Tamo gdje nema rata.* Vinkovci: Privlačica, 1993.

Ramet, Sabrina P. *Balkan Babel: Politics, Culture, and Religion in Yugoslavia.* Boulder, CO: Westview Press, 1992.

———. "Feminism in Yugoslavia." In Ramet, Sabrina Petra (ed.), *Social Currents in Eastern Europe,* 2nd ed. Boulder, CO: Westview Press, 1995.

———. *Nationalism and Federalism in Yugoslavia, 1962–1991,* 2nd ed. Bloomington: Indiana University Press, 1992.

Ramet, Sabrina P., and Ljubiša S. Adamovich. *Beyond Yugoslavia: Politics, Economics and Culture in a Shattered Community.* Boulder, CO: Westview Press, 1995.

Regional Environmental Center for Central and Eastern Europe. *Strategic Environmental Issues in Central and Eastern Europe,* vol. 2 Budapest: REC, August 1994.

Richardson, Mervyn. *The Effects of War on the Environment: Croatia.* London: Spon, 1995.

Rieff, David. *Slaughterhouse: Bosnia and the Failure of the West.* New York: Simon and Schuster, 1995.

Rogel, Carole. *The Breakup of Yugoslavia and the War in Bosnia.* Westport, CT: Greenwood Press, 1998.

Rohde, David W. *A Safe Area—Srebrenica: Europe's Worst Massacre since the Second World War.* London: Pilot, 1997.

Rose, Michael. "The Bosnia Experience." In Ramesh Thakur (ed.), *Past Imperfect, Future UNCertain: The United Nations at Fifty.* London: Macmillan, 1998.

Rupel, Dimitrij. "Slovenia's Shift from the Balkans to Central Europe." In Jill Benderly and Evan Kraft (eds.), *Independent Slovenia: Origins, Movements, Prospects.* New York: Macmillan, 1994.

Rusinow, Dennison (ed.). *Yugoslavia: A Fractured Federalism.* Washington, DC: Wilson Center Press, 1988.

Sadowski, Yahya M. *Is Chaos a Strategic Threat? Bosnia and Myths about Ethnic Conflict.* Washington, DC: Brookings Institution, 1997.

Said, Edward. *Orientalism.* Harmondsworth, Middlesex: Penguin Books, 1985.

Samary, Catherine. *Yugoslavia Dismembered.* New York: Monthly Review Press, 1995.

Schulze, Carl. *IFOR: Allied Forces in Bosnia* (pictorial). *Europa Militaria,* no. 22 London: Windrow and Greene, 1996.

Secretariat for Information. *The Law on Economic Reform in Yugoslavia.* Belgrade: Yugoslav Survey, 1990.

Sekelj, Laslo. *Yugoslavia: The Process of Disintegration,* transl. Vera Vukelić. Boulder, CO: Social Science Monographs, 1993.

Selenić, Slobodan. *Premeditated Murder.* New York: HarperCollins, 1996.

Sells, Michael A. *The Bridge Betrayed: Religion and Genocide in Bosnia.* Berkeley: University of California Press, 1996.

Seroka, Jim, and Vukašin Pavlović (eds.). *The Tragedy of Yugoslavia: The Failure of Democratic Transformation.* Armonk, NY: M. E. Sharpe, 1992.

Siber, Ivan, Daniel B. German, and Steve Millsaps. "Yugoslavia Divided: Nationalism, Ethnic Rivalry and War." *Politics and the Individual* 4, no. 1 (1994):85–93.

Silber, Laura, and Alan Little. *The Death of Yugoslavia.* London: Penguin, 1995.

Simmie, James, and Jože Dekleva (eds.). *Yugoslavia in Turmoil: After Self-Management.* London: Pinter, 1991.

Singleton, Fred. "Yugoslavia's Defence and Foreign Policy in the Context of Non-Alignment." In M. Milivojević, J. B. Allcock, and P. Maurer (eds.), *Yugoslavia's Security Dilemmas.* Oxford: Berg, 1988.

Singleton, Fred. *A Short History of the Yugoslav Peoples.* Cambridge University Press, 1985.

Stewart, Bob. *Broken Lives: A Personal View of the Bosnian Conflict.* London: HarperCollins, 1993.

Stiglmayer, Alexandra (ed.). *Mass Rape: The War against Women in Bosnia-Hercegovina.* Lincoln: University of Nebraska Press, 1994.

Stokes, Gale. *The Walls Came Tumbling Down: The Collapse of Communism in Eastern Europe.* New York and Oxford: Oxford University Press, 1993.

Stokes, Gale, John Lampe, Dennison Rusinow with Julie Mostov. "Instant History: Understanding the Wars of Yugoslav Succession." [review essay] *Slavic Review* 55, no.1 (Spring 1996):136–160.

Sugar, Peter F. (ed.). *Eastern European Nationalism in the Twentieth Century.* Washington, DC: American University Press, 1995.

Šušter, Željan. *Historical Dictionary of the Federal Republic of Yugoslavia.* Lanham, MD: Scarecrow Press, 1998.

Szajkowski, Bogdan (ed.), *Political Parties of Eastern Europe: Russia and the Successor States.* London: Longman, 1994.

Tanner, Marcus. *Croatia: A Nation Forged in War.* New Haven, CT: Yale University Press, 1997.

Thompson, Mark. *Forging War: The Media in Serbia, Croatia and Bosnia-Hercegovina.* London: International Centre against Censorship, 1994.

———. *A Paper House: The Ending of Yugoslavia.* London: Hutchinson, 1992.

The Times. *The Times Map of the Western Balkans; Showing the New States and Territories of the Former Yugoslav Federation and Surrounding Areas.* London: Times Books, 1993.

Todorova, Maria N. *Imagining the Balkans.* New York and Oxford: Oxford University Press, 1997.

Tomašić, Dinko. *Personality and Culture in Eastern European Politics.* New York: Stewart, 1948.

Tomšić, Vida. *Women in the Development of Socialist Self-Managing Yugoslavia.* Belgrade: Radnička Štampa, 1980.

Tudjman, Franjo. *Horrors of War: Historical Reality and Philosophy.* New York: M. Evans, 1997.

Udovički, Jasminka, and James Ridgeway (eds.). *Burn This House: The Making and Unmaking of Yugoslavia.* Durham, NC: Duke University Press, 1997.

———. *Yugoslavia's Ethnic Nightmare: The Inside Story of Europe's Unfolding Ordeal.* New York: Lawrence Hill, 1995.

Ugrešić, Dubravka. *Američki fikcionar.* Zagreb, 1993. *Have a Nice Day: From the Balkan War to the American Dream,* transl. C. Hawkesworth. London: Cape, 1994.

———. *The Culture of Lies,* transl. C. Hawkesworth. London: Weidenfeld and Nicolson, 1998.

Ullman, Richard H. (ed.). *The World and Yugoslavia's Wars.* New York: Council on Foreign Relations, 1996.

Vickers, Miranda. *Between Serb and Albanian: A History of Kosovo.* London: Hurst, 1998.

Vojnić, Dragomar. "The Economic Dimension of Yugoslavia's Demise." In Payam Akhavan and Robert Howse (eds.), *Yugoslavia, the Former and the Future: Reflections by Scholars from the Region.* Washington, DC: Brookings Institution, 1995.

Vulliamy, Ed. *Seasons in Hell: Understanding Bosnia's War.* New York and London: Simon and Schuster, 1994.

Woodward, Susan L. *Balkan Tragedy: Chaos and Dissolution after the Cold War.* Washington DC: Brookings Institution, 1995.

———. *Socialist Unemployment: The Political Economy of Yugoslavia.* Princeton University Press, 1995.

Zimmerman, Warren. "Memoirs of the Last American Ambassador for Yugoslavia." *Foreign Affairs* 74, no. 2 (March–April 1995):20.

———. *Origins of a Catastrophe: Yugoslavia and its Destroyers.* New York: Times Books, 1996.

Periodicals that have regularly covered the events and issues include:

Balkan Forum (Macedonia)
Bosnia Report (UK)
Foreign Affairs (U.S.)
South Slav Journal (UK)
Transitions: Changes in Post-Communist Societies (Czech Republic)
War Report/Yugofax (UK)

Newspapers that have reported on the conflict with consistently high quality include the *New York Times* (U.S.), the *Guardian* (UK) and *Le Monde* (France).

Yugoslavia and its aftermath continues to figure copiously on the Internet. This vehicle is especially valuable for current information not covered by newspapers or magazines, but the user should exercise caution in the context of unregulated sources of information.

Chronology

Abbreviations Used in Chronology

B-H	Bosnia-Hercegovina
CSCE	Conference on Security and Cooperation in Europe
DEMOS	Democratic Opposition of Slovenia
EC	European Community
EU	European Union
FRY	Federal Republic of Yugoslavia
GDR	German Democratic Republic
GNP	gross national product
HDZ	Hrvatska Demokratska Zajednica (Croatian Democratic Union)
HV	Hrvatska Vojska (Croatian Army)
IFOR	Implementation Force
IMF	International Monetary Fund
IMRO	International Macedonian Revolutionary Organization
IWCT	International War Crimes Tribunal
JNA	Jugoslavenska Narodna Armija (Yugoslav Peoples' Army)
LC	League of Communists
LCY	League of Communists of Yugoslavia
NAM	Nonaligned Movement
NATO	North Atlantic Treaty Organization
OIC	Organization of the Islamic Conference
OSCE	Organization for Security and Cooperation in Europe
PDP	Party for Democratic Prosperity
RRF	Rapid Reaction Force
RS	Republika Srpska
SDA	Stranka Demokratske Akcije (Party of Democratic Action)
SFOR	Stabilization Force
SFRY	Socialist Federal Republic of Yugoslavia
SPS	Socialisticka Partija Srbije (Socialist Party of Serbia)
UK	United Kingdom
UN	United Nations
UNCRO	United Nations Confidence Restoration Operation (Croatia)
UNPREDEP	United Nations Preventive Deployment
UNPROFOR	United Nations Protection Force
UNSC	United Nations Security Council
UNTAES	United Nations Transitional Administration for Eastern Slavonia
US	United States
VOP	Vance-Owen Plan
WEU	Western European Union

Events in Yugoslavia

1941

6 April The forces of the Axis invade Yugoslavia, drawing the country into World War II.

June German forces invade the Soviet Union; the Partizan uprising is launched in Yugoslavia.

1942

November The first meeting of the Anti-Fascist Council for the National Liberation of Yugoslavia (AVNOJ), in Bihać, suggests a federal system for postwar Yugoslavia.

1943

November The second meeting of AVNOJ, in Jajce, effectively establishes the Communists as leading the provisional government.

Events in the Surrounding World

Events in Yugoslavia

1944

October Soviet troops enter Yugoslavia and assist the Partizan army to liberate Belgrade.

1945

August A "Popular Front" government is established under Communist leadership.

1953

The concept of workers' self-management is introduced.

1961

The process of economic reform begins, with the first moves toward "market socialism."

1963

Constitutional reform introduces greater decentralization in the federation.

1968

Student demonstrations and strikes take place. Serious civil disorder develops in Kosovo.

1971–1972

The Croatian Spring and the rise and fall of the mass movement *(maspok)* in favor of greater independence for Croatia take place.

1974

Constitutional reform furthers the process of decentralization and proposes the collective presidency to take over on the death of President Tito.

1976

The introduction of the Law on Associated Labor launches the final and most cumbersome form of self-management.

1980

4 May President Tito dies.

1981

Serious disturbances in Kosovo are suppressed violently.

Events in the Surrounding World

1948

Yugoslavia is expelled from the Cominform.

1961

The Conference of the NAM is held in Belgrade; Yugoslav foreign policy becomes centrally defined in relation to the NAM.

1973

The world faces its first oil crisis.

1979

The second world oil crisis occurs.

1983

The IMF demands economic reform in Yugoslavia in relation to the latter's burden of foreign indebtedness.

Events in Yugoslavia

1986

January–February Serbs in Kosovo mount anti-Albanian demonstrations.

1987

July The Agrokomerc scandal breaks in Bosnia, involving Fikret Abdić in accusations of massive fraud and implicating several leading Bosnian Communists.

September Slobodan Milošević takes over at the head of the League of Communists of Serbia and launches his "antibureaucratic revolution."

October The Province of Kosovo is placed under martial law.

November The central committee of the Kosovo LC is purged of those with "counterrevolutionary views."

1988

The Serbian LC begins its attempt to revise the republic's constitution, curtailing the autonomy of its provinces, Kosovo and the Vojvodina.

September Massive demonstrations are held in several Serbian cities in support of Milošević's proposed constitutional changes.

October Following huge demonstrations in Novi Sad, the leadership of the LC in the Vojvodina resigns, to be replaced by nominees of Milošević. The presidium of the LC in Montenegro is also compelled to resign in the face of pro-Milošević demonstrations, and Momir Bulatović takes over.

October–November Massive protests are held in Kosovo, including a strike by miners of the Trepča complex, against the abrogation of the autonomy of the province and the forced resignations of Azem Vllasi and other Albanian Kosovar leaders.

30 December The federal government led by Branko Mikulić resigns, having lost a vote of no confidence in the federal assembly, opposed because of its program of economic reforms. Inflation reaches an annual rate of 250 percent.

1989

11 January The Democratic Alliance is launched in Ljubljana—the first political organization in postwar Yugoslavia to declare itself to be a "party." Leading figures of the LC in Montenegro are compelled to resign under pressure from popular demonstrations orchestrated by Slobodan Milošević.

19 January Ante Marković takes office as the federal prime minister (president of the federal executive council) of Yugoslavia, presenting a program of economic reform and restructuring. His government faces a balance of payments deficit of U.S.$1,600 million, annual inflation of 250 percent, and an international debt estimated at U.S.$19 billion.

Events in the Surrounding World

Events in Yugoslavia

20 January A new leadership of the LC is elected in the Vojvodina following the collective resignation of the presidency under pressure from supporters of Slobodan Milošević.

2 February The Movement for a Yugoslav Democratic Initiative is launched in Zagreb—the first and only effective federation-wide opposition group to emerge in the movement toward party pluralism.

14 February A major strike of miners at the Trepča complex near Kosovska Mitrovica, prompted by the ousting from the LC of popular Albanian leader Azem Vllasi, underscores growing social tension in Kosovo and reveals the political disunity of the League of Communists.

20 February A thousand Trepča miners begin a hunger strike deep in their mine. The next day students from the University of Priština begin a sit-in in support.

28 February The Croatian Democratic Union, the principal voice of anticommunist Croatian nationalism, is founded in Zagreb under the leadership of Franjo Tudjman.

28 March The Serbian assembly adopts a new constitutional structure including (1) the abolition in all but name of the autonomous provinces and (2) the subordination of those provinces to the republic. Further strikes take place, as well as public disturbances, involving Albanians in Kosovo. These types of events become more general during April.

April The Marković government unfolds the detail of its reform program, which includes severe cuts of the federal budget from 11.7 to 8.5 percent of GNP and curtailment of the monetary supply.

May Substantial price increases introduced under the economic reform spark a wave of strikes and demonstrations.

9 May Slobodan Milošević is elected as president of the Serbian republic under the new constitution. The formation of a "Milošević Commission" is announced, directed at the formulation of a rival economic strategy.

15 May Janez Drnovšek of Slovenia takes office as the new president of the collective state presidency of the federation.

June Strain grows throughout the month between the federal government (and its allies) and the Serbian government with respect to their divergent economic programs.

Events in the Surrounding World

1989

20 March At a meeting in Brussels, the EC announces its support for the Marković reform program, including the radical transformation of the financial and fiscal systems.

June Yugoslavia's ambassador to the United States, Živorad Kovačević, is withdrawn because of his failure to head off criticism in Congress of the infringement of human rights in Kosovo.

Events in Yugoslavia

28 June The 600th anniversary of the Battle of Kosovo is celebrated at Gazi Mestan (the site of the battle) by huge crowds.

July The debate about financial policy intensifies as the annual rate of inflation is estimated at 791 percent.

28 August Farmers hold a large demonstration in Belgrade to protest against their deteriorating standard of living.

September Worsening balance-of-payments figures are announced, intensifying debate about the pressing need to implement economic reform.

27 September The new Slovene constitution omits reference to the "leading role" of the League of Communists and reaffirms the republic's right of secession from the federation.

October Increases in retail prices of more than 45 percent for some commodities are announced in an attempt to diminish federal subsidies. The trial of Azem Vllasi and others on charges of "counterrevolution" begins. The remains of King Nikola and other members of the former Montenegrin royal family are returned from Italy to Cetinje for reburial.

November By the end of the month, annual inflation is estimated to have passed 2,000 percent.

1 December A "Meeting of Truth" planned by Serbs to take place in Ljubljana, protesting against Slovenia's critical attitude toward the federation, is thwarted by the republican authorities.

6 December Slobodan Milošević is elected president of Serbia by the republic's assembly.

13 December Ante Marković outlines his reform program in a special speech to senior officers of the JNA.

19 December The government announces its program for the stabilization of the dinar.

End of December By the end of the month, all the republican assemblies have reported agreement in principle with the reform program. By the end of the year, inflation reaches 2,700 percent.

1990

January The new convertible dinar is launched by the Marković government, and inflation is eliminated within three months.

Events in the Surrounding World

4–7 September The Ninth Summit of the NAM takes place in Belgrade.

23 October Senior officials of the World Bank visit Belgrade for discussions with the federal government, following which new credits of U.S.$800 million are announced.

7 November The government of the GDR resigns, and the Berlin Wall is breached.

Events in Yugoslavia

20–22 January The long-postponed fourteenth congress of the LCY opens in Belgrade, only to be adjourned indefinitely following the withdrawal of the Slovene delegation and others.

23 January The press announces that the LCY "no longer exists"; Marković declares that "Yugoslavia continues to function without the LCY."

24 January Following the violent breakup by police of a demonstration in Priština, there is a week of rioting throughout Kosovo, resulting in 27 deaths.

30 January The federal presidency announces "special measures" in Kosovo because of the security situation. For the first time, units of the JNA are fielded for civilian crowd control; Slovene and Croatian units of the security forces are withdrawn from the province.

February Founding assemblies take place for several newly formed parties expecting to compete in open elections.

4 March A mass meeting takes place in Petrova Gora in the Kordun region of Croatia, calling for the defense of the territorial integrity of Yugoslavia in the face of moves toward Croatian autonomy. The lack of federal response to this event meets with condemnation by the Croatian government on 13 March.

22 March In the wake of rumors of the poisoning of Albanian children, further massive demonstrations sweep Kosovo; 100 people are injured in Podujevo alone.

3 April The provincial premier and other ministers resign in Kosovo in protest against the brutality of the security forces.

18 April The "special measures" of 30 January are suspended in Kosovo, and security is passed to the Serbian republican authorities.

22 April The second round of the first multiparty elections in Slovenia returns a large majority in support of Communist leader Milan Kučan but places government in the hands of a coalition of six center-right parties (DEMOS). The Croatian elections return the HDZ to power with a massive majority.

24 April Azem Vllasi is released from custody.

6 May The second round of the first multiparty elections in Croatia confirms a substantial majority for the HDZ and Franjo Tudjman as president.

15 May Under the normal rules of rotation, Borisav Jović (a Serb and a close ally of Milošević) and Stipe

Events in the Surrounding World

1990

March Agreement is reached with the IMF on the granting of an 18-month stand-by credit of up to U.S.$600 million to support the SFRY's economic reform program.

Events in Yugoslavia

Suvar (from Croatia) take over as president and vice president, respectively, of the federal collective presidency, foreshadowing that body's difficulties in functioning.

30 May A specially convened congress of the LCY fails to produce a quorum after delegates from Croatia and Macedonia as well as Slovenia fail to appear. The League of Communists can be regarded as dead.

June The second round of Marković's reform proposals is launched, including proposals to privatize socially owned enterprises.

2 July The Slovene assembly affirms the republic's sovereignty within the federation. The unofficial Assembly of Kosovo meeting in Kačanik declares the "Republic of Kosova."

25 July The Croatian assembly adopts the amended constitution, including the introduction of controversial new state symbols.

End of July Following a demonstration of 100,000 people in the village of Srb, Croatian Serbs declare their autonomy from Croatia. The Serb National Council is formed in order to conduct a referendum on the future of Serb communities in the republic.

August The first barricades are erected in defense of the "Serbian autonomous regions" in Croatia. There is widespread disorder surrounding incidents connected to the referendum on Serb autonomy.

17 August Serb militias set up barricades on roads in the area of Benkovac.

19 August The referendum on the autonomy of the Serb regions in Croatia (the Krajina) takes place, with a large majority in favor of autonomy.

24 August In response to federal inactivity in the face of the Serb referendum in the Krajina, Stipe Šuvar's mandate as Croatian representative on the federal presidency is withdrawn on the grounds that he is insufficiently energetic in defending Croatian interests. He is replaced by Stipe Mesić of the HDZ.

3 September A general strike begins in Kosovo with a demonstration estimated at 200,000 people, protesting against the dismissal of Albanian officials and their replacement by Serbs.

7 September At a secret meeting in Kačanik, the Albanian representatives of the dissolved provincial assembly proclaim a new constitution for the "Republic of Kosova."

9 September The first of a series of public disturbances in Bosnia-Hercegovina takes place in Foča.

Events in the Surrounding World

2 August Iraq invades Kuwait, launching the Gulf War.

12 September The treaty marking the settlement of the international status of the reunified Germany is signed.

Events in Yugoslavia

Events in the Surrounding World

28 September The new Serbian constitution is adopted, abrogating the powers of the former autonomous provinces.

1 October The Serbian National Council proclaims the "Serbian Autonomous Region of the Krajina."

3 October Slovene and Croat representatives submit a new model for the federation to the federal presidency.

18 November The first free elections in Bosnia take place, returning nationalist parties to power.

December Reports emerge that Serbian banks have been conspiring to evade the provisions of reform legislation by issuing unsecured credits to ailing enterprises.

9 December The second round of multiparty elections in Macedonia returns Kiro Gligorov as president. Although the nationalist IMRO (Internal Macedonian Revolutionary Organization) emerges as the largest party in the assembly, it lacks an overall majority, and a nonparty "government of experts" takes office. In the last of the multiparty elections for new republican governments, Slobodan Milošević is returned as president with an overwhelming majority in the first round. Two weeks later the second round confirms the Socialist Party of Serbia as the governing party with more than three-fourths of the votes cast.

19 December Two of the Serb enclaves in Croatia (the Autonomous Region of the Krajina and the Autonomous Region of Slavonia, Baranja, and Western Srem) declare their unification in the Serb Republic of the Krajina, including a population of about 300,000. Milan Babić is elected as president.

22 December The new constitution is adopted in Croatia, declaring Croatia to be the "national state of the Croatian people."

23 December The League of Communists in Montenegro is returned to power with an unchallenged majority in multiparty elections. The government of Montenegro announces that it will not be seeking separate recognition from the EU. The Democratic League of Kosova announces that it will be seeking recognition for an independent Republic of Kosova. A referendum on Slovene independence returns a vote of yes. Renewed problems in the economy force a devaluation of the dinar.

1991

9 January The federal presidency orders the disbanding of all irregular forces and the surrender of illegally held weapons.

Events in Yugoslavia

20 January It becomes known that the Croatian government has imported weapons in order to arm its defense forces.

25 January The federal presidency orders the dissolution of the armed police reserve in Croatia. TV film is broadcast of Martin Špegelj's negotiations over the purchase of weapons for the Croatian government. A warrant for his arrest is issued on 31 January.

7 February Janez Drnovšek informs the federal presidency that Slovenia is commencing the formal process of dissociation from Yugoslavia.

16 February The arrival of units of the Croatian interior ministry forces in the Plitvice area is met with resistance by the local Serb population.

20 February The Slovene assembly adopts the new constitution as an independent state.

28 February The Serbian National Council declares the independence of the Krajina from Croatia and its intention to remain within Yugoslavia.

2–3 March Fighting breaks out in the Slavonian town of Pakrac and spreads to several locations along the Croatian-Bosnian border.

9 March Demonstrations organized by the opposition parties in Belgrade and supported massively by students are broken up violently by the JNA; two people are killed.

12–14 March The federal presidency refuses to adopt the proposal of the JNA high command to raise the combat readiness of the army. President Jovič resigns in protest on 15 March, followed by representatives of the Vojvodina and Montenegro.

18 March Crisis is provoked within the federal presidency when Serbia finally brings to an end the autonomy of the provinces of Kosovo and the Vojvodina but insists upon retaining three voices in the collective presidency. The use of the Albanian language in public documents is declared illegal. Throughout the rest of the year, the replacement of Albanians by ethnic Serbs in public offices gathers speed.

20 March The federal assembly refuses to accept Jović's resignation, and he returns to office.

28 March The first of a series of meetings of the presidents of the Yugoslav republics takes place in Split, but no agreement is reached.

31 March The situation in the Plitvice area deteriorates into open armed conflict between Croatian security forces and the local Serb militia.

Events in the Surrounding World

1991

3–4 April Growing international concern about the developments in Yugoslavia is reflected by the visit of a "troika" of EC ministers (from Italy,

Events in Yugoslavia

6 April The first armed clashes take place in Sarajevo and throughout Bosnia-Hercegovina, killing 14 people and wounding around 100.

7 April An assembly of Serb representatives takes place in Banja Luka and declares the independence of the Serbian Republic of Bosnia-Hercegovina. Biljana Plavšić and Nikola Koljević dissociate themselves from the official presidency of the republic.

25 April The Serb minority in Bosnia-Hercegovina declares its autonomy from the republic.

2 May Twelve Croatian policemen are killed in an ambush at Borovo Selo in Slavonia.

3 May Anti-Serb demonstrations in Split and Zadar degenerate into rioting. On 6 May a soldier of the JNA is killed.

9 May Special powers are finally granted to the JNA in an arrangement that effectively frees it from control by the federal government.

12 May A plebiscite of Serbs in Croatia declares a majority in favor of maintaining the union with Yugoslavia. The Serb nominees are then able to obstruct the accession of the Croatian representative, Stipe Mesić, to the chair of the federal presidency. After a week of intense and acrimonious negotiation, Mesić takes the chair.

13 May The National Council of the Sandžak is declared, with the aim of defending the interests of the Muslim population of the region.

19 May The official Croatian referendum on independence is boycotted by the Serbs and produces a massive majority in favor of an ambiguous resolution.

29 May A provisional government is announced for the Krajina, headed by Milan Babić.

3 June Presidents Kiro Gligorov and Alija Izetbegović announce a joint proposal for a confederal Yugoslavia of independent republics.

6 June The Gligorov-Iztebegović proposal is turned down by a meeting of the republican presidents in Sarajevo.

Events in the Surrounding World

Luxembourg, and the Netherlands) in order to clarify the situation.

29–30 May Jacques Santer (prime minister of Luxembourg) and Jacques Delors (president of the EC) visit Yugoslavia.

30–31 May The EC indicates that it would like to see a democratized and reformed Yugoslavia that does not change its internal and external borders and that resolves its problems without the use of force. It suggested that talks about the association of Yugoslavia with the EC could begin following the resolution of Yugoslavia's constitutional crisis. These views are reinforced by U.S. president Bush.

Events in Yugoslavia

12 June The Serb-majority region of eastern Hercegovina declares itself an autonomous region. Presidents Izetbegović, Milošević, and Tudjman meet in Split in a last attempt to negotiate a basis for a settlement to the Yugoslav crisis.

21 June A resolution based upon the Gligorov-Izetbegović proposal is adopted by the federal government. Slovenia hastily builds new border-crossing control posts on the Croatian border.

25–26 June The expected declarations of independence by Slovenia and Croatia are implemented. The Serb population of eastern Slavonia declares the setting up of a further autonomous region. Delegates from the two republics withdraw from the federal assembly. The federal government authorizes the removal of illegal border control posts.

27 June At Ormož and Jezersko, the first armed encounters take place between units of the JNA and Slovene Territorial Defense Force, launching the Ten Day War that secures Slovene independence.

28 June The federal government announces that control has been restored over the border posts in Slovenia and calls for a cease-fire.

29 June Agreement is reached between the federal prime minister and president, on the one hand, and the government of Slovenia, on the other, to withdraw units of the JNA to barracks.

2 July The government of Slovenia accepts proposals for the ending of hostilities in the republic.

7 July The presidents of Slovenia and Croatia and representatives of the federal government meet on the island of Brioni under EC sponsorship and negotiate the Brioni Accord, formally ending the war in Slovenia.

18 July The federal presidency announces the withdrawal of the JNA from Slovenia.

22–23 July The last of the "summits" of republican leaders takes place in Ohrid in a final attempt to

Events in the Surrounding World

19 June The CSCE Council of Ministers, meeting in Berlin, address the Yugoslav situation.

28 June–7 July The EC "troika" makes three visits to Yugoslavia, resulting in a cease-fire between the Slovene Territorial Defense Force and the JNA.

3–4 July Officials of the CSCE in Prague recommend the creation of an EC observer mission to monitor the cease-fire in Slovenia.

5 July EC foreign ministers impose an arms embargo on Yugoslavia and resolve to freeze further financial aid.

8 July The U.S. administration declares its preference to preserve the integrity of the Yugoslav state and endorses the EC arms embargo.

15 July The first of the EC monitors arrives in Slovenia.

Events in Yugoslavia

broker a solution to the disintegration of the federation.

30 July Stipe Mesić leaves the federal presidency in disagreement over the conditions for implementing a cease-fire.

31 July President Tudjman announces that legislation had been prepared to offer home rule to the "Autonomous Region of the Krajina"; proposals are published on 8 August.

August There is a steady escalation of armed conflict between Serbs and Croats in Croatia.

September Several "Serbian autonomous regions" are declared in Bosnia-Hercegovina. The Serbian government attempts to redress the "ethnic imbalance" in Kosovo by launching an unsuccessful colonization drive in the former province.

7 September The Macedonian government holds a referendum on the independence of the republic; this referendum is boycotted by the Albanian minority.

8 September A referendum in Macedonia returns a majority in favor of independence.

12 September Croatian representatives are withdrawn from federal institutions.

18 September Following the referendum of 8 September, Macedonia declares its independence.

Events in the Surrounding World

29 July EC foreign ministers offer to quadruple the number of EC observers and other staff and to extend the mission to Croatia upon the acceptance of a cease-fire.

2–4 August There is another visit of the EC "troika" to Yugoslavia—again unsuccessful.

7 August At its London meeting, the Council of the WEU discusses the possibility of its participation in monitoring.

8–9 August Senior officials of the CSCE meeting in Prague again consider the Yugoslav situation.

27 August An EC foreign ministers meeting in Brussels attributes responsibility for the fighting in Croatia to Serbia. Proposals are considered for a cease-fire followed by an international peace conference.

2 September A cease-fire is agreed to in Croatia, opening the way for the extension of the EC monitoring mission into the republic.

3–4 September The CSCE endorses the EC weapons embargo.

7 September Following a decision made by the EC foreign ministers at their meeting in The Hague on 3 September, a peace conference is convened, chaired by Lord Peter Carrington. A constitutional arbitration commission is also appointed. The EC takes over from the CSCE as the primary body responsible for international negotiation.

11–12 September EC monitors admit that their peace mission has failed and warn that they will leave Yugoslavia if their security cannot be assured.

Events in Yugoslavia

22 September An agreement is negotiated that permits the JNA to withdraw its besieged troops from barracks in Croatia. In addition, the siege of Dubrovnik commences.

30 September The Albanian population of Kosovo conduct their own referendum on independence from Yugoslavia, and return a massive vote in favor of independence.

8 October The three-month moratorium on the implementation of independence proposals agreed upon at Brioni expires, and Croatia and Slovenia sever relations with Yugoslavia. The Croatian government declares that Yugoslav law is no longer operative in Croatia and identifies the JNA as an "invading force." Slovenia launches its own currency, the *tolar.*

15 October The assembly of Bosnia-Hercegovina declares the sovereignty of the republic.

16 October The JNA ceases to use the Communist Party's five-pointed red star as its symbol.

31 October A much publicized "Convoy of Hope" reaches Dubrovnik with relief supplies, carrying Stipe Mesić and a number of celebrities.

Events in the Surrounding World

19 September After a succession of violations of Hungarian airspace by aircraft of the JNA, the Hungarian government offers to assist the EC in monitoring the border with Yugoslavia. Differences emerge between EC governments with respect to the handling of the Yugoslav crisis. Chancellor Kohl of Germany and President Mitterrand of France suggest the creation of a buffer zone in Croatia to be policed by a WEU force. The UK opposes an arrangement that might create a long-term commitment. The meeting of EU foreign ministers affirms that "no military intervention is contemplated," but a study by military experts is set in motion.

25 September Following a French initiative the UNSC adopts Resolution 713, calling for an arms embargo against Yugoslavia and the immediate cessation of hostilities. Sec.-Gen. Perez de Cuellar is requested to assist with mediation.

26 September The Hague conference establishes working groups to study constitutional solutions to the Yugoslav problem, the issue of economic relations between the republics, and the position of ethnic minorities.

18 October Proposals for the revision of the structure of the SFRY laid before the Hague conference are endorsed provisionally by five of the six republics and rejected by Serbia.

5 November A revised version of the Carrington plan is laid before the Hague conference, but no agreement is reached.

Events in Yugoslavia

9–10 November Serbs in Bosnia-Hercegovina hold their own referendum and return a large majority in favor of remaining within Yugoslavia.

17 November The siege of Vukovar ends with the fall of the town to Serb forces after 86 days. A cease-fire is negotiated in Dubrovnik, and the JNA withdraws from the area.

20 November The government of Bosnia-Hercegovina requests the deployment of UN troops in the republic.

2 December Voting in the second round of multiparty elections in Bosnia-Hercegovina confirms the distribution of candidates roughly in line with the ethnic division of the republic, leaving government in the hands of an uneasy agreement among the three main ethnic parties.

4 December The Croatian assembly approves a law on minorities, committing the republic to the acceptance of all international conventions on human rights and assuring cultural autonomy to minorities.

5 December Stipe Mesić is formally recalled from the federal presidency by the Croatian assembly.

Events in the Surrounding World

8 November The EC Council of Ministers, meeting in Rome, anounces trade sanctions against Yugoslavia and proposes a UN-enforced oil embargo.

10 November The United States declares its support for trade sanctions.

11 November The G-4 donor countries (France, Germany, the United Kingdom, and the United States) suspend aid to Yugoslavia.

15 November The EC announces economic sanctions against Serbia and Montenegro.

19 November At a meeting in Bonn, the WEU foreign ministers agree to the creation of naval "corridors" to permit the supply of humanitarian relief to Yugoslavia.

27 November The UNSC adopts Resolution 721, requesting a report on the feasibility of creating a peacekeeping force for Yugoslavia (conditional upon the success of a cease-fire).

2 December The EC foreign ministers vote to restore trade and credit agreements and to suspend aid sanctions against Yugoslavia, with the exception of Serbia and Montenegro.

3 December Boutros Boutros-Gali takes over from Perez de Cuellar as secretary-general of the UN.

10 December The EC heads-of-government meeting in Maastricht leads to an agreement in principle on recognizing the independence of the successor states to Yugoslavia. This agreement requires that the successor states meet certain conditions by 15 January and that a satisfactory report be issued from a commission headed by Robert Badinter.

15 December The UNSC votes to send a small monitoring force to Yugoslavia to prepare the way for the deployment of a peacekeeping force. It urges

Events in Yugoslavia

19 December The Serb Republic of the Krajina declares its independence and elects Milan Babić as its president.

20 December Federal prime minister Ante Marković resigns.

23 December Slovenia adopts its new constitution as an independent state.

24 December The assembly of the Serbian Autonomous Region of Slavonia, Baranja, and Western Srem votes to join the Serb Republic of the Krajina.

1992

6 January The Republic of Macedonia amends its constitution to meet the EU criteria for recognition. The amendments state that Macedonia has no territorial claims on other countries and renounce any interference in those countries' internal affairs.

8 January Gen. Veljko Kadijević resigns as Yugoslav defense secretary.

9 January An assembly representing the Serb population of Bosnia-Hercegovina renounces the government of the republic and declares an autonomous Serbian Republic.

11–12 January The ethnic Albanian minority in Macedonia conducts a referendum on autonomy, which returns a large majority in favor of secession.

Events in the Surrounding World

UN members to refrain from any action that might "exacerbate the situation."

23 December In spite of general agreement within the EC, Germany unilaterally recognizes the independence of Croatia and Slovenia at the deadline for receipt of applications, without waiting for the report of the Badinter Commission.

25 December The state presidency of Yugoslavia accepts proposals for the deployment of peacekeeping forces surrounding the Serb enclaves of the Krajina. Irregular forces are to be disarmed, and the JNA and Croatian national guard forces are to be withdrawn.

1992

7 January A helicopter transporting EC monitors is shot down by the Yugoslav air force, killing five. The UNSC approves the sending of an advanced force to prepare the way for the arrival of UN peacekeepers in Yugoslavia.

9 January The EC conference on Yugoslavia reconvenes in Brussels. EC foreign ministers lift sanctions against Montenegro. The EC arbitration commission headed by Robert Badinter recommends recognition of Macedonian independence, although a decision is deferred pending agreement about a name that satisfies the objection of Greece. Recognition of B-H is also deferred pending the holding of a referendum on the independence issue.

15 January The presidency of the EC announces its recognition of Croatia and Slovenia as independent states.

Events in Yugoslavia

25 January Boycotted by the Serb parties, the assembly of Bosnia-Hercegovina votes for a referendum on independence.

31 January–2 February After a three-day session, the Yugoslav presidency adopts the Vance Plan for peace, in spite of opposition on the part of the representatives of the Serb enclaves in Croatia and Bosnia-Hercegovina.

2 February Mate Boban replaces Stjepan Kljuić as head of the HDZ in Hercegovina. The JNA begins its withdrawal from Macedonia; the process is completed without incident on 26 March.

10 February On the recommendation of Milan Babić, the assembly of the Serb Republic of the Krajina (in Knin) votes to put the acceptance of the Vance Plan to a referendum.

16 February Milan Babić is ousted as president of the Krajina because of his reluctance to cooperate with the changing Croatian attitude toward international negotiation.

29 February–1 March In the referendum on the independence of Bosnia-Hercegovina, a turnout of 63 percent returns a vote of 99.4 percent in favor of independence, although the referendum is boycotted by the Bosnian Serbs. Fighting in the republic immediately intensifies.

1 March A referendum in Montenegro overwhelmingly supports continued association with a Yugoslav federation. The referendum also votes to restore the name of the capital Titograd to its pre-1945 form of Podgorica.

3 March The government of Bosnia-Hercegovina declares the republic's independence.

9–12 March A series of rallies against state control of the communications media are mounted in Belgrade.

17 March Macedonia and Slovenia agree to exchange ambassadors.

25 March President Alija Izetbegović calls on all citizens of the republic of B-H to reject the division of the republic along ethnic lines, saying that he had signed the 18 March agreement under pressure.

27 March The Serbian Republic of Bosnia-Hercegovina is formally proclaimed in Pale.

5–7April Armed clashes begin in the suburbs of Sarajevo. A 7,000-strong demonstration for peace is

Events in the Surrounding World

16 January EC monitors in Hungary begin surveillance of the border with Yugoslavia.

9 March The advance party of UNPROFOR arrives in Yugoslavia, commanded by Lt. Gen. Satish Nambiar.

18 March Following a meeting in Lisbon, the first of the agreements on the future of B-H is brokered by the EC negotiators, providing for the division of the country into 10 "cantons." This arrangement is repudiated on 26 March by the Muslim SDA.

Events in Yugoslavia

fired on by snipers. Altogether 14 people are killed and over 100 wounded.

7 April The independence of Bosnia-Hercegovina is declared. The Serb offensives begin in eastern Bosnia and the Krajina. President Izetbegović declares a state of emergency.

22 April The DEMOS government in Slovenia falls, to be replaced by a coalition led by the Liberal Democrats under Janez Drnovšek. The developing dispute with Croatia over territorial waters contributes to this change.

27 April The federal assembly endorses a new constitution for a Federal Republic of Yugoslavia, consisting of Serbia and Montenegro. Albanian and Magyar minorities distance themselves from the new constitution. The socialist federation can be said no longer to exist. Writer Dobrica Ćosić takes over as federal president; surprisingly, he chooses U.S. businessman Milan Panić as his prime minister.

24 May The unofficial Albanian government of Kosovo holds elections to an assembly; the government responds to this move by closing schools and other public institutions, dismissing Albanians from public office, and stepping up the colonization program.

27 May A mortar bomb attack in Sarajevo leaves 16 dead.

31 May An opposition rally in Belgrade is marked by the reading of a statement from the Orthodox hierarchy, which for the first time dissociates itself from the policy of the Milošević regime.

Events in the Surrounding World

6 April At a meeting in Luxembourg, the EC foreign ministers announce their recognition of an independent B-H but renew their deferral of recognition of Macedonia. The United States recognizes Croatia, Slovenia, and B-H.

7 April The UNSC recommends the full deployment of UNPROFOR.

28 April The UN agrees in principle to extend the remit of UNPROFOR to B-H.

2 May The EC foreign ministers, at a meeting in Guimares, issue an "action plan" for Yugoslavia and agree in principle to the recognition of Macedonia; however, they defer Macedonian recognition until a name can be selected that satisfies Greek objections.

12 May The UN secretary-general recommends that the headquarters of UNPROFOR should be transferred from Sarajevo to Zagreb because of the deteriorating security situation but that UN troops should not be deployed as peacekeepers in B-H.

30 May The UNSC adopts Resolution 757, imposing a range of mandatory sanctions against the FRY. During May the UN takes over from the EC as the principal agent of international negotiation over the future of Yugoslavia.

Events in Yugoslavia

20 June The Bosnian presidency declares that the republic is in a state of war.

28 June Aleksandar Karadjordjević, the pretender to the Serbian throne, visits Serbia for the first time and addresses a political rally.

July–August A Serb offensive develops attempting to link the Bosnian Krajina to eastern Bosnia. In the Yugoslav federation, relations between the federal government and that of Serbia deteriorate rapidly.

3 July The state of Herceg-Bosna is proclaimed in Grude.

16 July Following its defeat in a vote of no confidence in the Macedonian republican assembly, the IMRO-led "government of experts" resigns, to be replaced in August by a coalition of the former Communists and the Albanian PDP (Party of Democratic Prosperity).

23 July A joint defense committee is set up by the governments of Croatia and Bosnia-Hercegovina.

2 August Elections to the assembly take place in Croatia; the HDZ is returned to power but with a reduced majority.

Events in the Surrounding World

June An energetic round of international visits by newly elected Yugoslav prime minister Milan Panić, intended to reduce the severity of international sanctions, fails outright.

16 June Talks between Macedonian foreign minister Denko Malevski and Greek prime minister Konstantinos Mitsotakis fail to reach agreement on the name of the newly independent republic.

28 June French president François Mitterand visits Sarajevo, after which an agreement is reached that the airport will be handed over to UNPROFOR control.

10 July The WEU and NATO announce plans to cooperate in the policing of sanctions in the Adriatic Sea, although they recognize that they have no authority to stop vessels suspected of breaking sanctions.

13 July The UNSC endorses a recommendation by the secretary-general to send 500 troops to augment the force of 1,100 engaged in securing relief supplies to Sarajevo.

21 July Gen. Lewis MacKenzie, commanding the UN operation in Sarajevo, estimates that 40,000 UN troops will be needed around Sarajevo alone in order to enforce an effective peace.

August Greece closes its border with Macedonia in an attempt to compel the republic to abandon its claim on the name "Macedonia."

4 August The ICO, meeting in New York, passes a resolution advocating the use of force against Serbia (under Article 42 of the UN Charter) and the lifting of the arms embargo against B-H. A U.S.-sponsored resolution condemns the use of detention camps.

13 August The UNSC adopts Resolution 770, authorizing the use of "all measures necessary" in

Events in Yugoslavia

28 August UN economic sanctions are lifted against Slovenia.

4 September The Panić government in Belgrade survives a vote of no confidence.

19 October Serbian paramilitary forces seize control of the federal interior ministry in Belgrade as relations between the federal and republican governments reach their nadir.

Events in the Surrounding World

order to ensure the flow of humanitarian aid into Sarajevo. Several European governments express the view that caution is needed in escalating the use of force. Even so, over the following week, offers of troops to support the additional requirements of the UN are made by France, Spain, Italy, Belgium, and the UK.

25 August The UN General Assembly, under Chapter VII of its charter, authorizes the use of force in Yugoslavia where sanctions can be shown to have failed.

26–27 August The London Conference organized under the British presidency of the EC concludes with a communiqué that outlines the terms for a political settlement in Yugoslavia and confirms support for UN efforts to create a peacekeeping force.

28 August Following the expression of concern internationally about the use of the Danube River to breach sanctions against the FRY, ministers of the WEU agree upon measures to tighten security in the area. They also make provisions for an additional 5,000 troops to support the UN force.

3 September A new permanent conference on Yugoslavia, under cochairs Lord David Owen and Cyrus Vance (representing the EC and the UN, respectively), is inaugurated in Geneva.

6 September The Geneva conference issues a deadline of 12 September for the placing of specified categories of heavy weapons under UN supervision around Sarajevo and other specified areas.

14 September The UNSC agrees to expand UNPROFOR by an additional 6,000 troops (beyond the 1,500 in B-H and the 15,000 in Croatia). By the end of the year, 7,500 are in place in B-H and 15,000 in Croatia.

9 October The UNSC adopts Resolution 781, banning military flights within the airspace of B-H.

16 October In a communiqué issued after their meeting in Birmingham, the EC leaders warn that they will request that enforcement measures be taken by the UN should infractions against UNSC Resolution 781 continue.

28 October The Geneva conference formally agrees not to recommend the division of B-H into three ethnically based states, preferring a decentralized

Events in Yugoslavia

6 November Riots take place in Skopje that develop into an armed clash between the police and Albanians. The event is blamed upon an attempt by the Yugoslav secret service to destabilize Macedonia.

6 December Assembly elections in Slovenia confirm Milan Kučan's popularity as president and return the Liberal Democrat–led coalition to power.

20 December Elections to the Serbian assembly confirm Milošević's Socialists as the majority party but condemn Milošević to form a temporary coalition with Vojislav Šešelj's Radicals. The sound defeat of Milan Panić signals the end of the attempt to generate international legitimacy for the federal government.

Events in the Surrounding World

state based upon a number of provinces or cantons under the authority of a single central government.

6 November UNPROFOR units exchange fire with local forces as relief convoys come under attack.

12 November Albania, Bulgaria, and Yugoslavia issue declarations supporting a Greek proposal guaranteeing the existing borders of Macedonia.

16 November The UNSC passes Resolution 787, authorizing the stopping and searching of vessels in the Adriatic Sea suspected of breaking sanctions against Yugoslavia.

20 November The WEU and NATO both adopt rules governing the conduct of vessels operating on the Adriatic sanctions patrols.

25 November The ICO meeting in Istanbul expresses the growing concern of the Islamic countries for the situation in Bosnia.

1–2 December The ICO's Istanbul initiative continues with the approval for a plan by which countries of the ICO would become involved in the Yugoslav crisis, at a meeting in Jiddah.

8 December As a follow-up to the proposals for the "cantonization" of B-H, three competing sets of maps are placed before the Geneva conference.

10 December At their meeting in Brussels, the EC foreign ministers criticize Greece for allowing Greek companies to ship oil to Yugoslavia while withholding it from Macedonia.

11 December The UNSC authorizes the deployment of a small force of observers to Macedonia.

17 December Foreign ministers of the NATO countries agree to support action to enforce the UN ban on military flights over B-H, should they be required to do so.

18 December The UNSC condemns the detention and rape of Muslim women by Serb forces in B-H and calls for the inspection of such camps by EC observers.

20 December US president Bush and UK prime minister Major announce their agreement in Washington to support the UN resolution on the enforcement of a ban on military flights over B-H.

27 December French foreign minister Roland Dumas announces that France will also support UN efforts to enforce a military flight ban.

Events in Yugoslavia

1993

January A Muslim government counteroffensive against the Serbs is mounted in eastern Bosnia.

8 January Bosnian deputy prime minister Hakija Turaljić is murdered in Sarajevo, undermining government confidence in the UN forces.

10 January The Montenegrin elections return Momir Bulatović and the Socialists to power.

12 January Under heavy pressure from Serbian president Milošević and Yugoslav president Ćosić, Radovan Karadžić accepts provisionally the proposals of the Vance-Owen Plan.

19–20 January The assembly of the Serbian Republic in Pale accepts the general outline of the Vance-Owen Plan.

22 January Croat forces establish control over the strategic Maslenica Bridge. Retreating Serb units attempt unsuccessfully to blow up the Peruča Dam.

February A Serb offensive is mounted against several government-controlled enclaves in eastern Bosnia, including Srebrenica.

7 February Elections to the newly created Chamber of Districts in the Croatian assembly give 37 of the 67 seats to the HDZ.

22 February Croatian troops anticipate the expiration of the UN peacekeeping mandate in the Krajina and recover some territory in the "pink zones" from Serb control.

2 March After a protracted crisis based on disagreement between Serbs and Montenegrins, a

Events in the Surrounding World

1993

2 January Lord Owen and Cyrus Vance present the Vance-Owen Plan for a new constitutional settlement in Bosnia-Hercegovina. The plan is based upon the division of the country into 10 "cantons" united under a single republican government.

14 January The EC foreign ministers issue an ultimatum calling upon the Bosnian Serbs to accept the proposals of the VOP or risk complete economic and diplomatic isolation.

10 February The United States offers to become "actively and directly engaged" in the attempt to ensure peace in B-H, and Reginald Bartholemew (U.S. ambassador to NATO) is appointed special envoy to the peace talks, which transfer from Geneva to New York on 1 February. The U.S. administration endorses the VOP and advocates tighter enforcement of sanctions and the no-fly zone.

19 February The mandates of UNPROFOR and UNPREDEP are extended until the end of March.

March UN forces involved in the evacuation of Muslims from besieged areas are accused in the press of aiding and abetting "ethnic cleansing."

Events in Yugoslavia

new federal government finally takes over, headed by Radoje Kontić.

5 March In the face of growing public dissatisfaction, a coalition government takes over in Montenegro.

9 and 26 March Large demonstrations in Serbia protest against falling living standards.

12 March Yugoslavia's largest private bank (Jugoskandić) collapses.

29 March After a series of large strikes in protest against deteriorating economic conditions, a government reshuffle in Zagreb sees Nikica Valentić take over as prime minister.

4 April The Croatian Council of Defense (HVO) is created.

25–26 April The Serbian assembly in Pale rejects the amended version of the Vance-Owen Plan for Bosnia-Hercegovina.

Events in the Surrounding World

31 March The UNSC adopts Resolution 816, which permits NATO aircraft to shoot down planes violating the no-fly zone. UNPROFOR's mandate is extended for a further three months.

2 April NATO endorses the more active enforcement of the no-fly zone and specifies the rules of engagement. Throughout April the Clinton administration gradually begins to redefine its policy with respect to the former Yugoslavia, advocating the selective lifting of the arms embargo and the more determined use of air power.

8 April The Republic of Macedonia is admitted to the UN under a provisional title ("Former Yugoslav Republic of Macedonia") in response to Greek pressure. The German constitutional court authorizes the participation of German surveillance aircraft in support of the UN/NATO operations—the first post-1945 deployment of German troops outside its federal republic.

12 April NATO enforcement of the no-fly zone begins. Voting on a motion to tighten sanctions against the FRY in the UNSC is deferred until after the Russian referendum on the constitution on 25 April.

16 April Following the fall of Srebrenica to the Bosnian Serbs, UNSC Resolution 819 declares the town to be a "safe area." Srebrenica is accordingly demilitarized and handed back to B-H government control.

18 April The UNSC adopts Resolution 820, announcing additional economic sanctions against the FRY.

25 April The EC foreign ministers agree to double the number of sanctions monitors.

27 April Notwithstanding earlier resolutions on the importance of enforcing no-fly zones over B-H, the NATO meeting in Brussels makes it clear that NATO

Events in Yugoslavia

May The Croatian-Slovene border dispute develops.

1–2 May Radovan Karadžić signs the Vance-Owen Plan for B-H.

6 May The Serbian assembly in Pale refuses to ratify the Vance-Owen Plan and defers final consideration to a referendum to be held on 15–16 May. The Yugoslav federation imposes an embargo on the Bosnian Serbs aimed at forcing the latter's acceptance of the plan.

9 May The Croat-Muslim struggle for control of Mostar and the Neretva River Valley begins.

14 May A "Pan-Serb" assembly intended to demonstrate Serb solidarity takes place in Belgrade but is boycotted by the Bosnian Serbs. The occasion also provides a stage for a public display of the rift between Milošević and Šešelj.

15–16 May In a referendum, the Bosnian Serbs overwhelmingly (94 percent) reject the Vance-Owen Plan.

1 June After violent incidents in the Serbian assembly in Belgrade, riots break out in Belgrade. These outbreaks are controlled with great violence, and opposition leader Vukašin Drašković and others are arrested.

2 June Yugoslav president Dobrica Ćosić is attacked in the federal assembly for conducting an independent foreign policy and is ousted from office.

16 June At a meeting between Presidents Milošević and Tudjman, a plan is negotiated for partitioning Bosnia-Hercegovina into ethnic states.

Events in the Surrounding World

is reluctant to embark upon direct military intervention.

4 June Under Resolution 836 the UNSC authorizes the dispatch of additional troops to guarantee the security of the "safe areas." The resolution explicitly authorizes the use of armed force.

8 June Meeting in Luxembourg, the foreign ministers of the EU countries endorse the policy of "safe areas." NATO and the WEU hold the first joint session to deal with the coordination and enforcement of sanctions in the Adriatic Sea. Command and control are unified under the NATO structure.

10 June The NATO foreign ministers meet in Athens. Eighty combat aircraft are allocated to the Yugoslav operation. U.S. secretary of state Warren Christopher announces the dispatch of 300 U.S. troops to Macedonia. The WEU sets up a monitoring center at Calafat (Romania) to coordinate sanctions control along the Danube River. The UNSC adopts Resolution 837, deploying additional international observers of the sanctions operation along the Serbian/Bosnian border.

Events in Yugoslavia

25 June Zoran Lilić is elected as successor to Dobrica Ćosić as president of the Yugoslav federation.

July The Serb offensive on Mount Igman begins.

1 July Serbian opposition leader Vukašin Drašković starts a hunger strike in protest against his continuing detention without trial.

9 July Vukašin Drašković is released after more than a month in detention.

23 July In spite of the arms embargo, a large consignment of weapons destined for Bosnia-Hercegovina is discovered at Maribor airport.

28 July In conditions of increasing tension, the CSCE monitoring mission to Kosovo is terminated.

August Indicative of the measure of hyperinflation in Yugoslavia, a 500-million-dinar note is issued. The inflation rate reaches 2 percent per day by the year's end.

4 August Mount Igman is taken by Serb forces, tightening their control over Sarajevo.

Events in the Surrounding World

17 June Following the announcement of an agreement between Presidents Milošević and Tudjman for the partitioning of B-H along ethnic lines, Lord Owen concedes the failure of the VOP.

22 June The EU foreign ministers reaffirm the integrity of the Republic of B-H at their meeting in Copenhagen. The permanent conference on Yugoslavia resumes in Geneva but is suspended again the following day without achieving anything.

1 July Gen. Jean Cot replaces Gen. Lars-Eric Wahlgren as commander-in-chief of UNPROFOR in Zagreb.

7 July NATO adopts a detailed plan for air operations in B-H.

12 July The U.S. battalion arrives in Skopje in support of the 700 Scandinavian troops already assigned to UNPREDEP.

14 July The deployment of NATO aircraft to Italian bases begins.

30 July A motion from a group of NAM countries, which would have lifted the arms embargo with respect to the government of B-H, is defeated in the UNSC, although the United States votes for the resolution. The UNSC extends the mandate of UNPROFOR by another three months after objections from the government of Croatia.

At the Geneva conference, agreement is announced among the three parties to the conflict in B-H for the creation of a "Union of Republics of Bosnia-Hercegovina," composed of three constituent republics.

9 August The Geneva talks are suspended because of the withdrawal of President Izetbegović in protest against the continued deployment of Serb troops above Sarajevo. In Brussels NATO approves the principles governing the use of airstrikes in support of UNPROFOR troops.

Events in Yugoslavia

15 August Serb forces complete their evacuation of positions around Sarajevo, as agreed upon at the Geneva talks. The positions are taken over by UN forces.

24 August The Croatian Republic of Herceg-Bosna is proclaimed.

26 August A purge of senior officers in the Yugoslav Army takes place, intended to reinforce the position of those loyal to Milošević.

September Heavy fighting takes place in the vicinity of Karlovac. On 11 and 13 September, Zagreb itself is hit by rockets.

10–17 September Mutiny arises within the Serb armed forces based in Banja Luka.

20 September The Serbian assembly is dissolved before a vote of no confidence can be taken.

27 September Fikret Abdić proclaims the Autonomous Province of Western Bosnia in the "*Cazinska krajina.*"

29 September The assembly of Bosnia-Hercegovina rejects the Owen-Stoltenberg proposals for the division of the republic.

25 October A new government of Bosnia-Hercegovina is formed under the premiership of Haris Silajdžić.

Events in the Surrounding World

15 August Bosnian Serb troops complete their withdrawal from positions on Mounts Igman and Bjelašnica, overlooking Sarajevo. Their positions are taken by UN troops.

20 August The UN and EU mediators, Thorwald Stoltenberg and Lord Owen, respectively, submit to the Geneva conference a further plan for the tripartite division of B-H. This plan allocates 52 percent of the territory to a Serb republic, 30 percent to Bosnians, and 18 percent to Croats; it proposes special status for the cities of Sarajevo and Mostar, which are to be placed under UN and EU mandates respectively for a period of two years.

16 September Representatives of the governments of B-H, Bosnian Croat and Bosnian Serb representatives sign a provisional declaration in Geneva signaling their acceptance of some provisions of the Owen-Stoltenberg Plan, but they request further modifications.

21 September The proposed meeting at the Sarajevo airport at which the Owen-Stoltenberg Plan is expected to finally be endorsed is canceled because the assembly of B-H is unable to accept all of the plan's provisions.

4 October In the face of serious objections from Croatia, Resolution 871 is passed in the UNSC, extending the mandate of UNPROFOR in Croatia until March 1994.

10 October UNPROFOR commander-in-chief Cot publicly criticizes the conduct of both the UN and NATO toward the Yugoslav situation.

Events in Yugoslavia

31 October A sign of growing sentiment in Montenegro in favor of autonomy from Serbia is the enthronement of Antonije Avramović as the Orthodox Church's archimandrate at Ostrog.

19 December The Serbian general election leaves the SPS short of a majority, and Milošević is compelled to form a coalition with New Democracy, which deserts the opposition coalition.

1994

19 January Croatian and Yugoslav officials announce the beginning of the process of "normalization" in relations between the two countries.

24 January The Avramović economic reform is launched with the introduction of a "new dinar" in Yugoslavia. Two years of hyperinflation are ended.

5 February A mortar attack on Sarajevo kills 66.

8 February Mate Boban is deposed from the leadership of Herceg-Bosna and is replaced by Krešimir Zubak.

12–13 February The Albanian Party of Democratic Prosperity in Macedonia splits at its congress in Tetovo upon the desertion of a more radically nationalist wing.

22 February The new Serbian government takes over, headed by Mirko Marjanović.

23 February A cease-fire is negotiated between Bosnian government forces and the HVO. In Serbia the program of integrating Kosovo into Serbia continues with the dissolution of the Kosovo Academy of Sciences.

Events in the Surrounding World

1994

10–11 January The Brussels meeting of NATO leaders enunciates the principles governing possible NATO air intervention and the defense of "safe areas."

21 January The Russian Duma registers its strong reservations about NATO air intervention in Yugoslavia.

24 January French Gen. François Briquemont resigns as head of the UN force in B-H, saying that there is little point in continuing an impossible mission.

5 February Following an explosion in a Sarajevo marketplace, NATO announces an exclusion zone for heavy weapons surrounding the city. Enforcement begins on 17 February, with Russian troops deployed in the exclusion zone.

16 February Greek president Andreas Papandreou announces an intensification of Greek trade sanctions against Macedonia in response to the recognition of the Macedonian state by Russia and the United States. Greek action is subsequently challenged unsuccessfully by the EC in the European Court of Justice.

26 February Talks begin in Washington directed toward the elaboration of a common constitutional framework for Muslim-Croat cooperation; these talks bear fruit in an agreement announced the following month.

Events in Yugoslavia

28 March Janez Janša is dismissed as minister of defense in Slovenia following allegations of misuse of military police power. The withdrawal of his Social Democratic group from the ruling coalition precipitates within the Slovene government a crisis that is resolved only in September.

April The split within the HDZ deepens to the point that Stipe Mesić and Josip Manolić leave to found their own party.

4 April A Serb offensive is launched against the Bosnian government-controlled enclave of Goražde. In eastern Slavonia, however, a cease-fire comes into effect with the creation of a demilitarized buffer zone between Croatian and Serb forces.

28 April Milošević acts to assert his own authority in Serbia by abolishing the paramilitary Chetnik organization. Subsequently the organization's leader, Vojislav Šešelj, is sentenced to a short term of imprisonment.

May Informal and secret talks are reported to take place between the Serbian authorities and the LDK about the future of Kosovo.

30 May Croatia introduces its new currency—the *kuna.*

Events in the Surrounding World

28 February Four Serb fighter aircraft are shot down by NATO aircraft for infractions of the no-fly zone near Banja Luka. NATO forces also intervene in March in order to support the safe area of Goražde.

4 April Following protracted negotiations conducted by Russian special enjoy Vitalii Churkin, an agreement is announced on the establishment of a demilitarized buffer zone between Serb and Croat forces in eastern Slavonia.

10–11 April NATO forces bomb Serb ground defenses in the vicinity of Goražde in order to inhibit the assault on the city, which had been declared a safe area.

26 April The Contact Group (Britain, France, Russia, and the United States) is set up in order to coordinate diplomatic work toward the cessation of hostilities in B-H. The UN votes to send a further 6,500 troops to the region in order to support its work.

11 May The U.S. Senate votes in favor of lifting the arms embargo on the former Yugoslavia in support of the government of B-H (although the motion is not supported in a congressional vote on 1 July). There are already signs of policy disagreement within the Contact Group. The U.S. government dissents from the decision of a meeting of foreign ministers in Geneva on 13 May to award 51 percent of the territory of B-H to the Muslim-Croat Federation. During the following week, both British and French ministers speak of the possibility of withdrawing their troops from the region.

14 May The agreement resulting from the Washington talks is signed in Geneva by Croat representative Krešimir Zubak and Bosnian Haris Silajdžić.

Events in Yugoslavia

June Units of the Yugoslav Army take up positions on Macedonian territory north of Kriva Palanka in a border dispute with Macedonia. They withdraw in July.

8 June A general cease-fire negotiated for Bosnia-Hercegovina comes into effect, although it lasts less than a month.

10 June Following the sentencing of a group of Albanians on charges of organizing armed insurrection, the Albanian PDP begins a boycott of the Macedonian assembly.

21 June After protracted negotiation between Macedonian authorities and the Albanian minority, the controversial new census of the republic finally gets under way.

4 July The Federal Republic of Yugoslavia declares an economic embargo against the Bosnian Serbs.

13 July The Contact Group Plan is accepted by President Milošević. On 18 July it is also accepted by the Croat-Muslim assembly, but it is rejected by the Serb assembly in Pale.

20 August Fikret Abdić's stronghold in Velika Kladuša falls to the Bosnian army's Fifth Corps.

23 September The Croatian assembly votes to terminate the mandate of UNPROFOR.

3 October The Slovene-Croatian border dispute comes to a head with a vote in the Slovene assembly affirming the Slovene identity of the disputed area.

Events in the Surrounding World

14 June President Tudjman visits Sarajevo to emphasize his support for the new constitutional proposals.

16 June Talks between Italian prime minister Silvio Berlusconi and his Slovene counterpart, Janez Drnovšek, fail to reach agreement on the issue of Italian claims for compensating ethnic Italians displaced from Yugoslavia after 1945.

2 July Turkish troops are accepted as part of the UN contingent in B-H—the first such troops to serve in the region since the Austrian occupation of 1878.

6 July The Contact Group plan for B-H is presented; it is accepted by the assembly of B-H on 18 July. In spite of support from Belgrade for the plan, it is rejected by the Bosnia Serbs.

23 July The city of Mostar is placed under EU administration in an attempt to tackle one of the most serious disagreements between Muslims and Croats.

10–11 September Pope John Paul II visits Zagreb, bringing a message of reconciliation and forgiveness.

24 September After support has been secured from Belgrade for the international monitoring of the border with B-H, the UNSC announces the first selective and temporary suspension of economic sanctions against Yugoslavia.

Events in Yugoslavia

14 and 30 October New elections take place in Macedonia, returning a coalition government led by Branko Crvenkovski, following which the Albanian PDP returns to the governing coalition.

28 October Government forces based in the Bihać enclave begin a major offensive against the Serbs.

3 November Kupres falls to the HVO.

9 November The Bosnian Serbs, reinforced from the Croatian Krajina, launch a counteroffensive in the Bihać region, reaching the suburbs of the city between 23–24 November.

25 November A temporary cease-fire is agreed upon in the Bihać enclave, with a partial withdrawal of Serb forces.

2 December A section of the international highway through UN Sector West is opened to traffic.

1995

12 January President Tudjman gives notice that the mandate for UNPROFOR will not be renewed beyond the end of March.

9 February Albanian deputies walk out of the Macedonian assembly in protest of the lack of progress on the issue of the official use of the Albanian language. Later in the month, the government attempts to close the unofficial Albanian-language university opened near Tetovo.

6 March An agreement for cooperation between the Army of the Republic of Bosnia-Hercegovina and the HVO is signed.

23 March After protracted negotiations agreement is reached between Croatia and Slovenia over the future of the Krško nuclear power plant.

20–28 March The Bosnian army launches a major offensive on Mount Vlasić and Mount Majevica.

Events in the Surrounding World

20 December Following a visit by former U.S. president Jimmy Carter, a cease-fire is negotiated in the Bihać region, which holds for three months.

1995

4 January The UN presence in Yugoslavia is further enlarged when the UNSC votes for the addition of 6,000 troops to the 23,000 already serving in B-H.

12 January The "Zagreb Four" (Z-4) Group—the EU, UN, Russia, and the United States—is set up to promote resolution of the problem of the Serb secessionist areas.

12 March An agreement negotiated by U.S. vice president Al Gore is announced that enables the UN presence to continue in Croatia, although in deference to Croat sensibilities the UN operation is renamed UNCRO.

11 April The commander of the Russian unit serving with UNPROFOR is dismissed in connection with corruption charges. This move follows the earlier dismissal of 50 other UN personnel in similar circumstances.

Events in Yugoslavia

14–15 April A major public disagreement takes place revealing the division of opinion between Radovan Karadžić and Ratko Mladić.

May The HVO launches a major offensive toward Glamoč and Bosansko Grahovo.

1–2 May The HV launches Operation Flash in western Slavonia, reclaiming Sector West for the Croatian government.

25 May Bosnian Serb forces bombard Tuzla in retaliation against a NATO bombing of Serb forces that threatened the UN "safe areas." Seventy-one people are killed.

June Croatian forces take the strategically important Mount Dinara, enabling them to threaten Knin. The Serbian authorities begin a campaign to round up and return Bosnian-Serb men of military age to Bosnia.

14 June A major Bosnian government offensive is opened in the vicinity of Sarajevo, relieving pressure on communication routes to the city and briefly threatening Pale.

7–11 July The Bosnian Serb assault on Srebrenica finally results in the capture of the town.

14–26 July The government-controlled "safe area" of Žepa falls to Bosnian Serb forces.

22 July An agreement is signed that authorizes the HV to operate within Bosnia-Hercegovina in cooperation with government forces.

26 July Serb forces renew their attack on the Bihać enclave.

28 July Glamoč and Bosansko Grahovo are taken by the HV, laying the groundwork for Operation Storm.

3 August Internal crisis within the government of Bosnia-Hercegovina, brought about by the growing

Events in the Surrounding World

8 May UN commander Gen. Rupert Smith's request for air support against Serb targets is controversially overruled by UN special envoy Yasushi Akashi.

25–26 May Large airstrikes are launched by NATO against Bosnian Serb forces surrounding Sarajevo in response to increasing Serb pressure on the safe areas. In retaliation 370 UN personnel are taken hostage by the Serbs.

3 June At a meeting in Paris, NATO defense ministers authorize the creation of the Rapid Reaction Force (also known as the Mobile Theater Reserve) of 5,000 men, designed to increase the effectiveness of UN response to threats against its personnel.

12 June Swedish diplomat Carl Bildt takes over from Lord Owen as the EU mediator with responsibility for Yugoslavia.

16 June The UNSC votes for further troop reinforcements in addition to the creation of the RRF.

21 July A further meeting of the Contact Group takes place in London to review the deteriorating situation.

Events in Yugoslavia

conflict between Islamic and secular wings within the SDA.

4–9 August Operation Storm, mounted by the HV, results in the elimination of the remaining areas of Serb control in Croatia, except eastern Slavonia.

5 August Knin falls to the HV.

9 August Drvar na Uni is taken by advancing Croatian troops.

28 August A further mortar attack in Sarajevo kills 37 people.

30 August The Bosnian Serb assembly in Pale delegates negotiating power to President Milošević.

11 September A substantial offensive by government forces is launched in western and central Bosnia. Bosnian Serb forces are eventually pushed back east of Sanski Most.

19 September The HV declares the suspension of its operations in Bosnia-Hercegovina.

25 September The advancing forces of the HVO and the Bosnian army threaten Banja Luka.

3 October An attempt to assassinate Macedonian president Gligorov in Skopje fails.

12 October A general cease-fire comes into effect in Bosnia-Hercegovina.

29 October A general election takes place in Croatia. Although the HDZ is returned to power, surprisingly their majority is reduced.

11 November Agreement is reached between Muslim and Croat representation in Bosnia-Hercegovina for the unification and joint control of Mostar.

12 November Agreement is reached between the Croatian government and the Serb authorities in western Slavonia for the peaceful reintegration of the region into Croatia.

Events in the Surrounding World

1 September Operation Deliberate Force is launched against Bosnian Serb forces in response to the bombing of the Sarajevo marketplace.

13 September In New York, representatives of the governments of Macedonia and of Greece sign an agreement by which Greece agrees to lift the embargo against Macedonia in return for changes to the use of certain state symbols by the Macedonians.

5 October After a strenuous round of diplomatic activity, U.S. envoy Richard Holbrooke negotiates a general cease-fire.

1 November Peace talks convene in the United States at the Wright-Patterson Air Force Base, near Dayton, Ohio, eventually resulting in the settlement of the Bosnian war.

12 November At Erdut, UN mediator Thorvald Stoltenberg brokers an agreement between representatives of the Croatian government and the authorities in the Serb Krajina, providing for the establishment of a transitional administration (UNTAES) to supervise the return of Serb-occupied eastern Slavonia to normality.

Events in Yugoslavia

December Slovene privatization plans are brought to a halt after serious controversy opens over the reprivatization of forest land.

1996

January The first exchanges of ministerial visits between Croatia and the FRY take place, resulting in the signature of several normalization agreements.

15 January In his "state of the nation" address, President Tudjman tells the Croatian assembly that the costs of the war to Croatia are estimated at U.S.$27 billion.

21 January Prime Minister Haris Silajdžić resigns after disagreements within the government of B-H, especially between himself and President Izetbegović.

26 January The ruling coalition in Slovenia falls apart, but the Drnovšek government is able to function with the votes of minority parties.

February A series of assassinations of Serbian security personnel by members of the National Movement for the Liberation of Kosova and the Kosova Liberation Army result in a steady deterioration in ethnic relations in the former province and undermine tentative official talks between the unofficial Kosovar government and Belgrade.

23 February A new coalition government is formed in Skopje that once again includes the Albanian PDP.

April Haris Silajdžić founds the Party for Bosnia-Hercegovina.

26 April Agreement is signed in New York whereby the Croatian government accepts responsibility for a proportion of the international debt of the SFRY.

Events in the Surrounding World

14 November The successful conclusion of the Dayton peace negotiations is announced.

14 December The agreements reached at Dayton are formally signed at the Palace of Versailles outside Paris.

1996

19 January The establishment of the "zone of separation" between forces in B-H along the Inter-Entity Boundary Line is completed according to schedule.

15 March An international conference convenes in Ankara to address the modernization and rearmament of the Bosnian armed forces.

12–13 April The international community begins to address the problems of reconstruction in B-H by having a large conference of potential aid donors to the region, hosted by the World Bank and the EU.

7 May The first international war crimes trial since World War II opens at The Hague.

Events in Yugoslavia

14 May A joint defense ministry is set up uniting the HVO and the Bosnian army under a single command.

15 May RajkoKasagić is dismissed as prime minister of the RS following disagreements over the implementation of the Dayton Agreements. In spite of his supervision of a successful reform of the currency, Dragoslav Avramović is dismissed from his post as governor of the National Bank of Yugoslavia.

16 May Slovene foreign minister Goran Thaler resigns following a vote of no confidence in the assembly.

19 May UN High Representative Carl Bildt announces that he has received assurances about the withdrawal from public functions of Radovan Karadžić. The latter is replaced by Biljana Plavšić as president of the RS.

21 May The demilitarization process in eastern Slavonia begins.

12 June Mounting economic problems in the FRY lead to the reconstruction of the government.

29 June In spite of the publicized withdrawal of Radovan Karadžić from political life, he is reelected to the presidency of the Serbian Democratic Party in B-H.

30 June Following protracted negotiations under EU commissioner Hans Koschnick, municipal elections are finally held in Mostar, resulting in a multiethnic administration. The administration's work continues to be obstructed by nationalists on both sides.

15 August An agreement is signed in Zagreb bringing to an official end the republic of Herceg Bosna.

23 August Normal full diplomatic and consular arrangements between Croatia and the FRY come into effect. (Full international recognition comes into effect on 9 September.)

27 August Municipal elections throughout B-H are postponed by OSCE commissioner Robert Frowick.

Events in the Surrounding World

21 May UNTAES announces that the demilitarization of eastern Slavonia has begun. Because of concern over government measures against the media, the Council of Europe's Committee of Ministers defers admitting Croatia as a member. (The decision is reversed in November.)

18 June The UN suspends Operation Sharp Guard, the naval blockade against Yugoslavia designed to implement both economic sanctions against the Yugoslav federation and the general arms embargo.

11 July Warrants are issued by the IWCT for the arrest of Gen. Ratko Mladić and Radovan Karadžić.

27 August The head of the CSCE mission responsible for overseeing elections in B-H announces that municipal elections are to be postponed until the following year because of the slow progress toward the implementation of aspects of the Dayton Agreements.

Events in Yugoslavia

September The privatization process in Slovenia suffers a further setback when plans for the disposal of Litostroj, a large engineering company, fall apart.

2 September An agreement is signed between representatives of Kosovar Albanians and the Belgrade government to restore Albanian education in the former province. (There is no evidence of the plan's implementation by the year's end.)

14 September Elections take place across both entities of B-H (the Muslim-Croat federation and the Republika Srkska) to entity and federal assemblies. Nonethnic parties make encouraging gains.

5 October A new administration is inaugurated in Sarajevo following the elections of 14 September.

23 October Gen. Ratko Mladić and 80 other officers are "retired" from the armed forces of the RS in response to international pressure.

3 November Elections to the federal assembly of the FRY enable Slobodan Milošević's SPS to continue in government, although in coalition with two minor parties. There are allegations of extensive electoral fraud.

10 November General elections in Slovenia return a "hung parliament" (i.e., no clear ruling party), and six weeks are required for Prime Minister Drnovšek to put together a viable coalition.

20 November Dissatisfaction over government response to allegations of malpractice in the elections of 3 November result in large demonstrations throughout Serbia. These protests are sustained throughout the rest of the year, attracting on some occasions more than 200,000 participants.

5 December Responding to growing dissatisfaction among Montenegrins about the relationship between Montenegro and Serbia, Montenegrin president Momir Bulatović publicly criticizes the Belgrade government for its handling of the elections in November. This view is subsequently echoed by representatives of the Serbian Orthodox Church.

Events in the Surrounding World

1 October The UNSC votes in favor of withdrawing economic sanctions against the FRY, with the exception of an "outer wall" of financial sanctions.

21 November The first large consignment of material for the new army of B-H is delivered under the U.S. "Train and Equip" program.

27 November Because of continuing international concern about the stability of Macedonia, the UNSC votes to extend the mandate of UNPREDEP, although with reduced numbers.

Events in Yugoslavia

1997

January The protest rallies started in Belgrade in November continue through most of the month.

9 January Elections in Slovenia return Janez Drnovšek and his Liberals to government, although in coalition with Marijan Podobnik's Slovene People's Party.

24 January The Zagreb station Radio 101 finally wins a five-year legal battle with the authorities and is awarded a license. The long-running battle over the fate of the satirical weekly *Feral Tribune* continues.

February Outbreaks of violence are reported between Muslims and Croats in Mostar.

2–4 February In Belgrade, the police violently break up continued protest meetings over the contested results of November's elections.

11 February The Serbian assembly finally votes to reinstate the contested election results. Demonstrations among students continue over educational issues.

28 February Following protracted difficulties in establishing economic cooperation between the two entities in B-H, the Bosnian Serbs sign an agreement in Belgrade promoting "special ties" between the RS and Serbia.

19 March The rector of the University of Belgrade is compelled to resign in the face of popular protest.

25 March After attempts in Belgrade to restrict the private communications media through legislation, the Economic Court in Serbia permits the TV station BK to extend its range and the government withdraws its proposals.

11 April Serbian deputy minister of the enterior Radovan Stojičić is assassinated in Belgrade.

13 April Regional and local elections in Croatia include for the first time the formerly Serb-controlled districts of the Krajina. The HDZ is returned as the major party, although an unusual

Events in the Surrounding World

1997

January The mandate of UNTAES is extended to January 1998.

14 February The international Arbitration Commission for Brčko announces that it will defer its decision on the future of the town in view of the extreme sensitivity of the situation. Robert Ferrand takes over as UN commissioner.

19 March Greek foreign minister Theodoros Pangolos pays an official visit to Skopje.

26 March Agreement is reached with the "London Club" of international banks over Macedonia's share of the debt of the former Yugoslav federation. Subsequently, the IMF approves a U.S.$75 million structural adjustment loan to the republic.

9 April The UNSC votes to reduce the size of UNPREDEP in view of the improving situation in Macedonia.

12–13 April Pope John Paul II pays a pastoral visit to Sarajevo.

Events in Yugoslavia

feature of the elections is the right granted to Croats living outside of Croatia to participate in the vote.

15 April A central bank is established for B-H.

15 May A large demonstration in Skopje organized by IMRO expresses dissatisfaction with government handling of the economy, including the collapse of pyramid investment schemes. The Liberal Party withdraws from the ruling coalition on similar grounds.

26 May In a sensational interview with the Belgrade paper *Večernje Novosti,* Radovan Karadžić intimates that were he to appear before the IWCT his evidence would implicate the Serbian political leadership.

15 June Presidential elections in Croatia return Franjo Tudjman for another term of office, but OSCE observers criticize state control of the media.

28 June The conflict within the ruling Democratic Party in the RS deepens when Biljana Plavšić dismisses her interior minister, accusing him of supporting Radovan Karadžić. New elections to the RS assembly are called.

8 July After two months of controversy in Macedonia over the issue of the right of national minorities to fly flags on public occasions, new legislation fails to clarify the issue.

15 July In spite of continuing massive public dissatisfaction, Milošević is elected as president of the FRY, partly because of opposition ineptness and disagreement and partly because of low turnout. The same low turnout produces an invalid result in elections to the Serbian presidency. The SPS is compelled to govern through a coalition.

19 July Biljana Plavšić is expelled from her own party and forms the Serb National Alliance. She spends the summer under permanent guard by SFOR troops.

31 July Slovene foreign minister Goran Thaler resigns (for the second time!) over issues linked to Slovenia's application to join the EU.

Events in the Surrounding World

7 May The IWCT at The Hague delivers its first verdict, on Dušan Tadić, a Bosnian Serb accused of detention camp atrocities.

20 June Carl Bildt is replaced as UN High Representative for B-H by Carlos Westendorp.

1 July The government of B-H reaches agreement with the "London Club" of international banks over its share of the international debt of the former Yugoslav federation. The World Bank postpones a U.S.$30 million loan to Croatia because of the latter's lack of support for the Dayton process.

23–24 July The delayed conference of aid donors to B-H takes place and withholds aid to the RS.

Events in Yugoslavia

5 August President Tudjman's inauguration speech contains an impassioned demand that Croatia should never be permitted to join any union of Balkan states; it proposes several alterations to the constitution relating to the definition and status of national minorities.

9 August Dobroslav Paraga issues a formal request to the IWCT that President Tudjman, Gojko Šušak, and other leading Croatian political figures should be indicted for war crimes.

1 September After the publication of a self-incriminating interview in *Feral Tribune,* Miro Bajramović is arrested on war crimes charges.

13–14 September Municipal elections are finally held in B-H, with many refugees volunteering to return on buses to vote in the place of their original settlement. Muslim parties take control in Mostar and Srebrenica.

17 September The mayor of Gostivar is sentenced to a term of imprisonment for "fanning national, racial, and ethnic intolerance"—namely, flying the Albanian flag from the town hall. He is subsequently released without explanation.

18 September A bomb explodes in Mostar, injuring 30 people.

October There is widespread criticism in Belgrade of the government's sale of the Telecom state enterprise. A series of demonstrations begin in Kosovo against continuing Serb oppression of Albanians; these protests last throughout the rest of the year.

5 October A further attempt to elect a Serbian president fails, once again because of unconstitutionally low turnout. SPS candidate Zoran Lilić is beaten, however, by Vojislav Šešelj.

6 October After repeated international expressions of dissatisfaction over the low level of official Croatian cooperation with the IWCT, 10 leading suspects, including Dario Kordić, are arrested.

19 October After two rounds of voting, and following a major court case over the legitimacy of his candidacy, Milorad Djukanović defeats Momir Bulatović in elections to the Montenegrin presidency. This result is widely interpreted as a victory for those who favor greater independence for Montenegro.

Events in the Surrounding World

October Authorities from Albania and Macedonia meet to agree upon measures against arms smuggling.

1 October SFOR troops take over four TV transmitters because of their transmission of material loyal to Radovan Karadžić.

14 October Slovenia is elected to one of the nonpermanent seats on the UNSC. The republic's plans to distance itself fully from its Balkan neighbors are set back by its omission from the list of those Eastern European states that are to join NATO.

Events in Yugoslavia

24 October The general secretary of the Serbian party Yugoslav United Left is assassinated—the second such killing of persons close to Milošević in the year.

7 November Material published in the Sarajevo weekly *Dani* suggests that several figures in the political leadership of B-H may also have been implicated in war crimes.

11 November The rail link between Zagreb and Belgrade is reopened.

22–23 November The elections to the assembly of the RS enable Biljana Plavšić to form a government led by Social Democrat Milorad Dodik. In Slovenia, Milan Kučan is returned to the presidency of Slovenia for another term.

21 December After nearly a year of trying, a president of Serbia is finally elected when the SPS changes its candidate to Milan Miluntinović, thanks to a boycott of the election by Kosovo's Albanians.

29 December The struggle for free media expression in Croatia is made evident when the editor of the Croatian paper *Karlovački List* is beaten up.

Events in the Surrounding World

3–4 November At the summit of Balkan states in Crete, Croatia is not represented—but Macedonia is. A meeting between Albania's Fatos Nano and Slobodan Milošević fails to alleviate the situation in Kosovo.

26 November Commissioner Westendorp announces his belief that a UN presence will be necessary in B-H for two to three years beyond the target date for withdrawal in June 1998.

Appendix: The Dayton Agreements

Summary of the Dayton Agreements on Bosnia and Hercegovina: 22 November 1995

The General Framework Agreement

Identifies the parties to the Agreements (the Republic of Bosnia and Hercegovina, the Republic of Croatia, and the Federal Republic of Yugoslavia); recapitulates the history of previous relevant documents; and commits the parties to the conduct of their relations in accordance with the United Nations (UN) Charter, the Helsinki Final Act, and the principles and practices of the Organization for Security and Cooperation in Europe (OSCE). It affirms the political independence and territorial integrity of the Republic of Bosnia and Hercegovina. The parties then "welcome and endorse" each of the specific sets of arrangements that are set out in the accompanying Annexes, agreeing to "fully respect and promote fulfillment of the commitments made therein." The Federal Republic of Yugoslavia and the Republic of Bosnia and Hercegovina recognize each other as "sovereign independent states within their international borders." [Note that Croatia remains apart from this process of mutual recognition.]

Agreement on Military Aspects

This is by far the longest and most complex of the documents. The parties undertake to re-create as quickly as possible normal conditions of life in Bosnia and Hercegovina and "welcome the willingness of the international community to send to the region, for a period of approximately one year, a force to assist in the implementation" of the Agreements. The UN Security Council is invited to authorize the creation of a multinational Implementation Force (IFOR), to which is to be transferred the authority previously conferred upon the UN Protection Force (UNPROFOR), which will be responsible for the military aspects of the Agreements. It is understood that the North Atlantic Treaty Organization (NATO) may establish such a force (to be headed by a U.S. general) assisted by other states.

The parties agree to the cessation of hostilities and commit themselves to cooperation with IFOR. Provision is made for the withdrawal of foreign forces within 30 days and for the phased redeployment of the forces of the "Entities" (see Annex 4).

Phase 1 envisages withdrawal behind a "Zone of Separation" of approximately 2 kilometers to either side of the Cease-Fire Line within 30 days. Provision is made for a Zone of Separation around Sarajevo. A new road is to be opened along a specified route linking Goražde to Sarajevo.

Phase 2 deals with the transfer of control in those areas in which the Inter-Entity Boundary Line (see Annex 2) does not correspond to the Cease-Fire Line, expected to be completed within 91 days.

Phase 3, which is to be completed after 120 days, involves the general withdrawal to barracks and demobilization of all local forces, especially heavy weapons.

The rights of IFOR personnel are specified. Provision is made for the colocation of IFOR command posts with those of local forces. The prerogatives of the Commander of IFOR are enumerated.

A Joint Military Commission is established between the parties to the Agreements and the Commander of IFOR, and its operations are specified, including liaison with the civilian High Representative (see Annex 10). The functions of this Commission, however, are expressly consultative; full authority for the conduct and implementation of the military aspects of the Agreements rests with the Commander of IFOR, including the sanctioning of military action in the case of infractions against the Agreements.

Provision is made for the exchange of prisoners, which all parties are obligated to "release and transfer without delay."

The Agreements reached on 22 November incorporate a number of Annexes.

Agreements between Bosnia and Hercegovina, Croatia, the Federal Republic of Yugoslavia, and NATO (Annex 1A)

In addition to recording several key definitions of terms, the Agreements spell out the diplomatic, civil, and taxation status of NATO personnel, the scope of their legitimate activity, their rights of transit, and the conditions under which locals may be employed in NATO operations.

Agreement on Regional Stabilization (Annex 1b)
The parties to the Agreements are committed to certain measures to build confidence and security in the region, under the supervision of the OSCE. These measures include restrictions on the deployment of military forces; the disbanding of "special operations and armed civilian groups"; reduction of force levels; and the establishment of military liaison missions. The parties agree not to import additional weapons into the area, especially heavy weapons. Baselines for the reduction of forces are specified, and the OSCE is to supervise further arms control talks. Wider talks on the establishment of a regional arms balance "in and around the former Yugoslavia" are to take place under the auspices of the OSCE Forum on Security Cooperation.

Agreement on the Inter-Entity Boundary Line (Annex 2)
The boundary between the "Entities" (see Annex 4) is described in maps appended to the Agreements. The Annex sets out the procedures for marking the boundary, giving to IFOR the task of supervising a joint Commission of the parties that will conduct the delineation. Provision is made for the transfer of territory over a period of 45 days; for changes to be made in the boundary; and for the arbitration of disputes. In particular, the parties undertake to enter binding arbitration with respect to the delineation of the Brčko corridor, which is to be completed within one year. (Note that the much-discussed question of Serb access to the sea is not touched upon directly in the Agreements.)

Agreement on Elections (Annex 3)
The parties agree to the provision for free and fair elections to the Assemblies in the Republic of Bosnia and Hercegovina and in the two "Entities." These elections are to be monitored and conducted in accordance with criteria laid down by the OSCE, particularly complying with paragraphs 7 and 8 of the Copenhagen Document. Elections are also to take place for the Republican Presidency, the Presidencies of the "Entities," and for organs of local government. To this end the OSCE is invited to set up a Commission, which will ensure that elections take place, preferably within six months. The Agreement sets out the detailed mandate for this Commission. The franchise is to be based on universal adult suffrage and voting by secret ballot. Provisions are to be made to ensure that refugees and other displaced persons can vote in their original place of residence if they so choose.

Constitution of the Republic of Bosnia and Hercegovina (Annex 4)
"The Agreement enables Bosnia and Hercegovina to continue as a single state, with full respect for its sovereignty by its neighbors." Nevertheless, the newly constituted Republic of Bosnia and Hercegovina consists of two "Entities": (1) the Federation of Bosnia and Hercegovina and (2) the Republika Srpska. The Constitution specifies the range of rights available to the state's citizens. Its institutions consist of a three-person Presidency (one "Bosniac" and one Croat elected from the former entity, and one Serb from the latter); a Council of Ministers; a bicameral Parliamentary Assembly; a Constitutional Court; and a Central Bank. The Republic is responsible for external representation and affairs, including foreign trade; customs; monetary policy; international and inter-entity law enforcement; international and interentity transport and communications; coordination of the actions of the governments of the "Entities"; and execution of the decisions of the Parliamentary Assembly. It is answerable for its budget to the Parliamentary Assembly. After five years several other functions may revert to the Republican government, by agreement. (Note that there is no provision for the Republic's exclusive control over military matters, a unified taxation system, or general judiciary.)

Agreement on Arbitration (Annex 5)
This commits the "Entities" to engage in binding arbitration with respect to unresolved disputes between them.

Agreement on Human Rights (Annex 6)
This lists the rights that shall be available to citizens of the Republic. (A series of relevant international agreements on rights is also incorporated into the Constitution.) A Commission and Ombudsman for the supervision of human rights is established in Sarajevo. A Human Rights Chamber is also established, with equal representation from each of the "Entities," and the Council of Ministers of the Council of Europe. These organizations are obligated to report regularly on the human rights situation in the republic; to receive applications concerning the infringement of rights; and to make recommendations as to effective remedies where infractions of rights are demonstrated.

Agreement on Refugees and Displaced Persons (Annex 7)
This sets out the rights of refugees and displaced persons who have been deprived of their normal place of residence since 1991. In particular, these persons have the rights to return freely to their former place of residence and to have their property restored to them. The parties to the Agreement are obligated to create suitable conditions for the return of refugees; to cooperate with international organizations and monitoring bodies responsible for their welfare; and to assist in accounting for missing persons. An independent Commission for the return of displaced persons and refugees is to be established in Sarajevo; the terms and conditions of its work and organization are set out in the Annex.

Agreement on Commissions to Preserve National Monuments (Annex 8)

A Commission is established under the supervision of the Director-General of UNESCO (United Nations Educational, Social and Cultural Organization) with the responsibility of receiving petitions for the designation of property as being of cultural, historic, religious, or ethnic importance and as a National Monument. The significance and condition of these properties are then to be appraised, and the Commission will then decide upon the eligibility of these properties for designation as Monuments. Under Article VIII the officials of the localities in which Monuments are located are obligated to cooperate with the Commission and to take any action with respect to conservation.

Agreement on Public Corporations (Annex 9)

Public utilities—including transport, energy, and communications—within the Republic are to be the responsibility of public corporations, which are supervised by a Commission that is chaired by a representative of the EBRD (European Bank for Reconstruction and Development) and that includes representatives of the "Entities."

Agreement on High Representative (Annex 10)

A "High Representative" is to be responsible for overseeing at the most general level the implementation of the Agreements and relevant resolutions of the UN Security Council; the conduct of the several Commissions set up under the Agreements; the conduct of elections to representative bodies; and the liaison between the parties to the Agreements and various interested international organizations. In short, the High Representative is an all-purpose facilitator, troubleshooter, and negotiator whose responsibility is to ensure the smooth running of the normalization process. (The weight of the effective implementation of the Dayton Agreements rests jointly upon the shoulders of the High Representative and the Commander of IFOR.)

Agreement on the International Police Task Force (Annex 11)

To assist in the creation of a secure environment, the parties request the UN to set up an International Police Task Force (IPTF), which will be coordinated through the High Representative (Annex 10). The responsibilities of the IPTF are to provide advice, facilitation, and training to the police forces of the government of Bosnia and Hercegovina. In particular the Force is charged with assisting in the provision of safe conditions for the conduct of the elections (Annex 3). The parties to the Agreements are obligated to support the operation of the IPTF and to cooperate with its personnel.

Additional Materials (Annex 12)

An exchange of supporting letters between the major signatories constitutes an important annex to the main agreements, committing the signatories to the implementation of the Agreements; undertaking to ensure that additional forces are not introduced to the area; and specifying a range of further undertakings, generally in connection with the setting up of supporting diplomatic services.

The Agreements were accompanied by definitive maps. The political, economic, and above all military significance of the Dayton Agreements is fully evident only in relation to the detail regarding the demarcation between the Entities.

Index